APPLETONS'

CYCLOPÆDIA OF DRAWING,

DESIGNED AS

A TEXT-BOOK

FOR THE

MECHANIC, ARCHITECT, ENGINEER, AND SURVEYOR.

COMPRISING

GEOMETRICAL PROJECTION, MECHANICAL, ARCHITECTURAL, AND TOPOGRAPHICAL DRAWING, PERSPECTIVE AND ISOMETRY.

EDITED BY

W. E. WORTHEN.

NEW YORK:
D. APPLETON AND COMPANY,
346 & 348 BROADWAY.
1857.

PREFACE.

At the suggestion of the publishers this work was undertaken to form one of their series of Dictionaries and Cyclopædias. In this view, it has been the intention to make it a complete course of instruction and book of reference to the mechanic, architect and engineer. It has not therefore been confined to the explanation and illustration of the methods of projection, and the delineation of objects which might serve as copies to the draughtsman, matters of essential importance for the correct and intelligible representation of every form; but it contains the means of determining the amount and direction of strains, to which different parts of a machine or structure may be subjected, and the rules for disposing and proportioning of the material employed, to the safe and permanent resistance of those strains, with practical applications of the same. Thus while it supplies numerous illustrations in every department for the mere copyist, it also affords suggestions and aids to the mechanic in the execution of new designs. And although the arranging and properly proportioning alone of material in a suitable direction and adequately to the resistance of the strains to which it might be exposed, would produce a structure sufficient in point of strength for the purposes for which it is intended, yet as in many cases the disposition of the material may be applied not only practically, but also artistically, and adapted to the reception of ornament, under the head of Architectural Drawing the general characteristics of various styles have been treated of, and illustrated, with brief remarks on proportion and the application of color.

Within the last few years both here and abroad, a number of works have been published on "Practical Drawing," but no one work has illustrated all departments of the subject. In the mechanical, the works of M. Le Brun and M. M. Armengaud are the standard which have been made the basis of two English works, "The practical Draughtsman's Book of Industrial Design" and the "Engineer's and Machinist's Drawing Book." From the latter of these works we have drawn most of our chapters on Geometrical and Mechanical Drawing, and Shades and Shadows. In neither the French nor the English works has the science of architectural construction and drawing been adequately illustrated, nor has Topographical Drawing been treated of. In these two departments a varied selection has been made from the best authorities. In the Architectural, Ferguson and Garbett have been the most consulted; in the Topographical, Williams, Gillespie, Smith and Frome. The work will be found quite fully illustrated, and the drawings and engravings have been carefully executed, mostly under the supervision of Mr. H. Grassau.

Like most cyclopædias, this work claims for its articles but little of novelty or originality; the intention of the compiler was to collect within moderate compass as much valuable matter as possible, in practical Drawing and Design; and to this purpose he brings the experience of series of years in each of the departments treated. Practically, he has had means of knowing the necessities of the trade and of the profession, and trusts that the selection now made will be found useful for the purposes for which it was intended.—W.

TABLE OF CONTENTS.

GEOMETRICAL PROJECTION.

ARCHITECTURAL DRAWING.

SHADING AND SHADOWS.

TOPOGRAPHICAL DRAWING.

PERSPECTIVE DRAWING.

ISOMETRICAL DRAWING.

LIST OF PLATES.

GEOMETRICAL PROJECTION.

DRAWING OF MACHINERY.

ARCHITECTURAL DRAWING.

SHADING AND SHADOWS.

TOPOGRAPHICAL DRAWING.

PERSPECTIVE DRAWING.

ISOMETRICAL DRAWING.

APPLETONS'

CYCLOPÆDIA OF DRAWING.

GEOMETRICAL DEFINITIONS AND TECHNICALITIES.

A *point* is mere position without magnitude, as the intersection of two lines, or the centre of a circle.

Lines are measured by length merely, and may be *straight* or *curved.* Straight lines are generally designated by letters or figures at their extremities, as the line A——B, the line 1——2. Curved lines, by additional intermediate letters or figures, as the curved line ABC.

A *given point* or *given line* expresses a point or line of fixed position or dimension.

Surfaces or *superficies* are measured by length and breadth only. They may be *plane* or *curved.*

Solids are measured by length, breadth, and thickness. The extremities of *lines* are *points*, the boundaries of *surfaces* are *lines*, and the boundaries of *solids* are *surfaces.*

Parallel lines are lines in the same plane which are equally distant from each other at every part (fig. 1).

Fig. 1.

Horizontal lines are such as are parallel to the horizon, or *level.*

Vertical lines are such as are parallel to the position of a plumb-line suspended freely in a still atmosphere.

Inclined lines occupy an intermediate between horizontal and vertical lines. Also two lines which converge towards each other, and if produced, would meet or intersect, are said to incline to each other.

An *angle* is the opening between two straight lines which meet one another. "When several angles are at one point B, any one of them is expressed by three letters, of which the letter that is at the *vertex* of the angle, that is, at the point in which the straight lines that contain the angle meet one another, is put between the other two letters: Thus the angle which is contained by the straight lines, AB, CB, is named the angle ABC, or CBA; but if there be only one angle at a point, it may be expressed by a letter placed at that point; as the angle at E.'

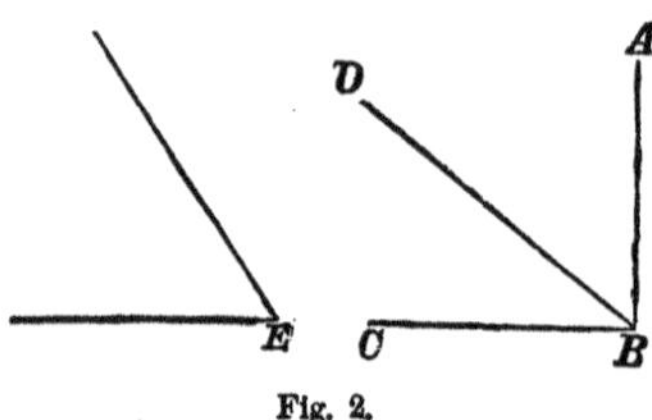

Fig. 2.

When a straight line standing on another straight line makes the adjacent angles equal to one another, each of the angles is called a *right angle;* and the straight lines are said to be *perpendicular* to each other (fig. 3).

An *obtuse angle* is that which is greater than a right angle (fig. 4).

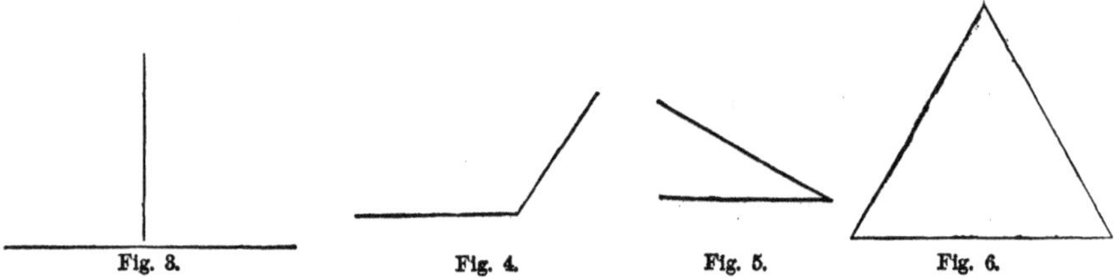
Fig. 3. Fig. 4. Fig. 5. Fig. 6.

An *acute angle* is that which is less than a right angle (fig. 5).

A *triangle* is a flat surface bounded by three straight lines; when the three sides are equal, the triangle is *equilateral;* when only two of its sides are equal, *isosceles;* when none equal, *scaline;* when one of the angles is a right angle, the triangle is *right angled*, and then the longest side, or that opposite the right angle is called the *hypothenuse.* The upper extremity of the triangle is called the *apex*, the bottom line the *base*, and the two other including lines the *sides*.

A *Quadrilateral* figure is a surface bounded by four straight lines.

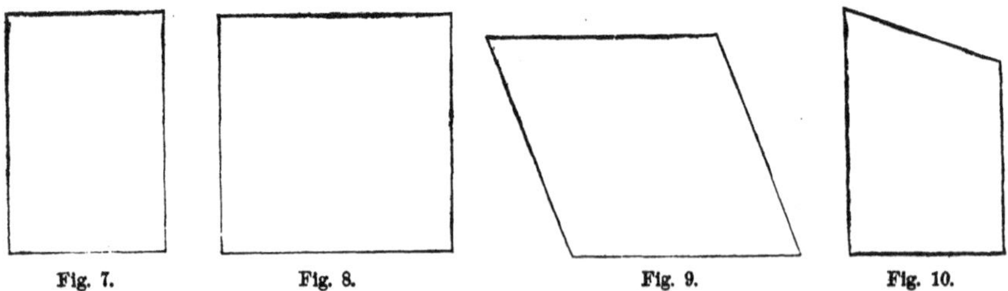
Fig. 7. Fig. 8. Fig. 9. Fig. 10.

When the opposite sides are parallel, it is a *parallelogram;* if its angles are right angles, it is a *rectangle* (fig. 7); if the sides are also equal, it is a *square* (fig. 8); if all the sides are equal, but the angles not right angles, it is a *rhombus* (fig. 9). A *trapezium* has only two of its sides parallel (fig. 10). A *diagonal* is a straight line joining two opposite angles of a figure.

Plane figures of more than four sides are called *polygons*. When the

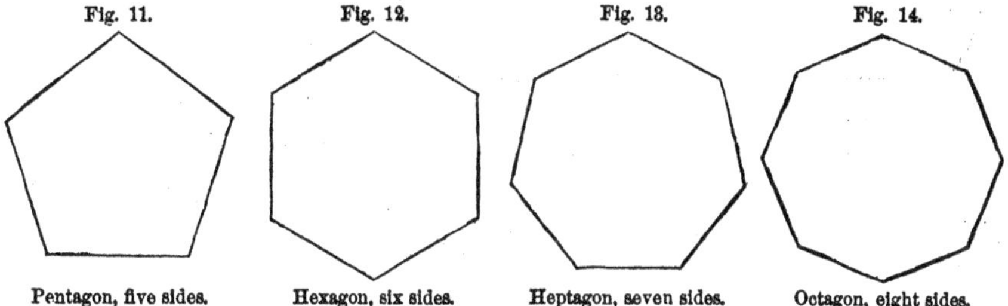

Fig. 11. Pentagon, five sides. Fig. 12. Hexagon, six sides. Fig. 13. Heptagon, seven sides. Fig. 14. Octagon, eight sides.

sides are equal, they are *regular polygons;* of which figs. 11–14 are examples, annexed to which are their respective designations.

A *circle* is a plane figure contained by one line, which is called the *circumference*, and is such that all straight lines, drawn from a certain point within the figure to the circumference, are equal to one another. And this point is called the *centre* of the circle.

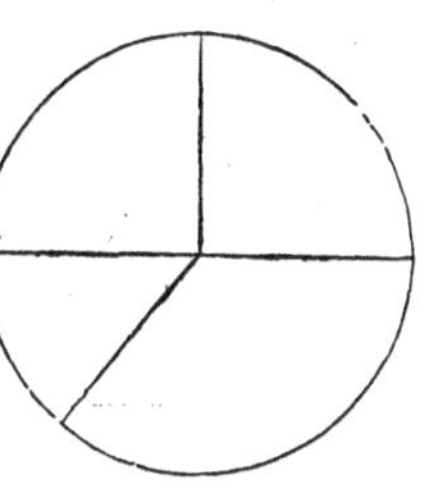

Fig. 15.

The term *circle* is very generally used for the circumference, and will be found to be employed in this work with this twofold meaning.

Any straight line drawn from the centre and terminating in the circumference is termed a *radius;* if drawn through the centre, and terminated at each end by the circumference, it is termed a *diameter*.

An *arc* of a circle is any part of the circumference.

A *sector* of a circle is the space enclosed by two radii and the intercepted arc. When the radii are at right angles, the space is called a *quadrant* as to one-fourth of a circle. Half a circle is called a *semicircle*.

A *chord* is a straight line joining the extremities of an arc, as *a b*. The space cut off by the chord is termed a *segment*.

A *tangent* to a circle or other curve is a straight line which touches it at only one point, as *c d* touching the circle at only *e*.

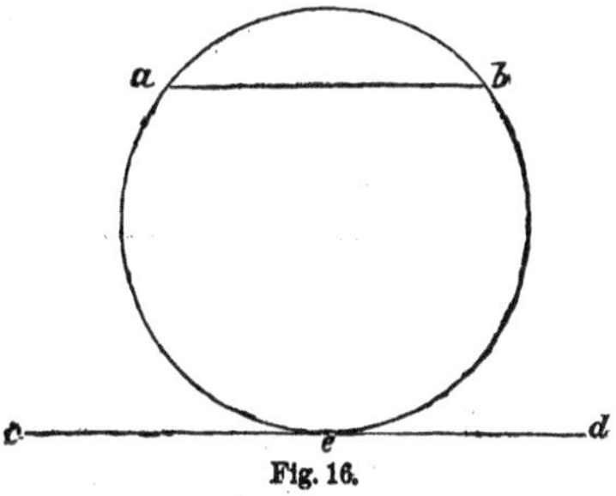

a b c e d

Fig. 16.

Circles are *concentric* when described from the same centres. *Eccentric* when described from different centres.

Triangular or other figures with a greater number of sides are *inscribed in* a circle, or *circumscribed by* it, when the vertex of all its angles are in the circumference (fig. 17).

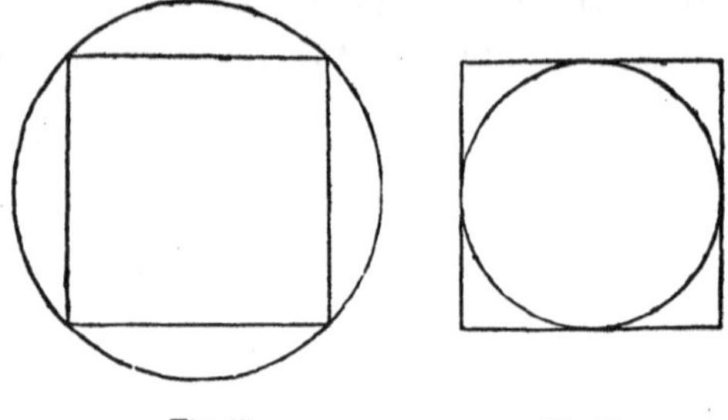

Fig. 17. Fig. 18.

A circle is *inscribed* in a straight-sided figure, when it is tangent to all the sides (fig. 18).

All regular polygons may be inscribed in circles, and circles may be inscribed in polygons; hence the facility with which polygons may be constructed.

For the measurement of angles, the circumference of a circle is divided into 360 equal arcs, called *degrees* °, which are again subdivided into minutes ′ and seconds ″; 60 minutes to a degree, and 60 seconds to a minute, the vertex of the angle being placed at the centre of the circle; the angle is measured by the arc enclosed between the sides. Thus the angle DCB is measured by the arc DB; the line DH, a line drawn from one extremity of the arc perpendicular to the radius passing through the other extremity is called the *sine* of the angle, GD is the *cosine*, HB the *versed sine*, AB the *tangent*, FE the *cotangent*, AC the *secant*, and CE the *cosecant*.

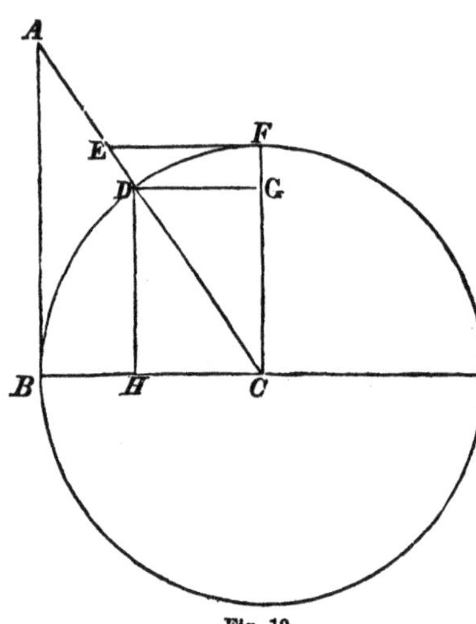

Fig. 19.

An *ellipse* is an oval-shaped curve from any point P in which, if straight lines be drawn to two fixed points FF′, their sum will be always the same. FF′ are the *foci*, the line passing through the foci is called the *transverse* axis, the line CD perpendicular to the centre of this line the *conjugate* axis.

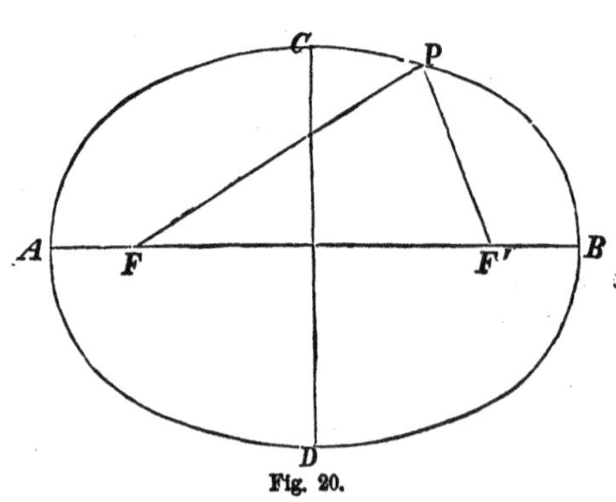

Fig. 20.

A *parabola* is a curve in which any point P is equally distant from a certain fixed point F and a straight line KK′; thus,

PF is always equal to PD—. F is called the *focus*, and the line KK′ the *directrix* (fig. 21).

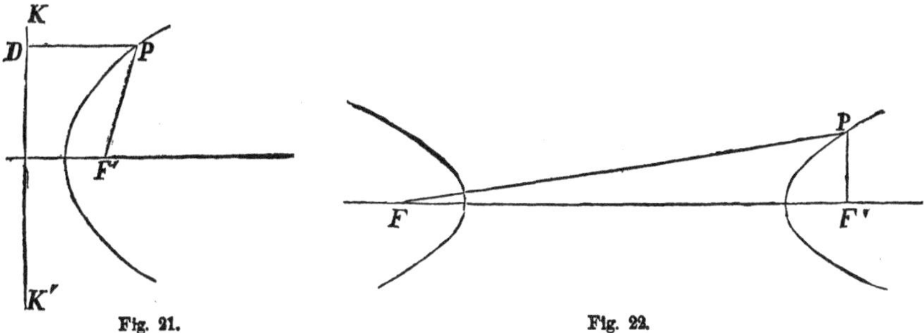

Fig. 21. Fig. 22.

An *hyperbola* is a curve from any point P in which, if two straight lines be drawn to two fixed points FF′ the *foci*, their difference shall always be the same (fig. 22).

A *cycloid* is the curve described by a point P in the circumference of

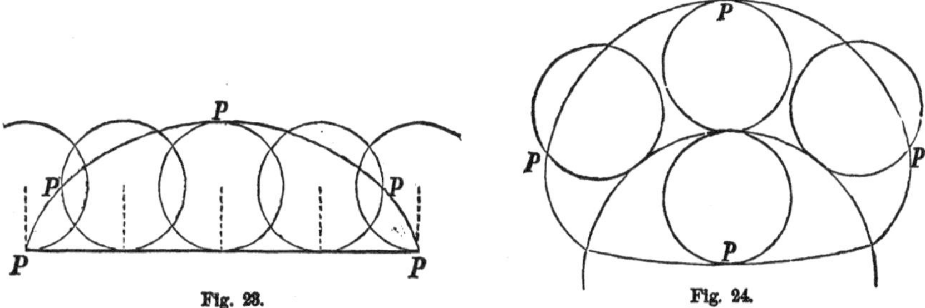

Fig. 23. Fig. 24.

a circle which rolls along an extended straight line until it has completed a revolution.

If the circle be rolled on the circumference of another circle, the curve then described by the point P is called an *epicycloid* (fig. 24).

Epicycloids are *external* or *internal*, according as the rolling or *generating* circle revolves on the outside or inside of the *fundamental* circle. The internal epicycloid is sometimes called a *hypocycloid*.

OF SOLIDS.

A *prism* is a solid of which the ends are equal, similar, and parallel straight-sided figures, and of which the other sides are parallelograms. When all the sides are squares, it is called a *cube* (fig. 25).

A *pyramid* is a solid having a straight-sided base, and triangular sides terminating in one point or vertex (fig. 26).

Prisms and pyramids are distinguished as triangular, quadrangular, pentagonal, hexagonal, &c., according as the base has three, four, five, six sides, &c.

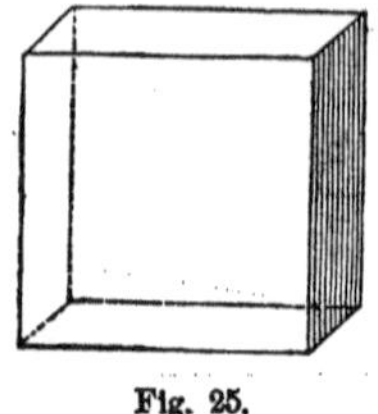
Fig. 25.

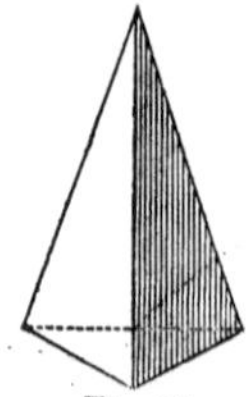
Fig. 26.

Fig. 27.

A *sphere* or *globe* (fig. 27), is a solid bounded by a uniformly curved surface, every point of which is equally distant from the *centre*, a point within the sphere. A line passing through the centre, and terminating both ways at the surface, is a *diameter*.

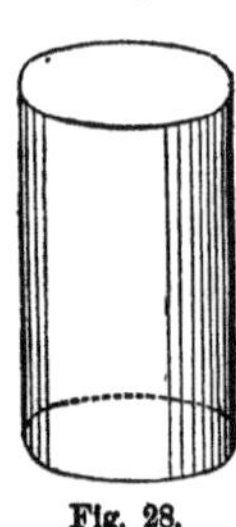
Fig. 28.

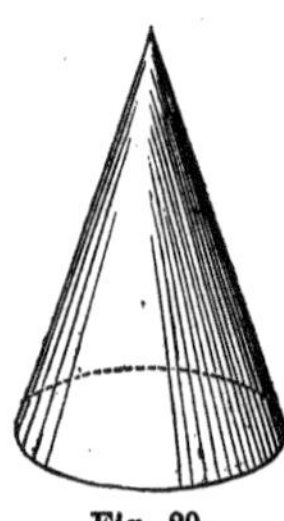
Fig. 29.

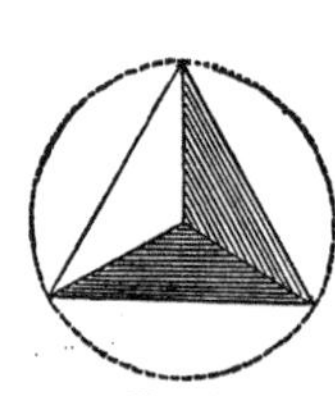
Fig. 30.

A *cylinder* is a round solid of uniform thickness, of which the ends are equal and parallel circles (fig. 28).

A *cone* is a round solid, with a circle for its base, and tapering uniformly to a point at the top (fig. 29).

When a solid is cut through transversely by a plane parallel to the base, the part cut off is a *segment*, and the part remaining is a *frustrum* of the solid. The latter term is usually limited to pyramids and cones.

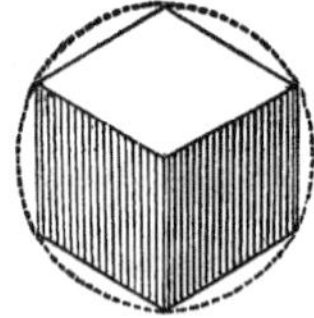
Fig. 31.

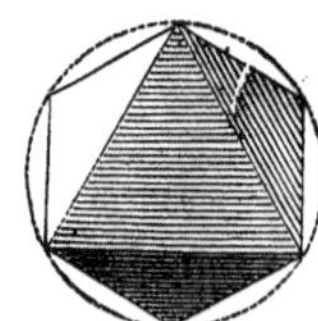
Fig. 32.

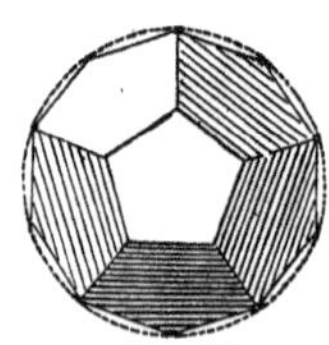
Fig. 33.

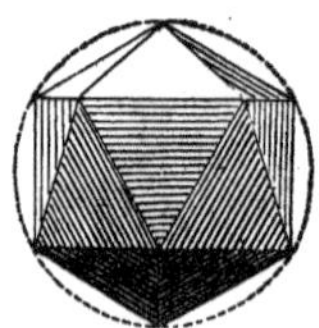
Fig. 34.

The *tetrahedron*, bounded by four equilateral triangles (fig. 30).

The *hexahedron*, or cube, bounded by six squares (fig. 31).

The *octahedron*, bounded by eight equilateral triangles (fig. 32).

The *dodecahedron*, bounded by twelve pentagons (fig. 33).

The *icosahedron*, bounded by twenty equilateral triangles (fig. 34).

Regular solids may be circumscribed by spheres, and spheres may be inscribed in regular solids.

DRAWING INSTRUMENTS.

Lead pencil.—Pencils are of various qualities, distinguished by letter marks, of which the most common in use by draftsmen are HH and HHH. The pencil used for drawing straight lines should be sharpened to a chisel edge; for making dots and marking points (.), the pencil should have a round sharp point. Pencil lines intended to be made permanent in ink, should be drawn quite delicately. The pencil should not be held tightly; a slight hold without slackness, inclined a little to the side toward which the line is drawn. Never extend the line beyond what is necessary, and avoid as much as possible the use of rubber, as it roughs the paper, making it difficult to trace a smooth line in ink, and readier to receive and retain dust.

The *common ruler* or *straight edge.*—Rulers should be of close-grained, thoroughly seasoned wood, such as mahogany, maple, pear, &c. They should be about ¼ of an inch thick, bevelled a little on one edge, and from 1 to 2½ inches wide, according to their length. Every draftsman should have at least two rulers, the shortest from 9 inches to a foot long, and the other as long as he may require in his drawing. As the accuracy of a drawing depends greatly on the straightness of the lines, the bevelled edge of the ruler should be perfectly straight. To test this, place a sheet of paper on a perfectly smooth board; insert two very fine needles in an upright position through the paper into the board, distant from each other nearly the length of the ruler to be tested; bring the edge of the ruler against these needles, and draw a line from one needle to the other; reverse the ruler, bringing the same edge on the opposite side and against the needles, and again draw a line. If the two lines coincide, the edge is straight; but if they disagree, the ruler is inaccurate. When one ruler has been tested, the other can be examined by placing their edges against the correct one, and holding them between the eye and the light.

Triangles are made of the same kinds of wood as the ruler, and somewhat thinner, and of various sizes. They should be right-angled, with acute angles of 45°, or of 60° and 30°. The most convenient size for general use measures from 3 to 6 inches on the side. A larger size from 8 to 10 inches long on the side is convenient for making drawings to a large scale. Circular openings are made in the body of the triangle for the insertion of the end of the finger to give facility in sliding the triangle on the paper. Triangles are sometimes made as large as 15 to 18 inches on the side; but in this case they are framed in three pieces of about 1¼ wide, leaving the centre of the triangle open. The value of the triangle in drawing perpendicular lines depends on the accuracy of the right angle. To test this (fig. 36), draw a line with an accurate ruler on paper. Place the right angle of the triangle near the centre of this line, and make one of the adjacent sides to coincide with the line; now draw a line along the other adjacent side, which, if the angle is strictly a right angle, will be perpendicular to the first line. Turn the triangle on this perpendicular side, bringing it into the position ABC′; if now the sides of the triangle agree with the line BC′ and AB, the angle is a right angle, and the sides straight. The straightness of the hypothenuse or longest side can be tested like a common ruler.

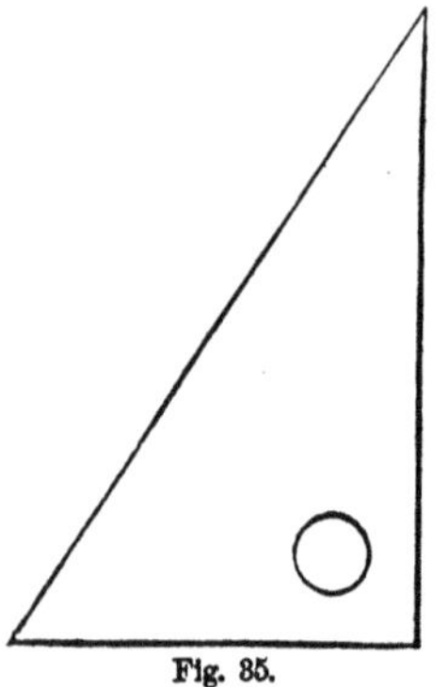
Fig. 35.

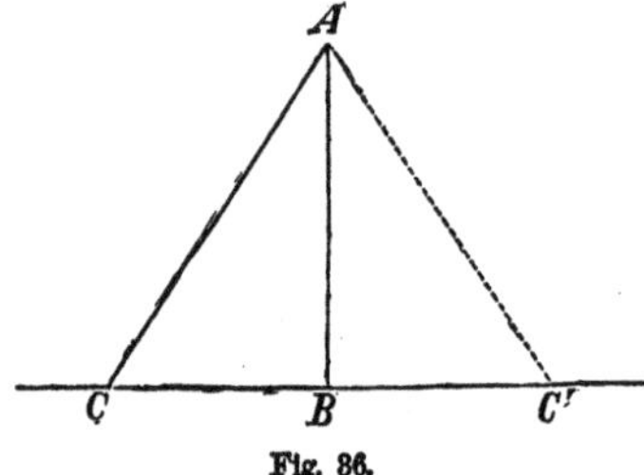

Fig. 36.

The triangle is used for the drawing of lines parallel or perpendicular to each other. Thus (fig. 37), if it were required to draw lines parallel and perpendicular to *c d*, place one side of the triangle so as to coincide accurately with the given line *c d;* keeping the triangle in this position with the right hand, bring the edge of the ruler against the hypothenuse of the triangle; if now the ruler be held securely by the left hand, the triangle may be slid along the edge of the ruler, and any line drawn along the upper side of the triangle will be parallel to the line *c d*, and the lines drawn along the other side of the triangle will be perpendicular to this same line; in this way a rectangle may be drawn through three given points without moving the position of the ruler.

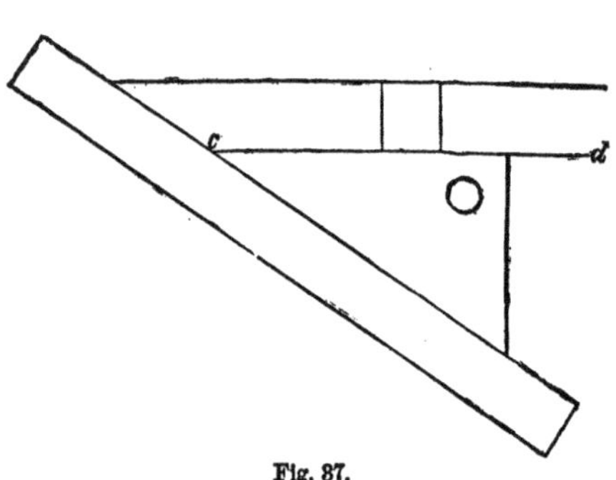

Fig. 37.

It is evident that for the drawing of parallel lines merely, either side may be brought in contact with the ruler; but the longer the side in contact, the more accurately may the parallelism be preserved in sliding the triangle.

The T *square* is a thin "straight edge" or ruler, *a*, fitted at one end with a stock, *b*, applied transversely at right angles. The stock being so formed as to fit and slide against one edge of the drawing board, the blade reaches over the surface, and presents an edge of its own at right angles to that of the board, by which parallel straight lines may be drawn upon the paper. To suit a 41-inch board, the blade should measure 40 inches long clear of the stock, or one inch shorter than the board, to remove risk of injury by overhanging at the end; it should be $2\frac{1}{2}$ inches broad by $\frac{3}{32}$ inch thick, as this section makes it sufficiently stiff laterally and vertically. The tip of the blade may be secured from splitting by binding it with a thin strip inserted in a saw-cut. The stock should be 14 inches long, to give sufficient bearing on the edge of the board, 2 inches broad and $\frac{5}{8}$ inch thick, in two equal thicknesses glued together. With a blade and stock of these sizes, a well proportioned T square may be made, and the stock will be heavy enough to act as a balance to the blade, and to relieve the operation of handling the square. The blade should be sunk flush into the upper half of the stock on the inside, and very exactly fitted. It should be inserted full breadth, as shown in the figure; notching and dovetailing is a mistake, as it weakens the blade, and adds nothing to the security. The lower half of the stock should be only $1\frac{3}{4}$ inches broad, to leave a $\frac{1}{4}$-inch check or lap, by which the upper half rests firmly on the board and secures the blade lying flatly on the paper.

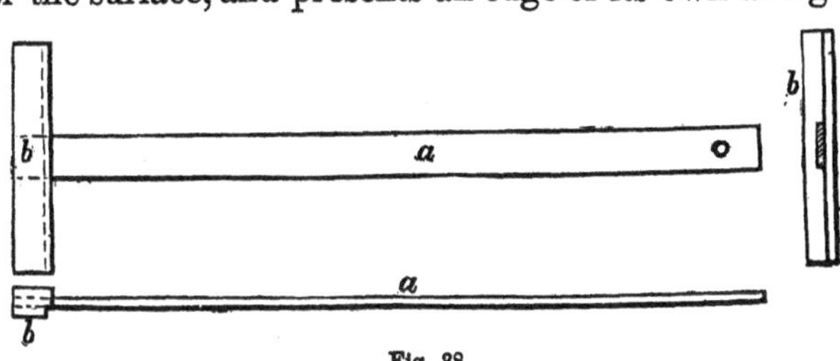

Fig. 38.

For the smaller sizes of board, reduce the proportions of both the blade and the stock.

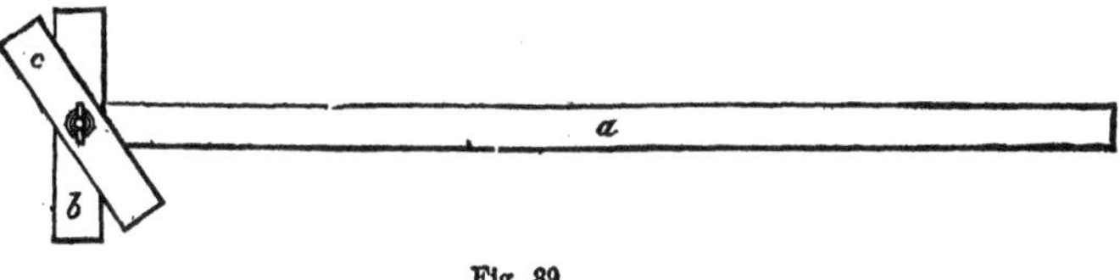

Fig. 39

One half of the stock, *c* (fig. 39), is in some cases made loose, to turn upon a brass swivel to any angle with the blade *a*, and to be clenched by a screwed nut and washer. The loose stock is useful for drawing parallel lines obliquely to the edges of the board, such as the threads of screws, oblique columns, and connecting-rods of steam-engines. A square of this sort should be rather as an addition to the fixed square, and used only when the bevel edge is required, as it is not so handy as the other.

The edges of the blade should be very slightly rounded, as the pen will thereby work the more freely. It is a mistake to chamfer the edges, that is, to plane them down to a very thin edge, as is sometimes done with the object of insuring a correct position of the lines; for the edge is easily damaged, and the pen is liable to catch the edge, and to leave ink upon it.

A small hole should be made in the blade near the end, by which the square may be hung up.

In many drawing cases will be found the parallel ruler (fig. 40), consisting of two rulers connected by two bars moving on pivots, and so adjusted that the rulers, as they open, form the sides of a parallelogram. The edge of one of the rulers being retained in a position coinciding with, or parallel to a given line; the other ruler may be moved, and lines drawn along its edge must also be parallel to the given line. This instrument is only useful in drawing small parallels, and in accuracy and convenience does not compare with the triangle and ruler or T square.

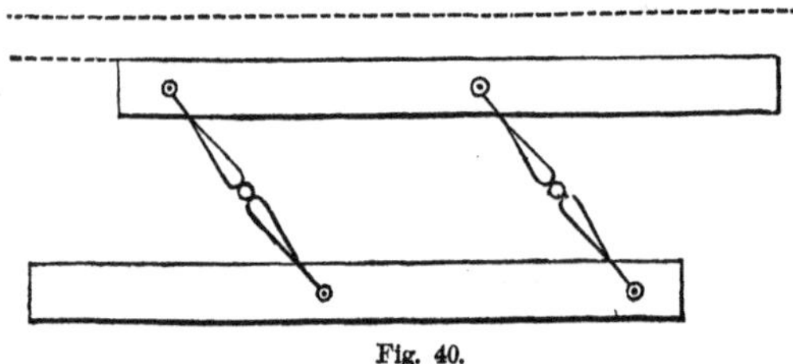

Fig. 40.

SWEEPS AND VARIABLE CURVES.

For drawing circular arcs of large radius, beyond the range of the ordinary compasses, thin slips of wood, termed sweeps, are usefully employed, of which one or both edges are cut to the required circle. For curves which are not circular, but variously elliptic or otherwise, "universal sweeps," made of thin wood, of variable curvature, are very serviceable. The two examples have been found from experience to meet almost all the requirements of ordinary drawing

Fig. 42. One fourth full size.

practice. Whatever be the nature of the curve, some portion of the universal sweep will be found to coincide with its commencement, and it can be continued throughout its extent by applying successively such parts of the sweep as are suitable, taking care, however, that the continuity is not injured by unskilful junction.

Fig. 42. One-fourth full size.

No varnish of any description should be applied to any of the wooden instruments used in drawing, as the best varnish will retain dust, and soil the paper. Use the wood in its natural state, keeping it carefully wiped. Various other materials besides wood have been used, as steel for the blades of the T square and the ruler; the objection is the liability to soil the paper. Glass is frequently used for the ruler and the triangle, and retains its correctness of edge and angle, but too heavy in use, and liable of course to fracture.

THE COMPASSES OR DIVIDERS.

The best compasses are constructed with joints of two different metals, as steel and brass, whereby the wear is more equal, and the motion of the legs uniform and steady, and not subject to sudden jerks in opening or shutting. This motion will occasionally require some adjustment to render it uniformly smooth, and to move stiffer or easier at pleasure, but so that they may keep steadily any position that may be given to them. This adjustment is performed by the application of a turnscrew to the axis of the joint. In the common compasses, a simple screw forms the axis, which may be turned with a screwdriver; but in the best made instruments, a steel pin passes through the joints, having at one end a head of brass riveted fast upon it, and on the other end a similar plate or nut is screwed, on a diameter of which are drilled two small holes for the application of a key (fig. 43). The points of a well made instrument should be of steel so tempered, as neither to be easily bent or blunted; not too fine and tapering, and yet meeting closely when the compasses are shut.

Fig. 43.

Instruction for using dividers, which are applied only to measure and transfer distances and dimensions, may appear superfluous; but there are a few simple directions which may save the young draughtsman much perplexity and loss of time. It is, of course, desirable to work the compasses in such a manner that, when the dimension is taken, it may suffer no disturbance in its transfer from the scale to the drawing. In order to this, the instrument is to be held by the head or joint, the forefinger resting on the top of the joint, and the thumb and second finger on either side. When held in this way, there is no pressure except on the head and centre, and the dimension between the points cannot be altered; but if the instrument be clumsily seized by a thumb on one leg, and two fingers on the other, the pressure, in the act of transference, must inevitably contract, in some small degree, the opening of the compasses; and if the dimension has to be set off several times, the probability is, that no two transfers will be exactly the same. And whilst it is all important to keep the dimension exact, it is also desirable to manipulate in such a way, when setting off the same dimension a number of times, that the point of position be never lost. Persons unaccustomed to the use of compasses, are very apt to turn them over and over in the *same* direction, when laying down a number of equal measures, and this necessitates a frequent change of the finger and thumb, which direct the movement of the instrument; the consequence is, either that the fixed leg is driven deep into the drawing, or it loses position. Now, if the movement be alternately above and below the line on which the distances are being set off, the compasses can be worked with great freedom and delicacy, and without any liability to shifting. If a straight line is drawn, and semicircles be described alternately above and below the line, it will show the path of the traversing foot. If the two movements are tried, the superiority of the one recommended will at once be discovered. The forefinger rests gently on the head; and the thumb and second finger, without changing from side to side, direct the movement for setting off any number of times that may be required.

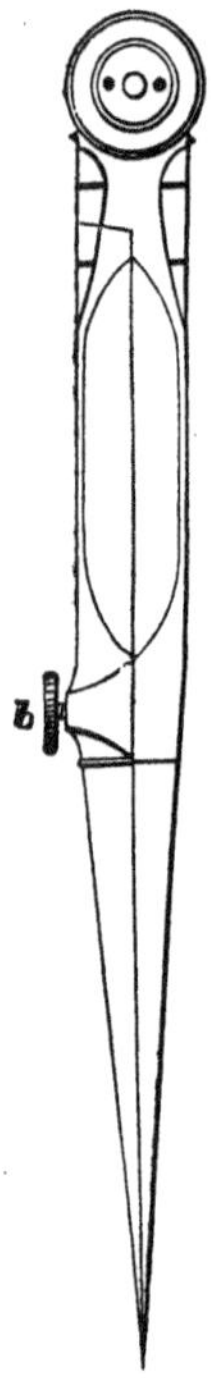

b

Fig. 44.

The *hair compasses* (fig. 44) is constructed in the same manner as the common compasses. The only difference consists in a contrivance, whereby the lower or point half of one shank can be moved a very small quantity either towards or from the other point, so that when the compasses are opened nearly to the required extent, by the help of the screw *b* the points may be set with great precision, which cannot be done so well by the motion of the joints alone.

Compasses with movable points (fig. 45) is a pair of compasses of which the point half of one of the legs is movable, to admit of adapting singly a pen, a pencil, or a dotting point. The pen point is used for drawing circles or arcs with ink. The pencil point is a a tube adapted to hold a piece of lead pencil for describing circles or arcs, and the dotting point consists of two blades, between which revolves a small wheel, with numerous points round its circumference, resembling the rowel of a spur. The space between the blades being supplied with Indian ink, as the compasses describe a circle or arc, each point, as the wheel revolves, will pass through the ink, and transfer it to the paper beneath, making equidistant dots in the circle which the compasses describe.

The movable points have a joint in them, just under that part which locks into the shank of the compasses, by which the part below the joint may be set perpendicular to the plane on which the lines are described, when the compasses are open.

An additional piece, called a lengthening bar, is frequently applied to these compasses, to enable them to strike larger circles, or measure greater extents than they otherwise could. The annexed engraving represents this instrument and its appendages.

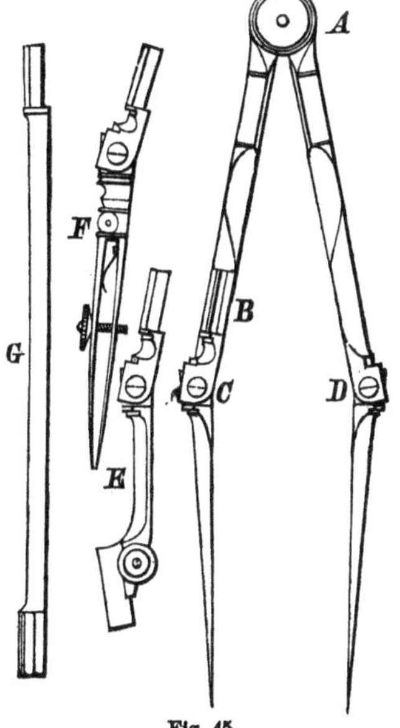

Fig. 45.

A, the compasses, with a movable point at B; C and D, the joints to set each point perpendicular to the paper; E, the pencil point; F, the pen point; G, the lengthening bar.

Bow compasses.—These are a small pair, either having a point for ink or pencil, used to describe small arcs or circles, which they do more conveniently than large compasses. Fig. 46 is adapted for describing arcs of a radius intermediate between those described by the above-named compasses, and those capable of being produced by the bows represented by fig. 47. In fig. 46, the legs can be opened a considerable width by the joint, whilst in fig. 47, the opening is limited, the two blades or legs being formed out of one solid piece of steel, and tempered so as to form a spring at the upper part; the spring of the two blades is then kept in obedience by an adjusting screw D, by which the two points may be set to any required degree of minuteness, and very small circles may be described with precision.

Fig. 46. 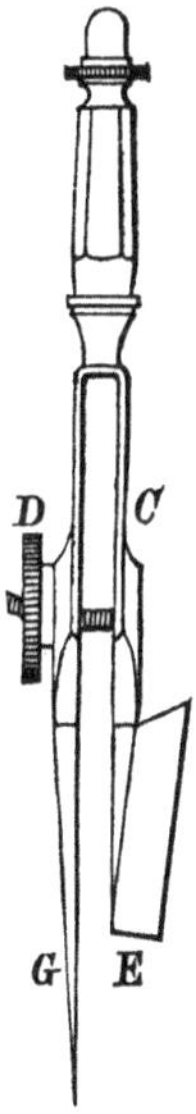 Fig. 47.

The pen bows (figs. 48, 49) are similar in their construction to the pencil bows. In fig. 49 there is a second joint A, by which, when the instrument is open for use, the pen may be set perpendicular, or nearly so, to the paper, which is essential in the use of the drawing pen.

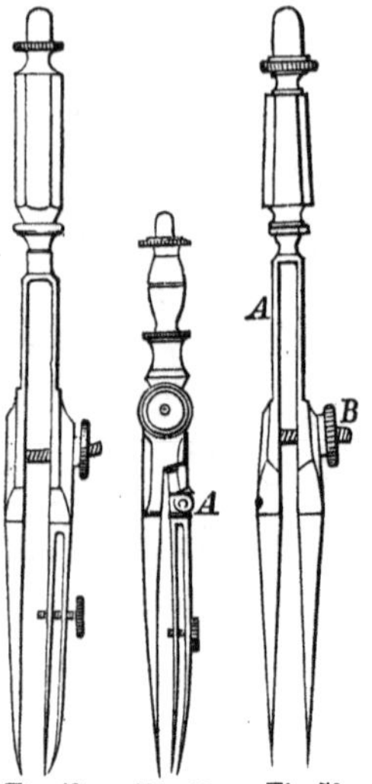

Similar to fig. 48 in their construction are the *spring dividers* (fig. 50), particularly useful for repeating divisions of a small but equal extent, a practice that has acquired the name of stepping.

Fig. 48. Fig. 49. Fig. 50.

The *drawing pen* (fig. 51) is used for drawing straight lines. It consists of two blades with steel points fixed to a handle; and they are so bent, that a sufficient cavity is left between them for the ink, when the ends of the steel points meet close together, or nearly so. The blades are set with the points more or less open by means of a millheaded screw, so as to draw lines of any required fineness or thickness. One of the blades is framed with a joint, so that by taking out the screw, the blades may be completely opened, and the points effectively cleaned after use. The ink is to be put between the blades by a common pen, and in using the pen it should be slightly inclined in the direction of the line to be drawn, and care should be taken that both points touch the paper; and these observations equally apply to the pen points of the compasses before described. The drawing pen should be kept close to the ruler or straight edge, and in the same direction during the whole operation of drawing the line. Care must be taken in holding the straight edge firmly with the left hand, that it does not change its position.

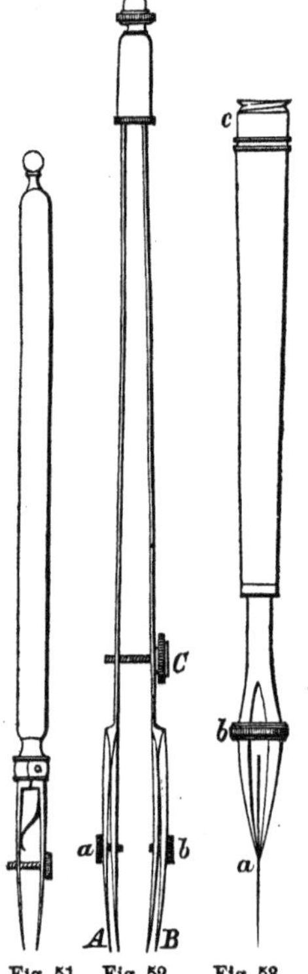

Fig. 51. Fig. 52. Fig. 53.

For drawing close parallel lines in mechanical and architectural drawings, or to represent canals or roads, a double pen (fig. 52) is frequently used, with an adjusting screw to set the pen to any required small distance. This is usually called the road pen. The best pricking point is a fine needle held in a pair of forceps (fig. 53). It is used to mark the intersection of lines, or to set off divisions from the plotting scale and protractor. This point may also be used to prick through a drawing upon an intended copy, or, the needle being reversed, the eye end forms a good tracing point.

For filling up the broad lines of borders, a goose quill is often used with a short nib and no slit (fig. 54). In drawing with this pen, incline

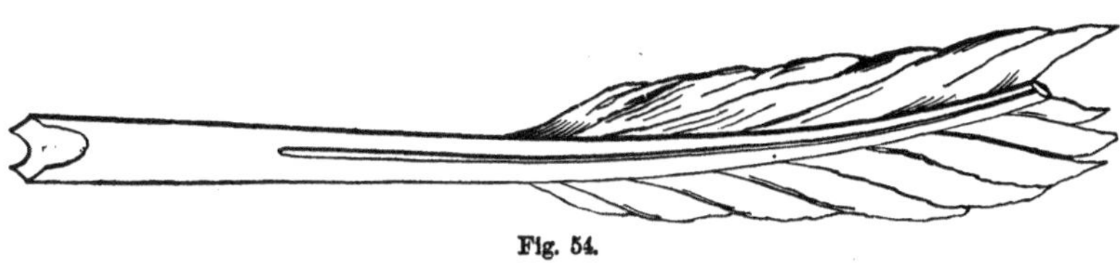

Fig. 54.

the drawing-board so that the ink will follow the pen, which prevents blots or the accumulation of too much ink at any one point.

The *dotting point* (fig. 55) resembles a drawing pen, except that the points are not so sharp. On the back blade, as seen in the engraving, is a pivot, on which may be placed a dotting wheel, *a*, resembling the rowel of a spur; the screw *b* is for opening the blades to remove the wheel for cleaning after use, or replacing it with one of another character of dot. The cap *c*, at the upper end of the instrument, is a box containing a variety of dotting wheels, each producing a different shaped dot. These are used as distinguishing marks for different classes of boundaries on maps; for instance, one kind of dot distinguishes *county* boundaries, another kind *town* boundaries, a third kind distinguishes that which is both a county and a town boundary, &c., &c. In using this instrument, the ink must be inserted between the blades above the dotting wheel, so that, as the wheel revolves, the points shall pass through the ink, each carrying with it a drop, and marking the paper as it passes. It sometimes happens that the wheel will revolve many times before it begins to deposit its ink on the drawing, thereby leaving the first part of the line altogether blank, and in attempting to go over it again, the first made dots are liable to get blotted. This evil may be mostly remedied by placing a piece of blank paper over the drawing to the very point the dotted line is to commence at, then begin with drawing the wheel over the blank paper first, so that by the time it will have arrived at the proper point of commencement, the ink may be expected to flow over the points of the wheel, and make the dotted line perfect as required.

Fig. 55.

Drawing pins (fig. 56) are used to hold paper down upon a drawing or other board in any required position, and in most cases answer better than heavy weights, which are frequently used for that purpose, as the board may be shifted from place

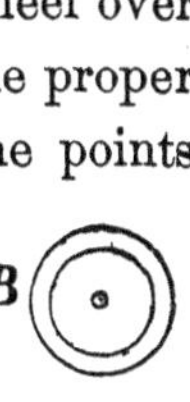

Fig. 56.

to place without moving the paper. They consist of a brass head, with a steel point at right angles to its plane. A represents it as seen edgewise, and B as seen from above.

SCALES.

Fig. 57 represents the usual scale to be found in the common boxes of drawing instruments. It contains, on its two sides, simply divided scales, a *diagonal scale* and a *protractor*. The simply divided scales consist of a series of equal divisions of an inch, which are numbered 1, 2, 3, &c., beginning from the second division on the left hand.

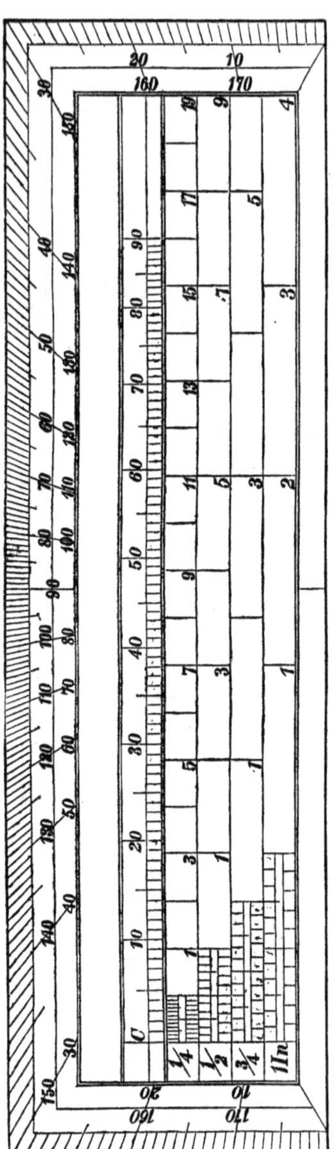

Fig. 57.

It will be seen (figs. 57, 58) that the different scales are marked 30, 35, 40, &c., and that the upper part of the left division in each is subdivided into twelve equal parts, and that the lower part of the same division is subdivided into ten equal parts. If now these last subdivisions or tenths be considered as units, one mile, or one chain, or one foot, then each primary division will represent ten units, ten miles, ten chains, or ten feet, and the scale is said to be 30, 35, 40 (according to the scale selected) miles, chains, or feet to the inch. Thus, suppose that it were required on a scale of 30 feet to the inch, to lay off 47 feet. On the scale marked 30, place one point of the compasses or dividers at 4, and bring the other point to the 7th lower subdivisions, counting from the right, and we have the distance required. Each of the primary divisions may be regarded as unit, one foot for instance; then the upper subdivisions are twelfths of a foot or inches, and the lower subdivisions tenths of an inch.

In fig. 57, the scales are marked at the

left, in., $\frac{1}{2}$, $\frac{1}{4}$, $\frac{1}{8}$, but the divisions and subdivisions are as above. In this fig., the primary divisions are one inch, $\frac{1}{2}$, $\frac{1}{4}$, and $\frac{1}{8}$ of an inch. These scales are more generally used for drawings of machinery and of architecture,

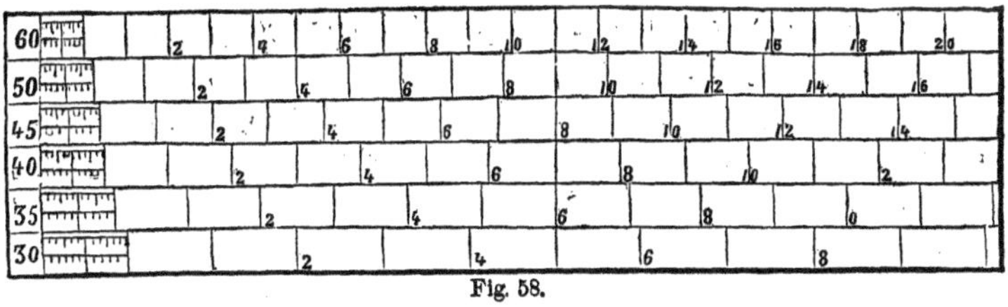

Fig. 58.

while fig. 58 are for topographical drawings. The application of these scales are similar to those already described. When the primary divisions are considered inches, then the drawings will be each full, $\frac{1}{2}$, $\frac{1}{4}$, or $\frac{1}{8}$ size, according to the scale adopted.

On the selection of the scale.—In all working architectural and mechanical drawings, use as large a scale as possible; neither depend, even in that case, that the mechanics employed in the construction will measure correctly, but write in the dimensions as far as practicable. For architectural plans, the scale of $\frac{1}{4}$ an inch to the foot is one of very general use, and convenient for the mechanic, as the common two-foot rule carried by all mechanics is subdivided into $\frac{1}{4}$ths, $\frac{1}{8}$ths, and sometimes sixteenths of an inch, and the distances on a drawing to this scale can therefore be easily measured by them. This fact should not be lost sight of in working drawings. When the dimensions are not written, make use of such scales that the distances may be measured by the division of the common two-foot rule; thus, in a scale of $\frac{1}{2}$ or $\frac{1}{4}$ full size, 6 inches or 3 inches represent one foot; in a scale of an inch to the foot or twelfth full size, each $\frac{1}{2}$ an inch represents 6 inches, $\frac{1}{4}$ 3 inches; but when $\frac{1}{3}$ or $\frac{1}{10}$ an inch to the foot, or any similar scale, is adopted, it is evident that these divisions cannot be taken by the two-foot rule. The scale should be written on every drawing, or the scale itself should be drawn on the margin. In topographical and geodesic drawings the latter is essential, as the scale adopted frequently has to be drawn for the specific purpose, and the paper itself contracts or expands with every atmospheric change, and the measurements will therefore not agree at all times with a detached scale; and moreover, a drawing laid down from such detached scale, of wood or ivory, will not be uniform throughout, for on a damp day the measurements will be too short, and on a dry day too long. Mr. Holtzapffel has sought to remedy this inconvenience by the introduction of *paper* scales; but all kinds of paper do not contract and expand equally, and the error is therefore only partially corrected by his ingenious substitution of one material for another.

Diagonal scales.—The simply divided scales give only two denominations, primaries and tenths, or twelfths; but more minute subdivision is attained by the diagonal scale, which consists of a number of primary divisions, one of which is divided into tenths, and subdivided into hundredths by diagonal lines (fig. 59). This scale is constructed in the following manner:—Eleven parallel lines are ruled, enclosing ten equal spaces; the length is set off into equal primary divisions, as DE, E1, &c.; the first DE is subdivided, and diagonals are then drawn from the subdivisions between A and B, to those between D and E, as shown in the diagram. Hence it is evident that at every parallel we get an additional tenth of the subdivisions, or a hundredth of the primaries, and can therefore obtain a measurement with great exactness to three places of figures. To take a measurement of (say) 168, we place one foot of the dividers on the primary 1, and carry it down to the ninth parallel, and then extend the other foot to the intersection of the diagonal, which falls from the subdivision 6, with the parallel that measures the eight-hundredth part (fig. 60). The primaries may of course be considered as yards, feet, or inches; and the subdivisions as tenths and hundredths of these respective denominations.

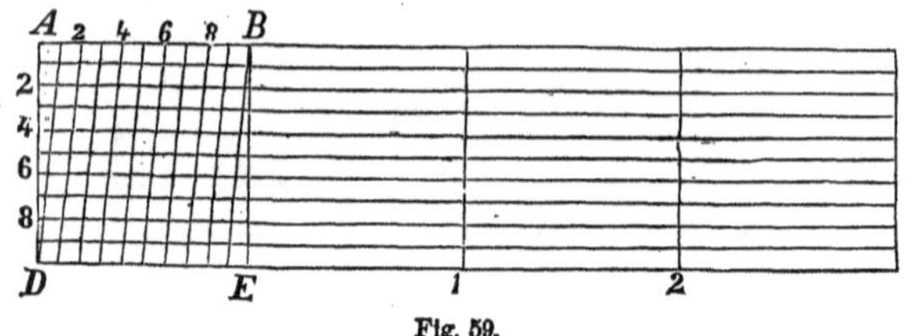

Fig. 59.

The diagonals may be applied to a scale where only one subdivision is required. Thus, if seven lines be (fig. 61) ruled, enclosing six equal spaces, and the length be divided into primaries, as AB, BC, &c., the first primary AB may be subdivided into twelfths by two diagonals running from 6, the middle of AB, to 12 and 0. We have here a very convenient scale of feet and inches. From C to 6 is 1 foot 6 inches; and from

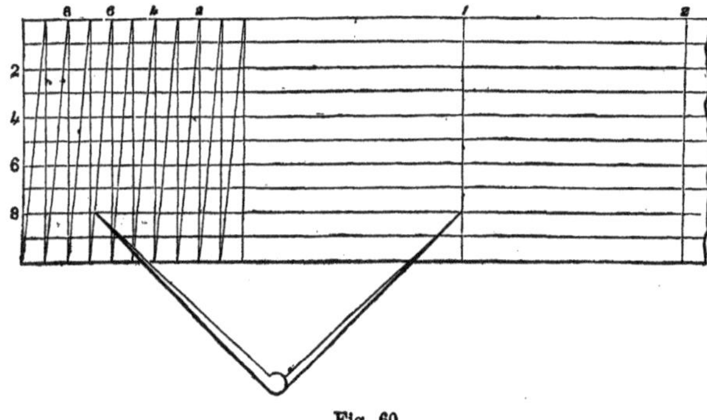

Fig. 60.

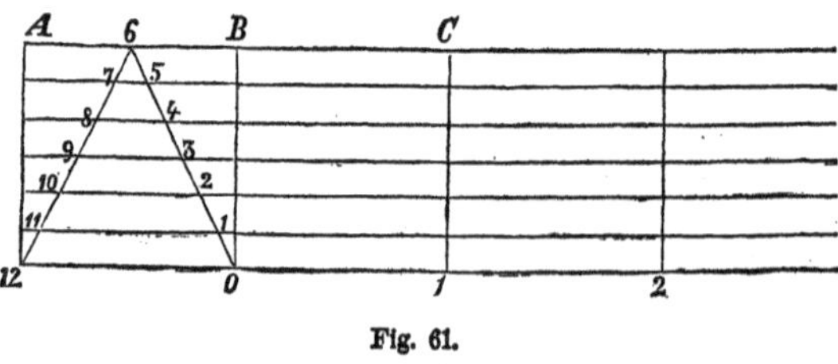

Fig. 61.

C on the several parallels to the various intersections of the diagonals, we obtain 1 foot and any number of inches from 1 to 12.

Plotting scales and rulers are scales of equal parts, with the divisions placed on a fiducial edge, by which any length may be pricked off on to the paper without using the compasses, whose points, by frequent use, destroy the fineness of the graduation.

On the scale (fig. 57) in common boxes of drawing instruments, the edge of one side is divided as a *protractor*, for the laying out of angles. The instrument, when by itself, consists of a semicircle of thin metal or

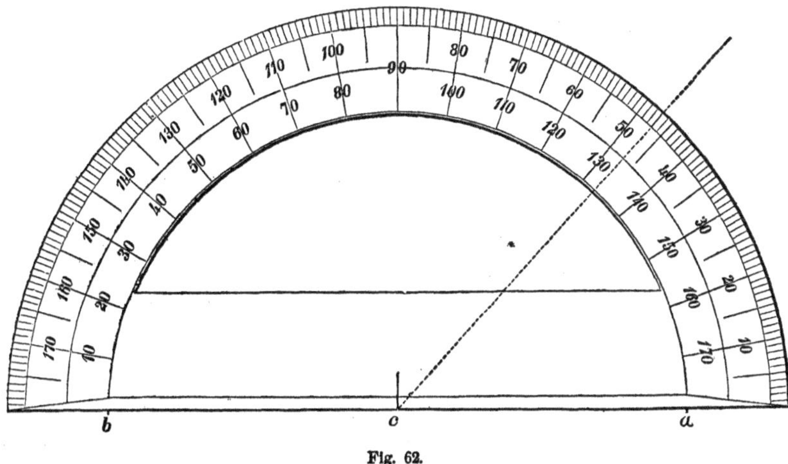

Fig. 62.

horn (fig. 62), whose circumference is divided into 180 equal parts or degrees (180°). In the larger protractors each of these divisions is subdivided.

Application of the protractor.—To lay off a given angle from a given point on a straight line, let the straight line *a b* of the protractor coincide with the given line, and the point *c* with the given point; now mark on the paper against the division on the periphery, coinciding with the angle required; remove the protractor, and draw a line through the given point, and the mark.

The instruments already described are those to be found in the usual cases of drawing instruments, and are sufficient for all the ordinary purpose of draughtsmen; but there are others adapted to special purpose, or of careful and elaborate workmanship, which are useful where great accuracy and finish are required, and of some of which descriptions will be given.

Vernier scales are preferred by some to the diagonal scale already described. To construct a vernier scale by which a number to three places may be taken, divide all the primary divisions into tenths, and number these subdivisions 1, 2, 3, from left to right. Take off now with the compasses eleven of these subdivisions, set the extent off backwards from the end of the first primary division, and it will reach beyond the beginning of this division, or zero point, a distance equal to one of the subdivisions. Now divide the extent thus set off into ten equal parts, marking the divisions on the opposite side of the divided line to the strokes marking the primary divisions and the subdivisions, and number them 1, 2, 3, &c., backwards from right to left. Then, since the extent of eleven subdivisions has been divided into ten equal parts, so that these ten parts exceed by one subdivision the extent of ten subdivisions, each one of these equal parts, or, as it may be called, one division of the vernier scale, exceeds one of the subdivisions by a tenth part of a subdivision, or a hundredth part of a primary division.

To take off the number 253 from this scale. Increase the first figure 2 by 1, making it 3; because the vernier scale commences at the end of the

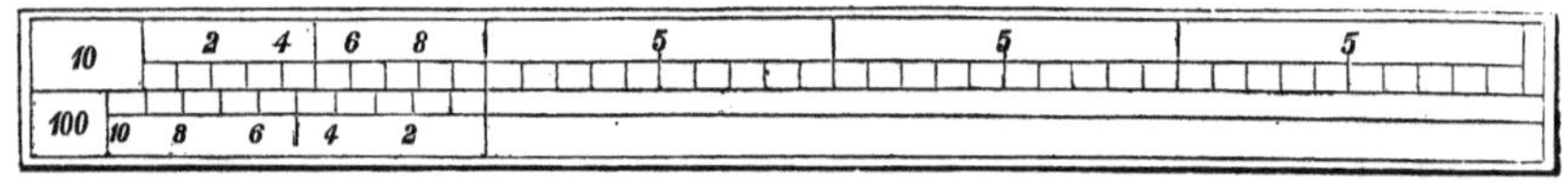

Fig. 63.

first primary division, and the primary divisions are measured from this point, and not from the zero point. The first thus increased with the second now represents 35 of the subdivisions from the zero point, from which the third figure, 3, must be subtracted, leaving 32; since three divisions of the vernier scale will contain three of these subdivisions, together with three-tenths of a subdivision. Place, then, one point of the compasses upon the third division of the vernier scale, and extend the other point to the 32d subdivision, or the second division beyond the 3d primary division, and laying down the distance between the points of the compass, it will represent 253, or 25·3, or 2·53, according as the primary divisions are taken as hundreds, tens, or units.

General rule.—To take off any number to three places of figures upon this vernier scale. Increase the first figure by one; subtract the third figure from the second, borrowing one from the first increased figure, if necessary, and extend the compasses from the division upon the vernier scale, indicated by the third figure, to the subdivision indicated by the number remaining after performing the above subtraction.

On some of the plain scales in the instrument boxes will be found divisions marked as in fig. 64. Many of the divisions here laid down have no application to drawing, according to the scope of this work; a brief explanation and application will therefore only be given. Under definitions and technicalities, the signification of the terms chords, tangents, sines, and secants, has been defined. The chord of 60° is equal to radius, or half

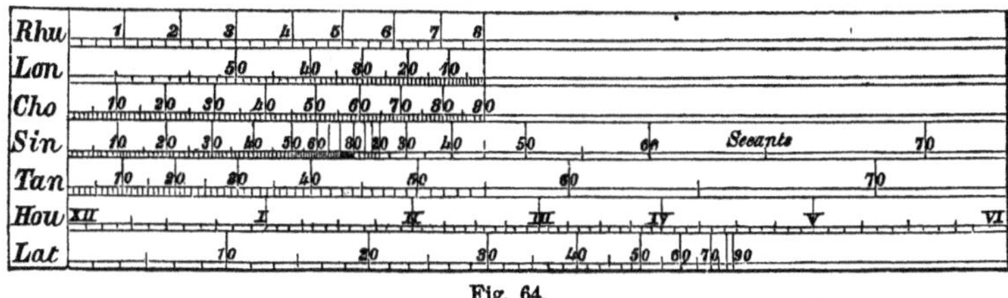

Fig. 64.

the diameter. The line of chords is used to set off an angle, or to measure an angle already laid down.

To set off an angle.—An angle of 35° for instance: open the compasses to the extent of 60° on the scale of chords, setting one point at A on the line A B, describe with the other point an arc; again with the compasses open to the extent of 35° on the scale, setting one point on B, describe an arc, cutting the arc B C; through this intersection and the point A, draw the line A C, and we have the angle C A B, 35°.

To measure the angle contained by the straight lines A B and A C already laid down. Open the compasses to the extent of 60° on the line of chords, as before, and with this radius describe the arc B C, cutting A B and A C, produced, if necessary, in the points B and C; then, extending the compasses from B to C, place one point of the compasses on the beginning or zero point, of the line of chords, and the other point will extend to the number upon this line, indicating the degrees in the angle B A C.

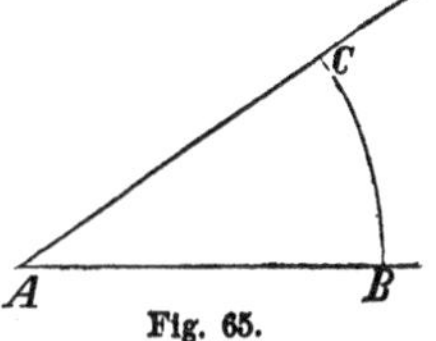

Fig. 65.

The lines of sines, secants, tangents, and semitangents are principally used for the several projections, or perspective representations, of the circles of the sphere, by means of which maps are constructed.

The line of rhumbs is a scale of the chords of the angles of deviation from the meridian denoted by the several points and quarter points of the compass, enabling the navigator, without computation, to lay down or measure a ship's course upon a chart.

The line of longitudes shows the number of equatorial miles in a degree of longitude on the parallels of latitude indicated by the degrees on the corresponding points of the line of chords. *Example.*—A ship in latitude 60° N. sailing E. 79 miles, required the difference of longitude between the beginning and end of her course. Opposite 60 on the line of chords stands 30 on the line of longitudes, which is, therefore, the number of equatorial miles in a degree of longitude at that latitude. Hence, as 30 : 79 : : 60 : 158 miles, the required difference of longitude.

The *sector* (fig. 66) consists of two flat rulers united by a central joint, and opening like a pair of compasses. It carries several plain scales on its faces, but its most important lines are in pairs, running accurately to the central joint.

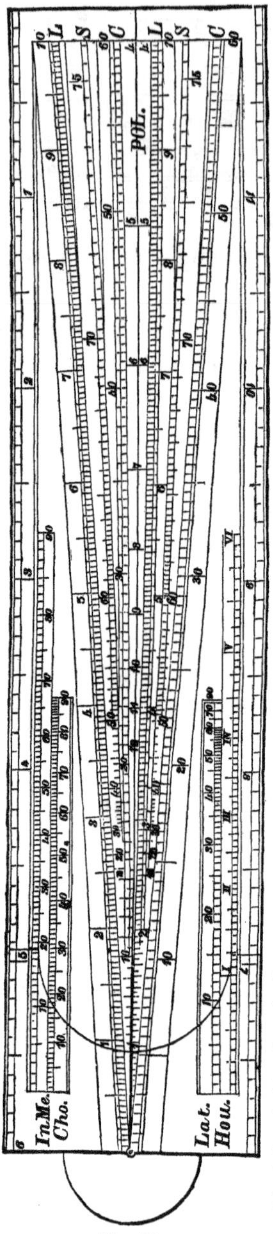

Plain scales on the sector.—On the outer edge of the sector is usually given a decimal scale from 1 to 100; and in connection with it, on one of the sides, a scale of inches and tenths. These are identical with the lines on the plain scale, previously mentioned, but the latter are more commodiously placed for use. On the other side we have logarithmic lines of numbers, sines, and tangents.

Sectoral double scales.—These are respectively named the Lines of Lines, Chords, Secants, Sines, and Tangents. These scales have one line on each ruler, and the two lines converge accurately in the central joint of the sector.

Fig. 66.

The principle on which the double scales are constructed is, that similar triangles have their like sides proportional. Let the lines A B, A C, represent the legs of the sector, and A D, A E, two equal sections from the centre; then, if the points B C and D E be connected, the lines B C and D E will be parallel; therefore, the triangles A B C, A D E, will be similar, and consequently the sides A B, B C, A D, D E, proportional, that is, as A B : B C :: A D : D E; so that if A D be the half, third, or fourth part of A B, then D E will be a half, third, or fourth part of B C; and the same holds of all the rest. Hence, if D E be the chord, sine, or tangent of any arc, or of any number of degrees to the radius A D, then B C will be the same to the radius A B. Thus at every opening of the sector, the *transverse* distances D E and C B from one ruler to another, are proportional to the *lateral* distances, measured on the lines A B, A C. It is to be observed, that all measures are to be taken from the inner lines, since these only run accurately to the centre.

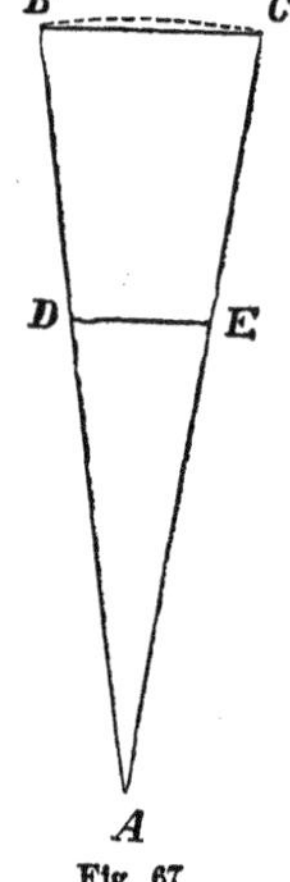

Fig. 67.

The line of lines, marked L on each leg of the sector.—This is a line of 10 primaries, each subdivided into tenths, thus making 100 divisions. Its use is, to divide a given line into any number of equal parts; to give accurate scale measures for the construction of a drawing; to form any required scale; to divide a given line in any assigned proportion; and to find third, fourth, and middle proportionals to given right lines.

To divide a given line into eight equal parts.—Take the line in the compasses, and open the sector so as to apply it transversely to 8 and 8, then the transverse from 1 to 1 will be the eighth part of the line.

To form any required scale of equal parts.—Take one inch in the compasses, and open the sector, till this extent becomes a transverse distance at the division indicating the number of parts in an inch of the required scale.

Example.—To adjust the sector as a scale of one inch to four chains.—Make one inch the transverse distance of 4 and 4; then the transverse distances of the other corresponding divisions and subdivisions will represent the number of chains and links indicated by these divisions: thus, the transverse distance from 3 to 3 will represent three chains.

To construct a scale of feet and inches in such a manner, that an extent of three inches shall represent twenty inches.—Make three inches a transverse distance between 10 and 10, and the transverse distance of 6 and 6 will represent 12 inches. Set off this extent, divide it into 12 equal parts, each of these divisions will represent inches. Place the figure 0 at the right, and set off again the extent of the whole twelve parts, from 0 to 1, 1 to 2, &c., to represent the feet.

Proportion.—Two lines being given, to find a third proportional.

Example.—The given lines = 2 and 6, a third proportional required. Take between the compasses the lateral distance of the second term 6 on any convenient scale, and open the sector until this distance becomes the transverse distance to the first term 2; then the transverse distance of the second term 6, measured upon the same scale as the former, will equal 18, the third proportional required.

Example.—to find a fourth proportional to the numbers 2, 6, and 10.

Take the lateral distance of the second term 6, from any convenient scale of equal parts, and open the sector until that quantity, or any aliquot part thereof, becomes the transverse distance of the first term 2, then the transverse distance of the third term 10, taken from the same scale of equal parts, will give 30, the fourth proportional required.

Line of Chords, marked C on each leg of the sector. The double scales of chords upon the sector are more useful than the single line of chords described on the plane scale; for on the sector, the radius with which the arc is to be described may be of any length less than the transverse distance of 60 and 60 when the legs are opened as far as the instrument will admit of. But with the chords on the plane scale, the arc described must be always of the same radius.

To protract an angle B A C, which shall contain a given number of degrees, suppose 36°.

Make the transverse distance of 60 and 60 equal to the length of the radius of the circle, and with that opening describe the arc B C.

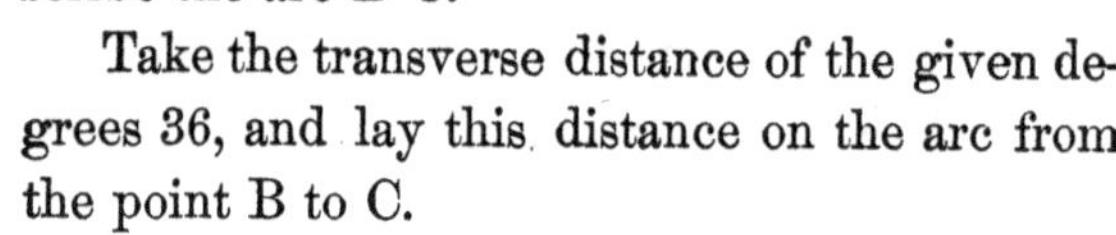

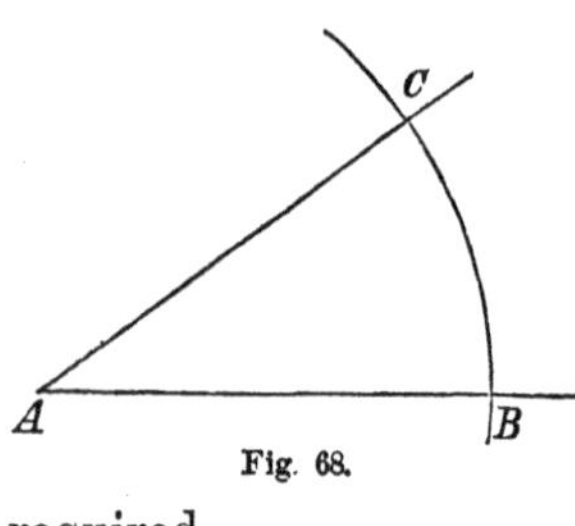

Fig. 68.

Take the transverse distance of the given degrees 36, and lay this distance on the arc from the point B to C.

From the centre A of the arc, draw A C, A B, and these two lines will contain the angle required.

To protract an angle of more than 60°, divide the required angle by 2 or 3, and set off as above twice or thrice the arc.

From what has been said about the protracting of an angle to contain a given number of degrees, it will easily be seen how to find the degrees (or measure) of an angle already laid down.

Line of Polygons.—The line of polygons is chiefly useful for the ready division of the circumference of a circle into any number of equal parts from 4 to 12; that is, as a ready means to inscribe regular polygons of any given number of sides, from 4 to 12, within a given circle. To do which, set off the radius of the given circle (which is always equal to the side of an inscribed hexagon) as the transverse distance of 6 and 6 upon the line of polygons. Then the transverse distance of 4 and 4 will be the side of a square; the transverse of 5 and 5 the side of a pentagon.

If it be required to form a polygon, upon a given right line set off the extent of the given line, as a transverse distance between the points upon the line of polygons, answering to the number of sides of which the polygon is to consist, as for a pentagon between 5 and 5, or for an octagon between 8 and 8; then the transverse distance between 6 and 6 will be the radius of a circle, whose circumference would be divided by the given line into the number of sides required.

All regular polygons, whose number of sides will exactly divide 360 (the number of degrees into which all circles are supposed to be divided) without a remainder, may likewise be set off upon the circumference of a circle by the line of chords. Thus, take the radius of the circle between the compasses, and open the sector till that extent becomes the transverse distance between 60 and 60 upon the line of chords; then having divided 360 by the required number of sides, the transverse distance between the numbers of the quotient will be the side of the polygon required. Thus, for an octagon, take the distance between 45 and 45; and for a polygon of 36 sides, take the distance between 10 and 10, &c.

Lines of sines, tangents and secants.—Given, the radius of a circle, required the sine and tangent of 28° 30′ *to that radius*—

Open the sector, so that the transverse distance of 90 and 90 on the sines, or of 45 and 45 on the tangents, may be equal to the given radius; then will the transverse distance of 28° 30′, taken from the sines, be the length of that sine to the given radius; or if taken from the tangents, will be the length of that tangent to the given radius.

But if the secant of 28° 30′ *was required*—

Make the given radius a transverse distance of 0 and 0, at the beginning of the line of secants, and then take the transverse distance of the degrees wanted, viz., 28° 30′.

A tangent greater than 45 *degrees* (*suppose* 60) *is found thus:*

Make the given radius a transverse distance to 45, and 45 at the beginning of the scale of upper tangents, and then the required degrees (60) may be taken from the scale.

Given the length of the sine, tangent, or secant of any degrees, to find the length of the radius to that sine, tangent, or secant.

Make the given length a transverse distance to its given degrees on its respective scale. Then

<table>
<tr><td>If a sine,</td><td rowspan="4">the transverse distance of</td><td>90 and 90 on the sines</td><td rowspan="4">will be the radius sought.</td></tr>
<tr><td>If a tangent under 45°,</td><td>45 and 45 on the tangents</td></tr>
<tr><td>If a tangent above 45°,</td><td>45 and 45 on the upper tangents</td></tr>
<tr><td>If a secant,</td><td>0 and 0 on the secants</td></tr>
</table>

To find the length of a versed sine to a given number of degrees, and a given radius.

Make the transverse distance of 90 and 90 on the sine equal to the given radius. Take the transverse distance of the complement of the sine of the given number of degrees. If the given number of degrees is less than 90, subtract the complement of the sine from the radius, the remainder will be the versed sine.

If the given number of degrees are more than 90, add the complement of the sine to the radius, and the sum will be the versed sine.

To open the legs of a sector, so that the corresponding double scales of lines, chords, sines, tangents, may make each a right angle.

On the line of lines, make the lateral distance 10, a transverse distance between 8 on one leg and 6 on the other leg.

On the line of sines, make the lateral distance 90, a transverse distance from 45 to 45, or from 40 to 50, or from 30 to 60, or from the sine of any degrees to their complement.

On the line of tangents, make the lateral distance of 45 a transverse distance between 30 and 30.

Marquois's scales (fig. 69).—These scales consist of a right-angled triangle, of which the hypothenuse or longest side is three times the length of the shortest, and a rectangular rule. Our figure, which is drawn one-third the actual size of the instruments from which it is taken, represents the triangle and a rule, as being used to draw a series of parallel lines. The rule is one foot long, and has, parallel to each of its edges, two scales, one placed close to the edge, and the other immediately

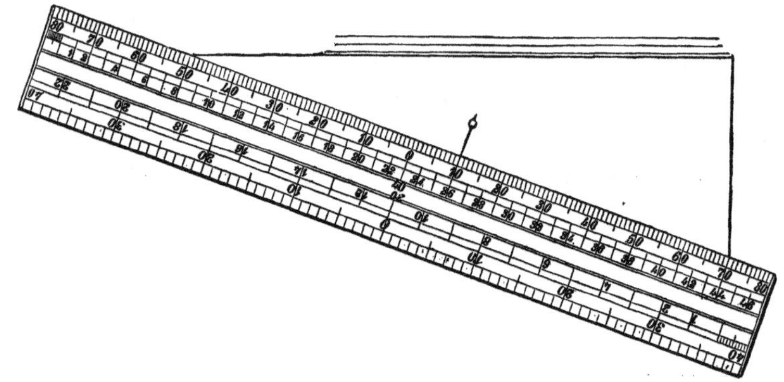

within this, the outer being termed the artificial, and the inner the natural scale. The divisions upon the outer scale are three times the length of those upon the inner scale, so as to bear the same proportion to each other that the longest side of the triangle bears to the shortest. In the artificial scales, the zero point is placed in the middle of the edge of the rule, and the primary divisions are numbered both ways from this point to the two ends of the rule, and are every one subdivided into ten equal parts, each of which is, consequently, three times the length of a subdivision of the corresponding natural scale.

The triangle has a short line drawn perpendicular to the hypothenuse near the middle of it, to serve as an index or pointer; and the longest of the other two sides has a sloped edge.

To draw a line parallel to a given line, at a given distance from it.—1. Having applied the given distance to the one of the natural scales which is found to measure it most conveniently, place the triangle with its sloped edge coincident with the given line, or rather at such small distance from it, that the pen or pencil passes directly over it when drawn along this edge. 2. Set the rule closely against the hypothenuse, making the zero point of the corresponding artificial scale coincide with the index upon the triangle. 3. Move the triangle along the rule, to the left or right according as the required line is to be above or below the given line, until the index coincides with the division or subdivision corresponding to the number of divisions or subdivisions of the natural scale, which measures the given distance; and the line drawn along the sloped edge in its new position will be the line required.

The natural scale may be used advantageously in setting off the distances in a drawing, and the corresponding artificial scale in drawing parallels at required distances.

The advantages of Marquois's scales are: 1st, that the sight is greatly assisted by the divisions on the artificial scale being so much larger than those of the natural scale to which the drawing is constructed; 2d, that any error in the setting of the index produces an error of but one-third the amount in the drawing.

If the triangle be accurately constructed, these scales may be advantageously used for dividing lines with accuracy and despatch.

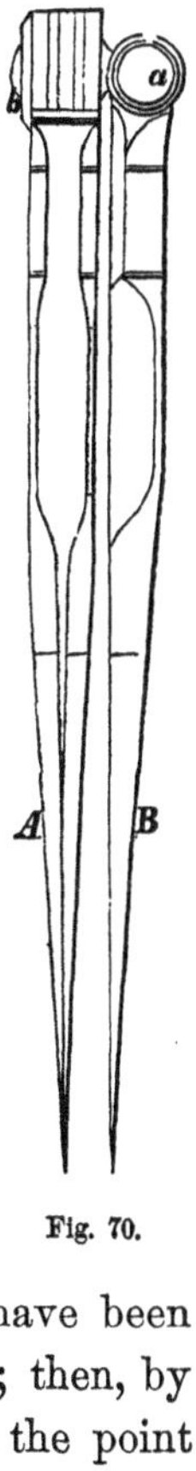

Triangular compasses.—Fig. 70 represents this instrument closed up. That which appears in the fig. as one limb A, consists of a pair of compasses of the ordinary construction. The single point limb B has a compass joint at *a*, by which its point may be opened at right angles to the plane of the pair of compasses A, when the three points will form a triangle. The compass joint *a* is firmly attached to the centre of the compasses A, which, by means of a nut and screw *b*, may be turned round without moving the limbs, of which it is the centre. The double motion thus given to the point limb B (both at right angles to, and parallel to the plane of the compasses A), partakes of the nature of a universal joint, and enables the three points of the instrument to be placed at the angular points of any shaped triangle whatever. This instrument is chiefly useful in transferring of points from one paper to another. The two points of the compasses A being set upon such points of the drawing as have been already copied, the third, B, is brought upon any other point; then, by applying the points A to the corresponding points on the copy, the point B will establish the other and new point on the copy.

Fig. 70.

Wholes and halves.—For copying and reducing drawing to half size, compasses called wholes and halves are used (fig. 71), in which the longer legs being twice the length of the shorter, when the former are opened to any given line, the shorter ones will be opened to the half of that line. By their means then, all the lines of a drawing may be reduced to one-half, or enlarged to double their length. These compasses are also useful for dividing lines by continual bisections.

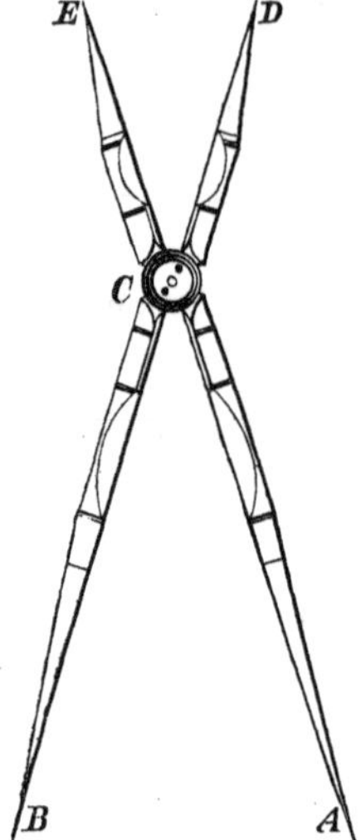

Fig. 71.

The *proportional* compasses (fig. 72) are somewhat similar in their construction to wholes and halves, but of more varied application. The principle is the same, with this difference, that the screw-joint C passes through slides moving in the slots of the bars, and admits of the centre being adjusted for various relative proportions between the openings A B and D E. Different sets of numbers are engraved on the outer faces of the bars, and by these the required proportions are obtained. The instrument must be closed for adjustment, and the nut C loosened; the slide is then moved in the groove, until a mark across it, named the index, coincides with the number required; which done, the nut is tightened again.

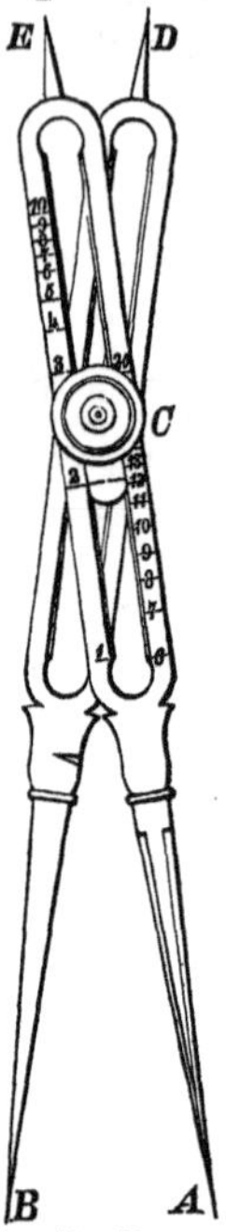

Fig. 72.

The scales usually engraved on these compasses are named Lines, Circles, Planes, and Solids.

The scale of lines is numbered from 1 to 10, and the index of the slide being brought to any one of these divisions, the distance D E will measure A B in that proportion. Thus, if the index be set to 4, D E will be contained four times in A B.

The line of circles extends from 1 to 20, and the index being set to (say) 10, D E will be the tenth part of the circumference of the circle, whose radius is A B.

The line of planes, or squares, determines the proportion of similar areas. Thus, if the index is placed at 3, and the side of any one square be taken by A B from a scale of equal parts, D E will be the side of another square of one-third the area. And if any number be brought to the index, and the same number be taken by A B from a scale of equal parts, D E will be the square root of that number. And in this latter case, D E will also be a mean proportional between any two numbers, whose product is equal to A B.

The line of solids expresses the proportion between cubes and spheres. Thus, if the index be set at 2, and the diameter of a sphere, or the side of a cube, be taken from a scale of equal parts by A B, then will D E be a diameter or side of a sphere or cube of half the solidity. And if the slide be set to (say) 8, and the same number be taken from a scale of equal parts, then will D E measure 2 on the same scale, or the cube root of 8.

Beam compasses (fig. 73).—When it is required to set off with accuracy distances of considerable extent, or describe arcs of over a foot radius, the beam compass is used. This instrument consists of a beam, A A, of any length required, generally made of well-seasoned mahogany; upon its

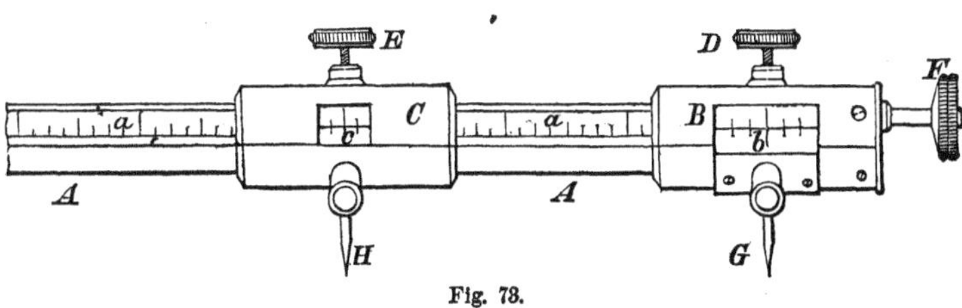

Fig. 73.

face is inlaid throughout its whole length a slip of holly or boxwood, *a a*, upon which are engraved the divisions or scale, either feet and decimals or inches and decimals, or whatever particular scale may be required; but ordinary beam compasses are constructed with a plain beam, with no scale whatever. Two brass boxes, B and C, are adapted to the beam; the latter may be moved, by sliding, to any part of its length, and fixed in position by tightening the clamp screw E. Connected with the brass boxes are the two points of the instrument G and H, which may have any extent of opening by sliding the box C along the beam, the other box, B, being firmly fixed at one extremity. The object to be attained in the use of this instrument, is the nice adjustment of the points G H to any definite distance apart; this is accomplished by two vernier or reading plates *b c*, each fixed at the side of an opening in the brass boxes to which they are attached, and afford the means of minutely subdividing the principal divisions *a a* on the beam, which appear through those openings. D is a clamp screw for a similar purpose as the screw E, namely, to fix the box B, and prevent motion in the point it carries after adjustment to position. F is a slow motion screw, by which the point G may be moved any very minute quantity for perfecting the setting of the instrument, after it has been set as nearly as possible by the hand alone.

The method of setting the instrument for use may be understood from the above description of its parts, and also by the following explanation of the method of examining and correcting the adjustment of the vernier *b*, which will occasionally get deranged; this verification must be done by means of a detached scale. Thus, suppose, for example, that our beam compass is divided to feet, inches, and tenths, and subdivided by the vernier to hundredths, &c. First set the zero division of the vernier to the zero of the principal divisions on the beam, by means of the slow motion screw F. This must be done very nicely. Then slide the box C, with its point G, till the zero on the vernier *c* exactly coincides with any principal division on the beam, as twelve inches or six inches, &c., which must also be done very accurately; then apply the points to a similar detached scale, and if the adjustment is perfect, the interval of the points G H will measure on it the distance to which they were set on the beam. If they do not by ever so small a quantity, it should be corrected by turning the screw F till the points exactly measure that quantity on the detached scale; then, by loosening the little screws which hold the vernier *b* in its place, the position of the vernier may be gradually changed, till its zero coincides with the zero on the beam, and then tightening the screws again, the adjustment will be complete.

Portable or turn-in compasses (fig. 74) forms in itself a complete portable case of drawing instruments, consisting of a large pair of compasses with movable points, which are also so contrived, that one forms in itself a small pencil bow, the other a pen bow; and when the whole instrument is put together and folded up, they occupy but a space three inches long, and may be carried in the pocket without being an incumbrance.

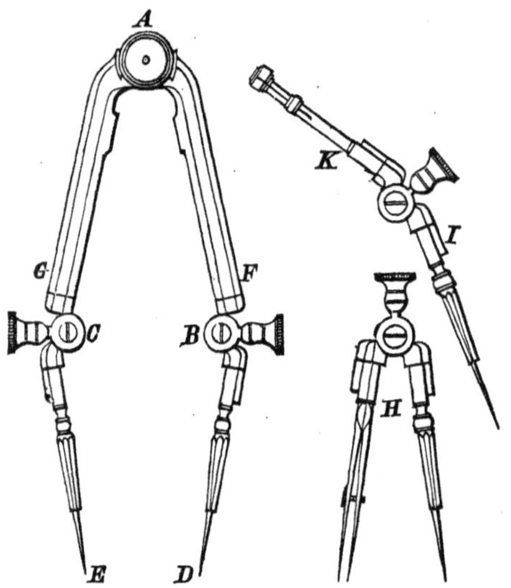

Fig. 74.

Fig. 74 represents the instrument when all its parts are together. The principal legs of the instrument are F and G, movable as usual by a joint at A. The lower joints, B and C, afford the means of setting the point limbs D and E perpendicular to the paper.

Each of the point limbs may be removed from the legs F and G, and by means of their joints B and C, form perfect instruments, the one a pen bow represented at H, and the other a pencil bow, shown at I K; the point limbs of these lesser instruments are all adapted to slide into the principal legs F and G of the larger one, which are made hollow for their reception.

It may easily be seen from the engraving, that by reversing either of the points in the principal instrument, it may be supplied with a pen or pencil as may be required, leaving the other fine or plain point E or D to act as a centre.

Mr. Brunel has introduced what are called Tubular Compasses, in which the upper part of the legs lengthens out like the slide of a telescope, thus giving greater extent of radius when required. The movable legs are double, having points at one end, and a pencil or pen at the other; and they move on pivots, so that the pen or pencil can be instantly substituted for the points, or *vice versa*, and that with the certainty of a perfect adjustment. The design is very ingenious, and offers many conveniences, but the instrument is too delicate for ordinary hands. Without extreme care it is soon disarranged.

Large screw dividers (fig. 75) are used for accurately dividing lines into a definite number of equal parts, or for setting off equal distances. A is the centre about which the legs A C and A B open or shut. B and C are joints, by which the point limbs may be set perpendicular as usual; the extent or opening between the points is regulated by a screw passing through a socket F, and terminated at the other extremity by a milled head E, by which the screw is turned round. Between this milled head and the nearest point limb is fixed what is called a micrometer head, decimally divided round its outer or cylindrical edge. One turn of the screw carries the micrometer head completely round; therefore, when part of a turn only is given to the screw, the divisions on the head show what fraction of a turn has been given, and if it be known what number of turns or threads of the screw are equal to one inch, the points of these compasses may be thus set to any small definite measure of length with the utmost precision. The index or zero for reading the fraction of a turn of the screw is marked on the point limb below B. Thus this instrument may be considered as a beam compass of small dimensions and minute accuracy.

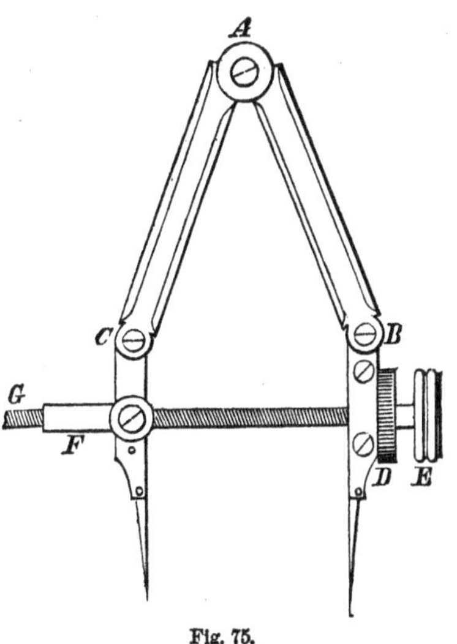

Fig. 75.

The circular protractor (fig. 76) is one of the best kind of protractors. It is a complete circle, A A, connected with its centre by four radii, *a a a a*. The centre is left open, and surrounded by a concentric ring or collar, *b*, which carries two radial bars, *c c*. To the extremity of one bar is a pinion, *d*, working in a toothed rack quite round the outer circumference of the protractor. To the opposite extremity of the other bar, *c*, is fixed a vernier, which subdivides the primary divisions on the protractor to single minutes, and by estimation to 30 seconds. This vernier is carried round the protractor by turning the pinion *d*. Upon each radial bar *c c*, is placed a branch *e e*, carrying at their extremities a fine steel pricker, whose points are kept above the surface of the paper by springs placed under their supports, which give way when the branches are pressed downwards, and allow the points to make the necessary punctures in the paper. The branches *e e* are attached to the bars *c c*, with a joint which admits of their being folded backwards over the instrument when not in use, and for packing in its case. The centre of the instrument is represented by the intersection of two lines drawn at right angles to each other on a piece of plate glass, which enables the person using it to place it, so that the centre, or intersection of the cross lines, may coincide with any given point on the plan. If the instrument is in correct order, a line connecting the fine pricking points with each other would pass through the centre of the instrument, as denoted by the before-mentioned intersection of the cross lines upon the glass. In using this instrument, the vernier should first be set to zero (or the division marked 360) on the divided limb, and then

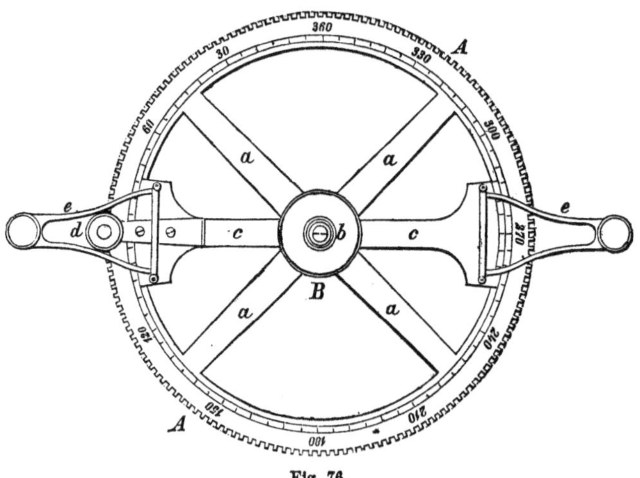

Fig. 76.

placed on the paper, so that the two fine steel points may be on the given line (from whence other and angular lines are to be drawn), and the centre of the instrument coincides with the given angular point on such line. This done, press the protractor gently down, which will fix it in position by means of very fine points on the under side. It is now ready to lay off the given angle, or any number of angles that may be required, which is done by turning the pinion *d* till the opposite vernier reads the required angle. Then press downwards the branches *e e*, which will cause the points to make punctures in the paper at opposite sides of the circle; which being afterwards connected, the line will pass through the given angular point, if the instrument was first correctly set. In this manner, at one setting of the instrument, a great number of angles may be laid off from the same point.

It is not essential that the centre be over the given point, when applied to the given line, provided the pricking points exactly fall upon the line, for the inclined line may be transferred to pass through the given angular point by a parallel ruler.

The *pentagraph* (fig. 77) is used for the copying of drawings either on

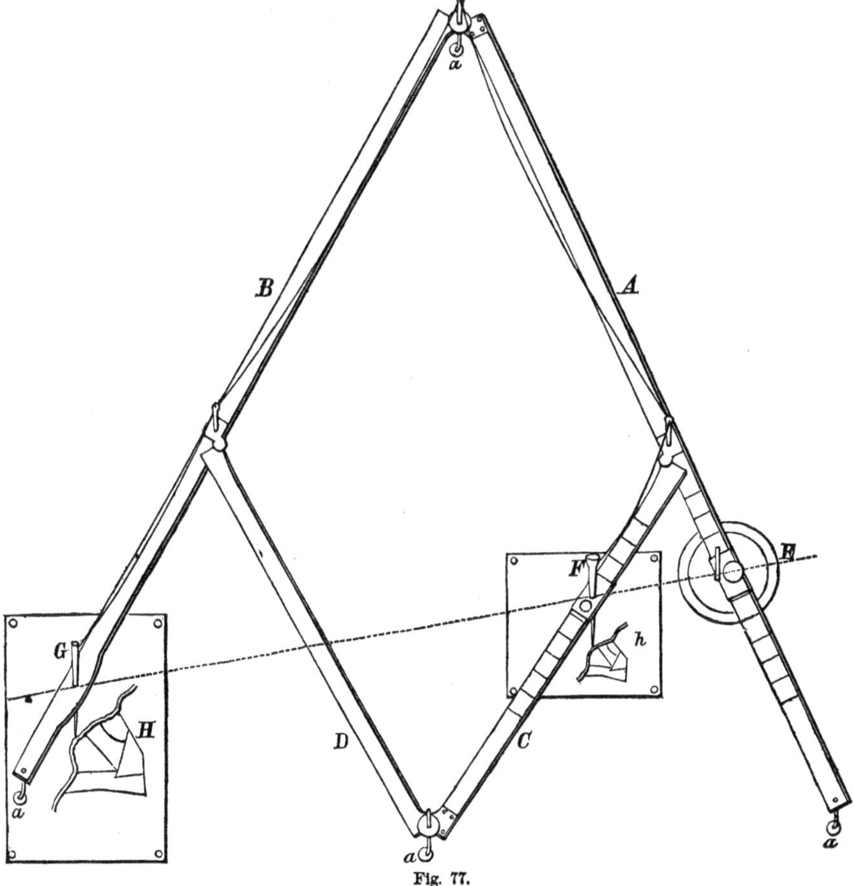

Fig. 77.

the same scale, on a reduced scale, or on an enlarged scale, as may be required. It is represented (fig. 77) as in the act of copying a plan H, upon a reduced scale *h*. The pentagraph consists of four rulers, A, B, C, and D, made of stout brass. The two longer rulers, A and B, are connected together by, and have a motion round a centre, shown at the upper part of the engraving. The two shorter rulers are, in like manner, connected with each other, and with the longer rulers. The whole instrument is supported by small pillars resting upon ivory castors, *a a a*, &c., which have a motion in all directions. The rulers A and C have each an equal number of similar divisions, marked $\frac{1}{4}$, $\frac{1}{2}$, &c.; and likewise a sliding index, E and F, which can be fixed to any divisions on the ruler by a milled-headed clamp screw shown in the engraving. The sliding indexes, E and F, have each of them a tube adapted to slide on a pin, rising from a heavy circular weight called the fulcrum, which acts as a centre for the whole instrument to turn upon when in use, or to receive a sliding holder with a pencil or a tracing point, as may be required.

To explain the method of using the instrument, the engraving represents the instrument in the act of reducing a plan to a scale of one half the original. For this purpose the tracing point is fixed in a socket at G, over the original drawing H. The pencil is placed in a similar tube or socket at F, over the paper, to receive the copy; and the fulcrum is fixed to that at E, the scale being one half the original. The sliding indices were first clamped at those divisions on the rulers marked $\frac{1}{2}$. The instrument being thus set for use, if correct, the three points, E, F, and G, will be in one straight line, as shown by the dotted line in the figure. This will invariably be the case at whatever division the indices may be set to. Now, if the tracing point G be passed delicately and steadily over every line of the plan H, a true copy, but of one half the scale of the original, will be marked by the pencil at F on the paper *h* beneath it. The fine thread represented as passing from the pencil quite round the further extremity of the instrument to the tracer at G, is to enable the draftsman at the tracing point to raise the pencil from the paper, whilst he passes the tracer from one part of the original to another, and prevents false lines being made on the copy. Likewise, it may be noticed, that the pencil holder F is represented as surmounted by a cup, which is for the purpose of putting some small shot in, to press the pencil heavier upon the paper, whenever such expedient may be found necessary.

If the object had been to enlarge the drawing to double its scale, then the tracer must have been placed at F, and the pencil at G. And if a copy be required, retaining the scale of the original, then the slides E and F must be placed at the divisions marked 1. The fulcrum must take the middle station, and the pencil and tracer those on the exterior rules A and B of the instrument.

The *camera lucida* is sometimes used for copying and reducing topographical drawings. A description of the use of this instrument will be found under the head of topographical drawing.

The drawing table and drawing board.—The usual size of the drawing table should be from 5 to 6 feet long, and 3 feet wide, of $1\frac{1}{2}$ or 2 inch white pine plank well seasoned, without any knots, closely joined, glued, dowelled, and clamped. It should be fixed on a strong firm frame and legs, and of such a height that the draughtsman, as he stands up, may not have to stoop to his work. The table is usually provided with a shallow drawer to hold paper or drawings. Drawing tables are made portable, by having two horses for their supports, and a movable drawing board for the top; this board is made similar to the top of the drawing table, but of inch boards, and barred at the ends. Various woods are used for the purposes, but white pine is by far the cheapest and best. Drawing boards should be made truly rectangular, and with perfectly straight sides for the use of the T square. Two sizes are sufficient for common purposes, 41 × 30 inches to carry double elephant paper with a margin, and 31 × 24 inches for imperial and smaller sizes. Boards smaller than this are too light and unsteady in handling.

Small boards are occasionally made, as loose panels fitting into a frame, flush on the drawing surface, with buttons on the back to secure it in position. The panel is mostly of white pine, with a hard-wood frame.

DRAWING PAPER.

Drawing paper, properly so called, is made to certain standard sizes as follows:—

Demy	20 inches	by	$15\frac{1}{4}$	inches.
Medium,	$22\frac{3}{4}$	"	$17\frac{1}{2}$	"
Royal,	24	"	$19\frac{1}{4}$	"
Super Royal,	$27\frac{1}{4}$	"	$19\frac{1}{4}$	"
Imperial,	30	"	22	"
Elephant,	28	"	23	"
Columbier,	35	"	$23\frac{1}{2}$	"
Atlas,	34	"	26	"
Double Elephant,	40	"	27	"
Antiquarian,	53	"	31	"
Emperor,	68	"	48	"

Of these, Double Elephant is the largest in common use by engineers, and it is the most generally useful size of sheet. Demy and Imperial are the only other sizes worth providing for a drawing establishment. Whatman's white paper is the quality most usually employed for finished drawings; it will bear wetting and stretching without injury, and when so treated, receives color readily. For ordinary working drawings, where damp-stretching is dispensed with, cartridge paper, of a coarser, harder, and tougher quality, is preferable. It bears the use of indiarubber better, receives ink on the original undamped surface more freely, shows a fully better line, and as it does not absorb very rapidly, tinting lies better and more evenly upon it. For delicate small-scale line-drawing, the thick blue paper, such as is used for ledgers, &c., imperial size, answers exceedingly well; but it does not bear damp-stretching without injury, and should be merely pinned or waxed down to the board. With good management, there is no ground to fear the shifting of the paper. Good letter paper receives light drawing very well; of course it does not bear much fatigue.

Large sheets, destined for rough usage and frequent reference, should be mounted on linen, previously damped, with a free application of paste.

Tracing paper is a preparation of tissue paper, transparent and qualified to receive ink lines and tinting without spreading. When placed over a drawing already executed, the drawing is distinctly visible through the paper, and may be copied or *traced* directly by the ink-instruments; thus an accurate copy may be made with great expedition. Tracings may be folded and stowed away very conveniently; but, for good service, they should be mounted on cloth, or on paper and cloth, with paste.

Tracing paper may be prepared from thick tissue paper, by sponging over one surface with a mixture of one part raw linseed oil and five spirits of turpentine; five gills of turpentine and one of oil will go over from forty to fifty sheets of paper.

Tracing cloth is a similar preparation of linen, and is preferable for its toughness and durability.

Mouth Glue, for the sticking of the edges of drawing paper to the board, is made of glue and sugar or molasses; it melts at the temperature of the mouth, and is convenient for the draughtsman.

Drawing paper may be fixed down on the drawing board by the pins at the corners, by weights, or by gluing the edges. The first is sufficient when no shading or coloring is to be applied, and if the sheet is not to be a very long time on the board; and it has the advantage of preserving the paper in its natural state. For shaded or tinted drawings, the paper must be damped and glued at the edges, as the partial wetting of paper, loose or fixed at the corners merely, by the water colors distorts the surface.

Damp-stretching is done as follows:—The edges of the paper should first be cut straight, and, as near as possible, at right angles with each other; also the sheet should be so much larger than the intended drawing and its margin, as to admit of being afterwards cut from the board, leaving the border by which it is attached thereto by glue or paste, as we shall next explain.

The paper must first be thoroughly and equally damped with a sponge and clean water, on the opposite side from that on which the drawing is to be made. When the paper absorbs the water, which may be seen by the wetted side becoming dim, as its surface is viewed slantwise against the light, it is to be laid on the drawing board with the wetted side downwards, and placed so that its edges may be nearly parallel with those of the board; otherwise, in using a T square, an inconvenience may be experienced. This done, lay a straight flat ruler on the paper, with its edge parallel to, and about half an inch from one of its edges. The ruler must now be held firm, while the said projecting half inch of paper be turned up along its edge; then, a piece of solid or mouth glue, having its edge partially dissolved by holding it in boiling or warm water for a few seconds, must be passed once or twice along the turned up edge of the paper, after which, by sliding the ruler over the glued border, it will be again laid flat, and the rule being pressed down upon it, that edge of the paper will adhere to the board. If sufficient glue has been applied, the ruler may be removed directly, and the edge finally rubbed down by an ivory book-knife, or by the bows of a common key, by rubbing on a slip of paper placed on the drawing paper, so that the surface of the latter may not be soiled, which will then firmly cement the paper to the board. This done, another but *adjoining* edge of the paper must be acted upon in like manner, and then the remaining edges in succession; we say the adjoining edges, because we have occasionally observed, that when the opposite and parallel edges have been laid down first, without continuing the process progressively round the board, a greater degree of care is required to prevent undulations in the paper as it dries.

Sometimes strong paste is used instead of glue; but as this takes a longer time to set, it is usual to wet the paper also on the upper surface to within an inch of the paste mark, care being taken not to rub or injure the surface in the process. The wetting of the paper in either case is done for the purpose of expanding it; and the edges being fixed to the board in its enlarged state, act as stretchers upon the paper, while it contracts in drying, which it should be allowed to do gradually. All creases or undulations by this means disappear from the surface, and it forms a smooth plane to receive the drawing.

To remove the paper after the drawing is finished, cut off inside the pasted edge, and remove the edge by warm water and the knife.

With panelled boards, the panel is taken out, and the frame inverted; the paper, being first damped on the back with a sponge slightly charged with water, is applied equally over the opening to leave equal margins, and is pressed and secured into its seat by the panel and bars.

MOUNTING PAPER AND DRAWINGS, VARNISHING, ETC.

In mounting paper upon canvas, the latter should be well stretched upon a smooth flat surface, being damped for that purpose, and its edges glued down, as was recommended in stretching drawing paper. Then with a brush spread strong paste upon the canvas, beating it in till the grain of the canvas be all filled up; for this, when dry, will prevent the canvas from shrinking when subsequently removed; then, having cut the edges of the paper straight, paste one side of every sheet, and lay them upon the canvas sheet by sheet, overlapping each other a small quantity. If the drawing paper is strong, it is best to let every sheet lie five or six minutes after the paste is put on it, for as the paste soaks in, the paper will stretch, and may be better spread smooth upon the canvas; whereas, if it be laid on before the paste has moistened the paper, it will stretch afterwards and rise in blisters when laid upon the canvas. The paper should not be cut off from its extended position till thoroughly dry, which should not be hastened, but left in a dry room to do so gradually, if time permit; if not, it may be exposed to the sun, unless in the winter season, when the help of a fire is necessary, provided it is not placed too near a scorching heat.

In joining two sheets of paper together by overlapping, it is necessary, in order to make a neat joint, to feather edge each sheet; this is done by carefully cutting with a knife half way through the paper near the edges, and on the sides which are to overlap each other; then strip off a feather-edged slip from each, which, if done dexterously, will form a very neat and efficient joint when put together.

For mounting and varnishing drawings or prints, stretch a piece of linen on a frame, to which give a coat of isinglass or common size, paste the back of drawing, which leave to soak, and then lay it on the linen. When dry, give it at least four coats of well made isinglass size, allowing it to dry between each coat. Take Canada balsam diluted with the best oil of turpentine, and with a clean brush give it a full flowing coat.

MANAGEMENT OF THE INSTRUMENTS.

In constructing preparatory pencil-drawings, it is advisable, as a rule of general application, to make no more lines upon the paper than are necessary to the completion of the drawing in ink; and also to make these lines just so dark as is consistent with the distinctness of the work. With respect to the first idea, it is of frequent application: in the case, for example, of the teeth of spur wheels, where, in many instances, all that is necessary to the drawing of their end view in ink are three circles, one of them for the pitch line, and the two others for the tops and bottoms of the teeth; and again, to draw the face view of the teeth, that is, in the edge view of the wheel, we have only to mark off by dividers the positions of the lines which compose the teeth, and draw four pencil lines for the two sides, and the top and bottom of the elevation. And here we may remark the inconvenience of that arbitrary rule, by which it is by some insisted that the pupil should lay down in pencil every line that is to be drawn, before finishing it in ink. It is often beneficial to ink in one part of a drawing, before touching other parts at all; it prevents confusion, makes the first part of easy reference, and allows of its being better done, as the surface of the paper inevitably contracts dust, and becomes otherwise soiled in the course of time, and therefore the sooner it is done with the better.

Circles and circular arcs should, in general, be inked in before straight lines, as the latter may be more readily drawn to join the former, than the former the latter. When a number of circles are to be described from one centre, the smaller should be inked first, while the centre is in better condition. When a centre is required to bear some fatigue, it should be protected with a thickness of stout card glued or pasted over it, to receive the compass-leg.

Indiarubber is the ordinary medium for cleaning a drawing, and for correcting errors in the pencil. For slight work it is quite suitable; that substance, however, operates to destroy the surface of the paper; and by repeated application, it so ruffles the surface, and imparts an unctuosity to it, as to spoil it for fine drawing, especially if ink shading or coloring is to be applied. It is much better to leave trivial errors alone, if corrections by the pencil may be made alongside without confusion; as it is, in such a case, time enough to clear away superfluous lines when the inking is finished.

For cleaning a drawing, a piece of bread two days old is preferable to indiarubber, as it cleans the surface well and does not injure it. When ink lines to any considerable extent have to be erased, a small piece of damped soft sponge may be rubbed over them till they disappear. As, however, this process is apt to discolor the paper, the sponge must be passed through clean water, and applied again to take up the straggling ink. For ordinary small erasures of ink lines, a sharp rounded pen-blade applied lightly and rapidly does well, and the surface may be smoothed down by the thumb-nail. In ordinary working drawings, a line may readily be taken out by damping it with a hair pencil, and quickly applying the indiarubber; and to smooth the surface so roughened, a light application of the knife is expedient. In drawings intended to be highly finished, particular pains should be taken to avoid the necessity for corrections, as every thing of this kind detracts from the appearance.

In using the square, the more convenient way is to draw the lines off the left edge with the right hand, holding the stock steadily but not very tightly against the edge of the board with the left hand. The convenience of the left edge for drawing by is obvious, as we are able to use the arms more freely, and we see exactly what we are doing.

To draw lines in ink with the least amount of trouble to himself, the mechanical draughtsman ought to take the greater amount of trouble with his tools. If they be well made, and of good stuff originally, they ought to last through three generations of draughtsmen; their working parts should be carefully preserved from injury, they should be kept well set, and, above all, scrupulously clean. The setting of instruments is a matter of some nicety, for which purpose a small oil-stone is convenient. To dress up the tips of the blades of the pen or of the bows, as they are usually worn unequally by the customary usage, they may be screwed up into contact in the first place, and passed along the stone, turning upon the point in a directly perpendicular plane, till they acquire an identical profile. Being next unscrewed and examined to ascertain the parts of unequal thickness round the nib, the blades are laid separately upon their backs on the stone, and rubbed down at the points, till they be brought up to an edge of uniform fineness. It is well to screw them together again, and to pass them over the stone once or twice more, to bring up any fault; to retouch them also on the outer and inner side of each blade, to remove barbs or frasing; and, finally, to draw them across the palm of the hand.

The China ink, which is commonly used for line-drawing, ought to be rubbed down in water to a certain degree, avoiding the sloppy aspect of light lining in drawings, and making the ink just so thick as to run freely from the pen. This medium degree may be judged of after a little practice by the appearance of the ink on the pallet. The best quality of ink has a soft feel when wetted and smoothed; free from grit or sediment, and musky. The rubbing of China ink in water tends to crack and break away the surface at the point; this may be prevented by shifting at intervals the position of the stick in the hand while being rubbed, and thus rounding the surface. Nor is it advisable, for the same reason, to bear very hard, as the mixture is otherwise more evenly made, and the enamel of the pallet is less rapidly worn off. When the ink, on being rubbed down, is likely to be for some time required, a considerable quantity of it should be prepared, as the water continually vaporises; it will thus continue for a longer time in a condition fit for application. The pen should be levelled in the ink, to take up a sufficient charge; and to induce the ink to enter the pen freely, the blades should be lightly breathed upon before immersion. After each application of ink, the outsides of the blades should be cleaned, to prevent any deposit of ink upon the edge of the squares.

To keep the blades of his *inkers* clean, is the first duty of a draughtsman who is to make a good piece of work. Pieces of blotting or unsized paper and cotton velvet, washleather, or even the sleeve of a coat, should always be at hand while a drawing is being inked. When a small piece of blotting paper is folded twice so as to present a corner, it may usefully be passed between the blades of the pen now and then, as the ink is liable to deposit at the point and obstruct the passage, particularly in fine lining; and for this purpose the pen must be unscrewed to admit the paper. But this process may be delayed by drawing the point of the pen over a piece of velvet, or even over the surface of thick blotting paper; either method clears the point for a time. As soon as any obstruction takes place, the pen should be immediately cleaned, as the trouble thus taken will always improve and expedite the work. If the pen should be laid down for a short time with the ink in it, it should be unscrewed to keep the points apart, and so prevent deposit; and when done with altogether for the occasion, it ought to be thoroughly cleaned at the nibs. This will preserve its edges and prevent rusting.

For the designing of machinery, it is very convenient to have some scale of reference by which to proportion the parts; for this purpose, a vertical and horizontal scale may be drawn on the walls of the room.

GEOMETRICAL PROBLEMS.

ON STRAIGHT LINES.

It is desirable that the beginner should construct the following problems, not copying them, but adopting some scale, which will give him the use of the scale, and imprint the problems on his memory.

Problem I.—*To draw a straight line through given points.*

Let A and B (fig. 78) be two given points, represented by the intersection of two lines, or pricked into the surface. Surround the points by small circles, when advisable for assisting to define their locality, as thus ⊙ ; place the straight edge at or so near the points, that the point of the pen or pencil may pass through them, and draw the line firmly and steadily.

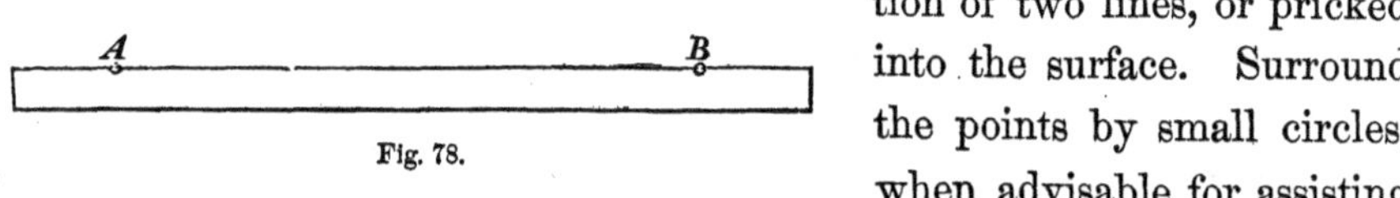

Fig. 78.

Lines in drawing are divided into several classes, as *full*, *broken*, *dotted*, and *broken* and *dotted*, &c.; these again are divided into *fine*, *medium*, and *heavy*, according to the breadth of the line (fig. 79).

The lines of a problem which are either given or are to be found, and the outlines of an object that can be seen from the point of view in which it is represented should be full, and either fine, medium, or heavy, according to the particular effect that the draughtsman wishes to give. The portions of the outline that are hidden from view, but which are requisite to give a complete idea of the object, should be dotted or broken.

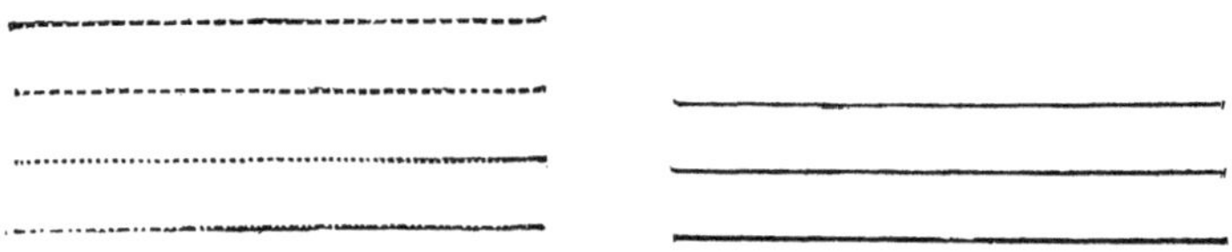

Fig. 79.

The other lines are used for conventional purposes by the draughtsman, as boundaries of parishes or estates, or to show a change in position of an object, &c., &c.

Prob. II.—*To set off a given distance along a straight line* C D, *from a given point* A *on it* (fig. 80).

Take off the given distance from the scale of equal parts with the dividers. Set one foot of the dividers on A, and bring the other foot upon the line, and mark the point B, either by pricking with the foot of the dividers, or by a small dot with the sharp point of a lead pencil.

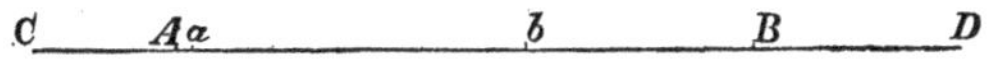

C A a b B D

Fig. 80.

When the distance as at A to be set off is too small to be taken off from the scale with accuracy, set off any convenient distance A *b* greater than the given distance; set off from *b* towards A, the length by which A *b* is greater than the given distance; the part A *a* will be the required distance.

To set off a number of distances on a straight line, set off their successive sums. Thus, to set off successively the distances = 10, 15, 20, set off as above 10, 25, and 45, always starting from the same point. The object of performing the operation in this manner is to avoid carrying forward any inaccuracy that might be made were the respective distances set off separately, one after the other. If the distances to be set off are equal, it will be more accurate to set off a distance equal either to the whole aggregate, or such a number of them as can be contained by the compasses, and then dividing the line into the required parts.

Prob. III.—*To divide a given line into two equal parts* (fig. 81).

Open the dividers to as near as possible half the given line, place one point of the dividers on the end of the line, bring the other point to the line, and turn on this point; if now the point of the dividers coincide with

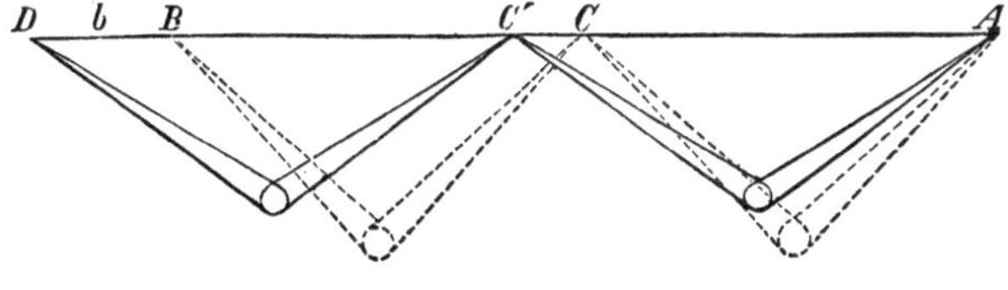

Fig. 81.

the other end of the line, we have the division required; but should the point of the dividers fall within or without the end of the line, divide this deficit or excess by the eye into two equal parts, and contract or open the dividers to this point, and apply them again as at first; perform the operation till the revolution of the compasses coincides with the given line. Thus (fig. 81), suppose it were required to divide the line A B into two equal parts, and the distance A C′ was the first guess or opening of the dividers; turning on the point C′, the point of the dividers that was at A falls on the point D beyond B, keeping the point of the dividers still on the point C′, open them till they embrace the distance C′ *b*, *b* being at or near as can be judged by the eye the centre of D B; begin again from the point A with the distance C′ *b* contained in the dividers, and apply the distance as at first, dividing the deficit or excess of the two revolutions, till the point of the dividers that was at A falls by revolution on B. The eye, by practice, becomes so accustomed to this means of division, that a plan may be reduced to half scale as quickly and with as little chance of mistake as by the proportional compasses.

To divide a line into any number of equal parts.—If the number is divisible by two, bisect the line, or divide it into two equal parts as above, and continue this as long as the number remaining is divisible by two; but when the number is uneven, measure the given line on the scale, divide numerically the length thus found by the number of parts into which it is to be divided, and take on the scale as accurately as possible the quotient thus obtained; apply this length successively on the line, and if the last distance set off does not agree with the extremity of the line; thus if, as in fig. 81, when the line is to be divided into two parts, the repeated length exceeds the line, divide this excess by the eye into as many parts as the given line is to be divided, and close the dividers so as to include a length less by one of these parts. If the point D should fall inside B, divide the deficit as before by the number of parts, but open the dividers by one of these parts.

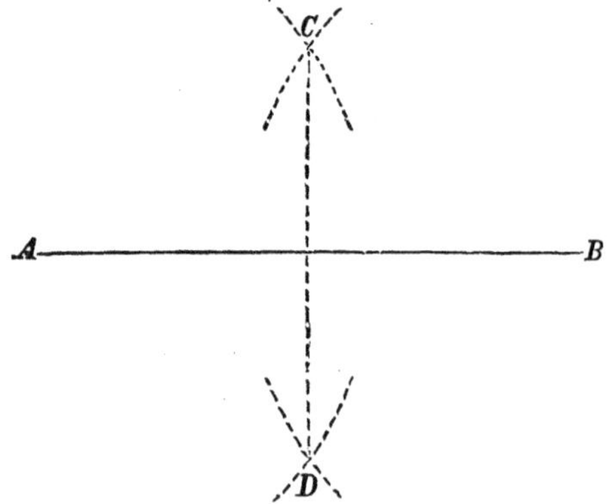

Fig. 82.

The above problems may be constructed geometrically as follows:—To *bisect* or divide into two equal parts a given line A B. From A and B, with any radius greater than half of A B, describe arcs intersecting each other above and below the given line, the line C D connecting these intersections will bisect A B, and also be perpendicular to it.

PROB. IV.—*To divide a given line into a given number of equal parts.*

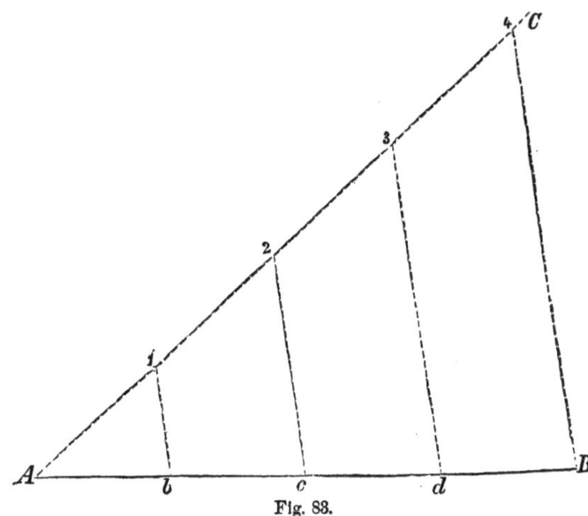

Fig. 83.

Let A B be the distance to be divided, for example, into four equal parts; draw the line A C, making an acute angle with A B; on A C lay off any four equal distances, each as near as may be to $\frac{1}{4}$ of A B, connect the last division 4 with B, and through the other points 1, 2, 3, draw lines parallel to 4 B, the intersections of these lines *b*, *c*, *d*, with the line A B, will divide it into four equal parts.

PROB. V.—*To draw a perpendicular to a straight line, from a point without it.*

1*st Method* (fig. 84).—From the point A, with a sufficient radius, cut the given line at F and G, and from these points describe arcs cutting at E; through E draw A E, which will be the perpendicular required. If there be no room below the line, the intersection may be taken above; that is, between the line and the given point. This mode is not, however, likely to be as exact in practice as the one given.

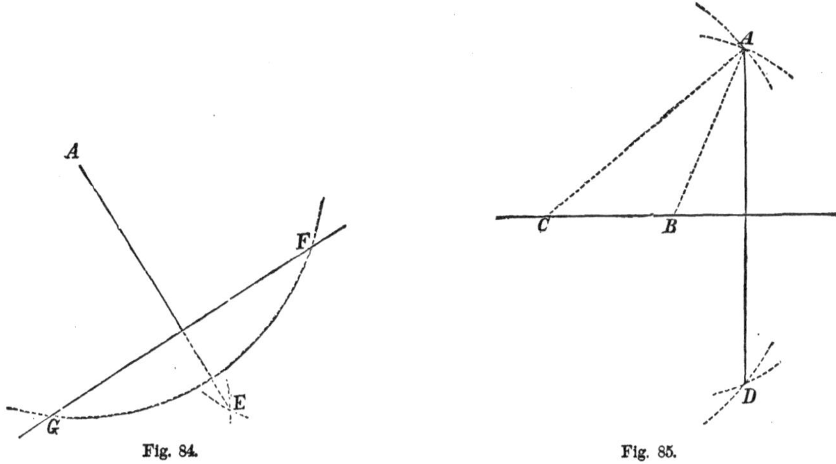

Fig. 84. Fig. 85.

2*d Method* (fig. 85).—From any two points B and C, at some distance apart, in the given line, and with radii B A, C A, respectively, describe arcs cutting at A and D. Draw the perpendicular required, A D. This method is useful where the given point is opposite the end of the line, or nearly so.

PROB. VI.—*To draw a perpendicular to a straight line from a given point* A *in that line.*

1*st Method* (fig. 86).—With any radius, from the given point A, in the given line B C, cut the line at B and C; with a greater radius describe arcs from B and C, cutting each other at D, and draw D A the perpendicular.

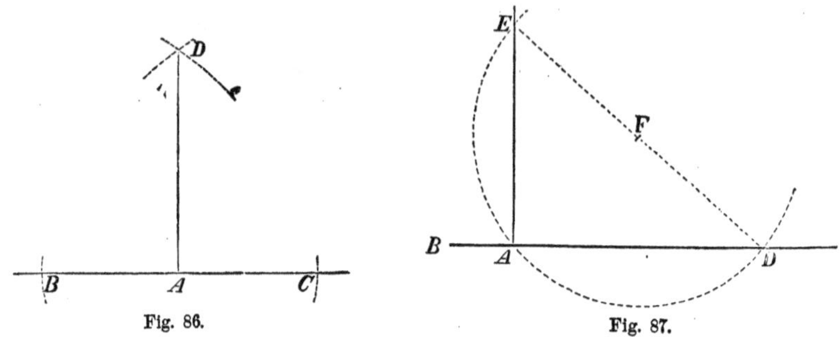

Fig. 86. Fig. 87.

2*d Method* (fig. 87).—From any centre F, above B C, describe a circle passing through the given point A, and cutting the given line at D; draw D F, and produce it to cut the circle at E; and draw A E the perpendicular. This method is useful when the point A is at or near one end; and in practice, it is expedient in the first place to strike out a preliminary arc, of any convenient radius, from the point A, as any point in that arc may be chosen for the centre F, with the certainty that the arc from this centre will pass through A, without the delay of adjusting the point of the compass to it. This expedient is of general use where an arc is to be passed through a given point, and particularly if the point of the pencil be round or misshapen, and therefore uncertain.

3*d Method* (fig. 88).—From A describe an arc E C, and from E, with the

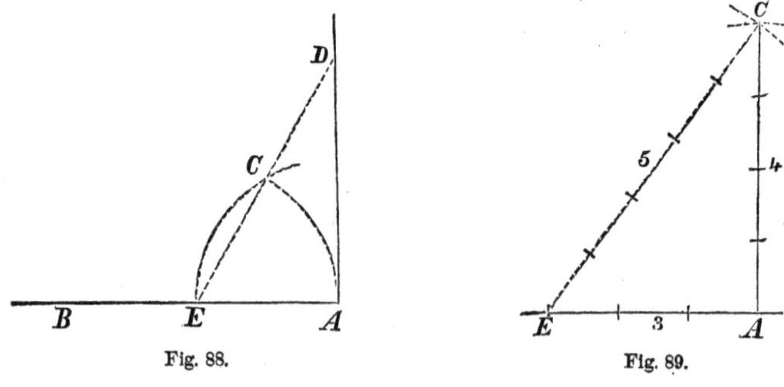

Fig. 88. Fig. 89.

same radius, the arc A C, cutting the other at C; through C draw a line E C D, and set off C D equal to C E, and through D draw A D the perpendicular required. This method, like the previous one, is useful when the point A is at one end.

4th Method (fig. 89).—From the given point A, set off a distance A E equal to three parts, by any scale; and on the centres A and E, with radii of four and five parts respectively, describe arcs intersecting at C. Draw A C for the perpendicular required. This method is most useful on very large scales, where straight edges are inapplicable, as in laying down perpendiculars or right angles on the ground; as in laying out the corners of houses, beams and girders may be set square with the sides of the houses: columns, and the like, may be set perpendicularly by the same method. The numbers 3, 4, 5, are, it is to be observed, taken to measure respectively—the base, the perpendicular, and the slant side of the triangle A E C. Any multiples of these numbers may be used with equal propriety, as 6, 8, 10, or 9, 12, 15, whether feet, yards, or any other measure of length.

Prob. VII.—*To draw a straight line parallel to a given line, at a given distance apart* (fig. 90).

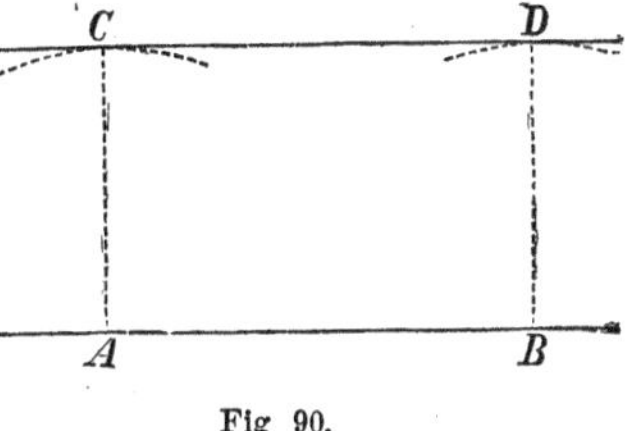

Fig 90.

From the centres A, B, in the given line, with the given distance as radius, describe arcs C, D; and draw the parallel line C D touching the arcs. The method of drawing tangents will be afterwards shown; meantime, in all ordinary cases, the line C D may be drawn by simply applying a straight edge by the eye.

Prob. VIII.—*To draw a parallel through a given point.*

1st Method (fig. 91).—With a radius equal to the distance of the given point C from the given line A B, describe the arc D from B, taken considerably distant from C; draw the parallel through C to touch the arc D.

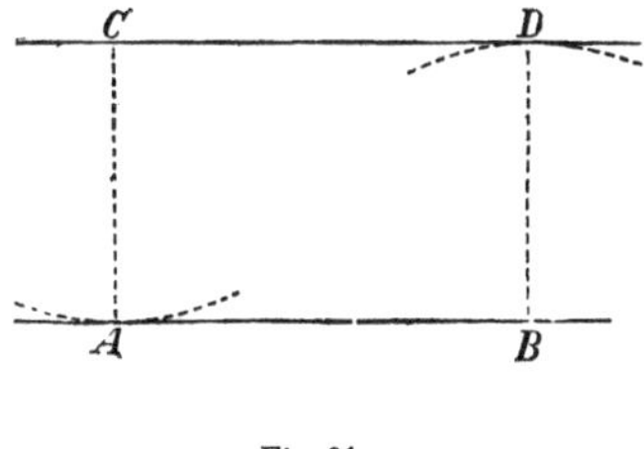

Fig. 91.

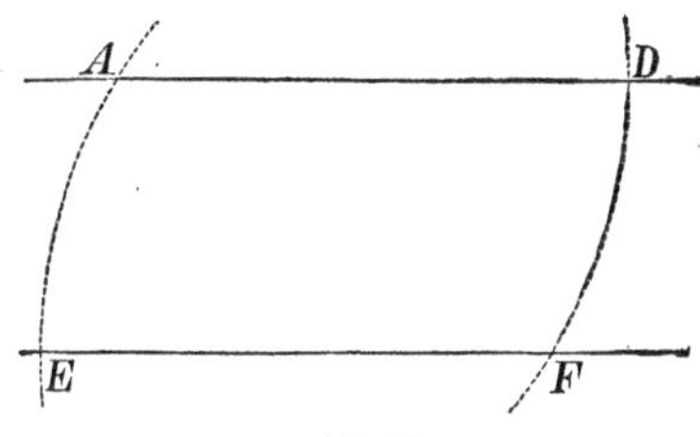

Fig. 92.

2d Method (fig. 92).—From A, the given point, describe the arc F D, cutting the given line at F; from F, with the same radius, describe the arc E A; and set off F D equal to E A. Draw the parallel through the points A, D.

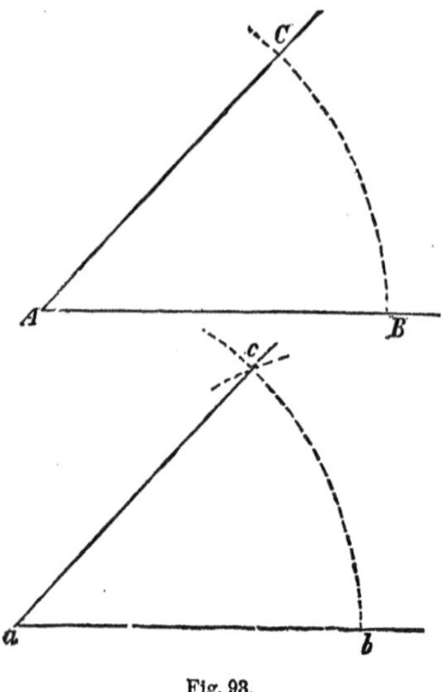

Fig. 93.

Prob. IX.—*To construct an angle equal to a given angle* (fig. 93).

Thus, on the line *a b* to construct an angle which shall be equal to the given angle C A B. With the dividers describe the arc C B; from the point *a*, with the same radius describe *c b;* with the dividers measure the length of the arc C B, and on *c b* lay off this distance; through *c* draw *c a*, and we have the required angle or opening *c a b*, equal to the given angle C A B.

Prob. X.—*From a point* A *of a given line* D E, *to draw a line making an angle of* 60° *with the given line* (fig. 94).

Take any convenient distance in the dividers, and from A describe the arc B C. From B, with the same distance, describe an arc, and mark the point C where the arcs cross. Draw the line A, C. This line will make with the given one the required angle of 60°.

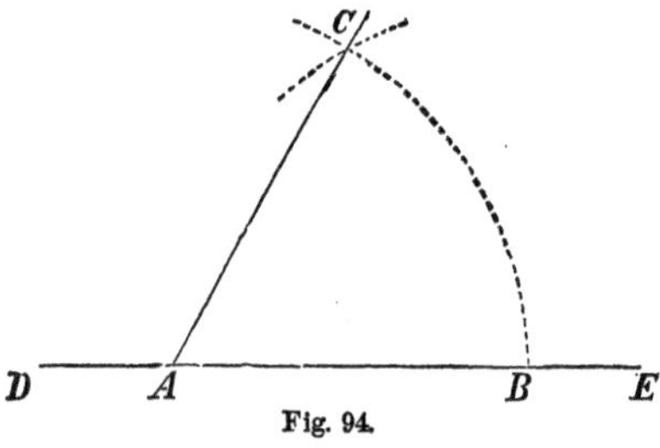

Fig. 94.

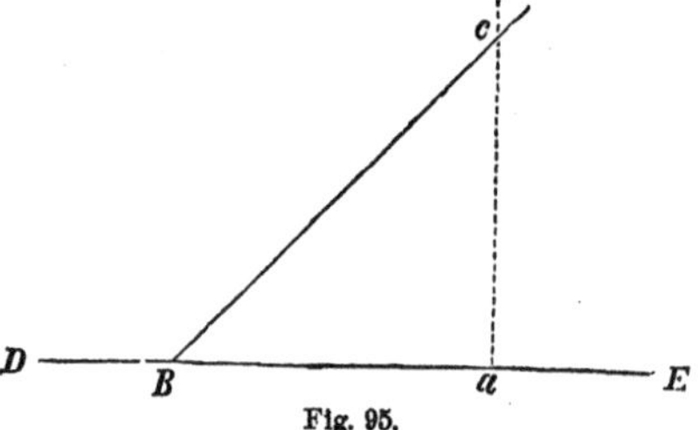

Fig. 95.

Prob. XI.—*From a point* B *on a given line* D E, *to draw a line making an angle of* 45° *with it* (fig. 95).

Set off any distance B *a*, along D E, from B. Construct a perpendicular to D E at *a*, and set off on this perpendicular *a c* equal to *a* B; draw through B *c* a line, which will make with D E the required angle of 45°.

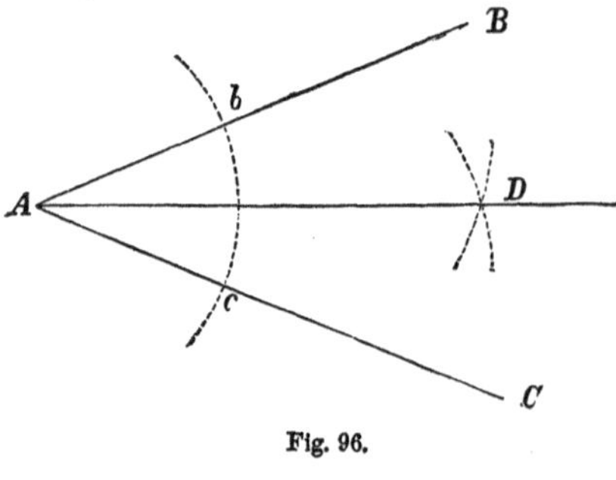

Fig. 96.

Prob. XII.—*To divide a given angle, as* B A C (fig. 96), *into two equal parts.*

From the point A, or vertex of the angle, with any radius describe an arc *b c*; from *b* and *c*, the intersections of the arc with the sides of the angle, with any radius greater than half the arc *b c*, describe two arcs intersecting each other, as at D; through A and D draw a line which will bisect or divide into two equal parts the angle B A C.

PROB. XIII.—*To bisect the angle contained between two lines, as* A B *and* C D (fig. 97), *when the intersecting point or vertex of the angle is not on the drawing.*

Set off a point *b* at any convenient distance from A B, and through this point draw a parallel to A B; at the same distance from C D draw a parallel; extend these parallels till they intersect at *c*; bisect the angle *b c d* by *c a*, which will also bisect the angle contained between the lines A B and C D.

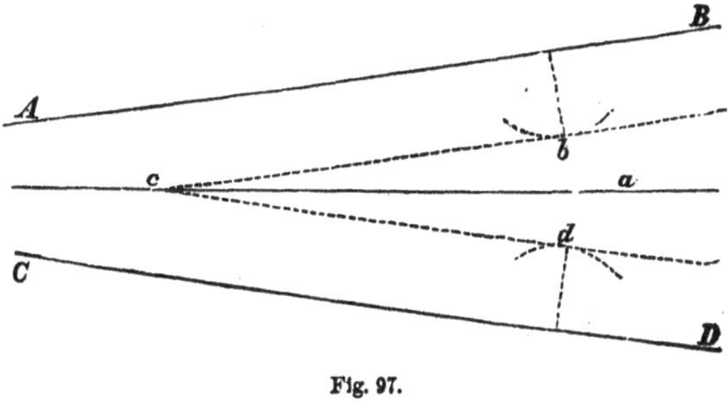

Fig. 97.

PROB. XIV.—*Through two given points, as* B *and* C (fig. 98), *to describe an arc of a circle with a given radius.*

From B and C, with an opening of the dividers equal to the given radius, describe two arcs crossing at A; from A, as a centre, with the same radius describe an arc which will be the one required. It is to be observed, that there are two points A, one above and one below the line B C, from which, as centres, arcs can be described with the given radius, and passing through B and C.

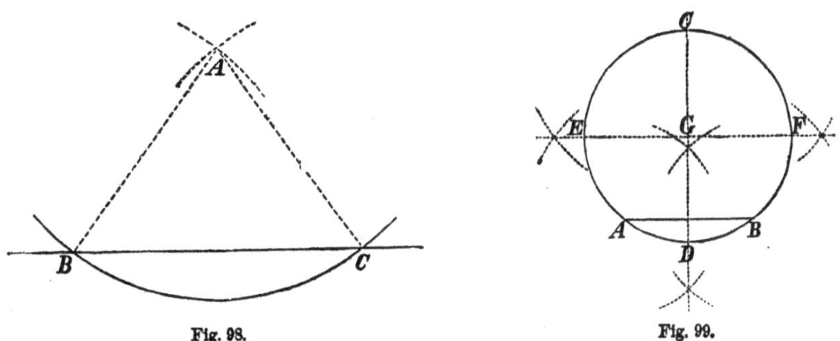

Fig. 98. Fig. 99.

PROB. XV.—*To find the centre of a given circle, or of an arc of a circle.*

Of a circle (fig. 99).—Draw the chord A B, bisect it by the perpendicular C D, whose extremities lie in the circumference, and bisect C D for the centre G of the circle.

Of an arc, or of a circumference (fig. 100).—Select the points A, B, C, in the circumference well apart; with one radius describe arcs from these three points, cutting each other; and draw the two lines D E, F G, through their intersections: the point O, where they cut, is the centre of the circle or arc.

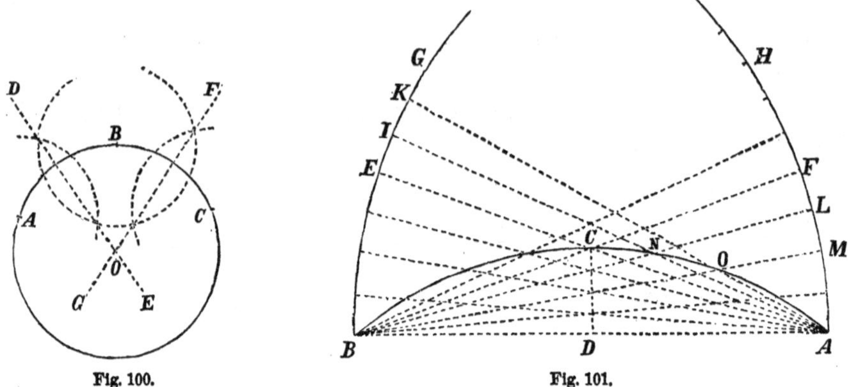

Fig. 100. Fig. 101.

Prob. XVI.—*To describe a circle passing through three given points.*

Join the given points A, B, C (fig. 100), and proceed as in last problem to find the centre O, from which the circle may be described.

This problem is of utility: in striking out the circular arches of bridges upon centering, when the span and rise are given; describing shallow pans, or dished covers of vessels; or finding the diameter of a fly-wheel, or any other object of large diameter, when only a part of the circumference is accessible.

Prob. XVII.—*To describe a circle passing through three given points, when the centre is not available.*

1*st Method* (fig. 101).—From the extreme points A B, as centres, describe arcs A H, B G. Through the third point C draw A E and B F, cutting the arcs. Divide A F and B E into any number of equal parts, and set off a series of equal parts of the same length on the upper portions of the arcs beyond the points E F. Draw straight lines B L, B M, &c., to the divisions in A F; and A I, A K, &c., to the divisions in E G: the successive intersections N, O, &c., of these lines, are points in the circle required, between the given points A and C, which may be filled in accordingly. Similarly, the remaining part of the curve B C may be described.

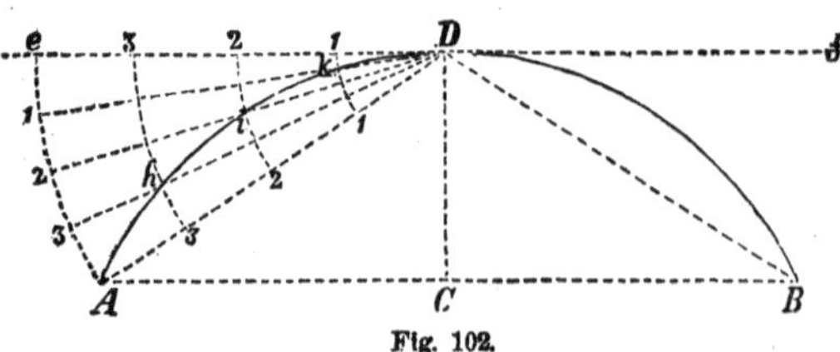

Fig. 102.

2*d Method* (fig. 102).—Let A, D, B, be the given points; draw AB, AD, DB, and *ef*, parallel to A B. Divide D A into a number of equal parts, 1, 2, 3, &c.,

and from D describe arcs through these points to meet *e f*. Divide the arc A *e* into the same number of equal parts, and draw straight lines from D to the points of division. The intersections of these lines successively with the arcs 1, 2, 3, &c., are points in the circle, which may be filled in as before.

Note.—The second method is not perfectly true, but sufficiently so for arcs less than one-fourth of a circle.

To describe the arc mechanically with three strips of board forming a triangle.—Insert two stiff pins or nails at A and B; place the strips as shown in fig. 103, one against the pins at A and B, and having D at their intersection; fasten the two strongly together at this point and at the base of the triangle by the third strip; placing the pencil at D, and keeping the edges against A and B, moving the triangle to the right and left, the pencil will describe the circle.

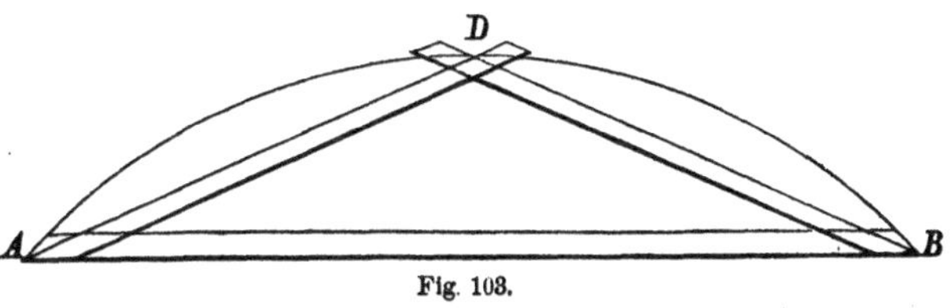

Fig. 103.

Prob. XVIII.—*To draw a tangent to a circle from a given point in the circumference.*

1*st Method.*—Through the given point A (fig. 104) draw the radial line A C, and the perpendicular F G for the tangent required.

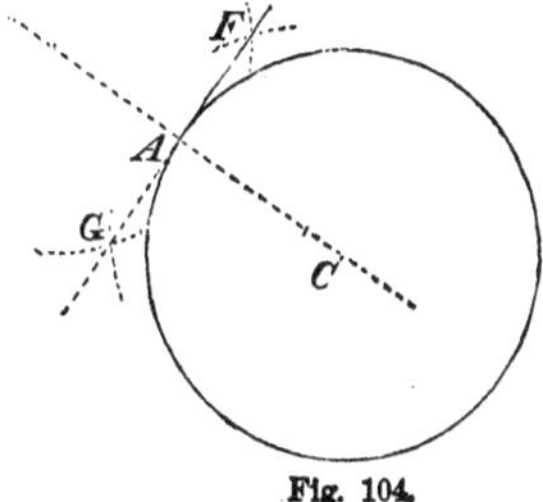

Fig. 104.

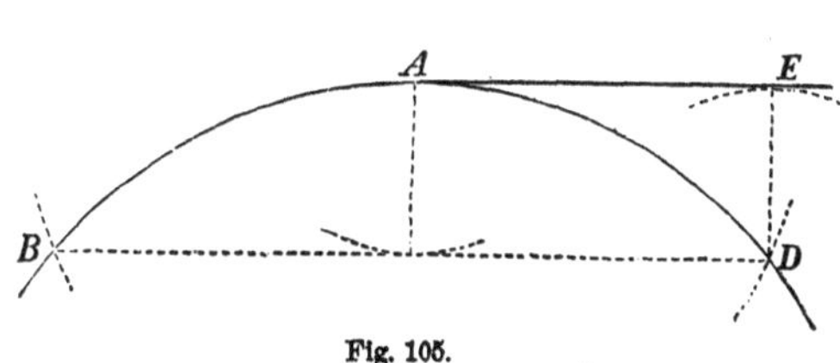

Fig. 105.

2*d Method.*—From A (fig. 105) set off equal segments, A B, A D; join B D, and draw A E parallel to it, for the tangent. This method is useful when the centre is inaccessible.

Prob. XIX.—*To draw tangents to a circle from a point without it* (fig. 106).

Draw A C from the given point A to the centre of the circle, bisect it at D, from D describe an arc through C, cutting the circle at E and F. Draw A E, A F for the required tangents.

To construct within the sides of an angle a circle tangent to these sides, at a given distance from the vertex.—In fig. 107, to describe a circle or arc tangent at *a* and *b*, equally distant from the vertex A; draw perpendiculars to A C at *a*, and to A B at *b*; the intersection of these will be the centre of the required circle.

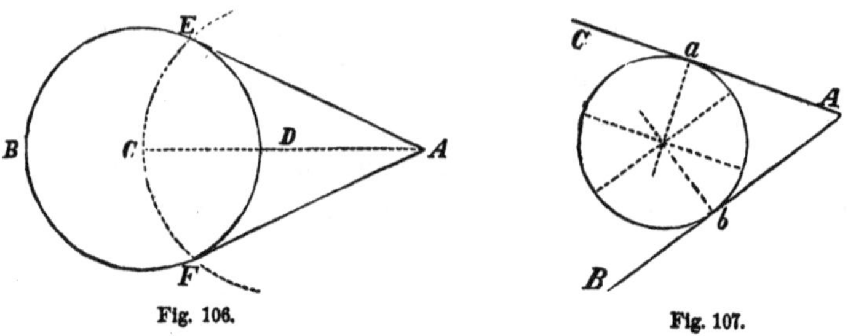

Fig. 106. Fig. 107.

In the same fig., *to find the centre, the radius being given*, and not the points *a* and *b*.—Draw parallels to A C and A B at a distance equal to the given radius, and their intersection will be the centre required.

Prob. XX.—*To describe a circle from a given point to touch a given circle* (figs. 108, 109).

D E being the given circle, and B the point, draw from B to the centre C, and produce it, if necessary, to cut the circle at A, and with B A as radius describe the circle F G, touching the given circle. The operation is the same whether the point B be within or without the circle.

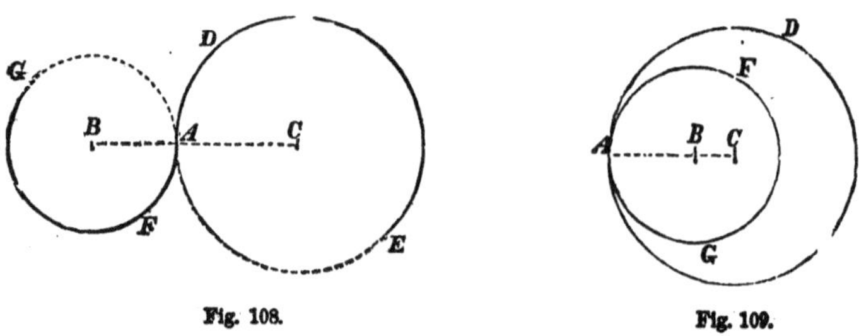

Fig. 108. Fig. 109.

It will be remarked that, in all cases of circles tangential to each other, their centres and their points of contact must lie in the same straight line.

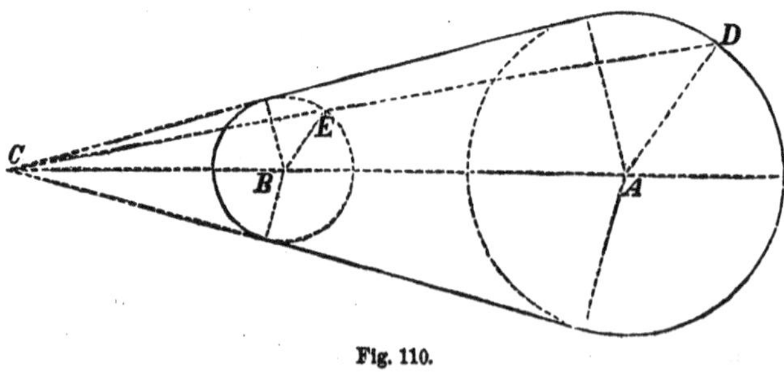

Fig. 110.

Prob. XXI.—*To draw tangents to two given circles.*

1*st Method* (fig. 110).—Draw the straight line A B C through the centres of the two given circles; from the centres A, B, draw parallel radii A D, B E, in the same direction; join D E, and produce it to meet the centre line at C, and from C draw tangents to one of the circles by Prob. XIX. Those tangents will touch *both* circles, as required.

2d Method (fig. 111).—Draw A B, and in the larger circle draw any radius A H, on which set off H G equal to the radius of the smaller circle;

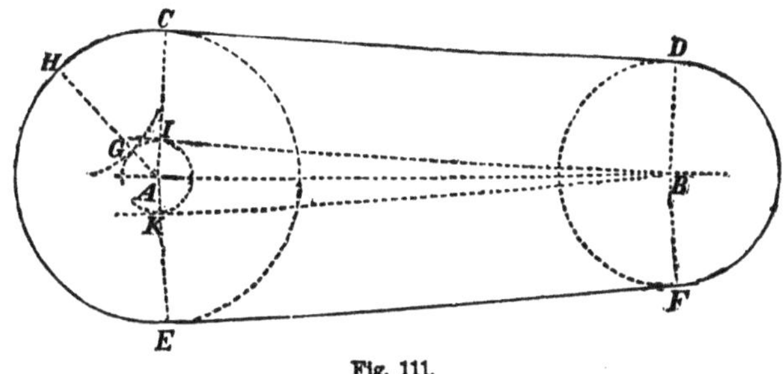

Fig. 111.

on A describe a circle with the radius A G, and draw tangents B I, B K, to this circle from the other centre B; from A and B draw perpendiculars to these tangents, and join C, D, and E, F, for the required tangents.

Note.—The second method is useful when the diameters of the circles are nearly equal.

PROB. XXII.—*Between two inclined lines to draw a series of circles touching these lines and touching each other* (fig. 112).

Bisect the inclination of the given lines A B, C D, by the line N O; this is the centre line of the circles to be inscribed. From a point P in this line draw the perpendicular P B to the line A B, and from P describe the circle B D touching the given lines and cutting the centre line at E; from E draw E F perpendicular to the centre line, cutting A B at F, and from F describe an arc E G, cutting A B at G;

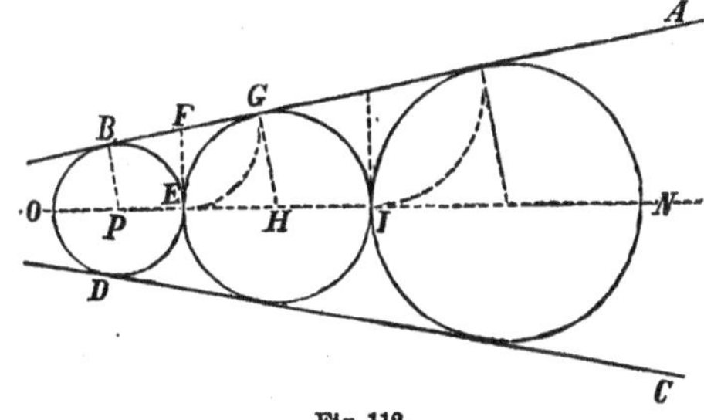

Fig. 112.

draw G H parallel to B P, giving H the centre of the second touching circle, described with the radius H E or H G. By a similar process the third circle I N is determined. And so on.

Inversely, the largest circle may be described first, and the smaller ones in succession.

Note.—This problem is of frequent use in scroll work.

PROB. XXIII.—*Between two inclined lines to draw a circular segment to fill up the angle, and touching the lines* (fig. 113).

Let A B, D E, be the inclined lines; bisect the inclination by the line F C, and draw the perpendicular A F D to define the limit within which the circle is to be drawn. Bisect the angles A and D by lines cutting at C, and from C with radius C F, draw the arc H F G as required.

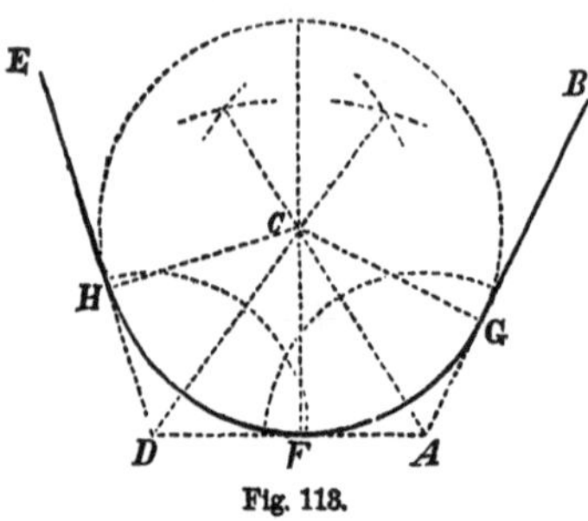

Fig. 113.

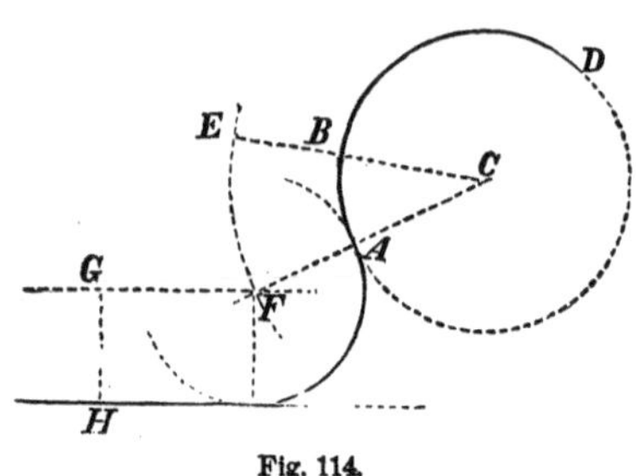

Fig. 114.

Prob. XXIV.—*To fill up the angle of a straight line and a circle, with a circular arc of a given radius* (fig. 114).

In the given circle A D draw a radius C B and produce it, set off B E equal to the radius of the required arc, and on the centre C with the radius C E, describe the arc E F. Draw G F parallel to the given line H I, at the distance G H equal to the radius of the required arc, and cutting the arc E F at F. Then F is the required centre; draw the perpendicular F I, and the radius F C cutting the circle at A, and with the radius F A or F I describe the arc A I as required.

Prob. XXV.—*To fill up the angle of a straight line and a circle, with a circular arc to join the circle at a given point* (fig. 115).

In the given circle draw the radius A and produce it; at A draw a tangent meeting the given line at D; bisect the angle A D E so formed with a line cutting the radius at F; and on the centre F describe the arc A E as required.

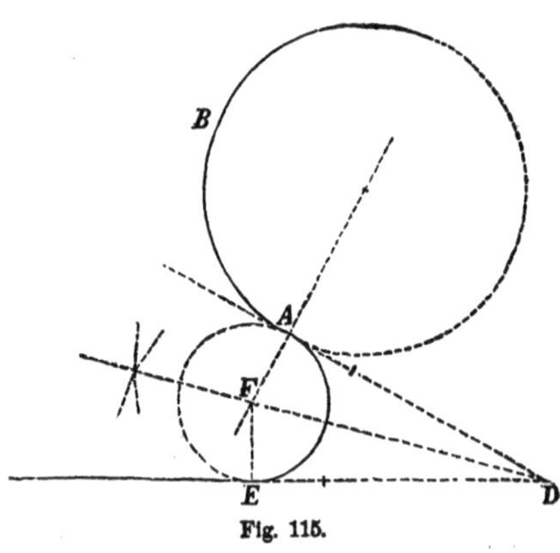

Fig. 115.

Prob. XXVI.—*To describe a circular arc joining two circles, and to touch one of them at a given point* (fig. 116).

Let A B and F G be the given circles, to be joined by an arc touching one of them at F. Draw the radius E F, and produce it both ways; set off F H equal to the radius A C of the other circle; join C H and bisect it with the perpendicular L I, cutting E F at I on the centre I; with radius I F describe the arc F as required.

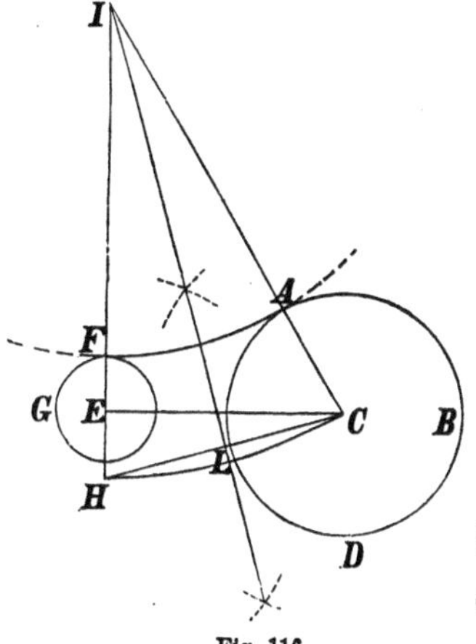

Fig. 116.

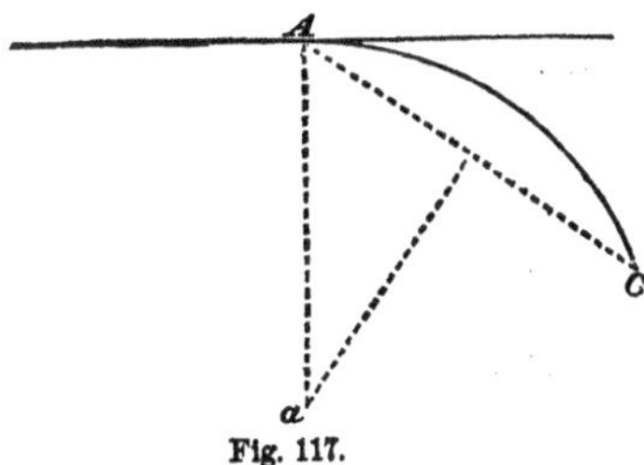

Fig. 117.

Prob. XXVII.—*To find the arc which shall be tangent to a given point* A *on a straight line, and pass through a given point outside the line* (fig. 117).

Erect at A a perpendicular to the given line; connect C A, and bisect it by a perpendicular; the intersection of the two perpendiculars at *a* will be the centre of the required arc.

Prob. XXVIII.—*To connect two parallel lines by a reversed curve composed of two arcs of equal radius, and tangent to the lines at given points,* as at A and B (fig. 118).

Join A B, and divide it into two equal parts at C; bisect C A and C B by perpendiculars; at A and B erect perpendiculars to the given lines, and the intersections *a* and *b* will be the centres of the arcs composing the required curve.

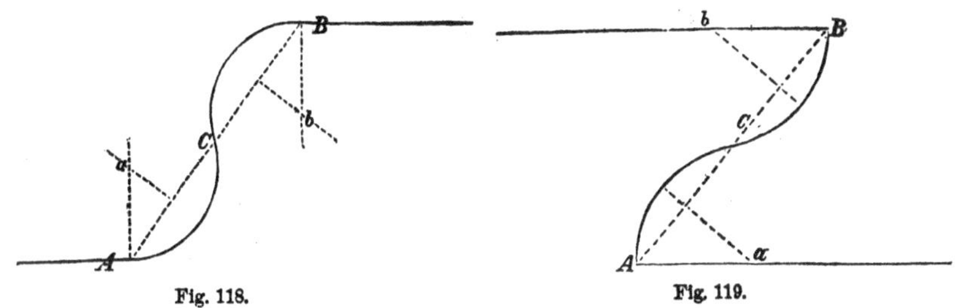

Fig. 118. Fig. 119.

Prob. XXIX.—*To join two given points,* as A and B (fig. 119), *in two given parallel lines by a reversed curve of two equal arcs, whose centres lie in the parallels.*

Join A B, and divide it in equal parts at C, as above. Bisect also A C and B C by perpendiculars; the intersections *a* and *b* of the parallel lines by these perpendiculars will be the centre of the required arcs.

Prob. XXX.—*On a given line,* as A B (fig. 120), *to construct a compound curve of three arcs of circles, the radii of the two side ones being equal and of a given length, and their centres in the given line; the central arc to pass through a given point,* as C, *on the perpendicular bisecting the given line, and tangent to the other two arcs.*

Draw the perpendicular C D; lay off A *a*, B *b*, and C *c*, each equal to the given radius of the side arcs; join *a c;* bisect *a c* by a perpendicular; the intersection of this line with the perpendicular C D will be the required centre of the central arc. Through *a* and *b* draw the lines D *e* and D *e'*; from *a* and *b* with the given radius, equal to *a* A, *b* B, describe the arcs A *e* and B *e'*, from D as a centre, with a radius equal to C D, and consequently by construction D *e* and D *e'*, describe the arc *e* C *e'*, and we have the compound curve required.

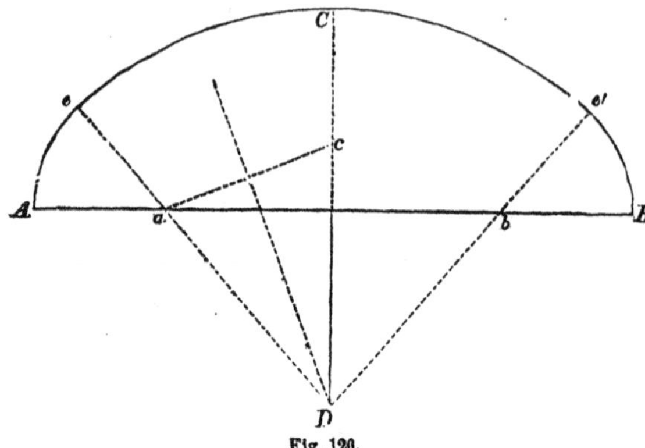

Fig. 120.

For the construction of compound curves of five arcs, see construction of ellipses, page 72.

PROBLEMS ON CIRCLES AND RECTILINEAR FIGURES.

PROB. XXXI.—*To construct a triangle upon a given straight line or base, the length of the two sides being given.*

First, an equilateral triangle (fig. 121). On the ends A B of the given line, with A B as radius, describe arcs cutting at C, and draw A C, B C; then A B C is the triangle required.

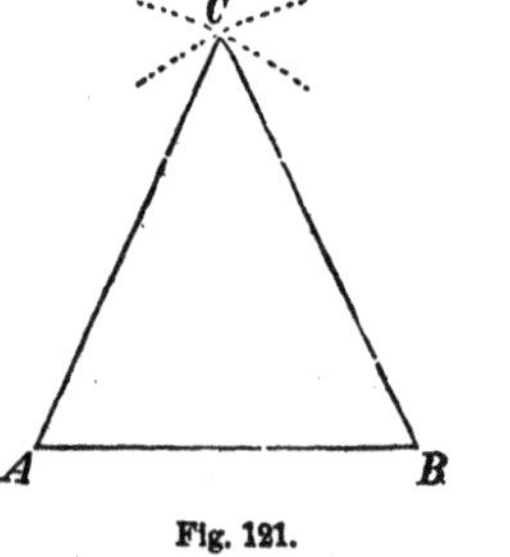

Fig. 121.

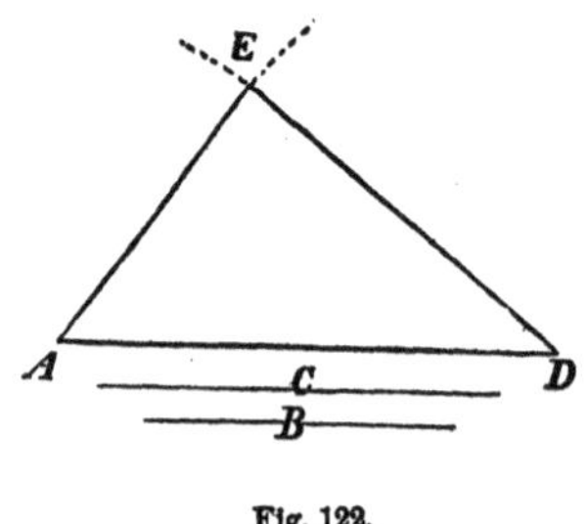

Fig. 122.

Second, when the sides are unequal (fig. 122). Let A D be the base, and B and C the two sides. On either end, as A, of the base-line, with the line B as radius, describe an arc; and on D, with C as radius, cut the arc at E. Draw A E, E D, then A E D is the triangle as required.

This construction is used also to find the position of a point, when its distances are given from two other given points, whether joined by a line or not.

PROB. XXXII.—*To construct a square or a rectangle upon a given straight line.*

First, a square (fig. 123). Let A B be the given line; on A and B as centres, with the radius A B, describe arcs cutting at C; on C, with the same radius, describe arcs cutting the others at D and E; and on D and E, cut these at F G. Draw A F, B G, cutting the arcs at H, I; and join H I to form the square as required.

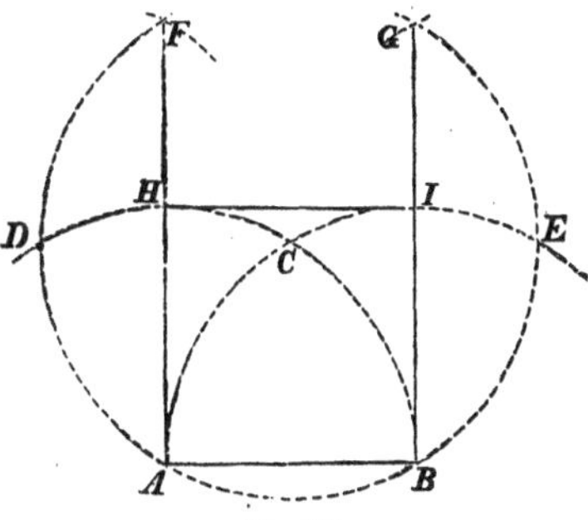

Fig. 123.

Second, a square or rectangle (fig. 124). To the base E F draw perpendiculars E H, F G, equal to the sides, and join G H to complete the rectangle.

When the centre lines of the square or rectangle are given, the figure may be described as follows:—

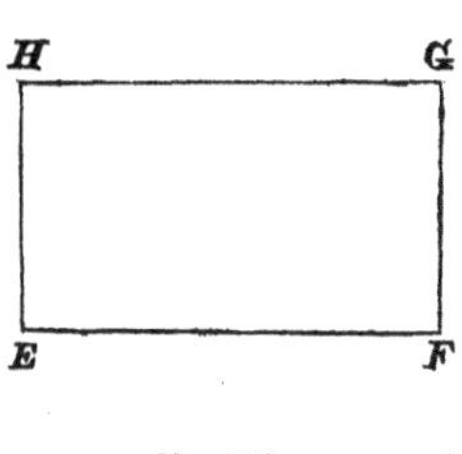

Fig. 124.

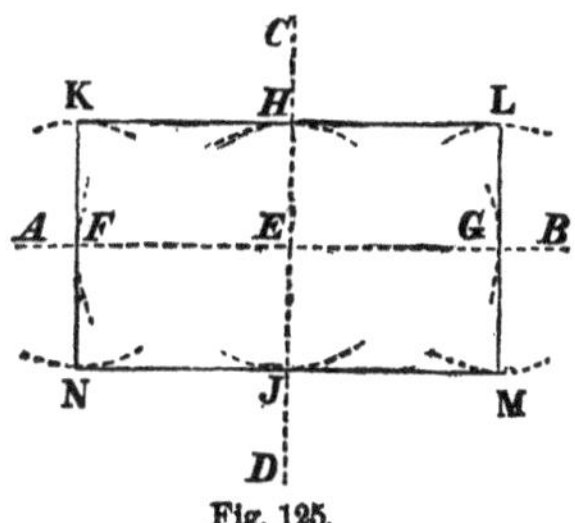

Fig. 125.

Let A B and C D (fig. 125) be the centre lines, perpendicular to each other, and E the middle point of the figure; set off E F, E G, equal each to the half length of the rectangle, and E H, E J, each equal to half the height. On the centres H, J, with a radius equal to the half length, describe arcs on both sides; and on F, G, with a radius of half the height, cut these arcs at K, L, M, N. Join the four intersections so formed, to complete the rectangle.

PROB. XXXIII.—*To construct a parallelogram, of which the sides and one of the angles are given* (fig. 126).

Let A and B be the lengths of the two sides, and C the angle; draw a straight line, and set off D E equal to A; from D draw D F equal to B, and forming an angle with D E equal to C; from E with D F as radius, describe an arc, and from F with D E as radius, cut the arc at G, and draw F G and E G, to complete the parallelogram. Or, the remaining sides may be drawn parallel to D E and D F, cutting at G, and the figure is thus completed.

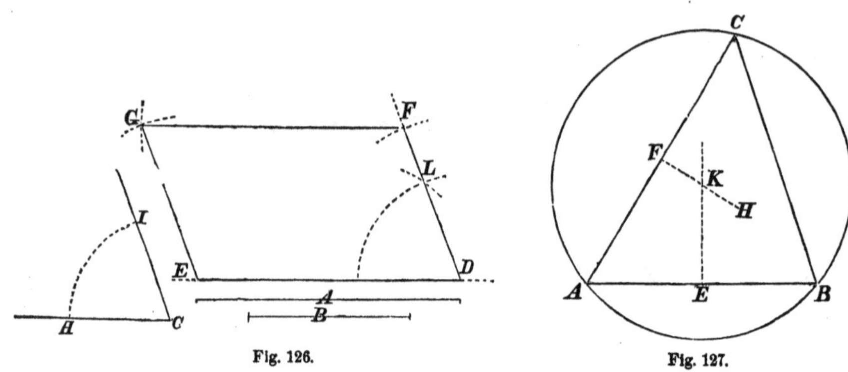

Fig. 126. Fig. 127.

Prob. XXXIV.—*To describe a circle about a triangle* (fig. 127).

Bisect two of the sides A B, A C, of the triangle at E, F; from these points draw perpendiculars cutting at K. From the centre K, with K A as radius, describe the circle A B C, as required.

Prob. XXXV.—*To inscribe a circle in a triangle* (fig. 128).

Bisect two of the angles A, C, of the triangle A B C, by lines cutting at D; from D draw a perpendicular D E to any side, as A C; and with D E as radius, from the centre D, describe the circle required.

When the triangle is equilateral, the centre of the circle is more easily found by bisecting two of the sides, and drawing perpendiculars, as in the previous problem. Or, draw a perpendicular from one of the angles to the opposite side, and from the side set off one-third of the length of the perpendicular.

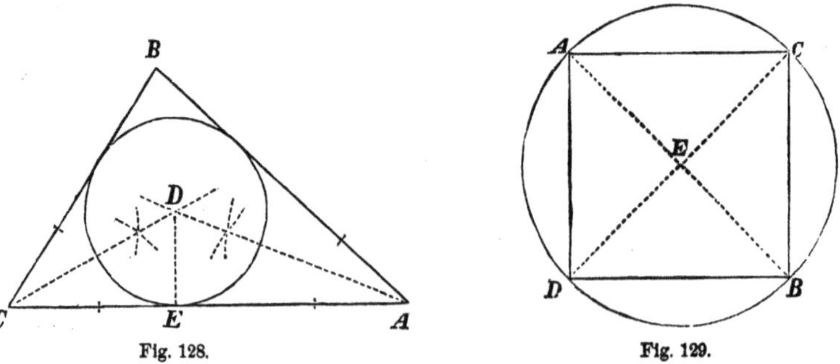

Fig. 128. Fig. 129.

Prob. XXXVI.—*To inscribe a square in a circle; and to describe a circle about a square* (fig. 129).

To inscribe the square. Draw two diameters A B, C D, at right angles, and join the points A, B, C, D, to form the square as required.

To describe the circle. Draw the diagonals A B, C D, of the given square, cutting at E; on E as a centre, with E A as radius, describe the circle as required.

In the same way, a circle may be described about a rectangle.

Prob. XXXVII.—*To inscribe a circle in a square; and to describe a square about a circle* (fig. 130).

To inscribe the circle. Draw the diagonals A B, C D, of the given square, cutting at E; draw the perpendicular E F to one of the sides, and with the radius E F, on the centre E, describe the circle.

To describe the square. Draw two diameters A B, C D, at right angles, and produce them; bisect the angle D E B at the centre by the diameter F G, and through F and G draw perpendiculars A C, B D, and join the points A, D, and B, C, where they cut the diagonals, to complete the square.

Prob. XXXVIII.—*To inscribe a pentagon in a circle* (fig. 131).

Draw two diameters A C, B D, at right angles; bisect A O at E, and

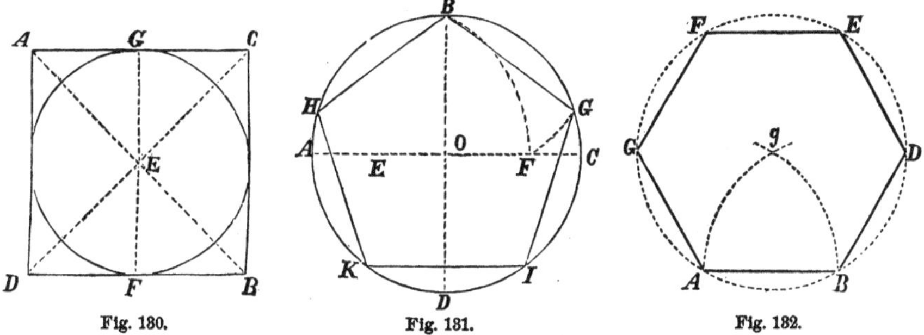

Fig. 130. Fig. 131. Fig. 132.

from E with radius E B, cut A C at F; from B, with radius B F, cut the circumference at G H, and with the same radius step round the circle to I and K; join the points so found to form the pentagon.

Prob. XXXIX.—*To construct a regular hexagon upon a given straight line* (fig 132).

From A and B, with a radius equal to the given line, describe arcs cutting at *g*; from *g*, with the radius *g* A, describe a circle; with the same radius set off from A the arcs A G, G F, and from B the arcs B D, D E. Join the points so found to form the hexagon.

Prob. XL.—*To inscribe a regular hexagon in a circle* (fig. 133).

Draw a diameter A B, from A and B as centres, with the radius of the circle A C, cut the circumference at D, E, F, G; draw straight lines A D, D E, &c., to form the hexagon.

The points of contact, D, E, &c., may also be found by setting off the radius six times upon the circumference.

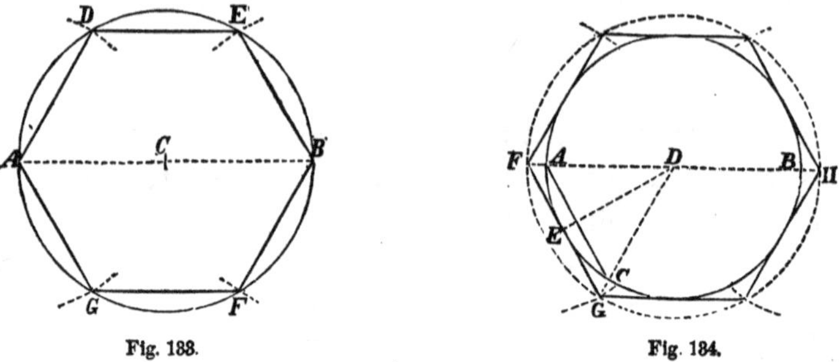

Fig. 133. Fig. 134.

Prob. XLI.—*To describe a regular hexagon about a circle* (fig. 134).

Draw a diameter A B of the given circle; with the radius A D from A as a centre, cut the circumference at C; join A C, and bisect it with the radius D E; through E draw F G parallel to A C, cutting the diameter at F, and with the radius D F describe the circle F H. Within this circle describe a regular hexagon by the preceding problem; the figure will touch the given circle as required.

Prob. XLII.—*To construct a regular octagon upon a given straight line* (fig. 135).

Produce the given line A B both ways, and draw perpendiculars A E, B F; bisect the external angles at A and B by the lines A H, B C, which make equal to A B; draw C D and H G parallel to A E and equal to A B; and from the centres G, D, with the radius A B, cut the perpendiculars at E,F, and draw E F to complete the octagon.

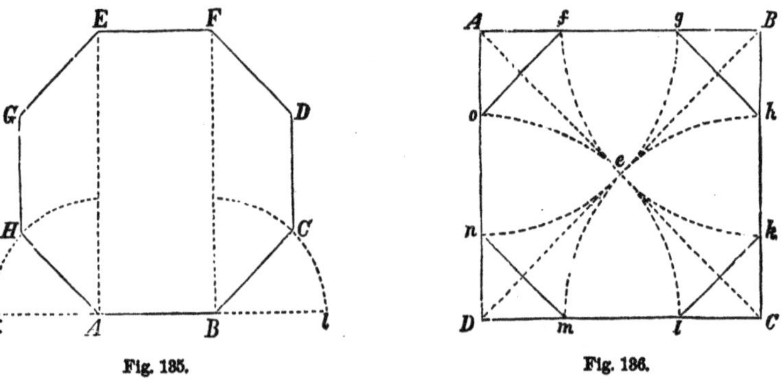

Fig. 135. Fig. 136.

Prob. XLIII.—*To convert a square into a regular octagon* (fig. 136).

Draw the diagonals of the square cutting at *e*; from the corners A, B, C, D, with A *e* as radius, describe arcs cutting the sides at *g h*, &c.; join the points so found to complete the octagon.

PROB. XLIV.—*To inscribe a regular octagon in a circle* (fig. 137).

Draw two diameters A C, B D, at right angles; bisect the arcs A B, B C, &c., at *e*, *f*, &c.; and join A *e*, *e* B, &c., for the inscribed figure.

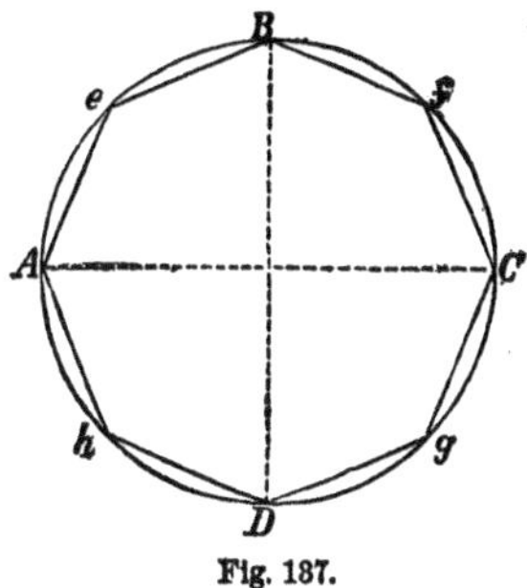

Fig. 137.

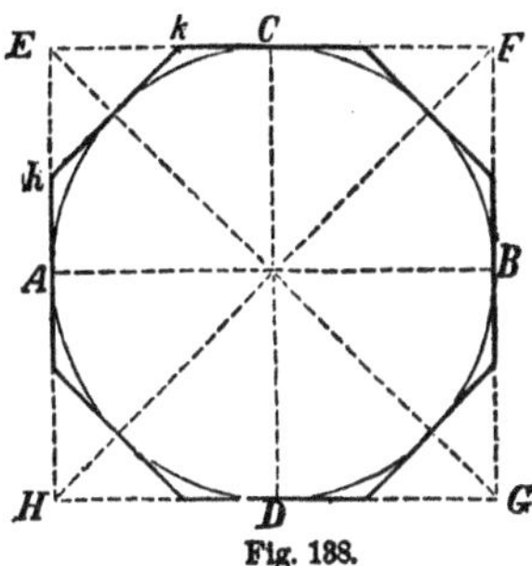

Fig. 138.

PROB. XLV.—*To describe a regular octagon about a circle* (fig. 138).

Describe a square about the given circle A B; draw perpendiculars *h k*, &c., to the diagonals, touching the circle. The octagon so formed is the figure required.

Or, to find the points *h*, *k*, &c., cut the sides from the corners of the square, as in Prob. XLIII.

PROB. XLVI.—*To inscribe a circle within a regular polygon.*

When the polygon has an even number of sides, as in fig. 139, bisect two opposite sides at A and B, draw A B, and bisect it at C by a diagonal D E drawn between opposite angles; with the radius C A describe the circle as required.

When the number of sides is odd, as in fig. 140, bisect two of the sides at A and B, and draw lines A E, B D, to the opposite angles, intersecting at C; from C with C A as radius, describe the circle as required.

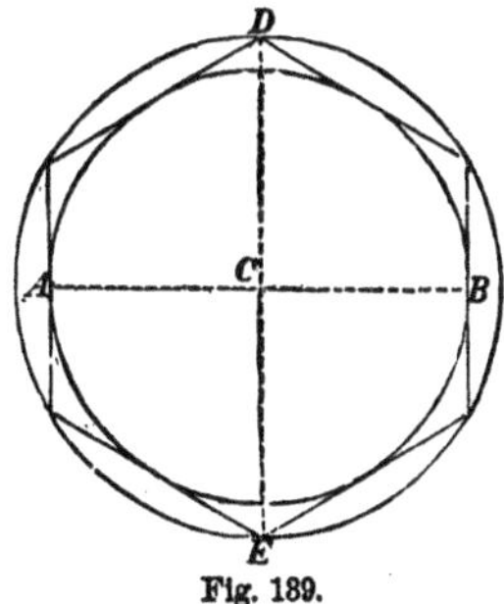

Fig. 139.

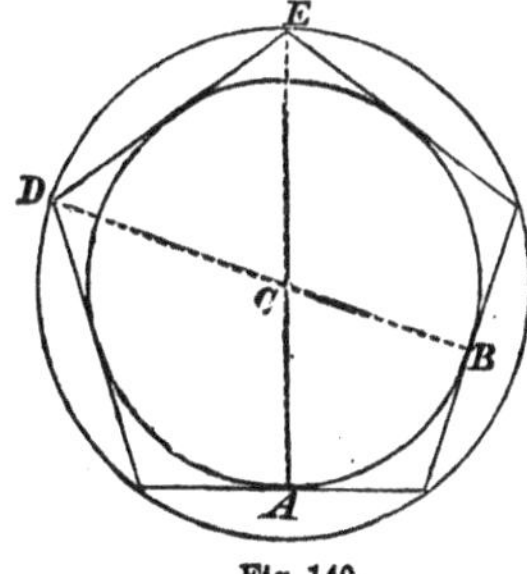

Fig. 140.

PROB. XLVII.—*To describe a circle without a regular polygon.*

When the number of sides is even, draw two diagonals from opposite angles, like D E (fig. 139), to intersect at C; and from C with C D as radius, describe the circle required.

When the number of sides is odd, find the centre C (fig. 140) as in last problem, and with C D as radius describe the circle.

The foregoing selection of problems on regular figures is the most useful in mechanical practice on that subject. Several other regular figures may be constructed from them by bisection of the arcs of the circumscribing circles. In this way a decagon, or ten-sided polygon, may be formed from the pentagon by the bisection of the arcs in Prob. XXXVIII., fig. 132. Inversely, an equilateral triangle may be inscribed by joining the alternate points of division found for a hexagon.

The constructions for inscribing regular polygons in circles are suitable also for dividing the circumference of a circle into a number of equal parts. To supply a means of dividing the circumference into *any* number of parts, including cases not provided for in the foregoing problems, the annexed table of angles relating to polygons, expressed in degrees, will be found of general utility. In this table, the angle at the centre is found by

TABLE OF POLYGONAL ANGLES.

Number of Sides of Regular Polygon; or number of equal parts of the circumference.	Angle at Centre.	Number of Sides of Regular Polygon.	Angle at Centre.
No.	Degrees.	No.	Degrees.
3	120	12	30
4	90	13	$27\frac{9}{13}$
5	72	14	$25\frac{5}{7}$
6	60	15	24
7	$51\frac{3}{7}$	16	$22\frac{1}{2}$
8	45	17	$21\frac{3}{17}$
9	40	18	20
10	36	19	$18\frac{18}{19}$
11	$32\frac{8}{11}$	20	18

dividing 360°, the number of degrees in a circle, by the number of sides in the polygon; and by setting off round the centre of the circle a succession of angles by means of the protractor, equal to the angle in the table due to a given number of sides: the radii so drawn will divide the circumference into the same number of parts. The triangles thus formed are termed the elementary triangles of the polygon.

PROB. XLVIII.—*To inscribe any regular polygon in a given circle; or to divide the circumference into a given number of equal parts, by means of the angle at the centre* (fig. 141).

Suppose the circle is to contain a hexagon, or is to be divided at the circumference into six equal parts. Find the angle at the centre for a hexagon, or 60°; draw any radius B C, and set off by a protractor or otherwise the angle at the centre C B D, equal to 60°; then the interval C D is one side of the figure, or segment of the circumference; and the remaining points of division may be found either by stepping along the circumference with the distance C D in the dividers, or by setting off the remaining five angles of 60° each round the centre.

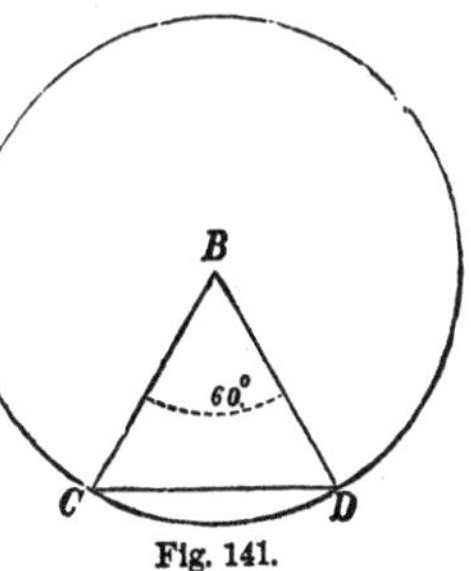

Fig. 141.

THE USE OF THE T SQUARE AND TRIANGLE IN THE CONSTRUCTION OF SOME OF THE FOREGOING PROBLEMS.

From the description of the T square it may be seen, that by sliding the stock along two contiguous edges of the board, the left hand and bottom edges, any number of parallel and perpendicular lines may be drawn. In so far, therefore, the T square supersedes the application of all the problems for drawing parallels and perpendiculars, coinciding in direction with the edges of the board; for the square need only be set with its edge coincident with the points through which the line is to be drawn, and the pen or pencil drawn along the edge will describe the line required. When the perpendiculars or upright lines are of short length, the triangle and ruler are used. For this purpose, the triangle of 60° is preferable to that of 45°, as it is longer and lighter.

When the lines to be drawn do not coincide in direction with the edges of the board, the square may be adjusted with its bevel stock to the obliquity required, and the lines may be drawn as before. This is probably the best plan when the oblique lines are numerous or extensive. In most cases, however, oblique lines are only occasional, and when their position is given, they may be drawn with a straight-edge. When the oblique parallels and perpendiculars are short, as in oblique framing, short rods or bars, bolt-heads, and the like, the combined use of the straight-edge and triangle is expedient. Square figures may be described on a given centre, at one setting of the straight-edge, as in the drawing of the head of a square nut *n* (fig. 142). From the given centre, with a radius equal

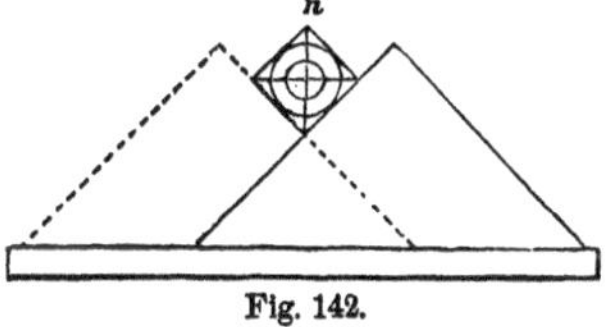

Fig. 142.

to half the side of the square, describe a circle, and with the aid of the triangle draw lines tangent to four sides.

To draw an octagon, apply the set-square of 45° to the corners, after completing a square figure, and draw tangents to the inscribed circle, as, for example, the line *h k* (fig. 138).

To draw an equilateral triangle upon a given line A B (fig. 143), it is only necessary to apply the slant edge of the set-square of 60° to each end

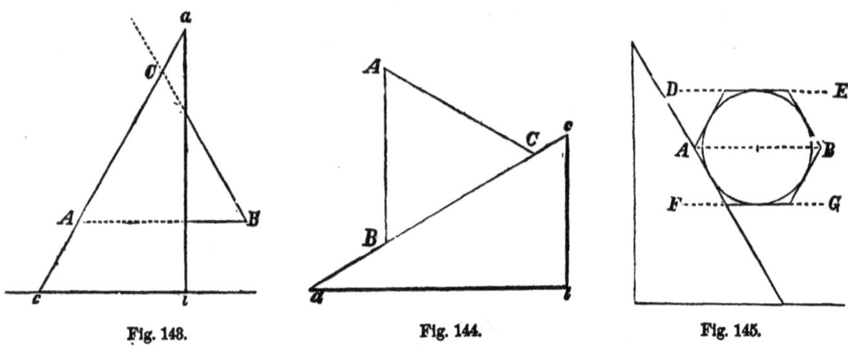

Fig. 143. Fig. 144. Fig. 145.

of the base, with the short side *b c* applied to the square-blade, and to draw the two sides A C, B C. If the given side A B be upright (fig. 144), apply the long side *a b* to the straight-edge, and draw as before.

To draw a regular hexagon about a circle, with two of its sides parallel to the lower edge of the board: draw the centre line A B (fig. 145), and the upper and lower sides D E, F G, touching the circle, and apply the triangle of 60° touching the circle for the four remaining sides, as shown in the figure.

When the hexagons are to be inscribed in the circle, first draw the centre line A B (fig. 133) as a diameter, and from the ends A, B, with the set-square, draw four sides cutting the circle at D, E, F, G, and join D E, F G.

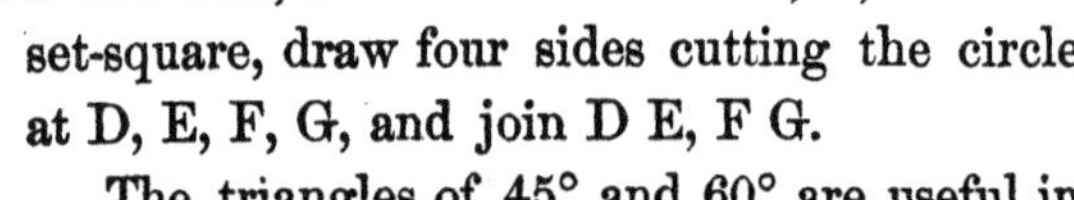

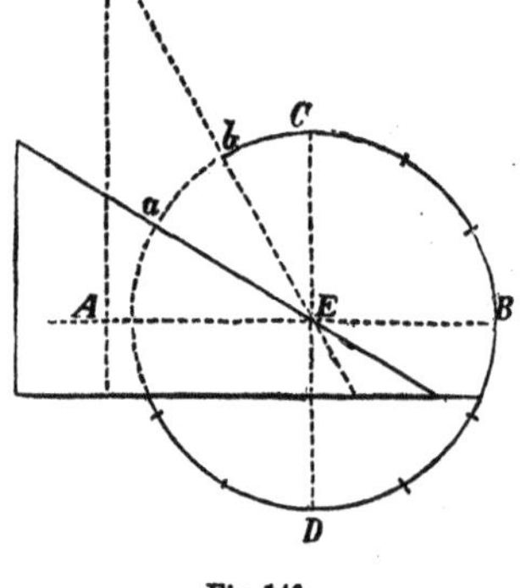

Fig. 146.

The triangles of 45° and 60° are useful in setting out the centre-lines of wheels with 3, 4, 6, 8, &c., arms, by drawing lines through the centre of the wheel. To set out 12 spokes in a wheel (fig. 146) :—Draw two diameters, A B, C D, parallel to the two edges of the board; in the quadrant A C, draw radii E *a*, E *b*, with the long and the short sides of the triangle against the square-blade. These will divide the quadrant equally; and the same construction being employed for the other quarters of the circle, 12 centre lines, equally distant, will be described. Should the triangle be large enough to embrace the whole circle at once, the opposite quadrants A C and B D may be divided with the same setting of the triangle.

A short method of dividing a line or surface into a number of equal parts is illustrated by fig. 147; and it is convenient where an ordinary rule does not evenly measure the dimension. Suppose the width A C is to be divided into seven equal parts, and that it measures $7\frac{3}{4}$ inches; an ordinary inch rule, it is plain, does not afford the subdivisions when applied directly; but if 14 inches of length, or double the number of parts, be applied obliquely across the space between the parallels A B, C D, so as to measure it exactly, then point off two-inch intervals on the edge of the rule, and in this way 7 equal subdivisions will be effected, through which parallels may be drawn.

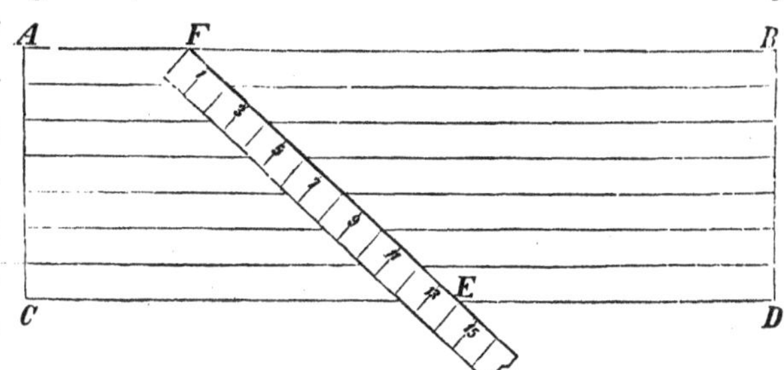

SIMPLE APPLICATIONS OF REGULAR FIGURES.

Prob. XLIX.—*To cover a surface with equilateral triangles, hexagons, or lozenges.*

Describe an equilateral triangle A B C, and produce the sides indefinitely. Set off from one angle A, equal intervals at *a*, *b*, *a′*, *b′*, &c., as required; and through these points draw parallels to each of the sides of the triangle. The area will be covered with triangles as required.

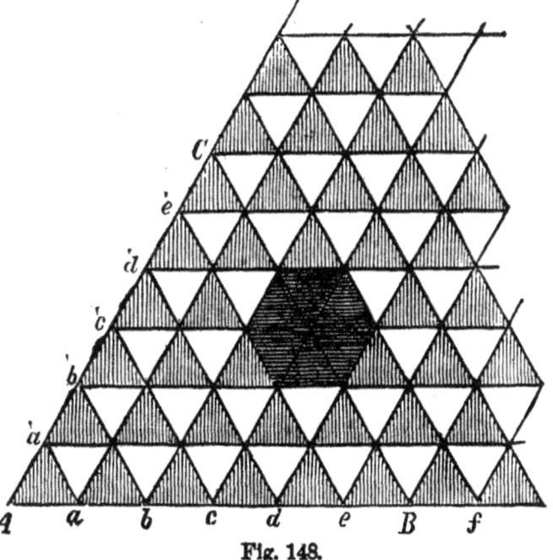

Fig. 148.

For hexagons, or equilateral triangles and hexagons on the same surface, or lozenges, group the triangles.

Prob. L.—*To cover a surface with octagons and squares.*

Draw two straight lines A B, A C, at right angles; set off equal intervals A *d*, *d e*, &c., on each line, equal to the breadth of the octagon to be described, and through these points draw parallels to the given lines, to

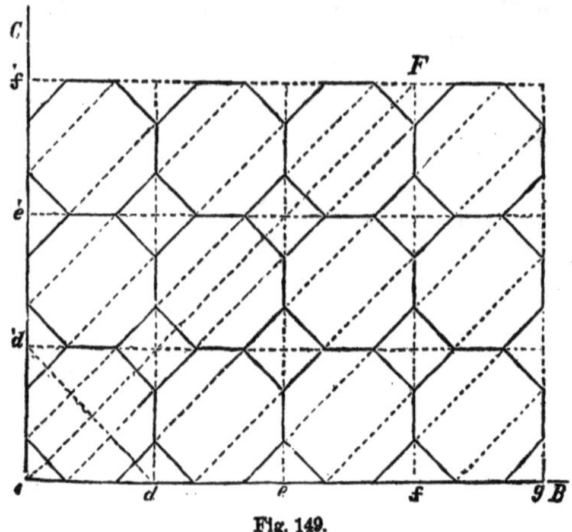

Fig. 149.

form squares. Within these squares construct octagons, by Probs. XLIII. or XLIV., and finish as in the figure.

PROBLEMS ON PROPORTIONAL LINES AND EQUIVALENT FIGURES.

Prob. LI.—*To divide a given straight line into two parts proportional to two given lines.*

Let A B (fig. 150) be the line to be divided; draw the straight line A D at any angle with A B, and set off A E, E D, equal to the other two given lines. Join D B, and draw C E parallel to it; this line divides A B at C in the required ratio.

Prob. LII.—*To divide a straight line into any number of parts of given proportions; or similarly to a given straight line.*

Let A B (fig. 151) be the line to be divided. Draw B G at any angle

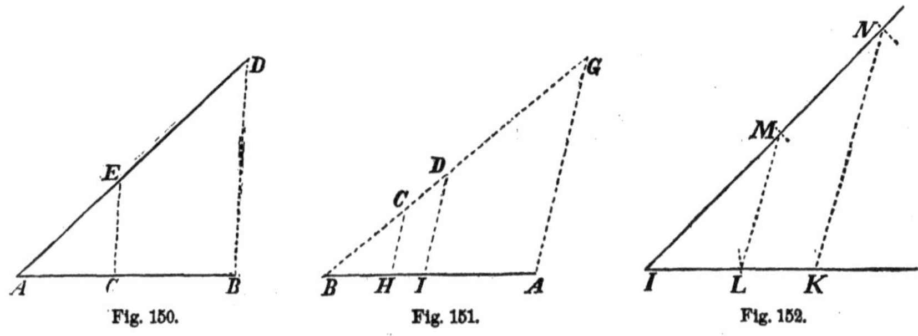

Fig. 150. Fig. 151. Fig. 152.

with it, and set off by any convenient scale, B C, C D, &c., to G, respectively, equal to the given divisions. Join A G, and from the points of division of B G draw parallels to A G, cutting it at H, I, &c. The parallels so drawn will divide A B as required.

PROB. LIII.—*To find a fourth proportional to three given lines.*

Draw two lines I K, I N (fig. 152), at any angle, and set off I M, I N, equal to the two first of the given lines, and set off I L equal to the third. Join L M, and draw N K parallel to it. Then I K is a fourth proportional as required.

The two first lines may be set off successively on the same line, as from I to M, and from M to N, and the third from I to L; then L K will be the fourth line required.

PROB. LIV.—*To find a mean proportional between two given lines* (fig. 153).

Let *a b* and *b c* be the given lines. Set off, on a straight line, A B, B C, equal to the given lines; bisect A C at D, and with D A as a radius describe the semicircle A E C; draw B E perpendicular to A C, meeting the circle at E. Then B E is the mean proportional required.

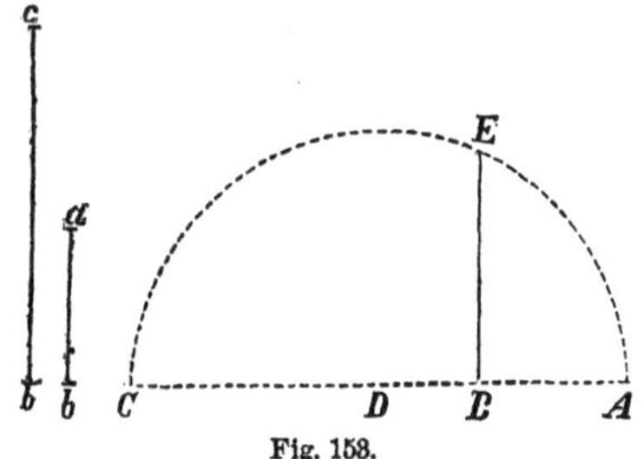

Fig. 153.

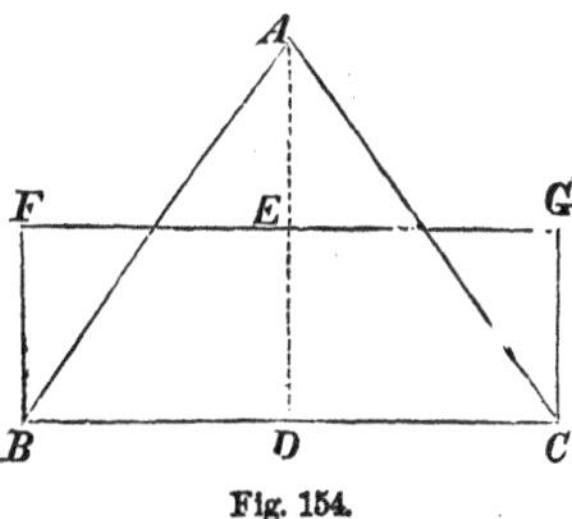

Fig. 154.

PROB. LV.—*To construct a triangle equal in area to a given rectangle.*

Bisect the base B C (fig. 154) of the rectangle at D, and draw the perpendicular D A equal to twice the height, D E, of the rectangle. Draw B A, A C; the triangle A B C is equal in area to the rectangle B G.

PROB. LVI.—*To construct a square equal to a given rectangle* (fig. 155).

Let A B C D be the rectangle; produce A B, and set off B E equal to the side B C of the rectangle; bisect A E at K, and describe a semicircle on A E; draw the perpendicular B H, cutting the circle at H, and on B H describe the square B G required.

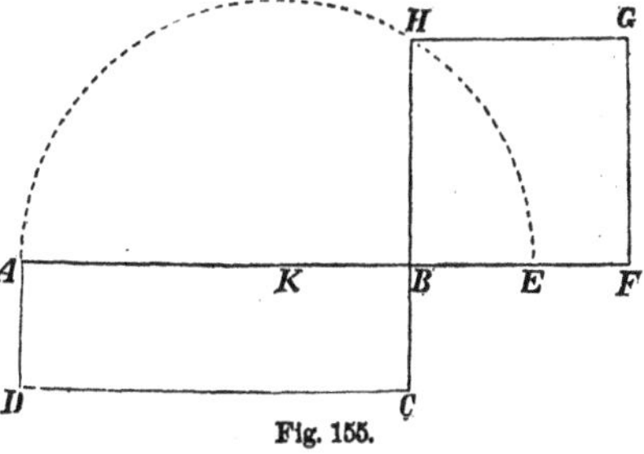

Fig. 155.

PROB. LVII.—*To construct a triangle equivalent to any regular polygon.*

Find the radius of the circle inscribed in the polygon. Set off on a right line a distance equal to half the sum of the sides of the polygon. This distance will be the base of the equivalent triangle, and the radius of the inscribed circle its perpendicular or altitude.

PROBLEMS ON THE ELLIPSE, THE PARABOLA, THE HYPERBOLA, THE CYCLOID, AND THE EPICYCLOID.

The Ellipse.

PROB. LVIII.—*To describe an ellipse, the length and breadth, or the two axes being given.*

1*st Method* (fig. 156).—Bisect the transverse axis A B at C, and through

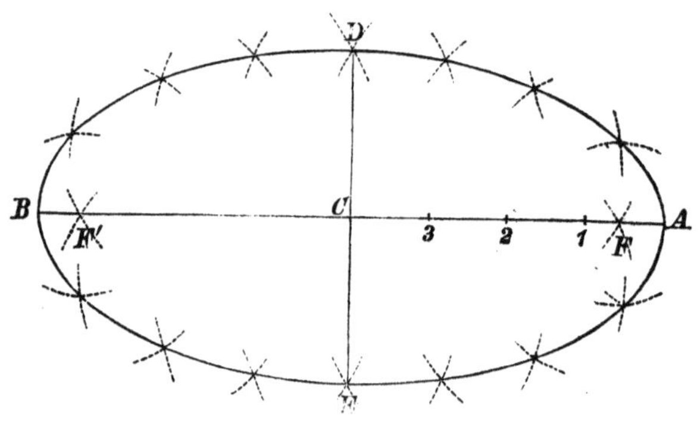

Fig. 156.

C draw the perpendicular D E, making C D and C E each equal to half the conjugate diameter. On D as a centre, with C A as radius, describe arcs cutting at F, F′, for the foci. Divide A C into a number of parts at the points 1, 2, 3, &c. With radius A 1 on F and F′ as centres, describe arcs; and with radius B 1, on the same centres, describe arcs intersecting the others as shown. Repeat the operation for the other divisions of the transverse axis. The series of intersections thus found will be points in the curve, and they may be as numerously found as is desirable; after which a curve traced through them will form the complete ellipse.

2*d Method* (fig. 157).—The two axes, A B, D E, being given. On A B and D E as diameters from the same centre C, describe circles F G, H I; take a convenient number of points, *a*, *b*, &c., in the semi-circumference A F B, and draw radii cutting the innner circle at *a′* *b′*, &c.; from *a*, *b*, &c., draw perpendiculars to A B, and from *a′*, *b′*, &c., draw parallels to

A B, cutting the respective perpendiculars at *n*, *o*, &c. The points of intersection so found are points in the curve.

3d Method (fig. 158). — Along the straight edge of a slip of stiff paper mark off a distance *a c* equal to A C, half the transverse axis; and from the same point, a distance *a b* equal to C D, half the conjugate axis. Place the slip so as to bring the point *b* on the line A B of the transverse axis, and the point *c* on the line D E; and set off on the drawing the position of the point *a*. Always keeping the point *b* on the transverse axis, and the point *c* on the conjugate axis, any required number of points may be found.

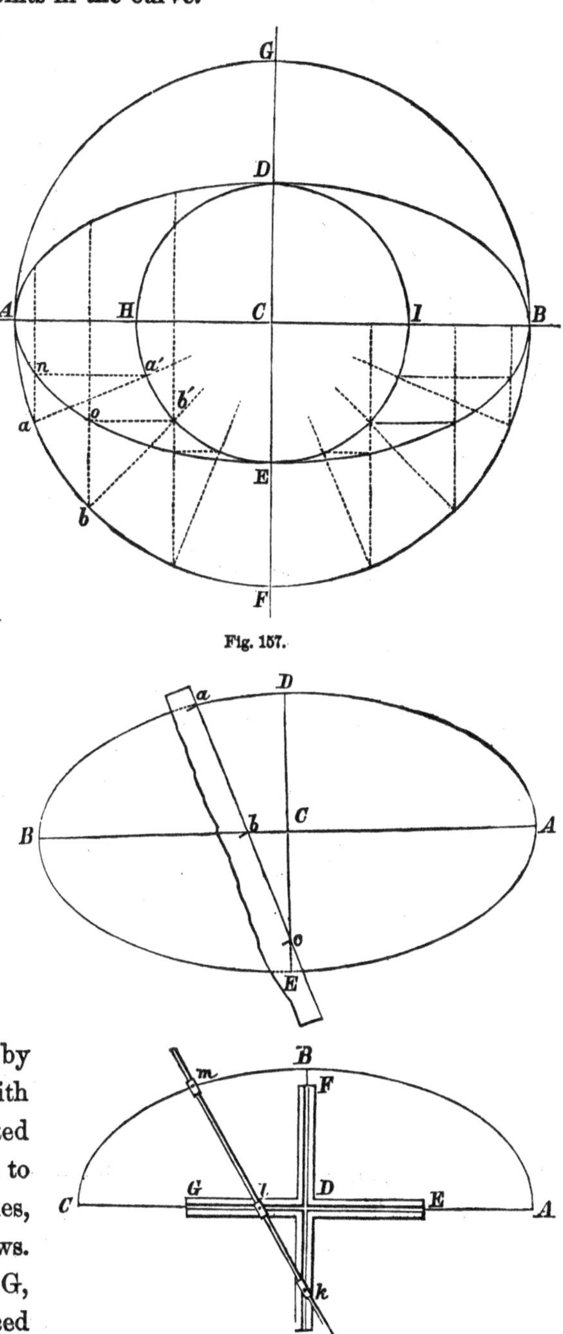

4th Method (fig. 159). —By the above method large curves may be described continuously by means of a bar *m k*, with steel points *m*, *l*, *k*, riveted into brass slides, adjusted to the length of the semi-axes, and fixed with set-screws. A rectangular cross E G, with guiding slots, is placed to coincide with the two axes of the ellipse A C and B H; by sliding the points *k*, *l*, in the slots, and carrying round the point *m*, the curve may be completely described. If desirable, of course, a pen or pencil may be fixed at *m*.

5th Method (fig. 160).—Given the two axes A B, C D; on the centre C, with A E as radius, describe an arc cutting A B at F and G, the foci; fix a couple of pins into the transverse axis at F and G, and loop on a thread or cord upon these, equal in length, when looped on, to A B, so as, when stretched, as per dot-line F C G, just to reach the extremity, C, of the conjugate axis. Place a pencil or draw-point inside the cord, as at H, and guiding the pencil in this way, keeping the cord equally on tension, pass round the two points F, G, and describe the curve as required.

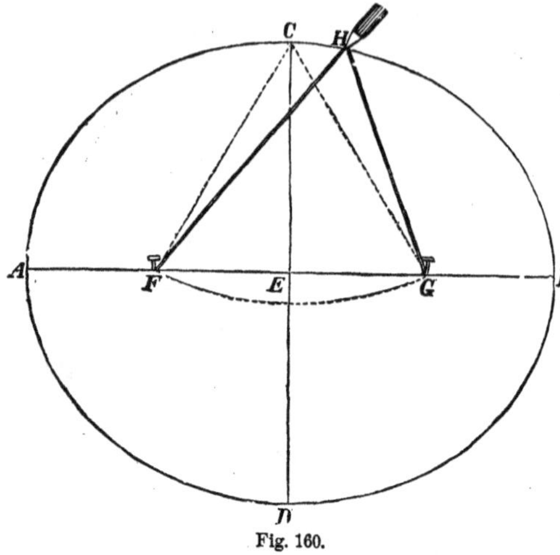

Fig. 160.

This method is employed in setting off elliptical garden-plots, walks, &c.

Prob. LIX.—*To draw a tangent to an ellipse through a given point in the curve* (fig. 161).

From the given point T draw straight lines to the foci F, F′; produce

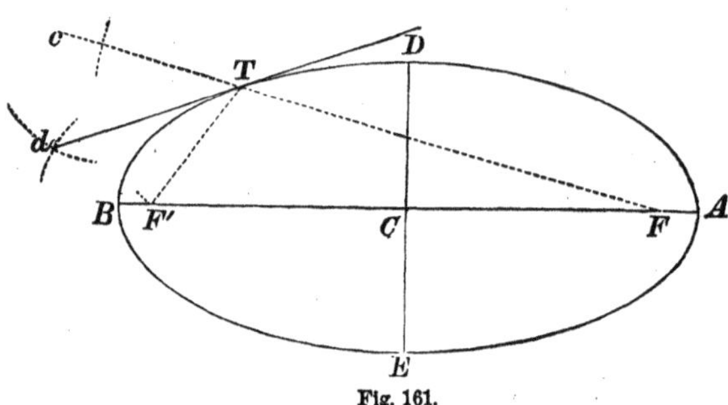

Fig. 161.

F T beyond the curve to *c*, and bisect the exterior angle *c* T F′ by the line T *d*. This line T *d* is the tangent required.

Prob. LX.—*To draw a tangent to an ellipse from a given point without the curve* (fig. 162).

From the given point T as centre, with a radius equal to its distance from the nearest focus F, describe an arc; from the other focus F′, with the transverse axis as radius, cut the arc at K, L, and draw K F′, L F′, cutting the curve at M, N; then the lines T M, T N, are tangents to the curve.

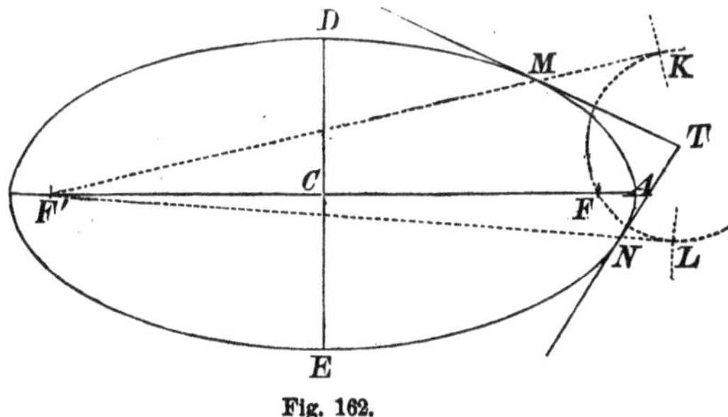

Fig. 162.

PROB. LXI.—*To describe an ellipse approximately, by means of circular arcs.*

First, with arcs of two radii (fig. 163). Take the difference of the transverse and conjugate axes, and set it off from the centre O to *a* and *c*, on O A and O C; draw *a c*, and set off half *a c* to *d*; draw *d i* parallel to *a c*,

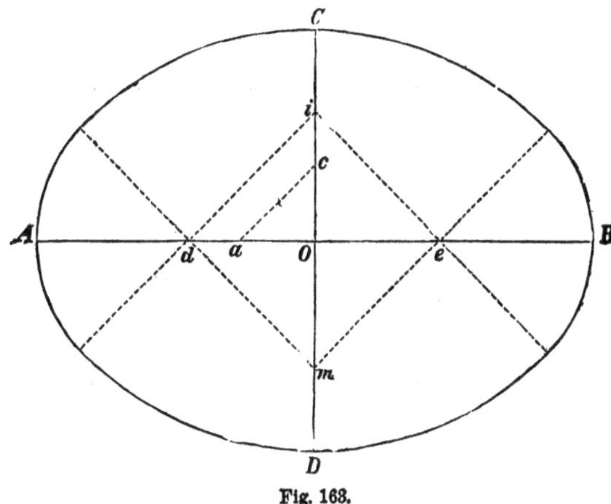

Fig. 163.

set off O *e* equal to O *d*, join *e i*, and draw *e m*, *d m*, parallels to *d i*, *i e*. On centre *m*, with radius *m* C, describe an arc through C, and from centre *i* describe an arc through D; on centre *d*, *e*, also, describe arcs through A and B. The four arcs thus described form approximately an ellipse. This method does not apply satisfactorily when the conjugate axis is less than two-thirds of the transverse axis.

Second, with arcs of three radii (fig. 164). On the transverse axis A B, draw the rectangle B G, equal in height to O C, half the conjugate axis. Draw G D perpendicular to A C; set off O K equal to O C, and on A K as a diameter, describe the semicircle A N K; draw a radius parallel to O C, intersecting the semicircle at N and the line G E at P; extend O C to L and to D; set off O M equal to P N, and on D as a centre, with a radius D M, describe an arc; from A and B as centres, with a radius O L,

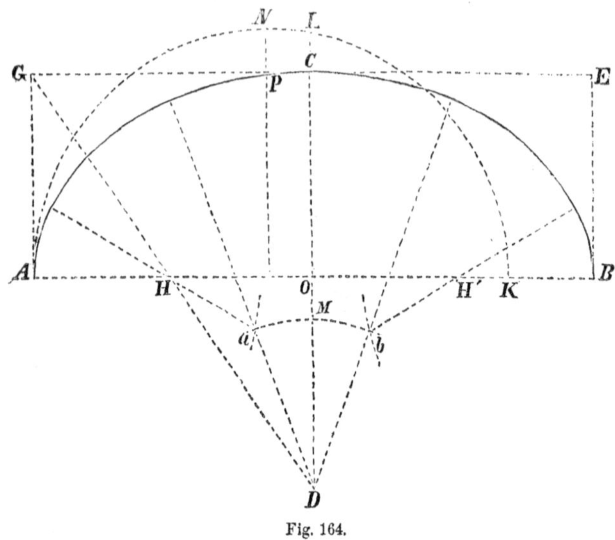

Fig. 164.

intersect this arc at a and b. The points H, a, D, b, H′, are the centres of the arcs required; produce the lines a H, D a, D b, b H′, and the spaces enclosed determine the lengths of each arc.

This process works well for nearly all proportions of ellipses. It is employed in striking out vaults and stone bridges.

The Parabola.

The *parabola* may be defined as an ellipse whose transverse axis is infinite; its characteristic is that every point in the curve is equally distant from the directrix E N and the focus F (fig. 165).

PROB. LXII.—*To construct a parabola when the focus and directrix are given.*

1*st Method* (fig. 165).—Through the focus F draw the axis A B perpendicular to the directrix E N, and bisect A F at e, then e is the vertex of the curve. Through a series of points C, D, E, on the directrix, draw parallels to A B; connect these points C, D, E, with the focus F, and bisect by perpendiculars the lines F C, F D, F E. The intersections of these perpendiculars with the parallels will give points in the curve C′ D′ E′, through which trace the parabola.

2*d Method* (fig. 166).—Place a straight edge to the directrix E N, and apply to it a square L E G; fasten at G one end of a cord, equal in length to E G; fix the other end to the focus F; slide the square steadily along

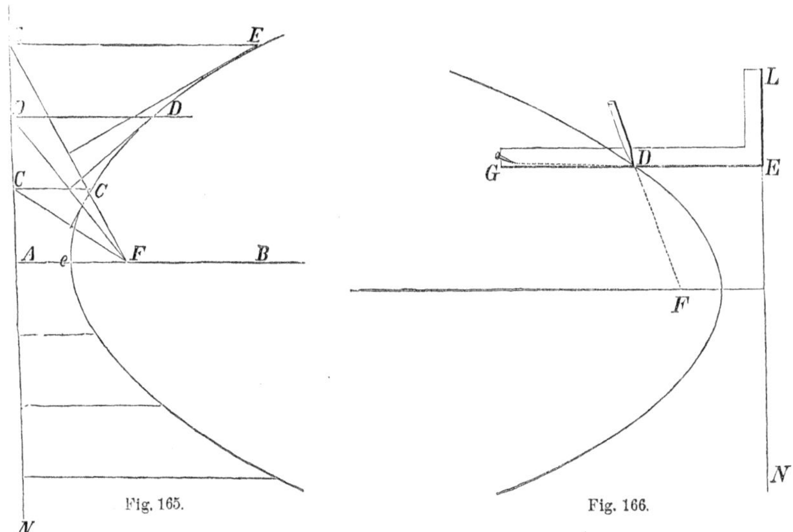

Fig. 165. Fig. 166.

the straight edge, holding the cord taut against the edge of the square by a pencil D, and it will describe the curve.

PROB. LXIII.—*To construct a parabola when the vertex* A, *the axis* A B, *and a point* M *of the curve are given* (fig. 167).

Construct the rectangle A B M C; divide M C into any number of equal parts, four for instance; divide A C in like manner; connect A 1, A 2, A 3; through 1′ 2′ 3′, draw parallels to the axis. The intersections I, II, III, of these lines are points in the required curve.

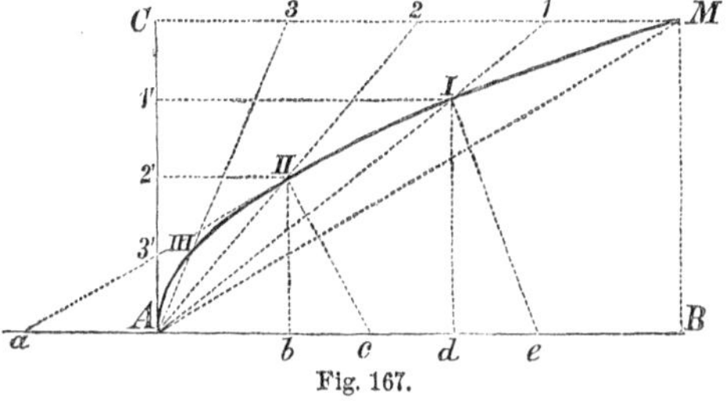

Fig. 167.

PROB. LXIV.—*To draw a tangent to a given point* II *of the parabola* (fig. 167).

From the given point II let fall a perpendicular on the axis at *b*; extend the axis to the left of A; make A *a* equal to A *b*; draw *a* II, and it is the tangent required.

The lines perpendicular to the tangent are called normals. *To find the normal to any point* I, *having the tangent to any other point* II.—Draw the normal II *c*; from I let fall a perpendicular I *d* on the axis A B; lay off *d e* equal to *b c*; connect I *e*, and we have the normal required. The tangent may be drawn at I by a perpendicular to the normal I *e*.

The Hyperbola.

An *hyperbola* is a curve from any point P in which, if two straight lines be drawn to two fixed points, F F′ the foci, their difference shall always be the same.

Prob. LXV.—*To describe an hyperbola* (fig. 168).

From one of the foci F, with an assumed radius, describe an arc, and from the other focus F′, with another radius exceeding the former by the given difference, describe two small arcs, cutting the first as at P and *p*. Let this operation be repeated with two new radii, taking care that the second shall exceed the first by the same difference as before, and two new points will be determined; and this determination of points in the curve may thus be continued till its track is obvious. By making use of the same radii, but transposing, that is, describing with the greater about F, and the less about F′, we have another series of points equally belonging to the hyperbola, and answering the definition; so that the hyperbola consists of two separate branches.

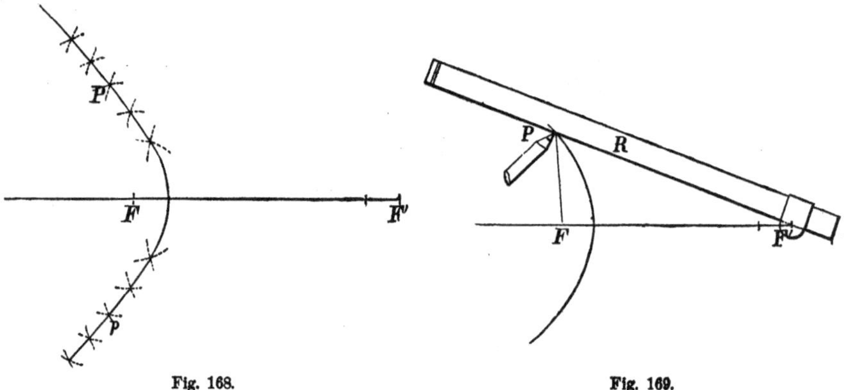

Fig. 168. Fig. 169.

The curve may be described mechanically (fig. 169).—By fixing a ruler to one focus F′, so that it may be turned round on this point, connect the extremity of the ruler R to the other focus F by a cord shorter than the whole length F R of the ruler by the given difference; then a pencil P keeping this cord always stretched, and at the same time pressing against the edge of the ruler, will, as the ruler revolves around F′, describe an hyperbola, of which F F′ are the foci, and the differences of distances from these points to every point in the curve will be the same.

Prob. LXVI.—*To draw a tangent to any point* P *of an hyperbola* (fig. 170).

On F′ P lay off P p equal to F P; connect F p, and from P let fall a perpendicular on this line F p, and it will be the tangent required.

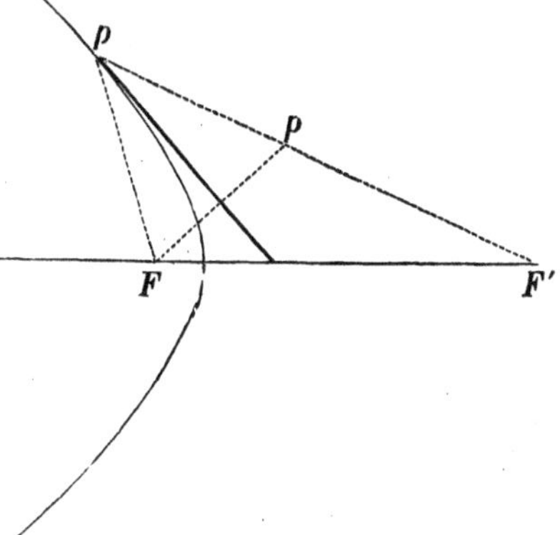

Fig. 170.

The three curves, the ellipse, the parabola, and the hyperbola, are called conic sections, as they are formed by the intersections of a plane with the surface of a cone (plate III).

If the cone be cut through both its sides by a plane not parallel to the base, the section is an ellipse; if the intersecting plane be parallel to the side of the cone, the section is a parabola; if the plane have such a position, that when produced it meets the opposite cone, the section is a hyperbola. The opposite cone is a reversed cone formed on the apex of the other by the continuation of its sides.

The Cycloid.

The *cycloid* is the curve described by a point in the circumference of a circle rolling on a straight line.

Prob. LXVII.—*To describe a cycloid* (fig. 171).

Draw the straight line A B as the base; describe the generating circle tangent to the centre of this line, and through the centre C draw the line E E parallel to the base; let fall a perpendicular from C upon the base;

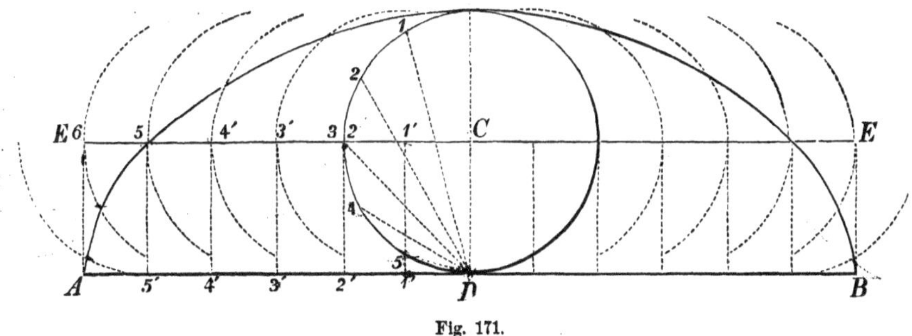

Fig. 171.

divide the semicircumference into any number of equal parts, for instance six; lay off on A B and C E distances C 1′, 1′ 2′ . . ., equal to the divisions of the circumference; draw the chords D 1, D 2 . . ., from the points 1′, 2′, 3′ . . . on the line C E, with radii equal to the generating circle, describe arcs;

from the points 1′, 2′, 3′, 4′, 5′ on the line B A, and with radii equal successively to the chords D 1, D 2, D 3, D 4, D 5, describe arcs cutting the preceding, and the intersections will be points of the curve required.

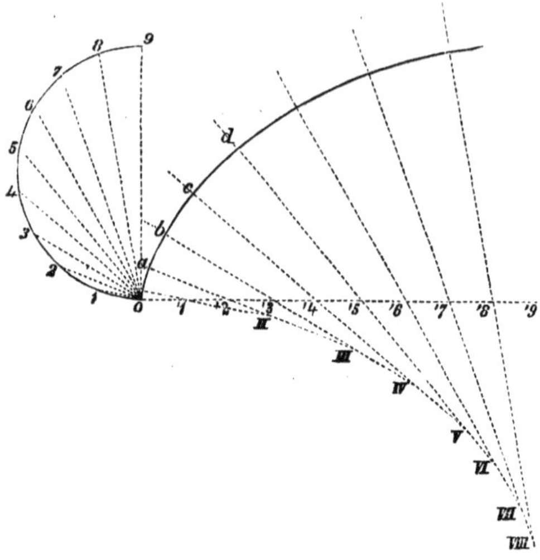

2d Method (fig. 172).—Let 0 9′ be the base line, 0 4 9 the half of the generating circle; divide the half circle into any number of equal parts, say 9, and draw the chord 0 1, 0 2, 0 3, &c.; lay off on the base 0 1′, 1′ 2′, 2′ 3′ . . . . , equal respectively to the length of one of the divisions of the half circle 0 1; draw through the points 1′, 2′, 3′ . . . . . lines parallel to the chords 0 1, 0 2, 0 3 . . . . ; the intersections I, II, III . . . . of these lines are centres of the arcs 0 *a*, *a b*, *b c* . . . . , of which the cycloid is composed.

The Epicycloid.

The *epicycloid* is formed by a point in the circumference of a circle revolving either externally or internally on the circumference of another circle as a base.

PROB. LXVIII.—*To describe an epicycloid.*

Let us in the first place take the exterior curve. Divide the circumference A B D (fig. 173) into a series of equal parts 1, 2, 3 . . . ., beginning from the point A; set off in the same manner, upon the circle A M, A N, the divisions 1′, 2′, 3′ . . . . equal to the divisions of the circumference A B D. Then, as the circle A B D rolls upon the circle A M A N, the points 1, 2, 3 will coincide successively with the points 1′, 2′, 3′; and, drawing radii from the point O through the points 1′, 2′, 3′, and also describing arcs of circles from the centre O, through the points 1, 2, 3, ..., they will intersect each other successively at the points *c*, *d*, *e* . . . . Take now the distance 1 to *c*, and set it off on the same arc from the point of intersection, *c*, of the radius A C; in like manner, set off the distance 2 to *d*, from *b* to A^2, and the distance 3 to *e* to A^3, and so on. Then the points A^1, A^2, A^3, will be so many points in the epicycloid; and their frequency may be increased at pleasure by shortening the divisions of the circular arcs. Thus the form of the curve may be determined to any amount of accuracy, and completed by tracing a line through the points found.

As the distances 1 to *c*, ... which are near the commencement of the curve, must be very short, it may, in some instances, be more convenient to set off the whole distance *i* to 1 from *c*, and in the same way the distance *b* to 2 from *d* to A^2, and so on. In this manner the form of the curve is the more likely to be accurately defined.

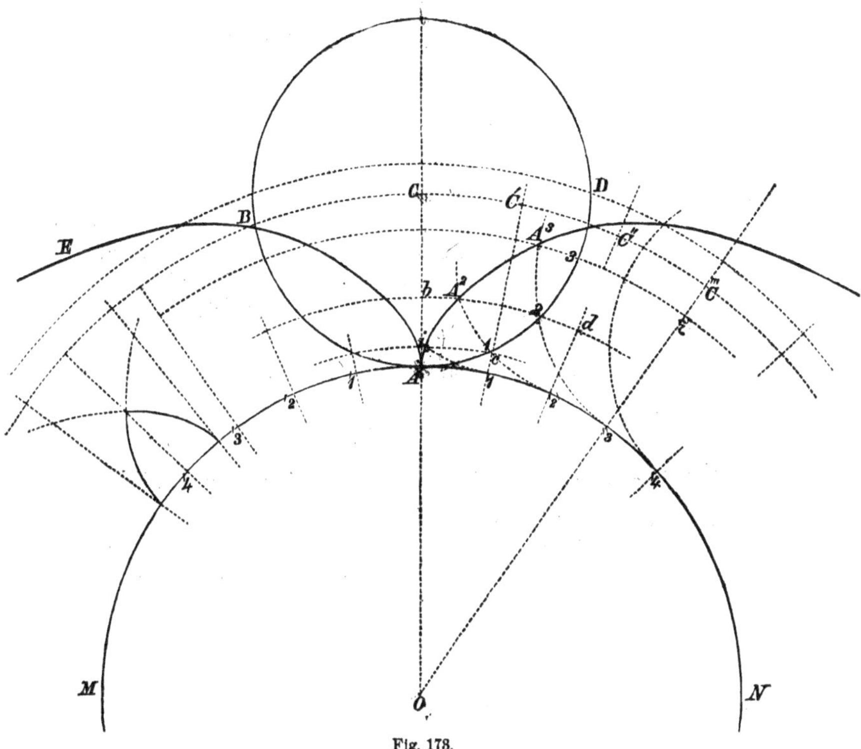

Fig. 173.

2*d Method.*—To find the points in the curve, find the positions of the centre of the rolling circle corresponding to the points of contact 1′, 2′, 3′, &c., which may be readily done by producing the radii from the centre O, through the points 1′, 2′, 3′, ... to cut the circle B C. From these centres describe arcs of a circle with the radius of C A, cutting the corresponding arcs described from the centre O, and passing through the points A^1, A^2, A^3, ... as before.

When the moving circle A B D is made to roll on the interior of the circumference A M, A N, as shown (fig. 174), the curve described by the point A is called an *interior epicycloid.* It may be constructed in the same way as in the preceding case, as may be easily understood, the same figures and letters of reference being used in both figures.

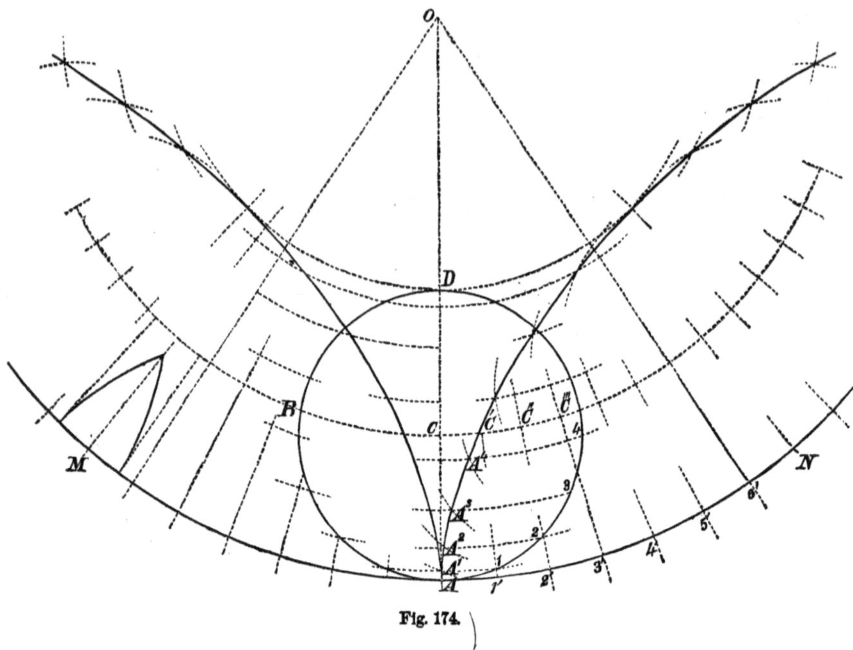

Fig. 174.

The Involute.

The *involute* is a curve traced by the extremity of a flexible line unwinding from the circumference of a circle.

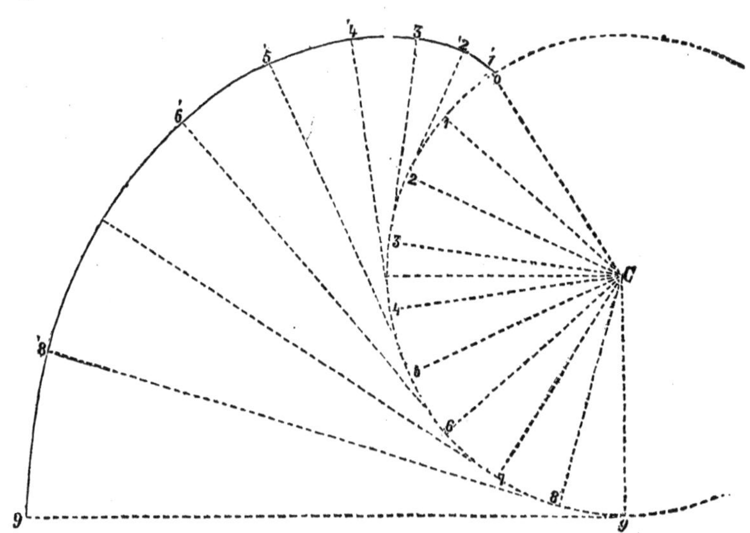

PROB. LXIX.—*To describe an involute.*

Divide the circumference of the given circle (fig. 175) into any number of equal parts, as 0, 1, 2, 3, 4, ... ; at each of these points draw tangents to the given circle; on the first of these lay off the distance 1 1′, equal to the arc 0 1; on the second lay off 2 2′, equal to twice the arc 0 1 or the arc 0 2: establish in a similar way the points 3′, 4′, 5′, ... as far as may be requisite, which are points in the curve required.

It may be remarked, that in all the problems in which curves have been determined by the position of points, that the more numerous the points thus fixed, the more accurately can the curve be drawn.

The involute curve may be described mechanically in several ways. Thus, let A (fig. 176) be the centre of a wheel for which the form of involute teeth is to be found. Let *m n a* be a thread lapped round its circumference, having a loop-hole at its extremity *a;* in this fix a pin, with which describe the curve or *involute a b . . . . h*, by unwinding the thread gradually from the circumference, and this curve will be the proper form for the teeth of a wheel of the given diameter.

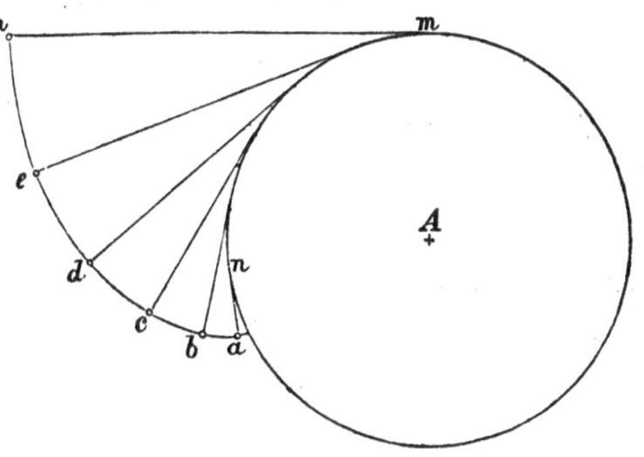

Fig. 176.

The Spiral.

The *spiral* is the involute of a circle produced beyond a single revolution.

Prob. LXX.—*To describe a spiral* (figs. 5 and 6, plate VII.)

Divide the circumference of the primary into any number of equal parts, say not less than eight. To these points of division *e*, *f*, *i*, &c., draw tangents, and from these points draw a succession of circular arcs; thus, from *e* as a centre, with the radius *e g*, equal to the arc *a e* reduced to a straight line, describe the arc *a g h;* from *f*, with the radius *b f*, describe the arc *g h;* from *i* the next arc, and so on. Continue the use of the centres successively and repeatedly to the extent of the revolutions required. Thus the point *a* in the fig. is used as a centre for three arcs, *b l*, *c m*, *d n*.

GEOMETRICAL PROJECTION.

Architectural and mechanical drawing is generally the delineation of bodies by geometrical or orthographic projection; the representation on a sheet of paper which has only two dimensions, length and breadth; solids which have three, length, breadth, and thickness.

Since the surfaces of all bodies may be considered as composed of points, the first step is to represent the position in space of a point, by referring it planes whose position is established. The projection of a point upon a plane is the foot of the perpendicular let fall from the point on the plane. If, therefore, on two planes not parallel to each other, whose positions are known, we have the projections of a point, the position of this point is completely determined by erecting perpendiculars from each plane at the projected points: their intersection will be the point.

If from every point of an indefinite straight line A B (fig. 177), placed in any manner in space, perpendiculars be let fall on a plane L M N O, whose position is given, then all the points in which these perpendiculars meet the plane will form another indefinite straight line *a b*: this line is called the projection of the line A B on this plane. Since two points are sufficient to determine a straight line, it is only necessary to project two points of the line, and the straight line drawn through the two projected points will be the projection of the given line. The projection of a straight line, itself perpendicular to the plane, is the point in which this perpendicular meets the plane.

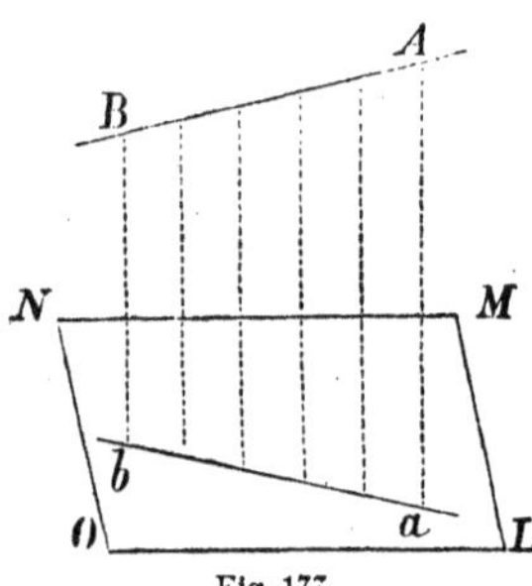

Fig. 177.

If the projections *a b* and *a′ b′* of a straight line on the two planes L M N O and L M P Q (fig. 178) are known, this line A B is determined; for if, through one of its projections *a b*, we suppose a plane drawn perpendicularly to LMNO, and if through a' b' another plane be drawn perpendicular to L M P Q, the intersection of the two planes will be the line A B.

To delineate a solid, as the form of a machine for instance, it must be referred to three series of dimensions, each of them at right angles to the plane of the other.

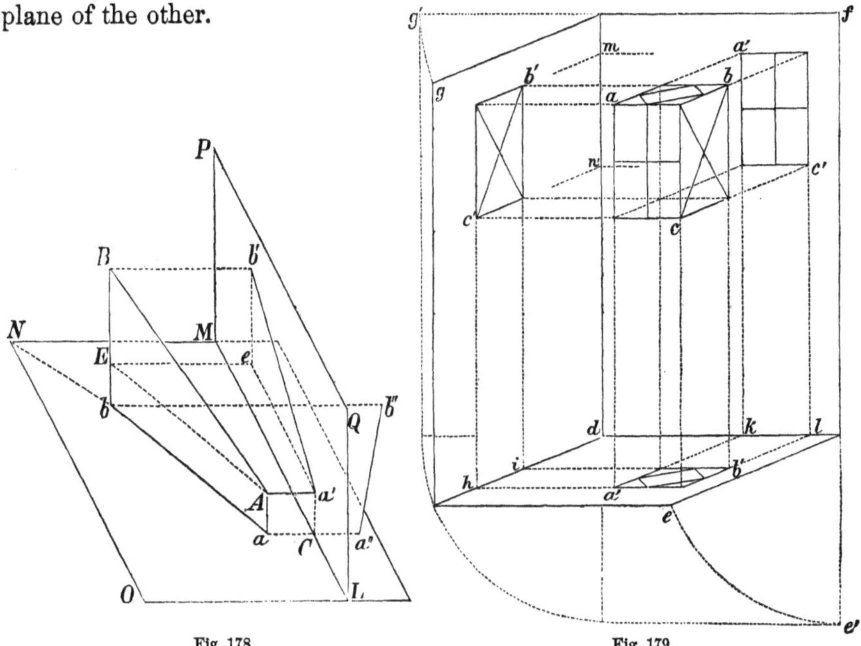

Fig. 178. Fig. 179.

Thus, let *a b c* (fig. 179) be a parallelopiped in an upright position, of which the plane *a b* is horizontal, and the planes *a c* and *c b* vertical. Let *d e*, *d f*, and *d g*, be the boundary planes of a cubical space in which the body *a b c* is placed; the sides of the body being parallel to those planes, each to each, let the figure of the parallelopiped be projected on these planes; for this purpose draw parallel lines from the angles of the body perpendicular to the planes, as indicated by the dotted lines; then upon the plane *d e* we shall have a' b', the projection of the surface *a b:* this is called the *plan* of the object. Upon the plane *d f* we have a' c', the projection of the surface *a c*, the *front elevation;* and upon the plane *d g*, the projection b' c' of the surface *b c*, the *side elevation*. Here, then, we have three distinct views of the regular solid *a b c* delineated on plane surfaces, which convey an accurate and sufficient idea of its form. Indeed, any two of these representations are sufficient as a description of the object. From the two figures a' c', b' c', for example, the third figure a' b' may be compounded, by merely drawing the vertical lines c' *h*, b' *i*, and a' *k*, c' *l*, to meet the plane *d e*, and by producing them horizontally till they meet and form the figure $a'\, b'$. Similarly, the figure $b'\, c'$ may be deduced from the other two by the aid of the lines h, i, from $a'\, b'$, and the lines m, n, from $a'\, c'$.

It is in this way that a third view of any piece of machinery is to be found from two given views; and in many cases two elevations, or one elevation and a plan, may afford a sufficiently complete idea of the construction of a machine. In other cases, many parts may be concealed by others in which they are enclosed; this suggests the occasional necessity of views of the interior, in which the machine is supposed to be cut across by planes, vertically or horizontally, so as properly to reveal its structure. Such views are termed *sections*, and, with reference to the *planes of section*, are denominated *vertical and horizontal sections.* To all such drawings is given the general title of *geometrical drawings*, as distinguished from perspective drawings.

By the aid of drawing instruments, measurements are transferable from one position to another; and there is no necessity for erecting three such planes as are supposed in fig. 179, upon which to execute drawings of a machine. In practice, the drawings are done upon one common surface, and we may readily suppose the plane $d\, g$ moved back into the position $d\, g'$, and $d\, e$ also moved to $d\, e'$, both of these positions being in the plane of $d\, f$. This being done, we have the three views depicted on one plane surface (fig. 180). In this figure, the same letters of reference are employed as in fig. 179; $d\, l$ and $d\, m$ are the ground and vertical lines. It is evident that the positions of the same points in $a'\, c'$ and $a'\, b'$ are in the same perpendicular from the ground line: that, in short, the position of a point in the plane may be found by applying the edge of the square to the same point as represented in the elevation. The same remark is applicable as between the two elevations. Hence the method of drawing several views of one machine upon the same surface of paper in strict agreement with each other.

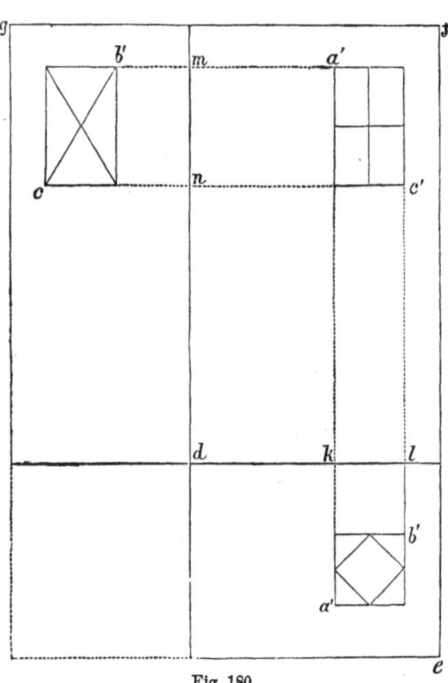

Fig. 180.

OF SHADE LINES.

In *outline drawings*, or drawings which consist simply of the lines employed to indicate the form of the object represented, the roundness, the flatness, or the obliquity of individual surfaces, is not indicated by the lines, although it may generally be inferred from the relation of different views of the same part. The direct significance of an outline drawing may, however, be considerably increased, by strengthening those lines which indicate the contours of surfaces resting in the shadow; and this distinction also improves the general appearance of the drawing. The strong lines, to produce the best effect, ought to be laid upon the sharp edges at the summits of salient angles; but bounding lines for curve surfaces should be drawn finely, and should be but slightly, if at all, strengthened on the

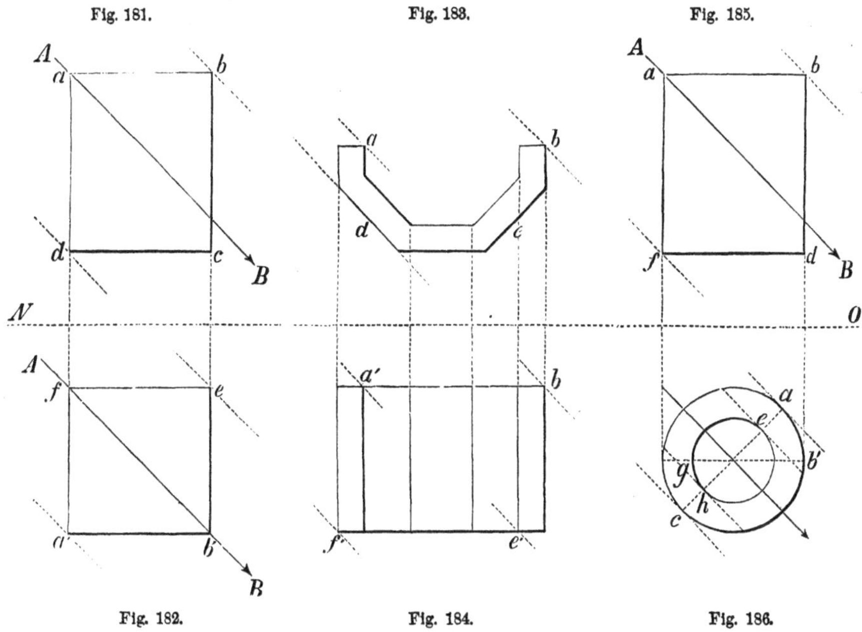

Fig. 181. Fig. 183. Fig. 185.

Fig. 182. Fig. 184. Fig. 186.

shade side. This distinction assists in contrasting flat and curve surfaces. To understand and apply the shade lines, however, we must know the direction in which the light is supposed to fall upon the object, and thence the locality of the shadows.

It is necessary for the explicitness of the drawing, that firstly, the light be supposed to fall upon the object in parallel lines, that all the parts may be shade-lined according to one uniform rule; secondly, that the light should be supposed to fall upon the object obliquely, as in this way both the horizontal and vertical lines may be relieved by shading. To distribute the shadows equally, the light is supposed to fall in directions forming an angle of 45° with both the horizontal and the vertical planes of projection. In general, the light should fall, as it were, from towards the upper left-hand corner of the sheet of paper, supposing it square, making also an angle of 45° with the surface.

To illustrate what has been stated, let *a b c d* and *a′ b′ e f* (figs. 181 and 182) represent the elevation and plan of a solid rectangular body, N O being the ground line. Let the direction of the light in both views be represented in projection by the arrows A B; these lines form the angle 45° with the line N O, and by drawing the parallels at *b*, *d*, *a′*, *e′*, so as to embrace the extreme contour, we may readily perceive the way in which the light falls upon the body: it falls upon three faces, namely, the two vertical faces *a′ f*, *f e*, and the top *a′ b′ e f*. Consequently, the intersections or lines at which these planes meet ought to be lightly drawn, namely, *a b*, *a d*; *a′ f* and *f e*. Again, the lateral planes represented by *b c*, *c d*, *b′ e′*, and *a′ b′*, are obviously in the shade, as no light falls upon them directly; and these lines are strengthened to express the distinction.

In figs. 183 and 184, the portion of the exterior from *b* by *c* to *d* is in the shade, while the rest is light; and the inverse is the case with the inner edges. A peculiarity, however, occurs at *d*, for here the edges, inner and outer, are parallel to the direction of the light. It is plain that the surfaces which come up to these edges will be in a medium shade, and that the lines at *d* should be of medium thickness.

Figs. 185 and 186 represent a hollow cylinder in projection. In the plan, two lines, *a*, *c*, drawn parallel to the direction of the light, and touching the exterior of the cylinder, define the semicircular outline *a b′ c*, which is thrown in the shade, and ought to be strengthened. The outlines *a* and *c* are, like the edges at *d* (fig. 183), parallel to the light, and the contour on each side gradually recedes and advances to the light. The thickness of the line should, therefore, be rather gradually reduced at the points *a*, *c*. In the elevation, the base-line *d f* should be shaded, and *b d* is often half-shaded, as it lies in a curve surface; more generally full-shaded.

If, again, the cylinder be hollow, presenting in plan the interior contour circle *e h*, then the semicircle *e g h* expresses the shady side of the interior, the light striking directly upon the oppposite semicircle.

These examples illustrate every case of shade-lining that occurs in outline drawings. The effect is enhanced by proportioning the thickness of the lines to the depth of the surfaces to which they belong, below the original surfaces from which the shadows arise.

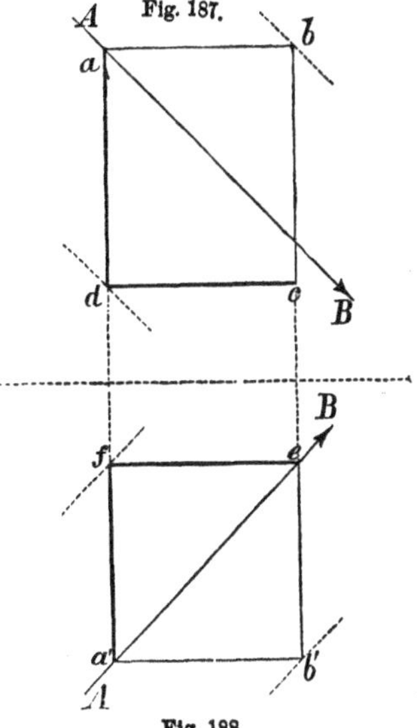

Fig. 187.

Fig. 188.

In the later French system of shading, the light is supposed, in *plan*, to strike towards the right hand upper corner, falling, as it were, in front of the objects; but in *elevation*, towards the right hand and foot of the sheet (figs. 188, 187).

It will be observed in the illustrations of this work, that in the tinted drawings, the shadow is thrown according to the French system; that is, the light is supposed to fall on the drawing over the left shoulder at an angle of 45°. But in outline drawings, on account of its greater simplicity, the more usual system of throwing the shade line one way, both in plan and elevation, is adopted.

PROJECTIONS OF SIMPLE BODIES.

Projections of a regular hexagonal pyramid (plate I).—It is evident that two distinct geometrical views are necessary to convey a complete idea of the form of the object: an elevation to represent the sides of the body, and to express its height; and a plan of the upper surface, to express the form horizontally.

It is to be observed that this body has an imaginary axis or *centre-line*, about which the same parts are equally distant; this is an essential characteristic of all symmetrical figures.

Draw a horizontal straight line L T through the centre of the sheet; this line will represent the ground line. Then draw a perpendicular Z Z′ to the ground line. For the sake of preserving the symmetry of the drawing, the centres of the lower range of figures are all in the same straight line M N, drawn parallel to the ground line.

Figs. 1, 2.—In delineating the pyramid, it is necessary, in the first place, to construct the plan. The point S′, where the line Z Z′ intersects the line M N, is to be taken as the centre of the figure, and from this point, with a radius equal to the side of the hexagon which forms the base of the pyramid, describe a circle, cutting M N in A′ and D′. From these points with the same radius, draw four arcs of circles, cutting the primary circle in four points. These six points being joined by straight lines, will form the figure A′ B′ C′ D′ E′ F′, which is the base of the pyramid; and the lines A′ D′, B′ E′, and C′ F′, will represent the projections of its edges fore-shortened as they would appear in the plan. If this operation has been correctly performed, the opposite sides of the hexagon should be parallel to each other and to one of the diagonals; this should be tested by the application of the square or other instrument proper for the purpose.

By the help of the plan obtained as above described, the vertical projection of the pyramid may be easily constructed. Since its base rests upon the horizontal plane, it must be projected vertically upon the ground line; therefore, from each of the angles at A′, B′, C′, and D′, raise perpendiculars to that line. The points of intersection, A, B, C, and D, are the true positions of all the angles of the base; and it only remains to determine the height of the pyramid, which is to be set off from the point G to S, and to draw S A, S B, S C, and S D, which are the only edges of the pyramid visible in the elevation. Of these it is to be remarked that S A and S D alone, being parallel to the vertical plane, are seen in their true length; and moreover, that from the assumed position of the solid under examination, the points F′ and E′ being situated in the lines B B′ and C C′, the lines S B and S C are each the projections of two edges of the pyramid.

Figs. 3 and 4.—*To construct the projections of the same pyramid, having its base set in an inclined position, but with its edges* S A *and* S D *still parallel to the vertical plane.*

It is evident, that with the exception of the inclination, the vertical projection of this solid is precisely the same as in the preceding example, and it is only necessary to copy fig. 1. For this purpose, after having fixed the position of the point D upon the ground line, draw through this point a straight line D A, making with L T an angle equal to the desired inclination of the base of the pyramid. Then set off the distance D A, fig. 1, from D to A, fig. 3; erect a perpendicular on the centre, and set off G S equal to the height of the pyramid. Transfer also from fig. 1 the distance B G and C G to the corresponding points in fig. 3, and complete the figure by drawing the straight lines A S, B S, C S, and D S.

In constructing the plan of the pyramid in this position, it is to be remarked, that since the edges S A and S D are still parallel to the vertical plane, and the point D remains unaltered, the projection of the point A will still be in the line M N. Its position at A′ (fig. 4) is determined by

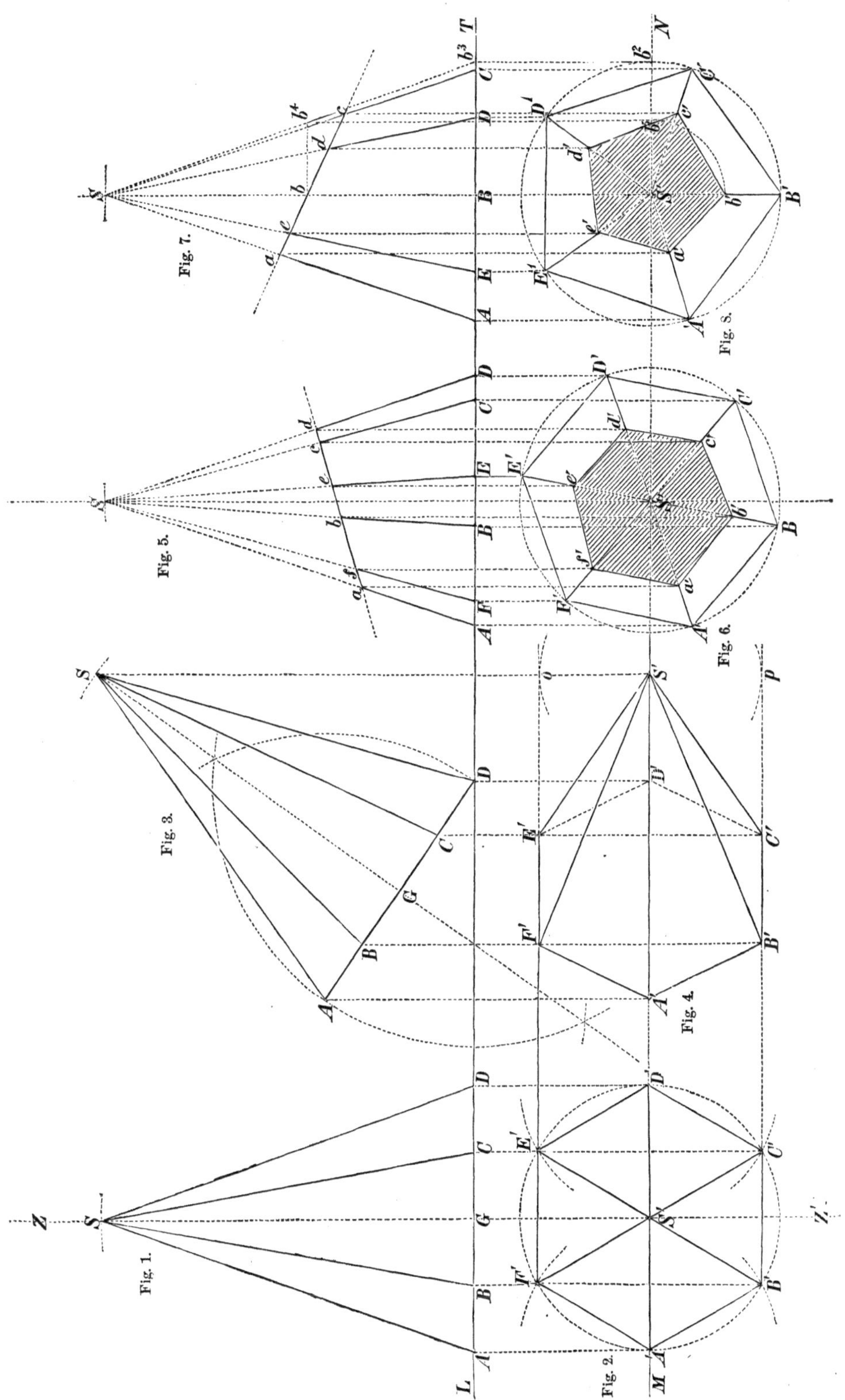
Fig. 1.
Fig. 2.
Fig. 3.
Fig. 4.
Fig. 5.
Fig. 6.
Fig. 7.
Fig. 8.

the intersection of the perpendicular A A′ with that line. The remaining points B′, C′, &c., in the projection of the base, are found in a similar manner, by the intersections of perpendiculars let fall from the corresponding points in the elevation, with lines drawn parallel to M N, at a distance (set off at *o*, *p*,) equal to the width of the base. By joining all the contiguous points, we obtain the figure A′ B′ C′ D′ E′ F′, representing the horizontal projection of the base, two of its sides, however, being dotted, as they must be supposed to be concealed by the body of the pyramid. The vertex S having been similarly projected to S′, and joined by straight lines to the several angles of the base, the projection of the solid is completed.

Figs. 5 and 6.—*To find the horizontal projection of a transverse section of the same pyramid, made by a plane perpendicular to the vertical, but inclined at an angle to the horizontal plane of projection; and let all the sides of the base be at an angle with the ground line.*

Having drawn the vertical S S′, the centre line of the figures, its point of intersection with the line M N is the centre of the plan. Since none of the sides of the base are to be parallel with the ground line, draw a diameter A′ D′ making the required angle with that line, and from the points A′ and D′ proceed to set out the angular points of the hexagon as in fig. 2. Then, in order to obtain the projections of the edges of the pyramid, join the angular points which are diametrically opposite; and, following the method pointed out in reference to fig. 1, project the figure thus obtained upon the vertical plane, as shown at fig. 5.

Now, if the cutting plane be represented by the line *a d* in the elevation, it is obvious that it will expose, as the section of the pyramid, a polygon whose angular points being the intersections of the various edges with the cutting plane, will be projected in perpendiculars drawn from the points where it meets these edges respectively. If, therefore, from the points *a*, *f*, *b*, &c., we let fall the perpendiculars *a a*′, *f f*′, *b b*′, &c., and join their contiguous points of intersection with the lines A′ D′, F′ C′, B′ E′, &c., we shall form a six-sided figure, which will represent the section required. The edges F S and E S being concealed in the elevation, but necessary for the construction of the plan, have been expressed in dotted lines, as also the portion of the pyramid situated above the cutting plane, which, though supposed to be removed, is necessary in order to draw the lines representing the edges. We have here introduced the ordinary method of expressing sections in purely line-drawings, by filling up the spaces comprised within their outlines with a quantity of parallel straight lines drawn at equal distances.

Figs. 7 and 8.—*To find the horizontal projection of the transverse section of a regular five-sided pyramid, cut by a plane perpendicular to the vertical, but inclined to the horizontal plane; and let one edge of the pyramid be in a plane perpendicular to both planes of projection.*

The plan of the pyramid is constructed by describing from the centre S′ a circle circumscribing the base, and from B′ dividing the circumference into five equal parts, and joining the contiguous points of division by straight lines to form the polygon A′ B′ C′ D′ E′, each of whose angles, being joined to the centre S′, shows the projections of the edges of the pyramid. Then, following the method above explained, we obtain the elevation and the horizontal projection of the section made by the plane *a c*. But that method will not suffice for the determination of the point *b*′, because the perpendicular let fall from the corresponding point *b*, in the elevation, coincides with the projection of the edge B S. Let the pyramid be supposed to be turned a quarter of a revolution round its axis; the line B′ S′ will then have assumed the position S′ b^2. Project the point b^2 to b^3, and join S b^3. Then, since the required point must also be conceived to have described a quarter of a circle in a plane parallel to the horizontal plane, and that its new position must be in the line S b^3, it is obvious that its vertical projection is the point b^4, the intersection of a horizontal line drawn through *b*, with that line. The distance *b* b^4, then, being transferred from S′ to *b*′, determines the position of the latter point in the plan; or, following a more methodical process, by projecting the point b^4 to b^5, and describing a circle from the centre S′ passing through b^5; its intersection with B′ S′ is the point sought.

PROJECTIONS OF A PRISM.

Plate II., figs. 1 and 2.—*Required to represent in plan and elevation a regular six-sided prism in an upright position.*

Lay down the ground line and centre line, and describe the hexagon as already directed. Project the plan thus delineated by perpendiculars to the ground line from each of its angular points; and since the prism is upright, these angular points themselves represent the horizontal projections of all its edges, and their elevations coincide with the perpendiculars A′ G, B′ H, &c. Set off from G to A the height of the prism, and through A draw A D parallel to the ground line. This will be the vertical projection of the upper surface. The edges being all parallel to the vertical plane, are, of course, seen in their actual length.

Figs. 3 and 4.—*To form the projections of the same prism, supposing it*

PLATE II.

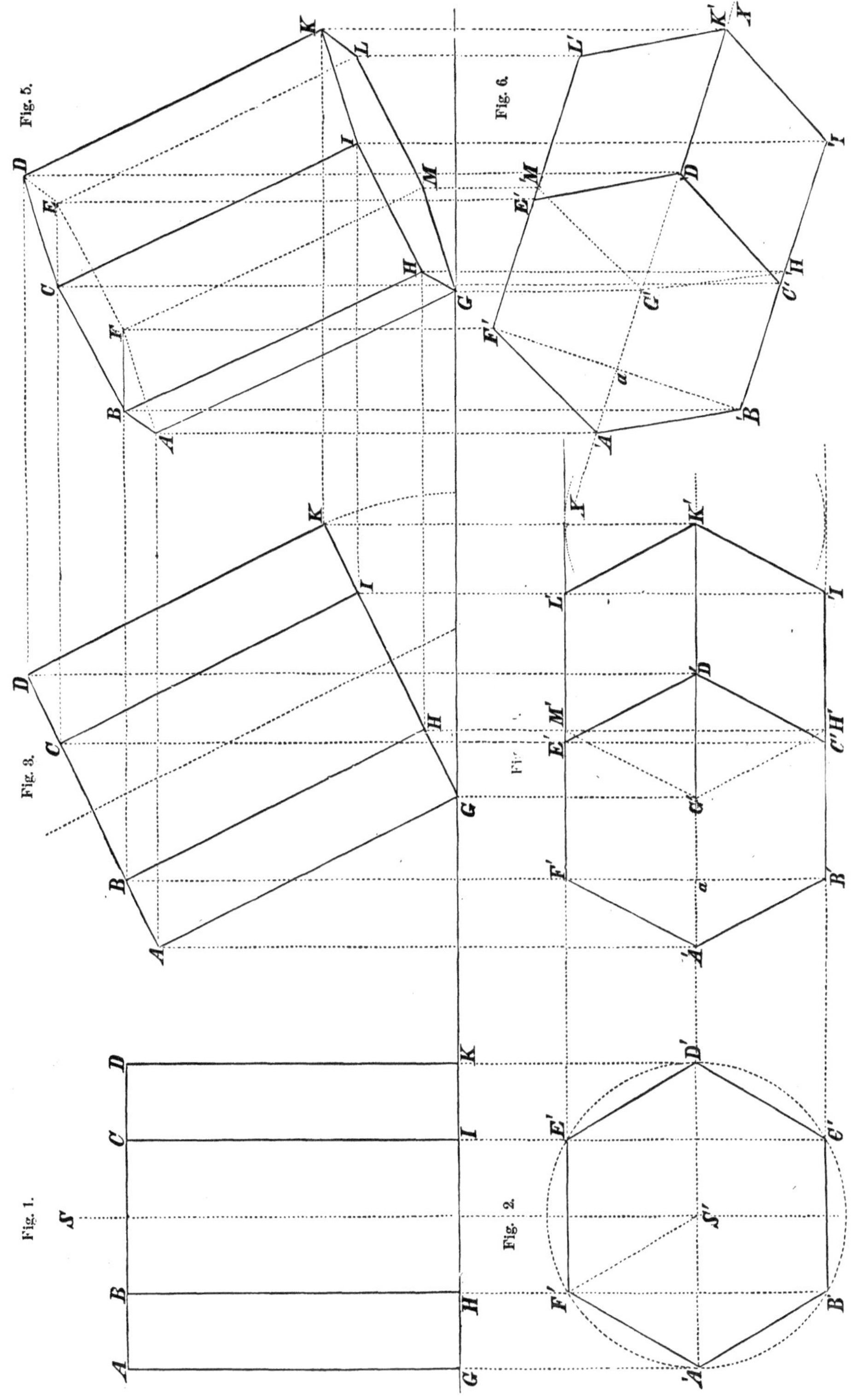

to have been moved round the point G, *in a plane parallel to the vertical plane.*

Copy the elevation (fig. 1) on an inclined base. Now, by letting fall perpendiculars from all the angles in the elevation, and joining the contiguous points of intersection with the horizontal lines appropriate to these points respectively, we obtain the polygon A′ B′ C′ D′ E′ F′ as the projection of the upper surface, and G′ H′ I′ K′ L′M′ as that of the base of the prism. Finally, it will be observed that all the edges are represented, in the horizontal projection, by equal straight lines, as D′ K′, A′ G′, &c., and that the sides A′ B′, G′ H′, &c., remain still parallel to each other, which will afford the means of verifying the accuracy of the drawings.

Figs. 5 and 6.—*Required the projections of the same prism set into a position inclined to both planes of projection.*

Assuming that the inclination of the prism upon the horizontal plane is the same as in the preceding figures for the sake of simplifying the operation, the first process is to copy fig. 4, which may be done by drawing a centre line X X, so as to form the required angle of the prism with the vertical plane; then, having set off upon this line a distance equal to A′ K′, fig. 4, transfer the distances A′ G′ and D′ K′ also to fig. 6; and in order to find the remaining angular points, make A′ *a* equal to the corresponding distance in fig. 4, and through *a* draw B′ F′ perpendicular to the centre line, and transfer the distances *a* B′, *a* F′. Through the points B′ and F′, draw straight lines parallel to A′ K′, and join A′ B′, A′ F′; and since we have already seen that all the other sides must be parallel to these, the figure is completed by drawing through the points G′, D′, and K′, straight lines parallel to A′ B′ and A′ F′ respectively.

Now, since the prism has been supposed to have preserved its former inclination to the horizontal plane, it is obvious that every point in it, such as A, has, in assuming its new position, simply moved in a horizontal plane, and will, therefore, be in the line A A parallel to the ground line, and since the same point has been projected to A′, fig. 6, it will also be in the perpendicular A′ A; the point of intersection A, fig. 5, is, therefore, its projection in the elevation. The remaining angular points in this view are all determined in the same manner by the aid of figs. 3 and 6; and having joined the contiguous points, and the corresponding angles of the upper and lower surface, we obtain the complete vertical projection of the prism in its doubly-inclined position.

CONSTRUCTION OF THE CONIC SECTIONS.

Plate III.—The *plan* of the cone (fig. 2) is simply a circle, described from the centre S′ of a diameter equal to that of the base. Its *elevation* (fig. 1) is an isosceles triangle, obtained by drawing tangents A′ A, B′ B, perpendicular to and intersecting the ground line; then set off upon the centre line the height C S, and join S A, S B. These lines are called the exterior *generatrices* of the cone.

Figs. 1 and 2.—*Given the projections of a cone, and the direction of a plane* X X, *cutting it perpendicularly to the vertical, and obliquely to the horizontal plane; required to find, first, the horizontal projection of this section; and, secondly, the outline of the ellipse thus formed.*

Through the vertex of the cone draw a line S E to any point within the base A B; let fall a perpendicular from E, cutting the circumference of the base in E′, and join E′ S′; then another perpendicular let fall from *e* will intersect E′ S′ in a point *e*′, which will be the horizontal projection of a point in the curve required; and so on for any required number of points.

The exterior generatrices A S and B S being both projected upon the line A′ B′, the extreme limits of the curve sought will be at the points *a*′ and *b*′ on that line, which are the projections of the points of intersection *a* and *b* of the cutting plane with the outlines of the cone. And since the line *a*′ *b*′ will obviously divide the curve symmetrically into two equal parts, the points *f*′, *g*′, *h*′, &c., will be readily obtained by setting off above that line, and on their respective perpendiculars, the distances $d' \, d^2$, $e' \, e^2$, &c. A sufficient number of points having thus been determined, the curve drawn through them (which will be found to be an ellipse) will be the outline of the section required.

This curve may be obtained by another method, depending on the principle that all sections of a cone by planes parallel to the base are circles. Thus, let the line F G represent a cutting plane; the section which it makes with the cone will be denoted on the horizontal projection by a circle drawn from the centre S′, with a radius equal to half the line F G; and by projecting the point of intersection H of the horizontal and oblique planes by a perpendicular H H′, and noting where this line cuts the circle above referred to, we obtain two points H′ and I′ in the curve required. By a similar construction, as exemplified in the drawings, any number of additional points may be found.

As the projection obtained by the preceding methods exhibits the sec-

PLATE III.

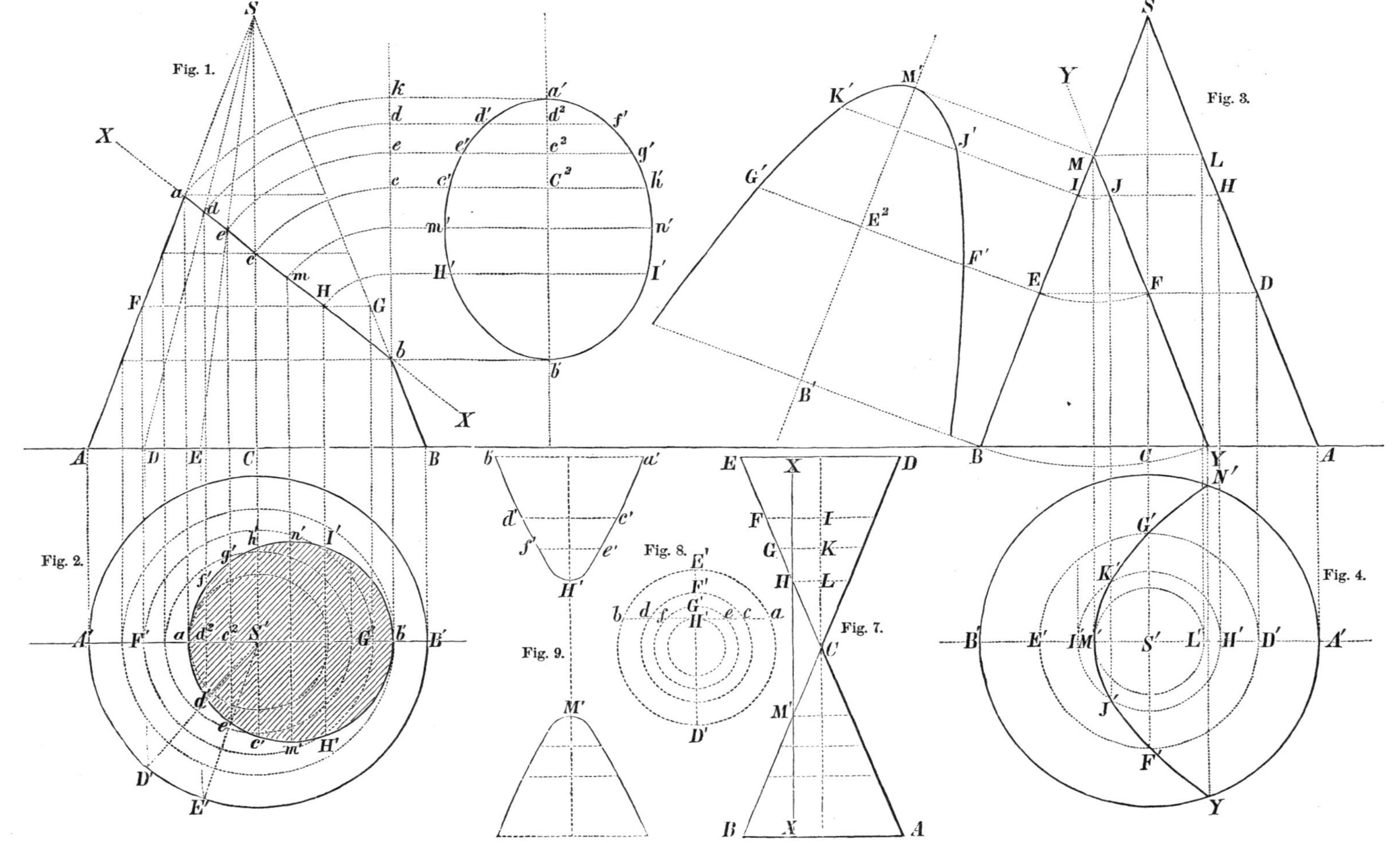

tion as fore-shortened, and not in its true dimensions, we shall now proceed to the consideration of the second question proposed. Let the cutting plane X X be conceived to turn upon the point *b*, so as to coincide with the vertical line *b k*, and (to avoid confusion of lines) let *b k* be transferred to *a′ b′*, which will represent, as before, the extreme limits of the curve required. Now, taking any point, such as *d*, it is obvious that in this new position of the cutting plane, it will be represented by d^2, and if the cutting plane were turned upon *a′ b′* as an axis till it is parallel to the vertical plane, the point which had been projected at d^2 would then have described round *a′ b′* an arc of a circle, whose radius is the distance d' d^2 (fig. 2). This distance, therefore, being set off at *d′* and *f′* on each side of *a′ b′*, gives two points in the curve sought. By a similar mode of operation any number of points may be obtained, through which, if a curve be drawn, it will be an ellipse of the true form and dimensions of the section.

Figs. 3 and 4.—*To find the horizontal projection and actual outline of the section of a cone, made by a plane* Y Y *parallel to one side or generatrix, and perpendicular to the vertical plane.*

Determine by the second method laid down in the preceding problem any number of points, as F′, G′, J′, K′, &c., in the curve representing the horizontal projection of the section specified. The horizontal plane passing through M gives only one point M′ (which is the vertex of the curve sought), because the circle which denotes the section that it makes with the cone is a tangent to the given plane.

In order to determine the actual outline of this curve, suppose the plane Y Y to turn as upon a pivot at M, until it has assumed the position M B, and transfer M B parallel to itself to M′ B′. The point F will thus have first described the arc F E till it reaches the point E, which is then projected to E^2; suppose the given plane, now represented by M′ B′, to turn upon that line as an axis, until it assumes a position parallel to the vertical plane, the point E^2, which is distant from the axis M′ B′ by the distance F′ S′ (fig. 4), will now be projected to F′ (fig. 3). The same distance F′ S′ set off on the other side of the axis M′ B′ gives another point G′ in the curve required, which is the *parabola.*

Figs. 7, 8, 9.—*To draw the vertical projection of the sections of two opposite cones made by a plane parallel to their axis.*

Let C E D and C B A be the two cones, and X X the position of the cutting plane (fig. 7). Project in plan either of the cones, as in fig. 8; from its centre, with a radius equal to L H, describe a circle, and draw the tangent *b a; b a* will be the horizontal projection of the cutting plane. Draw the line H′ M′ (fig. 9) parallel to the cutting plane; H′ M′ corresponding in position to the intersections H, M (fig. 7), of the plane with the cones. From H′ and M′ lay off distances equal to L K, K I, and the length of the cone, and through these points draw perpendiculars, as *f′ e′*, *d′ c′*, *b′ a′*, &c., which must be made equal to the chords *f e*, *d c*, *b a* (fig. 8), made by the cutting plane *a b*, with circles whose radii are G K, I F, and the radius of the base of the cone. Through the points *a′*, *c′*, *e′*, H′, *f′*, *d′*, *b′*, draw the curve, and we have the projection required. A similar construction will give the sectional projection of the opposite cone at M′. The curve thus found is the hyperbola.

PENETRATIONS OR INTERSECTIONS OF SOLIDS.

On examining the minor details of most machines, we find numerous examples of cylindrical and other forms, fitted to, and even appearing to pass through each other in a great variety of ways. The examples grouped in plates IV. and V. are selected with the view of exhibiting those cases which are of most frequent occurrence, and of elucidating general principles.

PENETRATIONS OF CYLINDERS.

Plate IV.—Figs. 1 and 2 represent the projections of two cylinders of unequal diameters meeting each other at right angles; one of which is denoted by the rectangle A B E D in the vertical, and by the circle A′ H′ B′ in the horizontal projections; while the other, which is supposed to be horizontal, is indicated in the former by the circle L P I N, and in the latter by the figure L′ I′ K′ M′. From the position of these two solids it is evident that the curves formed by their junction will be projected in the circles A′ H′ B′ and L P I N; and further, that such would also be the case even although their axes did not intersect each other.

But if the position of these bodies be changed into that represented at figs. 3 and 4, the lines of their intersection will assume in the vertical projection a totally different aspect, and may be accurately determined by the following construction.

Through any point taken upon the plan (fig. 4) draw a horizontal line *a′ b′*, which is to be considered as indicating a plane cutting both cylinders parallel to their axes; this plane would cut the vertical cylinder in lines drawn perpendicularly through the points *c′* and *d′*. To find the vertical projection of its intersection with the other cylinder, conceive its base I′ L′,

PLATE IV.

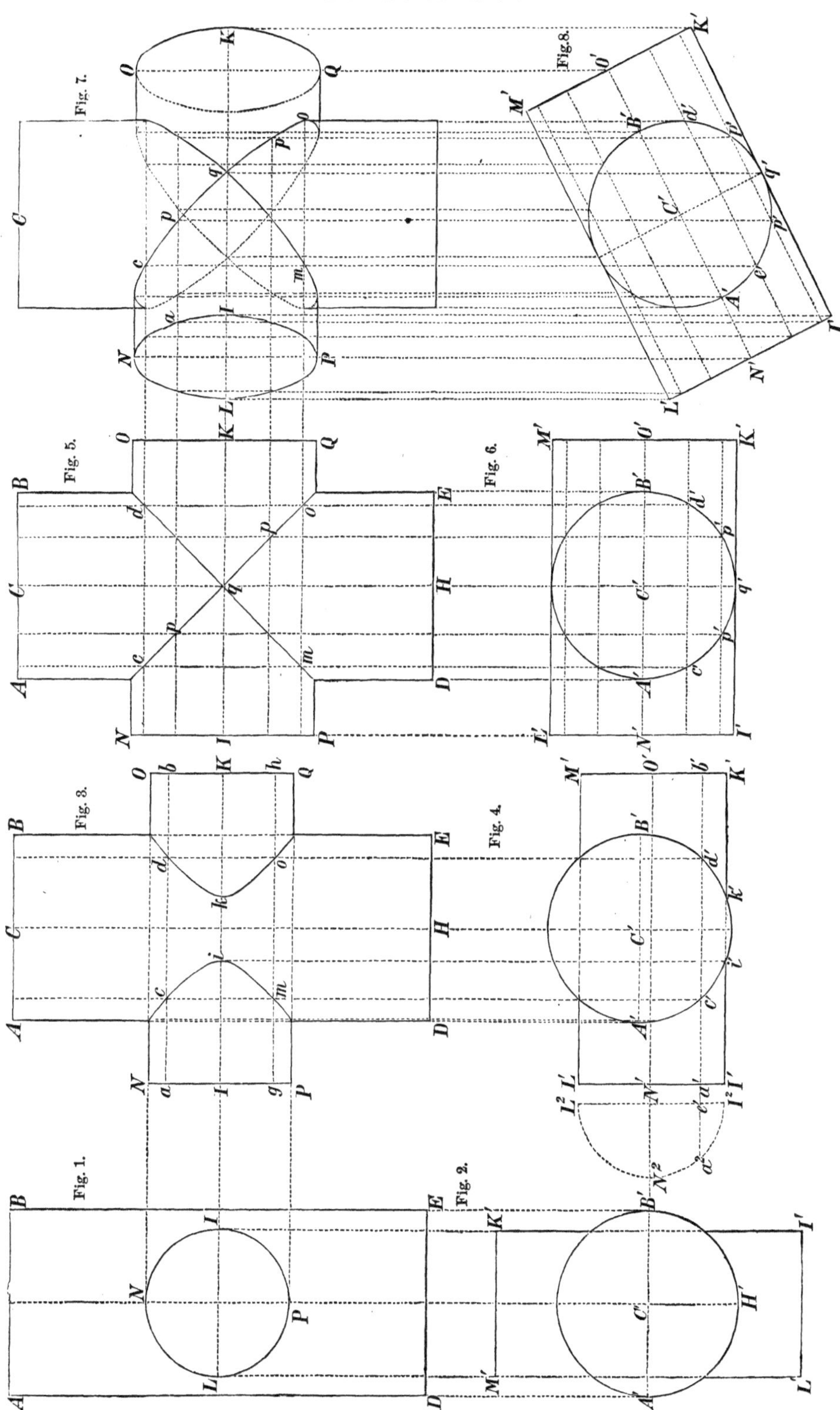

after being transferred to $I^2 L^2$, to be turned over parallel to the horizontal plane; this is expressed by simply drawing a circle of the diameter $I^2 L^2$; and producing the line $a' b'$ to a^2; then set off the distance $a^2 e'$ on each side of the axis I K, and draw straight lines through these points parallel to it. These lines $a\,b$, $g\,h$, denote the intersection of the plane $a' b'$ with the horizontal cylinder, and therefore the points c, d, m, o, where they cut the perpendiculars $c\,c'$, $d\,d'$, are points in the curve required. By laying down other planes similar to $a' b'$, and operating as before, any number of points may be obtained. The vertices i and k of the curves are obviously projected directly; and their extreme points are determined by the intersections of the outlines of both cylinders. When the cylinders are of unequal diameters, as in the present case, the curves of penetration are hyperbolas.

Figs. 5 and 6.—*When the diameters of the cylinders are equal*, and when they cut each other at right angles, the curves of penetration are projected vertically in straight lines perpendicular to each other, as in fig. 5, where the projections of some of the points are indicated in elevation and plan by the same letters of reference.

Figs. 7 and 8.—*To delineate the intersections of two cylinders of equal diameters at right angles, when one of the cylinders is inclined to the vertical plane.*

Supposing the two preceding figures to have been drawn, the projection c of any point such as c' may be ascertained by observing that it must be situated in the perpendicular $c' c$, and that since the distance of this point (projected at c in fig. 5) from the horizontal plane remains unaltered, it must also be in the horizontal line $c\,c$. Upon these principles all the points indicated by literal references in fig. 7 are determined; the curves of penetration resulting therefrom intersecting each other at two points projected upon the axial line L K, of which that marked q alone is seen. The ends of the horizontal cylinder are represented by ellipses, the construction of which will also be obvious on referring to the figures; and they do not require further consideration here.

PENETRATIONS OF CYLINDERS, CONES, AND SPHERES.

Plate V., figs. 1 and 2.—*To find the curves resulting from the intersection of two cylinders of unequal diameters, meeting at any angle.*

For the sake of simplicity, suppose the axes of both cylinders to be parallel to the vertical plane, and let A B E D and N O Q P be their projections upon that plane. In constructing, in the first place, their horizontal projection, observe that the upper end A B of the larger cylinder is represented by an ellipse A′ K′ B′ M′, which may easily be drawn by the help of the major axis K′ M′ equal to the diameter of the cylinder, and of the minor A′ B′, the projection of the diameter. The visible portion of the base of the cylinder being similarly represented by the semi-ellipse L′ D′ H′, its entire outline will be completed by drawing tangents L′ M′ and H′ K′. The upper extremity P N of the smaller cylinder will also be projected in the ellipse p' i' N′.

Now, suppose a plane, as a' g' (fig. 2), to pass through both cylinders parallel to their axes; it will cut the surface of the larger cylinder in two straight lines passing through the points f' and g' on the upper end of the cylinder; these lines will be represented in the elevation, by projecting the points f' and g' to f, g; and drawing $a\,f$ and $c\,g$ parallel to the axis. The plane a' g' will in like manner cut the smaller cylinder in two straight lines, which will be represented in the vertical projection by $d\,h$ and $e\,i$, and the intersections of these lines with $a\,f$ and $c\,g$ will give four points l, k, m, and n, in the curves of penetration. Of these points one only, that marked l, is visible in the plan, where it is denoted by l'.

Fig. 1.—*To find the curves of penetration in the elevation without the aid of the plan.*

Let the bases D E and Q O of both cylinders be conceived to be turned over into the vertical plane after being transferred to any convenient distance, as D² E² and Q² O², from the principal figure; they will then be represented by the circles D² H² E² and Q² G′ O². Now draw $a^2\,c^2$ parallel to D E, and at any suitable distance from the centre I; this line will represent the intersection of the base of the cylinder with a plane parallel to the axes of both, as before. The intersection of this plane with the base of the smaller cylinder will be found by setting off from R a distance Rp, equal to I o, and drawing through the point p a straight line parallel to Q O. It is obvious that the intersection of the supposed plane with the convex surfaces of the cylinders will be represented by the lines $a\,f$, $c\,g$, and $d\,h$, $e\,i$, drawn parallel to the axes of the respective cylinders through the points where the chords $a^2\,c^2$ and $d^2\,e^2$ cut the circles of their bases; and that, consequently, the intersections of these lines indicate points in the curves sought. These points may be multiplied indefinitely by conceiving other planes to pass through the cylinders, and operating as before.

Figs. 3 and 4.—*To find the curves of penetration of a cone and sphere.*

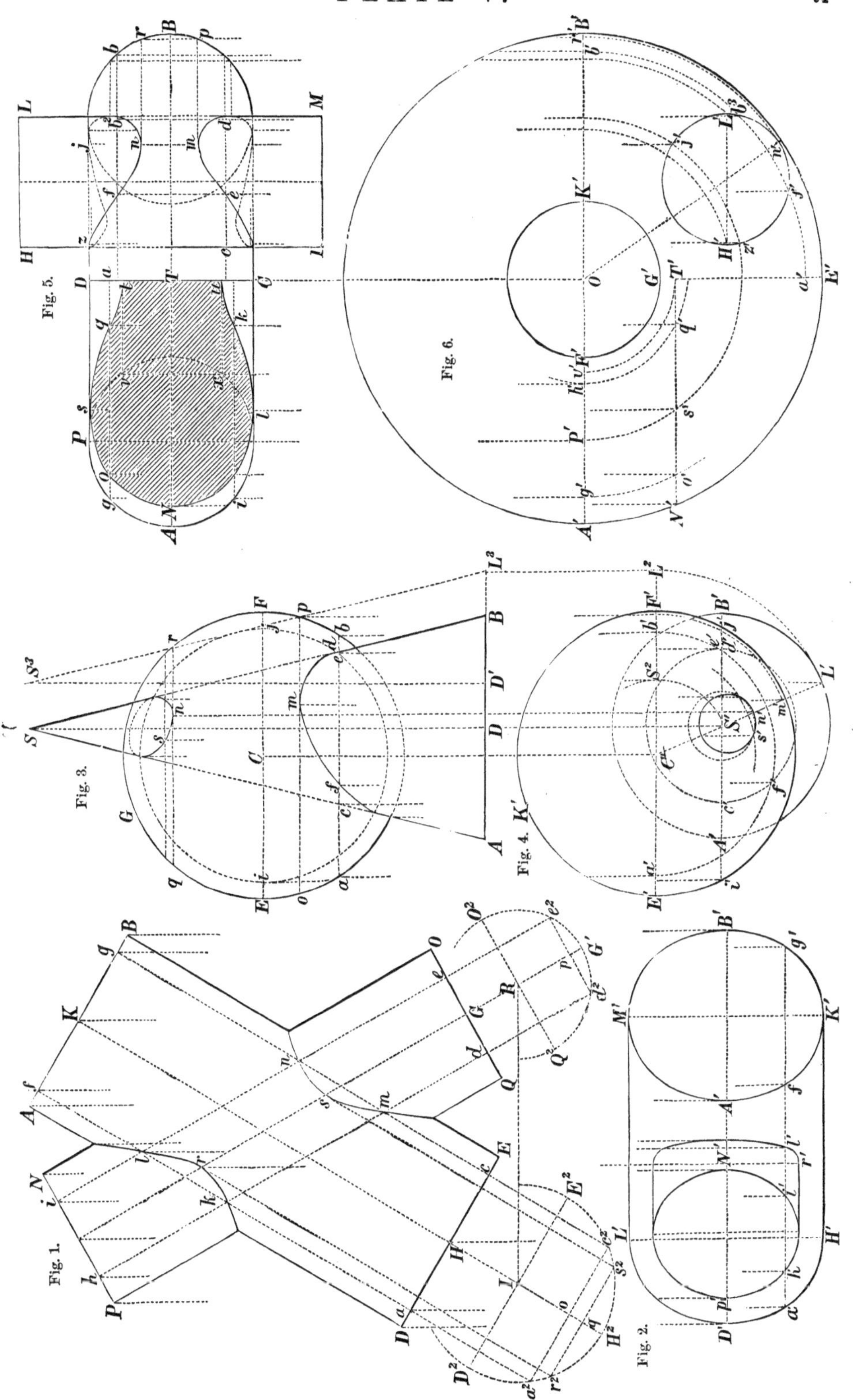
Fig. 1.
Fig. 2.
Fig. 3.
Fig. 4.
Fig. 5.
Fig. 6.

Let D S be the axis of the cone, A′ L′ B′ the circle of its base, and the triangle A B S its projection on the vertical plane; and let C, C′, be the projections of the centre, and the circles E′ K′ F′ and E G F those of the circumferences of the sphere.

This problem, like most others similar to it, can be solved only by the aid of imaginary intersecting planes. Let *a b* (fig. 3) represent the projection of a horizontal plane; it will cut the sphere in a circle whose diameter is *a b*, and which is to be drawn from the centre C′ in the plan. Its intersection with the cone is also a circle described from the centre S′ with the diameter *c d;* the points *e′* and *f′*, where these two circles cut each other, are the horizontal projections of two points in the lower curve, which is evidently entirely hidden by the sphere. The points referred to are projected vertically upon the line *a b* at *e* and *f*. The upper curve, which is seen in both projections, is obtained by a similar process; but it is to be observed that the horizontal cutting planes must be taken in such positions as to pass through both solids in circles which shall intersect each other. For our guidance in this respect it will be necessary, first, to determine the vertices *m* and *n* of the curves of penetration.

For this purpose, conceive a vertical plane passing through the axis of the cone and the centre of the sphere; its horizontal projection will be the straight line C′ L′ joining the centres of the two bodies. Let us also make the supposition that this plane is turned upon the line C C′ as on an axis, until it becomes parallel to the vertical plane; the points S′ and L′ will now have assumed the positions S^2 and L^2, and consequently the axis of the cone will be projected vertically in the line D′ S^3, and its side in S^3 L^3, cutting the sphere at the points *p* and *r*. Conceive the solids to have resumed their original relative positions, it is clear that the vertices or adjacent limiting points of the curves of penetration must be in the horizontal lines *p o* and *r q*, drawn through the points determined as above; their exact positions on these lines may be ascertained by projecting vertically the points *m′* and *n′*, where the arcs described by the points *p* and *r*, in restoring the cone to its first position, intersect the line S L.

It is of importance further, to ascertain the points at which the curves of penetration meet the outlines A S and S B of the cone. The plane which passes through these lines being projected horizontally in A′ B′, will cut the sphere in a circle whose diameter is *i′ j′;* this circle, described in the elevation from the centre C, will cut the sides A S and S B in four points at which the curves of penetration are tangents to the outlines of the cone.

Figs. 5 and 6.—*To find the lines of penetration of a cylinder and a cylindrical ring or torus.*

Let the circles A′ E′ B′, F′ G′ K′, represent the horizontal, and the figure A C B D the vertical projection of the torus, and let the circle H′ *f*′ L′, and the rectangle H I M L be the analogous projections of the cylinder, which passes perpendicularly through it. Conceive, as before, a plane *a b* (fig. 5), to pass horizontally through both solids; it will obviously cut the cylinder in a circle which will be projected in the base H′ *f*′ L′ itself, and the ring in two other circles, of which one only, part of which is represented by the arc *f*′ b^3 *b*′, will intersect the cylinder at the points *f*′ and b^3, which being projected vertically to fig. 5, will give two points *f* and b^2 in the upper curve of penetration.

Another horizontal plane, taken at the same distance *below* the centre line A B as that marked *a b* is above it, will evidently cut the ring in circles coinciding with those already obtained; consequently the points *f*′ and b^3 indicate points in the lower as well as in the upper curves of penetration, and are projected vertically at *d* and *e*. Thus, by laying down two planes at equal distances on each side of A B, by one operation four points in the curves required are determined.

To determine the vertices *m* and *n*, following the method explained in the preceding problem, draw a plane O *n*′, passing through the axis of the cylinder and the centre of the ring, and conceive this plane to be moved round the point O as on a hinge, until it has assumed the position O B′, parallel to the vertical plane; the point *n*′, representing the extreme outline of the cylinder in plan, will now be at *r*′, and being projected vertically, that outline will cut the ring in two points *p* and *r*, which would be the limits of the curves of penetration in the supposed relative position of the two solids; and by drawing the two horizontal lines *r n* and *p m*, and projecting the point *n*′ vertically, the intersections of these lines, the two points *m* and *n*, are the vertices of the curves in the actual position of the penetrating bodies.

The points at which the curves are tangents to the outlines H I and L M of the cylinder, may readily be found by describing arcs of circles from the centre O through the points H′ and L′, which represent these lines in the plan, and then proceeding, as above, to project the points thus obtained upon the elevation. Lastly, to determine the points, as *j*, *z*, &c., where the curves are tangents to the horizontal outlines of the ring, draw a circle P′ *s*′ *j*′ with a radius equal to that of the centre line of the ring, namely, P D; the points of intersection *z*′ and *j*′ are the horizontal projections of the points sought.

Required to represent the sections which would be made in the ring now before us, by two planes, one of which, N′ T′, *is parallel to the vertical plane, while the other,* T′ E′, *is perpendicular to both planes of projection.*

The section made by the last-named plane must obviously have its vertical projection in the line C D, which indicates the position of the plane; but the former will be represented in its actual form and dimensions in the elevation. To determine its outlines, let two horizontal planes *g q* and *i k*, equidistant from the centre line A B, be supposed to cut the ring; their lines of intersection with it will have their horizontal projections in the two circles *g′ o′* and *h′ q′* which cut the given plane N′ T′ in *o′* and *q′*. These points being projected vertically to *o*, *q*, *k*, &c., give four points in the curve required. The line N′ T′ cutting the circle A′ E′ B′ at N′, the projection N of this point is the extreme limit of the curve.

The circle P′ *s′ j′*, the centre line of the rim of the torus, is cut by the planes N′ T′ at the point *s′*, which being projected vertically upon the lines D P and C *l*, determines *s* and *l*, the points of contact of the curve with the horizontal outlines of the ring. Finally, the points *t* and *u* are obtained by drawing from the centre O a circle T′ *v′* tangent to the given plane, and projecting the point of intersection *v′* to the points *v* and *x*, which are then to be replaced upon C D by drawing the horizontals *v t* and *x u*.

PENETRATIONS OF CYLINDERS, PRISMS, SPHERES, AND CONES.

Plate VI., figs. 1 and 2.—*Required to delineate the lines of penetration of a sphere and a regular hexagonal prism whose axis passes through the centre of the sphere.*

The centres of the circles forming the two projections of the sphere are, according to the terms of the problem, upon the axis C C′ of the upright prism, which is projected horizontally in the regular hexagon D′ E′ F′ G′ H′ I′. Hence it follows, that as all the lateral faces of the prism are equidistant from the centre of the sphere, their lines of intersection with it will necessarily be circles of equal diameters. Now, the perpendicular face represented by the line E′ F′ in the plan, will meet the surface of the sphere in two circular arcs E F and L M (fig. 1), described from the centre C, with a radius equal to *c′ b′* or *a′ c′*. And the intersections of the two oblique faces D′ E′ and F′ G′ will obviously be each projected in two arcs of an ellipse whose major axis *d g* is equal to the diameter of the circle *a c b*, and the minor axis is the vertical projection of that diameter, as represented at *e′ f′* (fig. 2). But as it is necessary to draw small portions only of these curves, the following method may be employed.

Draw D G; through the points E, F, divide the portions E F and F G respectively into the same number of equal parts, and drawing perpendiculars through the points of division, set off from F G the distances from the corresponding points in E F to the circular arc E C F, as points in the elliptical arc required. The remaining elliptical arcs should be traced by the same method.

Figs. 3 and 4.—*Required to draw the lines of penetration of a cylinder and a sphere, the centre of the sphere being without the axis of the cylinder.*

Let the circle D′ E′ L′ be the projection of the base of the given cylinder, the elevation of which is shown at fig. 3, and let A B be the diameter of the given sphere. If a plane, as *c′ d′*, be drawn parallel to the vertical plane, it will evidently cut the cylinder in two straight lines G G′, H H′, parallel to the axis, and projected vertically from the points G′ and H′. This plane will also cut the sphere in a circle whose diameter is equal to *c′ d′*, and which is to be described from the centre C with a radius of half that line; its intersection with the lines G G′ and H H′ will give so many points in the curves sought, viz., G, H, I, K.

The planes *a′ b′* and *e′ f′*, which are tangents to the cylinder, furnish only two points respectively in the curves; of these points E and F alone are visible, the other two, L and M, being concealed by the solid; therefore, the planes drawn for the construction of the curves must be all taken between *a′ b′* and *e′ f′*. The plane which passes through the axis of the cylinder cuts the sphere in a circle whose projection upon the vertical plane will meet at the points D, N, and *g*, *h*, the outlines of the cylinder, to which the curves of penetration are tangents.

Figs. 5 and 6.—*To find the lines of penetration of a truncated cone and a prism.*

The straight line C D is the axis of a truncated cone, which is represented in the plan by two circles described from the centre C′; and the horizontal lines M N and M′ N′ are the projections of the axis of a prism of which the base is square, and the faces respectively parallel and perpendicular to the planes of projection.

In laying down the plan of this solid, it is supposed to be inverted, in order that the smaller end of the cone, and the lines of intersection of the lower surface F G of the prism may be exhibited. According to this arrangement, the letters A′ and B′ (fig. 6) ought, strictly speaking, to be marked at the points I′ and H′, and conversely; but as it is quite obvious that the part above M′ N′ is exactly symmetrical with that below it, the distribution of the letters of reference adopted in our figures can lead to no confusion.

PLATE VI.

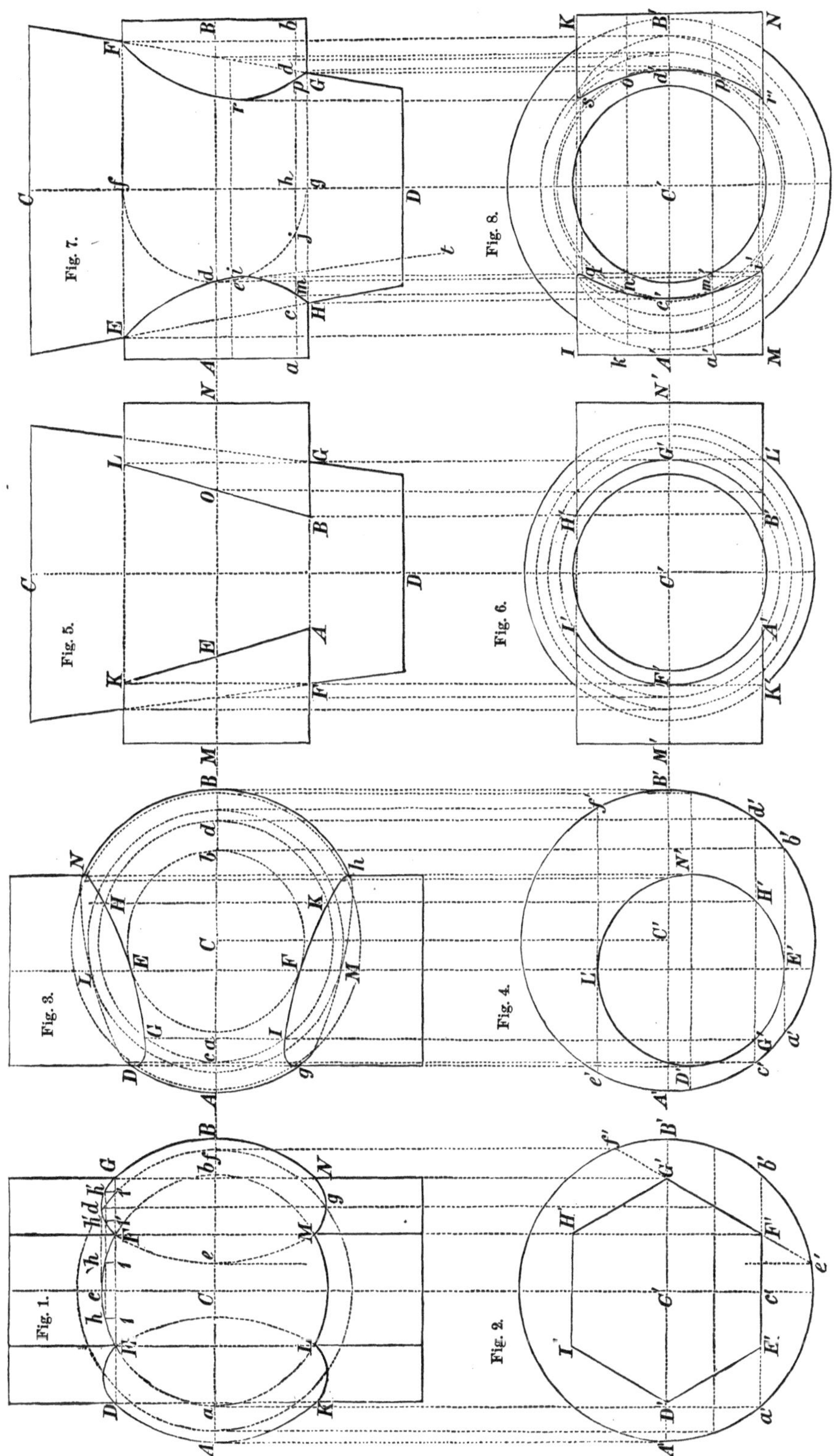

The intersection of the plane F G with the cone is projected horizontally in a circle described from the centre C′, with the diameter F′ G′. The arcs I′ F′ A′ and H′ G′ B′ are the only parts of this circle which require to be drawn.

Figs. 7 and 8.—*To describe the curves formed by the intersection of a cylinder with the frustum of a cone, the axes of the two solids cutting each other at right angles.*

The axes of the solids and their projections are laid down in the figures precisely as in the preceding example. The intersections of the outlines of the cone in the elevation with those of the cylinder, furnish, obviously, four points in the curves of penetration; these points are all projected horizontally upon the line A′ B′. Now, suppose a plane, as *a b* (fig. 7), to pass horizontally through both solids; its intersection with the cone will be a circle of the diameter *c d*, while the cylinder will be cut in two parallel straight lines, represented in the elevation by *a b*, and whose horizontal projection may be determined in the following manner:—Conceive a vertical plane *f g*, cutting the cylinder at right angles to its axis, and let the circle *g e f* thereby formed be described from the intersection of the axes of the two solids; the line *j h* will now represent, in this position of the section, the distance of one of the lines sought from the axis of the cylinder. Now set off this distance on both sides of the point A′, and through the points *k* and *a*′ thus obtained, draw straight lines parallel to A′ B′; the intersections of these lines with the circle drawn from the centre C′ of the diameter *c d* will give four points *m*′, *p*′, *n*, and *o*, which being projected vertically upon *a b*, determine two points *m* and *p* in the curves required.

In order to obtain the vertices or adjacent limiting points of the curves, draw from the vertex of the cone a straight line *t e*, touching the circle *g e f*, and let a horizontal plane be supposed to pass through the point of contact *e*. Proceed according to the method given above to determine the intersections of this plane with each of the solids in question, the four points *i*′, *r*′, *q*, and *s*, which being projected vertically upon the line *e r*, determine the vertices *i* and *r* required.

OF THE HELIX.

Plate VII.—*The Helix* is the curve described upon the surface of a cylinder by a point revolving round it, and at the same time moving parallel to its axis by a certain invariable distance during each revolution. This distance is called the *pitch* of the screw.

Figs. 1 and 2.—*Required to construct the helical curve described by the point* A *upon a cylinder projected horizontally in the circle* A′ C′ F′, *the pitch being represented by the line* A′ A³.

Divide the pitch A′ A³ into any number of equal parts, say eight; and through each point of division, 1, 2, 3, &c., draw straight lines parallel to the ground line. Then divide the circumference A′ C′ F′ into the same number of parts; the points of division B′, C′, E′, F′, &c., will be the horizontal projections of the different positions of the given point during its motion round the cylinder. Thus, when the point is at B′ in the plan, its vertical projection will be the point of intersection B of the perpendicular drawn through B′ and the horizontal drawn through the first point of division. Also, when the point arrives at C′ in the plan, its vertical projection is the point C, where the perpendicular drawn from C′ cuts the horizontal passing through the second point of division, and so on for all the remaining points. The curve A B C F A³ drawn through all the points thus obtained, is the helix required.

Figs. 1 and 2.—*To draw the vertical elevation of the solid contained between two helical surfaces and two concentric cylinders.*

A *helical surface* is generated by the revolution of a straight line round the axis of a cylinder; its outer end moving in a helix, and the line itself forming with the axis a constant and invariable angle.

Let A′ C′ F′ and K′ M′ O′ represent the concentric bases of the cylinders, whose common axis S T is vertical; the curve of the exterior helix A C F A³ is the first to be drawn according to the method above shown. Then having set off from A to A² the thickness of the required solid, draw through A² another helix equal and similar to the former. Now construct, as above, another helix, K C O, of the same pitch as the last, but on the interior cylinder; as also another, K² C² O², equal and parallel to the former. The lines A′ K′, B′ L′, C′ M′, &c., represent the horizontal projections of the various positions of the generating straight line, which, in the present example, has been supposed to be horizontal; and these lines are projected vertically at A K, B L, &c.

It will be observed, that in the position A K the generating line is projected in its actual length, and that at the position C′ M′ its vertical projection is the point C. The same remark applies to the generatrix of the second helix. The parts of both curves which are visible in the elevation may be easily determined by inspection.

Figs. 3 and 4.—*To determine the vertical projection of the solid formed by a sphere moving in a helical curve.*

Let A′ C′ E′ be the base of a cylinder, upon which the centre point C′

PLATE VII.

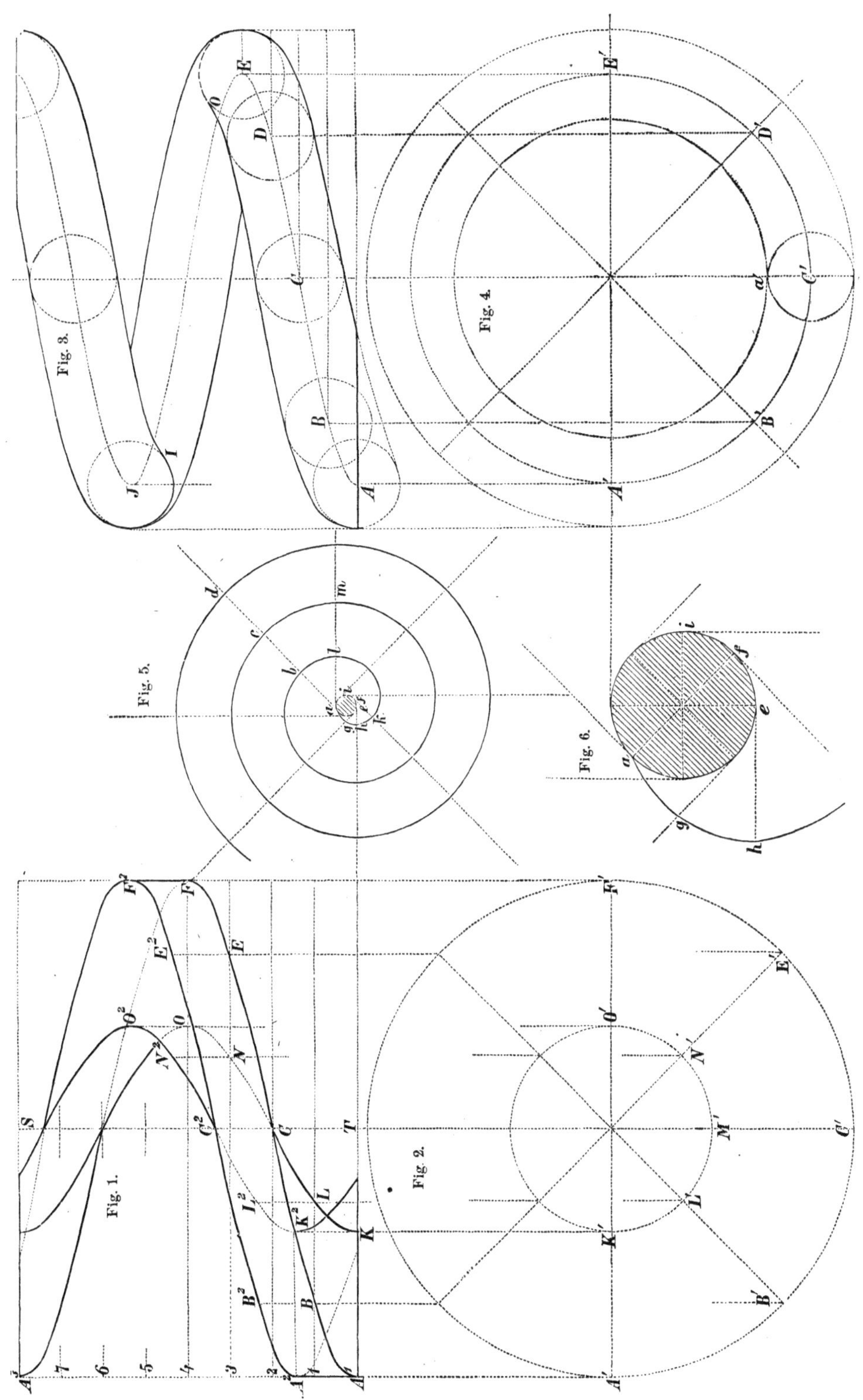

of a sphere whose radius is *a'* C' describes a helix, which is projected on the vertical plane in the curve A C E J. After determining as above the various points A, B, C, D . . . . . , in this curve, draw from each of these points as centres, circles with the radius *a'* C'; the circumferences of these circles will denote the various positions of the sphere during its motion round the cylinder; and if lines be drawn touching these circles, the curves thereby formed will constitute the figure required. One of these curves will disappear at O, which is its point of contact with the circle described from the point E, the intersection of the helix with the perpendicular E E'; it will again reappear at the point I when it becomes a tangent to the circle described from the point J in the prolongation of the line A A'. The exterior and interior circles (fig. 4) represent the horizontal projection of the solid in question.

The *conical* helix differs from the cylindrical one in that it is described on the surface of a cone instead of on that of a cylinder; but the construction differs but slightly from the one described. By following out the same principles, helices may be represented as lying upon spheres or any other surfaces of revolution.

In the arts are to be found numerous practical applications of the helical curve, as wood and machine screws, geers, and staircases, the construction of which will be still farther explained under their appropriate heads.

THE DEVELOPMENT OF SURFACES.

The *development* of the surface of a solid is the drawing or unrolling on a plane the form of its covering; and if that form be cut out of paper, it would exactly fit and cover the surface of the solid. Frequently in practice, the form of the surface of a solid is found by applying paper or thin sheet brass directly to the solid, and cutting it to fit. Tin and coppersmiths, boiler-makers, &c., are continually required to form from sheet metal forms analogous to solids; to execute which they should be able to construct geometrically the development of the surface of which they are to make the form.

The development of the surface of a plain cylinder is evidently but a plane sheet, of which the circumference is one dimension whilst its length is the other.

THE DEVELOPMENT OF THE SURFACE OF INTERSECTED CYLINDERS.

Plate VIII., figs. 1 and 2.—*To draw the surface of a cylinder formed by the intersection of another equal cylinder, as the knee of a stove pipe.*

Let A B C D be the elevation of the pipe or cylinder. Above A B describe the semicircle A′ 4′ B′ of the same diameter as the pipe; divide this semicircle into any number of equal parts, eight for instance; through these points 1′, 2′, 3′, &c., draw lines parallel to side A C of pipe, and touching the line C D of the intersection of the two cylinders. Lay off A″ B″ equal to the semicircle A′ 4′ B′, and divided into the same number of equal parts; through these points of division erect perpendiculars to A″ B″, and on these perpendiculars lay off the distances A″ C″, 1″ 1″, 2″ 2″, 3″ 3″, and so on, corresponding to A C, 1 1, 2 2, 3 3, &c., in preceding figure. Through the points C″, 1″, 2″, ——— D″, then draw connecting lines, and we have the developed surface required. It is to be remarked, that this gives but one half of the surface of the pipe, the other being exactly similar to it.

PLATE VIII.

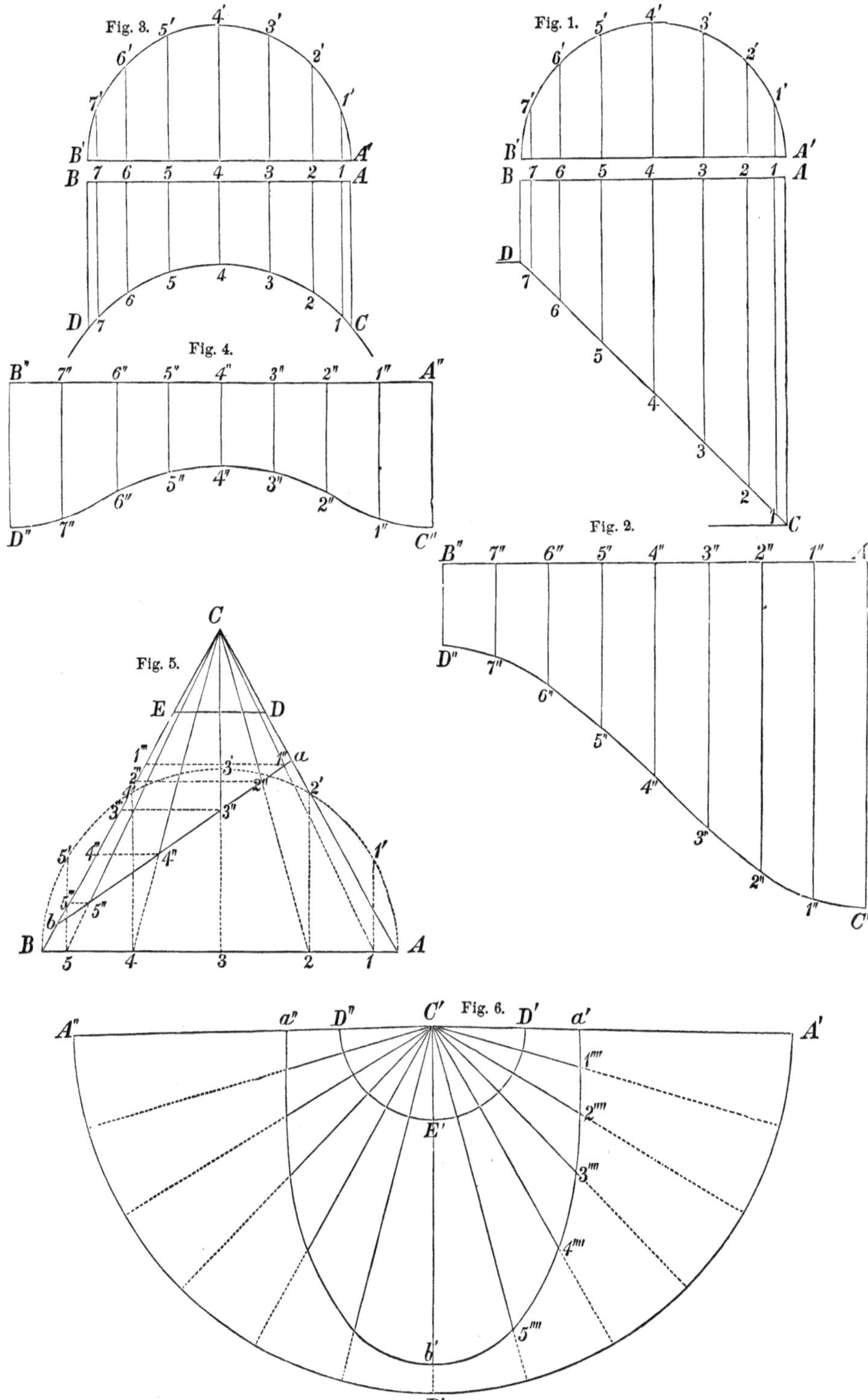

Figs. 3 and 4.—*To develop the surface of a cylinder intersected by another cylinder, as in the formation of a* T *pipe.*

The construction is similar to the preceding, and as the same letters and figures are preserved relatively, the demonstration will be easily understood from the foregoing.

The development of the surface of a right cone (figs. 5 and 6). From C′ (fig. 6) as a centre, with a radius C′ A′ equal to the inclined side A C of the cone (fig. 5), describe an arc of a circle A′ B′ A″; on this arc lay off the distance A′ B′ A″ equal to the circumference of the base of the cone; connect A′ C′ and C′ A″, and A′ B′ A″ C′ is the developed surface required.

To develop the surface of a frustrum of a cone, D A B E (fig. 5).

On fig. 6 develop the cut-off cone C D E as in preceding construction, and we have A′ B′ A″ D″ E′ D as the developed surface of the right frustrum.

To develop the surface of a frustrum of a cone, when the cutting plane a b (fig. 5) *is inclined to the base.*

On A B the base describe the semicircle A 3′ B; divide the semicircle into any number of equal parts, six for instance; from each point of division 1′, 2′, 3′, 4′, 5′, let fall perpendiculars to the base; at 1, 2, 3, 4, 5, connect each of these last points with the apex C. Divide now the arc A′ B′ (fig. 6) into six equal parts, or the arc A′ B′ A″ into twelve; each of these parts by the construction is equal to the arc A 1′, 1′ 2′ (fig. 5); connect these points of division with the point C′; on C′ A′ (fig. 6) take C′ *a*′ equal to C *a* of fig. 5, *a* being the point at which the plane cuts the inclined side of the cone; in the same way on C′ B′, lay off C′ *b*′ equal to C *b*.

It is evident that all the lines connecting the apex C with the base, included within the two inclined sides, are represented as less than their actual length in fig. 5, and must be projected on the inclined sides to determine their absolute dimensions; project, therefore, the points 1″, 2″, 3″, 4″, 5″, at which the cutting plane intersects the lines C 1, C 2, C 3, C 4, C 5, by drawing parallels to the base through these points to the inclined side C B′. On fig. 6 lay off C′ 1″″, C′ 2″″, &c., equal to C 1‴, C 2,‴, &c. (fig. 5); connect the points *a*′, 1″″, 2″″, —— *b*′, —— *a*″, and we have the developed surface *a*′ A′ B′ A″ *a*″ *b*′ required.

To develop the surface of a sphere or ball (figs. 189, 190).

It is evident that the surface cannot be accurately represented on a plane surface. It is done approximately by a number of gores. Let C A B (fig. 189) be the eighth of a hemisphere; on C D describe the quarter circle D A *c;* divide the arc into any number of equal parts, six for instance; from the points of division 1, 2, 3, . . . let fall perpendiculars on C D, and from the intersections with this line describe arcs 1′ 1″, 2′ 2″, 3′ 3″, ... cutting the line C B at 1″, 2″, 3″, ...; on the straight line C′ D′ (fig. 190), lay off C′ D′ equal to the arc D A *c*, with as many equal divi-

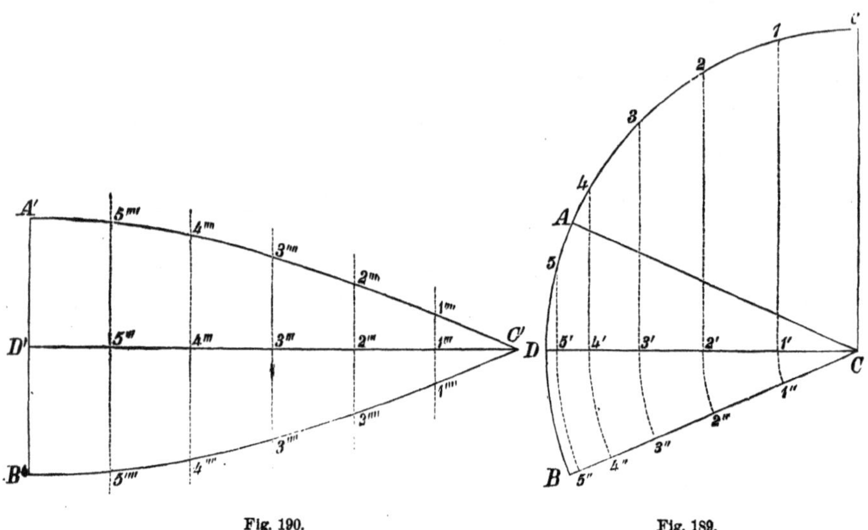

Fig. 190.

Fig. 189.

sions; then from either side of this line lay off 1‴ 1⁗, 2‴ 2⁗ . . . . D′ B′ equal to the arcs 1′ 1″, 2′ 2″, ... D B (fig. 189). Connect the points C′, 1⁗, 2⁗, ... and C′ A′ B′ is the developed surface.

It is to be remarked, that in the preceding demonstrations, the forms are described to cover the surface only; in construction, allowance is to be made for lap by the addition of margins on each side as necessary. It is found difficult in the formation of hemispherical ends of boilers, to bring all the gores together at the apex; it is usual, therefore, to make them, as shown (fig. 191), by cutting short the gores, and surmounting the centre with cap piece.

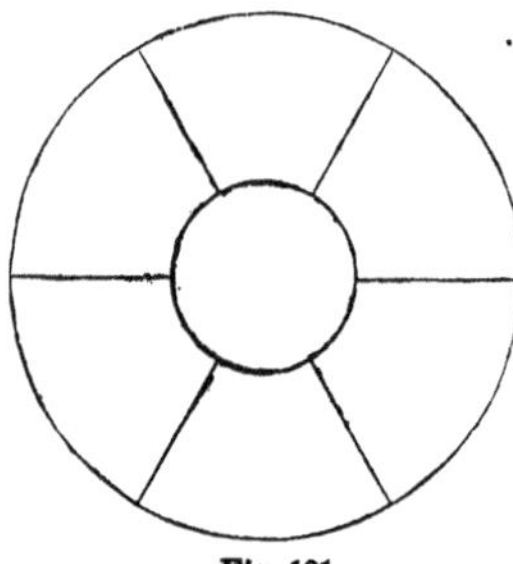

Fig. 191.

MECHANICS.

The profession of an architectural or mechanical draughtsman should embrace not merely the mere copying of examples which may be furnished him, but also the designing of new edifices and machines, in which he may draw from the results of his own experience; from good models, by collating suitable parts from divers designs; or by the rules of mechanics, proportioning the parts according to the magnitude and direction of the strains to which they are to be subject, and the materials of which they are to be composed; introducing as much of ornament as the subject may require.

Force is that which tends to cause or to destroy motion. The *direction of a force* is that in which this tendency is exerted; thus, gravity tends to draw bodies to the earth, and its direction is therefore vertical. Any number of forces which, being applied to a body, destroy one another's tendency to communicate motion to it, and thus hold it at rest, are said to be in equilibrium. *Two forces* cannot hold a body at rest unless they are equal to each other, and in opposite directions, and in the same straight line. To compare different forces, they are referred to some known standard, as for instance to pounds weight. For constructive purposes it is very convenient to represent forces by lines; in this way they can be represented both in magnitude and direction. Thus, if two forces act, for instance, on the point P in the direction P A and P B (fig. 192), by laying off from a scale of equal parts a distance corresponding in number to the pounds weight exerted by each force; thus, if the force exerted in the direction of P A would be represented numerically by 4 lbs., 4 cwt., or 4 tons, and that exerted in the direction P B be represented by 2 lbs., 2 cwt., or 2 tons, lay off from any convenient scale 4 equal parts on P A from P, and from the same scale 2 parts on P B, and

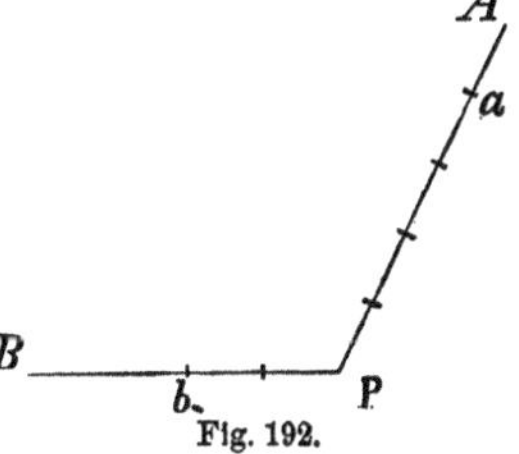

Fig. 192.

we have the two forces represented not only in direction but in magnitude. It is evident, that in this particular case the body cannot be at rest, as the two forces do not act in opposite directions, neither are they in the same straight line. A third force is necessary for equilibrium. We proceed to show how the magnitude and direction of this force may be determined.

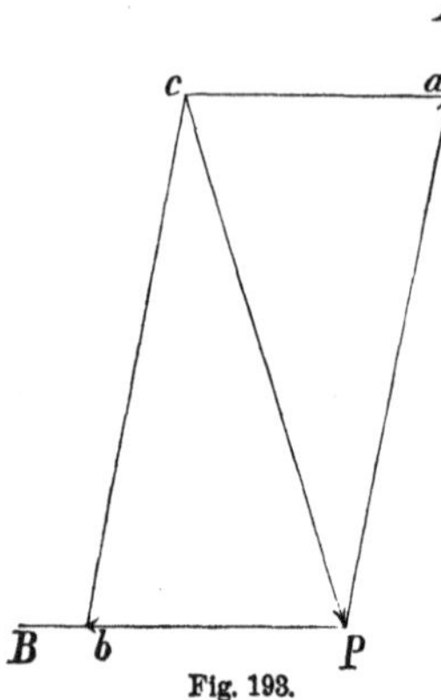

Fig. 193.

Through the extremities *a* and *b* (fig. 193), the distances laid off to represent the forces, draw two other lines, *a c* parallel to P *b*, and *b c* parallel to P *a*. The four will then form a parallelogram. Join the two opposite angles, P, *c*; then this line will represent, in magnitude and direction, the other, which will hold the other two at rest. Or stating this in general terms:—*If three forces acting on a point are in equilibrium, and lines be measured from this point in the direction of the forces, representing severally in length the relative amount of force exerted by them, then these lines will form the adjacent sides and diagonal of a parallelogram.* This is called the Law of the Parallelogram of Forces, which governs the equilibrium of any three forces, and the understanding of which is important for every one having charge of constructions either in machinery or architecture. The following simple and easy experiment will illustrate the principle. Let a small cord

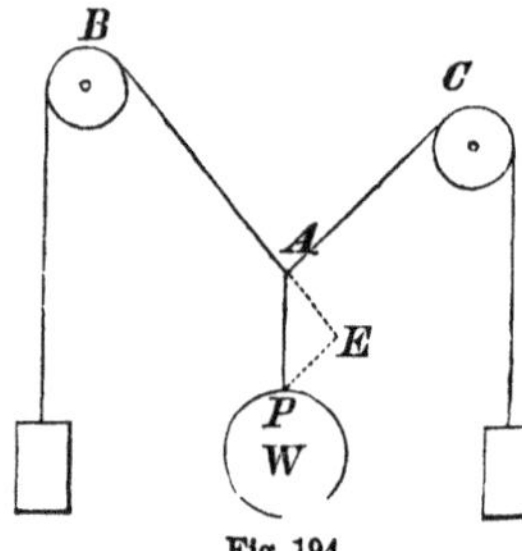

Fig. 194.

be passed over the pulleys B and C (fig. 194), and weights be attached to each end, and also one suspended from the centre at A, then the threads will assume a certain position dependent on the relation of the weights, and in this one position only will they balance each other; and if deranged by pulling, they will return to the same position when left at liberty. If this position be laid off on paper, and from a scale, lay off A P equal to the weight W, and the line P E drawn parallel to A C, and B A continued to E, then P E on the same scale would represent the weight suspended at C, and A E the weight at B. Thus, if a body be kept at rest by three forces, and any two of them be represented in magnitude and direction by two sides of a triangle, the third side will represent in magnitude and direction the other force. To extend this illustration still farther to any number of forces in the same plane: suspend a number of weights (fig. 195) over pulleys, and after they have assumed the position of rest, lay off the position of the lines on paper, making A a equal to the weight M; a b equal to N, and parallel to its direction A n; b c equal to O, and parallel to A o; c d equal to P, and parallel to A p; d e equal to Q, and parallel to a q; then the last force R will be in the direction and equal to the line A e, which completes the polygon. Hence, *if we represent in direction and magnitude any number of forces by the sides of a polygon, the force necessary to keep the others at rest will be represented by the line which completes the polygon.* This line is called the *resultant.*

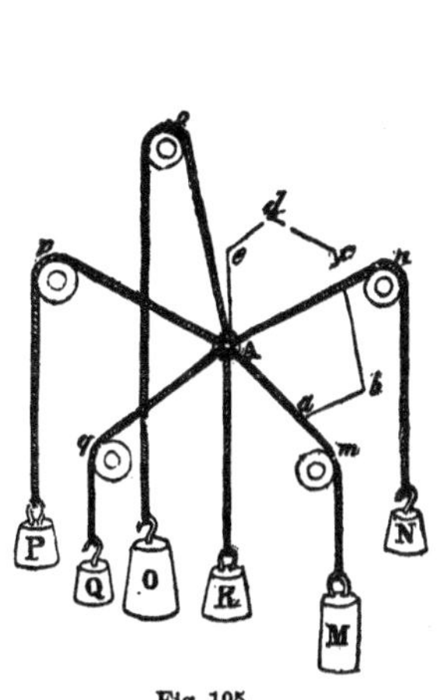

Fig. 195.

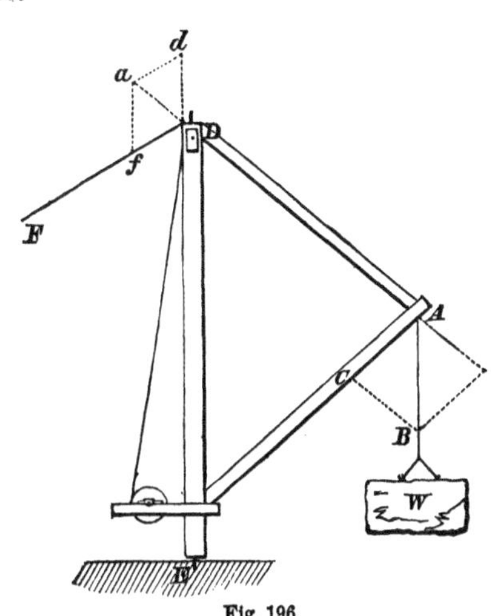

Fig. 196.

As a practical illustration of the application of the Parallelogram of Forces, take the raising of a weight by a crane or derrick (fig. 196). Represent by A B the weight W; draw C B parallel to the direction of the rope A D; C B will represent the strain on the rope A D, and A C the pressure in the direction of the line of the boom. The strain in the direction A D is supported by the guy D F, and the mast D E; represent by D a the strain on D A; then by constructing the parallelogram we have D f as the strain on the guy, and D d as the downward pressure or weight exerted on the top of the mast. By a similar construction, the pressure A C lengthways of the boom may be decomposed into a vertical pressure downwards on the step of the mast, and a horizontal thrust tending to displace it.

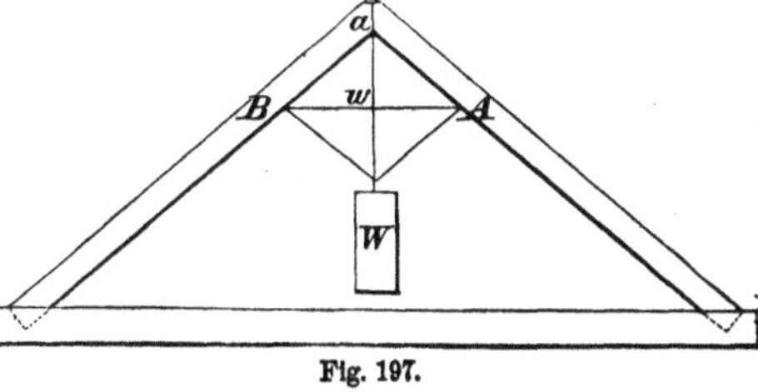

Fig. 197.

In the common roof truss (fig. 197), suspend a weight from the ridge representing it by a line, and construct the parallelogram by lines parallel to the direction of the rafters, and draw diagonals. Then *a* A will represent the pressure exerted against the end of the rafter A, which will be resolved at its foot into a downward pressure *a w*, and a thrust *w* A; in the same way the pressure on the other rafter becomes a weight, *a w*, and a thrust, *w* B. The thrust exerted by each rafter at its foot tends to break out its footing, or to tear asunder the tie; the amount of strain on the tie will be represented by either the lines *w* A or *w* B, and its tenacity must be sufficient to hold this weight with safety.

Fig. 198 represents a roof, of which the rafters have unequal pitches or inclinations, and consequently unequal pressures exerted against them.

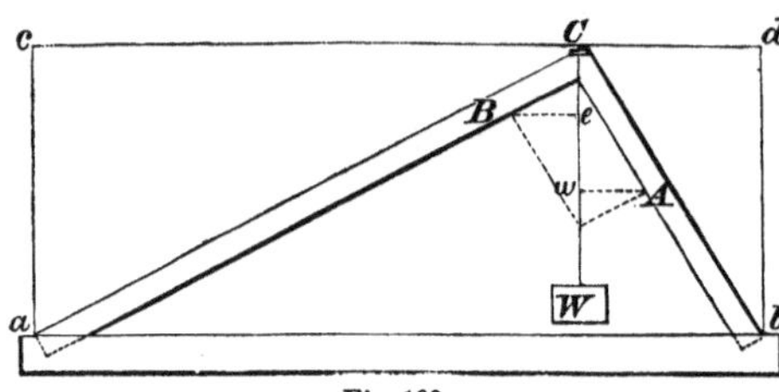

Fig. 198.

C A being the pressure on the rafter A, and C B on B, the weight supported at the foot *b* is represented by C *w*, on *a* by C *e*; the thrusts are equal, A *w* and B *e*, either of which is the strain on the tie. The weight supported at the end of the trusses is the inverse ratio of the distance at which the weight is supported from each end; thus if C *c* represent the weight at *b*, C *d* will represent the weight at *a*. The weight of the structure itself has not been regarded in the preceding estimates of the strains on the different parts.

It is evident that the weight or vertical pressure on the points of support can never exceed the suspended weight and the weight of the structure; but the horizontal strain may be increased or diminished by lowering or raising the point C. This is shown in the toggle-joint of the common hand-printing-press (fig. 199); thus the pressure on A and B increases, the nearer C approaches the straight line connecting them, and a small weight or pressure exerts an almost infinite force.

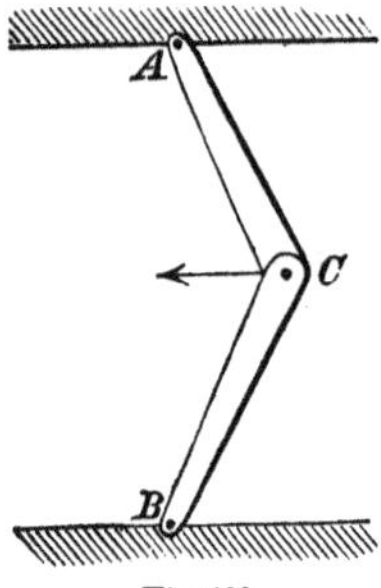

Fig. 199.

Parallel Forces.—Forces may act in lines parallel to each other, as in case of two horses harnessed abreast; and the resultant of any number of forces acting thus and in the same direction must be equal to the sum of the forces. But when two parallel forces act in opposite directions, they have no simple resultant, but their tendency is to rotation.

When two parallel but unequal forces, acting in the same direction, are balanced by a third, it must be equal to their sum, it must act in a contrary direction, and must be applied at a point nearer the greater than the less, inversely as their intensities. Thus (fig. 200), suppose the force or weight applied at A to be to that at B, as B *a* is to A *a*, *a* is the point of application of the third force. To find this point, suppose that the force A = 3 lbs., B = 8, then divide A B into 11 parts, and set off from B 3, and we have the point *a* of the application of the third force, which will be 11 lbs., the sum of the two, and acts in the opposite direction.

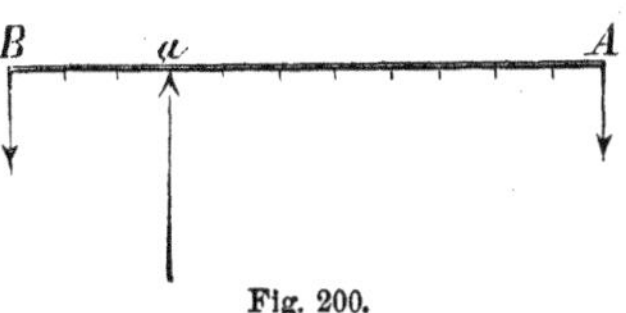

Fig. 200.

Now, the forces with which all bodies tend to fall to the earth may be considered *parallel;* hence, every body may be considered as acted on by a system of parallel forces, whose resultant may be found; and these forces, in all positions of the body, act on the same points in the same vertical direction. There is, therefore, in every body a point, through which the resultant always passes, in whatever position it is placed. This point is called the *centre of gravity* of the body. The centre of gravity of a uniform cylinder or prism is in its axis, and at the middle of its length; of a right cone or pyramid it is also in the axis, but at one-fourth the height from the base.

To ascertain mechanically the position of the centre of gravity of a body (figs. 201, 202). Suspend the body by a string from the point Q (fig. 201), and let Q R be the direction of the line when plumb; now the only forces by which the body is acted on are the weights of its different parts and the tension of the string; the former may be replaced by their resultant. Since the body is in equilibrium, the resultant and the tension must act in opposite directions, and in the same straight line Q R. But as the resultant must always pass through the centre of gravity, the centre of gravity must be in the line Q R. Mark the direction Q R, and suspend from another point P. The centre of gravity, by similar reasoning, must

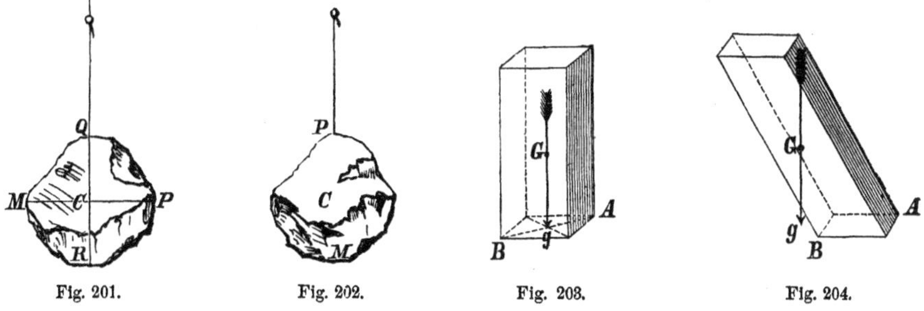

Fig. 201. Fig. 202. Fig. 203. Fig. 204.

be in the line P M, and can only be, therefore, at the intersection C of the two lines.

Another method.—Balance the body upon the edge of a bench till it be just on the point of falling off; then mark a line along it by the edge of the bench; do the same in another position of the body, and the point of intersection will be in a line corresponding to the place of the centre of gravity in the body.

A body, when placed on a horizontal plane, will fall over unless the vertical line passing through its centre of gravity fall within the base; thus in fig. 203, the body will stand firmly, whereas in fig. 204 it must manifestly tumble over. Persons who carry loads adjust their position so

Fig. 205.

Fig. 206.

Fig. 207.

that the common centre of gravity of the load H and of the body G shall fall within the area bounded by their feet (figs. 205, 206, 207).

The lower the centre of gravity, and the more extended the base, the more stable the position of the body, and the more difficult to be overturned.

THE MECHANICAL POWERS.

The simple machines or mechanical powers which enter as elements into the composition of all machinery are three, the *inclined plane*, the *lever*, and the *pulley;* to these some add the *toggle-joint* and *hydrostatic press*. The inclined plane includes the *incline*, the *wedge*, and the *screw;* the lever embraces the wheel-axle, being a modification of the same principle.

The incline.—When a body is drawn along a horizontal plane, the tractive force overcomes merely the friction of the surface, the weight is supported entirely by the plane. But when the plane is vertical, the whole weight is supported by the elevating power, and none by the plane. If, however, the body be drawn up an inclined plane, the power required is proportionate to the inclination of the plane and the direction of the force exerted. By the parallelogram of forces, decomposing the weight into an elevating force acting parallel to the plane and a pressure acting vertically to it, we form a triangle similar to the construction of the plane; that is, if we represent by $a\ c$ the length of the incline (fig. 208), the weight of the body, then the vertical line or height will represent the force acting parallel to the plane necessary to sustain the body, and the horizontal line or base will represent the pressure exerted perpendicular to the plane. Hence, the power acting parallel to the plane, we have the following rules:

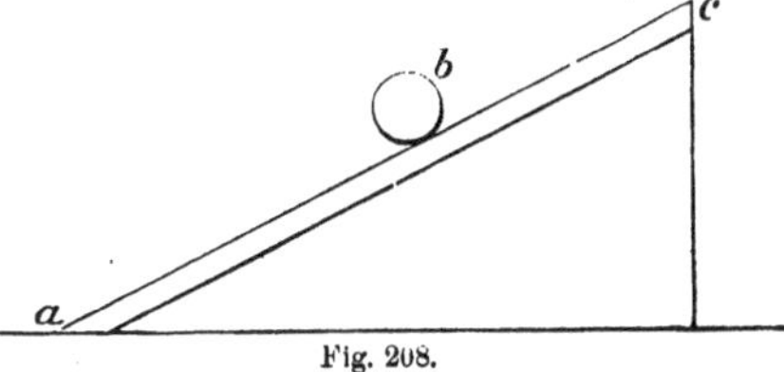

Fig. 208.

To find the power that will support a given weight, the length and height of the plane being known:

Multiply the weight by the height of the plane, and divide the product by its length.

Length of the plane, 54 inches; height of ditto, 18 inches; weight to be raised, 66 lbs.

Hence, $\frac{18 \text{ ins.} \times 66 \text{ lbs.}}{54 \text{ ins.}} = 22$ lbs., the power required to support the weight, and any other power greater than 22 lbs. will raise the body.

To find the weight that will be sustained by a known amount of power, the length and height of the plane being given:

Multiply the power by the length of the inclined plane, and divide the product by its height.

Length of the plane, 8 feet; height of ditto, 2 feet; power to be applied, 50 lbs.

$$\text{Hence, } \frac{8 \text{ feet} \times 50 \text{ lbs.}}{2 \text{ feet.}} = 200 \text{ lbs.}$$

The weight to the power, therefore, is as 200 to 50, or as 4 to 1.

To find the length of an inclined plane to raise a given weight, when its height, and the power to be applied, are known:

Multiply the height of the inclined plane by the weight, and divide the product by the power.

To find the height of an inclined plane necessary to sustain a given weight, its length, and the power to be applied, being known:

Multiply the length of the inclined plane by the power, and divide the product by the weight.

It is to be observed, that in the determination of the rules of mechanics, friction and the inertia are entirely left out of consideration.

The *wedge* is a movable incline, and when the power is applied continuously to the back, the force required to exert a determinate pressure may be determined by the same rules as for the incline. But the power is commonly imparted to this instrument by a succession of blows or strokes, or a percussive force. This force has not, as yet, been properly investigated, and we cannot, with propriety, assign a rule to the wedge under these conditions.

The *screw* is an inclined plane formed round the circumference of a cylinder. The *height* of the inclined plane is the distance from the upper surface of one thread of the screw to the upper surface of the next. The *length* is the extent of the spiral line between those surfaces, or in one revolution of the circumference.

Power is usually imparted to the screw through the interposition of the lever or winch. To calculate its power:

Divide the circumference described by the lever in its rotation by the interval or distance between two threads of the screw; the quotient will be the number of times the weight raised exceeds the power.

Circumference of circle = 48 inches; from thread to thread = $\frac{1}{2}$ inch. Hence, $48 \div \frac{1}{2} = 96$. The weight to the power is as 96 to 1.

To find the weight raised:

Multiply the circumference of the circle described by the lever or winch by the power that is to be applied, and divide the product by the distance between two threads of the screw.

Circumference of circle, 30 inches; from thread to thread, 1 inch; power to be applied 12 lbs.

Hence, $\frac{30 \text{ inches} \times 12 \text{ lbs.}}{1} = 360$ lbs. The weight raised will be 360 lbs.

Levers are of three classes, according to the relative positions of the power, weight, and fulcrum.

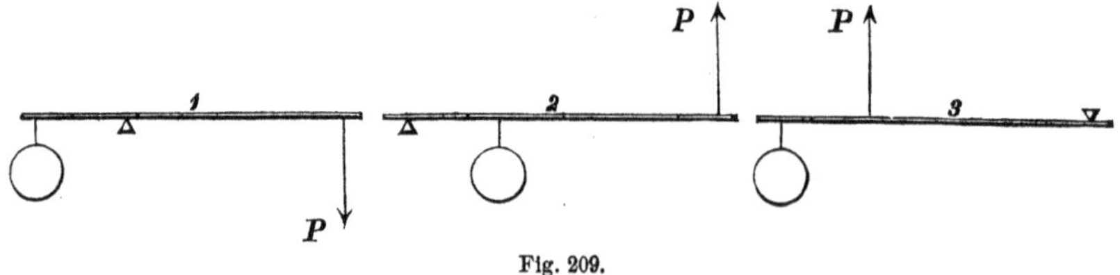

Fig. 209.

In the *lever of the first class*, the power is at one end of the bar, the weight at the other, and the fulcrum is placed somewhere in the intermediate space between them.

In the *lever of the second class*, the relative positions of the fulcrum and weight are changed.

In the *lever of the third class*, the weight changes place with the power.

The power and effect of the different kinds of lever may be thus determined:

To find the position of the fulcrum to support a given weight by a known amount of power:

Divide the weight to be supported by the power to be applied; the quotient will exhibit the difference of leverage necessary to support the weight in equilibrium.

Weight to be supported, 42 cwt.; power to be applied, 6 cwt.

$$\text{Hence, } 42 \div 6 = 7.$$

The distance from the power to the fulcrum, therefore, must be seven times greater than from the fulcrum to the weight.

To find the weight that will be supported by a known amount of power, the position of the fulcrum being given:

Multiply the distance between the power and the fulcrum by the power, and divide the product by the distance between the fulcrum and the weight.

A bar 10 feet long is arranged as a lever of the first kind.

From power to fulcrum, $8\frac{3}{4}$ feet; from fulcrum to weight, $1\frac{1}{4}$ foot; power to be applied, 40 lbs.

Hence, $\frac{8\frac{3}{4} \text{ feet} \times 40 \text{ lbs.}}{1\frac{1}{4} \text{ foot.}} = 280$ lbs. The weight supported, 280 lbs.

The same bar is arranged as a lever of the second kind.

From power to fulcrum, 10 feet; from weight to fulcrum, $1\frac{1}{4}$ foot; power to be applied, 40 lbs.

Hence, $\frac{10 \text{ feet} \times 40 \text{ lbs.}}{1\frac{1}{4} \text{ foot.}} = 320$ lbs. The weight supported, 320 lbs.

To find the power that will support a given weight, the position of the fulcrum being known:

Multiply the distance between the weight and the fulcrum by the weight to be raised, and divide the product by the distance between the fulcrum and the power.

Lever of the third kind:—from power to fulcrum, 1 foot; from weight to fulcrum, 10 feet; weight to be supported, 15 lbs.

Hence, $\frac{10 \text{ feet} \times 15 \text{ lbs.}}{1 \text{ foot.}} = 150$ lbs., the power required.

In the above examples we have considered weights or gravity as the acting forces; but should the forces not be parallel nor perpendicular to the lever, let fall from the fulcrum perpendiculars on the directions of the forces, and take these lines as the distances.

The *wheel and axle* is formed of a series of levers, so fixed on a fulcrum as an axis, that they can rotate or describe circles around it. The rules given for the lever are, therefore, applicable to the wheel and axle and the winch and axle; or thus.

As the radius of the wheel is to the radius of the axle, so is the weight to the power.

The *pulley* is of two kinds. The one consists of a series of cords attached to a beam and to one another; the other of a single cord, passing alternately over and under a series of sheeves or friction wheels.

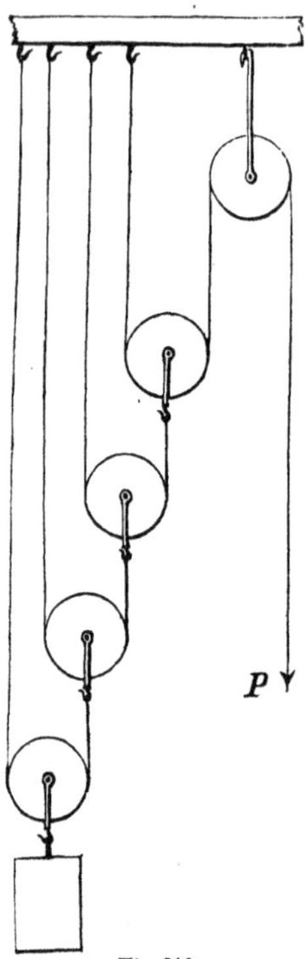

To find the *power* and *effect* of a pulley consisting of a series of cords:

Double the power at the first cord or point of suspension, and continue to double the amount at every subsequent suspension.

Required the weight that can be raised by one pound of power, the pulley having four cords.

1st cord—1 lb. × 2 = 2 lbs.
2d cord—2 lbs. × 2 = 4 lbs.
3d cord—4 lbs. × 2 = 8 lbs.
4th cord—8 lbs. × 2 = 16 lbs.

The weight that can be raised on the fourth cord is 16 lbs. (fig. 210).

Fig. 210.

To find the *power* and *effect* of a pulley, formed of a single cord, passing alternately over and under a series of sheeves.

Count the number of apparent lines connected with the lowest block of sheeves; these will indicate the difference between the power and the weight.

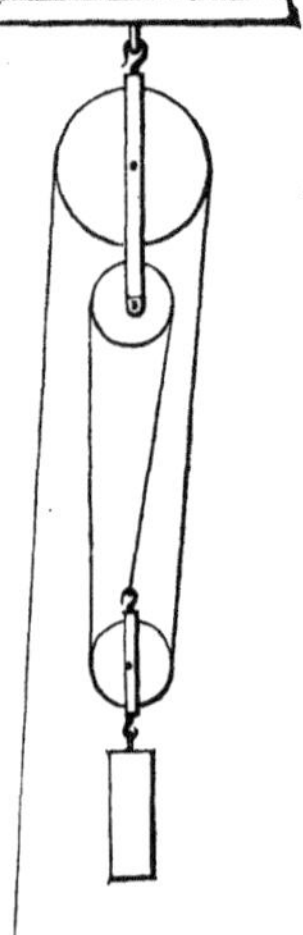

Fig. 211.

Required the weight that can be raised by 15 lbs. of power, the pulley having, apparently, three cords attached to the lowest block (fig. 211).

15 lbs. × 3 = 45 lbs., the weight.

FRICTION, AND THE LIMITING ANGLE OF RESISTANCE.

Suppose a mass A (fig. 212) be pressed upon another, B, by means of a force acting in a direction perpendicular to the common surface of the two bodies, and let a second force Q act also upon it in a direction parallel to this surface. Then, since the forces P and Q act in directions perpendicular to each other, they manifestly cannot counteract one another, and it would be expected that the body should move in the direction of the second force. This, however, is not always the case; except the force Q exceed a certain limit, no motion ensues. Some new force F, therefore, has been produced in the system, counteracting the force Q; that force is called friction. It acts always in a direction parallel to the surfaces in contact, *and is always for surfaces of the same nature the same fraction, or part of the force* P *by which these are pressed together*, whatever be the amount of that force, or whatever the extent of surfaces in contact. This fraction is called the coefficient of friction. Whilst it is thus the same for the same surfaces, whatever be the extent of the surfaces, or the force with which they are pressed together, it is different for different surfaces.

Construct the parallelogram of forces P P″ Q M (fig. 213). P″ M represent the resultant of the two forces P and Q. The actual friction is always a certain given fraction of P acting parallel to the impressed surface. Take M Q′ equal to this given fraction of P M, complete the parallelogram, and draw the diagonal P′ M. Since, then, M Q′ represents the friction of the body upon the plane, or the force called into action by P M, which opposes the motion of the body; since, moreover, Q M represents

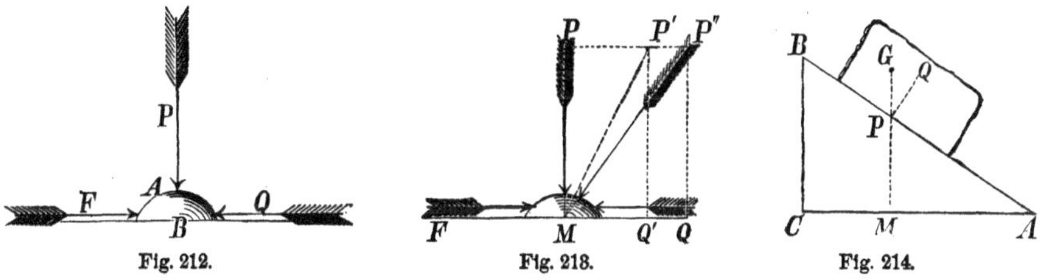

Fig. 212. Fig. 213. Fig. 214.

the force tending to produce motion, it follows that the body will or will not move, according as Q M is greater or less than M Q′, or as the angle P M P″ is greater or less than P′ M P. The angle P′ M P is called the limiting angle of resistance. It depends upon the coefficient of friction, and is therefore the same for the same surfaces, whatever be the actual amount of the impressed force P.

Hence it appears, that force impressed upon the surface of a solid body at rest, by the intervention of another solid body, will be destroyed, provided the angle which the direction of that force makes with the perpendicular to the surface does not exceed a certain angle called the limiting angle of the resistance at that surface, and this is true, however *great* the force may be. Also, that if the direction of the impressed force lie without this angle, it cannot be sustained by the resistance of the surfaces in contact, and that this is true, however *small* the force may be.

Suppose a heavy mass (fig. 214), whose centre of gravity is G, to be placed on an inclined plane A B. The whole pressure of the mass may be supposed to act in the direction of the vertical line G M, and this pressure will be just destroyed by the resistance of the surface of the plane when the angle G′ P Q, which G P makes with the perpendicular P Q, is equal to the limiting angle of resistance. A mass of any substance will, therefore, just be sustained on an inclined plane, without slipping, when the inclination of the plane is equal to the limiting angle of the resistance of the surfaces in contact; that is, when the angle B A C is equal to the angle G P Q.

EXPERIMENTS ON FRICTION, BY M. MORIN.

SURFACES OF CONTACT.	WITHOUT UNGUENTS.				UNCTUOUS SURFACES.			
	FRICTION OF MOTION.		FRICTION OF QUIESCENCE.		FRICTION OF MOTION.		FRICTION OF QUIESCENCE.	
	Co-efficient of friction.	Limiting angle of resistance.	Co-efficient of friction.	Limiting angle of resistance.	Co-efficient of friction.	Limiting angle of resistance.	Co-efficient of friction.	Limiting angle of resistance.
Oak upon oak, fibres parallel to the motion, ...	0.478	25° 33′	0.625	32° 1′	0.108	6° 10′	0.390	21° 19′
Oak upon oak, fibres of the moving body perpendicular to the motion,	0.324	17.58	0.540	28.23	0.143	8° 9′	0.314	17° 26′
Oak upon elm, fibres parallel, . .	0.246	13.50	0.376	20.37	0.136	7.45		
Elm upon elm, " " . .					0.140	7.59		
Wrought iron upon oak, . . .	0.619	31° 47′	0.619	31° 47′				
" " " wrought iron, .	0.138	7.52	0.137	7.49	0.177	10.3		
" " " cast " .	0.194	10° 59′	0.194·	10 59			0.118	6.44
" " " brass, . .	0.172	9.46			0.160	9.6		
Cast iron on elm, ...	0.195	11.3			0.125	7.8		
" " cast iron, . . .	0.152	8.39	0.162	9.13	0.144	8.12		
" " wrought iron, . .					0.143	8.9		
" " brass, ...	0.147	8.22			0.132	7.32		
Brass upon cast iron, . . .	0.217	12.15			0.107	6.7		
" " wrought iron, . .	0.161	9.9						
" " brass, ...	0.201	11.22			0.134	7.38	0.164	9.19
Leather oxhide, well tanned, on oak,	0.296	16.30						
" " on cast iron, wetted,					0.229	12.54	2.67	14.57
" belts on oaken drums, . .	0.27		0.47					
" " " cast iron pulleys, .	0.28							
Common building stones upon the same, ...	0.38 to 0.65	20.49—33.2	0.65—0.75	33.2—36.53				

From his experiments M. Morin found, that the friction of two surfaces which had been considerable time in contact was not only different in its amount, but in its nature, from the friction of surfaces in continuous motion; especially in this, that this friction of quiescence is subject to causes of variation and uncertainty, from which the friction of motion is exempt; but that the slightest jar or shock, the most imperceptible movement of the surfaces of contact, was sufficient to change the friction from the quiescent state into that which accompanies motion. Hence, as every machine or structure of whatever kind may be considered as subject to such shock or imperceptible motion, all questions of construction depending upon the state of friction should be referred to that which accompanies continuous motion. The friction of two surfaces outside the limits of abrasion is independent of the extent of superficies, and when in motion, of the velocity of the motion also.

There are three states in respect to friction into which the surfaces of bodies in contact may be made to pass; *one*, a state in which no unguent is present; *second*, a state in which the surfaces are unctuous, but intimately in contact; the *third*, a state in which the surfaces are separated by an entire stratum of the interposed unguent. From experiments on this last class Morin deduces, "that with the unguents olive oil and lard interposed in a continuous stratum between them, surfaces of wood on metal, metal on wood, wood on wood, and metal on metal, when in motion have all of them very nearly the same coefficient of friction, the value of that coefficient being in all cases included between 0.07 and 0.08, and the limiting angle of resistance between 4° and 4° 35′. For tallow as an unguent, the coefficient is the same as the above, except in case of metals upon metals, in which case the coefficient was found to be 0.10."

ON THE EQUILIBRIUM OF THE POLYGON OF RODS OR CORDS.

If we take all the forces excepting those which act upon the extremities of the polygon, and find the direction of their resultant, then the two extreme sides of the polygon being produced will meet this direction in the same point. Thus, in the polygon represented loaded with the weights P^1, P^2, P^3, if we find the vertical R T passing through the centre of gravity of these weights, and produce P A and P^6 B, these will meet R T in the same point T (fig. 215).

Similarly in the funicular curve or catenary (fig. 216), if we draw tangents at the points of suspension A and B, these, being in the direction of the forces sustaining the curve at these points, will meet when produced in the vertical line G T, passing through the centre of gravity G of the curve. Let G T represent the weight of the cord A B; draw G M and G N parallel to A T and B T; N T will represent the tension at A, and

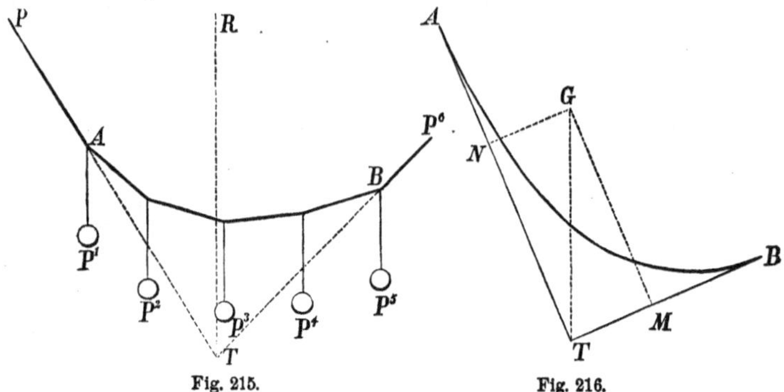

Fig. 215. Fig. 216.

M T the tension at B. Such a curved line is more liable to rupture, therefore, at the upper point of suspension. and in construction, when possible, should be of greater dimensions.

If a polygon of rods be reversed, that is, placed *upright* instead of *suspended*, the position in which it will stand is that which it will assume for itself when loaded with the same weights, and suspended. Hence, to determine the positions in which any number of beams should be arranged in a polygon, so as to support one another, the timbers of a gambrel roof for instance: let a cord be taken, and distances be measured along it, equal respectively in length to the sides of the polygon; let weights be attached to these, equal each to one half the sum of the weights of the two adjacent sides. Then the two ends of the string being held at a distance apart equal to the length of the base of the polygon, the form which the string will assume when hanging freely will be that in which the beams should be arranged.

To the continual equilibrium of an *upright* framework it *is* essential that its joints should be stiffened. Now this cannot be brought about by any peculiarity in the joint itself, for the different parts of such a joint, being situated exceedingly near to the centre about which each rod tends to move, are, on the principle of the lever, readily crushed by the action of a force, however slight, acting at the extremity of the rod. It is, therefore, requisite that each joint should be stiffened by subsidiary framing. And out of the necessity for this strengthening arises the greater economy of the suspended than the upright polygon or framing. In the *suspended* polygon or curve, the only precaution necessary is, that the parts should not *tear* asunder. In its *upright* position, their *flexibility* as well as the chance of their *compression*, must be guarded against.

The methods of giving rigidity to a system of rods are various. They all of them, however, resolve themselves directly or indirectly into the arrangement of the component rods in *triangles*. Of all simple geometrical figures, the triangle is the only one which cannot alter its form without at the same time altering the dimensions of its sides, and which cannot, therefore, yield, except by separating at its angles, or tearing its sides asunder. Hence, therefore, a triangle whose joints cannot separate, and whose sides are of sufficient strength, is perfectly rigid; and this can be asserted of no other plane figure whatever. Thus a parallelogram may have sides of infinite strength, and no force may be sufficient to tear its joints asunder, and yet may it be made to alter its form by the action of the slightest force impressed upon it. And this is true in a greater or less degree of all other four-sided figures and polygons. It is for these reasons that in all framing, care is taken to combine all the parts, as far as possible, in triangles; which being once done, we know that the rigidity of the system may be insured by giving the requisite strength to the timbers and joints.

The framing of a gate presents a very simple illustration of this principle. The outline of the form of the gate is that of a rectangular parallelogram. If, as in the accompanying figure (fig. 217), the parts which compose it had been arranged in directions parallel to its sides only, so

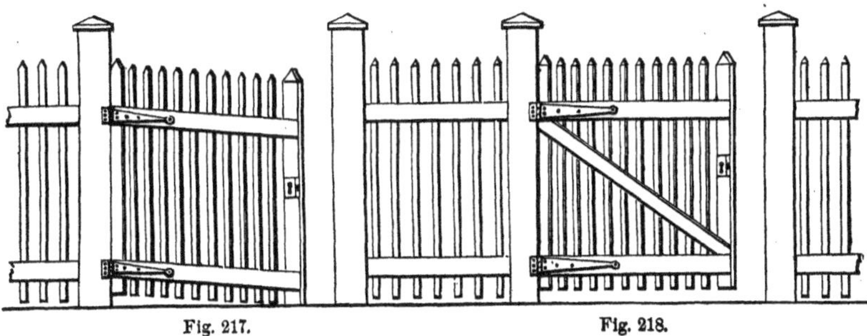

Fig. 217. Fig. 218.

that the whole frame should have been composed of elementary parallelograms, each component parallelogram, and, therefore, the whole frame of the gate, would readily have altered its form.

A bar placed *diagonally* across the gate remedies the evil, converting the elementary parts of the gate from parallelograms into *triangles*, and thus giving perfect rigidity to the frame (fig. 218).

Further illustrations of the principles of framing, together with the equilibrium of solid bodies in contact, as in the construction of retaining walls and arches, will be found under the head of Architectural Drawing.

THE MECHANICAL PROPERTIES OF MATERIALS.

To proportion properly the parts of a machine or edifice, the draughtsman should understand not only the kind of strain, the direction, and amount to which its different parts may be subjected, but also the nature and properties of the materials of which it may be composed, and their capability of resisting uninjured the required stress.

The forces to which materials in constructions are subjected are *compression*, *tension*, *flexure*, and *torsion*.

Parts of structures are usually subjected to a compressive force in the direction of their length, and when this dimension is less than a certain proportion (depending on the nature of the material) to its diameter or shortest side, rupture takes place from the absolute crushing of the parts. Woods have been found to resist a crushing force of from 2 to 10,000 lbs. per square inch of surface, varying with the kind of wood and selection of specimens. The various stones used in building will bear from 1 to 5 tons per square inch; brick, from ½ to 1½ tons; cast iron, from 38 to 65 tons; cast copper, 50 tons; cast lead, 3 tons. In the actual practice of construction, materials cannot with safety be subjected to any pressure approaching their ultimate strength. They are liable to various occasional and accidental pressures, and to others of a permanent kind resulting from settlement, and other causes, of which no previous account can be taken, for which allowance must nevertheless be made. Navier, from existing structures, deduces the rule that wood and stone should not be subjected to a strain over one-tenth of that which breaks them, and iron to not over one-fourth. Wood and iron, when used to resist a compressive force, are generally of such lengths in comparison with their sides or diameter, that rupture takes place partly from compression, partly from flexure. It has been found, that if the length of a circular post exceed eight times its diameter, that the tendency under pressure will be to bend; and the longer the pillar, the other dimensions remaining the same, the more this tendency developes itself.

The following table exhibits the pressure in lbs. per square inch which may be placed with safety on wooden posts of various lengths in proportion to their diameters, care being of course taken to select those that are not defective.

KIND OF WOOD.	PROPORTION OF LENGTH TO LEAST DIAMETER.			
	Above 8.	Above 12.	Above 24.	Above 48.
Sound oak, . .	425.	350.	210.	70.
Inferior " . .	270.	120.	70.	
Pitch pine, . .	530.	440.	265.	105.
Common pine, . .	140.	116	70.	

When the length of the post is intermediate between those given in the table, find the number by proportion; thus, for pitch pine post 18 times the length of its diameter, the number will be 352.5 lbs., which multiplied by the number of 39 inches of bearing surface of the post, will be a safe load.

For cast iron posts, the circular form is usually adopted, as being the strongest form for the same amount of material, the hollow pillar being in this respect preferable to the solid. Mr. Hodgkinson, from his experiments on cast iron pillars, deduces the following rules:

1*st.* In all long pillars of the same dimensions, the resistance to fracture by flexure is three times greater when the ends of the pillar are flat and firmly bedded, than when they are rounded and capable of moving. This shows the importance of having the ends of pillars turned square, and of having the ends of braces square and not rounded, as has been proposed and adopted by some architects.

2*d.* The strength of a pillar with one end round and the other flat, is the arithmetical mean between that of a pillar of the same dimensions, with both ends rounded and both ends flat.

3*d.* A long uniform pillar, with its ends firmly fixed, whether by discs or otherwise, has the same power to resist breaking as a pillar of the same diameter and half the length, with the ends rounded.

4*th.* Some little additional strength is given to a pillar by enlarging its diameter at the middle part; but this increase is not over one-seventh of the breaking weight.

5*th.* In cast iron pillars of the same length, the strength is as the 3.6 power of the diameter nearly.

6*th.* In cast iron pillars of the same diameter, the strength is inversely proportioned to the 1.7 power of the length.

The breaking weight of solid cylindrical cast iron pillars, with their ends flat and incapable of motion, is in tons $44 \times \frac{d^{3.6}}{l^{1.7}}$, l being the length in feet, d the diameter in inches. In hollow pillars the same rule applies, but for $d^{3.6}$ we use $D^{3.6}$ $d^{3.6}$, D being the external and d the internal diameter. For pillars with ends movable and rounded, one-third of the above formula will be the breaking weight.

TABLE I.—*Diameters to the* 3.6 *power.*

Inches.		Inches.		Inches.	
2.	12.125	5.25	391.36	8.	1782.9
2.5	27.076	5.5	462.71	8.25	1991.7
3.	52.196	5.75	543.01	8.5	2217.7
3.25	69.628	6.	632.91	8.75	2461.7
3.5	90.917	6.25	733.11	9.	2724.4
3.75	116.55	6.5	844.28	9.5	3309.8
4.	147.03	6.75	967.15	10.	3981.1
4.25	182.89	7.	1102.4	10.5	4745.5
4.5	224.68	7.25	1250.9	11.	5610.7
4.75	272.96	7.5	1413.3	11.5	6584.3
5.	328.32	7.75	1590.3	12.	7674.5

TABLE II.—*Lengths to the* 1.7 *power.*

Inches.		Inches.		Inches.	
1.	1.	9.	41.900	17.	123.53
2.	3.249	10.	50.119	18.	136.13
3.	6.473	11.	58.934	19.	149.24
4.	10.556	12.	68.329	20.	162.84
5.	15.426	13.	78.289	21.	176.92
6.	21.031	14.	88.801	22.	191.48
7.	27.332	15.	99.851	23.	206.51
8.	34.297	16.	111.43	24.	222.

Example.—To find the breaking weight of a hollow cast iron pillar with square ends, whose outside diameter is 6 inches; inside or core, $4\frac{1}{2}$; and length, 16 feet.

Then from Table I.:—Against 6. is 632.91; against 4.5, 224.68. $632.91 - 224.68 = 408.23$; $408.23 \times 44 = 17962.12$; dividing this by 111.43, the number against 16 in Table II., we have $\frac{17962.12}{111.43}$, $= 162$ tons very near of 2,240 lbs. each as the weight which would break this column.

The above formulas apply only to long pillars; that is, those whose length is at least 25 to 30 times their diameter, and the result arrived at is their ultimate strength; but the permanent load should not exceed one-fourth of the breaking weight. Short cylindrical pillars may be loaded perfectly safely with 10 tons to the square inch of area of base. It is, of course, important that the columns should be straight with a square base, so that the direction of the strain should be through the axis.

On the tensile strength of materials, when pulled in the direction of their length.

NAMES OF METALS.	Specific gravity.	Tensile strength per square inch in pounds.	Weight of cubic foot in pounds.
Copper, cast, ...	8.607	22.570	537.9
" wire, ...	8.607	61.228	
Iron, cast, ...	6.97 to 7.29	13 to 25.000	436. to 456.
" wrought bar, . .	7.6 to 7.8	20 to 80.000	475. to 487.
" cable, . . .		54 to 75.000	
" wire, . . .		86 to 113.000	
Lead, sheet, . . .	11.407	3 300	712.9
Tin, cast banca, . .	7.217	3.679	451.
" wire, ...		7.129	
Steel, soft, . . .	7.780	120.000	486.2
" cast, . . .		40.900	
Zinc, cast, . . .	7.215	2.900	451.
" sheet, . . .		16.616	

NAMES OF WOODS.	Specific gravity.	Tensile strength per square inch in pounds.	Weight of cubic foot in pounds.
Ash, ...	0.727	16 to 19.000	45.4
Beech, ...	0.696	17 to 22.000	43.5
Chestnut, ...	0.610	10 to 12.000	38.1
Cedar, ...	0.457	5 to 11.000	28.5
Elm, ...	0.554	13.000	34.6
Locust, ...		20.000	
Mahogany, ...	0.8 to 0.870	16 to 22.000	
" Spanish, . .	0.753	12.000	
Oak, white American, .		11.500	
" English, ...	0.7 to 0.76	8 to 20.000	43.7 to 47.5
Pine, pitch, ...	0.628	8 to 13.000	39.1
Spruce, ...	0.551	8.800	34.4

The above represent the absolute strength. Woods are seldom used for a tensile strain; but when so used, the size should be very much larger than that merely required to resist the strain, say at least ten times. Wrought iron is the material the most generally employed to resist a pulling force; and its elastic power in that capacity, or the load with which it may safely be trusted, is 8 to 10 tons per square inch for good iron.

TRANSVERSE STRENGTH OF MATERIALS.

The strength of a square or rectangular beam to resist lateral pressure, acting in a direction perpendicular to its length is as the breadth, and the square of the depth; and inversely as the length, or the distance from or between points of support. Thus a beam twice the breadth of another, other proportions being alike, has twice the strength; or twice the depth, four times the strength; but twice the length, only half the strength.

The general formula is $W = \frac{S\, b\, d^2}{l}$, in which W is the breaking weight; S, a number determined by experiment on different materials; b, the breadth, and d, the depth in inches; and l, the length in feet.

Value of S *for different materials.*

Wrought iron,	3,200 lbs.	Pitch pine,	550 lbs.
Cast "	2,500 "	White "	400 "
Oak, white,	580 "	Spruce,	350 "

To find the breaking weight of a beam supported at the ends and loaded in the centre: *Rule*—Multiply the constant S, for the material from the above table, by the breadth and square of the depth in inches, and divide the product by the length in feet.

Example.—What is the ultimate strength of a beam of white pine, 20 feet long, 8 inches wide, and 14 inches deep?

$$400 \times 8 \times 14^2 = 627.200. \quad \frac{627.200}{20} = 31.360 \text{ lbs.}$$

From the above formula we can determine either the breadth, depth, or length, the other quantities being known. To determine the depth; the weight, breadth, and length being known: Multiply the length in feet by the weight in pounds; also the tabular number S by the breadth in inches. Divide the first product by the last, and the square root of the quotient will be the required depth.

To find the depth of an oak timber 15 feet long and 6 inches wide, to support a weight of 10,000 lbs. In practice it is necessary to find a depth that would support this load permanently. Multiply the given weight by 6, and establish the depth on this basis; thus, to support 10,000 securely and permanently, find a beam whose ultimate strength is equal to 60,000 lbs.

$$15 \times 60000 = 900000. \qquad 580 \times 6 = 3480. \qquad \frac{900000}{3480} = 258.6$$

$\sqrt{258.6}$, = say 16 inches, the depth required.

When the load is not on the middle of the beam: Divide four times the product of the distance of the weight in feet from each bearing, by the whole distance between the points of support, and the quotient is the equivalent length of the beam loaded in the middle.

Suppose a beam 30 feet in length, with a load placed 9 feet from one end; required the equivalent length.

$$30 - 9 = 21. \quad \frac{21 \times 9 \times 4}{30} = 25.2 \text{ feet.}$$

When the load is distributed over the whole length of the beam, it will bear double the load which it would support in the middle; therefore, in calculations for the strength of a beam with distributed load, use double the tabular number S; if the ends of this beam are firmly fixed, use three times S. If loaded at the middle with ends firmly fixed, use $1\frac{1}{2}$ times S.

When a beam is fixed at one end, and the weight is placed on the other (fig. 218), use only one-fourth of the tabular number; if the load is distributed on a like beam, use one-half of S.

Ex.—To find the depth of a white pine beam 10 inches wide, projecting 5 feet from a wall, and capable of supporting with safety 2,000 lbs. Call the breaking weight 6 × 2.000 = 12.000 lbs.

$$5 \times 12.000 = 60.000. \quad \frac{400}{4} \times 10 = 1.000. \quad \frac{60.000}{1.000} = 60. \quad \sqrt{60} = 7.74 \text{ in.}$$

It is only necessary that the dimensions thus obtained be preserved at the points of greatest strain, that is, at A B (fig. 218). When the beam has two points of support, and the load is intermediate, the point of suspension of the weight is the point of greatest strain, and the beam may be reduced towards the points of support without breaking it.

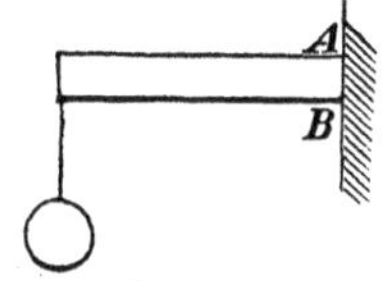

Fig. 218.

The forms of beams which afford equal strength throughout are parabolic (figs. 219, 220, 221), of which the axis A B and the vertex A are given, and the points M determined by calculations. Figs. 220, 221 are oftener used when the force is applied on alternate sides of A B.

If a beam be subjected to a transverse strain, one side is compressed, while the other side is extended; and therefore, where extension terminates and compression begins, there is a lamina or surface which is neither extended nor compressed, called the *neutral surface* or *neutral axis*. As the strains are proportional to the distance from this axis, the material of which the beam is composed should be concentrated as much as possible

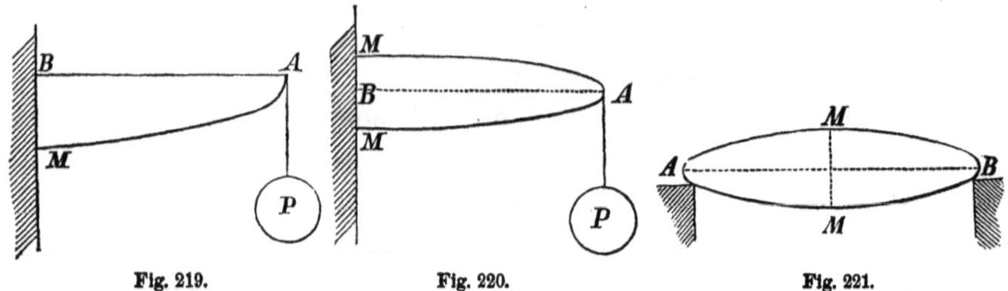

Fig. 219. Fig. 220. Fig. 221.

at the outer surface. Acting on these principles, Mr. Hodgkinson has determined the most economical form for cast-iron beams or girders, of which the section is given (fig. 222); it has been found, that the strength of cast-iron to resist compression is about six times that to resist extension; the top web is therefore made only one-sixth the area of the lower one. The depth of the beam is generally about $\frac{1}{16}$ of its length, the deeper of course the stronger; the thickness of the stem or the upright part should be from $\frac{1}{2}$ an inch to $1\frac{1}{2}$ inches, according to the size of the beam. The rule for finding the ultimate strength of beams of the above section

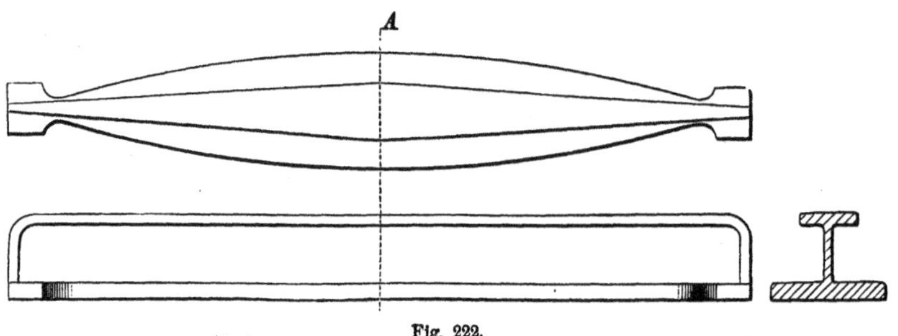

Fig. 222.

is:—Multiply the sectional area of the bottom flange in square inches by the depth of the beam in inches, and divide the product by the distance between the supports in feet, and 2.16 times the quotient will be the breaking weight in tons (2240 lbs.) As has already been shown above, the section thus determined need only be that of the greatest strain, and can be reduced towards the points of support, either by reducing the width of the flanges to a parabolic form (fig. 222), or by reducing the *thickness* of the bottom flange; the reduction of the girder in *depth* is not in general as economical or convenient.

For railway structures subject to an impulsive force, the upper flange should be ¼ of the lower one. For wrought iron beams, as this material affords less resistance to compression than tension, the top flange is generally made larger than the lower one in the proportion of 5 to 3. The following may be taken for the formula to determine the strength of solid wrought iron beams: $W = \frac{A\,d\,C}{l}$, in which W is the breaking weight, A the area of the section, d the depth, l the distance between the supports. C is a constant determined by experiment for each form of beam; for the beam shown in section (fig. 223) C is found to be about 40.000 lbs.

$$
\begin{aligned}
a &= 1. \text{ in.} \times 2.75 = 2.75 \text{ sq. in.} \\
b &= 8. \text{ “} \times 0.380 = 3.04 \text{ “} \\
c &= 0.42 \text{ “} \times 4.3 = 1.806 \text{ “} \\
d &= 9.42 \qquad A = 7.596 \text{ “}
\end{aligned}
$$

Fig. 223.

For wrought iron girders of large span, the box form is generally adopted.

Experiments on the transverse strength of rectangular tubes of wrought iron, supported at each end, and the weight laid on the middle.

Distance between the supports.	Weight of tubes between the supports.	Breaking weights, exclusive of the weights of the tubes.	External depth of the tubes.	External breadth of tubes.	Thickness of the plates of the tubes.
Feet.		Tons.	Inches.	Inches.	Inches.
30.0	42.62 cwt.	57.5	24	16	.525
7.5	72.36 lbs.	4.454	6	4	.1325
30.0	23.09 cwt.	22.84	24	16	.272
7.5	35.53 lbs.	1.409	6	4	.065
3.75	9.65 lbs.	1.1	3	2	.061
3.75	4.34 lbs.	.3	3	2	.03
45.0	130.36 cwt.	114.76	36	24	.75
3.75	9.65 lbs.	1.1	3	2	.061
30.0	39 cwt.	54.3	24	16	.50

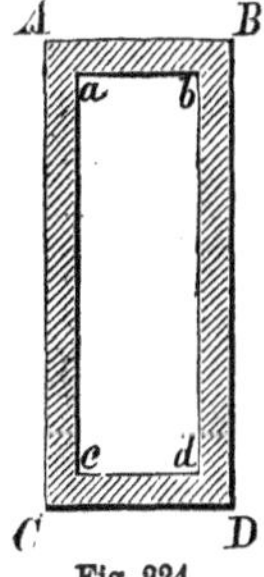

Fig. 224.

In several of these experiments, the tubes gave way by the metal at the top becoming wrinkled.

In similar tubes, the strength, and consequently the breaking weight, is proportioned to (1.9) power of the lineal dimensions.

Approximate formula for rivetted tubes:

$W = \frac{3}{4\,l\,D}\left\{ B\,D^3 - b\,d^3 \right\}$ the breaking weight in tons.

In which,

$A\ C = D$, and $a\ c = d$ in inches; b = length in feet.

$A\ B = B$, and $a\ b = b$ " "

If the thickness of the metal be equal to t inches completely round the section, then $b = B - 2\ t$, and $d = D - 2\ t$.

What is the breaking weight of a rectangular tube 40 feet long, depth 2 feet 6 inches, thickness of plate $\frac{1}{4}$ inch, and breadth 18 inches?

$$W = \frac{3}{4800}\left\{18 \times 30^3 - 17.5 \times 29.5^3\right\}$$

$$= \frac{1}{1600}\left\{486000 - 440167\right\} = 22.96 \text{ tons.}$$

It is found of iron beams and tubes, that they may be safely reduced in strength from the middle towards the extremities in the ratio indicated by theory.

It must be observed, that in the formula given for determining the strength of material, the force exerted is supposed to be dead weight or pressure, and that no consideration is paid to impulsive force, except such slight shocks as are incident to all structures. It is impossible to give rules to calculate the strength necessary to resist active forces, varying in intensity and frequency; we can only give instances of practical structures which have been found sufficient, as mere data on which to form judgment.* It must be remarked, that where rigidity is required, stiffness of beams, unlike their ultimate strength, is directly as the breadth, and the *cube* of their depth, and inversely as the *cube* of their length.

Detrusion.—The resistance to detrusion, or the force necessary to shear across any material, is called into play at the joints, and in the bolts of framings of timber and iron. The resistance of spruce to detrusion in the direction of its fibre, is about 600 lbs. per square inch; of cast iron to detrusion, about 73,000 lbs. per square inch; of wrought iron, 45 to 50,000 lbs.

Torsion.—When two forces act in opposite directions upon a body, tending to turn its extremities in different directions, or twist them, it is said to be subjected to torsion. Thus the main shaft of a steam-engine, at one end of which the power acts through a crank; which at the other is transmitted through a gear or pulley; the resistance which the load presents on the one hand, and on the other, the power applied to the crank, represent two forces, subjecting the shaft to the action of torsion.

When the torsion exceeds a certain limit, depending on the material

* For the girders of railway bridges, they should be of such dimensions as to bear a strain of two tons per foot in length.

and its form, the fibres are torn asunder, and the axles twisted off. For the determination of the size of axles subject to a twisting force, we deduce from Weisbach the following rule, allowing a five-fold security or strength above the absolute breaking twist: Multiply the weight in pounds by the leverage in inches, and divide the product by C determined for different forms and material, and the cube root of the product will be half the thickness of the axle, expressed by formula $r = \sqrt[3]{\frac{P\,a}{C}}$.

Value of C for	wrought and cast iron,		circular	section,	12,600	lbs.
"	"	"	square	"	15,000	"
"	"	wood,	circular	"	1,260	"
"	"	"	square	"	1,500	"

In the square section, the rule gives as the cube root of the product one-half the side of the square.

Example.—The shaft of a turbine exerts, through a toothed wheel of 30 inch pitch or 15 inch radius, a force of 2,500 lbs., what must be the diameter of the shaft?

$$2500 \times 15 = 37500. \qquad r = \sqrt[3]{\frac{37500}{12600}} = \sqrt[3]{\frac{375}{126}} = 1.44 \text{ inches.}$$

$$1.44 \times 2 = 2.88, \text{ say 3 inches, diameter required.}$$

The *length* of the axle subjected to torsion does not affect the actual amount of pressure required to produce rupture, but only the angle of torsion which precedes rupture, and therefore the space through which the pressure must be made to act. The ultimate strength of a long shaft to resist torsion may be sufficient, but its elasticity will be found to be too much.

To determine the degrees of the angle of torsion of a given shaft, multiply the load in pounds by the leverage, and also by the length of the shaft, between the points of the applied forces; and divide the product by the fourth power of the half diameter or half square, as the case may be, multiplied by a constant determined by experiment, and the quotient is the number of degrees in the angle, that is, $ang. = \frac{P\,a\,l}{C\,r^4}$.

Value of C.

	Circular section.	Square section.
Wood, ...	3500	5800
Cast iron, ...	160000	280000
Steel and wrought iron, .	280000	470000

Example.—If the distance of the toothed wheel from the water wheel in former experiment be 60 inches, what is the angle of torsion?

$$\frac{37.500 \times 60}{160.000\, r^4} = \frac{375 \times 6}{160 \times 1.44^4} = \frac{375 \times 6}{160 \times 4.28} = \frac{14.06}{4.28} = 3^\circ\, 3'.$$

An angle too considerable for practice; it should not exceed one degree. To calculate the size of the shaft, so that the angle is $\frac{1}{2}$ °, the formula becomes, $r = \sqrt[4]{\frac{P\,a\,l}{C \times \frac{1}{2}}}$; then in the above example,

$$\frac{37.500 \times 60}{160.000 \times \frac{1}{2}} = \frac{375 \times 60}{80} = \frac{375 \times 6}{8} = 281.25$$

$$\sqrt{281.25} = \sqrt{16.77} = 4.1.$$

$$4.1 \times 2 = 8.2, \text{ diameter of shaft.}$$

MECHANICAL WORK OR EFFECT.

To work, considered in the abstract, is to overcome, during any certain period of time, a continuously replaced resistance, or series of resistances.

Mechanical work is the effect of the simple action of a force upon a resistance which is directly opposed to it, and which it continuously destroys, giving motion in that direction to the point of application of the resistance. It follows from this definition, that the mechanical work or effect of any motor is the product of two indispensable quantities or terms:

First,—The effort, or pressure exerted.

Second,—The space passed through in a given time, or the velocity.

The amount of mechanical work increases directly as the increase of either of these terms, and in the proportion compounded of the two when both increase. If, for example, the pressure exerted be equal to 4 lbs., and the velocity one foot per second, the amount of work will be expressed by $4 \times 1 = 4$. If the velocity be double, the work becomes $4 \times 2 = 8$, or double also; and if, with the velocity double, or 2 feet per second, the pressure be doubled as well—that is, raised to 8 lbs.—the work will be $8 \times 2 = 16$ lbs. ft.

The unit of mechanical effect adopted in England and this country is the horse power, which is equal to 33,000 lbs. weight or pressure, raised or moved through a space of 1 foot in a minute of time. The corresponding unit employed in France is the kilogrammètre, which is equal to a kilogramme raised one mètre high in a second. The horse power is represented by 75 kilogrammètres; that is, 75 kilog. raised 1 mètre high per second. When we speak of small amounts of mechanical effect, it is generally said that they are equal to so many pounds raised so many feet high in some given time, as a minute for example. The *time* must always be expressed or understood. It is impossible to express or state intelligibly an amount of mechanical effect, without indicating all the three terms—pressure, distance, and time.

The motors generally employed in manufactures and industrial arts are of two kinds—living, as men and animals; and inanimate, as water and steam.

What may be termed the amount of a day's work, producible by men and animals, is the product of the force exerted, multiplied into the distance or space passed over, and the time during which the action is sustained. There will, however, in all cases be a certain proportion of effort, in relation to the velocity and duration which will yield the largest possible product or day's work for any one individual, and this product may be termed the maximum effect. In other words, a man will produce a greater mechanical effect by exerting a certain effort at a certain velocity, than he will by exerting a greater effort at a less velocity, or a less effort at a greater velocity, and the proportion of effort and velocity which will yield the maximum effect is different in different individuals.

In the manner and means in which the strength of men and animals is applied, there are three circumstances which demand attention:—

1*st.*—The power, when the strength of the animal is exerted against a resistance that is at rest.

2*d.*—The power, when the stationary resistance is overcome, and the animal is in motion. And,

3*d.*—The power, when the animal has attained the highest amount of its speed.

In the first case, the animal exerts not only its muscular force or strength, but at the same time a very considerable portion of its weight or gravity. The power, therefore, from these causes must be the greatest possible. In the second case, some portion of the power of the animal is withdrawn to maintain its own progressive motion; consequently the amount of useful labor varies with the variations of speed. In the third case, the power of the animal is wholly expended in maintaining its locomotion; it therefore can carry no weight.

The following table exhibits the average amount of mechanical effect produced by men and animals in different applications; the animal working with a mean velocity and effort during an average day's work, thereby producing the maximum effect.

Nature of the work.	Effort exerted.	Velocity per second.	Effect per second.	Duration.	Mechanical effect per day.
	Pounds.	Feet.		Hours.	
Man working at a lever, as in pumping, ...	10.5	3.5	37.45	8	1.078.560
" at a crank. Length of crank 16 to 18 inches; height of axis of shaft, 36 to 39 inches, . . .	17.	2.4	40.8	8	1.175.040
" tread-mill at level of axis, . .	128.	0.48	61.44	8	1.769.472
" " " at angle of 24° from the vertical, ...	25.⅔	2.25	57.75	8	1.663.200
" at a vertical capstan, ...	25 ½	1.9	48.45	8	1.395.360
Horse at a whim gin not less than 20 feet radius, ...	153.	2.9	443.7	8	12.778.560
Draught by traces, according to Gerstner: Weight.					
Man, ... 150	30.	2.5	75.	8	2.160.000
Horse, ... 600	120.	4.	480.	8	13.824.000
Mule, ... 500	100.	3.5	350.	8	10.080.000
Ox, ... 600	120.	2.5	300.	8	8.640.000

Gerstner also gives the following formula to calculate the effect of change of velocity.

$$P = (2 - \frac{v}{c})\,K.$$

K and c representing the effort and velocity per second, as given in the Table, v the assumed velocity, and P the resulting effect.

Example.—Suppose a horse to travel at the rate of 6 feet per second. What effort will he exert, and what will be the mechanical effect per second?

From the table we have $c = 4.$; $K = 120.$; v is assumed at 6; then

$$P = (2 - \frac{6}{4})\,120 = 60. = \text{effort}.$$

$$60 \times 6 = 360 \text{ ft. lbs. effect per second.}$$

It is evident that this formula will not apply to extreme values of P or v; yet it may be considered sufficiently near for most practical purposes, not very different from the mean, and is illustrative of the ill effects resulting from increase of velocity.

Water power.—Water acts as a moving power, or moves machines either by its weight, by pressure, or by impact; and is applied through various forms of wheels. The mechanical effect inherent in water is the product of its weight into the height from which it falls; but there are many losses incurred in its application to machinery, so that only a portion of the mechanical effect becomes available; that is, the efficiency of any water wheel is represented by a certain per-centage of the absolute effect of the water.

Example.—The quantity of water supplied to the mills at Lowell is 3,596 cubic feet per second; the net fall is 33 feet; the absolute dynamical effect of this water is:

$$3596 \times 33 \times 62.33 = 7.396.576 \text{ lbs. ft. per second.}$$

62.33 being the weight of a cubic foot of water, at 60° Fahr.; on an average it may be assumed, that a useful effect is derived equal to two-thirds of the total power of the water expended; two-thirds of 7.396.576, divided by 550, gives 8965.5 horse power as absolutely available. 550 lbs. 1 foot high per second represent a horse power, being equal to 33,000 lbs. 1 foot high per minute.

Steam is the elastic fluid into which water is converted by a continuous application of heat. It is used to produce mechanical action almost invariably by means of a piston movable in a cylinder. The horse power of a steam-engine is computed, by multiplying the area of the piston in square inches by the effective pressure in lbs. on each square inch of piston, and the product by velocity in feet through which the piston moves per minute, dividing this last product by 33,000.

The area of the piston is found by squaring the diameter, and multiplying the square by 0,7854.

Example.—Let the diameter of the piston be 18 inches, the effective pressure 45 lbs. per square inch, and the speed 300 feet per minute, what will be the horse power of the engine?

$$18 \times 18 \times 0{,}7854 = 254.46 \text{ square inches, area of piston.}$$

$$\frac{254.46 \times 45 \times 300}{33{,}000} = 104. \text{ horse power.}$$

To determine the effective pressure on the piston, recourse must be had to an indicator, and take the mean pressure, as shown on the diagram; the pressure on the boiler is readily known, but the steam in its passage to the cylinder is subject to various losses, as of wire-drawing, condensation, &c., so that frequently the pressure on the piston does not exceed two-thirds of that on the boiler. The boilers of most of our stationary engines are subjected to pressures of from 50 to 75 lbs. per square inch; the smaller engines, say less than 10 horse power, are generally worked with full steam; effective pressure from 30 to 60 lbs. Larger ones are generally worked expansively, cutting off at from one-half to one-sixth stroke. The principle of working steam expansively is as follows: If a cubic foot of air of the atmospheric density be compressed into the compass of half a cubic foot, its elasticity will be increased from 15 lbs. on the square inch to 30 lbs.; if the volume be enlarged to two cubic feet, the pressure will be one half, or $7\frac{1}{2}$ lbs. The same law holds in all other proportions for gases and vapors, provided their temperature is unchanged.

Thus, let E (fig. 225) be a cylinder, J the piston; let the cylinder be supposed to be divided in the direction of its length into any number of equal parts, say twenty, and let the diameter of the piston represent the initial pressure of the steam, which we call 1. If now the piston descend through 5 of the divisions, and the valve be then shut, the pressure at each subsequent position of the piston may be calculated by the law above given, and represented as shown in the figure. If the squares above the point, when the steam was cut off, be counted, they will be found to amount to 50, those below to about 68; so that while, by an expenditure of a quarter of cylinder full of steam, we get an amount of power represented by 50, we get 68 without any further expenditure, by merely permitting expansion. Practically, for large cylinders, it may be stated:

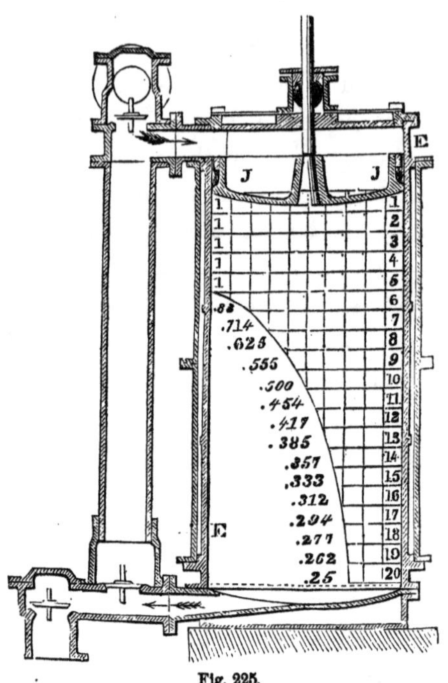

Fig. 225.

Cutting off at	Saves of fuel	Gains in effect
$\frac{1}{2}$ stroke,	41 per cent.	70 per cent.
$\frac{1}{4}$ "	58 "	$70 \times 2 = 140$ per cent.
$\frac{1}{8}$ "	68 "	$70 \times 3 = 210$ "

Mean pressure at different densities, and rate of expansion.

Initial pressure.	EXPANSION BY EIGHTHS.						
	$\frac{7}{8}$	$\frac{3}{4}$	$\frac{5}{8}$	$\frac{1}{2}$	$\frac{3}{8}$	$\frac{1}{4}$	
10	9.896	9.637	9.187	8.465	7.417	5.965	3.848
15	14.844	14.456	13.781	12.697	11.126	8.947	5.773
20	19.792	19.275	18.375	16.930	14.835	11.930	7.697
25	24.740	24.093	22.968	21.162	18.543	14.912	9.621
30	29.688	28.912	27.562	25.395	22.252	17.895	11.546
35	34.636	33.731	33.156	29.627	25.961	20.877	13.470
40	39.585	38.550	36.750	33.860	29.670	23.860	15.395
45	44.533	43.368	41.343	38.092	33.378	26.842	17.319
50	49.481	48.187	45.937	42.325	37.067	29.825	19.243

Water converted into steam under the pressure of the atmosphere, *i. e.*, 15 pounds per square inch, expands to 1700 times its volume; under double the pressure, or 30 pounds, the volume would be one-half; and this proportion would be strictly accurate but for the fact that the temperatures at which water boils in these cases are different.

In the following table are given the total pressure of steam in pounds per square inch, the corresponding temperature, and the number of cubic inches of steam which would be produced by one cubic inch of water.

Total pressure in pounds per square inch.	Corresponding temperature.	Cubic inches of steam produced by a cubic inch of water.	Total pressure in pounds per square inch.	Corresponding temperature.	Cubic inches of steam produced by a cubic inch of water.
14	209.1	1778	54	288.1	516
15	212.8	1669	55	289.3	508
20	228.5	1281	56	290.5	500
25	241.0	1044	57	291.7	492
30	251.6	883	58	292.9	484
35	260.9	767	59	294.2	477
40	269.1	679	60	295.6	470
45	276.4	610	61	296.9	463
46	277.8	598	62	298.1	456
47	279.2	586	63	299.2	449
48	280.5	575	64	300.3	443
49	281.9	564	65	301.3	437
50	283.2	554	66	302.4	431
51	284.4	544	67	303.4	425
52	285.7	534	68	304.4	419
53	286.9	525	69	305.4	414

It must be remarked, that in non-condensing engines, the effective pressure is the excess above the pressure of the atmosphere.

Table showing the weights, evaporative powers per weight, and bulk and character of fuels, from the report of Prof. Walter R. Johnson, 1844.

Designation of fuel.	Specific gravity.	Weight per cubic foot.	Water evaporat'd by one lb. of fuel.	Designation of fuel.	Specific gravity.	Weight per cubic foot.	Water evaporat'd by one lb. of fuel.
BITUMINOUS.		lbs.	lbs.	ANTHRACITE.		lbs.	lbs.
Cumberland, *maximum*	1.313	82.09	10.7	Peach Mountain, .	1.464	91.5	10.11
" *minimum*	1.337	83.28	9.44	Beaver Meadow, No. 5,	1.554	96.9	9.88
Blossburgh, . .	1.324	82.73	9.72	Lackawana, . .	1.421	88.8	9.79
Newcastle, . . .	1.257	78.54	8.66	Beaver Meadow, No. 3,	1.610	100.6	9.21
Pictou, . . .	1.318	82.83	8.41	Lehigh, . . .	1.500	93.8	8.93
Pittsburgh, . . .	1.252	78.37	8.20	COKE.			
Sydney, . . .	1.338	83.66	7.99	Natural Virginia, .	1.323	82.70	8.47
Liverpool, . . .	1.262	78.89	7.84	Cumberland, . .			8.99
Clover Hill, . .	1.285	80.36	7.67	WOOD.			
Cannelton, Ia. . .	1.273	79.[illegible]4	7.34				
Scotch, . . .	1.519	94.95	6.95	Dry Pine Wood, .		21.01	4.69

The above table exhibits the ultimate effects. As a safe estimate for practical values, a deduction (for the coals) of $\frac{14}{100}$ should be made.

From these two tables it is easy to calculate the amount of fuel which must be expended to produce a given power.

Example.—To find the consumption of water and fuel required by a high pressure engine, 12 inch cylinder, 4 feet stroke, the effective pressure on the piston being 40 lbs., and the number of double strokes 35 per min.

$$\text{Area of piston} = 12 \times 12 \times 0.7854 = 113.09.$$
$$\text{Velocity of piston} = 35 \times 8 = 280 \text{ ft. per min.}$$

Then, $113.09 \times 280 \times 12 = 379.982$ cubic inches of steam used during 1 minute, or $379.982 \times 60 = 22.798.920 \times 60$, consumption per hour. Looking in the first table against the pressure 55, that is 15, or atmosphere added to 40 given above, we find 508; dividing, therefore, 22.798.920 by 508, we have 44880, the number of cubic inches of water used per hour;

$$\frac{44880}{1728} = 26 \text{ cubic feet nearly.}$$

Multiplying this by the weight of a cubic foot of water,

$$26 \times 62.33 = 1620.58 \text{ lbs.}$$

Taking the safe estimate for the anthracites of the evaporation of 8 lbs. of water by 1 lb. of fuel, we have,

$$\frac{1620}{8} = 202.5 \text{ lbs. the consumption of coal per hour.}$$

On an average of boilers, 1 square foot of grate surface is allowed for the consumption of 14 lbs. of coal per hour, from 15 to 25 square feet of heating surface, and one-sixth of a square foot of flue at the base of the chimney. Continuing the previous example, we have

$$\frac{202.5}{14} = 14.5 \text{ square feet of fire grate.}$$

$$14.5 \times 20 = 290 \text{ square feet of heating surface.}$$

$$\frac{14.5}{6} = 2.42 \text{ square feet of flue.}$$

The horse power of the above engine would be

$$\frac{113{,}09 \times 280 \times 40}{33000} = 38.6 \text{ horse power.}$$

A portion of which power would be consumed in the driving of the engine itself, leaving about 35 horse power as effective on the first shaft.

DRAWING OF MACHINERY.

Having thus laid down the principles of geometrical projection, and the rules by which to proportion parts, according to the stress to which they may be subjected, we now proceed to the practical application ot the principles and rules in the drawing of machinery.

SHAFTING.

Shafts are made of wood, cast and wrought iron. Fig. 226 represents the sections of the usual forms. Wooden shafts are mostly of an octagonal or polyhedral form, and are seldom used but as shafts for water-wheels, but are not equal to those of cast iron except in cheapness, and are seldom adopted when the latter can be readily obtained. Cast iron is used for the shafts of water-wheels, and the heavier kinds of mill-work, when the strain is rather transverse than torsional. The most economical form for cast iron shafts is the tubular, but the more usual are the *feathered* shafts, that is, with a circular or square centre, and ribs running longitudinally. Wrought iron shafts are used for the main and counter shafts of mills, and for heavy shafts subject to torsional or to unequal stress and shocks, and is by far the best material for shafts. The more usual and the best form is the circular.

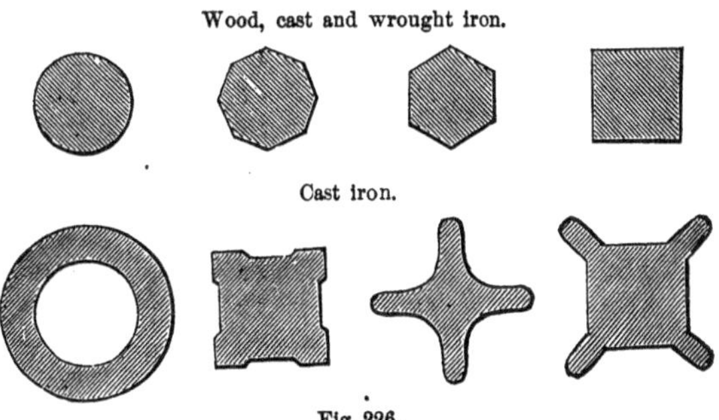

Fig. 226.

Shafts are termed first, second, and third movers; the first are the first recipients of power, as the jack-shaft from a water-wheel, or the fly-wheel shaft of engines; the second are the next in succession, distributing the power, as the main shafts of mills; and, third, the counters or shafts transmitting the power to the machines. The strain upon a shaft may be transverse, torsional, or both. In all breast, overshot, or undershot water-wheels, the jack-geer may be so placed that there will be no torsional strain on the shaft of the wheel; in many other shafts, no strain will be transmitted through the journal. In these cases, the size of the journal may be estimated from the transverse strain or weight to which it is subjected. The following table is taken from the *Practical Draughtsman*, calculated on this formula, $D = \sqrt[3]{w} \times .1938$, D being the diameter in inches, and w the weight to be sustained in lbs.

Table of the diameters of the journals of water-wheel and other shafts for heavy work.

Total load in pounds.	DIAM. OF JOURNAL IN INCHES.		Total load in pounds.	DIAM. OF JOURNAL IN INCHES.	
	Cast iron.	Wrought iron.		Cast iron.	Wrought iron.
1099.0	2	1.7	100156	9	7.7
2146.7	2½	2.1	117793	9½	8.1
3709.5	3	2.5	137388	10	8.6
5890.5	3½	3.0	158604	10½	9.0
8805.6	4	3.4	182864	11	9.4
12619.5	4½	3.8	208950	11½	9.9
17175.5	5	4.3	237296	12	10.3
22858.0	5½	4.7	268012	12½	10.7
29676.0	6	5.1	311666	13	11.2
37730.0	6½	5.6	338026	13½	11.6
43873.0	7	6.0	376993	14	12.0
58915.7	7½	6.4	418845	14½	12.5
70353.0	8	6.9	463685	15	12.9
84373.0	8½	7.3			

The length of the journal should be from once to twice the diameter. The size of the shaft at the point at which the load is applied may be determined from previous rules; but for all shafts less than three feet between bearings, the size as calculated for the journal need only be enlarged enough to cut the key-seat.

Plate IX.—Figs. 1, 2, 3, represent different views of a wooden water-wheel shaft. Fig. 1 shows at one end the side external elevation of the shaft, furnished with its iron ferules or collars, and its gudgeon at the other end. The shaft is shown in sections, giving the ferules in section, but showing the central spindle with its feathers in an external elevation. Generally, in longitudinal sections of objects enclosing one or more pieces,

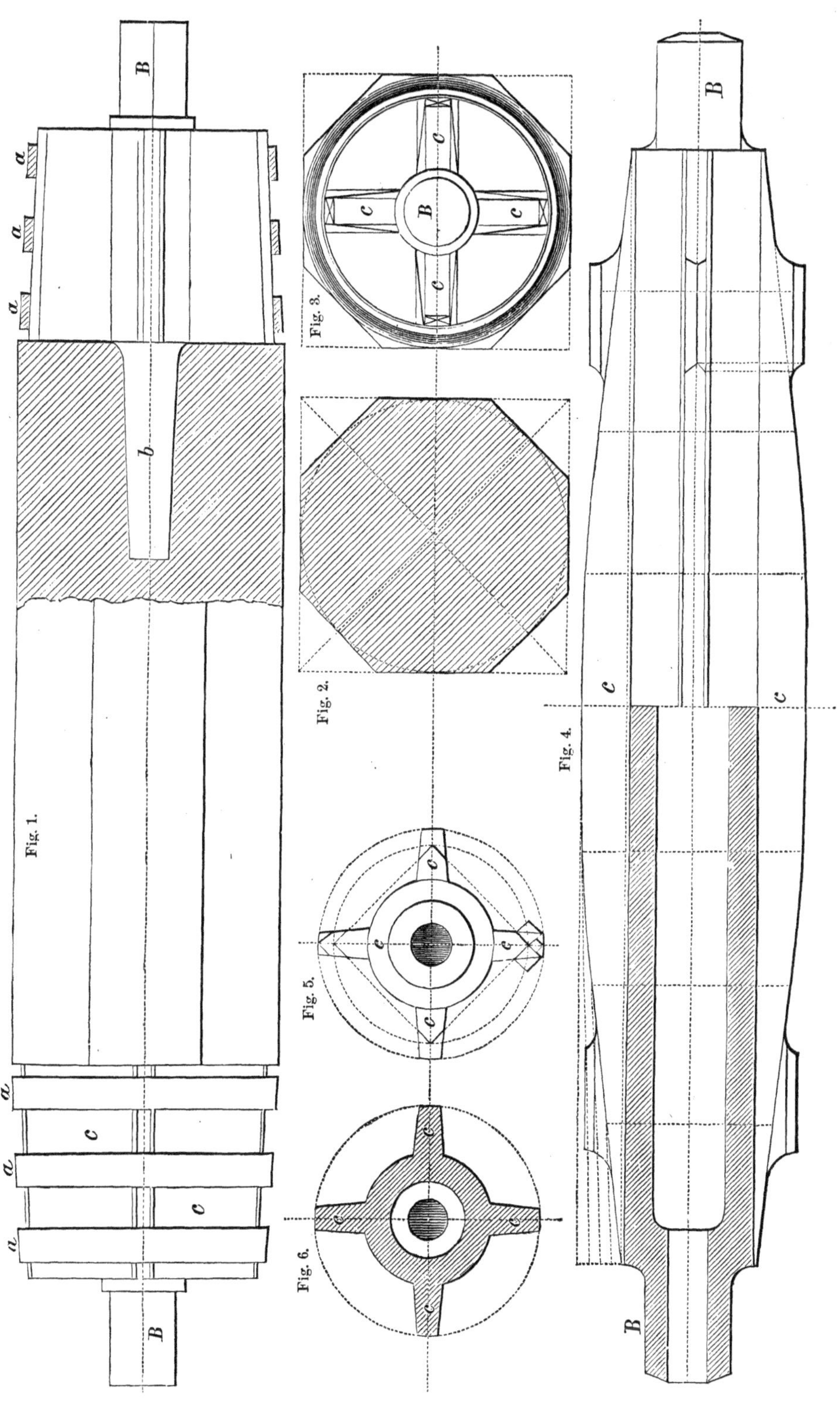
Fig. 1.
Fig. 2.
Fig. 3.
Fig. 4.
Fig. 5.
Fig. 6.
B
a
b
c

the innermost or central piece is not sectioned unless it has some internal peculiarity, the object of a section being to show and explain peculiarities, and being therefore unnecessary when the object is solid; on this account, bolts, nuts, and solid cylindrical shafts are seldom drawn in section. Fig. 2 is a cross or transverse section through the centre of the shaft, to show the outward octagonal form. Fig. 3 is an end view of the shaft, showing the fitting of the spindle B and its feathers into the end of the shaft, and the binding of the whole by ferules or hoops *a a*. From these views we understand, that this shaft is a long octagonal shaft of wood, oak or pine, of which the ends are rounded and slightly conical. The spindles B, which are let into the ends, are cast with four feathers or wings *c*. The tail-piece *b* is by many millwrights omitted. The ends of the beam are bored for the spindle, and grooved to receive the feathers; the casting is then driven into its place, hooped with hot ferules, and after this hard-wood wedges are driven in on each side of the feathers, and iron spikes are sometimes driven into the end of the wood.

Figs. 4, 5, 6, represent different views of a cast iron shaft of a water-wheel. Fig. 4 is an elevation of the shaft, with one half in section to show the form of the core; fig. 5, an end elevation; fig. 6, a section on the line *c c* across the centre. The body is cylindrical and hollow, and is cast with four feathers *c c*, disposed at right angles to each other, and of an external parabolic outline. Near the extremities of these feathers four projections are cast, for the attachment of the bosses of the water-wheel. These projections are made with facets, so as to form the corners of a circumscribing square, as shown in fig. 5, and they are planed to receive the keys by which they are fixed to the naves which are grooved to receive them. The shaft is cast in one entire piece, and the journals are turned.

Fig. 227 represents the section of a portion of a water-wheel, with a cast iron shaft, in use in this country, in which stiffness is given to the wheel by wooden trusses, and a tensional strain is given to the centre of the shaft. These shafts are cast circular in two lengths connected at the centre, with circular bosses on which the naves of the wheel are keyed.

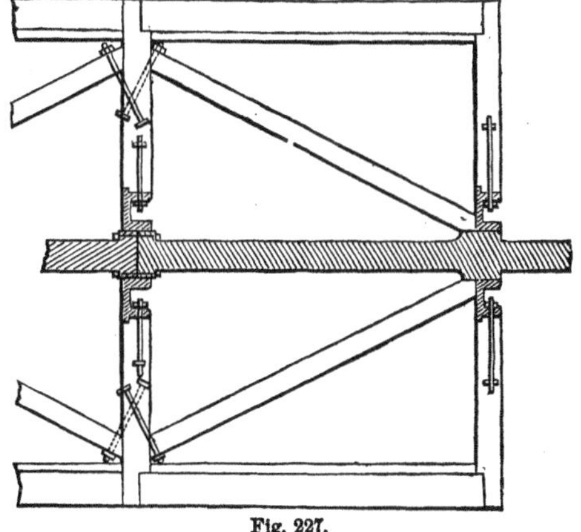
Fig. 227.

When the load upon a shaft is not central between the bearings, the size of the journals should be proportioned to the weight it will be required to support, which will be inversely as their distance from the centre of pressure.

Fig. 228 represents the fly-wheel shaft of a stationary engine. The parts of least diameter are the journals; their length is $1\frac{1}{4}$ times the diam-

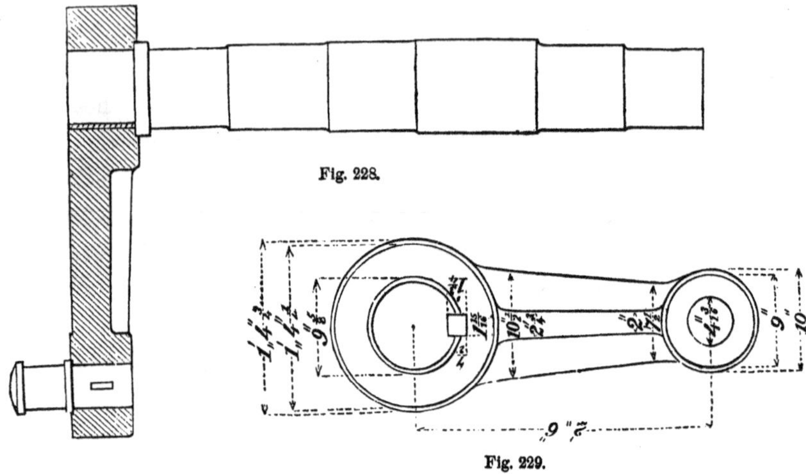

Fig. 228.

Fig. 229.

eter; the centre of the shaft is enlarged to receive the hub of the fly-wheel, and for convenience in driving the keys. Shafts of this form are mostly of wrought iron, the reduction being made by steps, as a convenience in swedging. Fig. 229 is a plan of the crank, from the wheel side.

The *torsional* strain on a shaft is as the power transmitted through it. It is evident, power being weight multiplied by velocity, that the greater the velocity of the shaft, the less the strain to transmit the same amount of power; and it is the modern practice to drive the shafts at high velocities, and reduce the weight of the geering. In first movers, the strain is often compound; and when the journals bear but little transverse strain, the determination of their size must depend entirely on their capacity to resist torsion. The formula given in the *Practical Draughtsman* for determining the proper diameter is:

$$d = \sqrt[3]{\frac{H\,P}{R} \times C.}$$

C being for cast iron, 1st movers, 419; 2d, 206; 3d, 106.
" wr'ght " " " 249; " 134; " 67.6.

Which formula is simplified and tabellated, so that it is only necessary to divide the number or revolutions of the shaft by the horse power, and find the diameter corresponding to the quotient in the table.

Table of diameters for shaft journals, calculated with reference to torsional strain.

Diameter in inches.	JOURNALS OF CAST-IRON SHAFTS.			JOURNALS OF WROUGHT-IRON SHAFTS.		
	First movers.	Second movers.	Third movers.	First movers.	Second movers.	Third movers.
1½	124.133	61.087	31.408	73.778	39.704	20.030
2	52.375	25.750	13.250	31.125	16.750	8.450
2½	26.816	13.190	6.790	15.872	8.576	4.327
3	15.519	7.630	3.922	9.222	4.963	2.504
3½	9.773	4.805	2.475	5.808	3.123	1.577
4	6.547	3.219	1.656	3.891	2.094	1.563
4½	4.598	2.266	1.163	2.732	1.475	.742
5	3.352	1.648	.848	1.992	1.072	.541
5½	2.519	1.239	.637	1.497	.806	.406
6	1.940	.954	.491	1.153	.620	.318
6½	1.526	.750	.386	.906	.488	.246
7	1.222	.601	.309	.726	.391	.197
7½	1.002	.493	.253	.595	.325	.162
8	.838	.402	.207	487.	.261	.130
8½	.682	.335	.173	.405	.218	.110
9	.575	.282	.145	.341	.184	.093
9½	.489	.240	.124	.290	.156	.079
10	.419	.206	.106	.249	.134	.068
10½	.362	.178	.092	.215	.116	.058
11	.314	.155	.079	.187	.101	.051
11½	.275	.135	.069	.163	.089	.044
12	.242	.119	.061	.144	.078	.039
12½	.214	.105	.054	.127	.068	.034
13	.191	.094	.049	.114	.061	.031
13½	.170	.084	.043	.101	.054	.027
14	.153	.075	.038	.091	.049	.024
14½	.137	.067	.035	.082	.044	.022
15	.124	.061	.031	.074	.039	.020
1	2	3	4	5	6	7

Example.—What must be the diameter of the journal of a wrought iron first mover, transmitting 30 horse power, and making 50 revolutions per minute?

$$\frac{50}{30} = 1.667.$$

1.667 in the table is intermediate between 1.992 and 1.497, corresponding to 5 and 5½, and should be about 5⅜ inches.

It is the common practice to make wrought iron 2d and 3d movers of an uniform diameter, without reduction at the journal; the shaft is prevented from sliding endways by collars keyed on. The usual length of main shafts is from 7 to 10 feet between bearings; and that they may run smooth, and not spring intermediately, it is desirable that they should never be less than 2 inches diameter, and that the pulleys or geers through which the power is transmitted to the next mover or to the machine should be as near as possible to the bearing.

Fig. 230 represents a line of shafting. A is an upright shaft; *a a*, bevel-geers; *b b*, bearings for the shaft; *c*, coupling or connection of the several pieces of shafting. These shafts are intended to be of wrought iron. No reduction is made for the journal, no bosses for pulleys or geers. As the power is distributed from this line of shafting, the torsional strain diminishes with the distance from the bevel-geers or first movers, and the

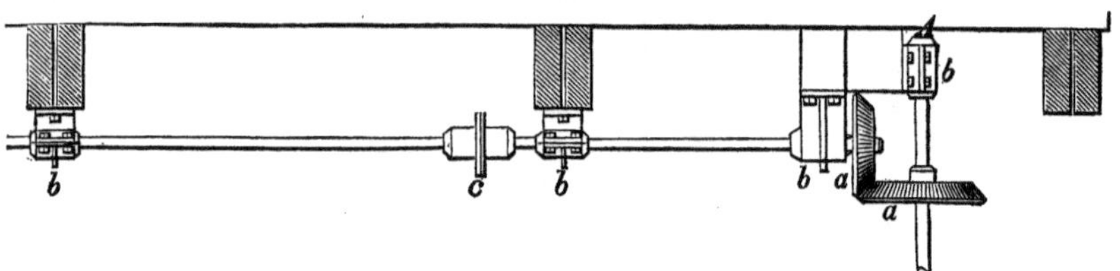

diameter of each piece of shafting may be reduced consecutively, if necessary; but uniformity will generally be found to be of more importance than a small saving of iron. The drawing given is of a scale large enough to order shafting by, but the dimension, should be written in. It is often usual in the order to the machinists merely to give the lengths of the shafts and diameters as thus:

× $2\frac{1}{2}$ in. 8 ft. × 8 ft. $2\frac{1}{2}$ in. × 6 ft. $2\frac{1}{4}$ in. ×

The × marks represent the bearings; the joints or couplings are generally made near the bearings, and it is also usual to bring the pulleys as near the bearings as possible. It frequently happens, therefore, that the coupling and pulley are needed at the same point; to remedy this, as the position of the pulley depends on the machine which it is required to drive, it frequently cannot be moved without considerable inconvenience or loss of room; the shaft will have, therefore, to be lengthened or shortened, to change position of coupling; or better, the coupling and pulley may be made together.

BEARINGS OR SUPPORTS FOR THE JOURNALS OF SHAFTS.

For upright shafts.—Footstep or step for an upright shaft.—Fig. 231 represents an elevation; fig. 232, a plan of the step. It consists of a foundation or bed-plate A, a box B, and a cap or socket C. The plate A is firmly fastened to the base on which it rests; in the case of heavy shafts, often to a base of granite. The box B is placed on A, the bearing surface being accurately bevelled, and fitted either by planing or chipping and

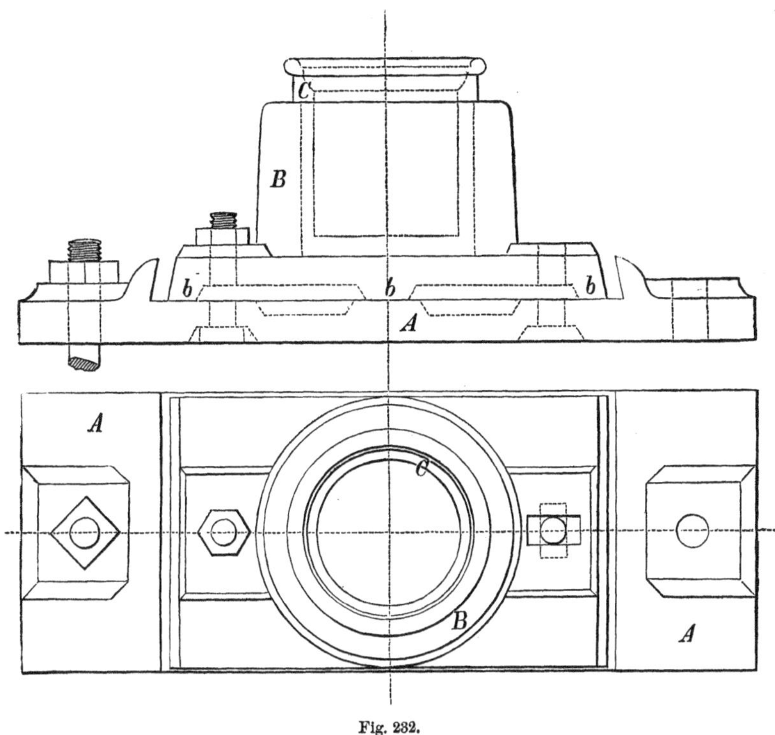

Fig. 232.

filing; *b*, *b*, *b*, are what are commonly called chipping-pieces, which are the bearing surfaces of the bottom of B. A and B are held together by two

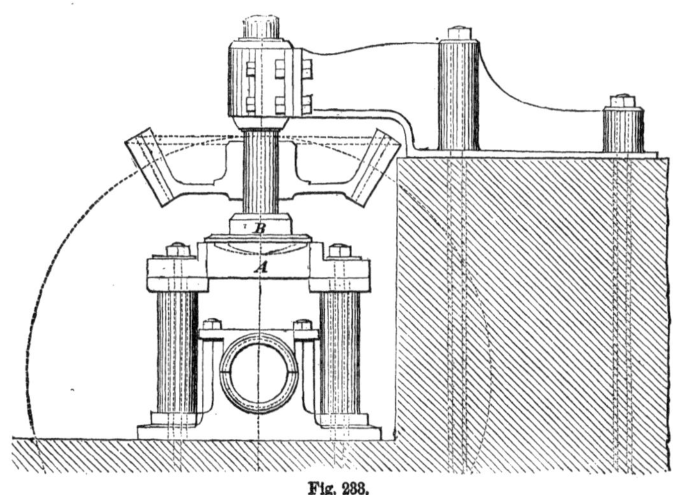

Fig. 233.

screws; the holes for these are cut oblong in the one plate at right angles to those of the other; this admits of the movement of the box in two directions to adjust nicely the lateral position of the shaft, after which, by means of the screws the two plates are clamped firmly to each other. C, the cup or bushing, which should be made of brass, slips into a socket in B. Frequently circular plates of steel are dropped into the bottom of this cup for the step of the shaft. The cup C, in case of its sticking to the shaft, will revolve with the shaft in the box B; if plates are used, these also admit of movement in the cup.

Fig. 233 represents the elevation of a bearing for an upright shaft, in which the shaft is held laterally by a box and bracket above the step. The step B is made larger than the shaft, so as to reduce the amount of wear incident to a heavy shaft. The end of the shaft, and the cup containing oil, are shown in dotted line. The bed-plate A rests on pillars, between which is placed a pillow-block or bearing for horizontal shaft.

Figs. 234, 235, represent the elevation and vertical section of the suspension bearing used by Mr. Boyden for the support of the shaft of his turbine wheels. It having been found difficult to supply oil to the step of such wheels, it was thought preferable by him to suspend the entire weight of wheel and shaft, where it could be easily attended to. The shaft (see section) is cut into necks, which rest on corresponding projections cast in the

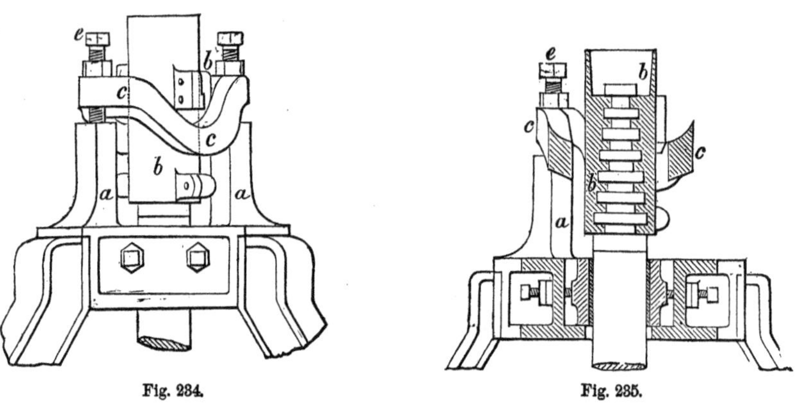

Fig. 234. Fig. 235.

box *b*; the spaces in the box are made somewhat larger than the necks of the shaft, to admit of Babbitting, as it is termed, the box; that is, the shaft being placed in its position in the box, Babbitt, or some other soft metal melted, is poured in round the shaft, and in this way accurate bearing surfaces are obtained; projections or holes are made in the box to hold the metal in its position. The box is suspended by lugs *b*, on gimbals *c*, similar to those used for mariners' compasses, which give a flexible bearing, so that the necks may not be strained by a slight sway of the shaft. The screws *e e* support the gimbals, consequently the shaft and wheel; by these screws the wheel can be raised or lowered, so as to adjust its position accurately; beneath the box will be seen a movable collar, to adjust the lateral position of shafts.

Figs. 236, 237 are the plan and elevation for the *step*, or rather *guide* (as it bears no weight), of the foot of the shaft of these same turbines. The plate A is firmly bolted to the floor of the wheel-pit; the cushions, C, holding the shaft, are either wooden or cast iron, and admit of lateral ad-

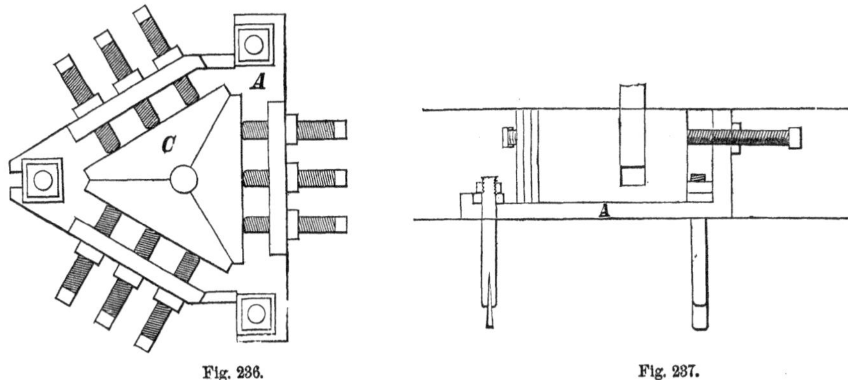

Fig. 236. Fig. 237.

justment by the three sets of set-screws. Wooden steps are often used to support the shafts of the smaller horizontal wheels beneath the surface of the water; the fibres of the wood are placed vertically, and afford a very excellent bearing surface. When cast iron or steel is used for the step, it is usual to encase the box, and supply oil by leading a pipe, sufficiently high above the surface of the water, to force the oil down.

For long upright shafts, it is very usual to suspend the upper portion by a suspension box, and to run the lower on a step, connecting the two portions by a loose sleeve or expansion coupling, to prevent the unequal mashing of the bevel wheels, incident to an alteration of the length of shaft by variations of temperature. The suspension is frequently made by a single collar at the top of the shaft.

When a horizontal shaft is supported from beneath, its bearing is usually called a *pillow* or *plumber-block*, or *standard;* if suspended, the supports are called *hangers*.

Figs. 238, 239 are the elevation and plan of a pillow-block. It consists of a base plate A, the body of the block B, and the box C. The plate, as in the step, is bolted securely to its base; the surface on which the block B rests being horizontal. A and B are connected by bolts passing through oblong holes, so as to adjust the position in either direction laterally. The

10

box or bush C is of brass, in two parts or halves, extending through the block, and forming a collar by which it is retained in its place. The cap of

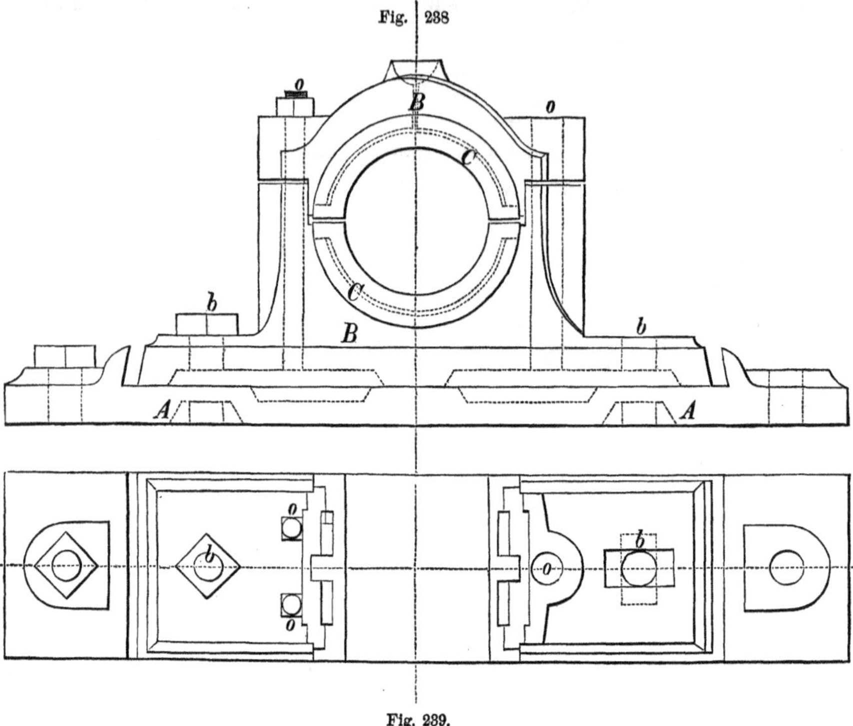

Fig. 238

Fig. 239.

the block is retained by the screws *o o o;* in the figure there are two screws on one side and one on the other; often four are used, two on each side, but most frequently but one on each side.

PROJECTIONS OF A STANDARD.

Plate X.—The standard is simply a modification of the pillow-block, being employed for the support of horizontal shafts at a considerable distance above the foundation-plate. Fig. 1 is a front elevation; fig. 2, a plan; and fig. 3, an end elevation of a standard. Like the pillow-block, the plate A is fastened to the foundation itself, and the upper surface is placed perfectly level in both directions. On these bearing surfaces *a a a* the body of the standard rests, and can be adjusted in position horizontally, and then clamped by screws to the foundation-plate, or keyed at the ends. Fig. 4 is a plan of the upper part of the standard with the cover off, showing the form of the box, with a babitted bearing surface.

Whilst drawing the front elevation, mark off on figs. 3 and 4 the out-

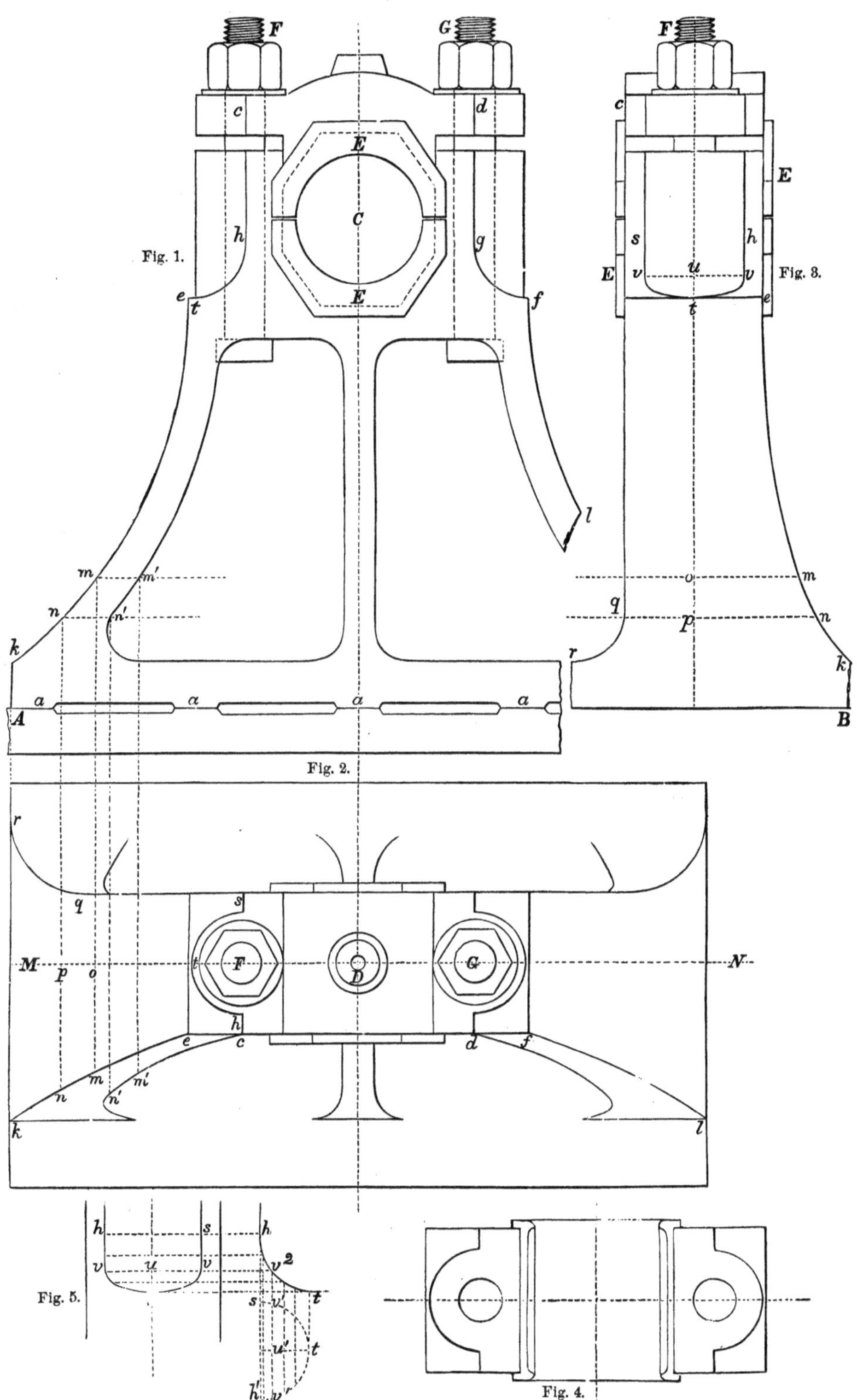
Fig. 1.
Fig. 2.
Fig. 3.
Fig. 4.
Fig. 5.

lines of all such parts as are immediately transferable by the help of the square and compasses, from one figure to the other. The outline $e\ k$ and $f\ l$ are arcs, whose centres lie in $e f$ produced, and pass through the points e, k and f, l. To find the projection of this arc upon the plan (fig. 2), draw through any points m and n, taken at pleasure upon the arc $e\ k$ (fig. 3), the horizontals $m\ m$, $n\ n$, and through m and n (fig. 1) draw $m\ m$ and $n\ n$ parallel to C D, then set off the distances $o\ m$ and $p\ n$ (fig. 3) to the corresponding points on the lower side of centre line M N (fig. 2): thus the curve $e\ m\ n\ k$ will be determined. By a similar method the curve $c\ m\ n'$ will be obtained, as also the projections of all such arcs as are denoted by $r\ q$ (fig. 3).

To draw on fig. 3 the $s\ t\ h$ (fig. 2), which is the line of penetration of two cylinders, a similar construction to the preceding may be adopted. But to avoid drawing too many lines on the figures, this projection is constructed (see fig. 5) on another part of the sheet, in which $s\ t\ h'$ represent the plan of the curve $s\ t\ h$ (fig. 2), and $h\ v^2\ t$ the elevation, as at fig. 1. Divide $h\ v^2\ t$ into any number of equal parts; let fall perpendiculars $h\ h'$ $v^2\ v'$ . . . from the points of division, and horizontal and parallel lines $h\ h$, $v^2\ v$ . . . ; lay off on each side from the half chords made on the semicircle, and we have the curve $h\ v\ t\ v\ s$, which may easily be transferred to its position in fig. 3.

It will be observed, that one side of the elevation (fig. 1) is represented as broken; this is often done in drawing, when the sides are uniform, and economy of space on the paper is required.

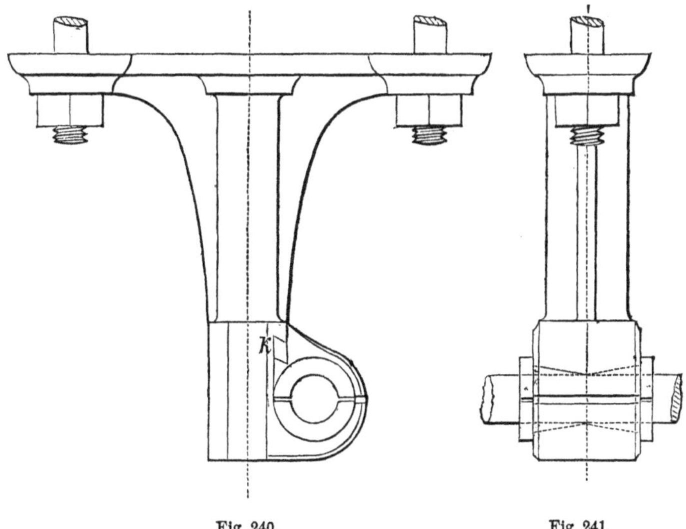

Fig. 240. Fig. 241.

Suspended bearings or *hangers* for horizontal shafts are divided into two general classes—side hangers (figs. 240, 241), and sprawl hangers (plate XI., fig. 1); the figures will sufficiently explain the distinction. The side hanger is the more convenient when it is required to remove the shaft, and when the strain is in one direction, against the upright part; they are generally used for the smaller shafts, but sprawl hangers affording a more firm support in both directions, are used as supports for all the heavier shafts. Hangers are bolted to the floor timbers, or to strips placed to sustain them, the centres of the boxes being placed accurately in line, both horizontally and laterally.

Plate XI.—Fig. 1 represents the elevation of a sprawl hanger; fig. 2, the plan looking from above, with cover of box off; fig. 3, a section on the line A B, fig. 1.

Fig. 4 represents the elevation of a bracket, or the support of a shaft bolted to an upright; the box is movable, and is adjusted laterally by the set-screws. Fig. 5 is a front elevation of the back plate cast on the post; it will be seen that the holes are oblong, to admit of the vertical adjustment of the bracket. Fig. 6 is a side elevation of the box; fig. 7, a section lengthways, showing aperture for grease, and the points which retain the babbit-metal lining in its place; fig. 8 is a plan of the bottom half of the box; fig. 9, plan of the top.

Fig. 242 represents different views of what may be called a *yoke-hanger*. Fig. 1 is a front and fig. 2 a side elevation; fig. 3 a plan of the hanger, looking up; and fig. 4 a plan of the yoke, looking down upon it. A is the plate which is fastened to the beam, E is the yoke, and B the stem of the yoke, cut with a thread so as to admit of a vertical adjustment; the box D of the shaft C is supported by two pointed set-screws passing through the jaws of the yoke; this affords a very flexible bearing, and a chance for lateral adjustment.

Couplings are the connections of shafts, and are varied in their construction and proportions often according to the mere whim of the mechanic making them.

The *Face Coupling* (fig. 242) is the one in most general use for the connecting of wrought iron shafts; it consists of two plates or discs with long strong hubs, through the centre of which holes are accurately drilled to fit the shaft; one-half is now drawn on to the shaft, and tightly keyed; the plates are faced square with the shaft, and the two faces are brought together by bolts. The number and size of the bolts depend upon the size of the shaft, never less than 4 for shafts less than 3 inches diameter, and more as the diameter increases; the size of the bolts varies from $\frac{5}{8}$ to $1\frac{1}{4}$ in. in diameter. The figure shows a usual proportion of parts for shafts of from 2 to 5 inches diameter; for larger than these, the proportion of the diameter of the disc to that of the shaft is too large.

PLATE XI.

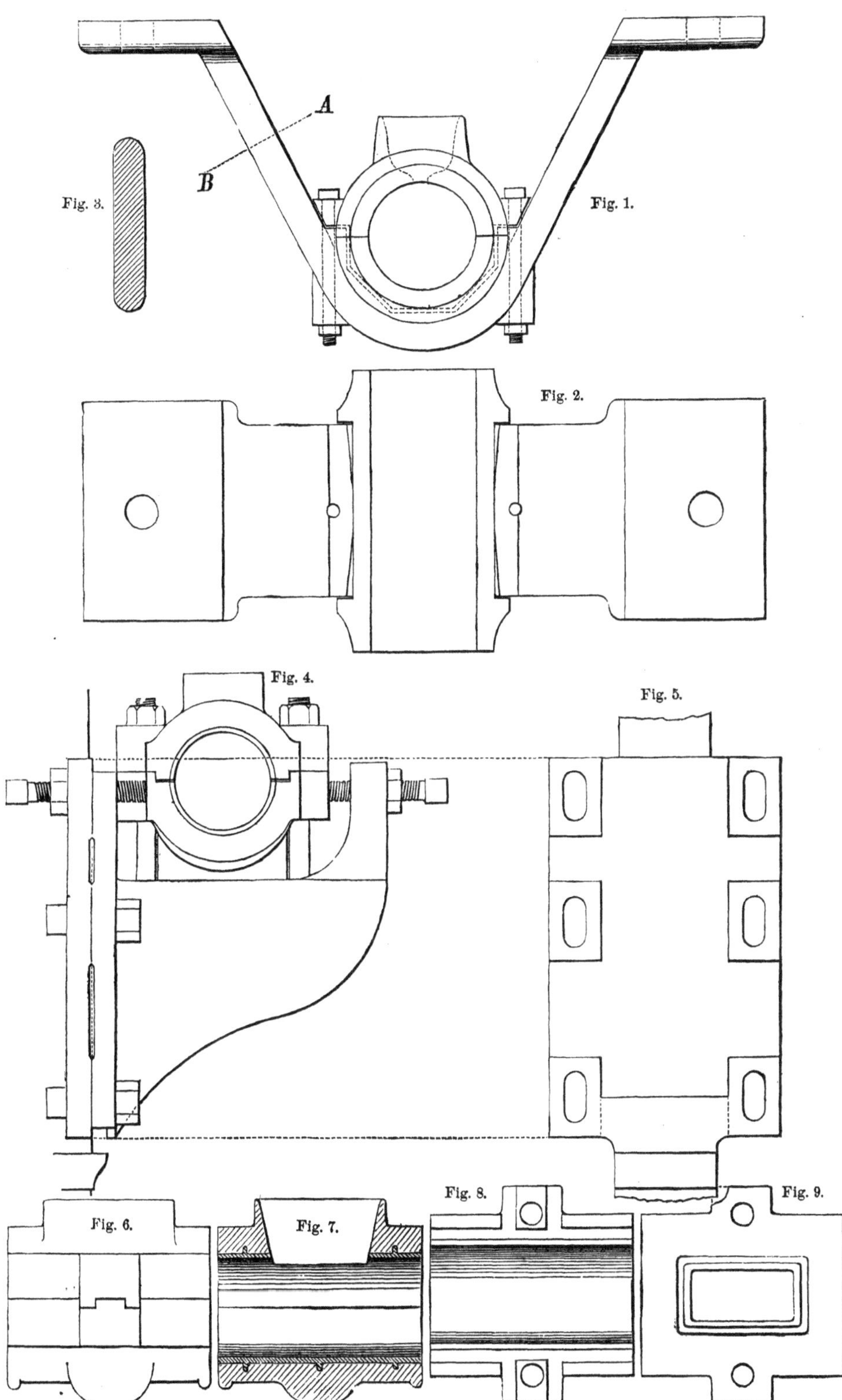

Fig. 243 is a rigid sleeve coupling for a cast iron shaft; it consists of a solid hub or ring of cast iron hooped with wrought iron; the shafts are made with bosses, the coupling is slipped on to one of the shafts, the ends

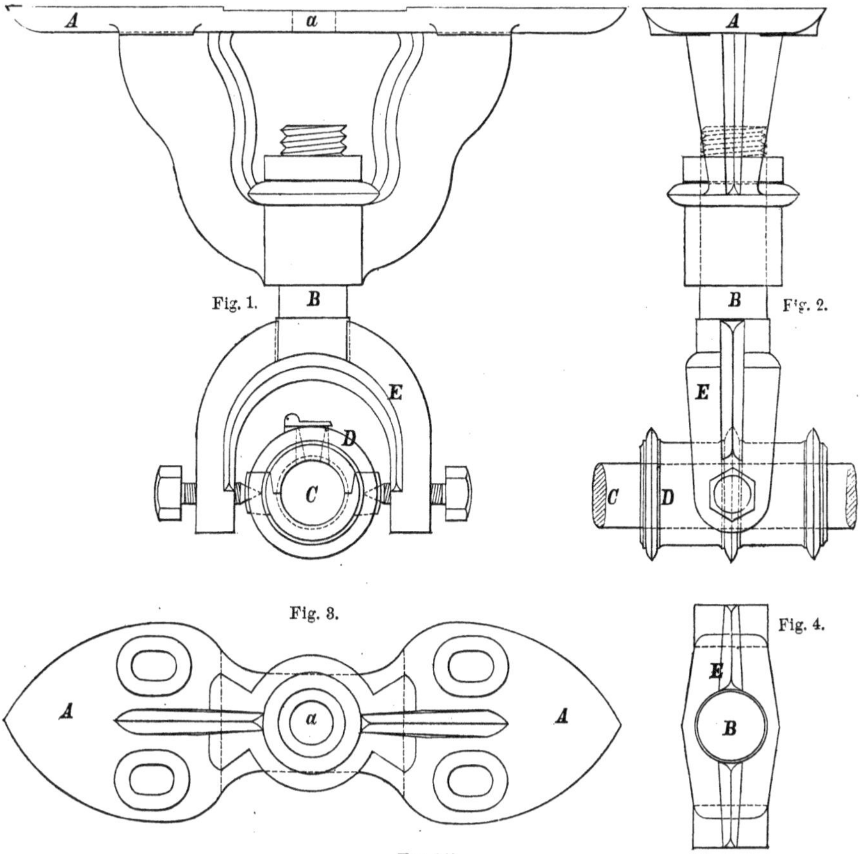

Fig. 1. Fig. 2. Fig. 3. Fig. 4.

Fig. 242.

of the two are then brought together; the coupling is now slipped back over the joint, and firmly keyed. This is an extremely rigid connection.

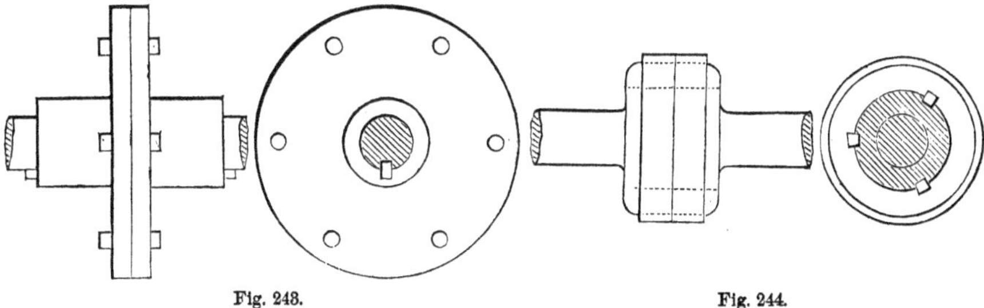

Fig. 243. Fig. 244.

Fig. 244 is a screw coupling, a very neat and excellent rigid coupling, for the connecting of wrought iron, more especially the lighter kinds. It will be observed that this coupling admits of rotation but in one direction, the one tending to bring the ends of the shafts towards each other, the reverse motion tends to unscrew and throw them apart, and uncouple them.

Fig. 245 is a clamp coupling for a square shaft.

In many cases it occurs that rigid couplings, such as we have given, are objectionable; they necessarily imply that, to run with the least strain

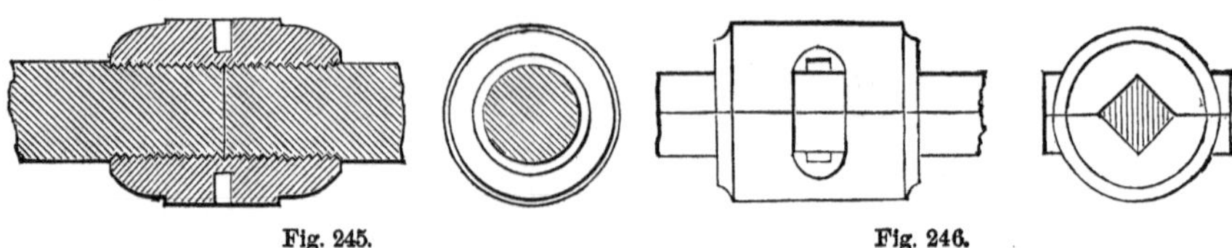
Fig. 245. Fig. 246.

possible, the bearings should be in accurate line; *any* displacement involves the springing of the shaft, and if considerably moved, fracture of shaft or coupling. Wherever, then, from any cause the allignment cannot be very nearly accurate, some coupling that admits of lateral movement should be adopted. The simplest of these is the *box* or *sleeve* coupling (fig. 246), sliding over the end of two square shafts, keyed to neither, but often held

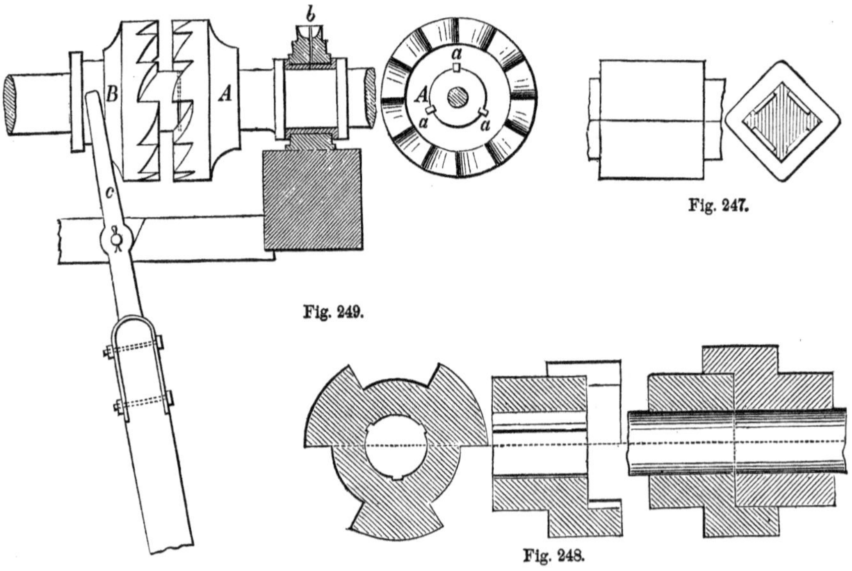

Fig. 247.

Fig. 249.

Fig. 248.

in place by a pin passing through the coupling into one of the shafts. For round shafts, the loose sleeve coupling is a pipe or hub, generally 4 to 6 times the diameter of the shaft in length, sliding on keys fixed on either shaft.

Fig. 247 represents a *horned* coupling. The two parts of the coupling are counterparts of each other, each firmly keyed to its respective shaft, but not fastened to each other; the horns of the one slip into the spaces of the other; if the faces of the horns are accurately fitted, it affords an excellent coupling, and is not perfectly rigid.

It often happens that some portion of a shaft or machine is required to be stopped whilst the rest of the machinery continues in motion. It is evident that, if one half of a horned coupling be not keyed to the shaft, but permitted to slide lengthways on the key,—the key being fixed in the shaft, forming in this case what is more usually called a feather,—by sliding back the half till the horns are entirely out of the spaces of the other half, communication of motion will cease from one shaft to the other.

Couplings are made on this principle, called *slide* or *clutch* couplings. As usually the motion is required but in one direction, the more general form of this coupling is given in fig. 249. A represents the half of the coupling that is keyed to the shaft, B the sliding half, *c* the handle or lever which communicates the sliding movement; the upper end of the lever terminates in a fork, enclosing the hub of the coupling, and fastened by two bolts or pins to a collar *c′* round the neck of the hub; *b* is a box or bearing for the shaft A to support B; the end of the shaft extends a slight distance into the coupling A. It will be observed that the horns are ratchet-shaped; by this form motion can be transmitted but in one direction; but should it be necessary to reverse the motion, it is necessary that the horns of the coupling be square. Shafts cannot be

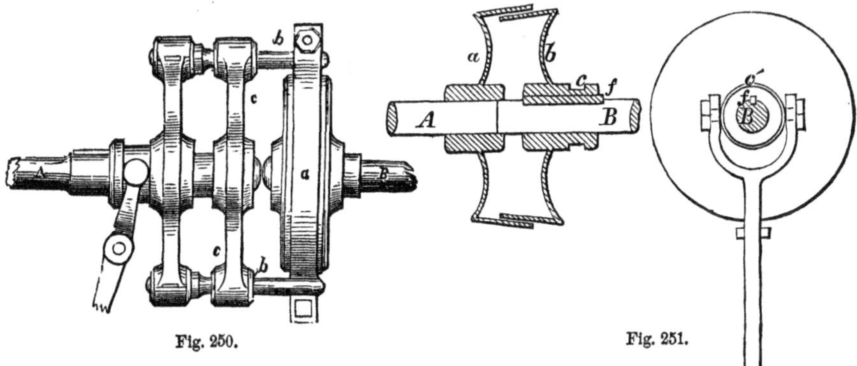

Fig. 250. Fig. 251.

engaged with this form of coupling while the shaft is in rapid motion, without great shock and injury to the machinery. To obviate this, other forms of coupling are requisite; one of these is represented (fig. 250). On the shaft B is fixed a drum or pulley, which is embraced by a friction band as tightly as may be found necessary; this band consists of two straps of iron, clamped together by bolts, leaving ends projecting on either side; the portion of the coupling on the shaft A is the common form of *bayonet* clutch; the part *c c* is fixed to the shaft, and affords a guide to the prongs or bayonets *b b*, as they slide in and out. Slipping these prongs forward, they are thrown into geer with the ears of the friction band; the shaft A being in motion, the band slips round on its pulley till the friction becomes equal to the resistance, and the pulley gradually attains the motion of the clutch.

But of all slide couplings to engage and disengage with the least shock, and at any speed, the *friction cone* coupling (fig. 251) is by far the best. It consists of an exterior and interior cone, *a*, *b*; *a* is fastened to the shaft A, whilst *b* slides in the usual way on the feather *f* of the shaft B; pressing *b* forward, its exterior surface is brought in contact with the interior conical surface of *a*; this should be done gradually; the surfaces of the two cones slip on each other till the friction overcomes the resistance, and motion is transmitted comparatively gradually, and without danger to the machinery. It must be observed, that the longer the taper of the cones, the more difficult the disengagement; but the more blunt the cones, the more difficult to keep the surfaces in contact. From the table given, page 116, it will be seen that the limiting angle of resistance for surfaces of cast iron upon cast iron is 8° 39′, and this angle with the line of shaft will give a very good angle for the surfaces of the cones of this material. When thrown into geer, the handle of the lever or *shipper* is slipped into a notch, that it may not be thrown out by accident.

Pulleys are used for the transmission of motion from one shaft to another by the means of belts; by them every change of velocity may be effected. The speed of the two shafts will be to each other in the inverse ratio of the diameter of their pulleys. Thus, if the driving shaft make 100 revolutions per minute, and the driving pulley be 18 inches in diameter, whilst the driven pulley is 12 inches, then,

$$12 : 18 :: 100 : 150;$$

that is, the driven shaft will make 150 revolutions per minute. Where there is a succession of shafts and pulleys, to find the velocity of the last driven shaft:—Multiply together all the diameters of the driving pulleys by the speed of the first shaft, and divide the product by the product of the diameters of all the driven pulleys.

Pulleys are made of cast iron and of every diameter, from 2 in. up to 20 ft. The number of arms vary according to the diameter; for less than 8 in. diameter the *plate* pulley is preferable (fig. 252); that is, the rim is attached to the hub by a plate; for pulleys of larger diameters, those with arms are used, never less than 4 in number. The arms are made either straight (fig. 253), or curved (fig. 254). When large pulleys are cast entire, it is better that the arms should be curved to admit of contraction in cooling; for the smaller it is unimportant.

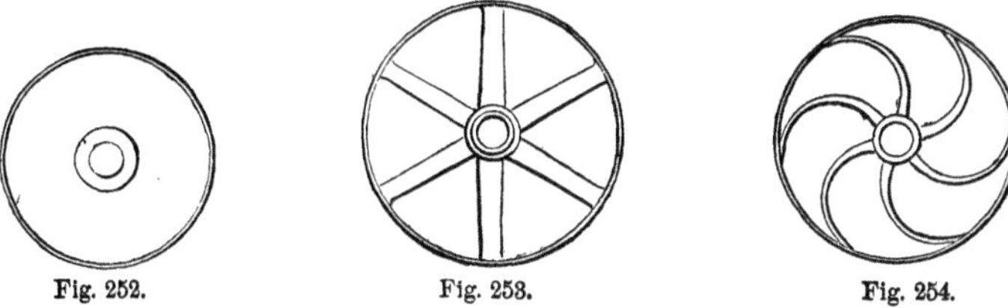

Fig. 252. Fig. 253. Fig. 254.

Fig. 255 represents a portion of the elevation of a pulley sufficient to show the proportion of the several parts, and fig. 256 a section of the same.

Fig. 255.

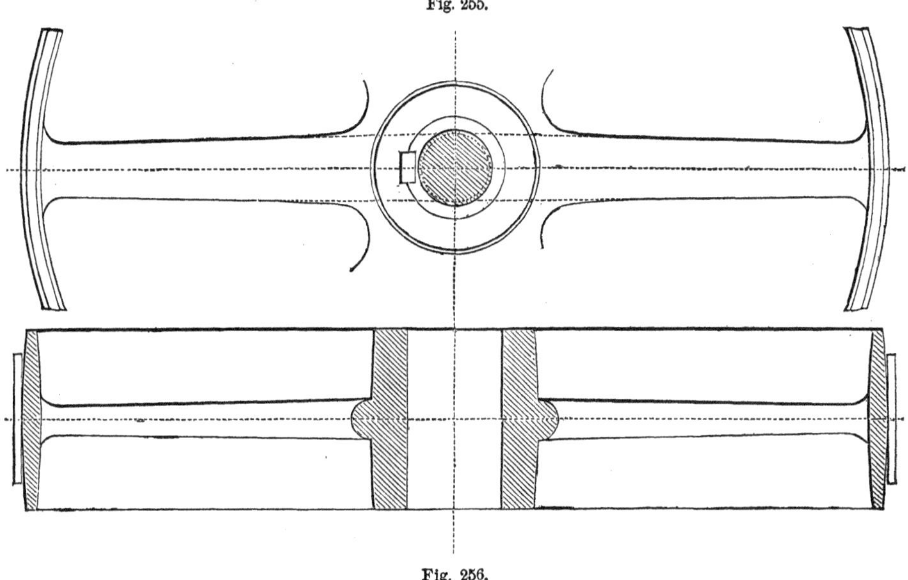

Fig. 256.

The parts may be compared proportionately with the diameter of shaft; thus the thickness of the hub is about $\frac{1}{2}$ the diameter of the shaft, this proportion is also used for the hubs of couplings; the width of the arms from $\frac{3}{4}$ to full diameter; the thickness half the width; the thickness of the rim from $\frac{1}{8}$ to $\frac{1}{6}$ the diameter; the length of hub the same as the width of face.

Fig. 257 represents a faced coupling pulley, an expedient sometimes adopted when a joint occurs where a pulley is also required, the two are then combined; the pulley is cast in halves—two plate pulleys, with plates at the side instead of central, faced and bolted together.

Fig. 257.

Wooden pulleys are commonly called *drums;* these are now but seldom used except for pulleys of very wide face. Fig. 258 represents one form of construction in elevation and longitudinal section. It consists of

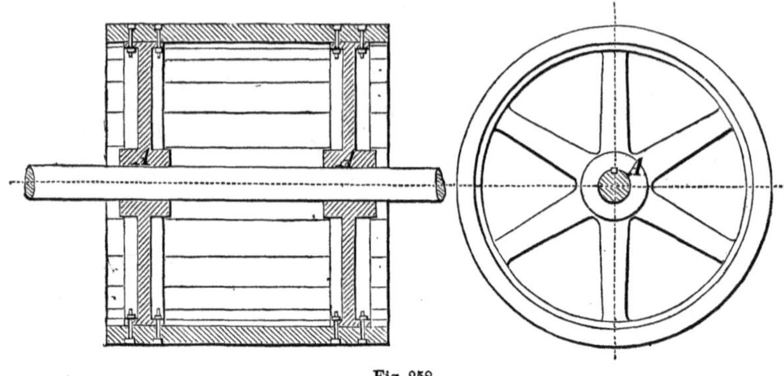

Fig. 258.

two cast iron pulleys A A, or *spiders*, with narrow rims; they are keyed on to the shaft at the required distance from each other, and plank or *lagging* is bolted on the rims to form the face of the drum; the heads of the bolts are sunk beneath the surface of the lagging, and the face is turned.

Fig. 259 represents a wooden pulley which may be termed a wooden plate pulley. The plate consists of sectors of inch boards firmly glued and nailed together, the joints of the boards being always broken. The face is then formed in a similar way, by nailing and gluing arcs of board one to another to the required width of face; these last should be of clear stuff. The whole is retained on the shaft by an iron hub, cast with a plate on one side, and another separate plate sliding on to the hub; the hub is placed in the centre of the pulley, the two plates are brought in contact

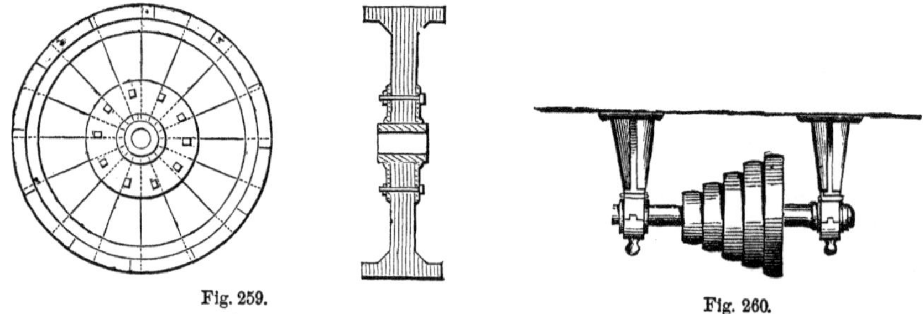
Fig. 259.

Fig. 260.

with the sides of the pulley, and bolted through; the face of the pulley is now turned in the lathe. A similar arrangement of hub is used for the hanging of *grindstones*.

Cone pulleys are used to change the speed of the driven shaft. Fig. 260 represents a cone pulley with its hangers; on the machine there is a similar set, but with ends reversed; that is, the large end of the hanging or driving-pulley connects with the small end of the pulley on the machine. At this time the maximum of velocity is attained on the driven shaft; but if the belt is at the opposite end, small pulley on to a large one, the speed is the minimum, the speed of the shafts being in the inverse ratio of the diameters of their pulleys. By this arrangement speed may be varied within any required limit. It is not necessary that the two pulleys should be counterparts of each other, but only that such proportions should be preserved, that the belt may be tight on whatever set it is placed.

The width of the face of the pulley depends upon the width of the belt necessary to transmit the power; it should exceed by about half an inch on each side the width of the belt for the ordinary sizes. To determine the width of the belt, determine first as near as possible the power required to be transmitted. The strain on the belt is determined by dividing the power to be transmitted by the velocity; thus, if a belt moving at a velocity of 1500 feet per min. be required to transmit 5 horse power; that is, $33000 \times 5 = 165000$ lbs. ft.; then $\frac{165000}{1500} = 110$ lbs., the strain on the belt to convey the power. In addition to this strain, it must be remarked, that the belt is stretched on the pulleys, so that it does not slip while conveying the power. The strain given above may be considered approximately as the difference of tension between the two sides. Morin gives the following Table to determine the strain on each side of the belt.

Portion of the circumference embraced by the belt.	VALUE OF K.			
	New belts on wooden drums.	Ordinary belts		Wet belts on iron pulleys.
		On wooden drums.	On iron pulleys.	
0.20	1.87	1.80	1.42	1.61
0.30	2.57	2.43	1.69	2.05
0.40	3.51	3.26	2.02	2.60
0.50	4.81	4.38	2.41	3.30
0.60	6.59	5.88	2.87	4.19
0.70	9.00	7.90	3.43	5.32
0.80	12.34	10.62	4.09	6.75
0.90	16.90	14.27	4.87	8.57
1.00	23.14	19.16	5.81	10.89

Application of the table.—Find in the table the value of K according to the given circumstances; from this number subtract unit or one, and divide the strain on the belt to convey the power by this remainder, and the quotient will be the minimum tension or that on the *slack* side. Add to this quotient 10 per cent. for friction due to shafting, or other causes. The tension on the leading or *tight* belt will be the above product added to the strain, as given by the power required to be conveyed.

Applying this to the example above of a strain on the belt of 110 lbs. with the ordinary belt embracing $\frac{1}{2}$ or 0.50 of the circumference, the value of K in the table is 2.41; subtract 1., = 1.41; 110 divided by 1.41 = 78 lbs.;

$78 + 10$ per cent. or $78 + 7.8 = 85.8$, the tension on the slack belt.
$85.8 + 110 = 195.8$, the tension on the tight belt.

Good belting of an ordinary thickness of $\frac{3}{16}$ of an inch should sustain a strain of 50 lbs. per inch of width without risk, and without serious wear for a considerable time. Therefore, in the example above, the belt moving at a velocity of 1500 feet per minute, required to transmit a power of five horses, should be $\frac{195.8}{50}$, or very nearly 4 inches in width.

For the engaging and disengaging of a machine, that is, for putting into or out of motion, the arrangement of a *fast-and-loose* pulley is adopted as simpler and better than the clutches before given. It consists merely of two pulleys in juxtaposition on the same axis, one fast, the other loose, so that the belt which transmits the motion may be shifted from one to the other. The face of the driving pulley, that is, the one on the driving shaft, ought to be equal in width to that of both the fast and loose pulleys. By making the face of the pulleys slightly convex, the belt is prevented from slipping off, as the tendency of a belt is always to the larger diameter.

When the belt is shifted, whilst in motion, to a new position on a drum or pulley, or from fast to loose pulley, or *vice versa*, the lateral pressure must be applied on the *advancing* side of the belt, on the side on which the belt is approaching the pulley, and not on the side on which it is running off. It is only necessary that a belt, to maintain its position, should have its advancing side in the plane of rotation of that section of the pulley on which it is required to remain, without regard to the retiring side. On this principle, motion may be conveyed by belts to shafts oblique to each other. Let A and B (fig. 261) be two shafts at right angles to each other, A vertical, B horizontal, so that the line run perpendicular to the direction of one axis is also perpendicular to the other, and let it be required to connect them by pulleys and a belt, that their direction of motion may be as shown by the arrows, their velocities will be

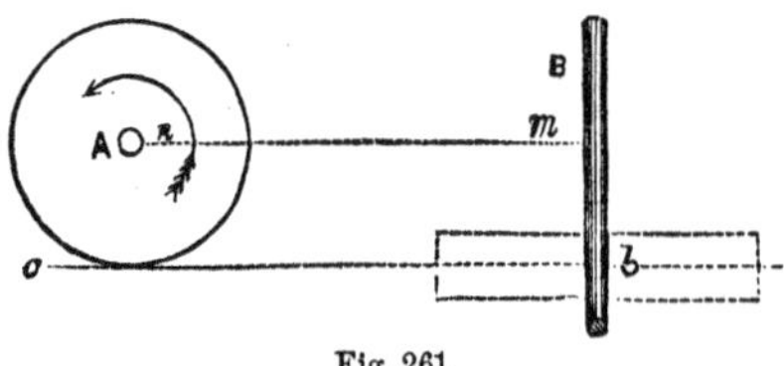

Fig. 261.

as 3 of A to 2 of B. On A describe the circumference of the pulley proposed on that shaft; to this circumference draw a tangent *a b* parallel to *m n*, this line will be the projection of the edge of the belt as it leaves A, and the centre of the belt as it approaches B; consequently, lay off the pulley *b* on each side of this line, and of a diameter proportional to the velocity required. To fix the position of the pulley on A, let fig. 262 be another view taken at right angles to fig. 261, and let the axis B have the direction of motion indicated by the arrow, then the circle of the pulley being described, and a tangent *a′ b′* drawn to it perpendicular to the axis B as before determined, the position of the pulley on the shaft A is likewise

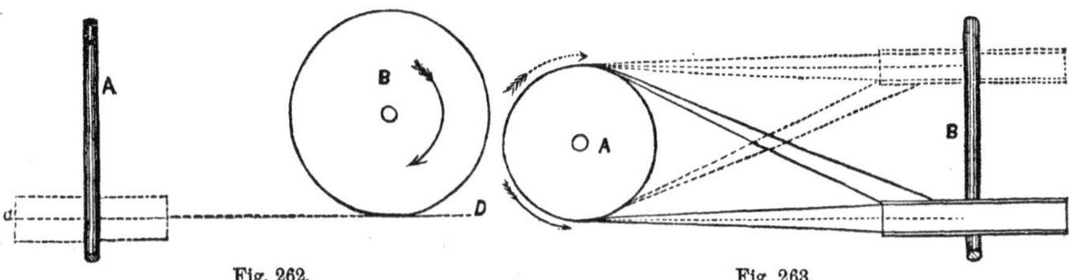

Fig. 262. Fig. 263.

The positions of the two pulleys are thus fixed in such a way, that the belt is always delivered by the pulley it is receding from, into the plane of rotation of the pulley towards which it is approaching. If the motion be reversed, the belt will run off; thus (fig. 263), if the motion of the shaft A is reversed, the pulley B must be placed in the position shown by the dotted lines.

It is not an essential condition that the shafts should be at right angles to each other to have motion transferred by a belt. They may be placed at any angle to each other, provided the shafts lie in parallel planes, so that the perpendicular drawn to one axis is perpendicular to the other. If otherwise, recourse must be had to guide-pulleys, which should be considerably convex on their face.

Geering.—The term geering, in general sense, is applied to all arrangements for the transmission of power; it is also used in a particular sense, as toothed geering.

Toothed geering may be divided into two great classes—*spur* and *bevel* wheels. In the former, the axes of the driving and driven wheels are parallel to each other; in the latter they may be situated at any angle: if of equal size and at right angles, they are called *mitre*-geers.

Spur wheels, strictly so called, consist of wheels of which the teeth are disposed at the outer periphery of the wheel (plate XIII.), in direction of radii from their centres.

Internal geering, in which the teeth are disposed in the interior periphery of the wheel, in direction of radii from their centres (plate XVI).

Rack geer and pinion are employed to convert a rotatory into a rectilinear motion, or *vice versa.* In this arrangement the pinion is a spur-wheel, acting on teeth placed along a straight bar (plate XV., fig. 1.)

Bevel-geering, strictly so called, consists of toothed wheels formed to work together in different planes, their teeth being disposed at an angle to the plane of their faces (plate XIV.)

Trundle-geer or *wheel* is constructed by inserting the extremities of a certain number of cylindrical pieces, called *staves*, into equi-distant holes formed near the circumferences of two parallel plates. The *trundle* or *lantern* is in mill-work made of wood, and is very useful when iron geers cannot be easily got or repaired. The trundle may be used either with a spur wheel to transmit motion to parallel shafts, or with *face* or *crown* wheels, to transmit motion to shafts at right angles to each other. *Face* or *crown* wheels are such as have their teeth perpendicular to the plane of their faces. The sides of the teeth should be radial, the outer edges cornered, and inserted in a single plate or disc, instead of two as the trundle.

On the transmission of motion.—The velocity of rotation of a driven wheel depends on its relative diameter to, and the velocity of the driving wheel with which, it is connected. Thus, if the diameter of the driven wheel be one-half that of the driver, then the driven wheel must make two revolutions for one of the driver. The driver is often called a *leader*, the driven a *follower*. Hence, to obtain the diameters of two wheels having the distances apart: Divide the distances between their centres into parts, inversely proportional to the number of revolutions which the wheels are to make in the same unit of time. Thus, let A and B (fig. 264) be the given centres, the ratio of their velocities being respectively *two* and *three;* if the line joining the centres A and B be divided into $2 + 3 = 5$ equal parts, that is, into as many equal parts as there are units in the terms of the given ratio, the radius of the wheel upon A will contain three of these parts, and the radius of the pinion on B will contain the remaining two parts.

In determining the size of a pair of bevels, we are not, however, limited to any particular diameters as when the axes are parallel; the wheels may be made of any convenient sizes, and the teeth consequently of any breadth, according to the stress they are intended to bear. The question is the mode of determining the *relative* sizes of the pair; and this resolves itself into a division of the angle included between the two axes inversely as the ratio of their angular velocities. Let B and C (fig. 265) be the position of the two given axes, and let them be prolonged till they meet in a point A. Further, let it be required that C make *seven* revolutions while B makes *four*. From

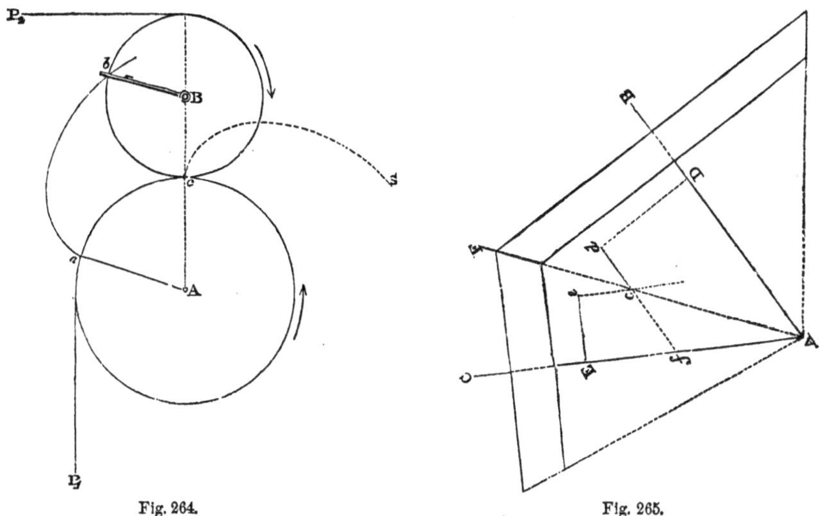

Fig. 264. Fig. 265.

any points D and E in the lines A B, A C, and perpendicular to them, draw D d and E e of lengths (from a scale of equal parts) inversely as the number of revolutions which the axes are severally required to make in the same unit of time. Thus, the angular velocity of axis B being 4 (fig. 265), and that of the axis C being 7, the line D d must be drawn $= 7$, and the line E $e = 4$. Then through d and e parallel with the axes A B and A C draw d c and e c till they meet in c. A straight line drawn from A through c will then make the required division of the angle B A C, and define the line of contact of the two cones, by means of which the two rolling frusta may be projected at any convenient distance from A.

Otherwise, having determined the relative perimeters, diameters, or radii, of the pair, then the lines D d and E e are to each other directly as these quantities.

The point c may also be found more directly thus: From A towards C in the axis A C, set off from a scale as many equal parts (A f) as there are units in the number (7) expressing the velocity of that axis; from the point f draw f c parallel to A B, and set off from the same scale as many parts (f c) as there are units in the number (4) expressing the velocity of the axis A B; then a line drawn from A through c, as before, will divide the angle as required.

The case in which the axes are neither parallel nor intersecting admits of solution by means of a pair of bevels upon an intermediate axis, so situated as to meet the others in any convenient points.

When the contiguity of the shafts is such as to permit of their being connected by a single pair, skewed bevels are sometimes employed.

When the axes are at right angles to each other, and do not intersect, the wheel and screw may be employed to connect them. The velocity of motion is in this arrangement immediately deduced from that of the screw, its number of threads, and the number of teeth in its geering wheel. Thus, if it be required to transmit the motion of one shaft to another contiguous, and at right angles to it—the angular motions being as 20 to 1; then, if the screw be a single-threaded one, the wheel must have 20 teeth; but if double-threaded, the number of teeth will be increased to 40, for 2 teeth will be passed at every revolution. If the velocities be as 2 to 1, the condition is, that the screw have half as many threads upon its barrel as there are teeth on the wheel; and if 1 to 1, the wheel and screw lose their distinctive characters: both become many-threaded screws under the form of wheels. Wheels of this sort may often be applied with peculiar advantage, especially in light geering; and when so applied, it is not essentially necessary that the axes be at right angles to each other any more than it is in bevel-geer.

If the screw have few threads compared with the number of teeth of the wheel, it must always assume the position of driver on account of the obliquity of the thread to the axis; and in this respect its action is analogous to that of a travelling rack, moving endwise one tooth, whilst the screw makes one revolution on its axis.

On the pitch of wheels.—The primary object aimed at in the construction of toothed-geer is the uniform transmission of the power, supposing that to be constant and equal. This implies that the one wheel ought to conduct the other, as if they simply touched in the plane, passing through both their centres. This plane is denoted by the line A B in fig. 264.

When this line—which is usually denominated the *line of centres*—is divided into two parts, A *c* and B *c*, proportional to the number of teeth formed upon the perimeters of the pinion and wheel, these two parts are *proportional* or *primitive radii* of the pair; and a circle being described from each centre passing through the common point *c*, limits what is called the *pitch line* or *circle;* that is, a circle described from the centre A, and another from the centre B, through the same point, are called, the first, the *pitch circle* or *pitch line* of the pinion, and the other of the wheel. They are also sometimes called the *primitive* and *proportional* circles. If the pitch circle be divided into as many equal parts as there are teeth to be given to the wheel, the length of one of these parts is termed the *pitch of the teeth.* One of these arcs comprehends a complete *tooth and space*, meaning by *space* the hollow opening between two contiguous teeth. In bevel and conical wheels, the pitch circle is the base of the frustum.

Rules.—I. To find the pitch of the teeth of a wheel, the diameter and number of teeth being given, divide the diameter D (in inches) by the number of teeth N, and multiply the quotient by 3.1416: the product is the pitch in inches or parts of an inch.

II. To find the diameter of a wheel, the number of teeth and pitch being given, divide the pitch by 3.1416, and multiply the quotient by the number of teeth.

III. To find the number of teeth, the diameter and pitch being given, divide 3.1416 by the pitch, and multiply the result by the diameter in inches.

In ordinary geering, the pitches most commonly in use range from 1 inch to 4 inches, increasing up to two inches by *eighths*, and beyond by *fourths* of an inch. Below inch the pitches decrease by *eighths* down to ¼ inch.

The rules given above may be greatly simplified by the use of the annexed table, which will be found very convenient when the diameter D is to be determined, the pitch P and number of teeth N being given; and conversely, when the diameter and pitch are given, to find the number of teeth.

	$D = \frac{P}{\pi} \times N.$	$N = \frac{\pi}{P} \times D$
Pitch in inches and parts of an inch.	RULE.—To find the diam. in inches, multiply the number of teeth by the tabular number answering to the given pitch.	RULE.—To find the number of teeth, multiply the given diameter in inches by the tabular number answering to the given pitch.
Values of P.	Values of $\frac{P}{\pi}$	Values of $\frac{\pi}{P}$
6	1.9095	.5236
5	1.5915	.6283
4½	1.4270	.6981
4	1.2732	.7854
3½	1.1141	.8976
3	.9547	1.0472
2¾	.8754	1.1333
2½	.7958	1.2566
2¼	.7135	1.3963
2	.6366	1.5708
1⅞	.5937	1.6755
1¾	.5570	1.7952
1⅝	.5141	1.9264
1½	.4774	2.0944
1⅜	.4377	2.2848
1¼	.3979	2.5132
1⅛	.3568	2.7926
1	.3183	3.1416
⅞	.2785	3.5904
¾	.2387	4.1888
⅝	.1989	5.0266
½	.1592	6.2832
⅜	.1194	8.3776
¼	.0796	12.5664

Ex. 1.—Given a wheel of 88 teeth, 2½-inch pitch, to find the diameter of the pitch circle. Here the tabular number in the second column answering to the given pitch is .7958, which multiplied by 88 gives 70.03 for the diameter required.

2. Given a wheel 33 inches diameter, 1¾-inch pitch, to find the number of teeth. The corresponding factor is 1.7952, which multiplied by 33, gives 59.242 for the number of teeth, that is, 59¼ teeth nearly. Now 59 would here be the nearest whole number, but as a wheel of 60 teeth may

be preferred for convenience of calculation of speeds, we may adopt that number, and find the diameter corresponding. The factor in the second column answering to $1\frac{3}{4}$ pitch is .557, and this multiplied by 60 gives 33.4 inches as the diameter which the wheel ought to have.

Another mode of sizing wheels in relation to their pitches, diameters, and number of teeth, is adopted in some machine shops, by dividing the diameter of the pitch circle into as many equal parts as there are teeth to be given to the wheel. To illustrate this by an arithmetical example, let it be assumed that a wheel of 20 inches diameter is required to have 40 teeth; then the *diametral* pitch,

$$\frac{20}{40} = \frac{1}{m} = \tfrac{1}{2} \text{ inch};$$

that is, the diameter being divided into equal parts corresponding in number to the number of teeth in the circumference of the wheel, the length of each of these parts is $\frac{1}{2}$ an inch, consequently $m = 2$; and according to the phraseology of the workshop, the wheel is said to be one of *two pitch*.

In this mode of sizing wheels, a few determined values are given to m, as 20, 16, 14, 12, 10, 9, 8, 7, 6, 5, 4, 3, 2, 1, which includes a variety of pitches from $\frac{1}{8}$ inch up to 3 inches, according to the following table, which shows the value of the circular pitches corresponding to the assigned values of m.

Values of m.	1	2	3	4	5	6	7	8	9	10	12	14	16	20
Corresponding circular pitch in decimals of an inch,	3.142	1.571	1.047	.785	.628	.524	.449	.393	349	314	262	.224	196	.157

As it is convenient to express all the dimensions in terms of the same unit, and the pitch being an appropriate quantity, it is nearly universally

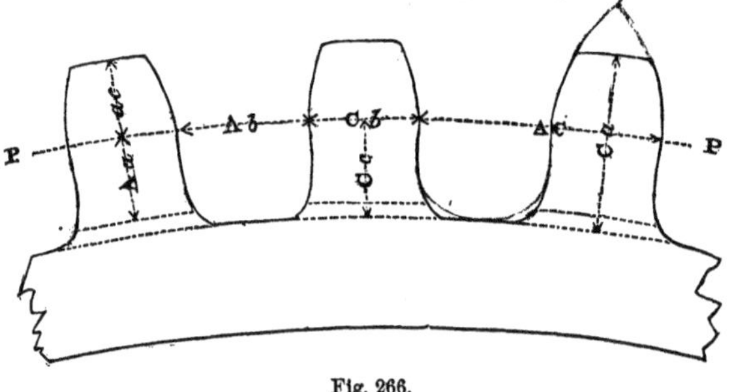

Fig. 266.

adopted as the term of comparison. The following are the proportions adopted by different workshops, some preferring one and some the other (fig. 266).

$A\ C$ =	Pitch of teeth,	= 1 pitch,	or = 15	parts.
$a\ c$ =	Depth to pitch line, P P,	= $\frac{3}{10}$ "	" = $5\frac{1}{2}$	"
$A\,a + a\,c$ =	Working depth of tooth,	= $\frac{6}{10}$ "	" = 11	"
$C\,c - A\,a$ =	Bottom clearance,	= $\frac{1}{10}$ "	" = 1	"
$C\ a$ =	Whole depth to root,	= $\frac{7}{10}$ "	" = 12	"
$C\ b$ =	Thickness of tooth,	= $\frac{5}{11}$ "	" = 7	"
$A\ b$ =	Width of space,	= $\frac{6}{11}$ "	" = 8	"

In practice, these proportions are often laid off in lines for the convenience of the workmen in the pattern shop, so that for any given pitch the other dimensions may at once be determined by means of the compasses. In figs. 267 and 268, two diagrams of that sort are given. Fig. 267 contains the proportions last enumerated, in which the pitch is supposed to be divided into 15 equal parts; and fig. 268 is constructed nearly according to the proportions first given, but embraces the recognised principle, that the relative amount of clearance ought to vary inversely as the pitch, wheels of small pitch requiring more clearance relatively than those in which the pitch is greater.

The construction of these scales is very simple. Thus, in fig. 267, let A B be divided into 15 equal parts, and draw B C perpendicular to it; and again divide B C into a determinate number of parts from B, actual measures of the pitches for which the scale is intended to be used; that is, B *a* = ½ inch; B *b* = 1 inch; B *c* = 2 inches, and so on, and join *a* and A, *b* and A, *c* and A, and so on. To complete the scale, draw 15 parallels to B C from the points numbered in the line A B, and also the two parallels T and U equidistant from the parallels on each side of them.

The scale is thus ready for use. To get from it the several proportions for a given pitch, say of three inches = B *d*, let the compasses be extended from the intersection of the parallel marked T, with the line A B, to the point where it intersects the line A *d;* this will be the part of the tooth from the pitch line to the point, and equivalent to 5½ parts of the pitch, (viz., of B *d*); similarly, the compasses being extended from the intersection of the parallel U with the line A B to its point of intersection of the line A *d*, will give the part of the length of the tooth from the pitch line to the root, and equivalent to 6½ parts of the pitch. For the whole length of the tooth (if wanted in one measurement), set the compasses to the point where the parallel marked 12 meets the line A B, and extend to its point of intersection of the line A *d* at *s*, the length is 12 parts of the pitch B *d;* the working depth is in like manner found from the parallel marked 11, the thickness from that marked 7, and the width of space from that marked 8.

The proportions for any other given pitch comprised in the scale are found in precisely the same way; and if the scale be well constructed, they may be measured off with the utmost accuracy and readiness. To save confusion, it is, however, better in practice to insert in the diagram only

Proportion scales for geering.

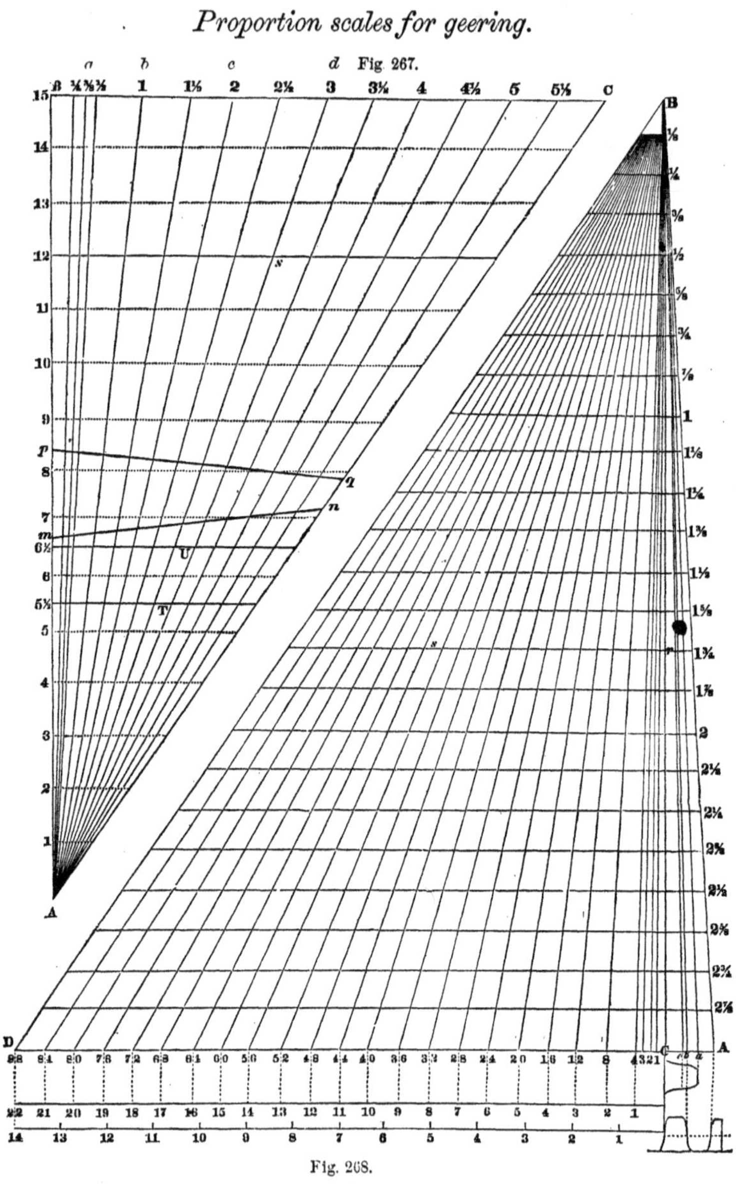

Fig 267.

Fig. 268.

those parallels, namely, T, U, 12, 11, 8, 7, which are required; the others are not requisite, and by inattention may lead to error.

The description of the scale as here given supposes that the lateral clearance is constantly 1-15th of the pitch; but as it is commonly desirable that this should vary slightly with the pitch, relatively increasing as the pitch decreases, two other lines, *m n* and *p q*, have been introduced into the scale, to enable such modification to be adopted should it be required. These lines are drawn at such angles as to give a clearance at 6 inches pitch of 1-18th, which is increased at $\frac{3}{4}$-inch pitch to 1-10th. From these lines the thickness and space are to be taken, instead of using the lines marked 7 and 8, setting the compasses in the points of intersection with the pitch lines, and extending perpendicularly to *the line* A B; in other words, the *shortest distance* from the point of intersection with the pitch line to the line A B is the required measure of the space when the line *p q* is taken, and of the thickness of tooth when the line *m n* is taken.

Fig. 268 is more complete than the one described; the principle of its construction is in effect the same, but its use is more extended, the diameter of the wheel being found from it simultaneously with the length and thickness of tooth, width of space, and clearances. The scale is adapted to wheels of all the pitches, from $\frac{1}{2}$ inch up to 3 inches. The mode of construction is this: having drawn the line A D of any convenient length, raise the perpendicular C B to it, also of any convenient length. On the line A D lay off the greatest pitch of the scale from C to A; then from C towards D lay off *seven* times the pitch *once* or *twice*, according to the sizes of wheels to which the scale is intended to be applied. In the scale given, double of seven times the pitch is laid off, namely, 42 inches; then each of these great divisions being subdivided into 11 equal parts, one of these parts will be equal to four teeth upon the radius of the wheel, so that the whole line C D will be divided into 88 radial pitches. Next on the line C B set off the pitches which may be required in the scale, and through these points draw the 24 parallels to A D, terminating in the lines A B and D B. Then each parallel measured from the line B C to its point of termination in B D is the radius of a wheel of 88 teeth of the particular pitch marked against it on the line A B. They also express the radii of wheels having less than 88 teeth when measured only to the corresponding point in the line joining B, and the divisional on C D, against which the number of teeth is marked. Thus, the radius of a wheel of 52 teeth and $1\frac{7}{8}$-inch pitch is $r\ s$ = 15 7-16th inches very nearly. (The true answer by the table, page 161, is $30.8724 \div 2 = 15.4362$ inches).

The scale may also be used when the number of teeth exceeds 88; for example, to find the radius of a wheel having 100 teeth. Thus, having found the radius answering to 88 teeth, upon the same parallel take off the measure answering to the difference 100 — 88 = 12 teeth; and the two measures together will be the radius required.

To adapt the scale to odd numbers of teeth, the first division on the right of C is divided into single radial pitches, so that the radius of any wheel may be measured off without having recourse to calculation of any kind. Thus, for example, if the wheel is intended to contain 50 teeth, the parallel, answering to the particular pitch, comprehended between 52 B and 2 B, will give the radius required, that is, a radius answering to 52 — 2 = 50 teeth; and any other number of teeth, when not marked against the base, may be found in the same way, observing that it is more convenient to subtract than to add in this use of the scale.

For the proportions of the teeth, set off C a = 7-*tenths* of the pitch, then will A a = 3-*tenths* of the pitch, which corresponds to the depth from the point of the tooth to the pitch line. Again, set off C b = 7-*fifteenths* of the 3-inch pitch, and 5-*elevenths* on the parallel against the 1-inch pitch; this will be the thickness of the tooth, allowing from a *fifteenth* for clearance on the largest pitch to a *tenth* on those from $\frac{7}{8}$-inch and under; and A b will be the width of space, including the clearance. Lines being drawn from those points to B complete the diagram, which will be found to contain all the proportions enumerated in the preceding table.

To use the scale, lay off the addendum of the tooth; that is, the length beyond the pitch line, equal to A a = $\frac{3}{10}$ pitch, and the same length marked off within the pitch line will give the whole working depth of the tooth, namely, 6-10ths pitch. Then with the measure C a = $\frac{7}{10}$ pitch in the compasses, mark off the whole length of the tooth, and this will allow 1-10th at bottom for clearance. Again, set off the thickness of tooth = C b, and the space = A b, which will contain the clearance for the particular pitch, varying from 1-15th to fully 1-10th on the small pitches. It is hardly necessary to observe, that these measurements must be taken upon the parallel corresponding to the particular pitch under consideration at the time.

The amount of bottom clearance is here presumed to be uniformly 1-10th of the pitch; but if it be thought advisable to make this vary, as in the case of the lateral clearance, it will then be necessary to insert a third line c B in the scale, and so related to a B that the space a c shall be throughout equal to the depth of tooth from the pitch circle to the root, and giving any bottom clearance that may be desired.

In relation to the strength of wheels, M. Morin gives it as a rule, that when the velocity of the pitch circle does not exceed five feet per second, the breadth of the tooth measured parallel to the axis ought to be equal to four times the thickness; but when the velocity is higher, the breadth ought to be equal to five thicknesses, the teeth being constantly greased. If the teeth be constantly wet, he recommends the breadth to be made equal to six thicknesses at all velocities.

With respect to the thickness of the tooth, it is plain that it must be dependent on the pressure which the tooth is required to sustain, and upon the nature of the material of which it is formed. We subjoin the following table for calculating the strength of cast iron wheels.

Stress in lbs. at the pitch circle.	Thickness of teeth.	Actual pitches to which the wheels would be made.
lbs.	inches.	inches.
400	0.50	1⅛ to 1¼
800	0.71	1⅜ " 1⅝
1200	0.87	1⅞ " 2
1600	1.00	2 " 2⅛
2000	1.12	2¼ " 2⅜
2400	1.22	2½ " 2⅝
2800	1.32	2⅝ " 2¾
3200	1.41	2⅞ " 3
3600	1.50	3⅛ " 3¼
4000	1.58	3¼ " 3⅜
4400	1.66	3⅜ " 3½
4800	1.73	3½ " 3⅝
5200	1.80	3⅝ " 3¾
5600	1.87	3⅞ " 4
6000	1.94	4 " 4¼

For teeth of wood add 50 per cent. to the thickness as given by Table.

When cast iron and wooden teeth work together, their action upon each other tends, in consequence of the elasticity of the wood, to maintain a more uniform distribution of the strain, and being at first commonly more accurately dressed, to prevent abrasion of wood by the iron, they work with much less friction, are less liable to shocks, and nearly exempt from accident by hard particles coming between the teeth.

The best practice, when a mortise and iron wheel are to work together, is to make both of the same pitch, and in the first instance, of the same thickness of tooth—the pitch being of course calculated for the wooden teeth; afterwards, to dress down the teeth of the iron wheel by the *chipping*-tool, or the geer-cutting machine and file, to the exact form and thickness, as given by the Table; that is, to a thickness in relation to the thickness of the wooden teeth, which shall have the ratio of 25 to 38. The following table may be useful in determining the relation of the dimensions of the teeth of wheels of the given pitches, and the power which they are capable of transmitting safely at the various speeds named.

To find the power which a wheel is capable of transmitting for other velocities than those in the table:—For 6 feet per second, double the result given for 3 feet; for 8 feet, double the result at 4 feet, and so on; and for lower velocities than those given, divide the tabular number by the ratio which they bear to those enumerated. Thus, for 2½ feet velocity, take half the result at 5 feet, and so of other velocities.

When a wheel and pinion, which differ very much in size, work together, the teeth of the latter, on account of their unequal thickness, are capable of sustaining much less pressure than the teeth of the wheel: they are in effect, if not in fact, much reduced in thickness; and in applying

Pitch.	Thickness of teeth.	Length of teeth.	Least breadth of teeth.	Velocity of the wheel at the pitch circle.				
				Three feet per second.	Four feet per second.	Five feet per second.	Seven feet per second.	Eleven feet per second.
Inches.	Inches.	Inches.	Inches.	H. P.	H. P.	H. P.	H. P.	H. P.
6	2.9	4.2	8.4	43.2	57.6	72.	100.2	158.4
5½	2.6	3.85	7.7	36.3	48.4	60.5	84.7	133.1
4	1.9	2.8	5.6	19.	25.5	32.	45.	70.5
3½	1.6	2.45	4.9	14.75	19.5	24.5	34.25	54.
3	1.4	2.1	4.2	11.	14.5	18.	25.	39.5
2½	1.2	1.75	3.5	7.5	10.	12.5	17.5	27.5
2	0.95	1.4	2.8	4.75	6.25	8.	11.	17.25
1¾	0.83	1.225	2.45	3.5	5.	6.25	8.5	13.5
1½	0.71	1.05	2.1	2.75	3.5	4.5	6.25	10.
1¼	0.59	0.875	1.75	2.	2.5	3.125	4.2	6.8
1⅛	0.53	0.7875	1.575	1.5	2.25	2.5	3.5	5.5
1	0.48	0.7	1.4	1.2	1.6	2.	2.8	4.4
⅞	0.41	0.6125	1.225	1.	1.4	1.75	2.5	3.8
¾	0.36	0.525	1.05	.7	.9	1.125	1.5	2.5
⅝	0.33	0.4375	0.875	.5	.625	.75	1.	1.7
½	0.24	0.35	0.7	.3	.4	.5	.7	1.1
⅜	0.18	0.2625	0.525	.2	.25	.3	.4	.6
¼	0.12	0.175	0.35	.075	.1	.125	.175	.275

rules to the calculation of the strength of wheels, the difference of size of the pair ought not to be overlooked, unless, as is indeed very common in practice, the deficiency of strength be made up to the pinion by a flange cast on one or both sides of the rim, of the same depth as the teeth, and binding these together like the staves of a trundle. In this case the pinion is commonly the stronger wheel of the pair.

In the construction of wheels, the problem which presents itself relative to the shape of the teeth is this, that the surfaces of mutual contact shall be so formed, that the wheels shall be made to turn by the intervention of the teeth, precisely as they would by the friction of their circumferences.

Fundamental principle.—In order that two circles A and B (fig. 269) may be made to revolve by the contact of the surfaces of the curves *m m* and *n n* of their teeth precisely as they would by the friction of their circumferences, it is necessary and sufficient that a line drawn from the point of contact *t* of the teeth to the point of contact *c* of the circumferences (pitch circles), should, in every position of the point *t*, be perpendicular to the surfaces of contact at that point; that is, in the language of mathematicians, that the straight line be a *normal* to both the curves *m m* and *n n*. The principle here announced exhibits a special application of one particular property of that curve known to mathematicians as the *epicycloid* (see page 76).

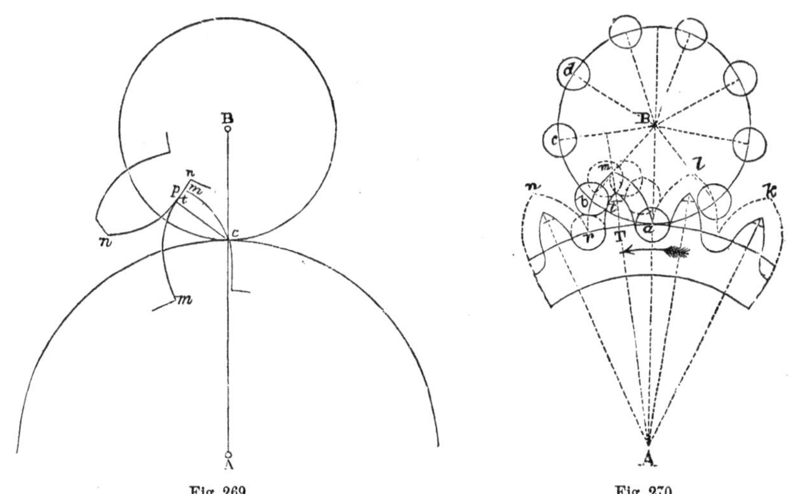

Fig. 269. Fig. 270.

Of epicycloidal teeth.—The simplest illustration of the action of epicycloidal teeth is when they are employed to drive a trundle, as represented in fig. 270. Let it be assumed that the staves of the trundle have no sensible thickness; that the distance of their centres apart, that is their *pitch*, and also their distance from the centre of the trundle, that is their pitch circle, are known. The pitch circles of the trundle and wheel being then drawn from their respective centres B and A, set off the pitches upon these circumferences, corresponding to the number of teeth in the wheel and number of staves in the trundle; let five pins *a b c*, &c., be fixed into the pitch circle of the trundle to represent the staves, and let a series of epicycloidal arcs be traced with a describing circle, equal in diameter to the radius of the pitch circle of the trundle, and meeting in the points *k l m n*, &c., alternately from right and left. If, now, motion be given to the wheel in the direction of the arrow, then the curved face *m r* will press against the pin *b*, and move it in the same direction; but as the motion continues, the pin will slide upwards till it reaches *m*, when the tooth and pin will quit contact. Before this happens, the next pin *a* will have come into contact with the face *a l* of the next tooth, which repeating the same action, will bring the succeeding pair into contact; and so on continually.

To allow of the required thickness of staves, it is sufficient to diminish the size of the teeth of the wheel by a quantity equal to the radius of the staves (sometimes increased by a certain fraction of the pitch for clearance), by drawing within the primary epicycloids at the required distance another series of curves parallel to these. In practice, a portion must be cut from the points of the teeth, and also a space must be cut out within the pitch circle of the driver, to allow the staves to pass; but no particular form is requisite, the condition to be attended to is simply to allow of sufficient space for the staves to pass without contact.

The action of a wheel and trundle being understood, it is easy to comprehend that of the teeth of a pair of wheels of the ordinary construction. Let A and B of fig. 271 be respectively the centres of a wheel and pinion of which the teeth are intended to be of the epicycloidal form, and A *c* and B *c* their primitive radii. To lay off the teeth of this pair, having determined the pitch and number of teeth in the wheel and pinion, let the pitch lines be divided into as many equal parts, setting out from the point of contact *c*, as there are teeth in them respectively. Let the thickness of the teeth be next set off, taking *c a* for the thickness of a tooth of the wheel, and *c b* for that of a tooth of the pinion. Upon the radii A *c* and B *c* as diameters describe two circles, having also their point of contact at *c* and their centres at X and Y. Now let the circle Y be made to roll upon the pitch line of the wheel, and a point in its circumference at *c* will describe the epicycloidal arc *c m*, and this curve determines the form of the point of the tooth of the wheel. In the same way describe the epicycloidal arc *c n*, by making the circle X to roll upon the pitch circle of the pinion, and this curve will determine the form of the part of the tooth of the pinion beyond the pitch line.

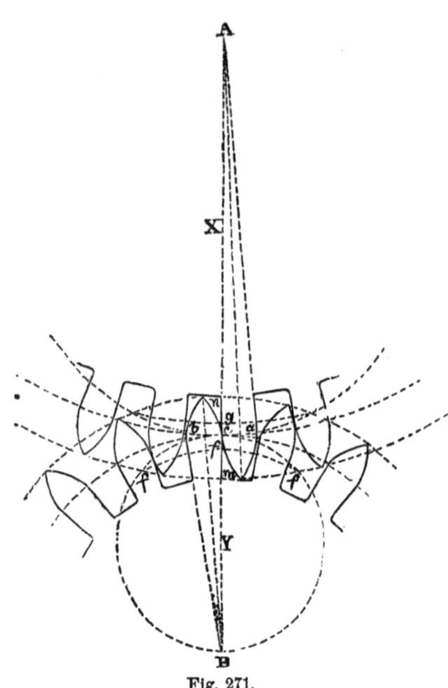

Fig. 271.

The curve *c m* of the tooth of the wheel is constantly in contact with the radius B *c*, and its point of contact is at the same time situated in the circumference of the circle X; the contact will therefore cease when the extremity *m* of the tooth becomes the point of contact; and this occurs when the point *m* has arrived at the circumference of Y. If, then, an arc of a circle be described from the centre A with the radius A *m*, its point *f* of intersection with the circumference of Y is that at which the tooth ought to cease to act, to secure uniformity of motion, and at the same instant that another new tooth advances into geer. The determination of the point *f* limits also the useful length of the flank; for if from B as a centre, with radius B *f*, an arc be described, the part *c f* of the radius *c* B is that which is in contact with the tooth till it arrives at the position B *f*, and consequently this is the useful length of the flank of the pinion. In the same manner it may be determined, that the useful length of the flank of the tooth of the wheel *c a* is the portion *c g*.

To find the form of the portions of the teeth within their respective pitch circles, it is usually considered enough that sufficient space for play be allowed whilst the tooth remains strong enough for its work. As every tooth moves between two flanks, and touches only one of them, the space may be bounded literally by radial lines prolonged towards the centre of the wheel. The bottom of the space being sufficiently removed' from the pitch circumference to allow the tops of the teeth of the pinion to pass round without touching them, may be described by arcs of a circle drawn from the centre. In practice, and especially when the teeth of the wheels are small, it is not usually considered necessary to apply strictly the form of the epicycloid to find curves of the teeth, but to define them approximately.

The forms of the teeth are also occasionally described by arcs, of which the radii are equal to the pitch, and with the centres taken upon the pitch lines. When the diameters of the wheels are not very unequal, and the teeth not thick, in many cases the curves of the teeth are described by arcs drawn from the centres of the adjacent teeth upon the pitch line. This gives a radius equal to the pitch, *plus* half the thickness of a tooth. In like manner, the sides of the teeth also are sometimes described by arcs from the centres of the adjacent teeth, giving a radius equal to the pitch, *minus* half the thickness of a tooth. This form of the tooth may be defective, in the case of a very small pinion having to transmit great pressure, as the extremities of the teeth may be too much reduced. In this case, the curves or faces of the teeth may be described with radii equal to three-fourths of the pitch; and if this be not sufficient curvature, radii equal to some smaller fraction of the pitch may be used. When, on the contrary, the pitch is large, and the pressure comparatively small, the teeth may be too short; this will be remedied by employing arcs, of which the radius is one and a half or twice the pitch. In practice, the ordinary mode in which epicycloidal teeth are set out is by the mechanical method of forming the pattern teeth by *templets* (figs. 272, 273, 274, 275).

Having determined the pitch of the teeth and the radius of the pitch circle, describe on a thin slip of wood—say $\frac{1}{8}$ in. thick—an arc of the pitch circle, and on another similar slip an arc of a circle equal to the diameter

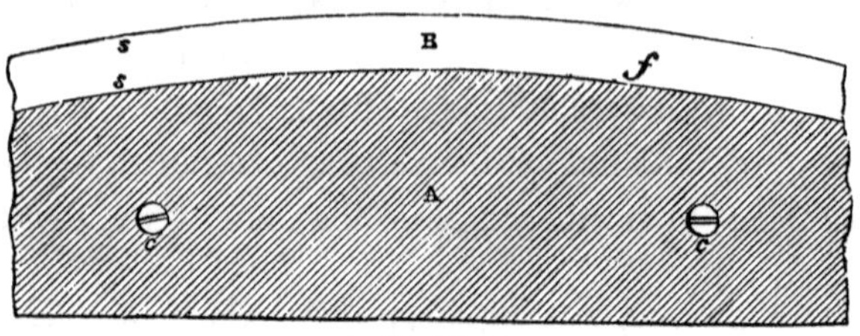

Fig. 272.

of the *wheel* to the points of the teeth. The slips are then cut to the circumferences of the circular arcs described upon them. These two pieces so prepared are fastened together by screws, as in the fig. 272; the piece

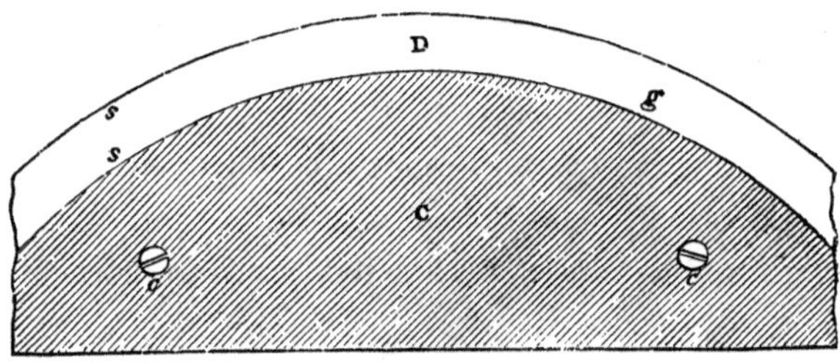

Fig. 273.

A, whose edge *s f* is an arc of the pitch circle, is fixed upon B, whose edge is an arc of the extreme circumference of the wheel, the space *s s* between those edges being in breadth equal to the length of the teeth from

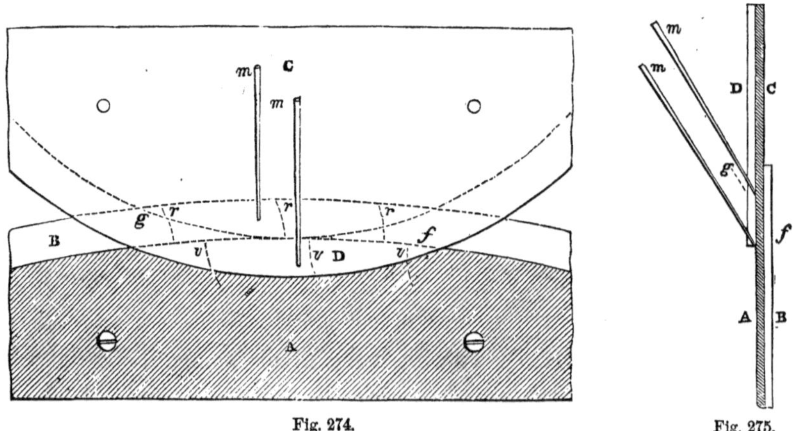

Fig. 274.

Fig. 275.

the pitch circle to the points. This done, a like templet is prepared for the *pinion* (fig. 273).

The pair of templets being thus prepared, two tracing points *m m* are inserted obliquely, and from behind into the piece D of the pinion templet. One of these points passes out at the edge of the piece C, and the other at the edge of the piece D, and the templets are then placed upon each other, as shown in figs. 274 and 275 annexed, so that the circumference of the piece C, that is the pitch circumference of the pinion, shall meet the circumference of the piece A, that is the pitch circumference of the wheel. If in this position the templets be made to roll upon each other through a certain arc, pressing them at the same time slightly together, the tracing points will mark two epicycloidal curves upon the pieces A and B, as *v* and *r*; of these two curves, that marked *v*, which is traced on the face of the piece A, will be the curve of the lower portion or flank, and that marked *r* will be the curve of the upper portion, or face of a tooth of the wheel. If now the thickness of the tooth be marked off on the edge of the piece C, that is, on the pitch circle, and the corresponding tracing point be made to coincide with that point, the curves of the opposite side of the tooth will be formed by making the templets roll together in the contrary direction. A complete outline of a tooth of the wheel is thus described, to which a pattern tooth may be cut and used to shape the teeth by in making the wheel pattern. Instead of forming pattern teeth, many prefer to lay off the teeth by circular arcs coinciding approximately with the epicycloidal arcs found by the templets.

The preceding mode of obtaining the curves of the teeth of a pair of wheels is faulty in as far as it gives a form of teeth smaller at the root than at the pitch circles, and also in the circumstance that a pair of wheels, formed in the manner described, will only work correctly with each other, and not with wheels of any other numbers, although of the same pitch. To obviate this, it is necessary to employ a modification of the ordinary practice.

Let a thin slip of wood be provided, and let an arc of the pitch circle be struck upon it; divide the slip into two portions through the line of this arc with a fine saw; one part, A, will have a *concave*, and the other, B, a corresponding *convex* circular edge. Describe an arc *d d* of the pitch circle upon a second board C D, upon which the pattern tooth is to be drawn. Fix the piece B upon the board, so that its circular edge may accurately coincide with the circumference of the arc *d d*. A portion of a circular plate D is next provided, of the same radius which it is proposed to give to the generating circle: this plate has a fine tracing point at *p* inserted into it, and projecting slightly from its under surface, and accurately coinciding with its circumference. Having set off the thickness of the tooth *a c* upon the pitch circle *d d*, so that twice this width increased by the clearance which it is desired the teeth should have, may be equal to the pitch, the generating circle D is made to roll upon the convex edge of B; meantime the point at p will trace upon the board the curve of the faces of the tooth, having caused the point to coincide successively with the two points a and c, and the circle to roll from right to left, and *vice versa*.

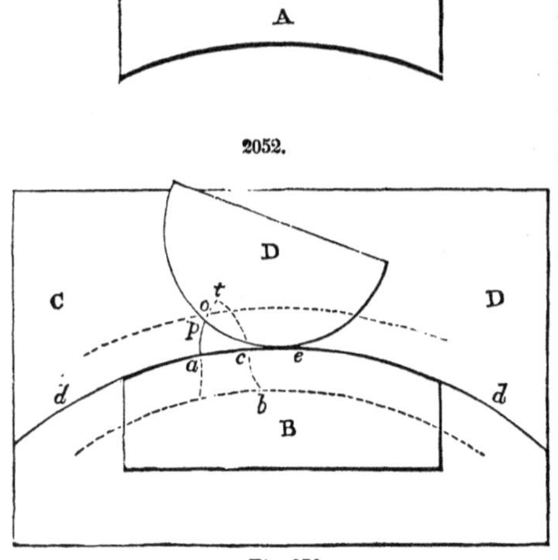

Fig. 276.

Let the piece B be now removed, and the piece A applied and fixed, so that its concave edge may accurately coincide with the circular arc d d; then, with the same circular plate D pressed against the concave edge of A, and made to roll upon it, the point at p, which is made as before to coincide successively with the points a and c, will trace upon the surface of the board C D the two hypocycloidal arcs a b, c b, which form the flanks of the tooth. The complete tooth, thus formed, will work correctly with the teeth similarly described upon any other wheel, provided the pitch of the teeth be the same, and the same generating circle D be used to strike the curves upon the two wheels. In this manner the general forms of the teeth of the pair are determined; and it only remains to cut them off at such lengths that they shall come into contact in the act of passing through the line of centres.

It has already been observed, that having found the epicycloidal curves of the teeth by means of the templets, a common method of proceeding is to find, by trial, a centre and small radius, by which the arc of a circle can be described that will coincide nearly with the templet-traced curve. A more commodious and certain method of determining the centre and radius of the approximate arc has been supplied by Prof. Willis in the construction of his *Odontograph*, manufactured by Messrs. Holtrapfel & Co., London, for description of which see *Appletons' Dictionary of Mechanics*, pp. 819, 820.

Involute teeth.—Involute teeth have the disadvantage of being, when in contact, too much inclined to the radius, by which an undue pressure is transferred to their axes. Their mutual friction is thereby little affected, but that of the axes is increased, and their journals are more speedily worn. But they have at the same time the advantage of working with more accuracy under derangement and incorrectness of fitting, and any pairs of them will work truly together in sets within certain limits, however different in diameters, the pitch being the same.

To describe this curve for the teeth of a pair, of which the radii of the pitch circles and pitch of the teeth are determined, we may employ the mode illustrated by fig. 277. Let A and B be the centres of the pair, and *e b* be their pitch lines; join A and B by a right line passing through *c;* from this last point draw *c d*, *c d*, perpendicular to the radials B *d*, A *d*, and cutting them in *d* and *d;* this line *d d* is then a common normal to the teeth in contact, and the perpendiculars A *d*, B *d*, are the radii of the involute circles which form the acting faces of the teeth.

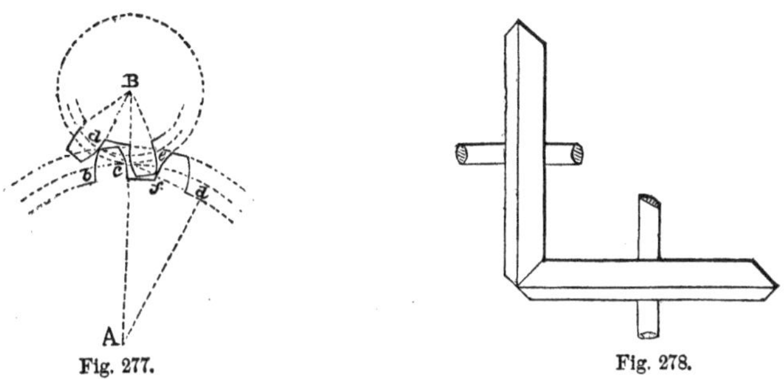

Fig. 277. Fig. 278.

Having thus elucidated the principles of the operation of toothed geering, and the form and proportions to be given to their parts, we proceed now to give complete drawings of different toothed wheels; premising, that except in case of working drawings to full size, arcs of circles are almost invariably used by the draughtsman to describe the forms of the teeth; and that in practice, too little attention is paid to the construction of epicycloidal and involute teeth. In many drawings details are unnecessary, and spur geers are represented by pulleys and bevel geers as in fig. 278, the pitch being written in in figures.

PROJECTIONS OF A SPUR WHEEL.

Plate XII.—To draw side elevation (fig. 1), an edge view (fig. 2), and a vertical section (fig. 3), of a spur wheel with 34 teeth, and a pitch of two inches:

Determine the radius of the pitch circle from table, page 161; against 2 in. we find in the second column .6366; .6366 × 54 = 34.38, the diameter. Draw the central line A C B and the perpendicular D E; on C as a centre, with a radius 17.19, describe the pitch circle, and divide it into 54 equal parts. To effect this division, without fraying by repeated trials that part of the paper on which the teeth are to be represented, describe from the same centre C′, with any convenient radius, a circle *a b c d;* with the same radius divide its circumference into six equal parts, and subdivide each sixth into nine equal parts, and draw radii to the centre C′; these radii will cut the pitch circle at the required number of points. Divide the pitch (2 in.) into 15 equal parts; mark off beyond the pitch circle a distance equal to $5\frac{1}{2}$ of these parts, and within it a distance equal to $6\frac{1}{2}$ parts (see page 163), and from the centre C describe circles passing through these points; these circles are projections of the cylinders bounding the points of the teeth and the roots of the spaces respectively.

In forming the outlines of the teeth, the radii which, by their intersections with the pitch circle, divide it into the required number of parts, may be taken as the centre lines of each tooth. The thickness of the tooth, measured on the pitch circle, is $\frac{7}{15}$ of the pitch, and the width of the space is equal to $\frac{8}{15}$. These distances being set off, take in the compasses the length of the pitch, and from the centre *g* describe a circular arc *h i;* and from the centre *j*, with the same radius, describe another arc *h k* touching the former; these arcs being terminated at the circles bounding the points of the teeth and the bottoms of the spaces respectively, form the curve of one side of a tooth. The other side is formed in a similar manner, by drawing from the centre *l* the arc *m n*, and from the centre *p* the arc *m o*, and so on for all the rest of the teeth.

The teeth having been thus completed, we proceed to the delineation of the rim, arms, and eye of the wheel. The thickness of the rim is usually made equal to that of the teeth, namely, $\frac{7}{15}$ of the pitch, which distance is accordingly set off on a radius within the circle of the bottoms of the spaces, and a circle is described from the centre C through the point *q* thus obtained. Within the rim, a strengthening feather *q r*, in depth about $\frac{3}{4}$ of the thickness of the rim, is generally formed, as shown in the plate. The *eye*, or central aperture for the reception of the shaft, is then drawn to the specified diameter, as also the circle representing the thickness of metal round the eye, which is usually made equal to the pitch of the wheel.

To draw the arms, from the centre C, with the radius C *u* equal to the pitch, describe a circle; draw all the radii, as C L, which are to form the centre lines of the arms, and set off the distance L *v*, equal to $\frac{2}{3}$ pitch, on each side of these radii at the inner circumference of the rim, and through all the points thus obtained draw tangents to the circle passing through *u*. The contiguous arms are rounded off into each other by arcs of circles,

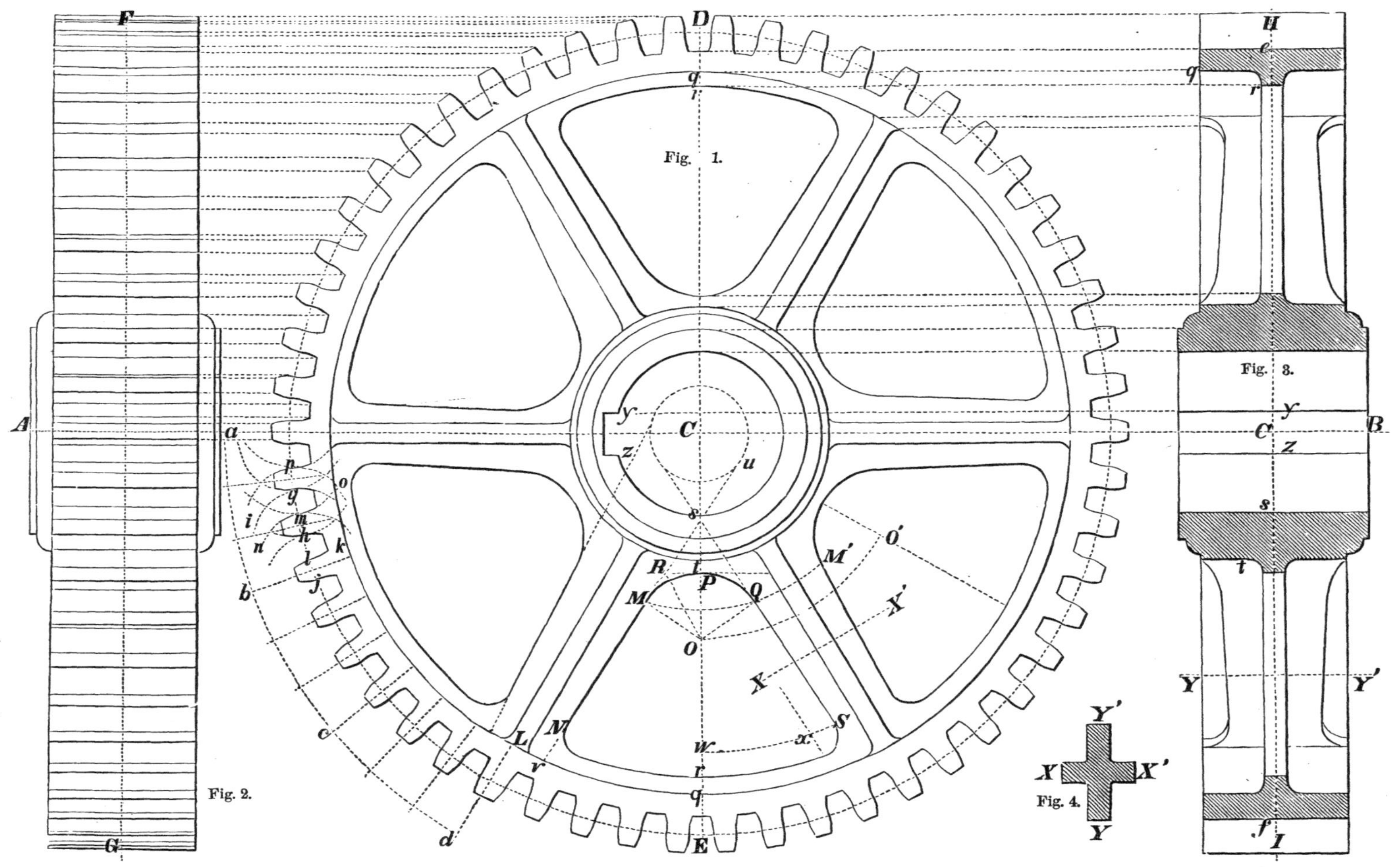
Fig. 1.
Fig. 2.
Fig. 3.
Fig. 4.

whose centres are obtained by the following construction:—Taking, for example, the arc M P Q, it is obvious that its centre is situated in the straight line C E which divides equally the interval between two contiguous arms. Having fixed the point P (which should be at the same distance from *t* as the breadth of the feather at the back of the rim) draw through it a perpendicular R P to the line C E; the question now becomes simply a geometrical problem, to draw a circle touching the three straight lines M N, P R, and S Q. Divide the angle P R M into two equal parts by the straight line R O, which cuts C E in the point O, the centre of the circle required; its radius is the line O M perpendicular to M N. If, now, a circle be drawn from the centre C, with the radius C O, its intersection with the radii bisecting all the intervals between the arms will give the remaining centres, such as O′, of the arcs required; and the circle passing similarly through M, marks all the points of contact M Q M′, &c. To draw the small arcs terminating the extremities of the arms, set off upon the line C E, within the point *r*, the required radius of the arcs, and from the centre C with a radius C *w* describe a circle; the distance *r w* being then transferred to the extremities of the arms at the points where they are cut by the circle, as at S *x*, will give the centres of the arcs required. Draw the central web of the arm by lines parallel to their radii, making the thickness about ¾ inch for wheel of about this size.

Having thus completed elevation, the construction of the edge view and vertical section becomes comparatively simple. Draw the perpendiculars F G and H I (figs. 2, 3) as central lines in the representations; set off on each side of these lines half the breadth of the teeth, and draw parallels; project the teeth of fig. 1 upon fig. 2, by drawing through all the visible angular points straight lines parallel to A B, and terminated at either extremity by the verticals representing the outlines of the breadth of the wheel; project in like manner the circles of the hub; lay off half length on each side of F G, and draw parallels to it. The section (fig. 3) is supposed to be made on the line D E of the elevation; project, as in fig. 2, those portions which will be visible in this section, and shade those parts which are in section. The arms are made tapering in width, and somewhat less than the face of the wheel.

Since the two projections (figs. 1 and 3) are not sufficient to exhibit fully the true form, a cross section of one of them is given at fig. 4; this section is supposed to be made by a plane passing through X X′ and Y Y′. The points *y*, *z*, in fig. 1, and corresponding lines in fig. 3, represent the edges of *key-seat.*

12

OBLIQUE PROJECTION OF A SPUR WHEEL.

Plate XIII.—In drawing a spur wheel or other object in an oblique position with respect to the vertical plane of projection, it is necessary, in the first place, to lay down the elevation and plan as if it were parallel to that plane, as represented at figs. 1 and 2. Then transfer the plan to fig. 4, giving it the same inclination with the ground line which the wheel ought to have in relation to the vertical plane; and assuming that the horizontal line A B represents the axis of the wheel, both in the parallel and oblique positions, the centre of its front face in the latter position will be determined by the intersection of a perpendicular raised from the point C′ (fig. 4) with that axis. Now it is obvious, that if we take any point, as *a* in fig. 1, the projection of that point on fig. 3 must be in the line *a a*, parallel to A B; and further, this point being projected at *a′* (fig. 4), it must be in the perpendicular *a′ a;* therefore the intersection of these two lines is the point required. Thus all the remaining points *b*, *c*, *d*, &c., may be obtained by the intersections of the perpendiculars raised from the points *b′*, *c′*, *d′*, &c. (fig. 4), respectively, with the horizontals drawn through the corresponding points in fig. 1. It will also be observed, that since the points *e* and *f*, in the further face of the wheel, have their projections in *a* and *b* (fig. 1), their oblique projections will be situated in the lines *a a* and *b b*, but they are also at *e* and *f;* consequently, the lines *e a* and *f b* are the oblique projections of the edges *a′ e′* and *b′ f′*. We have now to remark, that all the circles which, in the rectangular elevation (fig. 1), have been employed in the construction of this wheel, are projected in the oblique view into ellipses, the length and position of whose axes may be determined without any difficulty; tor since the plane F′ G′, in which these circles are situated, is vertical, the major axes of all the ellipses in question will obviously be perpendicular to the line A B, and equal to the diameters of the circles of which they are respectively the projections; and the minor axes, representing the horizontal diameters, will all coincide with the line A B. Thus, to obtain the ellipse into which the pitch circle is projected, it is only necessary to set off upon the vertical D E (fig. 3), above and below the point C, the radius of the pitch-circle, whose horizontal diameter *i j* being at *i′ j′* (fig. 4) is projected to *i j* (fig. 3); and thus having obtained the major and minor axes, the ellipse in question may easily be constructed. The intersection of the horizontal lines *g g*, *h h*, &c., with this circle gives the thickness of the teeth at the pitch line; and by projecting in the same manner the circles bounding the extremities and

PLATE XIII.

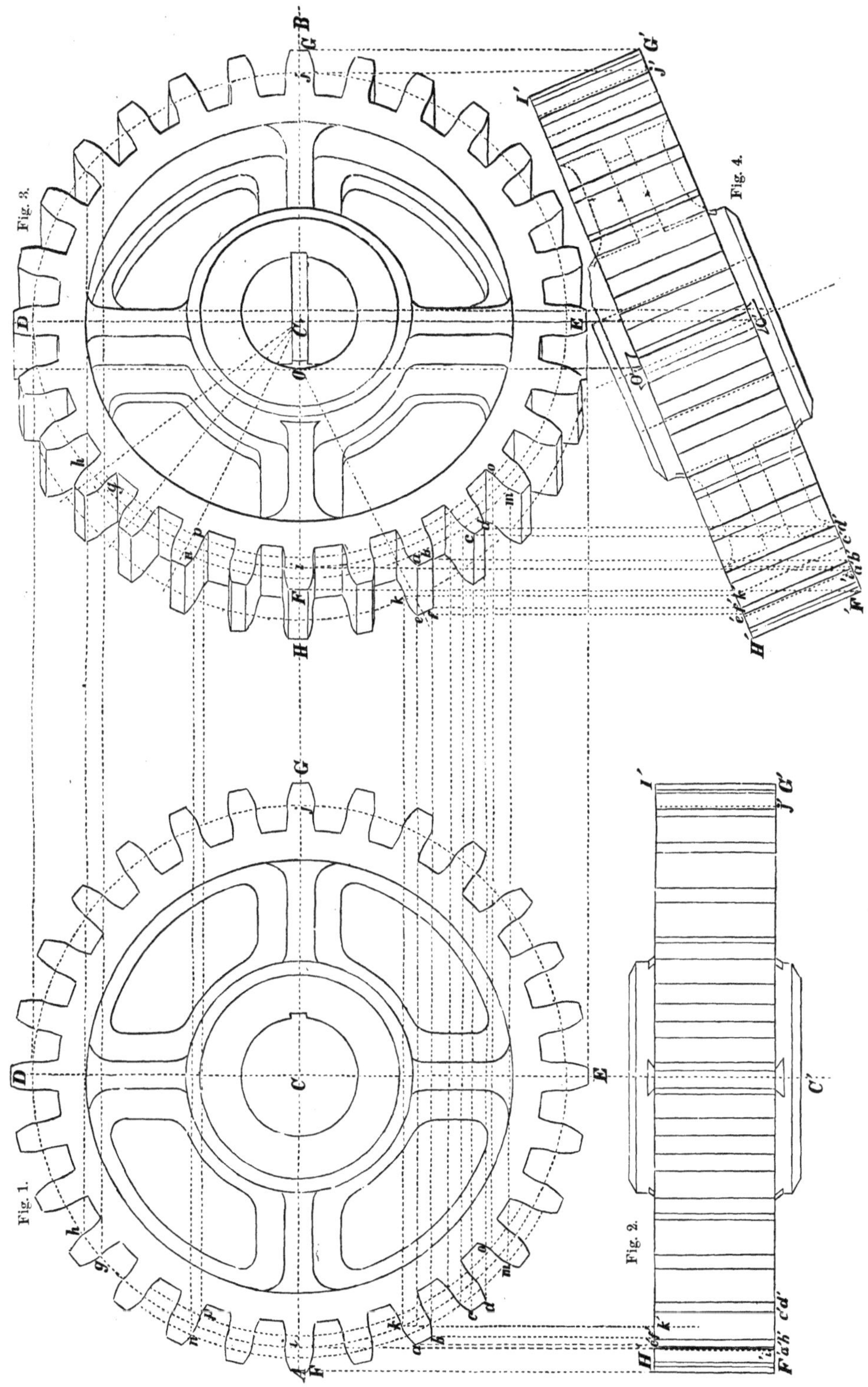

roots of the teeth, these points in each individual tooth may be determined by a similar process. But since, in cases where strict accuracy is required, a greater number of points is necessary for the construction of the curvature of the teeth, two additional circles *m n* and *o p* may be drawn on fig. 1, and projected to fig. 3, and the points of their intersection with the curves of the teeth projected to fig. 3, where the corresponding points are indicated by the same letters.

It is almost unnecessary to observe, that the instructions we have given for the drawing of the anterior face F′ G′ of the wheel are equally applicable to the posterior H′ I′, which is parallel to it, and in all respects the same; the common centre of all the circles in it being at O′ (fig. 4), is projected to O in fig. 3. Hence, it will be easy to construct the ellipses representing these circles in the oblique projection, and consequently to determine the points *e*, *f*, *k*, &c., in the curvature of the teeth; observing, that as their centre lines converge to C in the front face, they all tend to O in the remoter surface, which is, however, for the most part concealed by the former.

It would be superfluous to enter into any details regarding the construction of the oblique view of the rim, eye, and arms which are drawn upon precisely similar principles to those we have already so fully explained.

PROJECTIONS OF A BEVIL WHEEL.

Plate XIV.—Fig. 1 is a face view, fig. 2 an edge view, and fig. 3 a vertical transverse section. We have explained (page 159) the determination of the division of the angle of inclination of the axes of a pair of bevil wheels; their size and proportion are to be determined by the rules given for spur-wheels; thus, consider the base of the cone A B (figs. 2, 3) as the diameter of the pitch circle of a spur-wheel, and proportion the pitch, form, and breadth of teeth, according to the stress to which they are to be subjected.

Having determined and laid down, according to the required conditions, the axis O S of the primitive cone, the diameter A B of its base, the angle A S O which the side of the cone makes with the axis, and the straight lines A *o*, D *o*′, perpendicular to A S, and representing the sides of two cones, between which the breadth of the wheel (or length of the teeth) is comprised, the first operation is to divide the primitive circle, described with the radius A C, into a number of equal parts corresponding to the number of teeth or *pitch* of the wheel. Then upon the section (fig. 3), draw with the radius *o* A or *o* B, supposed to move parallel to itself, outside the figure a small portion of a circle, upon which construct the outlines of a tooth M, and of the rim of the wheel, with the same proportions and after the same manner as we have explained in reference to spur-wheels; set off from A and B the points *a*, *d*, and *f*, denoting respectively the distances from the pitch line to the points and roots of the teeth, and to the inside of the rim, and join these points to the vertex S of the primitive cone, terminating the lines of junction at the lines D *o*′, E *o*′; the figure *a b c d* will represent the lateral form of a tooth, and the figure *c d f e* a section of the rim of the wheel, by the aid of which the face view (fig. 1) may easily be constructed.

The points *a*, *b*, *c*, *d*, and *e*, having been projected upon the vertical diameter A′ B′, describe from the centre C′ a series of circles passing through the points thus obtained, and draw any radius, as C′ L, passing through the centre of a tooth. On either side of the point L set off the distances L *k*, L *l*, making up the thickness of the tooth M at the point, and indicate, in like manner, upon the circles passing through the points B′ and *d*′, its thickness at the pitch line and root; then draw radii through the points *i*, *l*, *k*, *g*, *m*, &c., terminating them respectively at the circles forming the projections of the corresponding parts at the inner extremity of the teeth; these radial lines will represent the rectilinear edges of all the teeth. The curvilinear outlines may be delineated by arcs of circles, tangents to the radii *g* C′ and *i* C′, and passing through the points obtained by the intersections of the radii and the various concentric circles. The radii of these circular arcs may in general, as in the case of spur wheels, be taken equal to the pitch, and their centres upon the interior and exterior pitch-circles; thus the points *g* and *i*, *n* and *o*, for example, are the centres for the arcs passing through the corresponding points in the next adjacent teeth, and *vice versa*.

The drawing of the teeth in the edge view (fig. 2), and of such portions of them as are visible in the section (fig. 3), is sufficiently explained by inspection of the lines of projection which we have partially introduced into the plate for this purpose. We have only to remark, that in the construction of these views, every point in the principal figure from which they are derived is situated upon the projection of the circle drawn from the centre C′, and passing through that point. Thus the points *g* and *i*, for example, situated upon the exterior pitch-circle, will be determined in fig. 2 by the intersection of their lines of projection with the base A B of the primitive cone; and the points *k* and *l* will be upon the straight line passing through *a a* (fig. 3), and so on. Farther, as the lateral edges of all the teeth in fig. 1 are radii of circles drawn from the centre C′, so in

PLATE XIV.

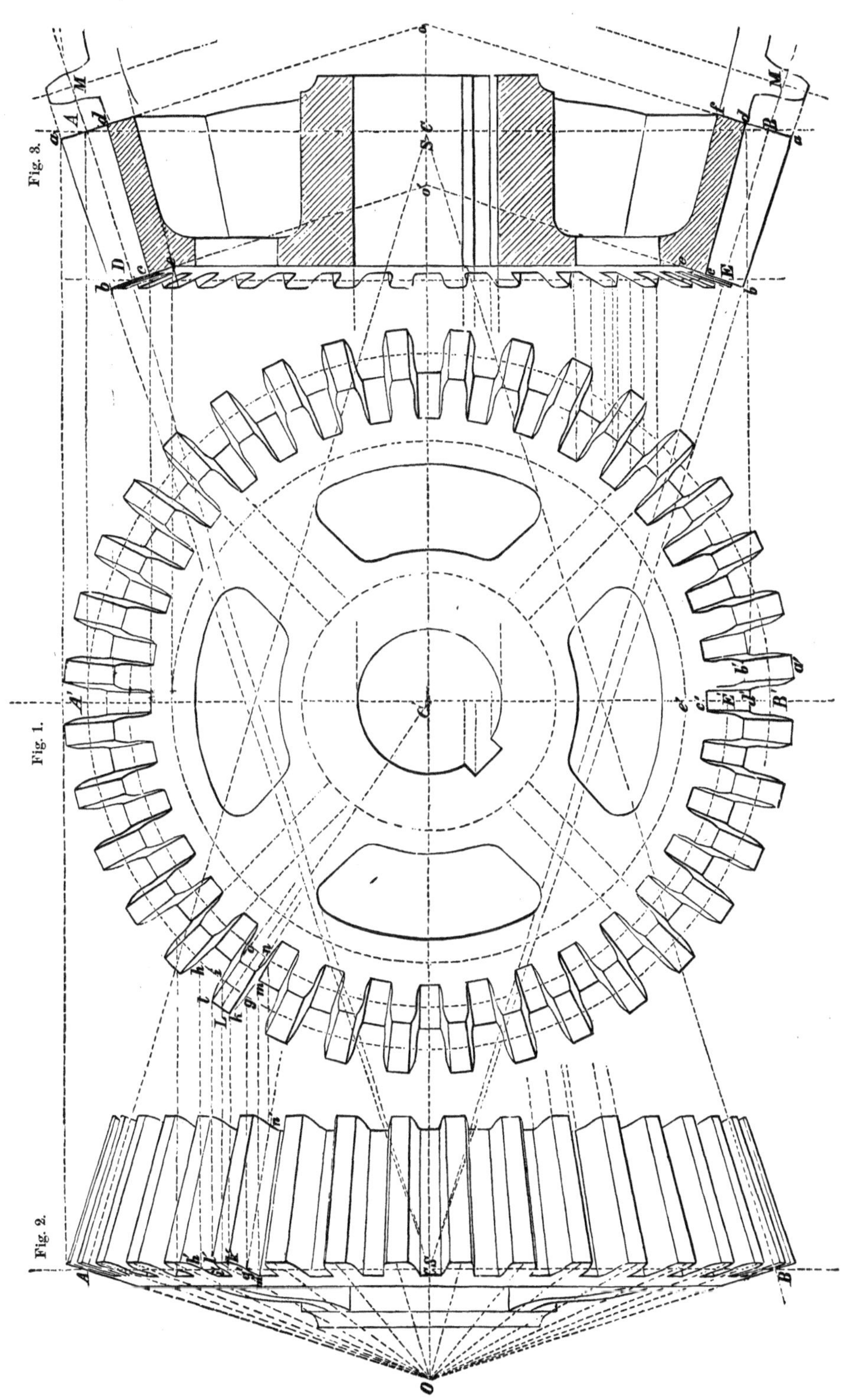

fig. 2 they are represented by lines drawn through the various points found as above for the outer extremities of the teeth, and converging towards the common apex S; while the centre-lines of the exterior and interior extremities themselves all tend to the points O and O′ respectively. This circumstance will suggest a mode of materially simplifying the operation of drawing the edge view of the teeth when the wheels are small, or executed to a small scale; and in all cases it affords a means of testing the accuracy of the operations, if the method of projecting numerous points be adopted.

Skew-bevels.—When the axes of wheels are inclined to each other, and yet do not meet in direction, and it is proposed to connect them by a single pair of bevels, the teeth must be inclined to the base of the frusta to

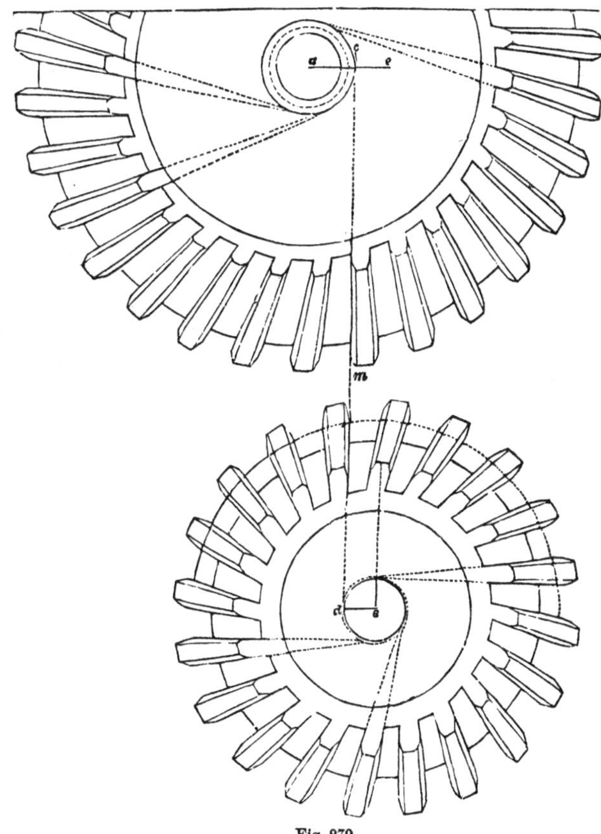

Fig. 279.

allow them to come into contact. Set off *a e* equal to the shortest distance between the axes, (called the *eccentricity*,) and divide it in *c*, so that *a c* is to *e c* as the mean radius of the frustum to the mean radius of that with which it is to work; draw *c m d* perpendicular to *a e*. The line *c m d* gives the direction of the teeth; and if from the centre *a*, with radius *a c*, a circle be described, the direction of any tooth of the wheel will be a tangent to it, as at *c*. Draw the line *d e* perpendicular to *c m d*, and with a radius *d e* equal to *c e* describe a circle; the direction of the teeth of the second wheel will be tangents to this last, as at *d*.

SYSTEM COMPOSED OF A PINION DRIVING A RACK.

Plate XV., fig. 1.—The pitch line M F of the rack, and the primitive circle A B D of the pinion being laid down touching one another, divide the latter into twice the number of equal parts that it is to have of teeth, and set off the common distance of these parts upon the line M N, as many times as may be required; this marks the thickness of the teeth and width of the spaces in the rack. Perpendiculars drawn through all these points to the solid part of the rack will represent the flanks of the teeth upon which those of the pinion are to be developed in succession. The curvature of these latter should be an involute A *c* of the circle A B D. The teeth might be cut off at the point of contact *d* upon the line M N, for at this position the tooth A begins its action upon that of the rack E; but it is better to allow a little more length; in other words, to describe the circle bounding the points of the teeth with a radius somewhat greater than C *d*.

With regard to the form of the spaces in the rack, all that is required is to set off from M N, as at the point *e*, a distance slightly greater than the difference A *a* of the radius of the pitch circle, and that of the circle limiting the points of the teeth, and through this point to draw a straight line F G parallel to M N. From this line the flanks of all the teeth of the rack spring, and their points are terminated by a portion of a cycloid A *b*, which, however, may in most instances be replaced by an arc of a circle. The depth of the spaces in the pinion obviously depends upon the height of this curved portion of the teeth; their outline is formed by a circle drawn from the centre C, with a radius a little less than the distance from this point to the straight line, bounding the upper surface of the teeth of the rack.

SYSTEM COMPOSED OF A RACK DRIVING A PINION.

In this case the construction is in all respects identical with that of the preceding example, with this exception, that the form proper to be given to the teeth of the rack is a cycloid generated by a point A in the circum-

PLATE XV.

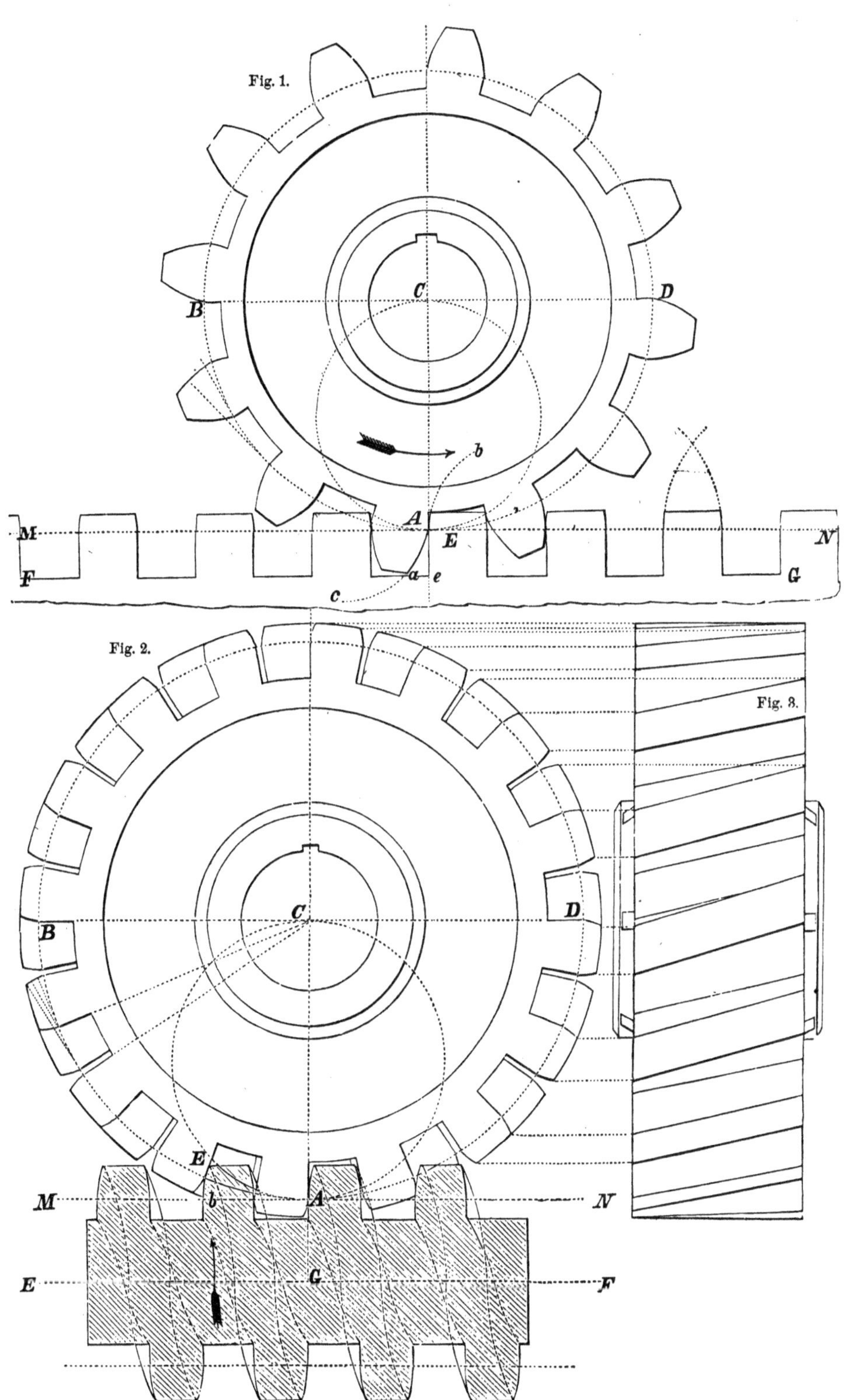

ference of the circle A E C, in rolling on the line M N. The curvature of the teeth of the pinion is an involute as before.

SYSTEM COMPOSED OF A WHEEL AND TANGENT, OR ENDLESS SCREW.

Fig. 2.—In the construction of this variety of geering, we must first fix upon the number of teeth in the wheel, and the distance of its centre from the axis of the screw. Then conceive a plane passing through the axis E F of the screw, parallel to the face of the wheel, and let C be the centre of its primitive circle. If now a perpendicular C G be drawn from C upon E F, and C A be taken as the radius of the pitch circle B A D of the wheel, the difference A G will represent the radius of a cylinder, which may be termed the *primitive cylinder* of the screw; and a line M N drawn through A, parallel to E F, will be a generatrix of that cylinder, which will serve the purpose of determining the form of the teeth.

The section having been made through the axis, the question obviously resolves itself into the case of a rack driving a pinion; consequently the curve of the teeth, or rather *thread*, of the screw should be simply a cycloid generated by a point in the circle A E C, described upon A C as a diameter, and rolling upon the straight line M N. It is to be remarked, further, that the outlines of the teeth are helical surfaces described about the cylinder forming the screw, with the pitch A *b* equal to the distance, measured upon the primitive scale, between the corresponding points of two contiguous teeth. These curves have been drawn on our figure, but being for the most part concealed, they are expressed by dotted lines. The teeth of the wheel are not, as in ordinary kinds of geering, set perpendicularly to the plane of its face, but at an angle, and with surfaces corresponding to the inclination and helical form of the thread of the screw. In some instances, the points of the teeth and bottoms of the spaces are formed of a concave outline adapted to the convexity of the screw, in order to present as much bearing surface as possible to its action. In this kind of geering, for obvious reasons, it is invariably the screw that imparts the motion.

Fig. 3 represents an edge elevation of the wheel, projected as in previous examples.

SYSTEM COMPOSED OF AN INTERNAL SPUR-WHEEL DRIVING A PINION.

Plate XVI., fig. 1.—The form of the teeth of the driving wheel is in this instance determined by the epicycloid described by a point in the circle A E C, rolling on the concave circumference of the primitive circle M A N.

The points of the teeth are to be cut off by a circle drawn from the centre of the internal wheel, and passing through the point E, which is indicated, as before, by the contact of the curve with the flank of the driven tooth.

The wheel being supposed to be invariably the driver, the curved portion of the teeth of the pinion may be very small. This curvature is a part of an epicycloid generated by a point in the circle M A N rolling upon B A D.

SYSTEM COMPOSED OF AN INTERNAL WHEEL DRIVEN BY A PINION.

Fig. 2.—This problem involves a circumstance which has not hitherto come under consideration, and which demands, consequently, a different mode of treatment from that employed in the preceding cases. The epicycloidal curve A *a*, generated by a point in the circle having the diameter A O, the radius of the circle M A N, and which rolls upon the circle B A D, cannot be developed upon the flank A *b*, the line described by the same point in the same circle in rolling upon the concave circumference M A N; and for this obvious reason, that that curve is situated *without* the circle B A D, while the flank, on the contrary, is *within* it. It becomes necessary, therefore, in order that the pinion may drive the wheel uniformly according to the required conditions, to form the teeth so that they shall act always upon one single point in those of the wheel. This may be most advantageously effected by taking for the curvature of the teeth of the pinion the epicycloid A *d* described by the point A in the circle M A N, rolling over the circle B A D. It will be observed that, as in the preceding examples, the tooth E of the pinion begins its action upon the tooth F of the wheel at the point of contact of their respective primitive circles, and that it is unnecessary that it should be continued beyond the point *c*, because the succeeding tooth H will then have been brought into action upon G; consequently the teeth of the wheel might be bounded by a circle passing through the point *c*. It is, however, one of the practical advantages which this species of geering has over wheels working externally, that the surfaces of contact of the wheel and pinion admit of being more easily increased; and by making the teeth somewhat longer than simple necessity demands, the strain may be diffused over two or more teeth at the same time. The flanks of the teeth of the wheel are formed by radii drawn to the centre O, and their points are rounded off to enable them to enter freely into the spaces of the pinion.

PLATE XVI.

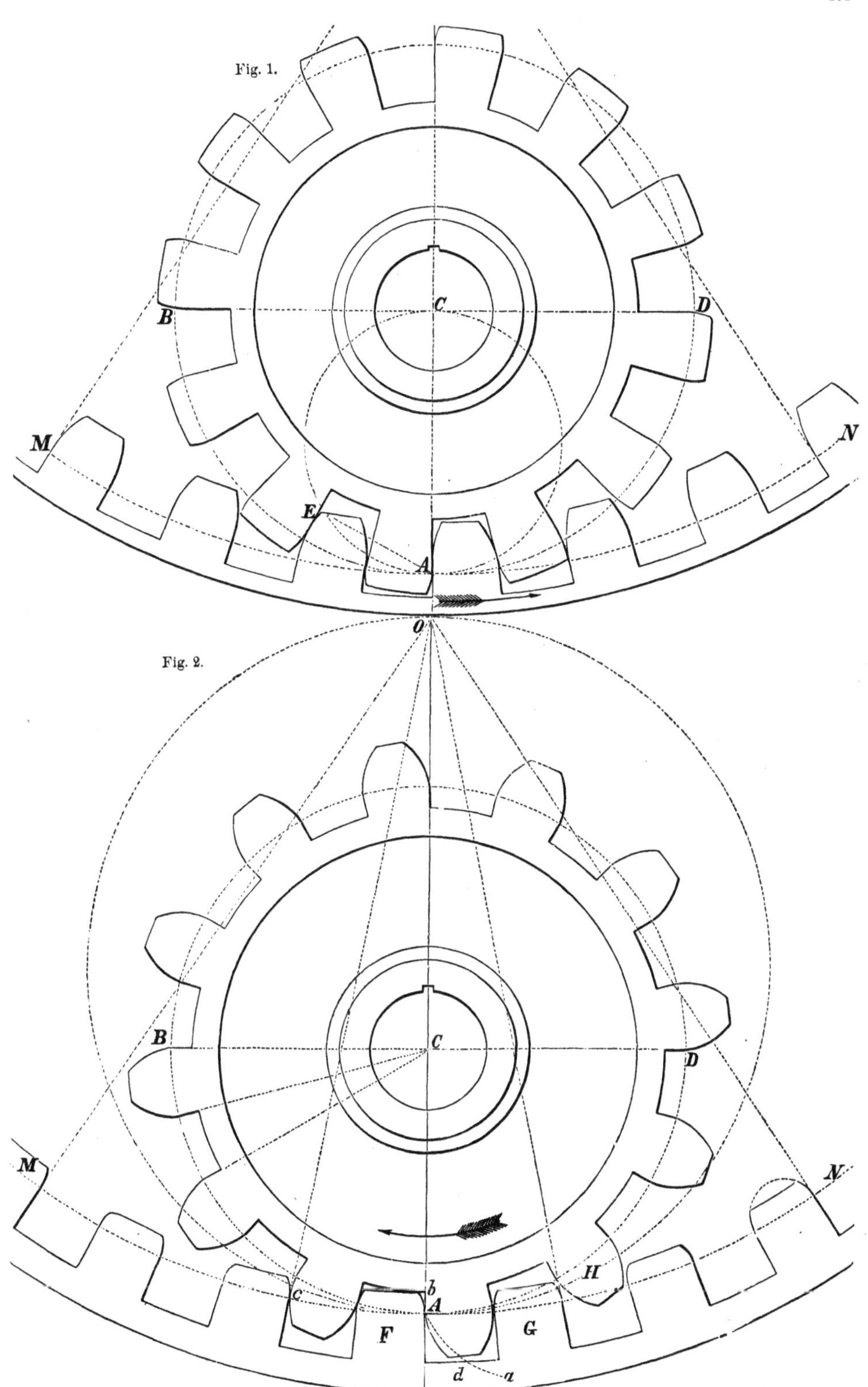

PLATE XVII.

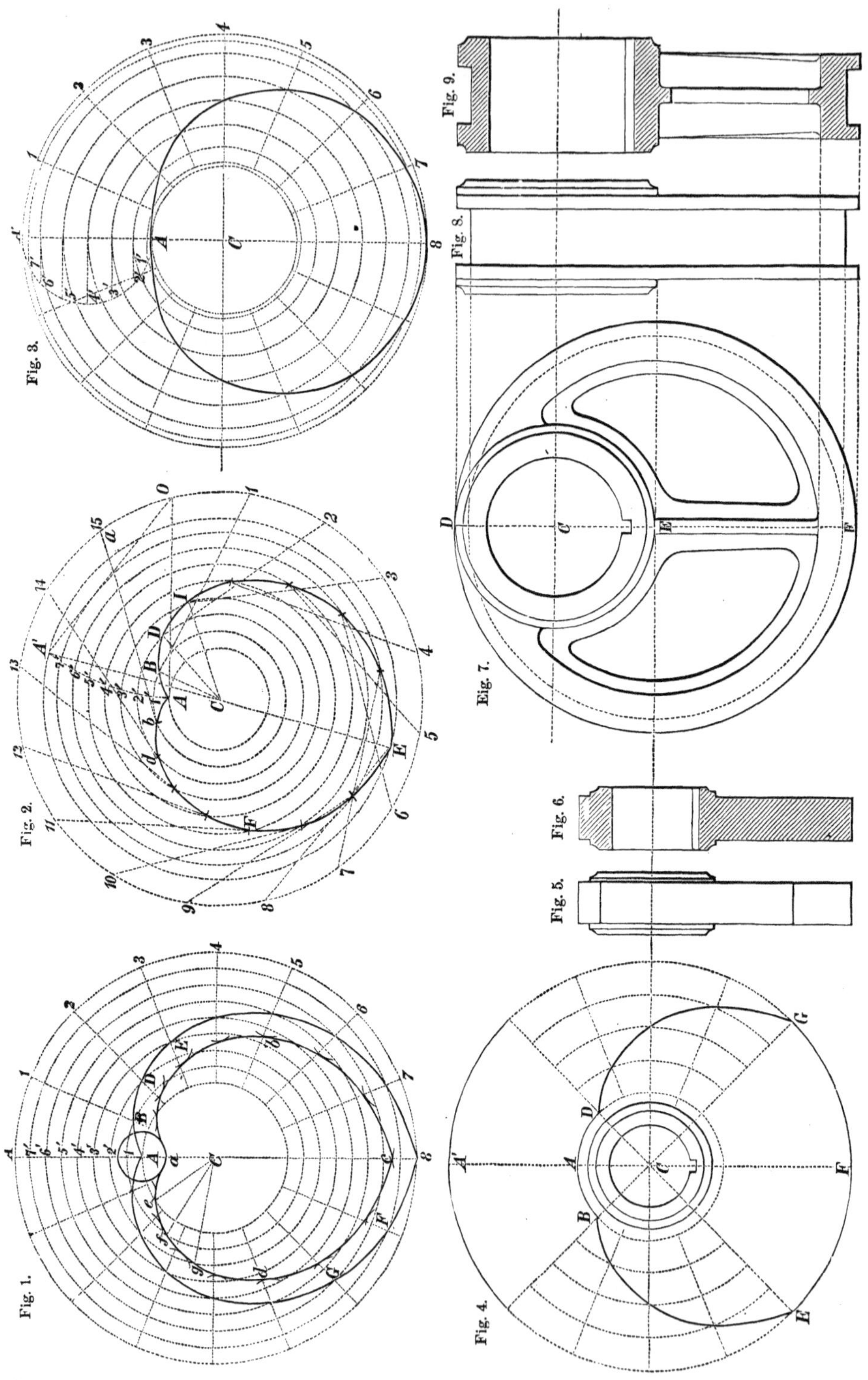

PROJECTIONS OF ECCENTRICS.

The term *eccentric* is applied in general to all such curves as are composed of points situated at unequal distances from a central point or axis. The ellipse, the curve called the *heart*, and even the circle itself, when supposed to be fixed upon an axis which does not pass through its centre, are examples of eccentric curves.

The object of such curves, which are of frequent occurrence in machinery, is to convert a rotatory into an alternating rectilinear motion; and their forms admit of an infinite variety, according to the nature of the motion desired to be imparted. Examples of their application occur in many arrangements of pumps, presses, valves of steam-engines, spinning and weaving machines, &c.

Fig. 1, plate XVII.—*To draw the eccentrical symmetrical curve called the heart, which is such as, when revolving with a uniform motion on its axis, to communicate to a movable point* A,*a uniform rectilinear motion of ascent and descent.*

Let C be the axis or centre of rotation upon which the eccentric is fixed, and which is supposed to revolve uniformly; and let A A′ be the distance which the point A is required to traverse during a half revolution of the eccentric. From the centre C, with radii respectively equal to C A and C A′, describe two circles; divide the greatest into any number of equal parts (say 16), and draw through these points of division the radii C 1, C 2, C 3, &c. Then divide the line A A′ into the same number of equal parts as are contained in the semicircle (that is, into 8 in the example now before us), and through all the points 1′, 2′, 3′, &c., draw circles concentric with the former; the points of their intersection B, D, E, &c., with the respective radii C 1, C 2, C 3, &c., are points in the curve required, its vertex being at the point 8.

It will now be obvious that when the axis, in its angular motion, shall have passed through one division, in other words, when the radius C 1 coincides with C A′, the point A, being urged upwards by the curvature of the revolving body on which it rests, will have taken the position indicated by 1′; and further, when the succeeding radius C 2 shall have assumed the same position, the point A will have been raised to 2′, and so on till it arrives at A′, after a half revolution of the eccentric. The remaining half A G F 8 of the eccentric, being exactly symmetrical with the other, will enable the point A to descend in precisely the same manner as it is elevated. It is thus manifest that this curve is fitted to impress a uniform motion upon the point A itself, but in practice a small friction roller is usually interposed between the surface of the eccentric and the piece which is to be actuated by it. Accordingly, the point A is to be taken as the centre of this roller, and the curve whose construction we have just explained is replaced by another similar to, and equidistant from it, which is drawn tangentially to arcs of circles described from the various points in the primary curve with the radius of the roller. This second curve is manifestly endowed with the same properties as the other; for, supposing the point *e*, for example, to coincide with A, if we cause the axis to revolve through a distance equal to one of the divisions the point *f*, which is the intersection of the curve with the circle whose radius is C 1′, will then obviously have assumed the position 1′; at the next portion of the revolution, the point *g* (which is such that the angle *f* C *g* is equal to *e* C *f*) will have arrived at 2′, and so on. Thus it is plain that the point *a* will be elevated and depressed uniformly by means of the second curve, in the same manner as that denoted by A is actuated by the first.

It is obvious that the movable point *a* must, in actual working, be held in contact with the surface of the eccentric; this is generally accomplished by the action of a weight or of a spring; but in forms similar to fig. 1, in which all the diameters, as A B, B F, D G, &c., are equal, two frictions connected and placed diametrically opposite each other may be used, which will be thus alternately and similarly impelled; in many cases an eccentric groove is cut, and the friction roll or point *a* is made to slide in this groove.

Fig. 2.—*To draw a double eccentric curve, which shall impart a uniform motion of ascent and descent to the point* A, *traversing an arc of a circle* A A′.

First, divide the given arc A A′ into any number of equal parts (8 in the present example), and from the common centre, or axis C of the eccentric, describe circles passing through each of the points of division 1′, 2′, 3′, &c. Divide also the circle passing through O, the centre of the arc A A′, into twice the number of equal parts; then taking up in the compasses the length A O, and placing one of the points at the division marked 1, describe an arc of a circle, which will cut at B the circle drawn with the radius C 1′; from the next point of division 2, mark off, in the same manner, the point D in the circle whose radius is C 2′, and so on. The points B, D, E, &c., thus obtained, are points in the curve required, which, supposing the eccentric to revolve uniformly, will possess the property of communicating to the point A a uniform motion of ascent and descent along the arc A A′. This admits of easy demonstration. The angle B C 1′ is half of 2′ C D, and consequently, when the point B has arrived at 1′, the radius C D, then coinciding with C B, will have passed through an angle equal to 1′ C B, and again, at the next point in the revolution, will coincide with C 2′. Therefore the portion B D of the curve will impel the given point through the arc 1′ 2′, in the same time and with the same velocity, as the part A B will have raised it from A to 1′. By a similar process of reasoning it will be manifest, that the angle 1′ C B being just one-third of 3′ C I, the point A will also traverse the space 2′ 3′ with a uniform motion.

By a glance at the figure it will be seen that this curve is not symmetrical; in other words, that the part A F E is not equal or similar to A D E. This may be accounted for by observing, that the arc *b* 1′, for instance, is equal to 1′ B, and consequently the point *b* (which is determined by the intersection of the circle passing through 1′ with the arc described from the centre 15) cannot be situated in the same position in relation to A as the point B, since the radius C A does not pass through 1′; the same remark applies to all the other arcs, *d* 2′, &c. It is not the less certain, however, that the part A F E of the eccentric will cause the given point to descend through the arc A′ A in the same uniform manner as it had been elevated by the part A D E.

In the two preceding examples of eccentrics it has been shown, that the point A moves through equal spaces in equal times, both in ascending and descending. In some cases, however, this is by no means desirable; thus, if the eccentric is destined to give motion to a mass of matter which offers considerable resistance, such a form would give rise to injurious and destructive shocks. In such cases, it is necessary so to regulate the curvature of the eccentric, that the point A shall move at the beginning and end of its stroke with diminished velocity; and that for this purpose, the space A A should be unequally divided, as in the example which comes next under notice.

Fig. 3.—*To draw a double and symmetrical eccentric curve, such as to cause the point* A *to move in a straight line, and with an unequal motion; the velocity of ascent being accelerated in a given ratio from the starting point to the vertex of the curve, and the velocity of descent being retarded in the same ratio.*

Upon A A′ as a diameter describe a semicircle, and divide it into any number of equal parts; draw from each point of division 1′, 2′, 3′, &c., perpendiculars upon C A′; and through the points of intersection 1^2, 2^2, 3^2, &c., draw circles having for their common centre the point C, which is to be joined, as before, to all the points of division on the circle (A′ 48.) The points of intersection of the concentric circles with the radii C 1, C 2, C 3, &c., are points in the curve required.

Fig. 4.—*To construct a double and symmetrical eccentric, which shall produce a uniform rectilinear motion, with periods of rest at the points nearest to, and farthest from, the axis of rotation.*

The lines in the figure above referred to indicate sufficiently plainly, without the aid of further description, the construction of the curve in question, which is simply a modification of the eccentric represented at Fig. 1. In the present example, the eccentric is adapted to allow the movable point A to remain in a state of rest during the first quarter of a revolution B D; then, during the second quarter, to cause it to traverse, with a uniform motion, a given straight line A A′, by means of the curve D G; again, during the next quarter E F G, to render it stationary at the elevation of the point A′; and finally, to allow it to subside along the curve B E, with the same uniform motion as it was elevated, to its original position, after having performed the entire revolution.

Fig. 5 represents an edge view of this eccentric, and fig. 6 a vertical section of it.

Figs. 7, 8, and 9, *a Circular Eccentric.*—These figures represent a model of a variety of the circular eccentric, which is the contrivance usually adopted in steam-engines for giving motion to the valves regulating the action of the steam upon the piston. The circular eccentric is simply a species of disc or pulley fixed upon the crank-shaft, or other rotating axis of an engine, in such a manner that the centre or axis of the shaft shall be at a given distance from the centre of the pulley. A ring or hoop, either formed entirely of, or lined with brass or gun metal, for the purpose of diminishing friction, is accurately fitted within projecting ledges on the outer circumference of the eccentric, so that the latter may revolve freely within it; this ring is connected by an inflexible rod with a system of levers, by which the valve is moved. It is evident, that as the shaft to which the eccentric is fixed revolves, an alternating rectilinear motion will be impressed upon the rod, its amount being determined by the eccentricity, or distance between the centre of the shaft and that of the exterior circle. The *throw* of the eccentric is twice the eccentricity C E; or it may be expressed as the diameter of the circle described by the point E. The nature of the alternating motion generated by the circular eccentric is identical with that of the crank, which might in many cases be advantageously substituted for it.

Fig. 8 is the edge view, fig. 9 the section of the eccentric, in this par-

PLATE XVIII.

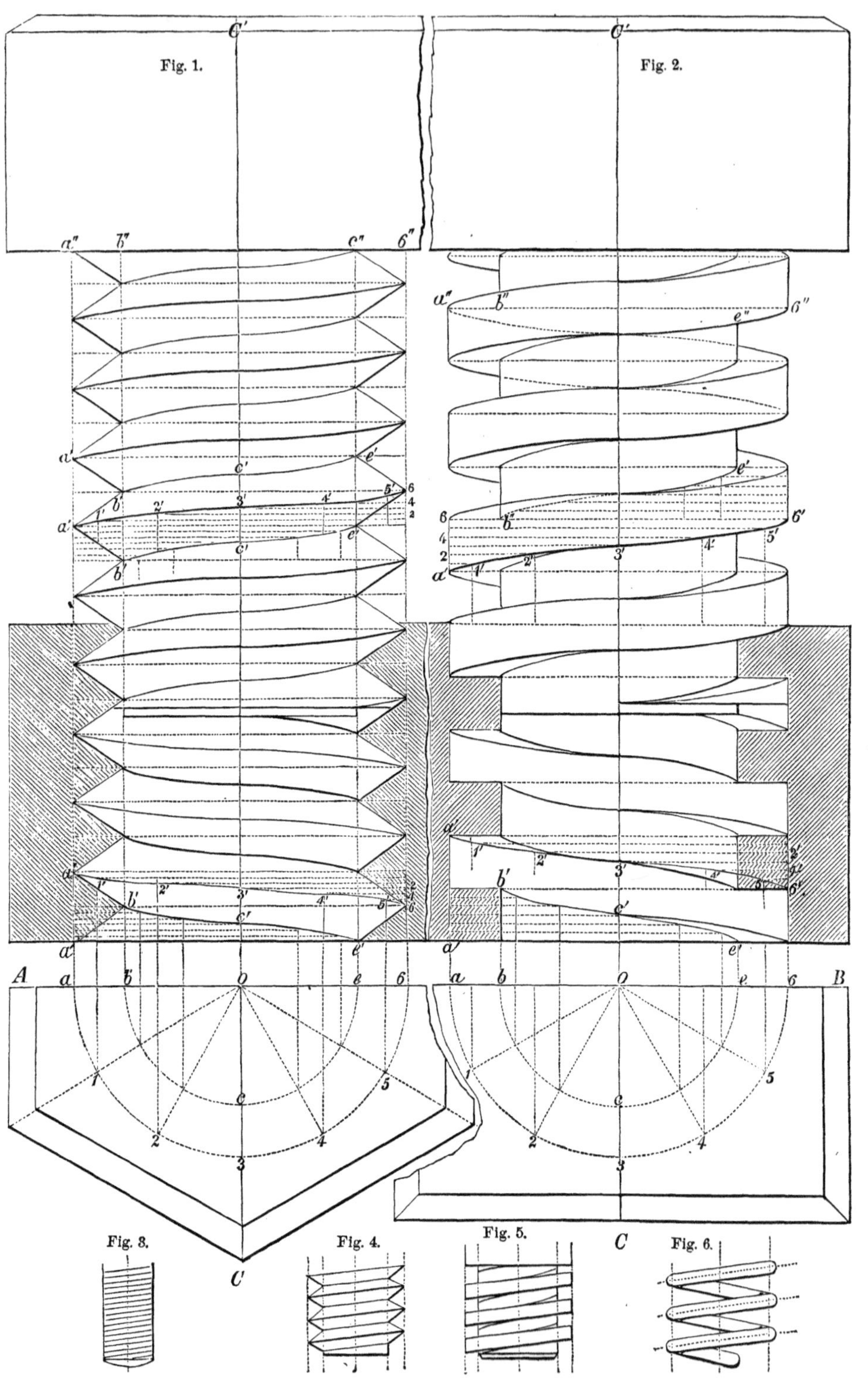

ticular example, formed in a single piece, and which can be applied only when the shaft to which it is to be attached is straight and uninterrupted by cranks, &c. The mode of representing the arm in fig. 9, which is a section on the line D F, is not strictly accurate, but is a license frequently practised in similar cases, and which is attended with obvious advantage.

In many machines, the eccentric is used for the raising of a weight a certain height and then letting it fall, as in the case of ore stampers, cloth beetles, trip hammers, and the valve rod of some steam engines. In these cases the eccentric may be considered as merely a single long tooth geer, in which commonly, on account of the uniformity of action, the *wiping* or rubbing surface is an involute curve, the boss of the eccentric being the generating circle.

In practice, the term *eccentric* is generally confined to the circular eccentric; all others, with exception of that last described, or *wypers*, being called *cams*.

DRAWING OF SCREWS.

The screw is a cylindrical piece of wood or metal, in the surface of which one or more helical grooves are formed. The *thread* of the screw is the solid portion left between the grooves; and the *pitch* of the screw is the distance, measured on a line parallel to the axis of the cylinder, between the two contiguous centres of the same thread.

Projections of a triangular-threaded screw and nut, plate XVIII., fig. 1. —Having drawn the ground line A B, and the centre lines C C′ of the figures, from O as a centre, with a radius equal to that of the exterior cylinders, describe the semicircle *a* 3 6; describe in like manner the semicircle *b c e* with the radius of the interior cylinder. Now draw the perpendiculars *a a″* and 6 6″, *b b″* and *e c″*, which will represent the vertical projections of the exterior and interior cylinders. Then divide the semicircle *a* 3 6 first described into any number of equal parts, say 6, and through each point draw radii, which will divide the interior semicircle similarly. On the line *a′ a″* set off the length of the pitch as many times as may be required; and through the points of division draw straight lines parallel to the ground line A B. Then divide each distance or pitch into twice the number of equal parts that the semicircles have been divided into, and following instructions already laid down (page 100), construct the helix *a′* 3′ 6 both in the screw and nut.

Having obtained the point *b′* by the intersection of the horizontal line passing through the middle division of *a′ a* with the perpendicular *b b″*, describe the helix b' c' e', which will represent the bottom of the groove. The apparent outlines of the screw and its nut will then be completed by drawing the lines b' a', a' b', &c., to the curves of the helices; these are not, strictly speaking, straight lines, but their deviation from the straight line is, in most instances, so small as to be imperceptible, and it is therefore unnecessary to complicate the drawing by introducing the method of determining them with rigorous exactness.

When a long series of threads have to be delineated, they should be drawn mechanically by means of a *mould* or *templet*, constructed in the following manner:—Take a small slip of thin wood or pasteboard, and draw upon it the helix a' 3′ 6 to the same scale as the drawing, and pare the slip carefully and accurately to this line. By applying this templet upon fig. 1, so that the points a' and 6 on the plate shall coincide with a' and 6 on the drawing, the curve a' 3′ 6 can be drawn mechanically, and so on for the remaining curves of the outer helix. The same templet may be employed to draw the corresponding curves in the screw-nut by simply inverting it; but for the interior helix a separate one must be cut, its outlines being laid off in the same manner.

Projections of a square-threaded screw and nut (fig. 2).—The depth of the thread is equal to its thickness, and this latter to the depth of the groove. The construction is similar to the preceding, and will be readily understood from the drawing, the same letters and figures marking relative parts. The parts of the curve concealed from view are shown in dotted lines.

It will be observed, that the heads and nuts of the screws are represented as broken, which is done for economy of space.

It is seldom necessary to delineate so exactly the outlines of screws, as they are generally drawn to a much smaller scale. Fig. 3 shows the simplest form by which a screw may be represented. Figs. 4, 5, 6, represent a triangular-threaded, a square-threaded screw, and a serpentine, in which the helical curves are replaced by straight lines, and these forms will be found sufficiently exact and graphic for most of the cases occurring in practice.

Screws may have two, three, or even a greater number of threads, according to the velocity which their action may be required to produce. *A double-threaded screw* is one in which the pitch of any individual helix includes two threads; a *three-threaded screw*, one in which it embraces three threads, and so on.

Size and proportion of bolts.—The diameter of the bolt depends, of course, on the strain to which it is to be subjected; but since the tensile strength of common bolts is reduced at least one quarter by the cutting of the thread, as a safe rule the tension ought not to exceed 4 tons on the square inch of section. It will be found economical often, where the bolt is long, to cut the thread on a larger wire, and weld the piece to a rod of the interior diameter of the screw. The section of the thread most approved of for strength and easy motion of the nut is the equilateral triangle, thus △, the bevelled sides being equal between themselves and to the base.

Diameter of bolts.	Threads in inch.	Short diameter of nut.	Diameter of bolts.	Threads in inch.	Short diameter of nut.
Inches.		Inches.	Inches.		Inches.
$\frac{1}{2}$	12	$\frac{7}{8}$	$1\frac{3}{4}$	5	$3\frac{1}{8}$
$\frac{5}{8}$	11	$1\frac{1}{16}$	$1\frac{7}{8}$	$4\frac{1}{2}$	$3\frac{3}{8}$
$\frac{3}{4}$	10	$1\frac{5}{16}$	2	$4\frac{1}{2}$	$3\frac{9}{16}$
$\frac{7}{8}$	$8\frac{3}{4}$	$1\frac{9}{16}$	$2\frac{1}{8}$	4	$3\frac{3}{4}$
1	8	$1\frac{3}{4}$	$2\frac{1}{4}$	4	4
$1\frac{1}{8}$	$7\frac{1}{2}$	2	$2\frac{3}{8}$	$3\frac{1}{2}$	$4\frac{1}{4}$
$1\frac{1}{4}$	7	$2\frac{1}{4}$	$2\frac{1}{2}$	$3\frac{1}{2}$	$4\frac{7}{16}$
$1\frac{3}{8}$	6	$2\frac{7}{16}$	$2\frac{5}{8}$	3	$4\frac{3}{4}$
$1\frac{1}{2}$	$5\frac{1}{2}$	$2\frac{11}{16}$	$2\frac{3}{4}$	3	$4\frac{15}{16}$
$1\frac{5}{8}$	5	$2\frac{7}{8}$	3	3	$5\frac{3}{8}$

The thickness of the nut should be equal to the diameter of the bolt. The head of the bolt is usually square; the nut may be of the same form, but as often is six-paned or *six square*. When the head of the bolt is in-

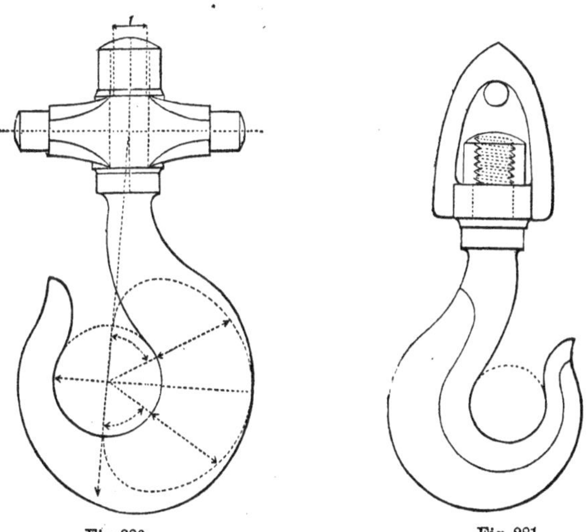

Fig. 280. Fig. 281.

tended to be *flush* or even with the surface of the piece into which the bolt is inserted, the inside of the head is made conical like the common wood-screw, or pyramidal, and it is then said to be countersunk. When bolts are employed in wood, *washers* are usually placed beneath the nut and head, to give a more extended bearing surface.

HOOKS.

Figs. 280 and 281 represent two wrought iron hooks, in which the material is distributed according to the strain to which the parts may be subjected. The following are the proportions on which fig. 280 is constructed:—Assuming the neck of the hook as the modulus or 1, the diameter of journals of the traverse are 1.1; width of traverse at centre, 2; distance from the centre of the hook to the centre of the traverse, 7.5; interior circle of the hook, 3.4; greatest thickness of the hook, 2.8. Assuming (fig. 281) the diameter of the wire of the chain as 1: interior circle of hook is 3.2, and greatest thickness of hook, 3.5.

FRAMES.

Plate XIX. represents the application of iron in the frames of tools.

Fig. 1 represents the cam-punch and shear; in this case, the force exerted whilst the machine is in the operation of punching or shearing, tends to open the jaws *a a;* and the tendency increases with the depth of the jaw, the strain obviously being the greatest at the inmost part of the jaw. The frame consists of a plate of cast iron, with two webs around its edges; the front web being subjected to a tensile strain, should be in the area of its section about six times that of the rear web which is subjected to a compressive force.

Fig. 2 is the side frame of a planing machine. The force here exerted is horizontal against the cutter, which can be raised or lowered at pleasure, according to the magnitude of the work to be planed; the upright has, therefore, to be braced, which is done in a curved form for beauty of outline.

Fig. 3 is a common jack-screw, in which the pressure is vertical; the base is made extended to give it stability.

Fig. 4 is a plan of the top plate, and fig. 5 the elevation of a hydraulic press. The top and bottom plates and platen are cast iron, the four rods are wrought iron; the strain upon the rods is tensile, and it is only necessary to give them such a size as to resist securely the power which may be required on the press. The plates are beams, supported at the four corners; subjected to a breaking strain, it will be evident that the bottom

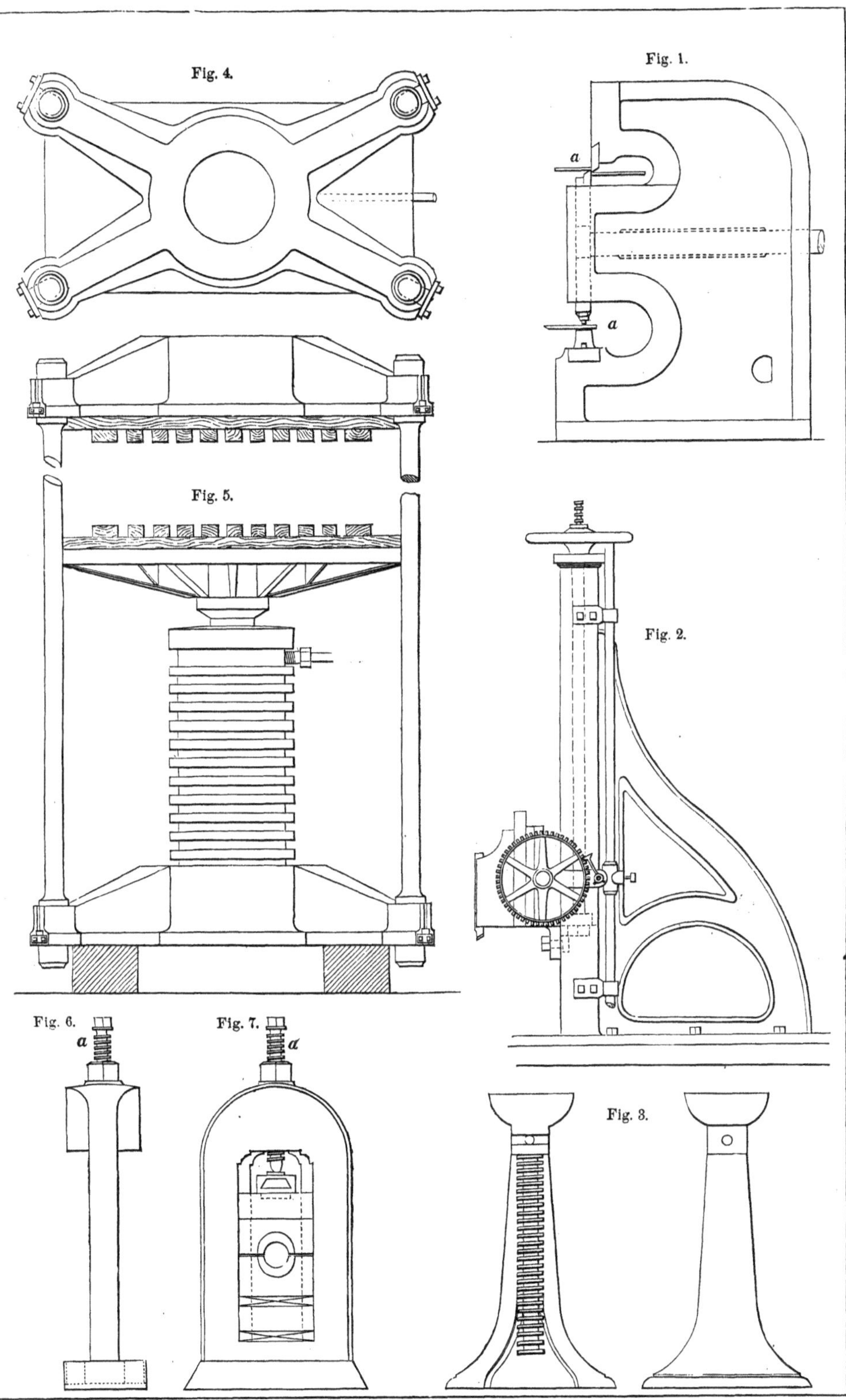
Fig. 4.
Fig. 1.
a
a
Fig. 5.
Fig. 2.
Fig. 6.
a
Fig. 7.
a'
Fig. 3.

plate is the strongest, as in this case the bottom of the plate being subjected to a tensile strain, is a flange or platen, and affords more material remote from the neutral axis than the ribs of the upper plate which are subjected to the tensile strain. The movable platen is braced by triangular wings or flanges radial from the piston. In this particular case the cylinder is cast iron hooped with wrought iron; it is very common to make the whole cylinder wrought iron.

Principle of the action of the hydrostatic press.—Let A B C D (fig. 282) epresent a vertical section of a cylindrical vessel filled with an incompressible non-elastic fluid, as water for instance; let E and F be two pistons of different magnitudes connected with the cylinder, and fitting closely their respective orifices; now, whatever pressure be exerted by the piston F on the fluid in the cylinder, it will be repeated on the piston E as many times as the area of the small piston is contained in the large piston; that is, if the area of F was 1 square inch, and the pressure exerted 10 lbs., and the piston E 100 square inches, then the pressure on E would be 10 × 100, or 1000 lbs. F corresponds to the plunger of the force-pump, E to the piston or ram of the press. The thickness of metal of the cylinder, if of cast-iron, should not be less than one-half the diameter of the ram. Adopting this as the rule, to find the entire pressure in tons which a cylinder can sustain, the diameter of the ram being given:

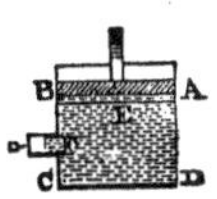

Fig. 282.

Multiply the square of the diameter in inches by 3, and the product will be the pressure in tons.

Or, the pressure in tons being given:

Divide the given pressure in tons by 3, and the square root of the quotient will be the diameter of the piston in inches. Thus, the diameter of the piston being 10 inches, the thickness of metal 5 inches, the pressure might be 10 × 10 × 3 = 300 tons.

Figs. 6 & 7 represent a *housing* for rolls. The screw *a* presses down upon the top of the box of the journal, and the effect is a tensile strain on the sides of the frame; but it must be remarked, that frames of this sort are subject to percussive and intermittent strain vastly exceeding the mere tensile strain, and proper allowance is to be made for this; and it is much better to depend in part on mass or on dead weight of material to resist such strains than upon cohesive strength merely.

Plate XX. represents the elevation of the frames of three classes of American marine engines.

Figs. 1 and 2 represent the frame-work of the *New World.* It is composed of four pieces of heavy pine timber *d d*, which are formed into two triangles, and inclined slightly laterally to each other (fig. 2); their lower ends rest on the keelsons, and upon their upper extremities are placed the pillow-block *c* of the working beam. They are solidly fastened together and to the boat by numerous horizontal and diagonal timbers, which are secured by wooden knees and keys, and are heavily bolted. The two front legs are bolted to flanges cast on the sides of the condenser, and the other end of the framing is attached to a large mass of timbers, which support the shaft pillow-block *b*. The framing is further steadied by two additional timbers, and rods running from the beam pillow-blocks outside the shaft to the keelsons of the boat; *a* represents the guides, which are bolted at the bottom to the cylinder flange, and retained in their vertical position by wrought iron braces connected with the framing. The entire fastening of the engine and its framing is so disposed as to reduce all the strains to direct ones of extension or compression on the fibres of the iron and wood employed in the construction. The height of the frame is 46 feet, width at bottom 31 feet.

Fig. 3 represents the side elevation of the frame of the side lever ocean steamer *Pacific*. In this frame the two large hollow pillow-blocks which sustain the shaft on each side of the cranks are supported by four wrought iron columns G G on the forward extremity of the bed-plate I, the centre of the shaft being 23 feet above the keelson. The pillow-blocks thus supported are connected by two strong inclined braces D to the cylinder, by means of solid facings cast with it on each side of the steam opening. The columns are connected by horizontal braces A A, composed of hollow tubes, through which bolts pass, and the frames of the two engines are connected at the same points by similar tubes, and also two diagonal horizontal braces cast together. Similar braces C C are used to connect each extremity of the pillow-blocks, and the two engine frames are connected by a horizontal wrought iron cross. To resist the tendency of the engines, in the rolling of the ship, to press the outer bearings, there are in a vertical transverse plan three wrought iron cross or diagonal braces F between the pillow-blocks and bed-plates. Four cross braces H and J connect the extremities of the cylinder and the frame. The cylinders are also connected by a horizontal tubular brace K. It will be thus seen that this frame is a system of bracing and cross-bracing, in which the material is most economically disposed to resist the various strains.

The bed-plate consists of a single casting, 32 feet long and 9 feet broad, which is securely fastened to the keelsons and ship's bottom; the diameter of the cylinder is 96 inches, and the stroke 9 feet.

Fig. 4 represents the side view of the frame of the inclined engines of

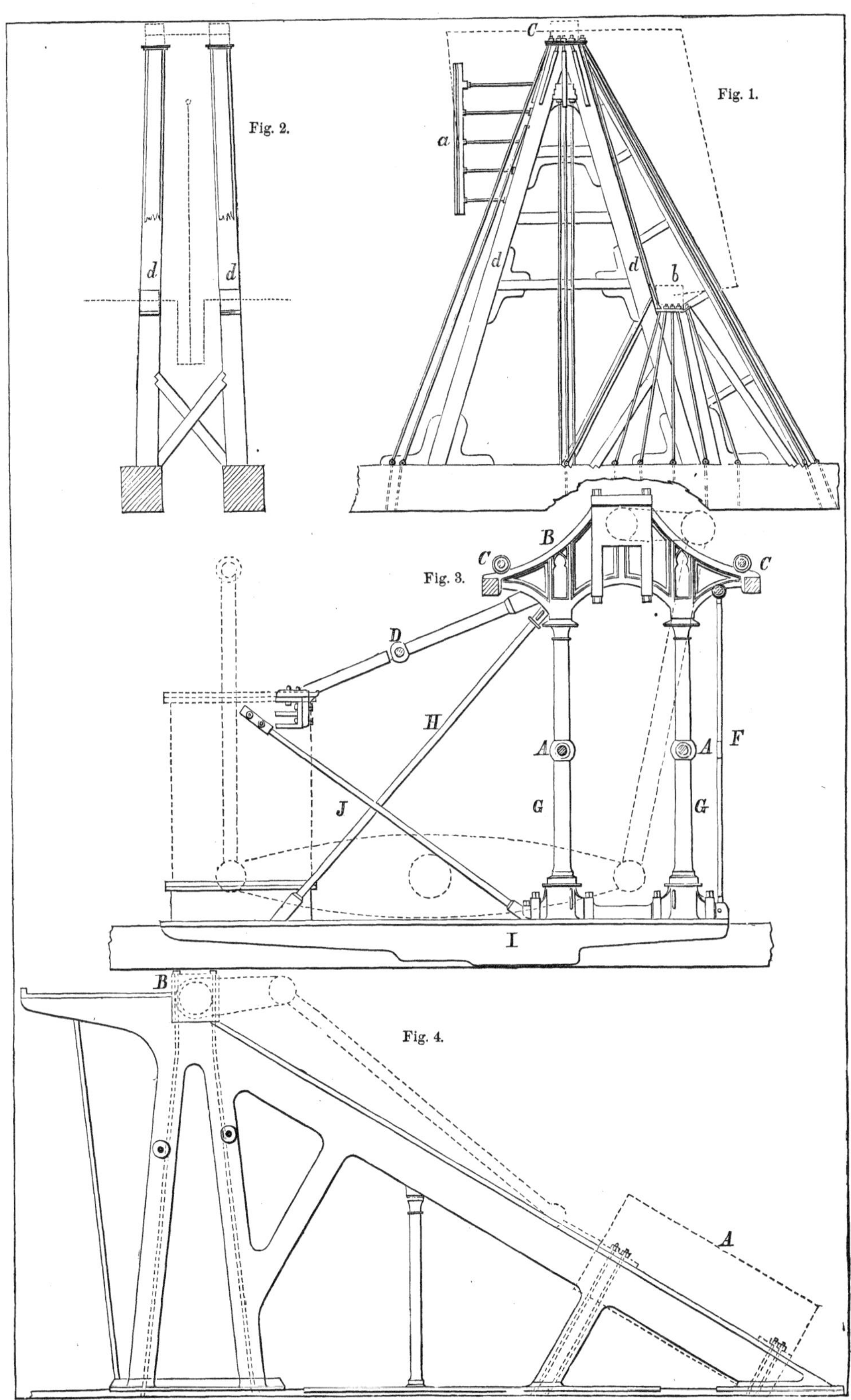
Fig. 1.
Fig. 2.
Fig. 3.
Fig. 4.
C
a
d
d
b
d
d
B
C
C
D
H
J
A
A
F
G
G
I
B
A

PLATE XXI.

Fig. 1.
A
b
C
b
b
C
b
A
Fig. 2.
a
a
a
a
Fig. 3.
B
B
Fig. 4.
Fig. 9.
Fig. 8.
Fig. 7.
a
a
Fig 6.
B
Fig. 5.
B

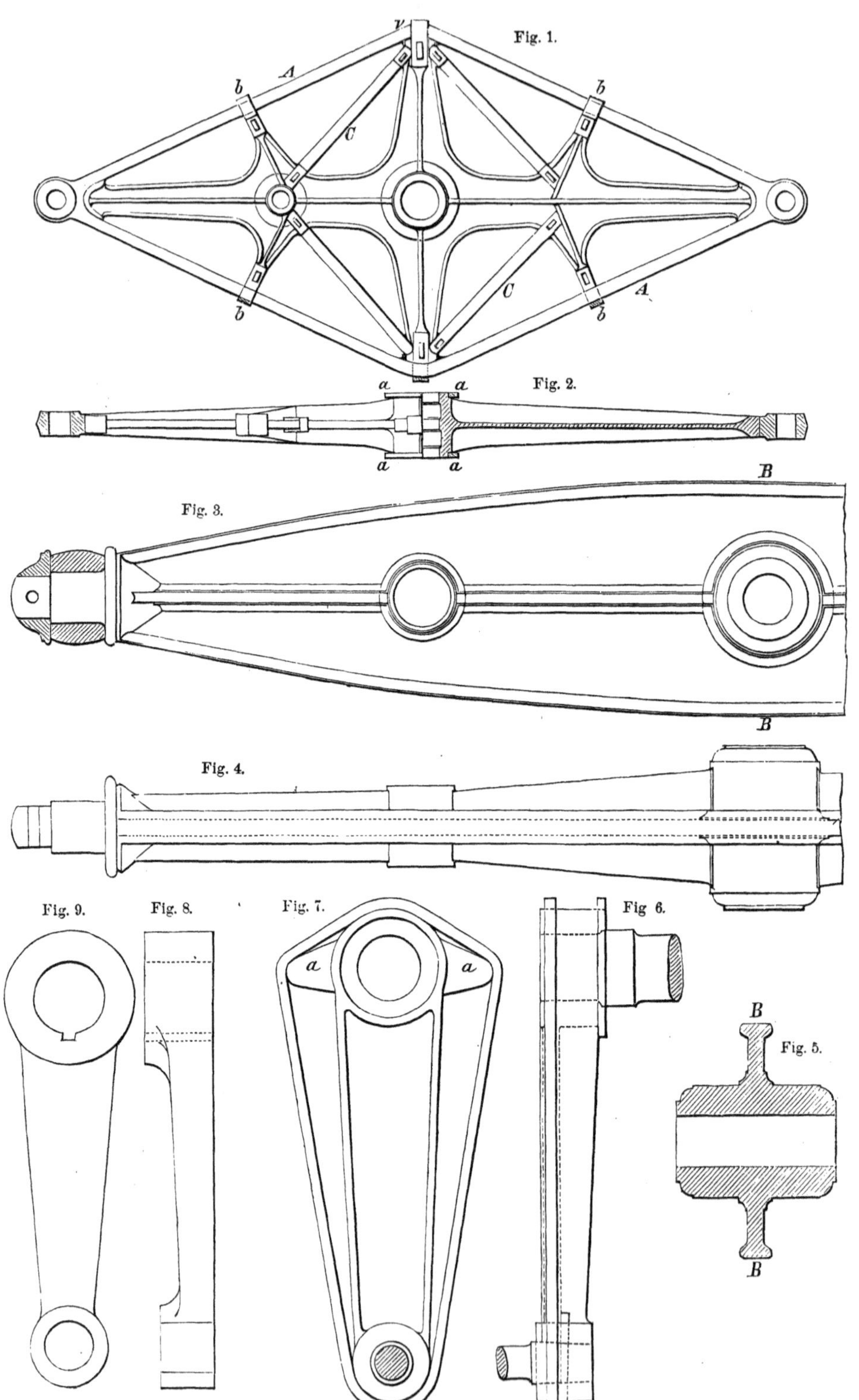

the war steamer *Susquehanna*. The cylinder A is rested between two triangular frames, on the inclination of the longest side, and is securely bolted to each frame. The two frames are connected together with braces similar to those of the *Pacific*, and the whole is securely bolted on to the keelsons and bottom of the ship. In this illustration, the main pieces of the frame are made of boiler iron, constructed like box girders; but in smaller engines, it is usual to make these parts of wood. The diameters of the cylinders are 5 feet 10 inches, the length of stroke 10 feet.

Plate XXI.—Fig. 1 represents the working-beam of the *New World*. It is composed of a skeleton frame of cast iron, round which a wrought iron strap A is fixed. This strap is forged in one piece, and its extreme ends are formed into large eyes, which are bored out to receive the end journals. The skeleton frame is a single casting, and contains the eyes for the main centre and air-pump journal; the centre hub is strengthened by wrought iron hoops *a a*, which are shrunk upon it. At the points of contact of the strap and skeleton, key-beds are prepared, into which the keys are carefully fitted and tightly driven; the keys are afterwards riveted over at both ends, which retains them in their places, as well as the strap on the skeleton frame. The strap is also secured to the frame by straps *b b* and keys. The skeleton frame is still further braced by wrought iron straps C C, which tie the middle of the long arms of the cross to the extremities of the shorter ones. This form of beam is that usually adopted for the engines of eastern American river boats; the proportions are somewhat varied, but the form is identical. The following are the dimensions of our illustration:—From centre to centre of end journals, 26 feet; this is somewhat less than the usual proportion to length of stroke, being but slightly less than double the stroke; length of centre hub, 26 inches; diameter of main centre eye, 15⅝; of eye for air-pump journal, 6¾; of end journal, 8⅛ inches.

Fig. 3 represents a side elevation; fig. 4, a plan; and fig. 5 a section of a cast iron working beam of an English stationary engine. It will be perceived that the outline of the beam is a parabola, it being in effect a beam supported at the centre and loaded at the extremities.

From the following table of practical examples from "Architecture of Machinery," we would assume as a safe rule for land engines, that the depth at centre should be the diameter of the cylinder, and the length of beam three times the length of stroke. Hence we can construct the outline, having for the vertex the extremity of the beam and the point B in the curve at the centre. The sectional area may be estimated from rules already given, knowing the load at the extremity, that is; the pressure on the piston, the weight of the same and its connections, and also the force required to drive the air-pump, estimated at the extremity of the lever. As an engine is subject to shocks, the load should be estimated as six times the absolute load. "Five per cent. of the nominal power of the engine may be considered the maximum of power required to drive the air-pump."—*Ed. Tredgold.*

Diameter of cylinder.	Length of stroke.	Description of work.	Length of beam from centre.	Depth at centre.	Sectional area.
inches.	ft. in.		ft. in.	inches.	square inches.
47⅞	8	Rolling,	12 4	48	240
40¾	7	Pumping,	10 4	36	162
39½	6 9	Blowing,	9 6	38½	96¼
36⅝	6 8	Rolling,	9 3	30	60
24¾	5	Mill work,	8	25	50
18½	4	"	6 10	22¼	50
42	4	Marine,	6 3	23	138
42	4 2	"	6 6	27	216
32	3	"	5	22	132

Figs. 6 and 7 represent a side and a front elevation of a crank, such as is usually adopted on the engines of American river boats. The main body of the crank is of cast iron, with two horns *a a* projecting from the central hub, and the whole is bound with a strap of wrought iron. It is evident that this form of crank gives the greatest amount of strength with the least material, and belongs to the same class of construction as the working beam (fig. 1). The eye of the crank is usually made one-fourth the diameter of the cylinder. The table from Redtenbacher here inserted gives the relative sizes of central and end eyes of cranks, depending on the proportion between the length of crank and the diameter of central eye. The first column exhibits the number of times the diameter of eye is contained in the length of crank; the other columns exhibit the diameter of crank-pin.

DIAMETER OF EYE, BEING UNITS.		
	For wrought iron shaft.	Cast iron shafts.
2	0.85	0.62
3	0.69	0.51
4	0.60	0.44
5	0.54	0.39
6	0.49	0.36
7	0.45	0.33
8	0.42	0.31
9	0.40	0.29
10	0.38	0.28
11	0.36	0.26
12	0.34	0.25
13	0.33	0.24

From this table may be determined for any crank the diameter of either eye, one being known, and the length of the crank.

Figs. 8, 9, a side view and front elevation of a wrought iron crank and their practical proportions; the eye for the crank-pin is a slightly conical hole, and the pin is made of a corresponding taper.

Plate XXII. represents steam-engine connecting-rods and their details.

Figs. 1, 2, represent the front and side elevation of a cast iron connect-

PLATE XXII.

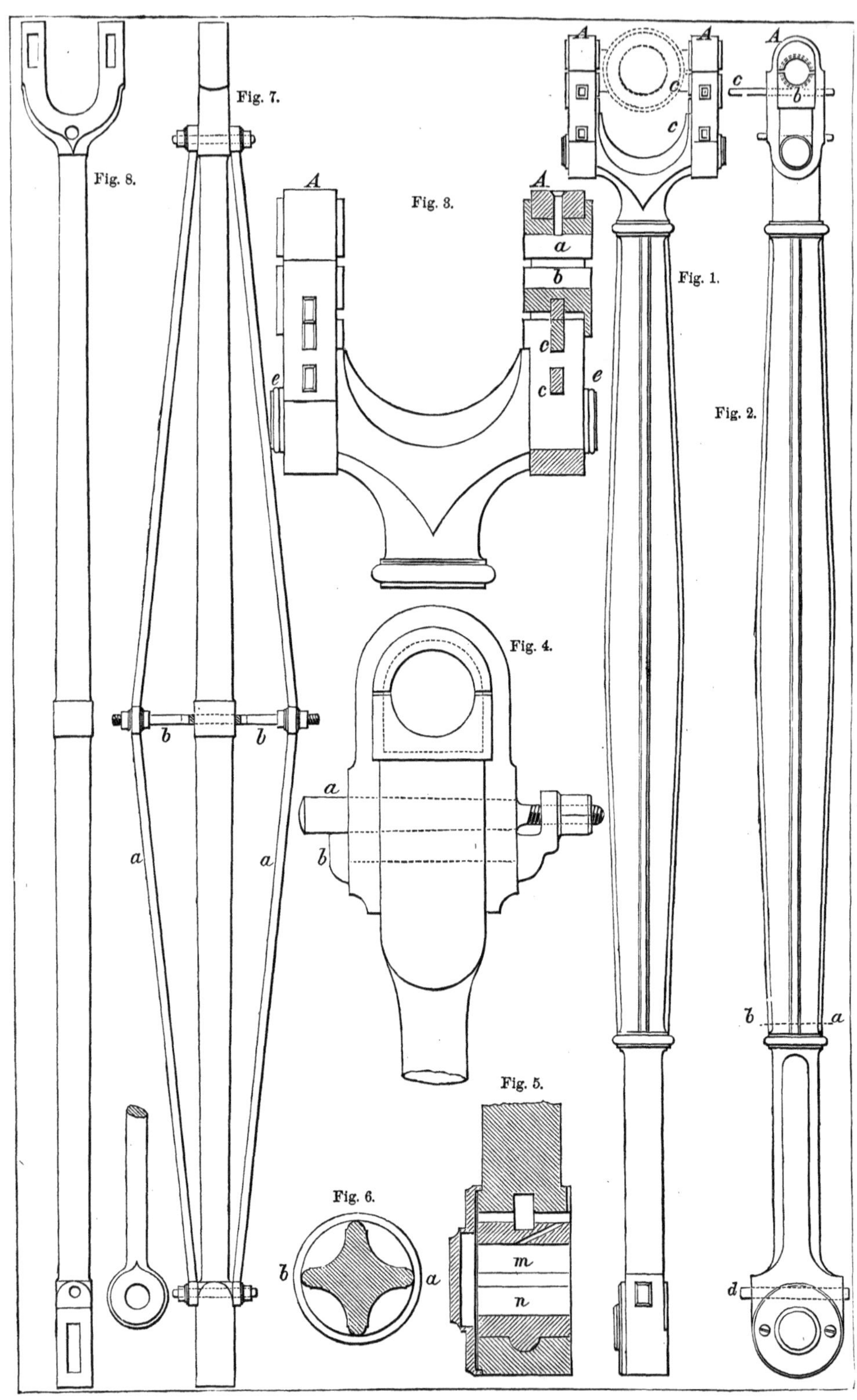

ing-rod. It is a bar, strengthened throughout the greater part of its length by four ribs or feathers, whose outlines in the direction of their length are parabolic curves. Its upper extremity is formed into two projecting arms, upon each of which a close wrought iron strap A is fixed by means of a key or cotter *c*. These straps are provided and formed for the reception of the brass bushes *a* and *b*, which are accurately fitted to the journals or bearings of the cross head.

The lower end of the connecting-rod is made of a form suitable for the reception of the brasses, and other adjusting mechanism necessary for the purpose of acting freely, but without play, upon the pin of the crank. In the present example, the end of the crank-pin is concealed by a slight brass cover or disc, fixed to the connecting-rod by two small, screw pins, which serves to protect the working surfaces from dust, and imparts an elegant finish to the whole.

In fig. 3 the ends of the connecting-rod are represented upon a scale of double the magnitude of the preceding figures. One of the upper links or straps, with its adjusting apparatus, is supposed to be cut by a vertical plane passing through the axes, so as to expose the interior arrangement. This section exhibits distinctly the mode of fixing the links upon the arms of the connecting-rod by means of the cotters *c*, *c*, and projecting discs *e*, *e*, cast upon the arms; as also the contrivance for retaining the brasses *a* and *b* in their places. Fig. 5, which is a vertical section, shows the corresponding provisions for the lower end of the rod; a small oblique hole for the introduction of oil will be observed in the upper brass *n*, while the lower *m* is formed with a spherical projection entering a concave recess in the cast iron, for the purpose of preventing its displacement by the friction of the crank-pin, which is regulated and adjusted by the cotter *d*.

Fig. 6 is a horizontal section on the line *a b*, showing the form of the body and feathers of the rod.

Fig. 4 represents the end of a connecting-rod, in which the arrangement for tightening the brasses consists of a gib *b* and cotter *a*. The small end of the cotter is made with a screw, which passing through a lug on the gib, is fitted with a nut, by means of which the cotter is adjusted and retained in any position required.

Figs. 7 and 8 represent the side and front elevation of a wrought iron connecting-rod, such as are generally used on American river boat engines. The extremities are fitted with brasses, straps, gibs, and cotters, similar to those already described. The peculiarity over the general English construction is the economy of material, and the means adopted to give the required stiffness. It consists of a double truss brace *a a* of round iron, which is fastened by bolts to the rod near each end; struts *b b*, cut with a screw, and furnished with nuts pass through the centre of the brace, by which means the braces are tightened.

The length of connecting-rods, as recommended by English mechanics, is three times that of the stroke; in this country shorter connecting-rods are used, twice the length of stroke being not an unusual proportion. The connecting-rod at its smallest part near the extremities is of the same diameter as the piston-rod; the boss in the centre is from 1 to 2 inches more.

ON THE LOCATION OF MACHINES.

In the arrangement of a manufactory or workshop, it is of the utmost importance to know how to place the machinery, both as to economy of space and also of working. Where a new building is to be constructed for a specific purpose of manufacture, it will be found the best to arrange the necessary machines as they should be, and then build the edifice to suit them. For defining the position of a machine, we merely need in outline the space it occupies in plan and elevation, and the position of the driven pulley or geer, and of the operative. To illustrate this subject, we have selected a two-story weaving room, of which fig. 283 is an elevation and plate XXIII. a plan.

In this example the building is rectangular, of a width and length to accommodate the required machinery. The illustration is confined to a few rooms in one angle, the rest being but a repeat of the same. The timbering and planking are the same as adopted at all our large manufacturing places. Beams 14 to 16 inches deep, and of little less width, placed from 8 to 9 feet apart from centre to centre, and floored with 3 to 4 inch plank dowelled or matched, with top floors and bottom sheathing. The form of construction being fixed, and the size of the building being determined for the number of looms, knowing the space they require for the machines and the alley ways; lay down the outlines of the building, and dot in, or draw in red or blue, the position and width of beams. This last is of importance, as it will be observed (fig. 283), that no driving-pulley can come beneath the beam, and also that this is the position for the hanger. Lay off now the width of the alleys and of the machines. The first alley, or nearest the wall, is a back alley; that is, where the operative does not stand, and so on alternate alleys. Draw the lines of shafting central to the alleys, as in this position the belts are least in the way. One operative usually tends four looms; they are therefore generally arranged in sets of four, two on each side of the alley, being placed as close to each other as possible, say one inch between the lathes, a small cross alley being left between them and the next set. Lay off now the required alley at the end of the room, and space off the length of two rows of looms with alleys at the end of alternate looms, and mark the position of the pulleys. It

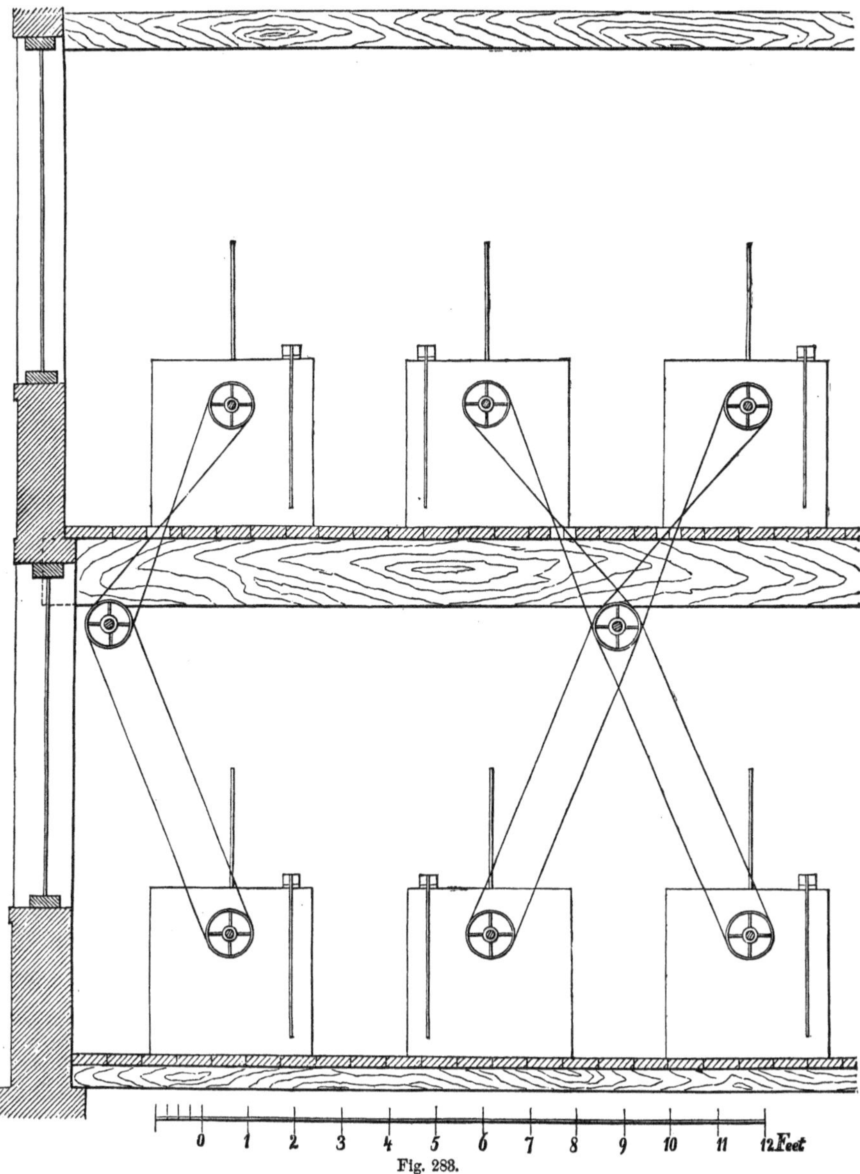

Fig. 288.

will be observed that looms are generally rights and lefts, so that the pulleys of both looms come in the space where there is no alley. Should the pulley come beneath a beam, the loom must be either moved to avoid it, or the pulley may be shifted to the opposite end of the loom. Parallel with the pulleys on the looms draw the driving-pulleys on the shafts, that is, *k* parallel with *k*, *b* with *b*, *f* with *f*, and so on. Proceed now to draw the third and fourth row of looms, since the second and third rows are driven from the same shaft; if they are placed on the same line, it will be impossible to drive both from the same end, and as this is important, we move the third row the width of the pulley *b*, and for the sake of uniformity, the fourth row also. Lay off now the length of looms and position of pulleys as before, and parallel with the pulleys the driving-pulleys on the shaft, that is *c* against *c*, *f* against *f*, and so on. Having in this way plotted in all the looms, every alternate set being on a line with the third and fourth row, we proceed now to lay down the position of the looms in the floor above; and since for economy of shafting it is usual to drive from the lines in the lower rooms, to avoid errors, interference of belts and pulleys, it is usual to plot the upper room on the same paper or board as the lower room, using either two different colored inks, or drawing the machines in one room in deep and in the other in light line, as shown in plate XXIV. If the width of the rooms are the same, the lateral lines of looms and alleys are the same, and it is only necessary, therefore, to fix the end lines. Now, as the first loom in the outer row of looms, in the lower room, occupies for its belt the position *k* on the shaft, the loom in the upper room must be moved either one way or the other to avoid this; thus the position *i* of the pulley on the loom must be made parallel to the pulley *i* on the shaft, so in the other looms *a* to *a*, *e* to *e*, *d* to *d*, and *b* to *b*.

Besides the plan, it is often necessary, and always conveniet, to draw a sectional elevation (as in fig. 283), of the rooms, with the relative positions of the driving pulleys and those on the machines, to determine suitably the length of the belts, and also to see that their position is in every way the most convenient possible. For instance, in the figure, one of the lower belts should have been a cross belt, and one of the upper ones straight: now had the belts to the second row of looms in the upper story, been drawn as they should have been, straight, the belt would have interfered a little with the alley, and it would have been better to have moved the driving shaft a trifle towards the wall.

From this illustration of the location of machines, knowing all the requirements, in a similar way any machinery may be arranged with economy of spaces, materials, power, and attendance. These two last items are of the more importance as they involve a daily expense, where the others are almost entirely the first outlay.

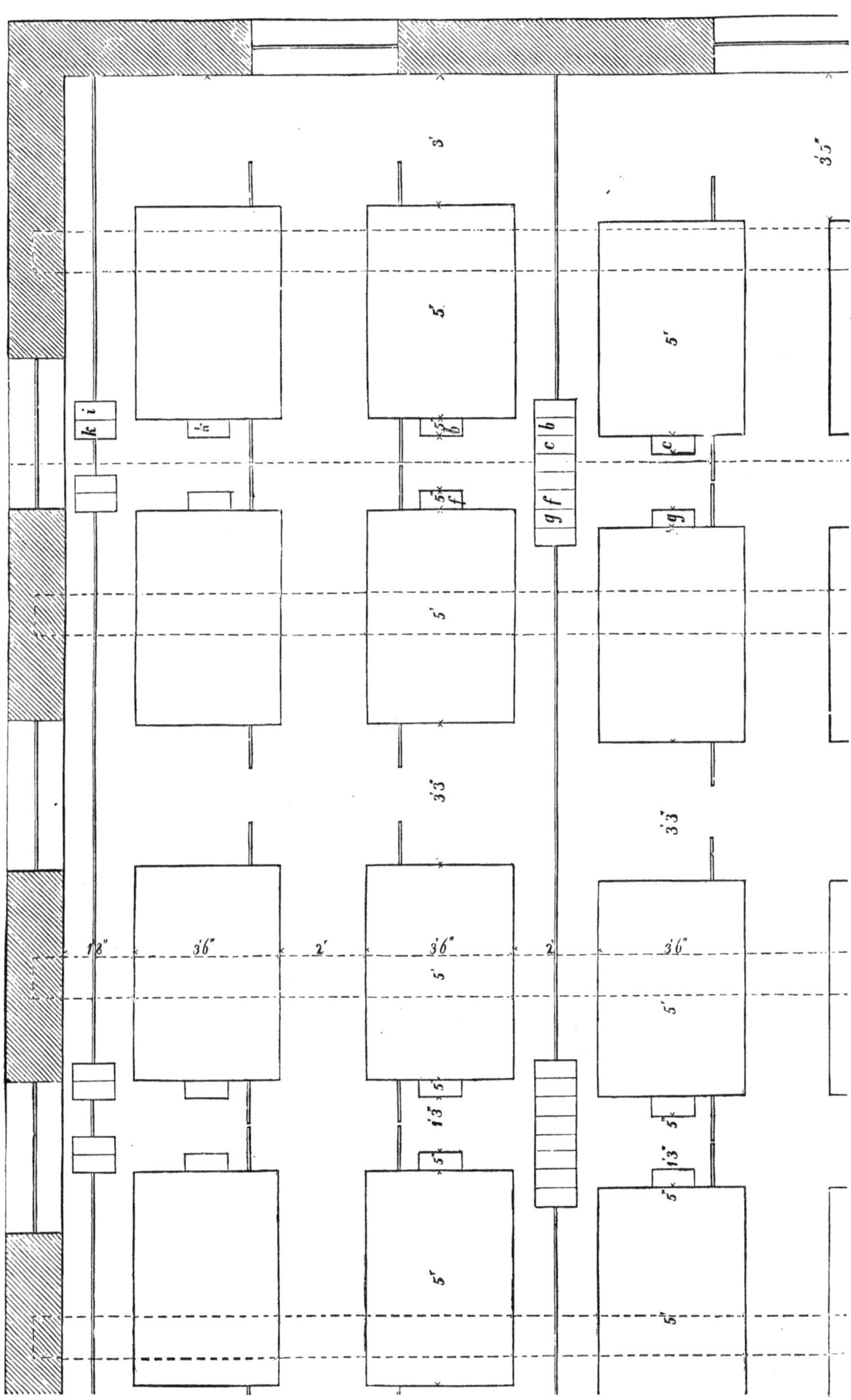
1'8"
3'6"
2'
5'
3'3"
1'3"

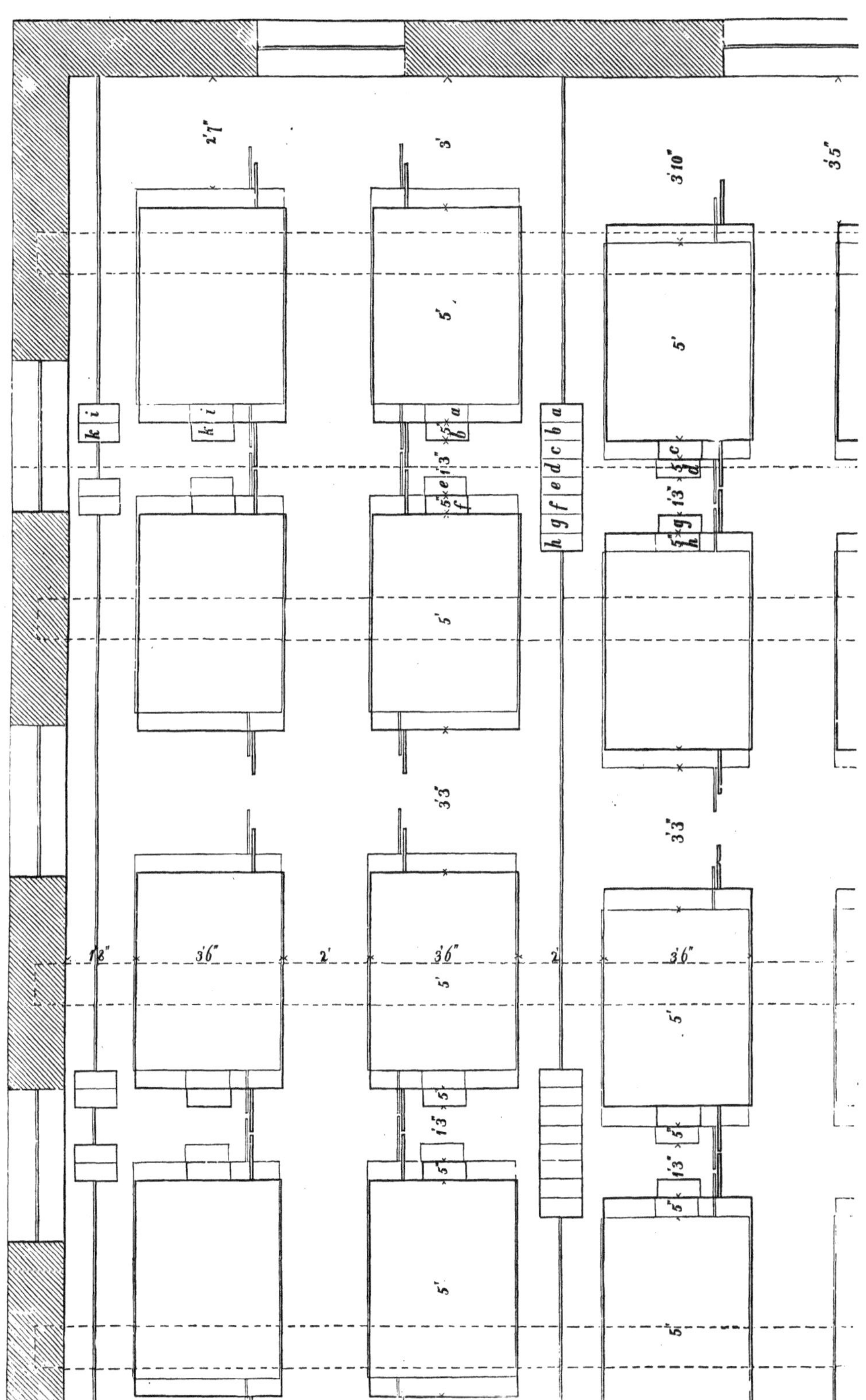
2'7"
3'
3'10"
3'5"
5'
k i
a b c d e f g h
13"
3'3"
3'6"
2'
1'8"

MACHINES.

Hitherto we have confined ourselves to geometrical projections, and to the delineation of parts of machines, we now proceed to give representations of complete machines, taken from actual constructions, together with a full description of their working, so that they may be not only copies for the mere draughtsman, but also examples to aid the engineer. Working Drawings are drawings in detail of the parts of a machine, generally in mere outline, or with but sufficient of shade to distinguish circular from flat parts. The drawings already given of parts of machines may be taken as illustrations of working drawings, but on a much smaller scale than in actual practice, it being usual to make them as near full size as possible with the dimensions written in, as many views of the parts in plan, elevation and section are given as may fully explain the construction.

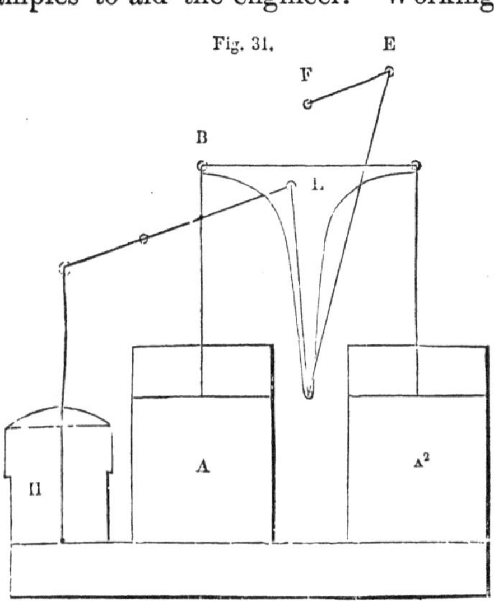

Fig. 31.

The working of a machine may often be illustrated by a very few lines —or a skeleton drawing, of which fig. 284 may be taken as an example, which represents the side elevation of Maudsley and Field's direct action double cylinder marine engine, A and A^2 being the cylinders, L the T plate connecting the two pistons, E the crank, F the wheel shaft, and H the air pump. Fig. 285 is the same engine with the cylinders, T plate and frame in outline, and the beams and connecting-rods in skeleton.

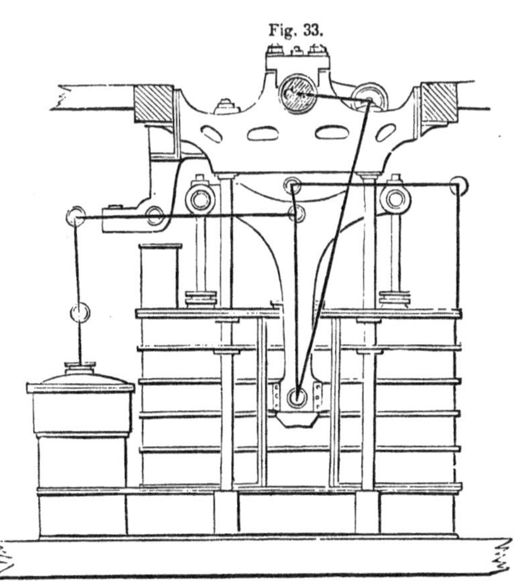
Fig. 33.

Plate XXV. fig. 1, is a sectional elevation through the centre of the cylinder of a Cornish Engine. Fig. 2 is a front elevation showing the valve geer.

A is the cylinder, enclosed in a jacket or casing of cast-iron, of such a diameter as to leave a clear space of one inch all around between it and the outside of the cylinder. This space communicates with the boilers by a pipe *a;* the boilers being so placed that the water line is at a lower level than the bottom of the cylinder, the water produced by condensation in the jacket finds its way back again to the boilers. The space *d*, under the bottom of the cylinder is kept constantly filled with steam by a branch from the pipe *a*.

In order to prevent radiation from the outside of the steam case, the whole is surrounded with an outer covering of wood (shown by dotted lines *b*,) leaving an interstice between the wood and the iron. This space is filled with some bad conductor of heat. The cylinder cover is fitted with a false lid or cap *c*, enclosing a thick layer of sawdust or other bad conductor, over the whole of the metal of the cover.

The stuffing box on the cylinder cover, through which the piston rod passes, is of peculiar construction. In the middle of the packing, and dividing it into two horizontal layers, a small chamber is formed by two brass rings *c c*, kept apart by small distance pieces. Into this chamber steam is admitted by a small pipe from the jacket of the cylinder, the object of the arrangement being to prevent any leakage of *air into* the cylinder.

C is the plug rod for working the valves and cataract. The plug rod is sometimes single and sometimes double, the latter in this instance. The two rods marked C 2, and C 3, 4, fig. 2, are connected at their upper extremity by joints with the back links of the parallel motion, and work through guides *i i*. The rod C 3, 4, is lengthened at its lower extremity for the purpose of working the lever of the cataract.

D is the top nozzle, shown on a larger scale and more fully figs. 3, 4, Plate XXVI. It contains three valves, viz. First; V^1, the *governor* or *regulating* valve, for regulating the admission of steam into the chamber *k k* of the nozzle. The motion of the governor valve is commanded by a handle placed within reach of the engine-man, and connected by a rod *f* and lever *g*, with the stalk of the valve. The rod has a micrometer screw on its upper end, which works into a united socket attached to the end of the lever *g*, and thereby raises or lowers the valve. Second; V^2, the *steam valve*, for admitting steam into the cylinder. When this valve is raised (the governor valve being supposed open also), the steam finds a passage through it, from the nozzle chamber *k k*, into the space *l*, and

PLATE XXV.

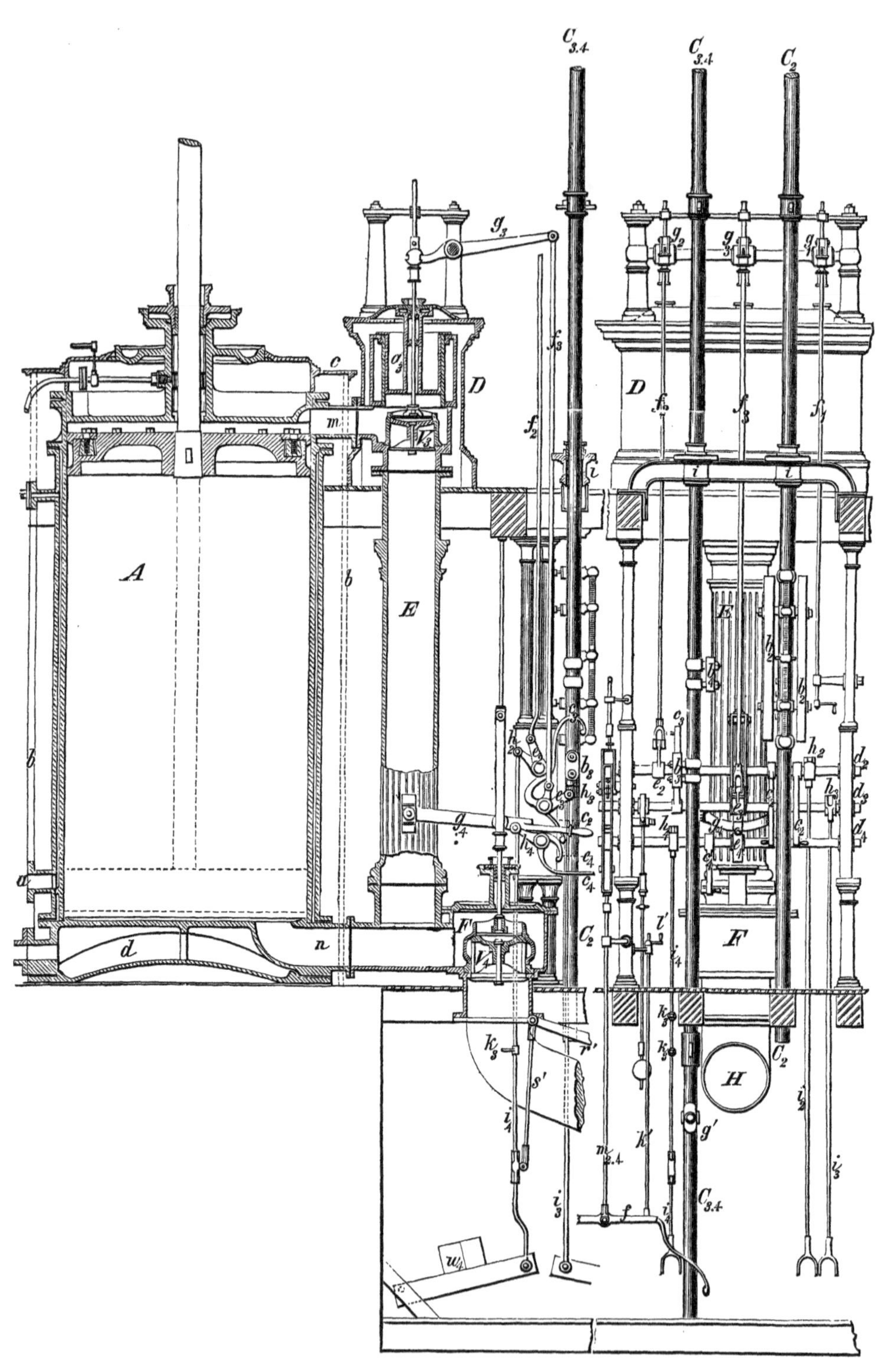

PLATE XXVI.

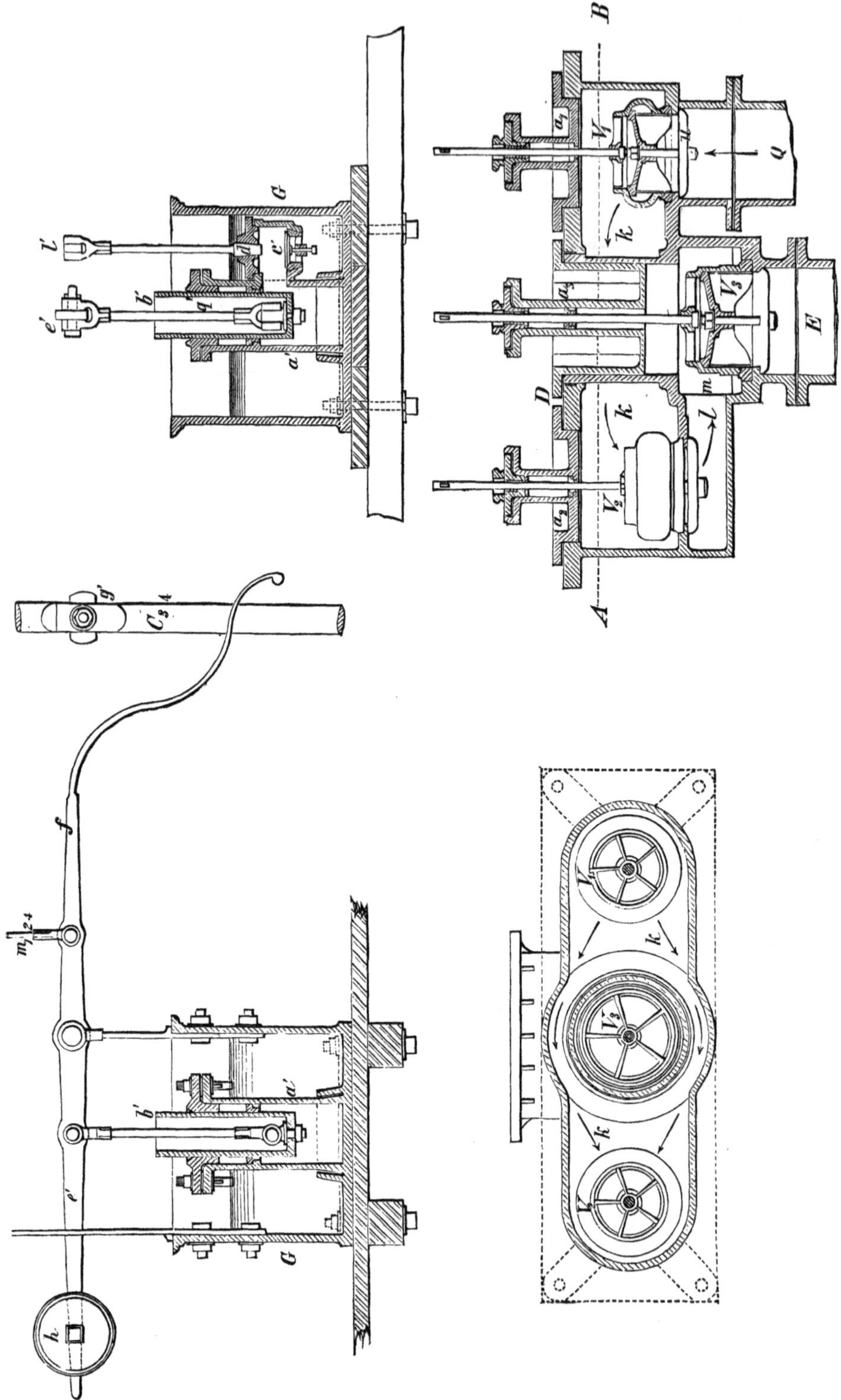

thence by the upper steam port *m* into the upper part of the cylinder; the piston therefore descends, and the engine commences its in-door stroke.

Third; V^3, situated in the middle of the nozzle, is the *equilibrium valve*. When this valve is opened the steam above the piston finds its way by the *equilibrium* pipe E, and the lower port *n*, into the lower part of the cylinder, until an *equilibrium* is restored between the pressures above and beneath the piston, which is then drawn upwards by the preponderating weight of the rods hung at the outer end of the beam. The top nozzle is, like the cylinder jacket, enveloped in an external casing.

F is the bottom nozzle; it contains V^4, the exhaustion valve, for opening or closing the communication between the lower part of the cylinder and the condenser. The nozzle chamber above the valve communicates with the cylinder by the lower port *n*, while to the *bottom* of the nozzle, under the valve, is attached the eduction pipe H. The four valves are double-beat valves, so called from their having two beating faces.

G is the cataract, fully shown in two sections, figs. 1, 2, Plate XXVI., the use of which is to regulate the period of opening the steam and exhaustion valves. It consists of a barrel in which works a plunger, being in fact simply a small plunger forcing pump. The *inlet* is by a valve *c'* opening freely upwards, but the *outlet* is contracted at pleasure by a moveable plug *d'*. The pump is placed in a cistern of water G, and the plunger is attached by a joint to the arm *e'* of the lever *e' f*. When the plug rod $C_{3\cdot4}$, has descended nearly to the bottom of its stroke, a tappet *g'* upon the lower part of it strikes the end of the lever and thus raises the plunger, the water entering freely through the valve *c'*. When the stroke is finished, and the plug rod begins to ascend, the tappet *g'* quits the lever, and the weight *h'*, which is fixed upon the arm *e'*, and has been raised by the preceding motion, becomes in its turn the motive power, tending to expel the water from the pump, by forcing the plunger down. But the inlet valve before *c'*, is closed, and the only exit for the water is by the aperture left round the regulating plug *d'*. It is evident therefore that the interval between the time the tappet *g'* leaves the cataract lever, and the commencement of the next stroke, depends upon the time occupied by the descent of the cataract plunger, and ultimately upon the degree of opening given to the regulating plug *d*. This can be adjusted with great nicety by means of a micrometer screw and handle *i* (fig. 1 Plate XXV.,) connected with the regulating plug by the rod *t* and lever *l*.

The parts of the cataract being all circular, the two sections given at right angles to each other, are all that are necessary to complete its construction, and in this respect, therefore, are sufficient working drawings.

Plate XXVII. fig. 1, is a longitudinal section of a locomotive boiler, and fig. 2 an interior view of the smoke box.

The steam space C at the fire end of the boiler is half globe shaped, and surmounted by a dome. The object of the dome is to carry the steam as high as possible above the water line before its introduction into the steam pipe *p*, in order that the water held in suspension near the surface of the water, may not be carried over into the cylinders. The steam pipe traverses the length of the boiler, and in the smoke box branches off to each cylinder; *l* is the regulating or throttle valve, worked by the handle which passes out through a stuffing box in the end of the boiler; *j* is the fire box, surrounded on all sides except at bottom with a water space; the top or crown sheet of the fire box is strengthened by pieces of iron, and the flat sides are securely bolted together. The tube sheet is sufficiently stayed by the tubes themselves; this sheet is often made of copper, as are the side sheets, from 6 to 7 inches below, to about the same height above the coal line, in locomotive boilers burning anthracite or bituminous coal; *q q* are the fire tubes varying in different boilers from $1\frac{1}{4}$ to 3 inches in diameter and from 7 to 14 feet in length; the longer the tube the larger the diameter. H H are the cylinders, *x x* the steam chests; *u u* the exhaust pipes, which are connected together, and pass up into the centre of the smoke stack or chimney. The exhaust furnishes by its blast draught to the chimney, and if the outlet be contracted, the greater the force of the issuing steam, and the stronger the draught; but of course the greater the back pressure in the cylinders.

Plate XXVIII. is the front elevation, and Plate XXIX. is the side elevation and section through air-pump of one of the oscillating engines of the Golden Gate, in which *a* is the main shaft, *b* crank-pin, *c* cylinder, *d* trunnions on which the cylinder oscillates to accommodate itself to the motion of the crank. *e*, stuffing-box on the cylinder head. This is made as long as practicable, to give as much bearing as possible for oscillating the cylinder. *f f*, belt-passage connecting the trunnion with *g g*, side pipe. *h h*, valve-stems connecting with the balance puppet-valves, in *i i* valve-chests. The lower valve on the right or steam side is concealed by *j*, air-pump. The air-pump bucket is provided with India-rubber valves, and is worked by *k*, crank on the intermediate shaft. *l l*, condenser. There are two condensers and two air-pumps, they are located between the cylinders and inclined towards each other, one only being represented.

The passage *f f*, together with the side pipes, valve-chests, and appurtenances, are fixed to the cylinder, and oscillate with it, the steam being received through one trunnion, and allowed to escape to the condenser

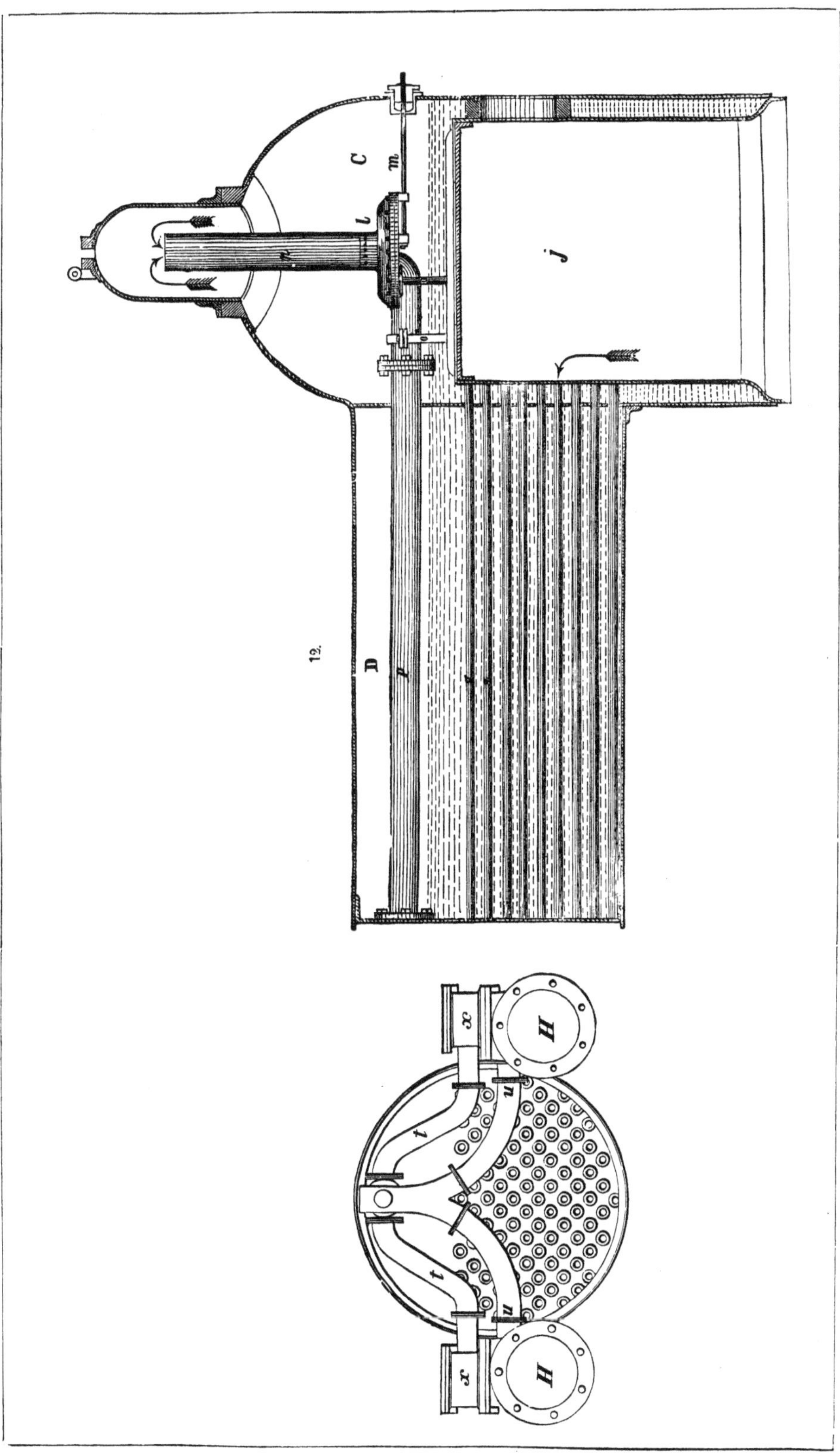
12.
C
m
l
n
j
D
p
t
t
u
u
x
x
H
H

through the opposite one. *m* is an injection cock, admitting the water upon a scattering plate in the condenser.

The valves are worked by the toes *o o* in the usual manner. The rock-shafts *p p* receive motion partly from the movement of the cylinder, and partly from the eccentric. Levers are permanently attached to the trip-shafts *q q*, the ends of which work in a slotted piece curved to the centre of the trunnion. This piece is guided, as represented in the engraving, by vertical rods sliding in bushes attached to the fixed framing, and is connected by a rod to the starting-lever *r*; all the levers for working by hand being so balanced, that the engineer with one hand can work the engine up to the usual speed.

The cut-off valve is placed outside the trunnion, and is a balance puppet-valve, worked by the ordinary cam motion, and so arranged as to act either as cut-off or throttle, or both, the levers being placed within reach of the engineer when working the engine.

Plate XXX. is a vertical section through the centre of a TURBINE WHEEL, and the axis of the supply pipe.* Plate XXXI. is a plan of the Turbine and wheelpit. Fig. 1, Plate XXXII., is a plan of the whole wheel, the guides and garniture. This Turbine was constructed for the Tremont Manufacturing. Co. at Lowell, by Mr. James B. Francis, and contains most of Mr. Boyden's improvements. Its expenditure of water under 13 feet head and fall, is about 139 cubic feet per second, and its ratio of useful effect to the power expended, about 79 per cent.

B, the surface of the water in the wheelpit, represented at the lowest height at which the turbine is intended to operate. C, the masonry of the wheelpit. D, the floor of the wheelpit. To resist the great upward pressure which takes place when the wheelpit is kept dry by pumps, three cast-iron beams are placed across the pit, the ends extending about a foot under the walls on each side; on these are laid thick planks, which are firmly secured to the cast-iron beams by bolts. To protect the thick planking from being worn out by the constant action of the water, they are covered with a flooring of one inch boards. E, the wrought-iron supply pipe. This is constructed of plate iron three-eighths of an inch thick, riveted together. The supply pipe is furnished with the man hole and ventilating pipe G, and the leak box H, to catch the leakage of the head gate, whenever it is closed for repairs of the wheel.

The lower end of the supply pipe is formed by the cast-iron curbs I I I. The curbs are supported from the wheelpit floor by four columns, resting

* By permission of the author we take the following plates and description from the standard work, "Lowell Hydraulic Experiments."

on the cast-iron beam, O; the beams N′, rest immediately upon the columns, and the curb upon the beams, the latter projecting over the columns far enough for that purpose. The beams N′ also act as braces from the wheelpit wall to the curb, and are strongly bolted at each end.

K, the disc. This is of cast-iron, and is turned smooth on the upper surface, and also on its circumference. It is suspended from the upper curb I, by means of the disc pipes M M. The disc carries on its upper surface, thirty-three guides (fig. 1, Plate XXXII.), for the purpose of giving the water entering the wheel, proper directions. They are made of Russian plate iron, one-tenth of an inch in thickness, secured to the disc by tenons, riveted on the under side. The upper corners of the guides, near the wheel, are connected by the garniture L, which is intended to diminish the contraction of the streams entering the wheel, when the regulating gate is fully raised. The garniture is composed of thirty-three pieces of cast-iron, carefully fitted to fill the spaces between the guides; they are strongly riveted to the guides and to each other.

The upper flange of the disc pipe is furnished with adjusting screws, by which the weight is supported upon the upper curb. The escape of water between the upper curb and the upper flange of the disc pipe, is prevented by a band of leather on the outside, which is retained in its place by the wrought-iron ring P. The top of the disc pipe, just below the upper flange, has two wings, fitting into recesses in the top of the curb, to prevent the disc from rotating in the opposite direction to the wheel.

R, R, the regulating gate. Represented, Plate XXX., as fully raised. The gate is of cast-iron; the upper part of the cylinder is stiffened by a rib, to which are attached three brackets, S, S. To these brackets are attached wrought-iron rods, by which the gate is raised or lowered. To one of the rods is attached the rack V. The other two rods are attached by means of links, to the levers T T. The other ends of these levers carry geered arch heads, into which, and into the rack V, work three pinions, W, of equal pitch and size, fastened to the same shaft, so arranged that by the revolution of the pinion shaft, the gate is moved up or down, equally on all sides. The shaft on which the pinions are fastened, is driven by the worm wheel X; this is driven by the worm *a*, either by the governor Y, or the hand wheel Z. The shaft on which the worm *a* is fastened, is furnished with movable couplings, which, when the speed gate is at any intermediate points between its highest aud lowest positions, are retained in place by spiral springs; in either of the extreme positions, the couplings are separated by means of a lever moved by pins in the rack V; by this means, both the regulator and hand wheel are prevented from moving the gate in one direction, when the gate has attained either extreme position. If, however, the regulator or hand wheel should be moved in the opposite direction, the couplings would catch, and the gate would be moved. The weight of the gate is counterbalanced by weights attached to the levers T T, and by the intervention of a lever to the rack V.

b b, the wheel, consists of a central plate of cast-iron, and two crowns, *c c*, of the same material to which the buckets are attached. The buckets are forty-four in number, made of Russian plate iron, $\frac{9}{64}$ of an inch in thickness, and are secured to the crowns by grooves cut in the crowns of the exact form of the buckets, and by tenons entered into the mortises in both crowns, and riveted on the opposite sides.

d.d, the vertical shaft, of wrought-iron, runs upon a series of collars, resting upon corresponding projections in the suspension box *e'*. The part of the shaft on which the collars are placed, is made separate from the main shaft, and is pinned to it at *f*, by means of a socket in the top of the main shaft, which receives a corresponding part of the collar piece. The collars are made of cast steel; they are separately screwed on, and keyed to a wrought-iron spindle.

The suspension box is made in two parts, to admit of its being taken off and put on the shaft; it is lined with Babbit metal. It is found that bearings thus lined will carry from fifty to a hundred pounds to the square inch, with every appearance of durability.

f' f', the upper and lower bearings are of cast-iron, lined with Babbit metal, adjustable horizontally by means of screws. The suspension box *e'*, rests upon the gimbal *g*. The gimbal itself is supported on the frame *h h* by adjusting screws, which give the means of raising and lowering the suspension box, and with it, the vertical shaft and wheel. The lower end of the shaft is fitted with a cast-steel pin, *i*. This is retained in its place by the step, which is made in three parts, and lined with case-hardened wrought-iron.

The weight of the wheel, upright shaft, and bevel geer, is supported by means of the suspension box *e'* on the frame *k*, which rests upon the long beams *m*, reaching across the wheelpit, and supported at the ends by the masonry, and also at intermediate points by the braces *n n*.

Mr. Francis deduces the following rules for proportioning turbines:

The sum of the shortest distances between the buckets, should be equal to the diameter of the wheel.

The height of the orifices at the circumference of the wheel, should be equal to one-tenth of the diameter of the wheel.

The width of the crowns should be four times the shortest distance between the buckets.

The sum of the shortest distances between the curved guides, taken near the wheel, should be equal to the interior diameter of the wheel.

The number of buckets is, to a certain extent, arbitrary. As a guide in practice, to be controlled by particular circumstances, and limited to diameters of not less than two feet, the number of buckets should be three times the diameter in feet, plus thirty. The Tremont Turbine is 8½ feet in diameter, and according to the proposed rule, should have fifty-five buckets instead of forty-four. The number of the guides is also to a certain extent arbitrary; the practice at Lowell has been, usually, to have from a half to three-fourths of the number of buckets.

As turbines are generally used, a velocity of the interior circumference of the wheel, of about fifty-six per cent. of that due to the fall acting upon the wheel, appears most suitable.

To lay out the curve of the buckets.

Referring to Plate XXXII., fig. 2, the number of buckets, N, having been determined by the preceding rules, set off the arc $g\,i = \frac{\pi D}{N}$. Let $\omega = g\,h$, the shortest distance between the buckets: t the thickness of the metal forming the buckets. Make the arc $g\,k = 5\omega$. Draw the radius $o\,k$, intersecting the interior circumference of the wheel at l; the point l will be the inner extremity of the bucket. Draw the directrix $l\,m$ tangent to the inner circumference of the wheel. Draw the arc $o\,n$, with the radius $\omega + t$, from i, as a centre; the other directrix $g\,p$, must be found by trial, the required conditions being, that, when the line $m\,l$ is revolved round to the position $g\,t$, the point m being constantly on the directrix $g\,p$, and another point at the distance $m\,g = r\,s$, from the extremity of the line describing the bucket, being constantly on the directrix $m\,l$, the curve described shall just touch the arc $n\,o$. A convenient line for a first approximation, may be drawn by making the angle $O\,g\,p = 11°$. After determining the directrix according to the preceding method, if the angle $O\,g\,p$ should be greater than 12°, or less than 10°, the length of the arc $g\,k$ should be changed, to bring the angle within these limits.

The trace adopted for the corresponding guides is as follows:—The number n having been determined, divide the circle in which the extremities of the guides are found, into n equal parts, $v\,w$, $w\,x$, &c. Put ω' for the width between two adjoining guides, and t' for the thickness of the metal forming the guides. We have by rule, $\omega' = \frac{d}{n}$. With w' as a centre, and the radius $\omega' + t'$, draw the arc $y\,z$; and with x as a centre, and the radius $2(\omega' + t')$, draw the arc $a'\,b'$. Through v draw the portion of a circle $v\,c'$, touching the arcs $y\,z$ and $a'\,b'$; this will be the curve for the essential part of the guide. The remainder of the guide, $c'\,d'$, should be drawn tangent to the curve $c'\,v$; a convenient radius is one that would cause the curve $c'\,d'$, if continued, to pass through the centre O.

For further and still more elaborate drawings of machinery see "Shading and Shadows."

o
p
b
c
a
z
x
w
y
v
t
t
t
l
m
r
r
r
s
s
s
h
o
g
k
i

ARCHITECTURAL DRAWING.

The art of architecture consists in the designing of a building, so as to be most suitable and convenient for the purposes for which it is intended; in selecting and disposing of the materials of which it is composed, so as to withstand securely and permanently the strains and wear to which they may be subjected; and arranging the parts so as to produce the most artistic effect consistent with the use of the building, and applying to it such appropriate ornament as may express the purpose, and harmonize with the construction.

The art of architecture, according to Ferguson's *Hand-Book of Architecture*, should combine the art of the engineer with that of the architect. "The art of the engineer consists in selecting the best and most appropriate materials for the object he has in view, and using these in the most scientific manner, so as to insure an economical but satisfactory result. Where the engineer leaves off, the art of the architect begins. His object is to arrange the materials of the engineer, not so much with regard to economical as to artistic effects, and by light and shade, and outline, to produce that which in itself shall be permanently beautiful. He then adds ornament, which by its meaning doubles the effect of the disposition he has just made, and by its elegance throws a charm over the whole composition. Viewed in this light, it is evident that there are none of the objects which are usually delegated to the civil engineer which may not be brought within the province of the architect; a bridge, an aqueduct, a pier, are all legitimate subjects for architectural ornament.

It is not necessary that the engineer should know any thing of architecture, though it certainly would be better in most instances if he did; but, on the other hand, it is indispensably necessary that the architect should understand construction. Without that knowledge he cannot design; but it would be well if, in most cases, he could delegate the mechanical part of his task to the engineer, and so restrict himself entirely to the artistic arrangement and ornamentation of his design. A building may be said to be architectural in the proportion in which the ornamental or artistic purposes are allowed to prevail over the mechanical; and an object of engineering, where the utilitarian exigencies of the design are allowed to prevail over the artistic. But it is nowhere possible to draw the line sharply between the two, nor is it desirable to do so. Architecture can never descend too low, nor need it ever be afraid of ornamenting too mean objects; while, on the other hand, good engineering is absolutely indispensable to a satisfactory architectural effect of any class. The one is the prose, the other is the poetry of the art of building."

Since, then, the basis on which the architect must build is the art of the engineer, we continue a former chapter on the *Strength of Materials* with examples of the forms and principles of construction.

FOUNDATIONS.

In preparing the foundation for any building, there are two sources of failure which must be carefully guarded against: viz., inequality of settlement, and lateral escape of the supporting material; and if these radical defects can be guarded against, there is scarcely any situation in which a good foundation may not be obtained. It is, therefore, important, that previous to the commencement of the work, soundings should be taken to ascertain the nature of the soil and the lay of the strata, to determine the kind of foundation; and the more important and weighty the superstructure, the more careful and deeper the examination.

Natural foundations.—The best foundation is a *natural* one, such as a stratum of rock or compact gravel. If circumstances prevent the work being commenced from the same level throughout, the ground must be carefully *benched out*, i. e., cut into horizontal steps, so that the courses may all be perfectly level. It must also be borne in mind, that all work will settle more or less, according to the perfection of the joints, and therefore in these cases it is best to bring up the foundations to a uniform level with large blocks of stone or with concrete, before commencing the superstructure, which would otherwise settle most over the deepest parts, on account of the greater number of mortar joints, and thus cause unsightly fractures. Foundations in soil should be excavated to a depth below the action of frost.

Artificial foundations.—Where the ground in its natural state is too soft to bear the weight of the proposed structure, recourse must be had to artificial means of support, and, in doing this, whatever mode of construction be adopted, the principle must always be that of extending the bearing surface as much as possible. There are many ways of doing this—as by a thick layer of concrete or béton (fig. 1), or by layers of planking, or by a net-work of timber, or by increasing width of wall, or these different methods may be combined. The weight may also be distributed over the entire area of the foundation by inverted arches. The use of timber is objectionable where it cannot be kept constantly wet, as alternations of dryness and moisture soon cause it to rot, and for such localities concrete is to be preferred.

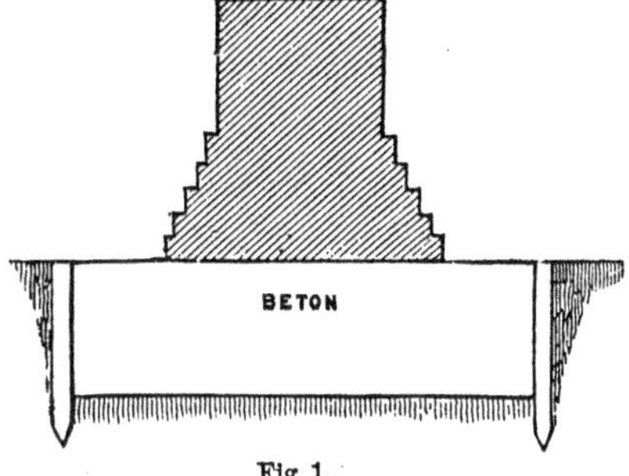

Fig. 1.

In the case of a foundation partly natural and partly artificial, the utmost care and circumspection are required to avoid fractures in the superstructure; and it cannot be too strongly impressed that it is not an *unyielding*, but a *uniform yielding* foundation that is required, and that it is not the *amount* so much as the *inequality* of settlement that does the mischief.

To prevent the lateral escape of the supporting material, when building in running sand or soft clay, which would ooze out from below the work, and allow the superstructure to sink, in addition to protecting the surface with planking, concrete, or timber, it is often necessary to enclose the whole area of the foundation with piles of timber or plank driven close together; this is called *sheet-piling*

Where there is a hard stratum below the soft ground, but at too great a depth to allow of the solid work being brought up from it without greater

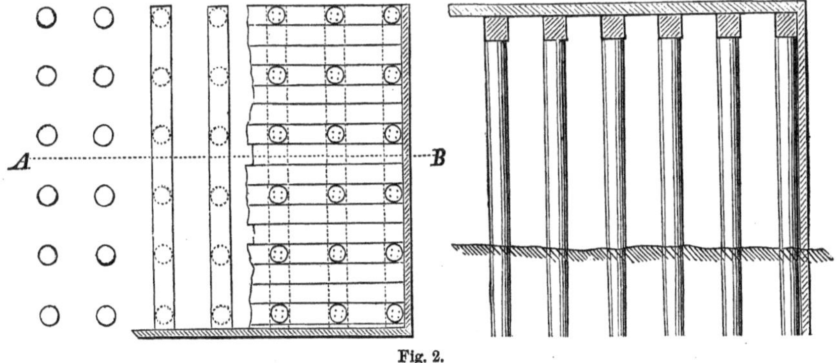

Fig. 2.

expense than the circumstances of the case will allow, it is usual to drive down wooden piles (fig. 2), often shod with iron, until their bottoms are firmly fixed in the hard ground. The upper ends of the piles are then cut off level, and covered with a platform of timber, on which the work is built in the usual way. The piles are generally of about 1 foot diameter, and are driven at distances of from 2 to 3 feet from centre to centre.

Where a firm foundation is required to be formed in a situation where no firm bottom can be found within an available depth, piles are driven, to consolidate the mass, a few feet apart over the whole area of the foundation, which is surrounded by a row of sheet-piling to prevent the escape of the soil; the space between the pile-heads is then filled to the depth of several feet with stones or concrete, and the whole is covered with a timber platform on which to commence the solid work.

Foundations beneath the surface of water, as for the foundations of piers and abutments of bridges, are formed by piles, by throwing down masses of stone until the mass reaches the surface of the water, by caisson, or by enclosing the space within a coffer-dam, and proceeding as in common foundations.

A caïsson is a chest of timber which is floated over the site of the work, and being kept in its place, is loaded with stone until it rests firmly on the ground. In some cases the stone is merely thrown in, the regular masonry commencing with the top of the caisson, which is sunk a little below the level of low water, so that the whole wood-work may be always covered, and the caisson remains as part of the structure. In others the masonry is built on the bottom of the caisson, and when the work reaches the level of the water, the sides of the caisson are removed.

Foundations under water are frequently executed with blocks of béton or hydraulic concrete, which has the property of setting under water. The site of the work is first enclosed with a row of sheet-piling, which protects the béton from disturbance until it has set. The French engineers have used béton in the works at Algiers, in large blocks of 324 cubic feet, which were floated out and allowed to drop into their places from slings. This method, which proved perfectly successful, was adopted in consequence of the smaller blocks first used being displaced and destroyed by the force of the sea.

WALLS.

The requisite precaution having been taken to secure a safe foundation for the structure, the next subject to be taken into consideration is the substance and proportions of the walls.

Walls of permanent structures are almost exclusively composed of either stone or brick, or both, and are included in one general term as *masonry*.

Fig. 3 represents the front of a wall called the face; fig. 4, a section; and fig. 5, the view of rear, or the *backing*. The interior of the wall is

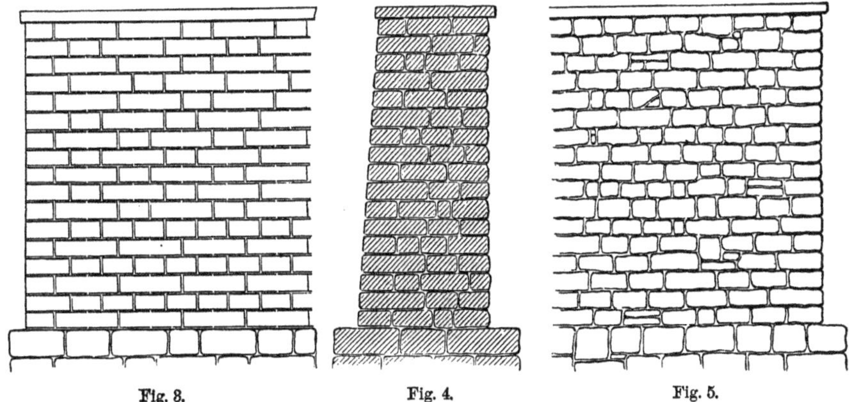

Fig. 3. Fig. 4. Fig. 5.

called the *filling*. The term *course* is applied to each horizontal layer of stone or brick; if all the stones in a layer are of equal thickness, it is termed *regular* coursing. *Footings* are the lower projecting courses (figs. 3 and 4) resting on the foundation, usually not less than double the width of the wall above in walls of buildings; but for other walls, the width depends on the nature of the foundation. Rock foundations need no extra width of wall. *String* courses, or *belting*, are upper courses projecting slightly beyond the face of the wall. *Coping* is the top courses, usually got out in considerable lengths in comparison with the stones in the rest of the work.

The *bed* of a stone or brick is the bottom surface on which it rests; the *build* is the upper surface on which the stone above is placed; the interstices between the stones are termed *joints*. *Stretchers* are stones or brick which have their length disposed lengthways of the wall; *headers* have their length crossways. *Quoins* are the corners of a wall. *Bond* is the lapping of the stones or brick on each other in the construction, so as to tie the separate pieces together. Three classes of bond are shown in the face (fig. 3); the lowest six courses consist of alternate courses of headers and stretchers, the next six courses above have alternate headers and stretchers in the same course, and in the remaining courses a header occurs at every third stone; this is the most usual bond. Headers should not be placed one above the other in alternate courses.

Figs. 6 and 7 represent brick bonds ;—fig. 6, the old English bond, and

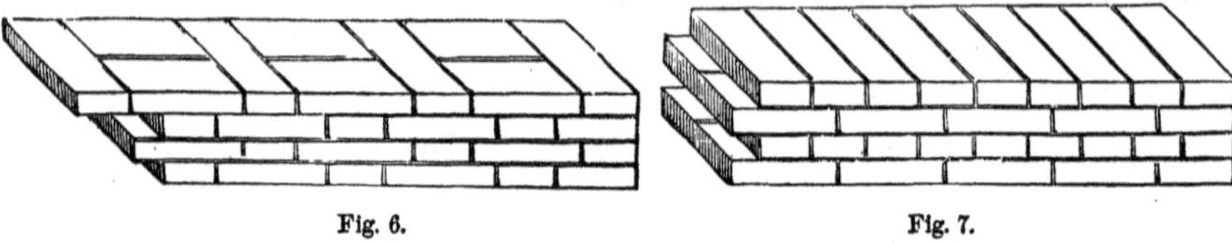

Fig. 6. Fig. 7.

fig. 7, the Flemish bond. The most common bond in this country is to lay a certain number of stretching courses, and then a heading course. The fire-law of New York requires brick work to be built with headers every five courses, but every seventh course a heading course is more commonly used. In all masonry, no vertical joint should extend through two courses, but the vertical joints should be as near as possible midway between those below; in other words, *break joint* with them.

Walls are composed of stones laid either with or without mortar. The latter is called *dry* masonry; *rough* wall is dry work of rough stones; if laid in mortar, it is called *rubble* work, but frequently this term is made to include all rough work. Cut stone is called *ashler;* thus (figs. 3, 4, 5), the face is ashler, the backing rubble. Rubble may be either *coursed* or *uncoursed.*

On the thickness of walls.—Retaining-walls are such as sustain a lateral pressure from an embankment or a head of water (figs. 8 and 9). The width of a retaining wall depends upon the height of the embankment which it may have to sustain, and the kind of earth of which it is composed, (the steeper the natural slope at which the earth would stand, the less the thrust against the wall,) and the comparative weight of the earth and of the masonry. The formula given by Morin for ordinary earths and masonry is $b = 0.285\ h + h'$; that is, to find the breadth of a wall laid in mortar, multiply the whole height of the embankment above the footing by $\frac{285}{1000}$; for dry walls make the thickness one-fourth more.

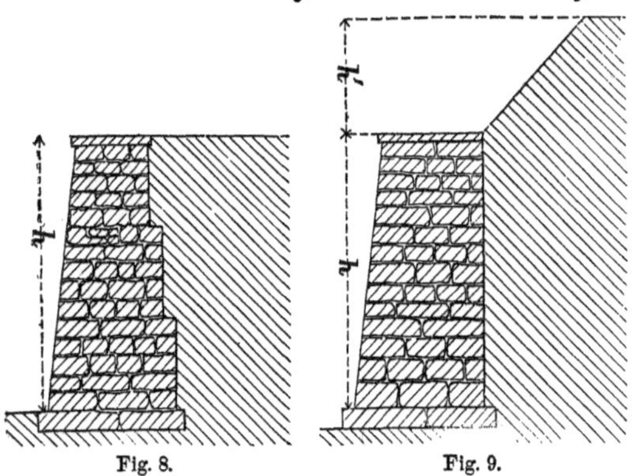

Fig. 8. Fig. 9.

Most retaining or brick walls have an inclination or *batter* to the face, sometimes also the same in the back, but *offsets* (fig. 8) are more common. The usual batter is from 1 to 3 inches horizontal for each foot vertical. To determine the thickness of a wall having a batter, "determine the width

PLATE I.

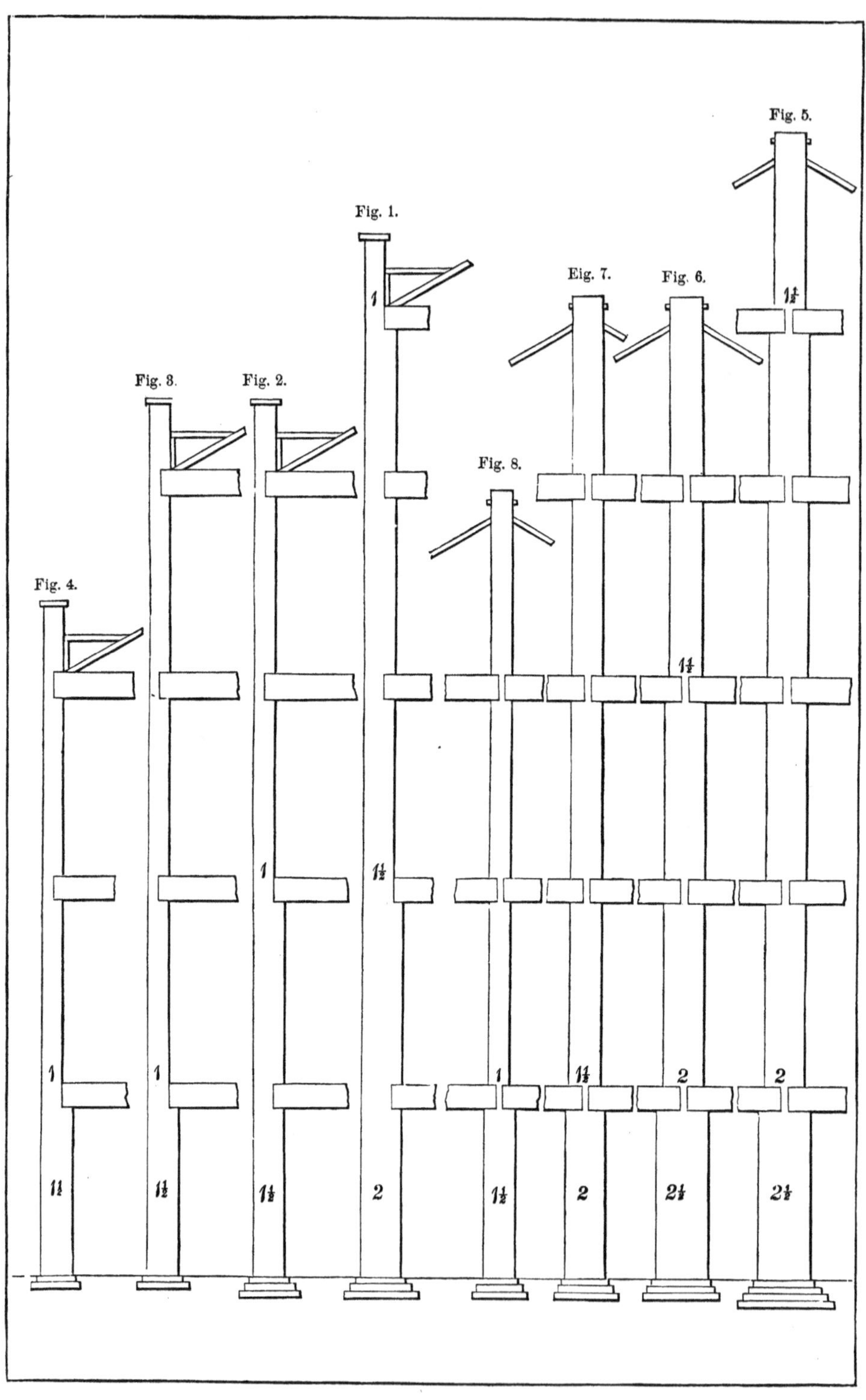

by our former rule, and make this the width at one-ninth of the height above the base."—*Morin.*

The footings or *trench* walls, as they are often termed, of a retaining-wall should be sunk below the action of the frost, and are generally about one foot wider than the wall, offsetting 6 inches both face and back.

Walls of buildings.—Figs. 1, 2, 3, 4, plate I., represent the thickness of *external* brick walls to the first, second, third, and fourth-rate buildings, as provided by the Building Act for the city of London. Figs. 5, 6, 7, 8, show the same with respect to party-walls. The figures 1, 1½, 2, 2½, represent the number of lengths of brick in the wall. The following table gives the way in which buildings are rated in Liverpool, not differing, constructively, materially from that of London.

HEIGHTS AND WIDTHS OF BUILDINGS.			
First-rate dwelling-house.	Second-rate dwelling-house.	Third-rate dwelling-house.	Fourth-rate dwelling-house.
Exceeding forty-four feet in height, or twenty-seven feet front.	Not exceeding forty-four feet in height, or twenty-seven feet front.	Not exceeding thirty-six feet in height, or twenty-one feet front.	Not exceeding thirty-two feet in height, or fifteen feet front.

"Every brewery, distillery, manufactory, or warehouse, of whatever height or extent of frontage, is considered to be a first-rate building, the external walls of which are in their respective stories to be 2½, 2, and 1½ bricks in thickness, and the party-walls of 2 and 1½ bricks.

"When the foundations of any building shall not be upon rock, such foundations to have footing courses under the same."

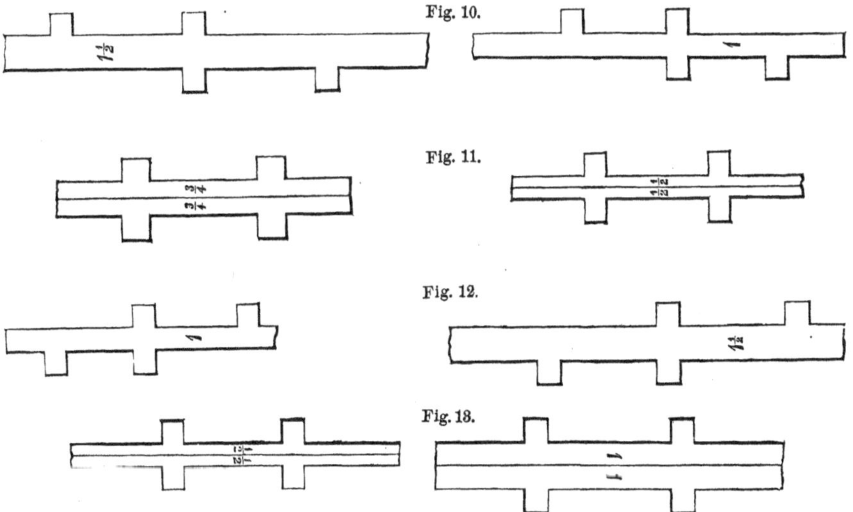

Figs. 10, 11, 12, 13, represent the position of the chimneys and thickness of chimney-backs in party-walls, according to the several rates; viz., fig. 10 (first-rate), basement, 1½ brick, all above, 1 brick thick. Fig. 11 shows the thickness when the chimneys are placed back to back in party-walls of first-rate buildings.

Fig. 12 shows the dimensions of second, third, and fourth-rate buildings, and fig. 13 the same when back to back.

The following is the Building Act in New York in regard to the thickness of walls:

"The outside walls of all dwelling-houses, stores, storehouses, and other buildings, shall be not less than eight inches thick; and all such outside walls as shall exceed thirty-five feet in height from the level of the sidewalk to the peak or highest point thereof, and all party-walls, shall be not less than twelve inches thick. And all walls, whether outside, party, or partition walls, of any such dwelling-house, store or storehouse, or other building other than a dwelling-house, which shall exceed fifty feet in height from the level of the sidewalk to the peak or highest point thereof, shall not be less than sixteen inches thick to the under side of the second tier of beams above the level of the sidewalk: provided said under side of said second tier of beams be not less than twenty feet from the level of the sidewalk; but should the under side of said second tier of beams be less than twenty feet from the level of the said sidewalk, said walls shall be sixteen inches thick to the under side of the third tier of beams above the said level.

"Every cellar, pier, column, post, and pillar, built of rubble, stone, or brick, shall at intervals of not more than three feet have built into it a stone of not less than three inches thick, and of a diameter each way equal to the diameter of the pier, column, post, or pillar."

From the above acts we can establish the necessary thickness of walls for the usual buildings in a city; but for detached manufactories and workshops it is usual to adopt a somewhat greater thickness for the walls; thus, for cotton factories of five stories, the first story is generally two feet, the second and third twenty inches, and the fourth and fifth 16 inches. Walls built of rubble should also be somewhat thicker than those of brick—on an average at least one quarter thicker, but depending on the character of the stone. Walls of entirely cut stone are stronger than brick of the same dimensions, but are unusual; the common form of cut-work is to make the face ashler, and back up with rubble or brick.

Mortar is a mixture of lime or cement, or both, with water and sand. In the preparation of good mortar, the materials should be well selected; the sand sharp and clean, the proportions properly preserved, and the whole intimately mixed. As a general rule, the lime or cement should be sufficiently fine to cover all the grains of sand, and, at the same time, with the thinnest possible stratum. Practically, about three to four cubic feet of sand are added to one cubic foot of half liquid lime, for fat limes; lean lime may not bear more than half this sand. Cement is generally mixed with sand in proportions of one to three, but in situations where a quick set is necessary, in equal proportions.

Arches.—Arches are of various shapes, as,

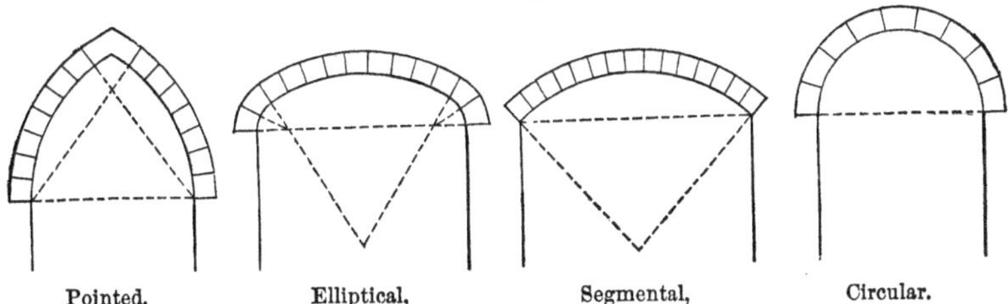

The outer surface of the arch is called the *extrados* or *back* of the arch, the inner or concave surface the *intrados* or the *soffit;* the joints of all arches should be perpendicular to the surface of the soffits. The stones are called *arch stones* or *voussoirs.* The first course on each side are termed *springers*, which rest on the *imposts* or *abutments.* In case of a segmental arch, the course beneath the springers are called *skew-backs.* The extreme width between springers is called the *span* of the arch, and the versed sine of the curve of the soffit the *rise* of the arch. The highest portion of the arch is called the *crown*, and the centre course of voussoirs the *key-course.* The side portions of arches between the springing and the crown, are termed *haunches* or *flanks.* All arches should be well sustained by backing on the haunches, called *spandrel*-backing. The line of intersection of arches cutting across each other transversely is called a *groin*, and the arches themselves *groined arches.*

That the voussoirs of an arch may resist crushing, they must have a certain depth proportioned to the pressure of the arch; and as this in-

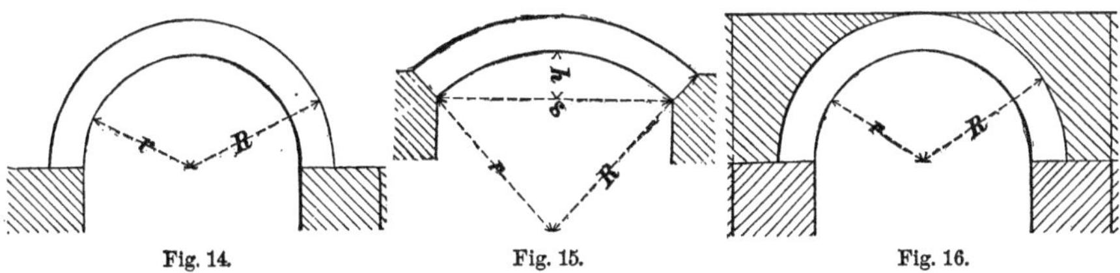

Fig. 14. Fig. 15. Fig. 16.

creases from the curve towards the springing, the depth of the voussoirs should likewise increase from the crown to the springing. Peronnet has given as a rule for the depth at the crown the formula $d = .07\,r + 1$ foot, in which formula r is the greatest radius of curvature of the intrados. This formula is applicable to arches less than fifty feet radius; but beyond this it gives greater dimensions than in ordinary practice. In order to facilitate investigations on the stability of arches of the more usual forms, M. Petit calculated a series of tables, of which we give the abstract for circular arches, as the class occurring most frequently in practice.

CO-EFFICIENT OF HORIZONTAL THRUST AT THE CROWN.

Ratio of the Radii $\frac{R}{r}$	Fig. 14.	Fig. 16.	Fig. 15.					
			$s = 4\,h$, $\frac{r}{h} = 2.5$	$s = 5\,h$, $\frac{r}{h} = 3,\ 265$	$s = 6\,h$, $\frac{r}{h} = 5$	$s = 6\,h$, $\frac{r}{h} = 8.5$	$s = 10\,h$, $\frac{r}{h} = 13$	$s = 16\,h$, $\frac{r}{h} = 32.5$
1.50	0.191	0.217						
1.45	0.168	0.192						
1.40	0.162	0.169	0.154	0.147	0.147	0.147	0.045	
1.35	0.153	0.147	0.148	0.130	0.126	0.126	0.124	
1.30	0.143	0.143	0.137	0.123	0.106	0.106	0.104	
1.25	0.128	0.139	0.126	0.114	0.100	0.086	0.084	0.072
1.20	0.111	0.131	0.110	0.102	0.091	0.070	0.066	0.056
1.15	0.092	0.119	0.091	0.086	0.079	0.063	0.049	0.041
1.10	0.068	0.103	0.067	0.065	0.062	0.052	0.042	0.027
1.05	0.038	0.082	0.038	0.038	0.037	0.034	0.029	0.019

To find the thickness of abutment necessary to support the thrust of the arch, multiply the co-efficient found in the table for the particular case by 3.8, and the square root of the product multiplied by the radius, r, of the intrados, will give the extreme thickness of the abutment.

Example.—What is the horizontal thrust, and what the thickness of abutment necessary to support an arch of ten feet span and two feet rise?

$$\frac{s}{h} = \frac{10}{2}, \text{ therefore } s = 5h.$$

$$\frac{r}{h} = \frac{r}{2} = 3.625 \qquad r = 3.625 \times 2 = 7.25 \text{ ft.}$$

By Peronnet's formula, $d = 0.07 \times 7.25 + 1 = 1.50.$

$$\text{R} = 7.25 + 1.50 = 8.75$$

$$\frac{\text{R}}{r} = \frac{8.75}{7.25} = 1.20$$

By the table against 1.20, under the the column $s = 5\ h$, we find 0.102 as the co-efficient of thrust, 150 lbs. being taken as the average weight of a cubic foot of masonry, the absolute thrust per square foot of surface is

$$0.102 \times 150 \times \overline{7.25}^2 = 804 \text{ lbs.}$$

$$\sqrt{0.102 \times 3.8} \times 7.25 = 4.50 \text{ feet, thickness of abutment.}$$

The formula gives the thickness of abutment, supposing the height infinite; for low abutments, the thickness may be reduced, for common spans, about ten per cent.

The following table gives the dimensions of the arches of a selection of bridges of European construction.

LOCATION.	Material.	Form of Arch.	Span.	Rise.	Depth at crown.	Depth at spring.
			ft. in.	ft. in.	ft. in.	ft. in.
Manchester and Birmingham Railroad,	Brick,	Semicircular,	18	9	1 6	uniform.
" " "	"	"	63	31 6	3	"
London and Brighton "	"	"	30	15	1 6	2 3
" Blackwall "	"	Segmental,	87	16	4 1½	uniform.
Great Western "	"	Elliptical,	128	24 3	5	7 1½
Orleans and Tours "	Stone,	Semicircular,	27 7		2 7½	uniform.
Stirling Bridge, ...	"	Segmental,	60	13 6½	3 6	4 6
Carlisle "	"	Elliptical,	65	21	3 9	7 4
Staines "	"	Segmental,	74	9 3	2 4	5 6
Hutcheson "	"	"	79	13 6	3 6	4 6
Jena "	"	"	71 9	10 9	5	

For smaller culverts of 15 to 30 feet span, the usual construction is to make the arch from 1 foot 6 inches to 2 feet deep. Arches in stone are seldom turned less than 1 foot deep, whatever may be the span; brick arches for less than 10 feet span are generally 8 inches, and this depth is required by building acts.

Fig. 17 represents a section of the Croton aqueduct in an open rock cut. The bottom is raised with concrete to the proper height and form for the inverted arch of a simple course of brick. The side walls are of stone laid in cement, plastered and faced with a single course of brick. The arch is semicircular, of brick, two courses thick, with spandril backing nearly to the level of the crown, and the earth filled in on top.

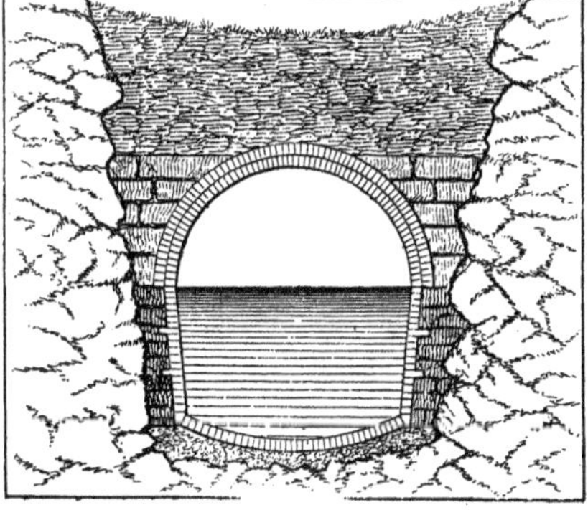

Fig. 17.

FRAMING.

Framing is the art of arranging beams for the various purposes to which they are applied in structures. Timber and iron are the only materials in common use for frames.

Wooden beams are usually represented longitudinally both in elevation and in section by their outlines merely, or in end view by rectangles with diagonals from opposite corners (fig. 18), and in end section by the usual diagonal lines in one direction across the face. Sometimes in more finished drawings, or when a distinction is to be marked between different materials, the grain of the wood is represented as in figs. 19 and 20, a side and end elevation of a beam.

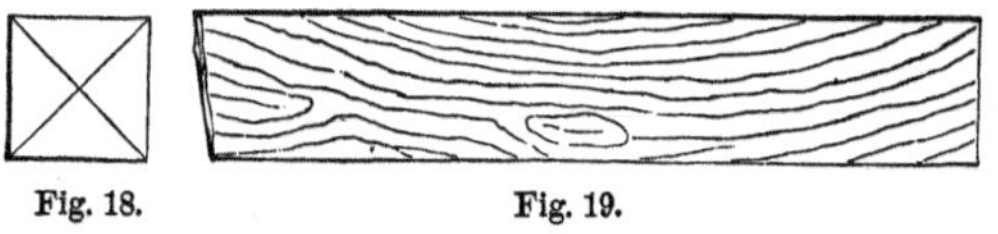

Fig. 18. Fig. 19. Fig. 20.

Flooring.—The timbers which support the flooring-boards and ceiling of a room are called the naked flooring.

The simplest form of flooring, and the one usually adopted in the construction of city houses and stores is represented in plan and section, fig. 21. It consists of a single series of beams or deep joists, reaching from wall to wall. As a lateral brace between each set of beams, a system of

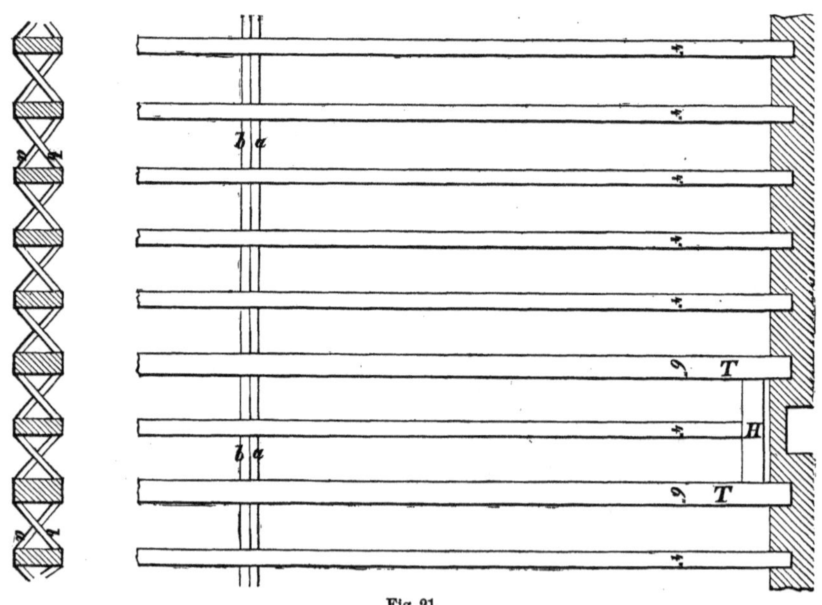

Fig. 21.

bridging is adopted, of which the best is the *herring-bone* bridging, formed of short pieces of joists about 2 × 4, crossing each other, and nailed securely to the top and bottoms of the several beams, represented by *a* and *b* in fig. 21, and whereever a flue occurs, or a stairway or well-hole prevents one or more joists from resting on the wall, a *trimmer* or *header*, H, is framed across the space into the outer beams or *trimmer-beams* T T, and the beams cut off, or *tail-beams* are framed into the trimmer.

Whenever the distances between the walls exceed the length that can safely be given to joists in one piece, an intermediate beam or girder, running longitudinally, is introduced, into which the joists are framed (fig. 22). Very often the joists are merely notched on to beams. Flooring is still further varied, by framing with girders longitudinally; beams crossways, and framed into or resting on the girders; and joists framed into the beams, running the same direction as the girders. It is evident, that when the joists are not flush or level with the bottom of the beams or girders, either that in the finish the beams will show, or that ceiling-joists or furrings will have to be introduced.

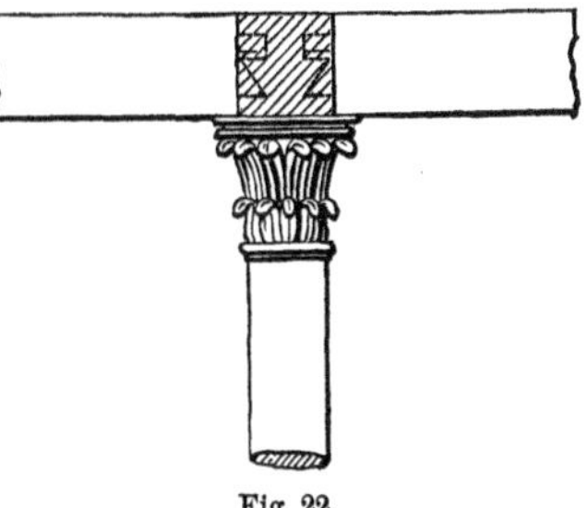

Fig. 22.

On the size of joists.—The following dimensions, taken in part from the Liverpool Building Act, may be considered as safe sizes for ordinary constructions, the distances from centre to centre being one foot.

Joists in floors, clear bearing

Exceeding	7	feet,	and not exceeding	10	feet,	to be not less	than	6 × 2	inches.
"	10	"	"	12	"	"	"	6 × 2½	"
"	12	"	"	14½	"	"	"	7 × 2½	"
"	14½	"	"	16	"	"	"	8 × 2½	"
"	16	"	"	18	"	"	"	9 × 2¾	"
"	18	"	"	20	"	"	"	10 × 2¾	"
"	20	"	"	22	"	"	"	11 × 3	"
"	22	"	"	24	"	"	"	12 × 3	"

It is to be observed that lumber is seldom sawed to dimensions of fractions of an inch; we must therefore adopt a width of an integral inch, and proportion the distances from centre to centre, according to the increase or decrease of width given to the joists.

Trimmers and headers should be of greater width than the joists, depending on the length of the former, and the amount cut from the laid beams or the dimensions of the opening. The New York Building Act requires all trimmers should be hung in stirrup irons (fig. 23), and not framed in. It also re-

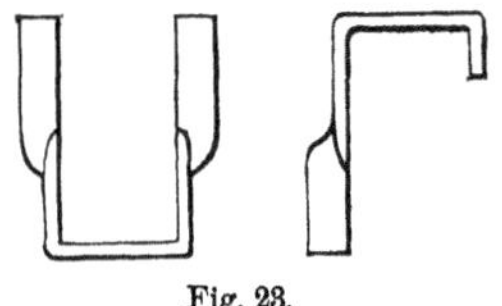

Fig. 23.

quires all girders to be not less than 10 by 12 inches square, and that the posts supporting them, shall be placed at intervals of not more than 10 feet.

Floors.—In New York it is usual to lay single floors, of tongued and grooved boards, but in the Eastern States, double floors are more common; the first floor consists of an inferior quality of boards, unmatched, laid during the progress of the work as a sort of staging for the carpenter and mason, and in finishing, a second course is laid on them of better material, generally tongued and grooved, but sometimes only jointed. Ceilings should always be furred; that is, laths should never be nailed directly to the joists; the usual furrings are of inch board, two inches wide, and twelve inches from centre to centre, nailed across from joist to joist.

Fig. 24. represents a section of a mill floor. The girders or beams, generally in pairs with a space of about an inch between them, are placed at a distance of from seven to nine feet from centre to centre, and are of from twelve to sixteen inches in depth. On these, a rough plank floor of from three to four inches thick is laid; the plank are *dowelled* together, that is, put together with pins or *dowels*, like a barrel head. Above the plank is laid the usual top floor, and beneath a sheathing of thin boards.

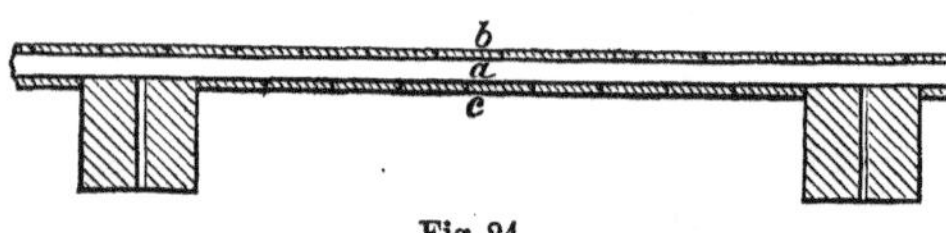

Fig. 24.

For extended bearings and for heavy loads, it is often found necessary to truss the girders or beams. Fig. 25 represents a bracing truss of wrought iron between a double girder; often a simple piece of arched iron is let into the wood, half on each side, and the beams bolted strongly together. Fig. 26 represents a truss by suspension; in this case, the strength depends upon the cohesive force of the iron.

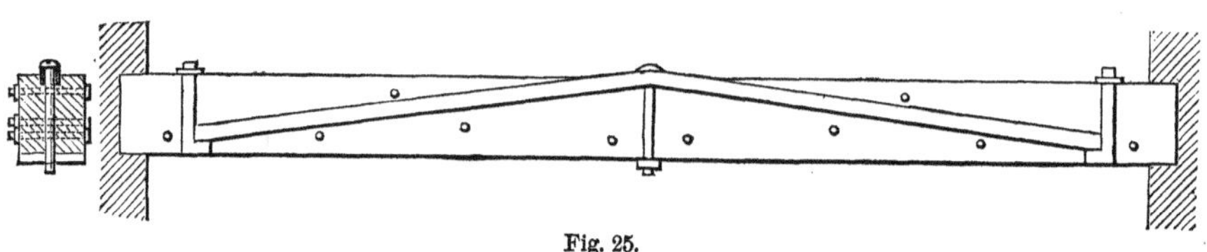

Fig. 25.

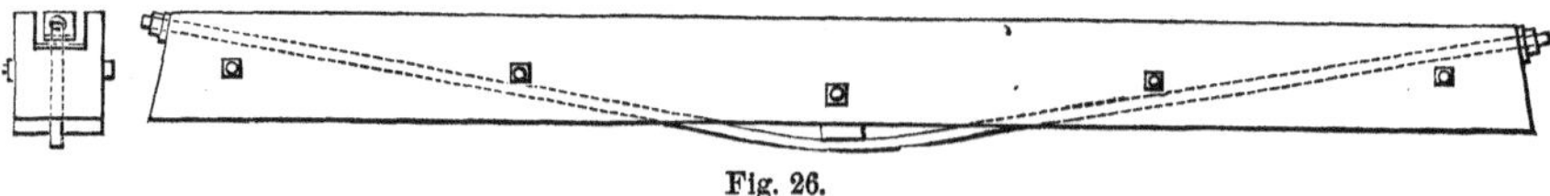

Fig. 26.

Fire-proof floors.—Fig. 27 represents a section of the fire-proof flooring

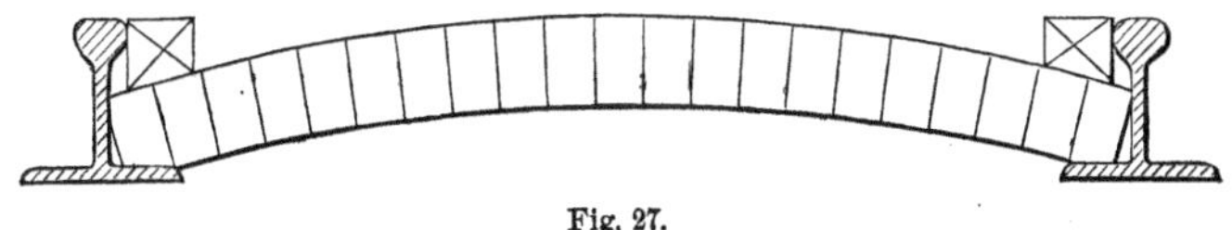

Fig. 27.

constructed by Cooper & Hewitt. The girders or beams are of wrought iron, with arches of a single course of brick in cement between them, resting on their lower flanches. The seven-inch deep beams are placed at a distance of from three to five feet from centre to centre; extreme width of span, between side walls, fifteen feet. Strips of plank are fastened lengthways at the side or on top of the beams, to receive the floor. Furrings for the ceiling may be attached crossways to the bottom of the beams, or the soffits of the arches may be plastered without any preparation.

Fig. 28 represents a section of one of the French systems of fire-proof floors. It consists of I girders, placed at a distance of one metre (39.38 inches), from centre to centre, slightly *cambered* or curved upwards in the centre; the depth of the girders to depend upon the span. Stirrups of cast iron are slid upon the girders, into which the ends of flat iron joists, set edgeways, pass and are secured by pins; the ends of the joists take a bearing also on the bottom flånges of the girders. The joists are placed at a distance of one metre from centre to centre. Upon the joists rest rods of square iron, which in this way form a *grillage* for the support of a species of rough cast and the ceiling. By this and other very similar systems, the French have succeeded in reducing the cost of such floors to that of wooden ones.

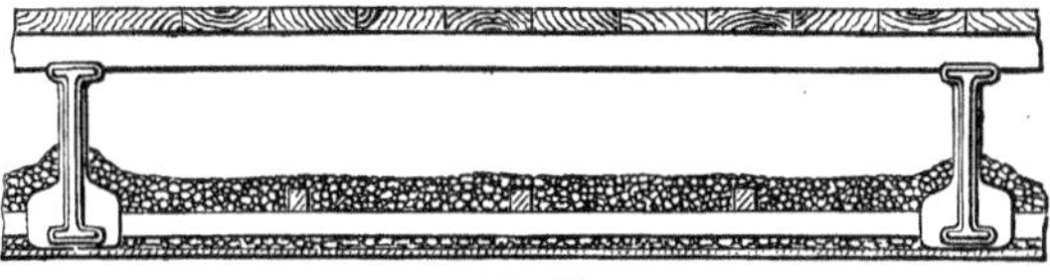

Fig. 28.

Floors are sometimes constructed of brick in single or in groined arches, the thrust being opposed by the weight of the abutments, but owing to its expensiveness, and the amount of room occupied by the material, this kind of construction is not at present very common in edifices.

Partitions are usually simply studs set at intervals of twelve or sixteen inches, these spaces being adapted to the length of the lath (forty-eight inches). The sizes of the studs are generally 2 × 4, 3 × 5, or 3 × 6 inches, according to the height of the partition; for any high partitions, greater depth may be required for the studs, but three inches will be sufficient width. Partitions should be bridged like floors with herring-bone bridging.

Fig. 29 represents the frame of the side of a wooden house, in which A A are the *posts*, B the *plate*, C C *girts* or *interties*, D D *braces*, E sill, F *window posts* or *studs*, G G *studs*.

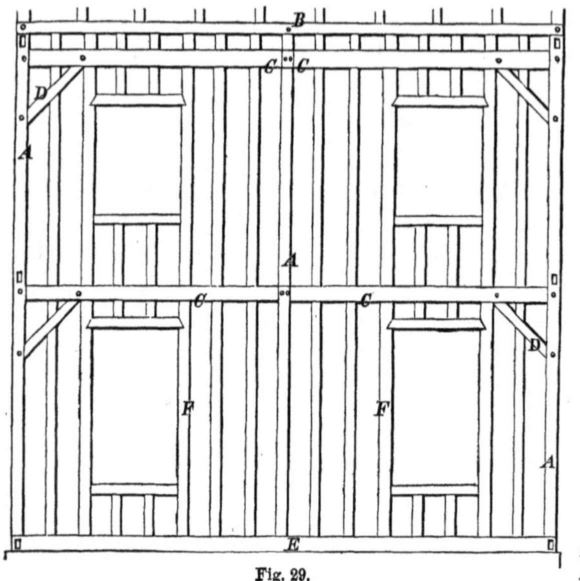

Fig. 29.

Usual dimensions of timber for frame of common dwelling houses:—sills 6 × 8, posts 4 × 8, studs 2 × 4 or 3 × 4, girts 6 × the depth of floor joists, plates 4 × 6, the floor joists (J fig. 30), are notched into the girts; more frequently the girts are omitted. The studs are of the same length as the posts, and the floor joists are supported by a board, *a*, 3 or 4 × 1 let into the studs (fig. 31), and firmly nailed; the joists are also nailed strongly to the studs. The posts and studs are *tenoned* into the sills and girts. Fig. 32 represents a *tenon*, *b c*, in side and end elevation, and *mortice*, *a;* the portions of the end of the stud resting on the beam are called the *shoulders* of the tenon.

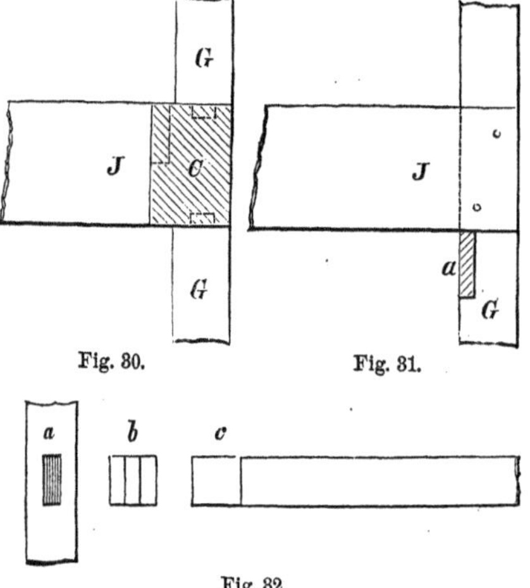

Fig. 30. Fig. 31.

Fig. 32.

Roofs.—The roofs of city dwellings and stores are generally flat, that is, with but very little inclination, from half an inch to two inches per foot, merely sufficient to discharge the water. The beams are laid from wall to wall, the same as floor timbers, but usually of less depth, or at greater distances between centres, and with one or two rows of bridging. The roof is laid with tongued and grooved boards, and mostly covered with tin.

Figs. 1, 2, 3, Plate II., represent side or portions of side elevations of the usual form of framed roofs. The same letters refer to the same parts in all the figures of the plate. T T are the *tie* beams, R R the *main rafters*,

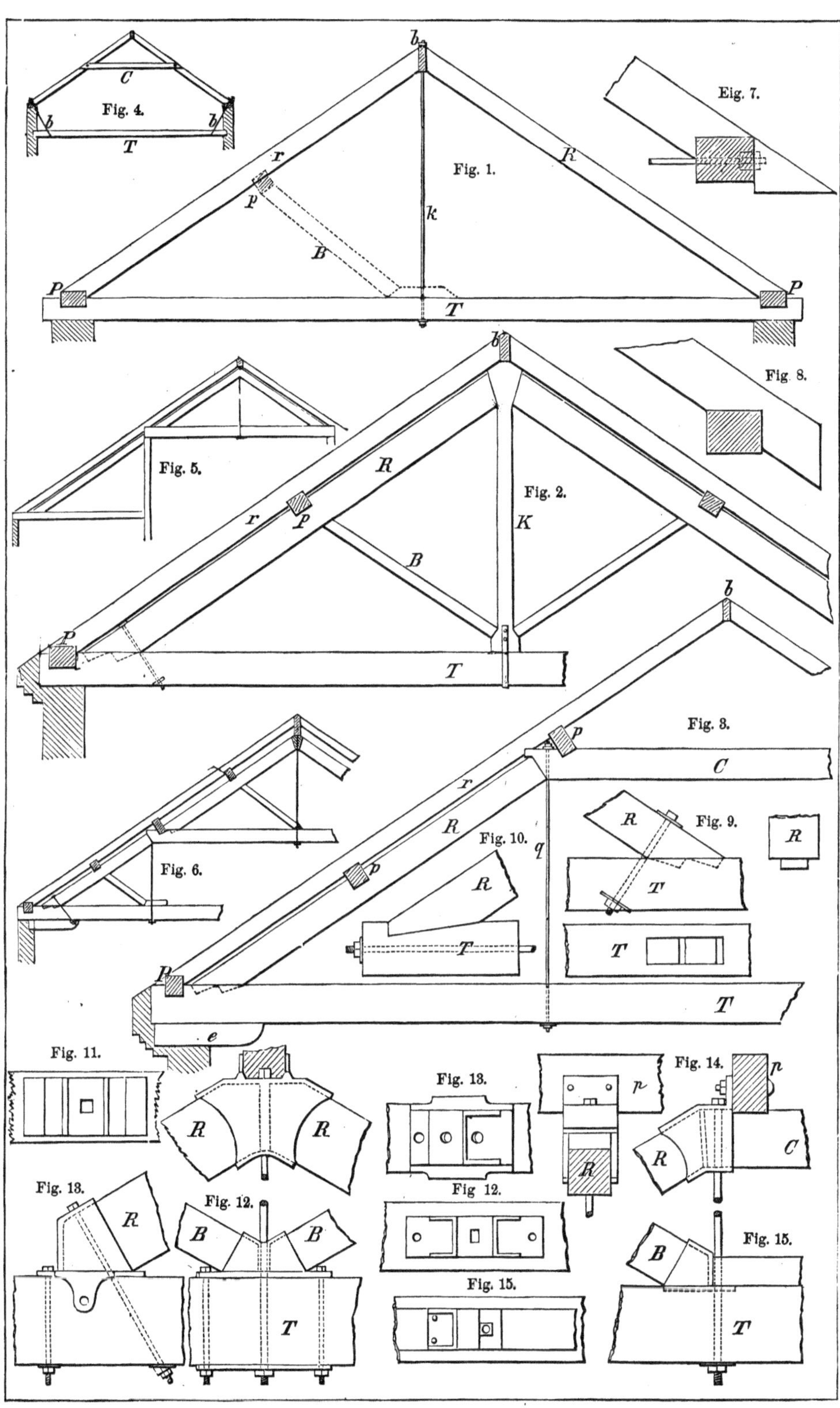
Fig. 1.
Fig. 2.
Fig. 3.
Fig. 4.
Fig. 5.
Fig. 6.
Eig. 7.
Fig. 8.
Fig. 9.
Fig. 10.
Fig. 11.
Fig. 12.
Fig. 13.
Fig. 14.
Fig. 15.

r r the *jack rafters*, P P the *plates*, *p p* the purlines, K K the *king posts*, *k k king bolts*, *q q queen bolts*, both are called *suspension* bolts, C C the *collar* or *straining* beams, B B *braces* or *studs*, *b b* ridge boards, *c c* corbels.

The *pitch* of the roof is the inclination of the rafters, and is usually designated in reference to the span as $\frac{1}{4}$, $\frac{1}{3}$, $\frac{3}{8}$, &c., pitch, that is, the height of the ridge above the plate is $\frac{1}{4}$, $\frac{1}{3}$, $\frac{3}{8}$, &c, of the span of the roof at the level of the plate. The higher the pitch of the roof, the less the thrust against the side walls, the less likely the snow or water to lodge, and consequently, the tighter the roof. For roofs covered with shingles or slate, in this portion of the country, it is not advisable to use less than $\frac{1}{4}$ pitch; above that, the pitch should be adapted to the style of architecture adopted. The pitch in most common use is $\frac{1}{3}$ the span.

Fig. 1 represents the simplest framed roof; it consists of rafters, resting upon a plate framed into the ceiling beam; this beam is supported by a suspension-rod, *k*, from the ridge, but if supported from below, this rod may be omitted. This form of construction is sufficient for any roof of less than 25 feet span, and of the usual pitch, and may be used for a 40 feet span by increasing the depth of the rafters to 12 inches; deep rafters should always be bridged. By the introduction of a purline extending beneath the centre of the rafter, supported by a brace to the foot of the suspension rod, as shown in dotted line, the depth of the rafters may obviously be reduced. It often happens that the king-bolt may interfere with the occupancy of the attic; in that case the beam is otherwise supported. Again, it may be necessary that the tie beam, which is also a ceiling and floor beam, should be below the plate some 2 to 4 feet; in that case, the thrust of the roof is resisted (fig. 4) by bolts, *b b*, passing through the plate and the beam, and by a collar plank, *C*, spiked on the sides of the rafters, high enough above the beam to afford good head room. For roofs $\frac{3}{8}$ pitch and under 20 feet span, the bolts are unnecessary, the collar alone being sufficient.

Fig. 2 represents a roof, a larger span than fig. 1; the frame may be made very strong and safe for roofs of 60 feet span. King-bolts or suspension-rods are now oftener used than posts, with a small triangular block of hard wood or iron, at the foot of the bolts, for the support of the braces. The objection to this form of roof is that the framing occupies all the space in the attic; on this account the form, fig. 3, is preferred for roofs of the same span, and is also applicable to roofs of at least 75 feet span, by the addition of a brace to the rafter from the foot of the queen-bolt. The collar beam (fig. 6), is also trussed by the framing similar to fig. 2. In the older roofs, queen posts are used (fig. 33), with the foot secured by straps or joint bolts to the tie beam. In many church and barn roofs the tie beam is cut off (fig. 5, Plate II.), the queen post being supported on a post, or itself extending to the base, with a short tie rod framed into it from the plate.

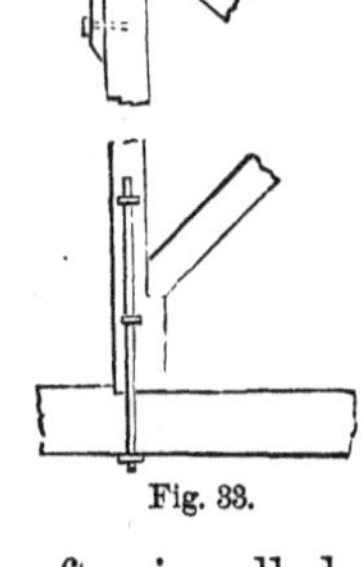
Fig. 33.

Figs. 7 and 8, Plate II., represent the foot of a rafter on an enlarged scale. In fig. 7, the face of the rafter does not project beyond the face of the plate; the coving is formed by a small triangular, or any desirable form of plank, framed into the plate. The form given to the foot of the rafter is called a *crow foot*. In fig. 8, the rafter itself projects beyond the plate to form the coving. Fig. 9 represents a front and side elevation and plan of the foot of a main rafter, showing the form of tenon, in this case double; a bolt passing through the rafter and beam retains the foot of the former in its place. Fig. 10 represents the side elevation of the foot of a main rafter with only a small portion of the beam, the remainder being supplied by a rod. In fig. 7, of a similar construction to fig. 1, the tie rod passes directly through the plate. In general, when neither ceiling nor flooring is supported by the tie beam, a rod is preferable.

Roofs are now very neatly and strongly framed by the introduction of cast-iron shoes and abutting plates for the ends of the braces and rafters. Fig. 11 represents the elevation and plan of a cast-iron king head for a roof similar to fig. 2. Fig. 12, that of the brace shoe; fig. 13, that of the rafter shoe for the same roof. Fig. 14, the front and side elevation of the queen head of roof similar to fig. 3, and fig. 15, elevation and plan of queen brace shoe.

Fig. 34 represents the section of a rafter shoe for a tie rod; the side flanches are shown in dotted line.

Fig. 34.

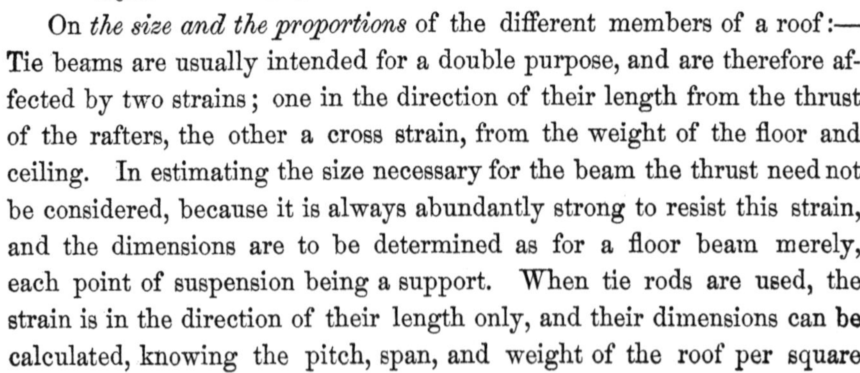

On *the size and the proportions* of the different members of a roof:— Tie beams are usually intended for a double purpose, and are therefore affected by two strains; one in the direction of their length from the thrust of the rafters, the other a cross strain, from the weight of the floor and ceiling. In estimating the size necessary for the beam the thrust need not be considered, because it is always abundantly strong to resist this strain, and the dimensions are to be determined as for a floor beam merely, each point of suspension being a support. When tie rods are used, the strain is in the direction of their length only, and their dimensions can be calculated, knowing the pitch, span, and weight of the roof per square foot, and the distance apart of the ties, or the amount of surface retained by each tie.

Rule.—Multiply one half the weight by one half the span, and divide the product by the pitch.

Example.—What is the strain upon the tie rod of a roof 40 feet span and 15 feet pitch?

The weight of the wood-work of a roof may be estimated at 35 lbs. per cubic foot, or on an average at about 9 lbs. per foot square, slate at 7 to 9 lbs., shingles at $1\frac{1}{2}$ to 2 lbs. The force of the wind may be assumed at 15 lbs. per square foot. The excess of strength in the timbers of the roof as allowed in all calculations, will be sufficient for any accidental and transient force beyond this. If, therefore, the roof be like fig. 1, Plate II., without ceiling beneath, and retained by a tie rod, we may consider as the weight per square foot for a slate roof: $9 + 7 + 15 = 31$ lbs. The length of the rafter is $\sqrt{20^2 + 15^2} = 25$ feet; hence, if the tie rods are 10 feet apart, the amount of surface on each incline supported by the tie is $25 \times 10 = 250$ square feet, which multiplied by the weight per square foot, or $250 \times 31 = 7750$ lbs.; applying the rule, $\frac{7750}{2} \times 20 \div 15 = 5166$ lbs., the thrust on the tie rod. If we estimate the strength of wrought-iron at 10,000 lbs. per square inch of section, or 8,000 lbs. when a thread is cut upon the end, then, $\frac{5166}{8000} = 0.646$ square inches, or a rod a little exceeding $\frac{7}{8}$ of an inch in diameter.

The rafters (fig. 1, Plate II.), may be considered as jack rafters of long bearings, or as a beam supporting transversely the weight of the roof, and the accidental pressures, and may be estimated by resolving the direction of these pressures into a line perpendicular to the direction of the rafters.

Main rafters, as in figs. 2 and 3. The pressure on main rafters is in the direction of their length, when they are supported by braces at or very near the points where the purlines rest; but in addition to the weight of the roof, they support a portion of the weight of the tie beam, and whatever may be dependent upon it. If the frame is like fig. 2, that is, with a king-bolt or post, and the weight is uniformly distributed upon the beam, then one half the weight is supported by the bolt or post, and consequently by the rafter, and the other half by the side walls. Under the same circumstances, the suspension rods (fig. 3), support each $\frac{1}{3}$ of the weight of the beam, &c., and the side walls each $\frac{1}{6}$. But in general, where the attic is made use of, the load is not uniformly distributed, by far the greatest part is suspended upon the rods.

To find the pressure on the main rafter. Multiply one half the weight of the roof, and that portion of the weight of the beam and its load which may depend upon it, by the length of the rafter, and divide the product by the pitch.

Example.—What is the pressure upon the main rafter of a slate roof of 56 feet span, 21 feet pitch, frames 10 feet between centres, and form like fig. 3, with an uniformly distributed load on the beam of 8,400 lbs., and a load between the suspension rods of 10,000 lbs.

The length of rafter is $\sqrt{28^2 + 21^2} = 35$ feet.

Assuming the load per square foot upon the rafter the same as the preceding example,

then $35 \times 31 \times 10 = 10{,}850$ lbs., $\frac{1}{2}$ the weight of roof.

$\frac{1}{3}$ of the uniform weight $\frac{8400}{3} = 2{,}800$ lbs.

$\frac{1}{2}$ the weight between rods $\frac{10000}{2} = 5{,}000$ lbs.

Total, 18,650 lbs.

$$\frac{18650 \times 35}{21} = 31{,}083 \text{ lbs.}$$

If we now assume the resistance of wood at 740 lbs. per square inch,* or 600 lbs. for length exceeding 13 times their thickness,

$$\frac{31083}{600} = 52.59 \text{ square inches of section.}$$

The proportion of the depth to the width is generally about 10 to 8 or 5 to 4.

Hence $\sqrt{\frac{52}{20}} \times 5 = 1.62 \times 5 = 8.1$ inches = depth.

$1.62 \times 4 = 6.5$ inches = width.

Gwilt, in his Architecture, recommends the following dimensions for portions of a roof:

* Weisbach.

SPAN.	FORM OF ROOF.	RAFTERS.	BRACES.	POSTS.	COLL'R BEAMS.
feet.		inches.	inches.	inches.	inches.
25	Fig. 2, Plate II.	5 × 4	5 × 3	5 × 5	
30	" "	6 × 4	6 × 3	6 × 6	
35	Fig. 3, "	5 × 4	4 × 2	4 × 4	7 × 4
45	" "	6 × 5	5 × 3	6 × 6	7 × 6
50	2 Sets of Queen Posts	8 × 6	5 × 3	{ 8 × 8 8 × 4 }	9 × 6
60	" "	8 × 8	6 × 3	{ 10 × 8 10 × 4 }	11 × 6

These dimensions, for rafters, are somewhat less than the usual practice in this country; no calculations seem to have been made for using the attic. An average of common roofs here, would give the following dimensions nearly: 30 feet span, 8 × 5 inches; 40 feet, 9 × 6; 50 feet, 10 × 7; 60 feet, 11 × 8; collar beams the same size as main rafters. Roof frames from 8 to 12 feet from centre to centre.

Dimensions for jack rafters 15 to 18 inches apart.

For a bearing of 6 feet,	3 × 2½ inches.
" " 8 "	4 × 3 "
" " 10 "	5 × 3 "
" " 12 "	6 × 3 "
" " 20 "	10 × 3 "

Purlines:

LENGTH OF BEARING.	DISTANCES APART IN FEET.			
feet.	6	8	10	12
6½	6 × 3½	6½ × 4	7 × 5	8 × 5
8	7 × 5	8 × 5	9 × 5	9 × 6
10	9 × 5	10 × 5	10 × 6	11 × 6
12	10 × 6	11 × 6	12 × 7	13 × 8

The pressure on the plates is transverse from the thrust of the rafters, but in all forms except fig. 1, owing to the notching of the rafters on the purlines, this pressure is inconsiderable. The usual size of plates for figs. 1 and 2, is 6 × 6 inches. For forms, fig. 1, the size depends on the magnitude of roof, and the distance between the ties. The width in all such cases to be greater than the depth; 4 to 6 inches may be taken as the depth, 8 to 12 for the width.

Joints.—As timber cannot always be obtained of sufficient length for the different portions of a frame, it is often necessary to unite two or more pieces together by the ends, called scarfing or lapping. Figs. 35 and 36 are the most common means of lapping or halving, which methods may be employed when there is not much longitudinal compression or extension. When such an effect is to be provided for, the upper as well as the lower timber should be let into each other. Figs. 37, 38, 39, 40, 41, are differ-

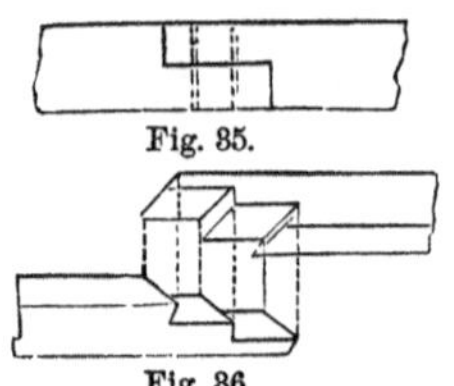

Fig. 35. Fig. 36.

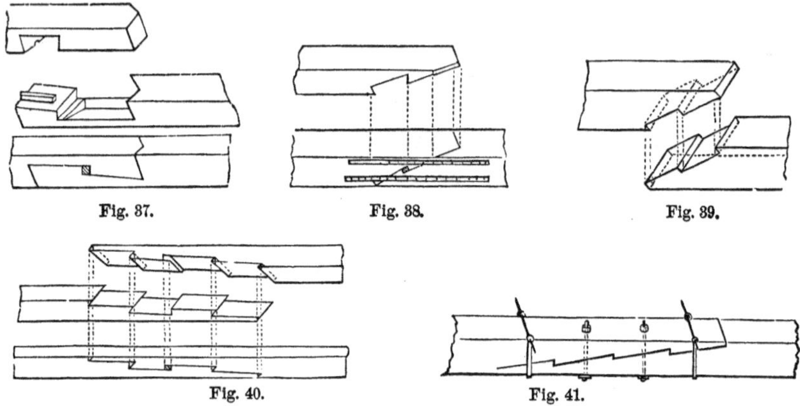

Fig. 37. Fig. 38. Fig. 39. Fig. 40. Fig. 41.

ent methods to obtain this result. In figs. 37, 38, the joint is brought to a bearing by a key driven in tight. Fig. 39 represents a scarf suited for a beam supported at this joint by a post, and where there is tensile strain, the timber should be joint-bolted or anchored. The centre of the post should be beneath the extreme edge of the lower joint. Figs. 40 and 41 are long scarfs, in which the parts are bolted through and strapped, suited for tie beams. Joints are also often made by abutting the pieces together and bolting splicing pieces on each side; still further security is given by cutting grooves in both timbers and pieces and driving in keys.

Circular Roofs.—The rafters of cylindrical roofs may be constructed of strips of boards cut to the width of the rafter, bent into the form of the proposed arc, and nailed together to the depth required for the size of the roof. The plate extends the whole length of the building; the foot of the rafters are nailed or bolted to the plate, and ties, either of wood or iron, as often as may be necessary, retain the thrust. For a 50 feet span, of 6 feet rise, the rafters may be 10 × 4 inches, and 15 inches apart; such a roof being very flat on top, must be covered with metal. Very large cylindrical roofs are constructed of trusses, those of Howe's bridge (fig. 52), the suspension rod being radial, and the lower and upper chords concentric; such roofs are nearly semicircular. The ends of each truss are retained by tie bolts, and purlines are used to support the rafters; but in general

PLATE III.

Fig. 1.
Fig. 2.
Fig. 3.
Fig. 4.
Fig. 5.
Fig. 6.
Fig. 7.
Fig. 8.
Fig. 9.
Fig. 10.
Fig. 12.
Fig. 13.

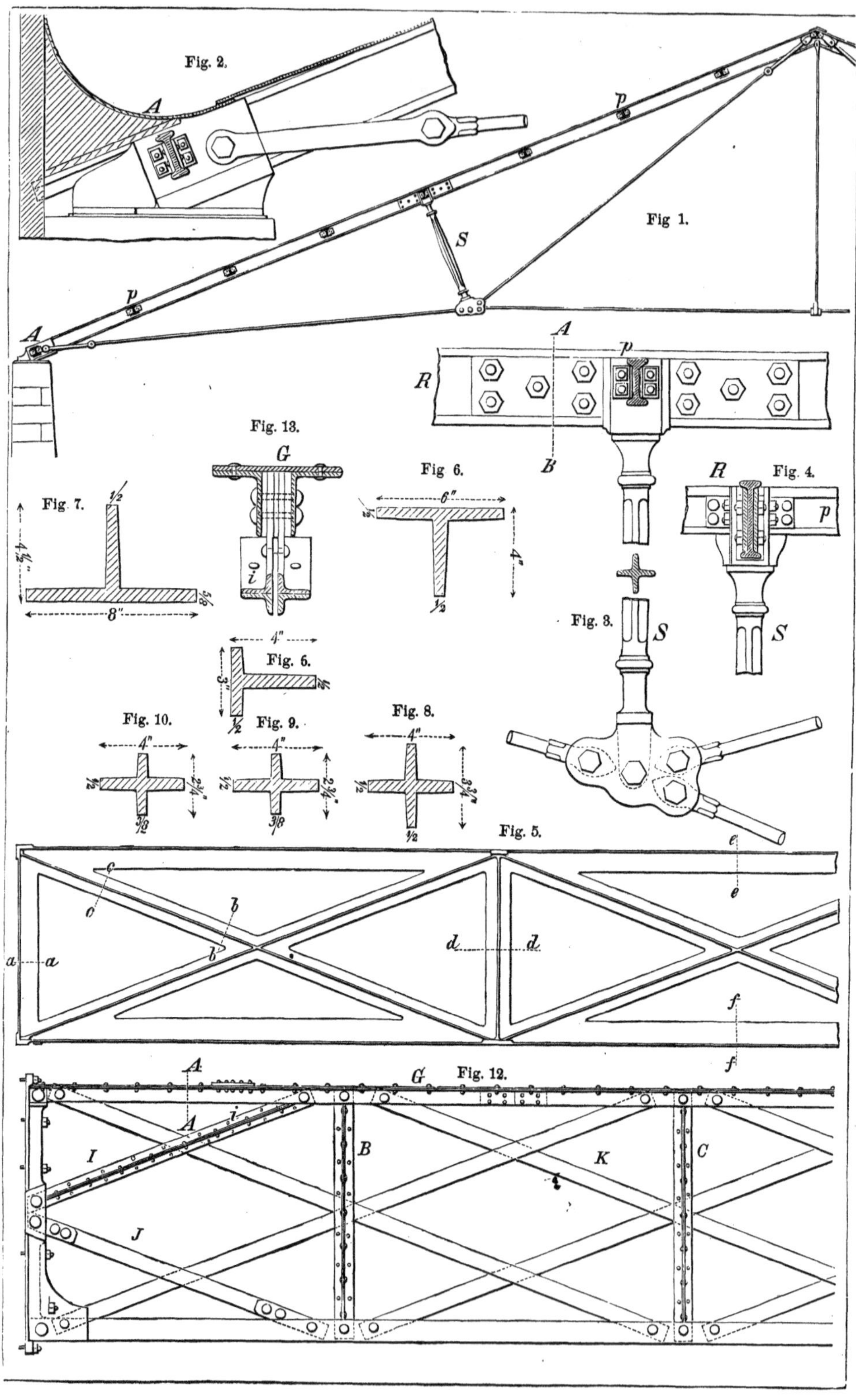

such roofs are for railroad station houses, and no rafters are used, corrugated iron being placed from purline to purline. Roofs of less than 30 feet span are often made of corrugated iron alone, curved into a suitable arc, and tied by bolts passing through the iron about 2 to 4 feet above the eaves.

Iron Roofs.—Plate III., fig. 1, represents the half elevation of an iron roof of a forge at Paris; figs. 2, 3, 4, details on a larger scale. This is a common form of iron roof, consisting of main rafters, R, of the I section, fig. 4, trussed by a suspension rod, and tied by another rod. The purlines are also of I iron, secured to the rafters by pieces of angle iron on each side; and the roof is covered with either plate iron resting on jack rafters, or corrugated iron extending from purline to purline. The rafter shoe, A, and the strut, S, are of cast iron, all the other portions of the roof are of wrought iron.

The surface covered by this particular roof, is 53 metres (164 feet) long, and 30 metres (98½ feet) wide. There are 11 frames, including the two at the ends, which form the gables.

The following are the details of the dimensions and weights of the different parts:

	lbs.
2 rafters, 0.72 feet deep, length together, 99.1 feet,	1,751
5 rods, 0.13 feet diameter, " " 131.4 "	882
16 bolts, "	79
8 bridle-straps, 0.24 × .05	123
2 pieces, .046 thick, connecting the rafters at the ridge, } 4 " " at the foot of the strut }	88
4 " .036 thick, uniting the rafters at the junction in the strut—together with their bolts and nuts,	176
2 cast iron struts,	308
2 rafter shoes,	287
Total of one frame,	3,695
16 purlines, 1 ridge iron, each 0.46 deep, 17.2 long,	2,985
Bolts for the same,	64
16 jack rafters, I iron, 0.16 deep,	2,489
Weight of iron covering, including laps, per square foot,	2.88

The weight of iron in this roof could be reduced by substituting corrugated iron for the covering, even of less weight per square foot, and omitting the jack rafters.

Roofs are sometimes made with deep corrugated main rafters with flat iron between, or purlines and corrugated iron for the covering. The great objection to iron roofs, lies in the condensation of the interior air by the outer cold, or, as it is termed, sweating; on this account they are seldom used for other buildings than boiler houses or depots, except a ceiling be made below to prevent the contact of the air inside with the iron.

Fig. 5 is an elevation of nearly two of the three panels of one of the cast iron girders for connecting the columns, and carrying the transverse main gutters, which supported the roof of the English Crystal Palace. Figs. 6, 7, 8, 9, 10, 11, sections of various parts on an enlarged scale.

The depth of the girder was 3 feet, and its length was 23 ft. 3¾ inches. The sectional area of the bottom rail and flange in the centre (fig. 7), was 6¼ square inches; the width of both bottom and top rail (fig. 6), was reduced to 3 inches at their extremities. It will be observed that the section of the braces and ties are such as to give great stiffness, and the section of the braces at *b b* (fig. 8), is greater than at *c c* (fig. 9); the section of the tie (fig. 10), is the same as the brace at *c c;* they are all formed with a *draft*, that is, with a taper from the centre to the outside of from $\frac{1}{32}$ to $\frac{1}{16}$ of an inch on a side, according to the depth of the feather.

The weight of these girders was about 1,000 lbs., and they were proved by a pressure of 9 tons, distributed on the centre panel.

A second series of girders were made of similar form to fig. 5, but of increased dimensions in the section of their parts. Their weight averaged about 1,350 lbs., and they were proved, as above, to 15 tons.

A third series, of increased section of parts, weighed about 2,000 lbs., and were proved to 22½ tons.

Fig. 12 represents an elevation of two of the nine panels of one of the wrought iron trusses which carry the lead flat and arched roof across the nave of the Crystal Palace. These trusses are 72 feet long and 6 feet deep. The top rail G, shown in section fig. 13, consists of two angle irons 4½ inches deep, 3½ inches wide, and ⅜ of an inch thick, with a plate 9 inches wide and ⅜ thick, riveted on top. A space of 2 inches is left between the angle irons. The angle irons are in five lengths, and are connected by eight ¾ rivets passing through them, and through a plate or plates introduced between them. The top plate is in seven lengths, connected by ½ inch rivets, through the angle irons, the plate, and a joint plate. The top plate is riveted to the angle irons by ½ inch countersunk rivets, 5 inches apart. The bottom rail consists of two flat wrought iron bars, 6 inches deep, with a 2 inch space between them. It is in four lengths, jointed by six 1 inch rivets passing through joint plates 6 × 18 × $\frac{15}{16}$ inches on the outside, and three plates 17 × ⅔ inches. The bars forming the central lengths of the bottom rail are ⅞ of an inch thick, and those forming the side lengths are ⅝ of an inch thick.

The end standards are of cast iron, 3¼ inches wide, 4 inches deep, and

1 inch thick, of a T form of section, secured to the column by six $1\frac{1}{8}$ inch bolts. The standard is 2 inches thick at top and bottom where it receives the rails. Two sockets are formed in the middle, to receive the diagonals I and J. I, being exposed to compression, is made of four angle irons, $2\frac{1}{4} \times 2\frac{1}{4} \times \frac{7}{16}$ inch, riveted together in pairs with $\frac{1}{2}$ inch rivets. The diagonal J is formed of two bars, $4\frac{1}{2} \times \frac{1}{2}$ inch, and is secured at each end by a $1\frac{3}{8}$ inch rivet. The ends are thickened by short plates riveted to them to make up in a measure the loss of strength from the large rivet hole. The diagonal K is formed of two bars $4\frac{1}{2}$ inches deep by 1 inch thick, and is fixed at each end by a 2 inch bolt and nut. The other diagonals, being exposed to much less strain, are formed of single bars $4\frac{1}{2} \times \frac{1}{4}$ inch, and are secured at each end by a 1 inch rivet.

The standards B and C consist each of four angle irons, $2\frac{1}{4} \times 2\frac{1}{4} \times \frac{1}{4}$ inch, riveted together in pairs, and the two pairs riveted together with six small cast iron distance pieces between them. The next standard, that is, the third from each end, but not shown in the drawing, is of cast iron. It is of + section, being at the centre 6 × 6 inches, thickness of metal $\frac{3}{4}$ to $\frac{7}{8}$ of an inch. The base, which rests upon the base of the bottom rail, is 18 × 4 inches, and the top is 18 × 3 inches. Triangular projections enter the top and bottom rail, where they are secured by 1 inch rivets. In the centre is a socket or slot through which pass the two light diagonals. The main strength of the truss consists in the top and bottom rails, the diagonals I, J, K, the first wrought iron standard, B, and the cast iron standard, D.

On the General Principles of Bracing.—Let fig. 42 be the elevation of a common roof truss, and let a weight, W, be placed at the foot of one of the suspension rods. Now, if the construction consisted merely of the rafter C′ B, and the collar-beam C′ C, resting against some fixed point, then the point B would support the whole downward pressure of the weight; but in consequence of the connection of the parts of the frame, the pressure must be resolved into components in the direction C′ A and C′ B, C′ *b* will represent the pressure in the direction C′ B, C′ *w* the portion of the weight supported at B, C′ *a* the pressure in the direction C′ A, and *w* W the portion of the weight supported on A. The same resolution obtains to determine the direction and amount of force exerted on a bridge truss of any number of panels, by a weight placed at any point of its length (fig. 43.) In either case, the

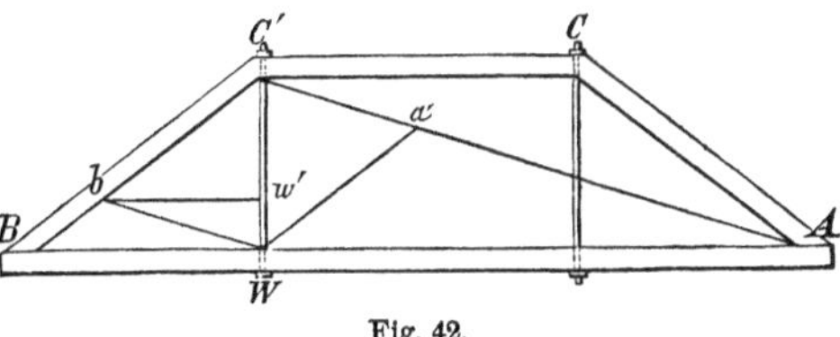

Fig. 42.

effect of the oblique form C′ A, upon the angle C, is evidently to force

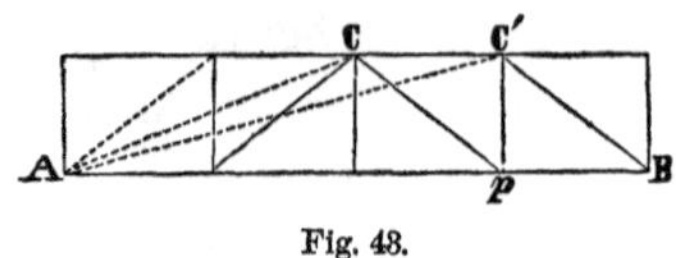

Fig. 43.

it upwards; that is, a weight placed at one side of the frame has, as in case of the arch, a tendency to raise the other side. The effect of this upward force is a tension on a portion of the braces, according to the position of the weight; but as braces, from the manner in which they are usually connected with the frame, are not capable of opposing any force of extension, it follows that the only resistance is that which is due to the weight of a part of the structure.

Figs. 44 and 45 illustrate the results of overloading at single points such forms of construction.

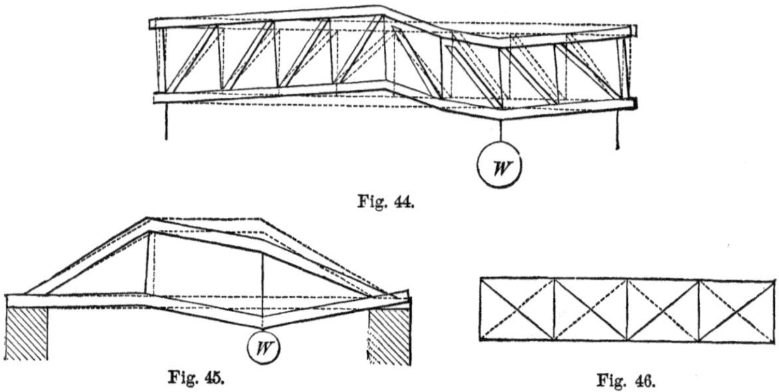

Fig. 44.

Fig. 45.

Fig. 46.

To remedy this effect, if *counter* braces be introduced, as shown in dotted lines (fig. 46), the tendency of a weight moving across the structure is to compress the counters and extend the braces. But since, as we have said, braces are not usually framed, especially in wooden structures, to resist a tensile strain, it is necessary to overcome this force in another way; that is, by introducing wedges between the end of the counter braces and the joints against which they abut, or by means of the counters and the suspension rods, in any way straining the structure so that there may be an additional compression upon the brace more than the upward or tensile force exerted by any passing weight. In this case, therefore, the passage of a load would produce no additional strain upon any of the timbers, but would tend to relieve the counters. The counter braces do not, of course, assist in sustaining the weight of the structure; on the contrary, the greater the weight of the structure itself, the more will the counter braces be relieved.

If instead of the counter braces, the braces themselves are made to act both as tie and as a strut, as has been done sometimes in iron bridges and trusses, then the upward force will be counteracted by the tension of the brace, but in general counter braces are preferable, as it is better that the force exerted against any portion of the structure should always be in one direction.

It follows, from what has been shown of the effect of a variable load, that no bridge, either straight or arched, intended for the passage of heavy vehicles or trains, should ever be without counter braces or diagonal ties, and that only in the case of roofs or aqueducts of similar construction, when the load is uniform, or very small in comparison with the weight of the structure itself.

On the Truss by Tension Rod (fig. 47).—Since the limit of the elas-

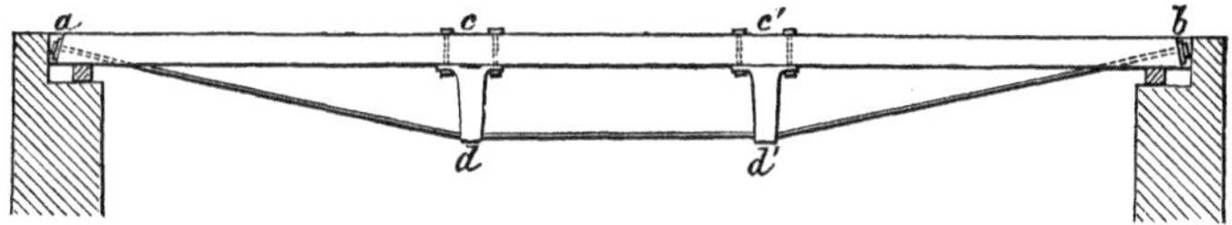

Fig. 47.

ticity of iron is very small in comparison with wood, when iron is thus used to truss timber, the rods must break before the beam reaches the deflection that the weight should produce. It is evident, therefore, that in construction the beam should not be cambered by the tension of the rod, but that the top of the beam should be arched, and be permitted to settle with the weight before it strains the rod at all. In general, the rods should be depended on to resist the whole of the tension, and act as the lower chords of an ordinary bridge; in this way the calculation becomes very simple and furnishes safe practical results. Thus (fig. 47.), to estimate the strain upon the suspension rod, multiply the weight supported at the point c or c' by the length of the rod $a\,d$ or $d'\,b$, and divide the product by the length of the strut $c\,d$. The length of the rod and of the strut, may be measured from any horizontal line which completes the triangle.

Example.—What must be the tension on the rod of a truss 40 ft. span, supporting a load uniformly distributed of 80,000 lbs.; the struts $c\,d$, $c'\,d'$, being 3 feet, and the middle interval 12 feet, and the end ones 14 feet each? Then each point c, c', supports $\frac{12}{2} + \frac{14}{2} \div 40$ or $\frac{13}{40}$ of the weight, and the side walls $\frac{7}{40}$ each.

$$\frac{13}{40} \times 80{,}000 = 26{,}000, \text{ weight on } c \text{ or } c'.$$

$$\sqrt{14^2 + 3^2} = 14.32, \text{ length of rod.}$$

$$\frac{26000 \times 14.32}{3} = 124{,}106 \text{ lbs., tension of rod.}$$

$$\frac{124106}{8000} = 15.5 \text{ sq. inches necessary to resist this tension.}$$

Suppose a system to be composed of a series of suspension trusses, as

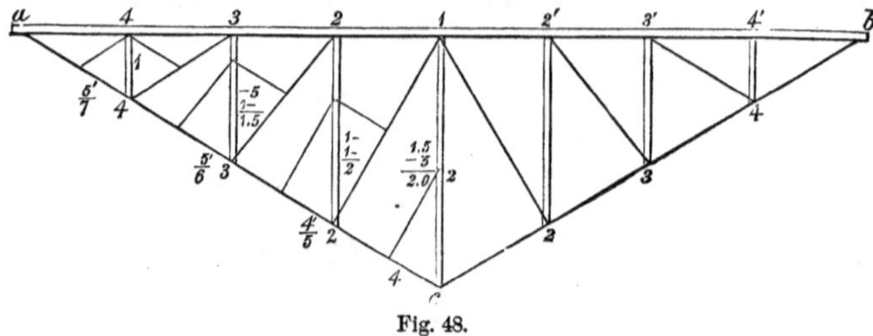

Fig. 48.

in fig. 48, in which the load is uniformly distributed. If we represent the load at each of the points, 4, 3, 2, 1, 2′, &c., by 1, the load at 4 will be supported $\frac{1}{2}$ upon a and $\frac{1}{2}$ upon 3; hence the strut 3 will have to support a load of $1 + .5 = 1.5$; of this, $\frac{2}{3}$ will be supported by 2 and $\frac{1}{3}$ by a; $\frac{2}{3}$ of $1.5 = 1$, $1+1 = 2$, load on strut 2; $\frac{3}{4}$ of this load, or 1.5, will be supported at 1, and since from the opposite side there is an equal force exerted at 1, therefore the strut 1 supports $1 + 1.5 + 1.5 = 4$; the tension on the rod $c\,2$ is 4; on 2 3, $4 + 1 = 5$; on 3 4, $5 + 1 = 6$; on 4 a, $6 + 1 = 7$; and the rod should therefore be increased in strength in these proportions from the central point c, to the point of suspension, a. The tension on the rods 3 4, 2 3, 1 2, may be easily resolved from their direction and the load upon the several struts.

If this construction be reversed, the parts which now act as ties must be made as braces, and braces, ties; then we have a roof truss, and the force exerted on the several parts may be estimated in a similar way as for the suspension truss.

It is evident that neither of these constructions would serve for a bridge truss, subject to the passage of heavy loads, but is only fit to support uniform and equally distributed loads.

To frame a construction so that it may be completely braced, that is, under the action of any arrangement of forces; the angles must not admit of alteration, and consequently the shape cannot. The form should be resolvable into either of the following elements:—Figs. 49, 50, 51.

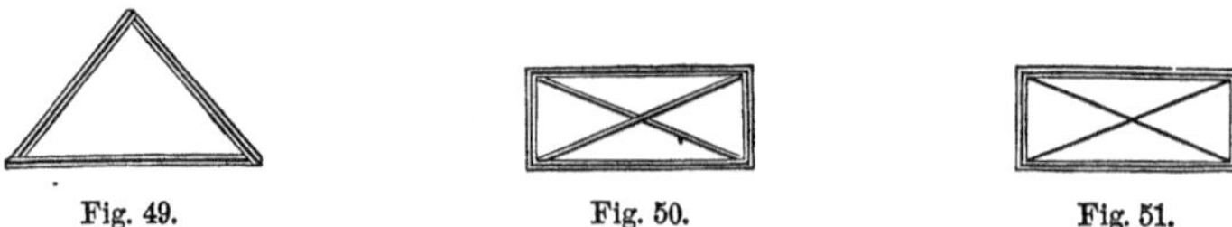

Fig. 49. Fig. 50. Fig. 51.

In these figures, lines ══════ represent parts required to resist compression; lines ────── parts to resist tension only; lines ▬▬▬▬▬▬ parts to resist both tension and compression.

It is evident that in a triangle (fig. 49.), an angle cannot increase or diminish, without the opposite angles also increasing or diminishing. In the form fig. 50, a diagonal must diminish; in fig. 51 a diagonal must extend, in order that any change of form may take place. Consequently all these forms are completely braced, as each does not permit of an effect taking place, which would necessarily result from a change of figure. Hence also, any system composed of these forms, properly connected, breaking joint as it were into each other, must be braced to resist the action of forces in any direction; but as in general all bridge trusses are formed merely to resist a downward pressure, the action on the top chord being always compression, it is not necessary that these chords should act in both capacities.

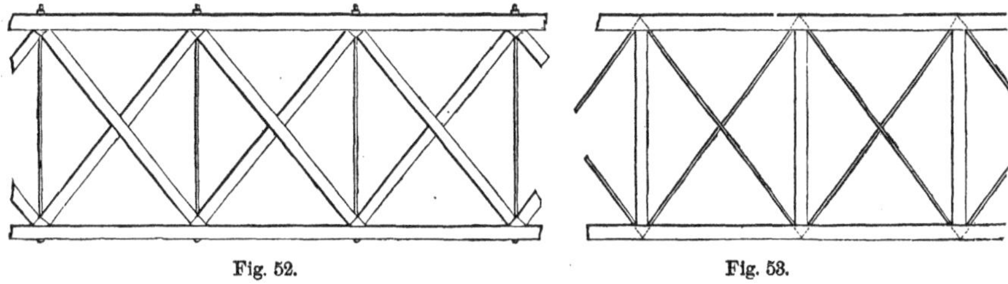

Fig. 52. Fig. 53.

We instance figs. 52 and 53, as illustrative of two systems of bridge trussing, the one being an elevation of Howe's bridge truss, the other of Pratt's. There are many other forms of trussing, but sufficient has been said to explain the principles of most constructions. For farther illustration, we would refer to Haupt on Bridge Construction.

DRAWING.

In the earlier chapters of this work we have given descriptions of the usual variety of drawing instruments and their use, and it is to be presumed that the reader is sufficiently acquainted with their management to construct, with but little explanation, most architectural drawings.

It has been observed, that the first thing to be done towards the execution of a drawing is to determine the scale upon which the drawing is to be made. The usual scale for plans and elevations in architectural drawings is either four feet or eight feet to the inch, and especially in all working drawings it is necessary that the scale should be such that it can be measured with the common two-foot rule, whose divisions are in eighths or sixteenths of an inch. Working details are generally drawn on coarse paper, and on as large a scale as possible, often full size. In our own illustrations, the size of the page has confined us to scales much smaller than should be recommended in practice, and the learner, in copying them, should in no case adopt the same scale, but select one for himself.

Plate IV., represents the plans, end and side elevation, and section of a house.

To construct these, select a scale of say 4 feet to the inch, and commence with the plan fig. 1. Lay off a base line A B on this measure of 20 feet for the length of the house, and erect perpendiculars at the extremities thus measured. Lay off 16 feet for the width on each of the perpendiculars, and connect these points, the line will be parallel to A B, and the outline of the house will be defined. The thickness of the wall for a house of this size, if of brick, will be 8 inches for wall and 2 inches for furring and plastering, or 10 inches; if of wood, the studs should be 2 × 4; 1½ inches for outside boarding and 1 for lath and plaster, or 6½ in total. Lay off now on the inside of the outline the thickness of the wall, and draw the interior lines. Lay off now the partitions marking the rooms; these partitions may be represented by a single line or by two lines. The thickness of partition for such an edifice will be from 4 to 5 inches. The dimensions, as generally marked, should be from outside lines to centres of partitions, or from centres to centres of partitions, as much more determinate for the carpenter to work from than dimensions in the clear, that is, between partitions, or actual space in the rooms. Lay off now the position of the windows, which are to be 3 feet wide. It is to be observed that we must strive in general to preserve uniformity both in inside and outside appearance. Here we wish the front window to be, as near as possible, in the centre of the room, and also, on the outside, to be uniform with the position of the door. The side of the door may be 4 feet from the end of the house; mark its position and width; but the side of the window, if in the centre of the room, will be 5 feet 4 inches from the opposite corner; make it 5 feet, and lay off the window in the rear opposite to the front window. The openings for windows are distinguished from those for doors by straight lines drawn across the aperture. The window in the end of the house, to present an uniform appearance outside, should be in the centre, and this position will also suit the purpose for which the room is designed, a blank corner being necessary for the bed. Lay off now the position of the fireplace in the centre of the end of the room and of the structure, the opening to be 3 feet, the width of the jambs 8 inches each, and the width of the back 2 feet 4 inches. Draw lines for a partition flush with the face of the chimney to one side of the room, with an opening for a door to be for a closet or pantry; all the inside doors to be 2 feet 10 inches wide, and to be represented by openings in the partitions merely. Lay

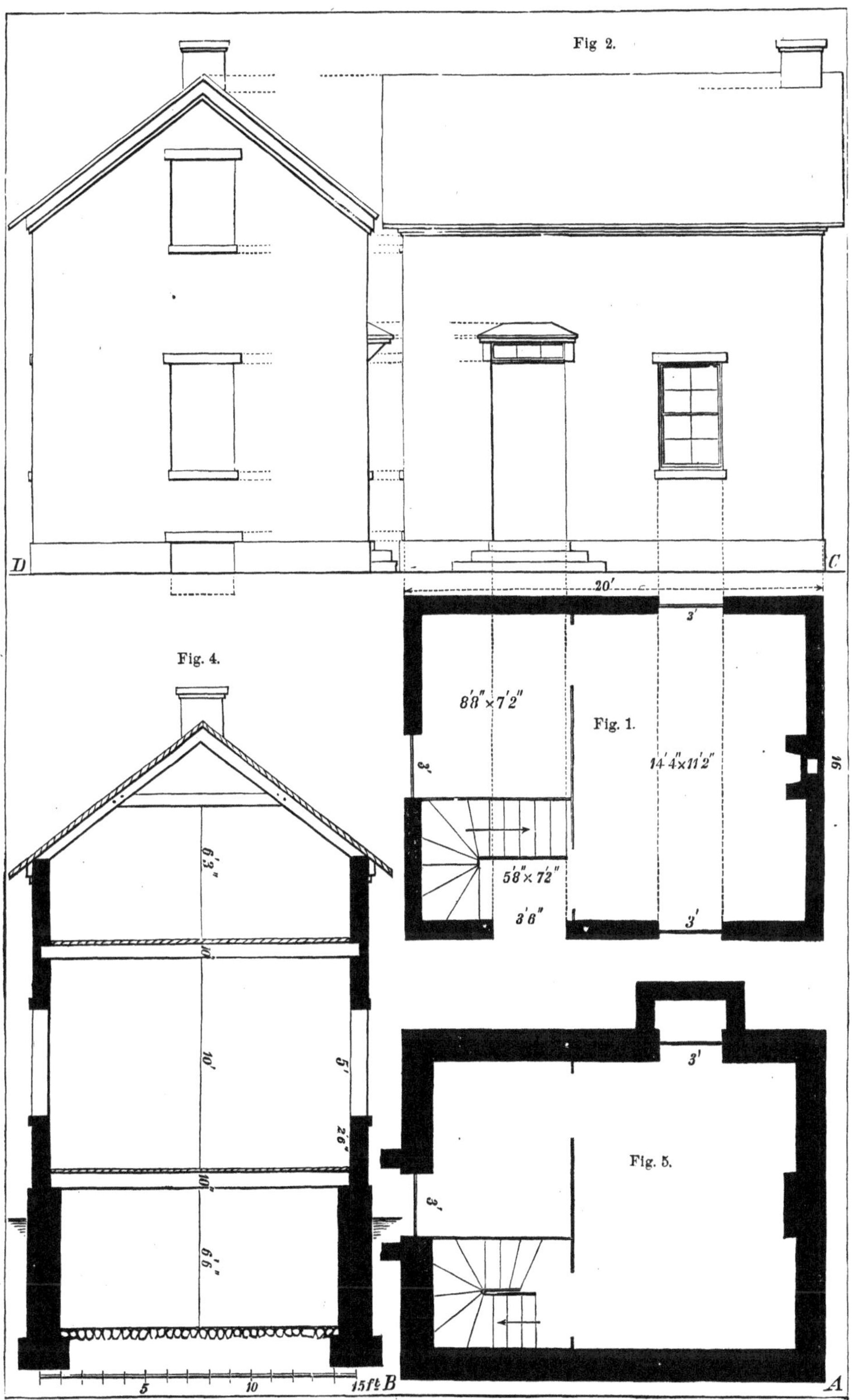
Fig 2.
D
C
20'
Fig. 4.
8'8"×7'2"
Fig. 1.
14'4"×11'2"
16
3'
3'
5'8"×7'2"
3'6"
3'
6'3"
10"
10'
5'
2'6"
10"
6'6"
Fig. 5.
3'
3'
5
10
15 ft.
B
A

off the stairs, as shown in the lobby, 2 feet 9 inches long. Now fill in the space between the interior and exterior outlines of the walls and partition in black, leaving the openings for the doors and windows without color, and the plan is complete. The filling is not necessary, but it adds considerably to the distinctness, and is more explanatory to persons not conversant with drawings, than leaving it in plain outline.

To construct the front elevation (fig. 2), project the various points or position of the corners, window and door, as shown on the plan, and extend the lines of projection as high as may be necessary above the line E D; on these lines mark off the height of window and door, the height of the eaves in projecting must be determined from the end elevation; finish the window and door with lines to represent caps and sills, and whatever other lines may be necessary for the style of finish of the drawing. On the line C D erect also the outlines of the end elevation, taking the horizontal dimensions from the plan, and projecting, as far as possible, the vertical ones from the front elevation. Establish the ridge of the roof by setting off the height of the pitch on the centre line above the eaves, and draw the various lines to represent the boarding and cornice. Draw the chimney in the centre above the ridge. It is to be observed that this chimney is at the opposite end of the house, and may be represented in lighter lines than the rest of the drawing. The base of the chimney and the eaves are to be projected on the front elevation. It is to be observed that many lines may be projected, either from the front to the side elevation, or vice versa; the true way is to construct both elevations together.

The outline of the section (fig. 4), may be taken from the end elevation or may be constructed directly from the dimensions. The roof is constructed of the plainest form, as being of very moderate span, and the attic may be finished for occupation. The dimensions given in this particular instance, in all the figures, is such as would be sufficient for the class of building and purposes for which it is designed. The learner will copy the details as laid down, but on the scale which has been adopted.

The cellar plan (fig. 5), is easily deduced from the ground or first floor plan (fig. 1).

Plate V., represents plans of familiar forms of houses, all drawn to the same scale, as illustrations to the student, and as examples to be copied on a larger scale. The same letters of reference are used, on all the plans, for rooms intended for similar purposes. Thus, K K designate kitchens, cooking rooms, or laundries, D D eating rooms, S S sleeping rooms, P P drawing rooms, parlors, or libraries, *p p* pantries, china or store closets, or clothes-presses, *c c* water-closets and bath rooms.

The plans and elevations given in Plate IV. represent as small a dwelling house as there should be occasion for building. Fig. 1, Plate V., is the first floor plan of a house containing one room more, which may be used either as an eating or drawing room. Figs. 2 and 2′, are the first and second floor plans of a still larger house. Fig. 3 is the floor plan of the same house differently arranged, the kitchen being in the basement. Fig. 4, the same, with an L in the rear for the kitchen. These plans are all of square houses, and although not picturesque in their elevations, are yet very convenient and economical structures; they are intended for the country. The sheds and back offices should be beneath a different roof, but attached or not to the main building as may be desired.

Figs. 5, 6, and 7, are first floor plans of houses of a different outline, but yet uniform, or nearly so; in subsequent plates will be found illustrations of more varied forms of houses. In the cities, houses are mostly confined to one form in their general outline, a rectangle. Figs. 8 and 9 may be taken as the usual type of New York City houses. Figs. 8, 8′, 8″, are the basement, first, and second floor plans of a Basement house, three rooms deep. There is usually a cellar beneath the basement, but in some cases there are front vaults, entered beneath the steps to the front door; the entrance to the basement itself is also beneath the steps. The front room of the basement may be used as an eating room, for the servants' sleeping room, billiards or library. The usual dining room is on the first floor; a dumb waiter being placed in the butler's pantry *p*, for convenience in transporting dishes to and from the kitchen. The objection to three room deep houses is that the central room is too dark, being lighted by sash folding doors between that and the front or rear rooms or both. Fig. 8‴ is a modification to avoid this objection, the dining room, or tea room as it is generally called, being built as L, so that there is at least one window in the central room opening directly out-doors. Figs. 9, 9′, 9″, 9‴, are plans of the several floors of an English Basement house so called, distinguished from the former in that the principal floor is up one flight of stairs. The first story or basement, is but one or two steps above the street, and contains the dining room, with its butler's pantry and dumb waiter, a small sitting room, with, in some cases, a small bed room in the room in the rear of it. The kitchen is situated beneath the dining room, in the sub-basement. The grade of the yard is in general some few steps above the floor of the kitchen. Vaults for coal and provisions are excavated either beneath the pavement in front or beneath the yard. The advantages of this form of house are the small sitting room on the first floor, which in small families, and in the winter months, is the most fre-

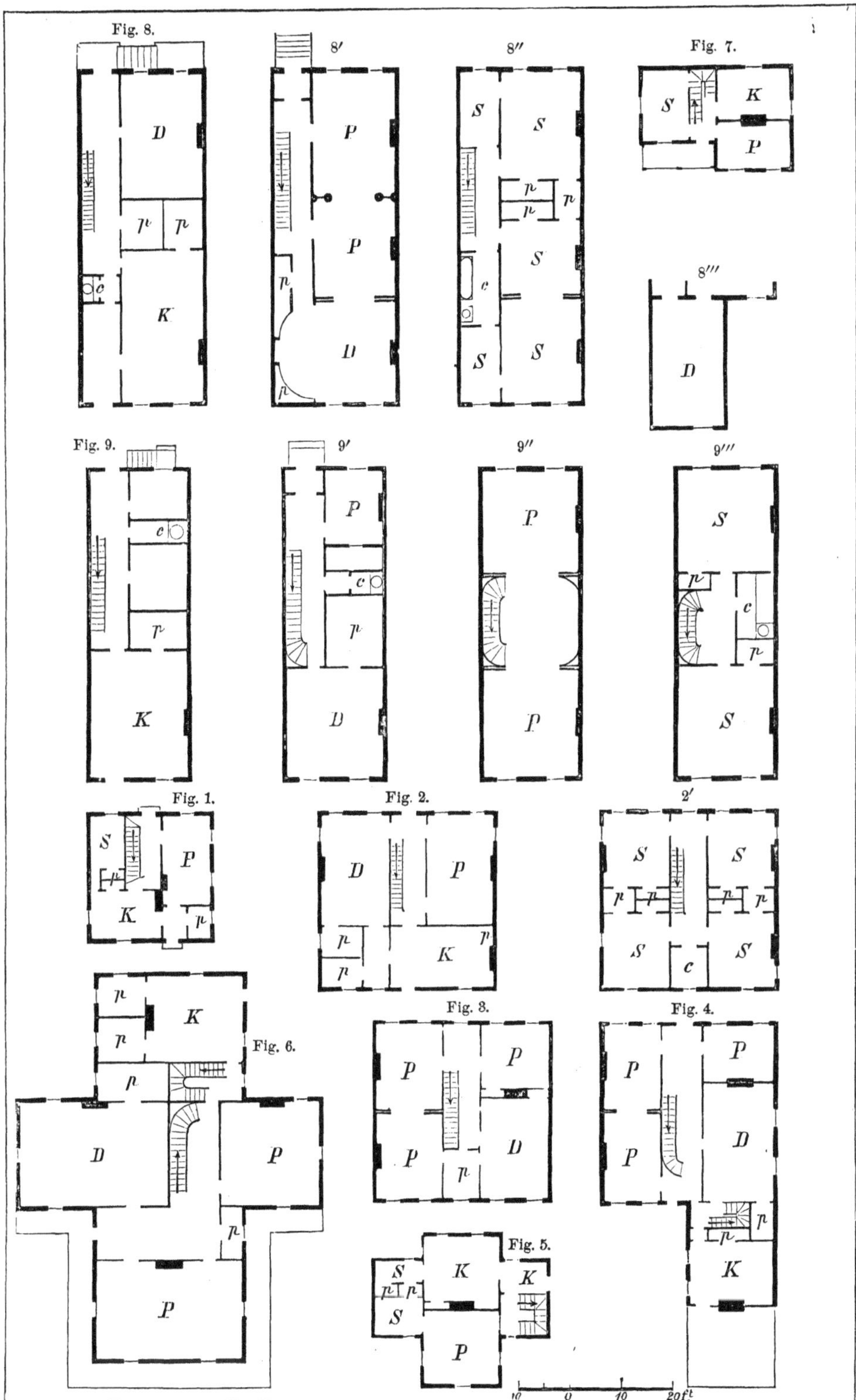
Fig. 8.
8′
8″
Fig. 7.
8‴
Fig. 9.
9′
9″
9‴
Fig. 1.
Fig. 2.
2′
Fig. 6.
Fig. 3.
Fig. 4.
Fig. 5.
10 0 10 20ft

quently occupied of any in the house; the spaciousness of its dining room and parlors in proportion to the width of the house, which is often but 16 feet 8 inches in width, or three houses to two lots, and not unfrequently of even a less width. The objections to the house are the stairs, which it is necessary to traverse in passing from the dining rooms or kitchen to the sleeping rooms, but this objection would, of course, lie against any house of narrow dimensions, where floor space is supplied by height.

On the Size and Proportion of Rooms in general.—"Proportion and ornament," according to Ferguson, "are the two most important resources at the command of the architect, the former enabling him to construct ornamentally, the latter to ornament his construction." A proportion to be good, must be modified by every varying exigence of a design, it is of course impossible to lay down any general rules which shall hold good in all cases; but a few of its principles are obvious enough. To take first the simplest form of the proposition, let us suppose a room built, which shall be an exact cube—of say 20 feet each way—such a proportion must be bad and inartistic; (and besides,) the height is too great for the other dimensions. As a general rule, a square in plan is least pleasing. It is always better that one side should be longer than the other, so as to give a little variety to the design. Once and a half the width has been often recommended, and with every increase of length an increase of height is not only allowable, but indispensable. Some such rule as the following meets most cases: "The height of the room ought to be equal to half its width plus the square root of its length;" but if the height exceed the width the effect is to make the room look narrow; again, by increasing the length we diminish, apparently, the other two dimensions. This, however, is merely speaking of plain rooms with plain walls; it is evident that it will be impossible, in any house, to construct all the rooms and passages to conform to any one rule of proportion, nor is it necessary, for in many rooms it would not add to their convenience, which is often the most desirable end; and if required, the unpleasing dimensions may be counteracted by the art of the architect, for it is easy to increase the apparent height by strongly marked vertical lines, or bring it down by horizontal ones. Thus if the walls of two rooms of the same dimensions be covered with the same strongly marked striped paper, in one case the stripes being vertical, and in the other horizontal, the apparent dimensions will be altered very considerably. So also a deep bold cornice diminishes the apparent height of a room. If the room is too long for its other dimensions, this can be remedied by breaks in the walls, by the introduction of pilasters, &c. So also, as to the external dimensions of a wall, if the length is too great it is to be remedied by projections, or by breaking up the lengths into divisions. This will be understood by reference to elevations of "Country Houses," Plates XXIII to XXVI. In this view, as variety in form adds greatly to the picturesque, it is far better in designing a country house, where one is not restricted to room, to mark out the rooms to the size which we wish them to be, cutting out slips of paper of the dimensions, according to some scale, to arrange them then in as convenient an order as possible, and again modifying the arrangement by the necessities of construction and economy. Thus the more the enclosing surface, in proportion to the included area, the greater the number of chimneys, unnecessary extent of passages; all of course conduce to an excess of expense. Again, the kitchen should be of convenient access to the dining room, both should have large and commodious pantries, and all rooms should have an access from a passage, without being compelled to pass through another room; this is particularly applicable to the communication of the kitchen with the front door. Outside doors for common and indiscriminate access should open into passages and never into important rooms.

As to the size of the different rooms, they must of course depend on the purposes to which they are to be applied, the class of house, and the number of occupants. To commence with the kitchen, for the poorer class of houses it is also used as an eating room, and should therefore be of considerable size to answer both purposes; for the richer houses, size is necessary for the convenience of the work; in New York City houses the average will be found to be about 16 × 20 feet, for medium houses in the country they are in general less, say 12 × 16. A back kitchen, scullery, or laundry, should be attached to the kitchen, and may serve as a passage way to out of doors.

The dining or eating rooms.—The width of dining tables vary from 3 to 5 feet 6 inches, the space occupied by the chair and person sitting at the table is about 18 inches on each side; the table space, for comfort, should be not less than 2 feet for each person at the sides of the table, and considerable more at the head and foot; hence we may calculate the space that will be necessary for the family and its visitors, at the table. If we now allow a farther space of 2 feet at each side for passages, and some 3 to 5 at the head for the extra tables or chairs, we can mark out the minimum of space required: but, if possible, do not confine the dining room to meagre limits, unless for very small families; let not the parties be lost in the extent of space, nor let them appear crowded.

The show room parlors, if there are any intended for such in the house, may be made according to the rules given above, not square, but the length about once and a half the width; if much longer than this, break up the walls by transoms or projections. As to the particular dimensions no rules can be given, it must depend on every person's taste and means. 20 × 16 may be considered a fair medium size for a regular living room parlor, not a drawing room. The same size will answer very well for a sleeping room. The usual width of single beds is 2 feet 8 inches, of three-quarter 3 feet 6 inches, of whole 4 feet 6 inches, the length 6 feet 6 inches, so that if adequate means of ventilation are provided, it is easy to see into how small quarters persons may be thrust. The bed should not stand too near the fire, nor between two windows; its most convenient position is head against an interior wall, with a space on each side of at least 2 feet.

Pantries.—Closets for crockery should not be less than 14 inches in width in the clear; for the hanging up of clothes, not less than 18 inches, and should be attached to every bed room. For medium houses, the closets of large sleeping rooms should be at least 3 feet wide, with hanging room, and drawers and shelves. There should also be blanket closets, for the storing of blankets and linen; these should be accessible from the entries, and may be in the attic. Store closets should also be arranged for groceries and sweetmeats.

Passages.—The front entries are usually 6 feet wide in the clear; common passage ways are usually 3 feet wide; these are what are required, but ample passages give an important effect to the appearance of the houses. The width of principal stairs should be not less than 3 feet, and all first class houses, especially those not provided with water-closets and slop sinks on the chamber floor, should have two pair of stairs, a front and a back pair; the back stairs may not necessarily be over 2 feet 6 inches in width.

The Height of Stories.—It is usual to make the height of all the rooms on each floor equal, it can be avoided by furring down, or by the breaking up of the stories, by the introduction of a mezzonine or intermediate story over the smaller rooms. Both remedies are objectionable; the more artistic way is to obviate the appearance of disproportionate height by means stated above.

The average height of the stories for such city dwellings as we have given plans of are: cellar 6 feet 6 inches, common basement 8 to 9 feet, English basement 9 to 10, principal story 12 to 15, first chamber floor 10 to 12, other chamber floors 8 to 10 feet, all in the clear. For country houses the smaller of the dimensions are more commonly used. Attic stories are sometimes but a trifle over 6 feet in height, but are of course objectionable.

Details of parts. Stairs consist of the *tread* or *step* on which we set our feet, and *risers*, upright pieces supporting the treads—each tread and riser forms a stair. If the treads are parallel they are called *fliers*, if less at one end than the other, they are called *winders;* in figs. 1 and 3, Plate V., both kinds are shown. Any wide step, for the purpose of resting, is called a *landing*. The height from the top of the nearest step to the ceiling above, is called the *headway*. The edge of the step which is rounded is called a *nosing*, as fig. 6, Plate V.; if a small hollow *b* be glued in the angle of the nosing and riser, it is called a *moulded* nosing. The pieces which support the ends of the stairs are called strings, that against the wall the *wall string*, the other the *outer string*. Besides the strings, pieces of timber are framed and placed beneath the fliers, called *carriages.* The opening on plan (which must occur between the outer strings, if they are not perpendicular over each other), is called the *well hole*, A, fig. 3, Plate VI.

The breadth of stairs in general use is from 9 to 12 inches. In the best staircases, the breadth should never be less than 12 inches, nor more than 15. The height of the riser should be the more, the less the width of the tread; for a 15 inch tread the riser should be 5 inches high, for 12 inches, $6\frac{1}{2}$, for 9 inches, 8. In laying out the plan of stairs, having determined the starting point either at bottom or top as the case may be, find exactly the height of the story; divide this by the height you suppose the riser should be. Thus (fig. 1), if the height of the story and thickness of floor be 9 feet, and we suppose the riser should be about 7 inches high,

then $$108 \text{ inches, divided by } 7 = 15\tfrac{3}{7}.$$

It is clear that there must be an even number of steps, either 16 or 15; to be near to what we have supposed to be the height of the riser, adopt 15,

then $$\tfrac{108}{15} = 7\tfrac{3}{15} \text{ inches, height of riser.}$$

For this particular case we assume the breadth of the step as 10 inches, and the length at 3 feet, a very usual length, seldom exceeding 4 feet in the best staircases of private houses.

Lay off (fig. 1), the outside of the stairs, two parallel lines 3 feet apart, and space off from the point of beginning 14 treads of 10 inches each, and draw the cross parallel lines, and we have the plan of the stairs. It is to be observed that the number of treads is always one less than the number of risers, the reason of which will appear by observing the elevation, fig. 2.

To construct the elevation, the line of the stair in plan may be projected, and the height be divided into the number of risers, 15 of $7\frac{1}{5}$ inches each, and cross parallels drawn through these points.

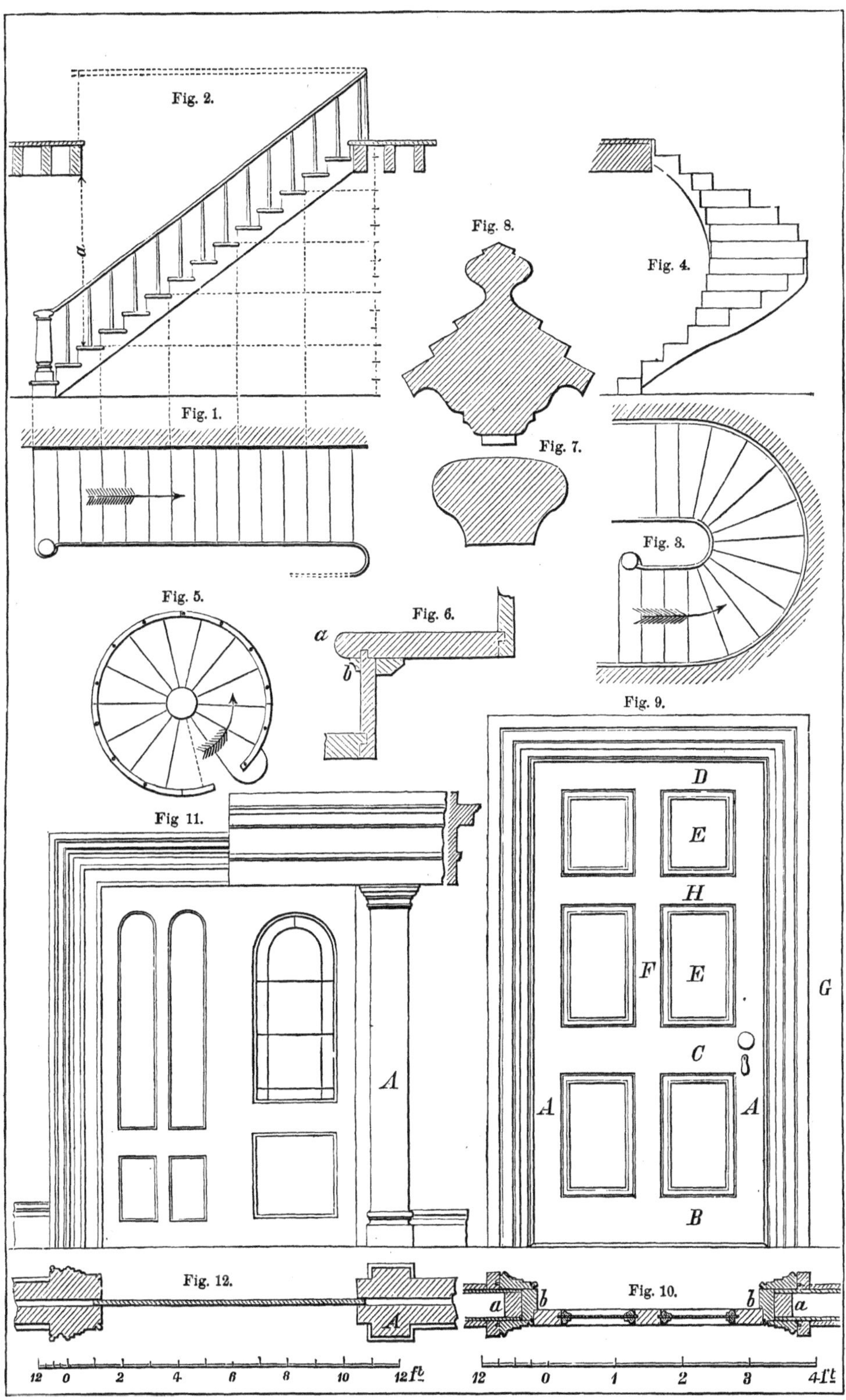
Fig. 2.
a
Fig. 8.
Fig. 4.
Fig. 1.
Fig. 7.
Fig. 3.
Fig. 5.
Fig. 6.
a
b
Fig. 9.
Fig 11.
D
E
H
F
E
G
C
A
A
A
B
Fig. 12.
A
Fig. 10.
a
b
b
a
12 0 2 4 6 8 10 12 ft.
12 0 1 2 3 4 ft.

When the stairs are circular, or consist in part of winders and fliers, as in fig. 3, the width of the tread of the winders should be measured on the central line. The construction of the elevation of a circular flight may be understood from figs. 3 and 4.

The drawing of elevation of stairs is in general necessary, to determine the opening necessary to be framed in the upper floor, to secure proper headway. Thus (fig. 2), the distance between the nearest stair and the ceiling, at *a*, should not be less than 6 feet; a more ample space improves the looks of the stairway; but if we are confined in our limits, this will determine the position of one trimmer, the other will be of course at the top of the stairs. When one flight is placed over another, the space required for timber and plastering, under the steps, is about 6 inches for ordinary stairs.

Fig. 5 represents a circular flight of stairs without a well hole, the narrow ends of the winders being mortised into a central shaft or *newel.* The same term is also applied to the first *baluster* or post of the *hand rail.* The objection to all circular stairs of this form, or with a small well hole, is that there is too much difference between the width of the tread, but a small portion being of a suitable size. The handsomest and easiest stairs are straight *runs*, divided into landings, intermediate of the stories, and either continuing then in the same line, or turning at right angles, or making a full return.

The top of the hand rail should, in general, be about 2 feet 10 inches above the nosing, and should follow the general line of the steps. The angles of the head rail should always be eased off, as shown at the top and bottom in fig. 2. A common form of the hand rail is shown (fig. 7); to serve the purpose for which in part it is designed, that is, of affording an assistance in ascending or descending, it should not be wider than the grasp of the hand, and where for architectural effect a more massive form may be necessary, it is very convenient, and may be very ornamental, to have a sort of double form, that is, a smaller one planted on top of the larger, as in fig. 8.

Doors.—Fig. 9 represents the elevation, and fig. 10 the horizontal section of a common inside door. A A are the *stiles*, B, C, H, D, the *bottom*, *lock*, *parting*, and *top rail*, E the *panels*, and F the *muntin ;* the combination of mouldings and offsets around the door, G, is called the *architrave ;* in the section, *a a* are the partition studs, *b b* the door *jambs*.

With regard to the proportions of internal doors, they should depend in some degree on the size of the apartments; in a small room a large door always gives it a diminutive appearance, but doors leading from the same entry, which are brought into the same view, should be of uniform height. The smaller doors which are found on sale are 2 ft. 4 in. × 6 feet; for water closets, or very small pantries, they are sometimes made as narrow as 20 inches, but any less height than 6 feet will not afford requisite head room. 2 ft. 9 in. × 7 ft., 3 ft. × 7 ft. 6 in., or 3 ft. 6 in. × 8 ft., are well proportioned 6 panelled doors. But the apparent proportions of a door may be varied by the omission of the parting rail, making the door 4 panelled, or narrowed still more by the omission of the lock rail, making a 2 panelled door. Sometimes the muntin is omitted, making but one panel; but this of course will not add to the appearance of width, but the reverse. Wide panels are objectionable, as they are apt to shrink from the mouldings and crack.

When the width of the door exceeds 5 feet, it is generally made in two parts, each part being hung to its side of the frame, or one part hung to the other, so as to fold back like a shutter; or the parts may be made to slide back into pockets or grooves in the partition, as shown in plan and horizontal section, figs. 11 and 12. One of the doors in the drawing is shown as a sash door, the other close panels, so as to give two illustrations in the same diagram; the same may be said of the architrave. It may be unnecessary to say that in construction both sides and doors should be uniform. The upper panels of the close door may be made of glass; the finish around this half of the door is with an architrave, as in fig. 9, but with different mouldings. The finish over the other half of the door is an entablature, supported by pilasters A, commonly called by carpenters antæ, though not correctly so, the antæ being pilasters at the end of a projecting wall.

Figs. 1 and 2, Plate VII., are the elevation and horizontal section of an antæ finished outside door, with *side lights* C C, and a *top*, *fan*, or *transom light* B. The bar A is called a transom, and this term is applied generally to horizontal bars extending across openings, or even across rooms.

Fig. 3 is the elevation of an outside folding door. The plan (fig. 4), shows a vestibule V, and an interior door. The outer doors, when open, fold back into the pockets or recesses, *p p*, in the wall. This is the present usual form of doors for first-class houses in this city. The fan lights are made semicircular, and also the head of the upper panels of the door; these panels in the interior or vestibule door are of glass.

Windows are apertures for the admission of light to the building, for ventilation, and for looking out. When used for the admission of light only, the sashes may be stationary, as they sometimes are in churches, but

PLATE VII.

Fig. 1.
B
A
C
C
Fig. 2.
Fig. 3.
Fig. 4.
p
V
p
Fig. 5.
A
H
T
p
M
a
B
p
S
W
Fig. 6.
w
F
C
p
w
C'
D
D
A
Fig. 8.
Fig. 7.
H
T
M
B
d
S
W
12
9
6
3
0
1ft

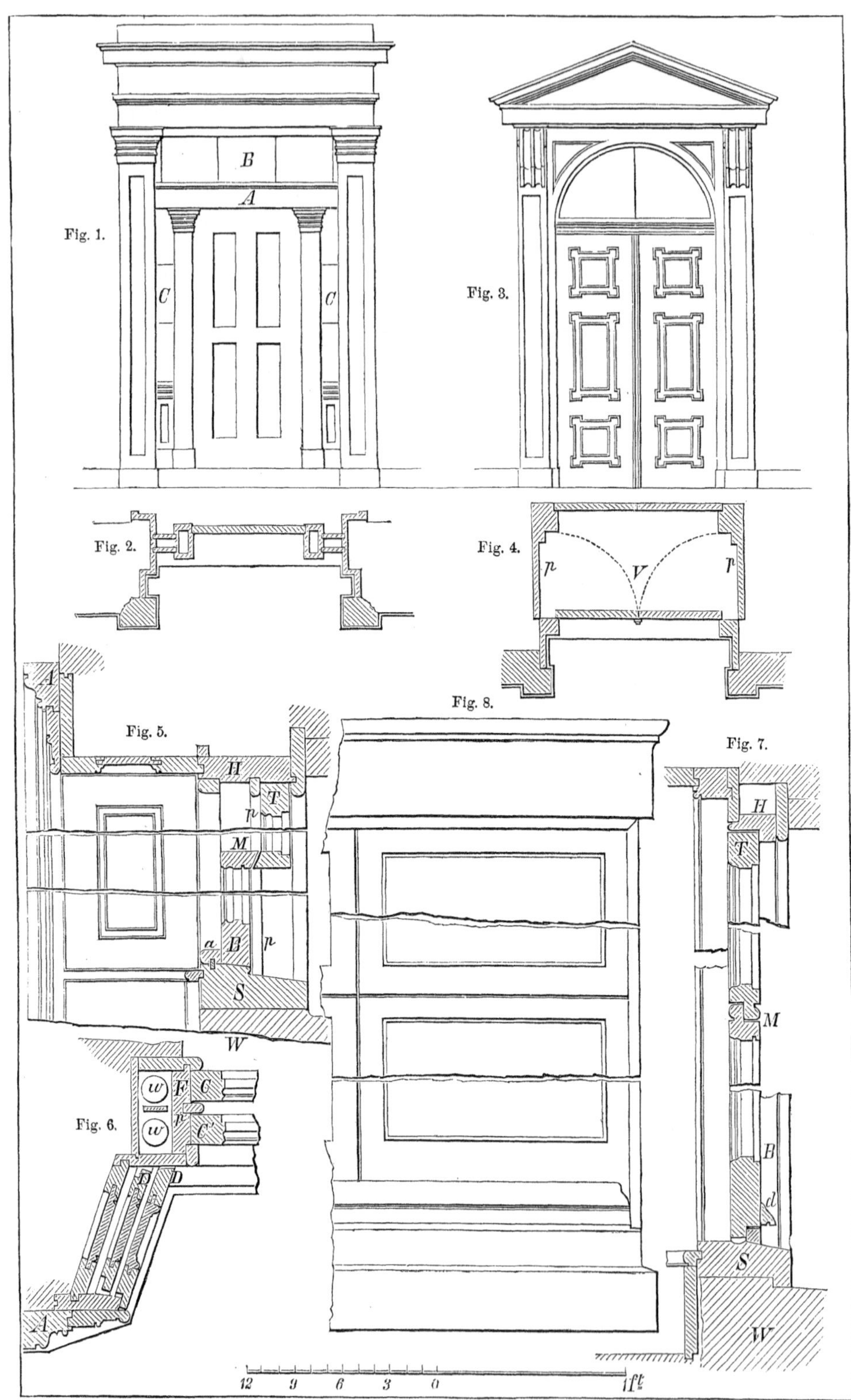

for most positions they are intended for all these purposes, and therefore the sashes are made to open, either by sliding vertically, or laterally, or like doors.

The first is the common form of window, the sashes are generally balanced by weights; the second, except in a cheap form in mechanics' shops, are seldom used; the third are called casements, or French windows.

Figs. 5 and 6 represent the parts of the common sash window and its shutters, broken, so as to show the details on a large scale. The general outside appearance of this window is familiar, and represented simply in the elevations, Plate IV. Fig. 5, Plate VII., is the elevation of the window and shutter, in which S designates the sill of the sash frame, W the stone sill, with a wash to discharge the water, B is the bottom rail of the sash, M the meeting rails, and T the top rail, H is the head of the sash frame, A the architrave similar to that around doors. In the sectional plan, *C C′* are the *window stiles*, F the *pulley stile*, *w w* the sash weights, *p* the parting strip, and D D double fold shutters. Sash windows for dwellings are almost always made with twelve lights, six in each sash. The height of the window must of course depend on the height of the room, Unless the windows begin from, or nearly from, the floor, the point *a* (fig. 5), may be fixed at a height of about 30 inches above the floor, and the top of the window sufficiently below the ceiling to allow space for the architrave or other finish above the window, and for the cornice of the room, if there be any; a little space between these adds to the effect. For common windows, the width of the sash is 4 inches more than that of the glass, and the height 6 inches more; thus the sash of a window 3 lights wide and 4 lights high, of 12 × 16 glass, is 3 feet 4 inches wide, and 5 feet 10 inches high. In plate glass windows more width is taken for the stiles and rails. The most usual sizes of glass are 7 × 9, 8 × 10, 9 × 12, 10 × 12, 10 × 14, 11 × 15, 12 × 16, 12 × 18, 12 × 20, 14 × 20, but glass may be had of intermediate or of much larger sizes. Plate glass, either polished or rough, may be had of size as large as 14 × 7 feet.

Fig. 7 represents the elevation of half of a French window, the same letters designate similar parts as in fig. 5. A transom bar is often framed between the meeting rails, and in this case the upper sash may be movable; in the fig. it is fixed. An upright, called a *mullion*, is often introduced in the centre, against which the sash shuts. Fig. 8 is a section of the elevation, fig. 9 of the plan.

For convenience of egress and ingress, the lower sashes should not be less than 5 feet 6 inches high, that is, when the window opens on a stoop or balcony. It will be seen that in both forms of sash the bottom rail is the widest, and that for the same aperture the French window admits the least light. The chief objection to this window lies in the difficulty of keeping out the rain at the bottom in a driving storm. To obviate this, the small moulding *d*, with a drip or undercut, is nailed to the bottom rail; but the more effectual means is the patent weather strip, the same as used on outside doors.

The most simple exterior finish for windows in brick or stone houses, is a plain stone cap and sill, the height of the cap for common apertures being from four to five courses of brick, and the sill three courses, the latter always to project from one to two inches beyond the line of brickwork. Usually in wooden structures, and often in stone and brick, an architrave is formed around the window (figs. 54, and 55). For brick houses the facings are made of stone. The architrave should not project so much as to interfere with the shutting back of the blinds. Blinds are commonly three-eighths of an inch narrower, and one inch longer than the sash.

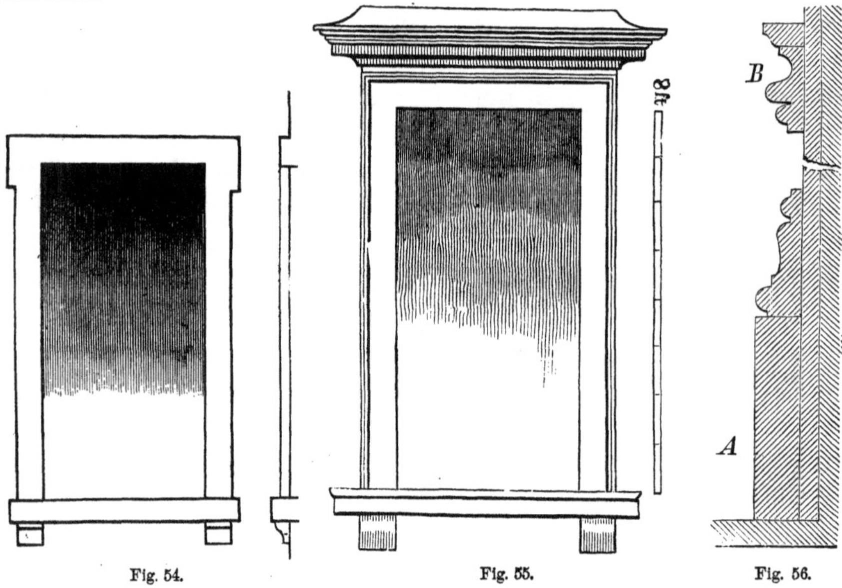

Fig. 54. Fig. 55. Fig. 56.

Fig. 56 represents a section of the finish around the bottom of the wall of a room. A, is the base, consisting of a plain strip or skirting, with a moulding above it. B, is the surbase or chain rail; between these, it is not unusual to have a panelled or plain board, called the dado. The rough plastering is usually continued to the floor, the skirting and surbase are then nailed on, the hard finish is next put on, and lastly the base moulding. The panels of the dado are imitated in oil or distemper; the surbase is seldom used but in dining rooms or offices.

For the finish of the angle of the wall and ceiling, the cornice adds often to the architectural effect. It consists of a series of mouldings similar to the style of finish of the houses, extending around the room. Fig. 57 exhibits the section of quite a simple one. The effect of the cornice is to diminish the apparent height of the room; for low rooms, if adopted, it should extend in width on the ceiling, and but little in depth on the wall, and the reverse where an opposite effect is desired.

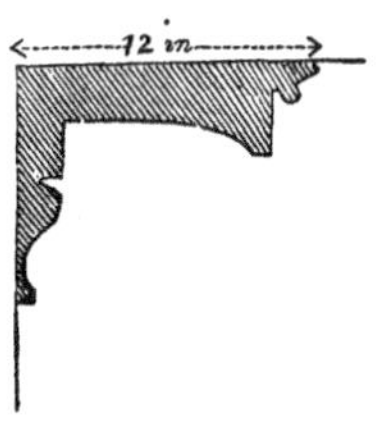

Fig. 57.

Fire-Places.—Fire-places for wood are made with flaring jambs of the form shown in plan, fig. 58; the depth from 1 foot to 15 inches, the width of opening in front from 2 feet 6 inches to 4 feet, according to the size of the room to be warmed; height 2 feet 3 inches to 2 feet 9 inches, the width of back about 8 inches less than in front; but at present fire-places for wood are seldom used, stoves and grates having superseded the fire-place. The space requisite for the largest grate need not exceed 2 feet in

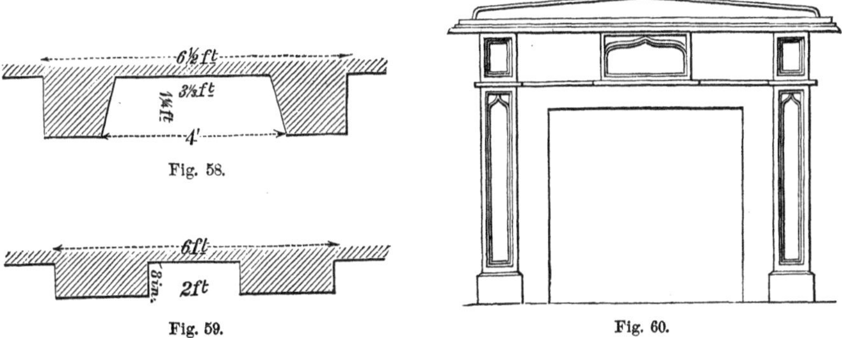

Fig. 58.

Fig. 59.

Fig. 60.

width by 8 inches in depth. The requisite depth is given by the projection of the grate, and of the mantel-piece. Fig. 60 represents the elevation of a mantel-piece of very usual proportions. The length of the mantel is 5 feet 5 inches, the width at base 4 feet 6 inches, the height of opening 2 feet 7 inches, and width 2 feet 9 inches. A portion of this opening is covered by the iron sides or architrave of the grate, and the actual open space would not probably exceed 18 inches in width by 2 feet in height. The sizes of flues are 8 × 8, 4 × 12, and 8 × 12 inches. In brick or stone houses the flues are formed in the thickness of the wall, but when distinct they have an outside shell of a half brick or 4 inches. The flues of different fire-places should be distinct, those from the lower stories pass up through the jambs of the upper fire-places, and keeping side by side with but half a brick between them, are topped out, sometimes in a cluster, but more generally in a single line; forming a chimney 16 inches in width by a length according to the number of the flues. The usual finish of the top of the chimney is by a stone cap and several projecting courses of brick, as shown in fig. 61, or some similar form. The chimney is often made to add considerably to the architectural effect in its finish, as will be seen in Plates XXII to XXV.

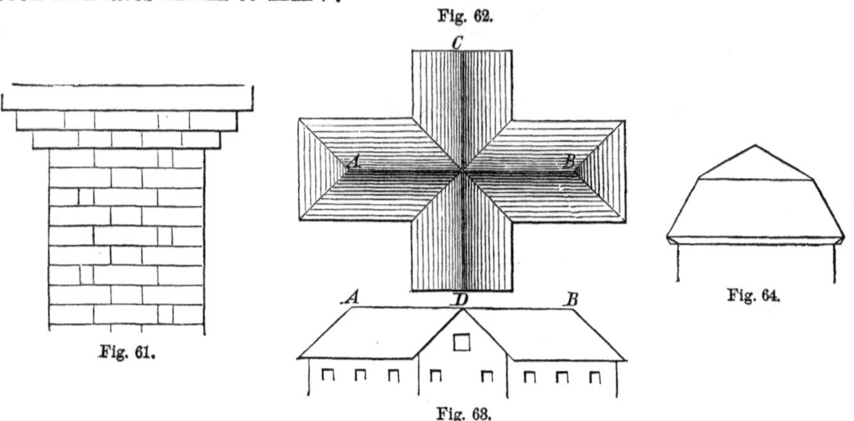

Fig. 61. Fig. 62. Fig. 63. Fig. 64.

Roof.—The general principles of the construction of roofs has been already treated of. A front, and end elevation or gable is given, Plate IV. But many roofs, especially of square houses, are hipped; that is, the roof slopes on all sides to the eaves, as shown in elevation, fig. 63, at A and B the ends of the house; at C and D there are gables. Fig. 62 represents the plan of the same; lines are drawn parallel with the eaves, to show as it were the lap of the shingles or slates, and are generally drawn heavier or closer together at the ridge. Fig. 64 represents the elevation of a gambrel or Mansarde roof, the principle of the construction of which is given, p. 118.

The eaves of roofs are finished with entablatures, consisting of various mouldings or members appropriate to the style of architecture of the structure. The gutters or eaves troughs are generally formed in the cornice (fig. 66), but sometimes they are formed into the depth of the rafter,

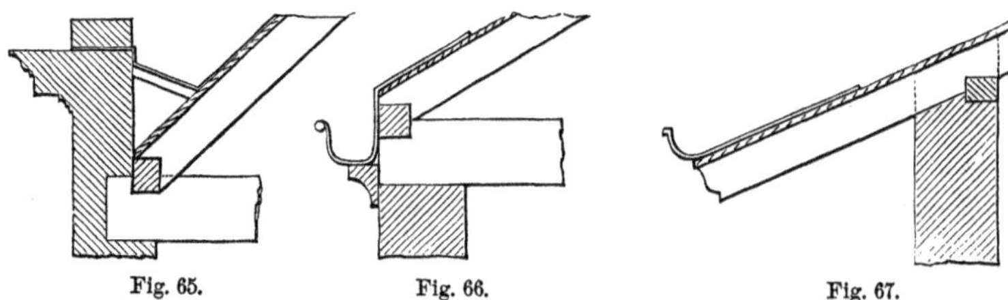
Fig. 65. Fig. 66. Fig. 67.

sometimes on top of the roof (fig. 67), and sometimes by raising a parapet (fig. 65), and forming a *valley*, rather a gutter. It is desirable, however, that the overflow of the gutter should flow over the outer edge, and not back between it and the roof.

It will have been observed that for the finish of most of the parts of an edifice, mouldings are found necessary; so much so, that they should be classed among useful rather than ornamental members. These mouldings are drawn either directly or indirectly from the Grecian orders of architecture.

The regular mouldings are eight in number: Fillet or Band, Torus, Astragal or Bead, Ovolo, Cavetto, Cyma Recta or Ogee, Cyma Reversa or Talon, Scotia.

To construct a Fillet.—The *fillet*, *a* (fig. 68), is the smallest rectangular member employed in any composition of mouldings. When it stands on a flat surface, its projection is usually made equal to its height. It is employed to separate members.

To describe a Torus, or an Astragal.—The *torus* and *astragal* are semicircles in form projecting from vertical diameters, as in fig. 69.

Fig. 68. Fig. 69.

Bisect the vertical diameter *a b*, on which the figure is projected; on the centre *c*, describe a semicircle with *c a* as radius. The astragal is described like the torus, and is distinguished from it in the same order by being made smaller. The torus is generally employed in the bases of columns; the astragal, in both the base and capital.

To describe an Ovolo.—The *ovolo* is a member strong at the extremity, and intended to support. The Roman ovolo consists of a quadrant or a less portion of a circle; the Greek ovolo is elliptic.

First, the Roman ovolo. When the projection is equal to the height. Draw *a b* for the height, and *b c* at right angles and equal to it, for the projection. On the centre *b* describe the quadrant *c a*.

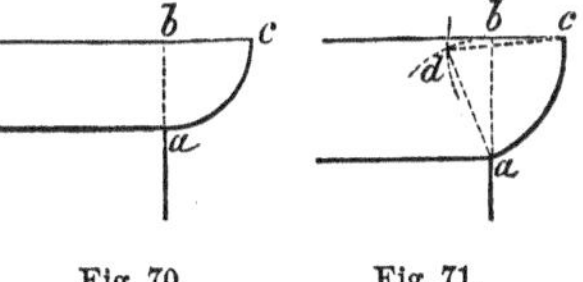

Fig. 70. Fig. 71.

When the projection is less than the height. Draw *a b* and *b c* (fig. 71), as before, equal to the height and the projection. On centres *a* and *c*, with radius *a b*, describe arcs cutting at *d*; and on *d* with same radius describe the arc *a c* to form the ovolo.

Second, the Greek ovolo. Draw *d f* from the lower end of the proposed curve, at the required inclination; draw the vertical *g e f* to define the projection, the point *e* being the extreme point of the curve. Draw *e h* parallel to *d f*, and draw the vertical *d h k*, such that *d h* is equal to

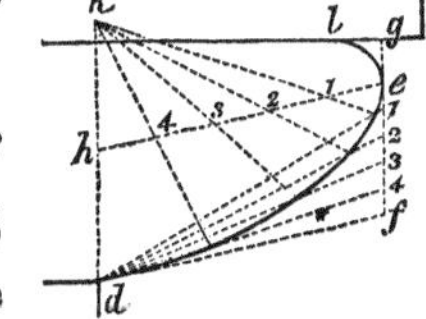

Fig. 72.

hk. Divide eh and ef into the same number of equal parts; from d draw straight lines to the points of division in ef, and from k draw lines to meet those others successively. The intersections so found are points in the curve, which may be traced accordingly.

To describe a Cavetto.—The *cavetto* is described like the Roman ovolo: by circular arcs, as shown in figs. 73 and 74. Sometimes it is composed of two circular arcs united (fig. 75); set off be, two-thirds of the projection, draw the vertical bd equal to be, and on d describe the arc bi. Join ed and produce it to p; draw in perpendicular to ed, set off no equal to ni, and draw the horizontal line op meeting ep; on p describe the arc io to complete the curve.

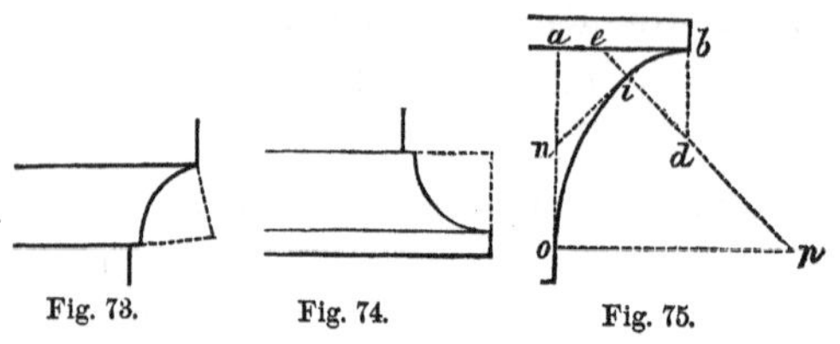

Fig. 73. Fig. 74. Fig. 75.

To describe a Cyma recta, or Ogee.—The *ogee* (fig. 76), is compounded of a concave and a convex surface. Join a and b, the extremities of the curve, and bisect ab at c; on a, c, as centres, with the radius a, c, describe arcs cutting at d; and on b, c, describe arcs cutting at e. On d and e, as centres, describe the arcs ac, cb, composing the moulding.

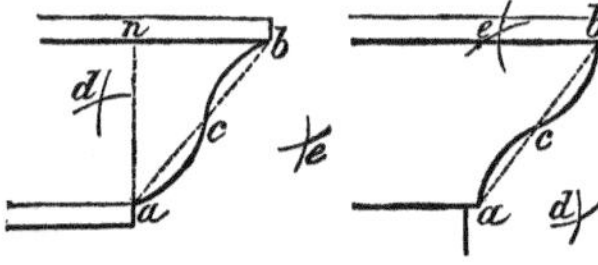

Fig. 76. Fig. 77.

To describe a Cyma reversa, or Talon.—The *talon* (fig. 77), like the ogee, is a compound curve, and is distinguished from the other by having

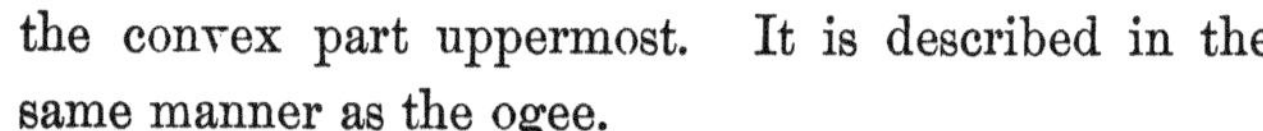
the convex part uppermost. It is described in the same manner as the ogee.

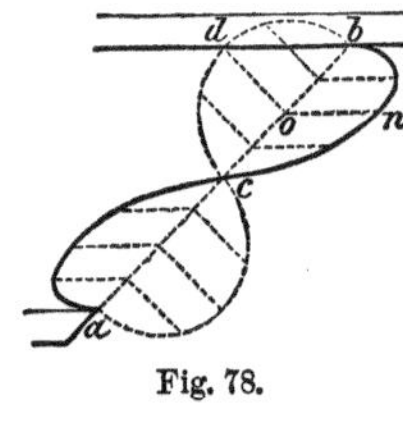

Fig. 78.

Note.—If the curve be required to be made quicker, a shorter radius than ac must be employed. The projection of the moulding nb (fig. 76), is usually equal to the height an.

Second, the Greek talon. Join the extreme points a, b (fig. 78); bisect ab at c, and on ac, cb, describe semicircles. Draw perpendiculars do, &c., from a number of points in ac, cb, meeting the circumferences; and from the same points set off horizontal lines equal to the respective perpendiculars: on equal to od for example. The curve line bna, traced through the ends of the lines, will be the contour of the moulding.

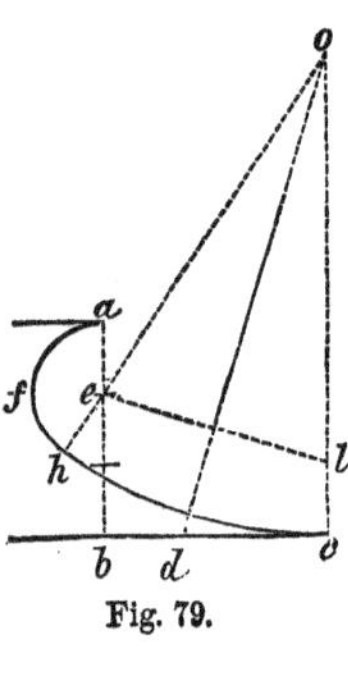

Fig. 79.

To describe a Scotia.—Divide the perpendicular ab (fig. 79), into three equal parts; and with the first, ae, as radius, and on centre *e*, describe the arc *a f h;* on the perpendicular *c o*, set off *c l* equal to *a e*, join *e l* and bisect it by the perpendicular *o d*, meeting *c o* at *o*. On centre *o*, with radius *o c*, describe the arc *c h* to complete the figure.

ORDERS OF ARCHITECTURE.

Order, in architecture, is a system or assemblage of parts subject to certain uniform established proportions, regulated by the office each part has to perform. An order may be said to be the genus, whereof the species are Tuscan, Doric, Ionic, Corinthian, and Composite; and consists of two essential parts: a column and entablature.

These are subdivided, the first into three parts, namely: the base, the shaft, and the capital. The second also into three parts, namely: the architrave, or chief beam, C, Plate VIII., which stands immediately on the column; the frieze B, which lies on the architrave; and the cornice A, which is the crowning or uppermost member of an order. In the subdivisions certain horizontal members are used, which from the curved form of their edges are called mouldings, the construction of which has already been explained, and their application may be seen on the Plate; thus *a* is the ogee, *b* the corona, *c* the ovolo, *d* the cavetto, which with fillets compose the cornice, *f f* the fasciæ. The capital of the column consists of the upper member or abacus *g*, the ovolo moulding *c*, the astragal *i i*, and the neck *h*. The base consists of the torus *k*, and the plinth *l*. The character of an order is displayed, not only in its column, but in its general forms and detail, whereof the column is, as it were, the regulator; the expression being of strength, grace, elegance, lightness, or richness. Though a building be without columns, it is nevertheless said to be of an order, if its details be regulated according to the method prescribed for such order.

In all the orders a similar unit of reference is adopted for the construction of their various parts. Thus, the lower diameter of the column is taken as the proportional measure for all other parts and members, for which purpose it is subdivided into sixty parts, called minutes, or into two modules of thirty minutes each. Being proportional measures, modules and minutes are not fixed ones like feet and inches, but are variable as to the actual dimensions which they express—larger or smaller, according to the actual size of the diameter of the column. For instance, if the diameter be just five feet, a minute, being one-sixtieth, will be exactly one inch.

Therefore before commencing to draw an elevation of any one of the orders, determine the diameter of the column, and from that form a scale of equal parts, by sixty divisions, and then lay off the widths and heights of the different members according to the proportions of the required order as marked in the body or on the sides of the plates.

Plate VIII. presents an illustration of the Tuscan order, considered by architects as a spurious or plain sort of Doric, and hardly entitled to remark as a distinct order. E, in the frieze corresponding to the triglyph, illustrates still further the connection of the two orders; but by many architects this member is not introduced. Fig. 1 is an elevation of capital and entablature, fig. 2 of the base, and fig. 3 of a detached capital. Our example is constructed according to the rules given by Vincent Scamozzi.

Examples of two capitals are given, differing merely in the number of mouldings in the abacus. In fact, this introduction of simple mouldings is about the only variety allowable in the order. Ornament is not admitted, nor are the pillars ever fluted.

A slightly convex curvature, or entasis, is given in execution to the outline of the shaft of a column, by classic architects, just sufficient to counteract and correct its appearance, or fancied appearance, of curvature in a contrary direction (*i. e.*, concavely), which might else take place, and cause the middle of the shaft to appear thinner than it really is.

Fig. 4 represents the form of a half column from the Pantheon at Rome. In fig. 5, another example of entasis, the lower third of the shaft is uniformly cylindrical; the two upper thirds are divided into seven equal parts. On the semicircle shown in the figure, is a chord cut off parallel to the diameter, the length of which is fifty-two parts, only one-half being shown. Divide that part, *a*, *b*, of the circumference between the diameter and chord into seven equal parts, and draw parallel lines from each division to those of the upper part of the column, which will give the diameter of the shaft at each division; by increasing the number of the divisions, more diameters for different parts of the shaft may be found.

Plate IX. exhibits an example of the Doric order, from the temple of Minerva in the Island of Egina. The dimensions are given in parts of the diameter, as in the preceding plate, and the same capital letters denote corresponding parts. Fig. 1 is an elevation of the capital and the entablature. Fig. 2 of the base, and a part of the Podium. Fig. 3 shows the forms of the flutes at the top of the shaft, and fig. 4 at the base. Fig. 5, the outline of the capital on an enlarged scale.

The Doric order may be said to be the original of the Greek orders,

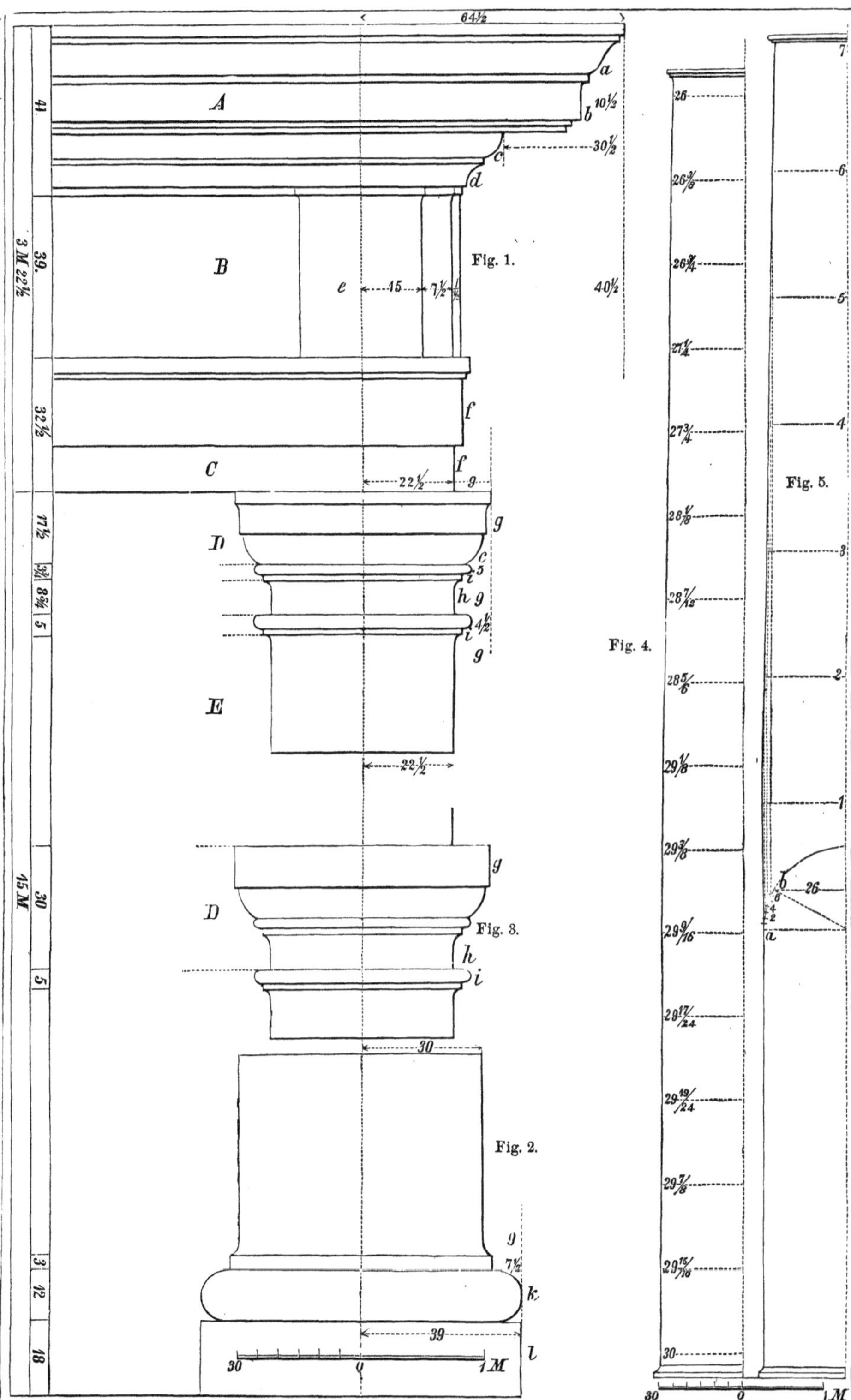
64½
a
b 10½
30½
c
d
A
41
B
39.
3 M 22½
e
15
7½
Fig. 1.
40½
C
f
32½
22½
g
D
17½
h
i
E
Fig. 2.
Fig. 3.
Fig. 4.
Fig. 5.
15 M
30
5
3
12
18
k
l
39
30 0 1 M
26
26⅜
26¾
27¼
27¾
28⅛
28 7/12
28⅚
29⅛
29⅜
29 9/16
29 17/24
29 49/24
29⅞
29 15/16
30
7
6
5
4
3
2
1

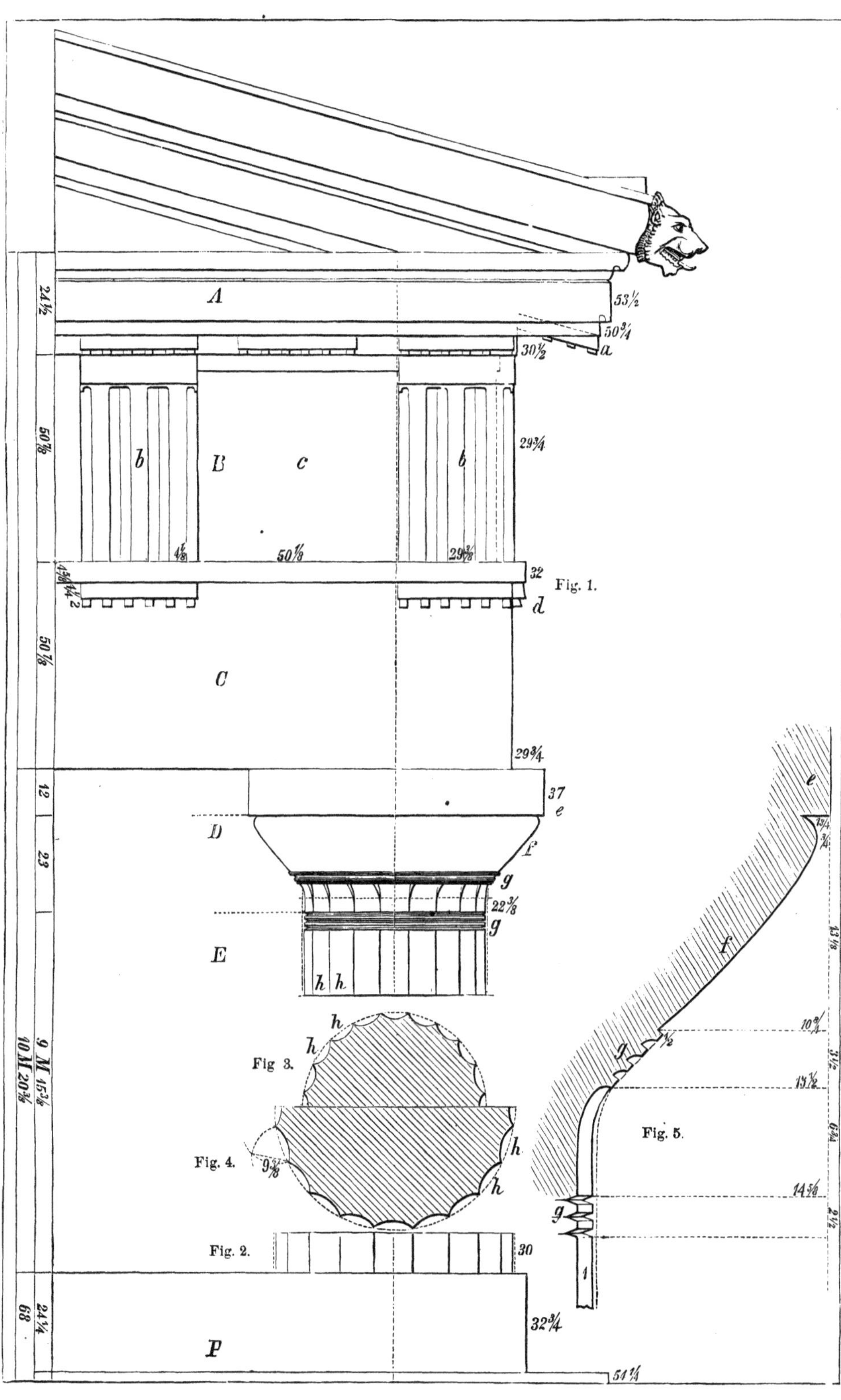
A
B
C
D
E
P
b
c
d
e
f
g
h
Fig. 1.
Fig. 2.
Fig 3.
Fig. 4.
Fig. 5.
53½
50¾
30½
29¾
50⅛
32
37
22⅜
30
32¾
54¼
24½
12
23
68
24¼

PLATE X.

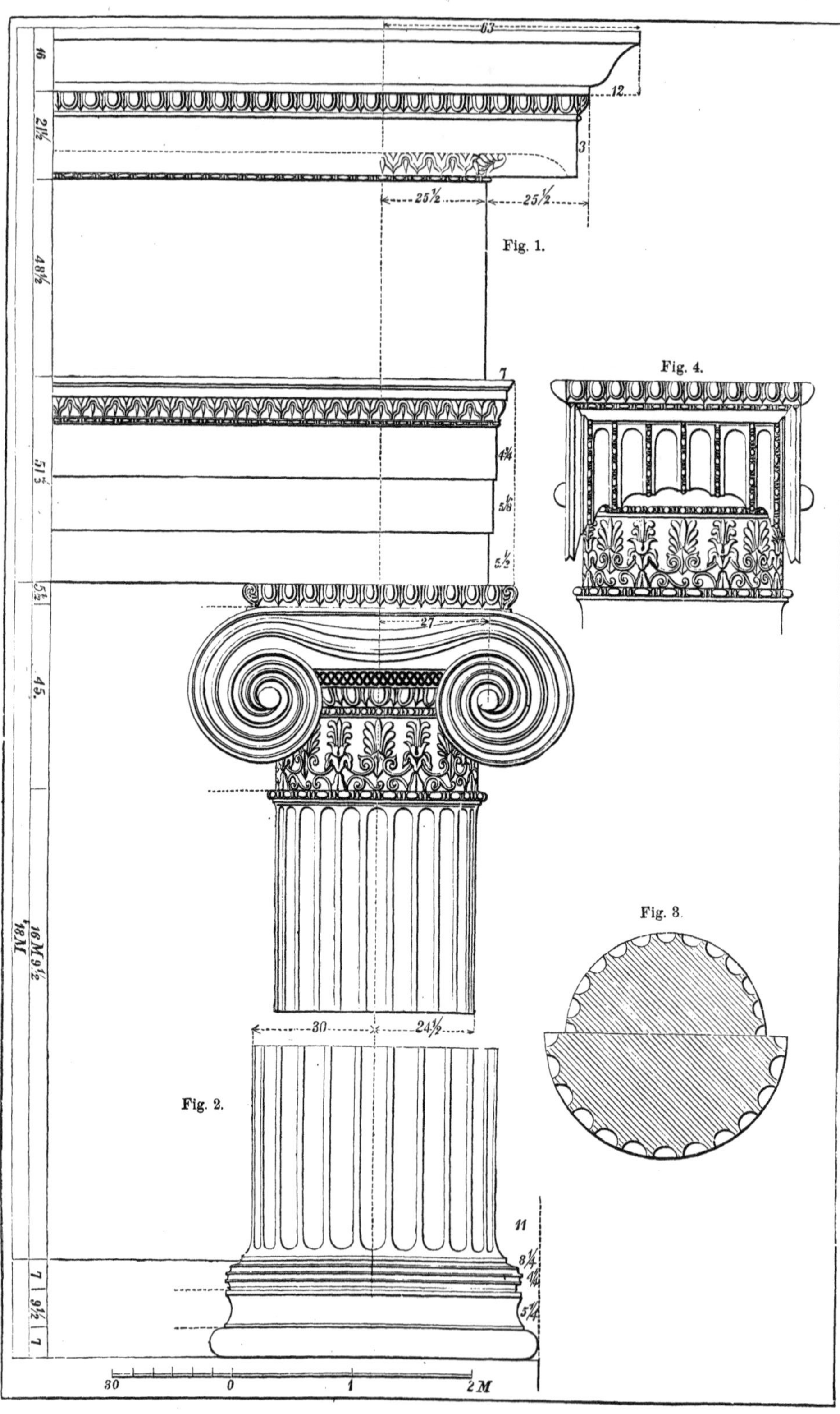

Fig. 1.

Fig. 2.

Fig. 3.

Fig. 4.

of which there are properly but three: the Doric, Ionic, and Corinthian, which differ in the proportion of their parts, and in some of the ornaments or mouldings. Of the Doric, the mutules *a a*, the triglyphs *b b*, the guttæ or drops *d d* of the entablature, the echinus *f*, and the annulets *g g* of the capital, may be considered characteristic. With regard to the arrangement of the triglyphs, one is placed over every column, and one or more intermediately over every *intercolumn* (or span between two columns), at such a distance from each other that the metopes *c*, or spaces between the triglyphs, are square.

In the best Greek examples of the order, there is only a single triglyph over each intercolumn. One peculiarity of the Grecian Doric frieze is, that the end triglyphs, instead of being, like the others, in the same axis or central line as the columns beneath, are placed quite up to the edge or outer angle of the frieze. The mutules are thin plates or shallow blocks attached to the under side or soffit of the corona, over each triglyph and each metope, with the former of which they correspond in breadth, and their soffits or under-surfaces are wrought into three rows of guttæ or drops, conical or otherwise shaped, each row consisting of six guttæ, or the same number as those beneath each triglyph. Though a few exceptions to the contrary exist, the shaft of the Doric column was generally what is technically called fluted. The number of channels is either sixteen or twenty, afterwards increased in the other orders to twenty-four; for they are invariably of an even number, capable of being divided by four; so that there shall always be a centre flute on each side of the column.

Plate X. presents an example of the Ionic order, taken from the temple of Minerva Polias at Athens. Fig. 1 is an elevation of capital and entablature, fig. 2 of the base, fig. 3 is a half of the plan of the column at the base and the top, fig. 4 an elevation of the side of the capital. In the proportions of its shaft, which are more slender, and the addition of a base, it differs from the Doric; but the capital is the indicial mark of the order, by which it is immediately recognized. It is far more complex and irregular than the other orders of capitals; instead of showing four equal sides, it exhibits two fronts, with spirals or volutes parallel to the architrave, and narrower *baluster* sides (fig. 4), as they are termed, beneath the architrave.

When a colonnade was continued in front and along the flanks of the building, this form of capital in the end column occasioned an offensive irregularity; for while all the other columns on the flanks showed the volutes, the end one showed the baluster side. It was necessary that the end column should, therefore, have two adjoining volute faces, which was effected by placing the volute at the angle diagonally, so as to obtain there two voluted surfaces placed immediately back to back. This same diagonal disposition of the volutes is employed for all the capitals alike, in Roman and Italian examples of this order.

The capital admits of great diversity of character and decoration—it sometimes is without necking, sometimes with; which may either be plain or decorated, to suit the entire design. The capital may also be modified in its proportions, first as regards its general proportion to the column; secondly, as regards the size of the volutes compared with the width of the face. In the best Greek examples, the volutes are much bolder than in the Roman. The *spirals* also of the volutes may be either single or manifold, and the eye or centre of the spiral may be made larger or smaller, flat or convex, or curved as a rosette.

Plate XI. represents an example of the Corinthian order, from the Arch of Hadrian, at Athens. This order is distinguished from the Ionic, more by its deep and foliaged capital than by its proportions,—the columns of both have bases differing but little from each other, and their shafts are fluted in the same manner.

Although the order itself is the most delicate and lightest of the three, the capital is the largest, being considerably more than a diameter in height, varying in different examples from one to one and a half diameter, upon the average about a diameter and a quarter.

The capital has two rows of leaves, eight in each row, so disposed that of the taller ones, composing the upper row, one comes in the middle, beneath each face of the abacus, and the lower leaves *alternate* with the upper ones, coming between the stems of the latter; so that in the first or lower tier of leaves there is in the middle of each face, a space between two leaves occupied by the stem of the central leaf above them. Over these two rows is a third series of eight leaves, turned so as to support the small volutes which, in turn, support the angles of the abacus. Besides these outer volutes, which are invariably turned diagonally, as in the four-faced Ionic capital, there are two other smaller ones, termed *caulicoli*, which meet each other beneath a flower on the face of the abacus. The abacus itself is not, properly speaking, a square, although it may be said to be so in its general form. But instead of being straight, the sides of the abacus are concave in plan, being curved outwards so as to produce a sharp point at each corner, which is usually cut off.

Fig. 80.

Fig. 80 represents one of the capitals of the Tower of the Winds, show-

PLATE XI.

ing the earliest formation of the Corinthian capital. In this example the abacus is square, and the upper row of leaves of the kind called *water leaves*, from their resemblance to those of water plants, being broad and flat, and merely carved upon the vase or body of the capital.

The proper Corinthian base differs from that of the usual Ionic or Attic, in having two smaller scotiæ, separated by two astragals: however, both kinds are employed indiscriminately. The shaft is fluted, in general, similarly to that of the Ionic column, but sometimes the flutes are *cabled* as it is called, that is, the channels are hollowed out for only about two-thirds of the upper part of the shaft, and the remainder cut so that each channel has the appearance of being partly filled up by a round staff or piece of rope, whence the term *cabling*.

The cornice is very much larger than in the other orders,—larger as to height, and consequently as to projection also.

From this greatly increased depth of cornice, it consists of a greater number of mouldings beneath the corona, for that and the cymatium over it invariably retain their places as the crowning members of the whole series of mouldings. In our illustration, square blocks or *dentels* are introduced, but often to the dentels is added a row of *modillions*, immediately beneath and supporting the corona. These modillions are ornamental blocks, curved in their under surface somewhat after the manner of the letter S turned thus, ∽; and between them and the dentels, and also below the latter, are other mouldings, sometimes cut, at others left plain. Sometimes a plain uncut *dentel band* is substituted for dentels; sometimes, in simpler cornices, that is omitted altogether, and plainer blocks are employed instead of modillions; or else both dentels and modillions are omitted. The dentel is not peculiar to this order, but is considered as more properly belonging to the Ionic.

The Composite Order is hardly to be considered as a distinct order, being but a union of the Ionic and Corinthian. Its capital consists of a Roman Ionic one, super-imposed upon a Corinthian foliaged base, in which the leaves are without stalks, placed directly upon the body of the vase. In general, the entablature is Corinthian—but in a few examples it is Ionic.

Although columns and entablatures do not of themselves, properly speaking, constitute an order, except they enter into the organization of a structure; yet, as the Greek edifices as such, are almost entirely inapplicable to purposes of the present day, we have confined our illustrations of the orders to the pillars and entablatures merely, remarking, that however the Greek temples differed from each other as to the treatment of the order adopted, the number of columns and mere particulars of that kind, they resemble each other. Not only were their plans invariably parallelograms, but alike also as to proportion, forming a double square, or being about twice as much in length as in breadth. The number of the columns iu front was invariably an even one, as otherwise there would be no intercolumn; but on the flanks of the edifice, where there was no entrance, the number of intercolumns was an even, and that of the columns an uneven one, so that a column came in the centre of these side elevations.

As to the mode in which the front influenced the sides, by determining the number of columns for them, the established rule seems to have been to give the flanks twice as many intercolumns as there were columns at each end: thus the Parthenon, which is octastyle or eight columns in front, has sixteen intercolumns, and consequently seventeen columns, on each flank. In like manner, a hexastyle temple would have twelve intercolumns and thirteen columns on each side.

In the Doric order, the distances between the columns is governed entirely by the triglyphs of the frieze, so that there can be no medium between monotriglyphic and ditriglyphic intercolumniation, accordingly as there is either one or two triglyphs over each intercolumn. But in the other orders there is no such restriction; in them the intercolumns may be made wider or narrower, as circumstances require, from one diameter and a quarter to a half in width. *Close spacing* carries with it the expression of both richness and strength, whilst wide spacing produces an effect of openness and lightness, but also partakes of meagreness and weakness, owing to the want of sufficient apparent support for the entablature.

Another mode of columniation and intercolumniation which has sometimes been practised by Modern Architects, consists in coupling the columns and making a wide intercolumn between every pair of columns, so that as regards the average proportion between solids and voids, that disposition does not differ from what it would be were the columns placed singly. Supercolumniation, or the system of piling up orders, or different stages of columns one above another, was employed for such structures merely as were upon too large a scale to admit of the application of columns at all as their decoration, otherwise than by disposing them in tiers. This method was afterwards adopted by the Architects of the Palladian School. Sometimes all the three orders are employed in as many tiers of columns or pilasters. In other cases, the two extreme orders,—that is, the Doric and Corinthian,—are brought together; in other cases but a single order.

In one or two instances the Greeks employed human figures to support entablatures or beams; the female figures or Caryatides, are almost uniformly represented in an erect attitude, without any apparent effort to sustain any burden or load; whilst the male figures, Telamones or Atlantes, manifestly display strength and muscular action. Besides entire figures, either Hermes' pillars or Termini are occasionally used as substitutes for columns of the usual form, when required to be only on a small, at least a moderate scale. The first mentioned consist of a square shaft with a bust or human head for its capital; the latter of a half-length figure rising out of, or terminating in, a square shaft tapering downwards. Hermes' pillars seem to be in great favor with modern German architects, they having not unfrequently employed them for the decoration of windows.

The Greek orders may be considered as the rudiments of modern architecture, but the forms of their buildings are almost entirely inapplicable to modern purposes. The Romans developed and matured the Corinthian order, and also worked out a freer and more complex and comprehensive system of architecture. They introduced circular forms and curves not only in elevation and section, but in plan; and while, among the Greeks, architecture was confined almost exclusively to external appearance and effect, in the hands of the Romans it was made to minister to internal display also. The true Roman order consists, not in any of the columnar ordinances, but in an arrangement of two pillars placed at a distance from one another nearly equal to their own height, and having a very long entablature, which, in consequence, required to be supported in the centre by an arch springing from piers. This, as will be seen from fig. 1, Plate XII. was, in fact, merely a screen of Grecian architecture placed in front of an arcade. Though not without a certain richness of effect, still as used by the Romans, these two systems remain too distinctly dissimilar for the result to be pleasing, and their use necessitated certain supplemental arrangements by no means agreeable. In the first place the columns had to be mounted on pedestals, or otherwise an entablature proportional to their size would have been too heavy and too important for a thing so useless and so avowedly a mere ornament. A projecting keystone was also introduced into the arch. This was unobjectionable in itself, but when projecting so far as to do the duty of an intermediate capital, it overpowered the arch without being equal to the work required of it. The Romans used these arcades with all the three orders, frequently one over the other, and tried various expedients to harmonize the construction with the ornamentation, but without much effect. They seem always to have felt the discordance as a blemish, and at last got rid of it, removing the pier altogether, and substituting in its place the pillar taken down from its pedestal. This of course was not effected at once, but was the result of many trials and expedients. One of the earliest of these is observed in the Ionic Temple of Concord, in which a concealed arch is thrown from the head of each pillar, but above the entablature, so as to take the whole weight of the superstructure from off the cornice between the pillars. When once this was done it was perceived that so deep an entablature was no longer required, and that it might be either wholly omitted, as was sometimes done, in the centre intercolumniation, or at all events very much attenuated. There is an old temple at Talavera, in Spain, which is a good example of the former expedient; and the Church of the Holy Sepulchre, built by Constantine at Jerusalem, is a remarkable example of the latter. There, the architrave is cut off so as merely to form a block over each of the pillars, and the frieze and cornice only are carried across from one of these blocks to the other, while a bold arch is thrown from pillar to pillar over these, so as to take any weight from off a member which has at last become a mere ornamental part of the style.

Figs. 2, 3 and 4, Plate XII., from the Palace of Diocletian at Spalatro, are illustrations of the different modes of treatment of the arch and entablature.

Perhaps the most satisfactory works of the Romans are those which we consider as belonging to civil engineering rather than to architecture; their aqueducts and viaducts, all of which, admirably conceived and executed, have furnished practical examples for modern constructions, of which the High Bridge across Harlem River may be taken as an illustration.

The whole history of Roman architecture is that of a style in course of transition, beginning with purely Pagan or Grecian, and passing into a style almost wholly Christian. The first form which Christian art took in emancipating itself from the Pagan was the Romanesque, which afterwards branched off into the Byzantine and the Gothic.

The Romanesque and Byzantine, as far as regards the architectural features, are almost synoymous; in the earlier centuries there is an ornamental distinction, the Romanesque being simply a debasement of Roman art—the Byzantine being the art combined with the symbolic elements introduced by the new Christian religion. As commonly used, the dome is also considered a characteristic of the Byzantine, but this will be found among Roman examples. In its widest signification, the Romanesque is applied to all the earlier round arch developments, in contradistinction to the Gothic or later pointed arch varieties of the North. In this view the Norman is included in the Romanesque, and this distinction will be sufficient for our purpose.

The general characteristics of the Gothic are these: it is essentially

Fig. 1.
Fig. 2.
Fig. 3.
Fig. 4.
Fig. 5.
Fig. 6.
Fig. 7.
Fig. 8.
Fig. 9.
Fig. 10.
Fig. 11.
Fig. 12.
Fig. 13.
Fig. 14.
Fig. 15.
Fig. 16.

pointed or vertical in its tendency, and its details geometrical, in its window tracery, in its openings, in its cluster of shafts and bases, in its suits of mouldings, and by the universal absence of the dome, and the substitution of the pointed for the round arch.

The Romanesque pillars are mostly round or square, and if square, generally set evenly, whilst the Gothic square pillar is set diagonally.

Figs. 5, 6, 7, 8 and 9, Plate XII., represent sections of Gothic pillars; fig. 10 is half of one of the great western piers of the Cathedral of Bourges, measuring 8 feet on each side.

Figs. 11 and 12 are the elevations of capitals and bases and the sections of Gothic pillars, one from Salisbury, the other from Lincoln Cathedral. Fig. 13 is a Byzantine capital from the church of St. Sophia at Constantinople; fig. 14 one from the palace at Gelnhausen; fig. 15, a Norman one, from Winchester Cathedral, and fig. 16 a Gothic capital and base from Lincoln Cathedral.

Mouldings.—"All classical architecture, and the Romanesque which is legitimately descended from it, is composed of bold independent shafts, plain or fluted, with bold detached capitals forming arcades or colonnades where they are needed, and of walls whose apertures are surrounded by courses of parallel lines called mouldings, and have neither shafts nor capitals. The shaft system and moulding system are entirely separate, the Gothic architects confounded the two; they clustered the shafts till they looked like a group of mouldings, they shod and capitalled the mouldings till they looked like a group of shafts."

Gothic Mouldings appear in almost every conceivable position; from the bases of piers and piers themselves, to the ribs of the fretted vaults which they sustain, scarce a member occurs which is incapable of receiving consistent decoration by this elegant method.

Jamb Mouldings.—In the earliest examples of Norman doorways, the jambs are mostly simply squared back from the walls; recessed jambs succeeded, and are common in both Norman and Gothic architecture; and when thus raised detached shafts were placed in each angle (fig. 81). In the later styles, the shafts were almost invariably attached to the structure. The angles themselves were often cut or chamfered off, and the mouldings attached to the chamfer plane. The arrangement of window jambs during the successive periods was in close accordance with that of doorways.

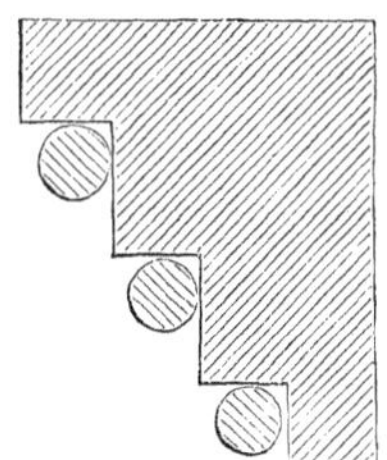
Fig. 81.

In the richer examples small shafts were introduced, which, rising up to the springing of the window, carried one or several of the arch mouldings.

Yet mouldings are not nevertheless essential accessories; many windows of the richest tracery have their mullions and jambs composed of simple chamfers.

Arch Mouldings, even when not continuous, partook of the same general arrangement as those in the jambs, with greater richness of detail. When shafts were employed, they carried groups of mouldings more elaborate than those of the jambs, though still falling on the same planes.

Capitals were either moulded, or carved with foliage, animals, &c.; they always consisted of three distinct parts (fig. 82), the head mould A, the bell B, and the neck mould C. In Norman examples the head mould was almost invariably square; in the later styles it is circular, or corresponding to the form of the pillar.

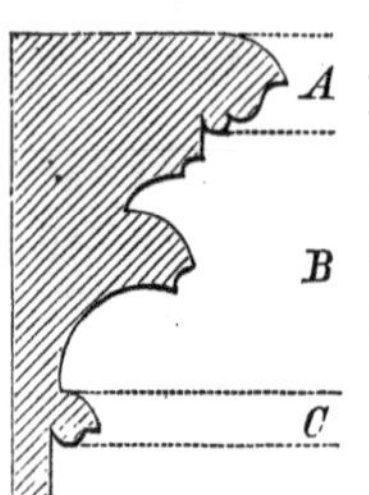

Fig. 82.

Bases consist of the plinth and the base mouldings. The plinth was square in the Norman style, afterwards octagonal, then assuming the form of the base mouldings, it bent in and out with the outline of the pier. Base mouldings were also extensively used round the buttresses, towers and walls of churches.

String Courses.—The most usual and perhaps essential position of the string course is under the windows. In the Norman styles they were usually heavy in the outline, and displayed no particular beauty of arrangement. In the later styles they were remarkably light and elegant; from restraint or horizontality, they now rose close under the sill of the window, and then suddenly dropping to accommodate themselves to the arch of a low doorway, and again rising to run immediately under the adjoining window. In this way, the string courses frequently served the purpose of a *drip stone* or hood moulding over doors; occasionally the hood mould was continued from one window to the other. But in the later styles they were generally terminated in heads, flowers, or some quaint device, or simply returned at the springing of the arch.

Cornices are not an essential feature in Gothic architecture. In the Norman and early English styles, the cornice was a sort of enlarged string course formed by the projection of the upper part of the wall, which was supported on brackets or *corbels*, and hence termed the corbel table.

The earliest moulding in Norman work, is a circular bead strip worked out of the edges of a recessed arch, called a circular *bowtel* (fig. 83). From a circular form the bowtel soon became pointed, and, by an easy transition, into the bowtel of one, two, or three fillets, all of which, with their numerous varieties, performed important parts in the Gothic moulding system.

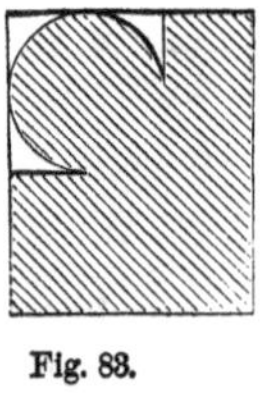

Fig. 83.

Fig. 84 is the *scroll* moulding, being, in fact, a simple filleted bowtel, with the fillet undeveloped on one side, as shown by the dotted lines. If this moulding be cut in half, through the centre of the fillet, we have on the developed side the moulding now termed by carpenters the rule joint, which, by rounding off the corners by reverse curves, becomes the wave moulding.

Fig. 84.

The ogee is also used very generally in Gothic architecture, both single and double, the latter formed by the junction of two ogees.

Figs. 85 and 86 are examples of groupings of mouldings, fig. 85 being of the earlier Gothic, the filleted bowtel with alternate hollows, fig. 86, of the perpendicular style, the hollow in the one case being made prominent, and dividing individual mouldings; in the latter insignificant, and as a separation of groups of mouldings.

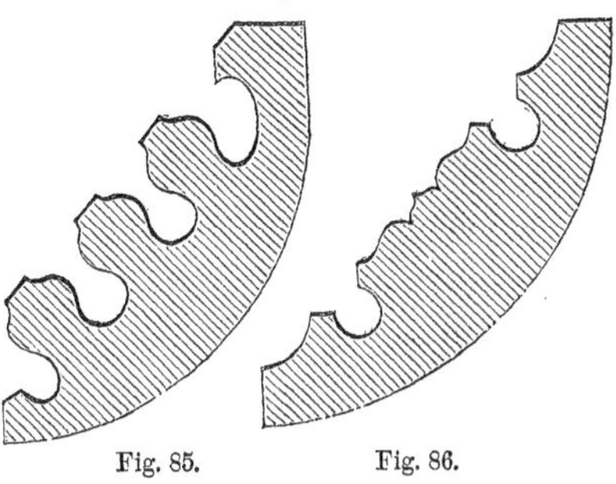
Fig. 85. Fig. 86.

Arches are generally divided into the triangular-headed arch, the round-headed arch, and the pointed arch. Of round-headed arches there are four kinds, the semicircular, segmental, the stilted, and the horse-shoe.

The stilted arch, fig. 87, is semicircular, but the sides are carried downwards in a straight line below the spring of the curve, till they rest upon the imposts. In the horse-shoe arch, the sides are also carried down below the centre, but follow the same curve (fig. 88).

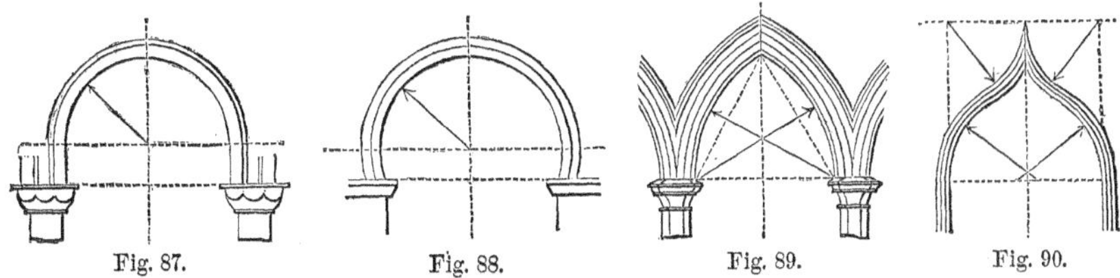
Fig. 87. Fig. 88. Fig. 89. Fig. 90.

The pointed arch may be divided into two classes, those described from two centres, and those described from four. Of the first class there are three kinds, the equilateral, the lancet, and the obtuse. The equilateral (fig. 89), is formed of two segments of a circle, of which the radii are equal to the breadth of the arch. The radii of the lancet segment are longer than the width of the arch, and of the obtuse, shorter.

Of the complex arches, there is the Ogee (fig. 90), and the Tudor (fig. 92). The Tudor arch is described from four centres, two on a level with the spring and two below it.

Of foiled arches, there are the round-headed trefoil (fig. 91), the pointed trefoil (fig. 93), and the square-headed trefoil arch (fig. 94).

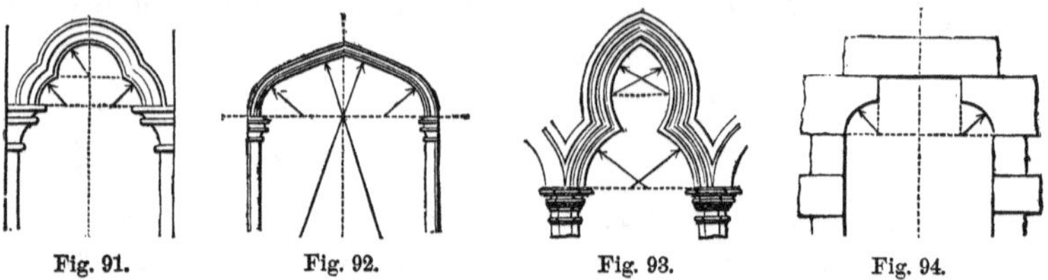

Fig. 91. Fig. 92. Fig. 93. Fig. 94.

The semi-circular arch is the Roman Byzantine and Norman arch, the ogee and horse-shoe is the profile of many Turkish and Moorish domes, the pointed and foliated arches are Gothic.

Domes and Vaults.—Both domes and vaults are found in Roman works, but with the decline of Roman power the art of vaulting was lost, and the chürches of all Roman Christendom remained with nothing but timber roofs. But among the Greek Christians, or Byzantines, it was retained, or else re-invented; but the Greek vaulting consisted wholly of spherical surfaces, whilst the Roman consisted of cylindrical ones. Figs. 95 and 96 illustrate this distinction, fig. 95 being the elevation of a Roman cylindrical cross vault, and fig. 96, the elevation of the roof of the church

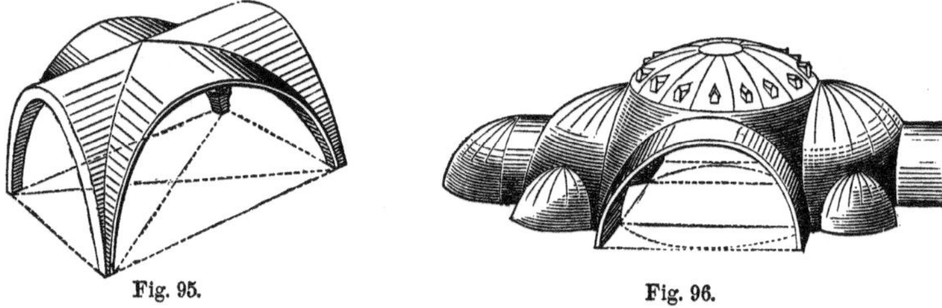

Fig. 95. Fig. 96.

of St. Sophia at Constantinople; and the sprouting of domes out of domes continues to characterize the Byzantine style, both in Greek churches and Turkish mosques, down to the present day. This system of vaulting has also been adopted in St. Paul's, London, and at St. Genevieve, Paris. As a constructive expedient the cross vault is to be preferred, as the whole pressure and thrust are collected in four definite resultants, applied at the angles only, so that it might be supported by four flying buttresses, no matter how slender, provided they were placed in the direction of these resultants, and were strong enough not to be crushed by the pressure.

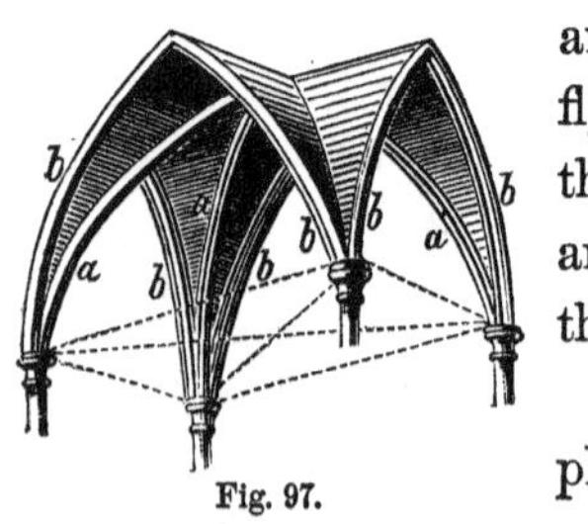

Fig. 97.

Fig. 97 represents a compartment of the simplest Gothic vaulting, *a*, *a*, groin ribs, *b*, *b*, *b*, side ribs.

The Romans introduced side ribs, appearing

on the inside as flat bands, and harmonizing with the similar form of pilasters in the walls, but they never used groin ribs; the Gothic builders introduced these, and deepened the Roman ribs. The impenetration of vaults, either round or pointed, produces elliptical groin lines, or else lines of double curvature. Yet the early Gothic architects rarely made their groin ribs elliptical, and never deviating from a vertical plane. These ribs were usually simple pointed arches of circular curvature, thrown diagonally across the space to be groined, and the four side arches were equally simple, the only care being that all the arches should have their vertices at the same level. The shell between, therefore, was no regular geometric surface. The strength depended on the ribs, and the shell was made quite light, often not more than six inches, while Roman vaults of the same span would have been three or four feet. The difference of principle being, that the Romans made their vault *surfaces* geometrically regular, and left the groins to take their chance; while the early Gothic architects made their groins geometrically regular, and let the intermediate surfaces take their chance.

In the next step the groin ribs were elliptical, and when intermediate ribs or *tiercerons* were inserted, these ribs had also elliptical curvatures, but different from the groins, in order that the vault of cut stone built upon them might have a regular cylindrical surface. In augmenting the number of tiercerons, and making them ramify, combinations of circular arcs were substituted for the elliptic curves; the surfaces of these vaults could not be cylindrical, but the ribs were placed very near each other, in order that the portion of the vault between each pair might practically be almost cylindrical. In the formation of the compound circular ribs three conditions were to be observed:—1st, that the two arcs should have a common tangent at the point of meeting. 2d. That the feet of all the ribs should have the same radius, up to the level at which they completely separate from each other. 3d. That from this point upwards, their curvatures should be so adjusted as to make them all meet their fellows on the same horizontal plane, so that all the ridges of the vaults may be on one level.

The geometrical difficulty of such works led to what is called *fan tracery vaulting*. If similar arches spring from each side of the pillars (fig. 97), it is easy to perceive that the portion of vault springing from each pillar would have the form of an inverted concave-sided pyramid, its horizontal section at every level being square. Now the later architects converted this section into a circle, the four-sided pyramid became a conoid, and all the ribs forming the conoidal surface became alike in curvature, so that they all might be made simple circular arcs; these ribs are continued with unaltered curvature till they meet and form the ridge; but in this case the ridges are not level, but gradually descend every way from the centre point (fig. 98).

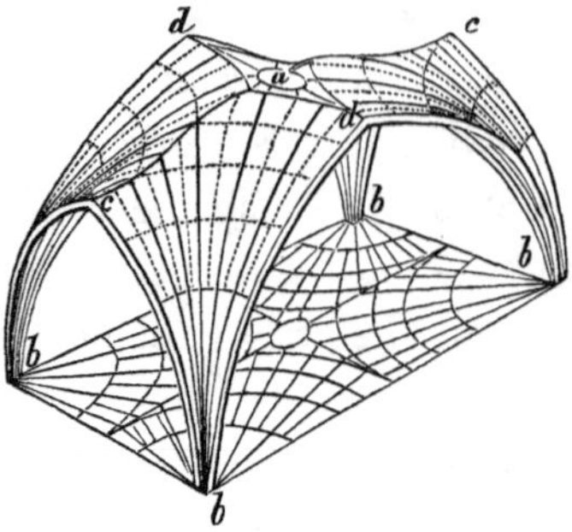

Fig. 98.

In the figure this is not fully carried out, for no rib is continued higher than those over the longer sides of the compartment, so that a small lozenge is still left, with a boss at its centre. When the span of the main arch *b a*, was large in proportion to that of *b c*, the arch *b c* became a very acute lancet arch, and scarcely admitting windows of an elegant or sufficient size. To obviate this, the compound curve was again introduced, and the ribs were made less curved in their upper parts than in the lower. Hence the four-centred or Tudor arches.

The four-centred arch is not necessarily flat or depressed, it can be made of any proportion, high or low, and always with a decided angle at the vertex. In general, the angular extent of the lower curve is not more than 65°, nor less than 45°. The radius of the upper curve varies from twice to more than six times the radius of the lower, but generally speaking, the greater their disproportion, the less pleasing is the sudden change of curvature. The projecting points of the trefoil arch are sometimes called cusps, often introduced for ornament merely, but serving constructively both in vaults and arches, as a load for the sides, to prevent them rising from the pressure on the crown. This property of arches has been explained, depending on the principle (p. 118), that if a polygon of rods be reversed, the position in which it will stand is that which it will assume for itself when loaded with the same weights and suspended; and perhaps the equilibrium of some of the boldest vaultings was insured by experiments on systems of rods representing the ribs inverted; and for any architect who may wish to introduce pendants or cusps in his vaultings, this rule of trial will be found particularly useful.

As vaultings, in general, were contrived to collect the whole pressure of each compartment into four single resultants, at the points of springing, leaving the walls so completely unloaded that they are required only as enclosures or screens, they might be entirely omitted or replaced by windows. Indeed, the real supporting walls are broken into narrow slips, placed at right angles to the outline of the building, and called *buttresses*. As to the *enclosing* walls, being not for support, they may be placed as the architect pleases, either at the outer or inner edge of the buttresses. The one method, being that adopted by the French architects, gave to their interiors those deep recesses, whilst the other, or English method, served only to produce external play of light and shade.

The Norman buttress resembles a flat pilaster, being a mass of masonry with a broad face, slightly projecting from the wall. They are, generally, of but one stage, rising no higher than the cornice, under which they often, but not always, finish with a slope. Sometimes they are carried up to, and terminate in, the corbel table.

Fig. 1, Plate XIII., represents a buttress in two stages, with simple slopes as set-offs; this example is somewhat narrower and projects more than the Norman buttress.

Fig. 2 is a buttress of the Early English style, having a plain triangular or pedimental head. The angles were sometimes chamfered off, and sometimes ornamented with slender shafts. In buttresses of different stages, the triangular head or gable is used as a finish for the intermediate stages.

In the Decorated style, the outer surfaces of the buttresses are ornamented with niches, as in fig. 3. In the Perpendicular style, the outer surface is often partially or wholly covered with panel-work tracery (fig. 4).

It has been said that the buttress was a constructive expedient to resist the thrust of vaulting, but to resist the thrust of the principal vault, or that over the nave or central part of the church, buttresses of the requisite depth would have filled up the side aisles entirely. To obviate this, the system of flying buttresses was adopted, that is, the connection of the interior with the outer buttress, by an arch or system of arches, as shown in fig. 5. To add weight, and consequently solidity, to the outer piers, they were surmounted by pinnacles, rendering them thus a sufficiently steady abutment to the flying arches, which, in their turn, abutted the central vaults.

An easy transition leads us from pinnacles to spires, the latter being but the perfect development of the former, and each requiring the assistance of the other in producing a thoroughly harmonious effect. Yet the spire never was a constructive expedient, or useful in any way. From the tower, the spire arose first as a wooden roof, and as height was one of the great objects to be attained, it was carried to an elevation beyond the mere requirements of a protection against the weather.

The earlier towers of the Romanesque style were constructed without spires. All are square in plan, and extremely similar in design. Fig. 6,

Plate XIII., is an elevation of the tower attached to the church of Sta. Maria, in Cosmedin, and is one of the best and most complete examples of this style. Its dimensions are small, being but 15 feet broad and 110 feet high; a sufficiency of height, where buildings are not generally tall, to give prominence, without overpowering other objects, which renders these towers not only beautiful structures in themselves, but singularly appropriate ornaments to the buildings to which they were attached. These towers are the types of the later Italian campaniles, or bell-towers, most generally attached to some angle of churches, but sometimes detached, yet so placed that they still form a part of the church design. Sometimes they are but civic constructions, as belfries, or towers of defence. In design, the Gothic towers differ from the Italian campaniles. The campanile is square, carried up without break or offset, to two-thirds, at least, of its intended height; it is generally solid to a considerable height, or with only such openings as serve to admit light to the staircases. Above this solid part one round window is introduced in each face, in the next story, two, in the one above this, three, then four, and lastly, five, the lights being separated by slight piers, so that the upper story is, virtually, an open loggia.

The Gothic towers have projecting buttresses, frequent offsets, lofty spires, and a general pyramidal form. Fig. 7 is the front elevation of a simple English Gothic tower; here the plain pyramidal roof, rising at an equal slope on each of the four sides, is intersected by an octagonal spire of steep pitch. The first spires were simple quadrangular pyramids, afterwards the angles were cut off, and they became octagonal, and this is the general Gothic form of spire. Often instead of intersecting the square roof as in the figure, the octagonal spire rests upon a square base, and the angles of the tower are carried up by pinnacles, or the sides by battlements, or by both, as in fig. 8, to soften the transition between the perpendicular and sloping part.

In general the spires of English churches are more lofty than those on the Continent. The angle at the apex in the former being about 10° and in the latter, about 15°. The apex angle of the spires of Chichester and Lichfield, are from 12° to 13°, or a mean between the two proportions, and according to Ferguson, more pleasing than either; although having more lofty spires, yet the English construction is much more massive in appearance, than the Continental; the apertures are less numerous, and the surfaces are less cut up, and covered with ornaments. The spires of Friberg Church and many others on the Continent are made open work, a precedent followed sometimes in this country, but not in the same material—wood

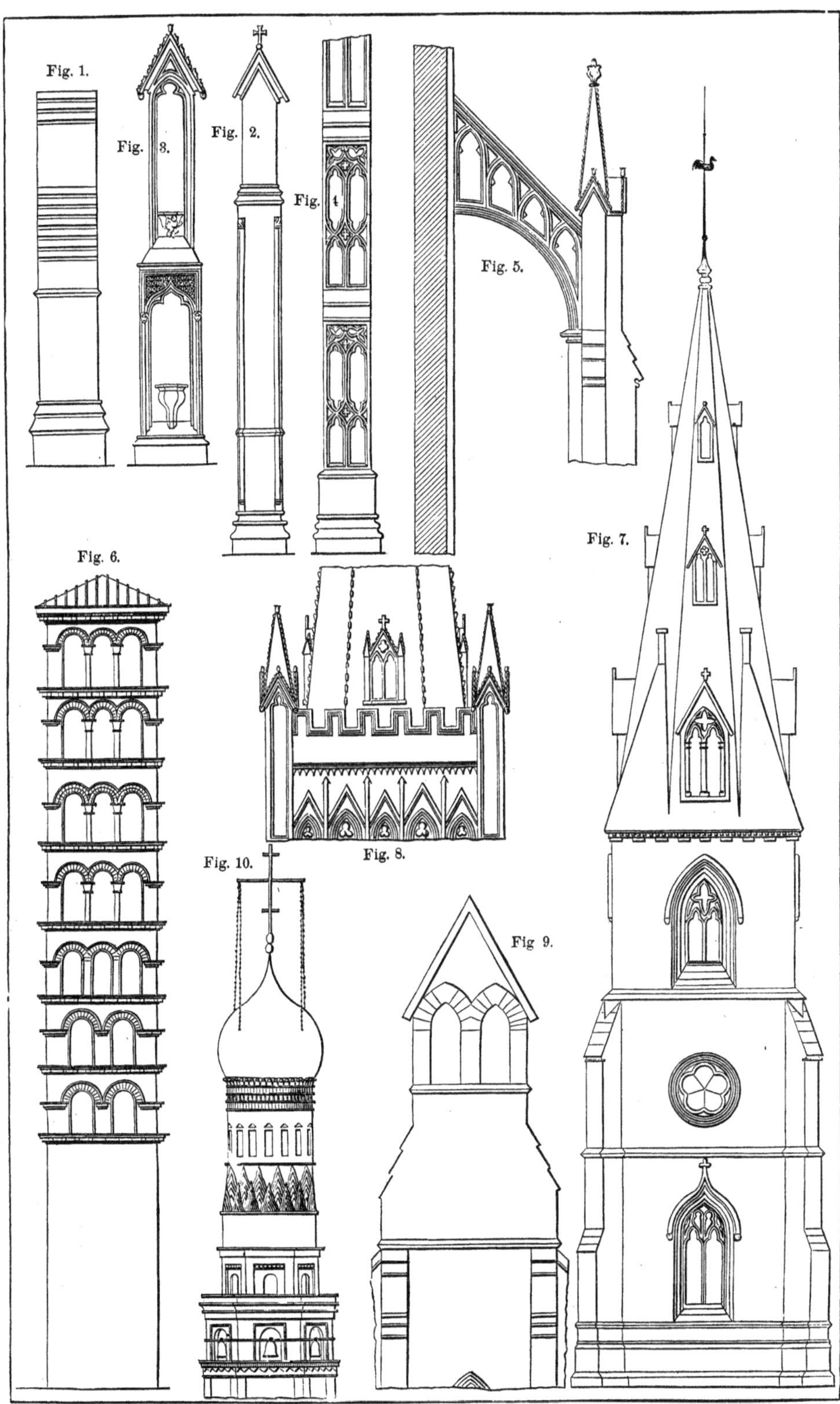
Fig. 1.
Fig. 3.
Fig. 2.
Fig. 4
Fig. 5.
Fig. 7.
Fig. 6.
Fig. 8.
Fig. 10.
Fig 9.

rather than stone. In cast iron, the same effect would be obtained at a less cost, and equally durable with stone.

Sometimes the central spires of the tower were omitted; each of the pinnacles at the angles being converted as it were into spires. Sometimes the tower is abruptly ended by mere battlements around its sides. In the poorer churches, a bell-cot was made to serve the purpose of a bell tower; this was formed by carrying up the gable wall, as in fig. 9, and making apertures for the reception of the bell. When the wall was not of the requisite thickness, the cot was either supported by buttresses from beneath, or the corbels were projected from each side of the wall.

Fig. 10 represents the upper portion of the tower of Ivan Veliki at Moscow. The Russian towers are generally constructed independent of their churches, and are intended for the reception of their massive bells.

Windows.—Before the use of painted glass, very small apertures sufficed for the introduction of the required quantity of light into a church; as a consequence the windows of the Romanesque churches were generally small, and devoid of tracery. Again, as the Byzantine architects adorned their walls with paintings, they could not make use of stained glass; neither in their climate, did they require large apertures; they followed in general form the Romanesque window, apertures with circular heads, either single or in groups (fig. 1, Plate XIV. or fig. 6, Plate XIII.). The Norman windows were also small, each consisting of a single light, semicircular in the head, and placed as high as possible above the ground; at first splayed on the inside only, afterwàrds the windows began to be recessed with mouldings and jamb shafts in the angles, as in fig. 2.

The Lancet in general use in the early Gothic period was of the simplest arrangement: in these windows the glass was brought within three or four inches of the outside of the wall, and the openings were widely splayed in the interior. The proportions of these windows vary considerably; in some the height being but five times the width, in others as much as eleven; eight or nine times may be taken as the average. Lancet windows occur singly: in groups of two, three, five and seven, rarely of four and six. The triplet, fig. 3, is the most beautiful arrangement of lancet windows. It was customary to mark with greater importance the central light, by giving it additional height, and in most cases increased width also. In some examples the windows of a lancet triplet are placed within one dripstone forming a single arch, thus bearing a strong resemblance to a single three-light window. The first approximation to tracery appears to have been the piercing of the space over a double lancet window comprised within a single dripstone; in place of the customary simple arch head, in some examples of lancet windows, the head of the light is foiled.

From the combination and foiling, or cusping, of distinct lancets, a single window divided by mullions and tracery derives its origin.

A traceried window may be justly regarded as a distinctive characteristic of Gothic architecture. With the decided establishment of the principle of window tracery, it became a recognized constructive arrangement to recess the mullions from the face of the wall in which the window arch was pierced, and the fine effect thus produced was, as the art advanced, speedily enhanced by the introduction of distinct orders of mullions, and by recessing certain portions of the tracery from the face of the primary mullions and their corresponding tracery bars. The tracery bars are those portions of the masonry of the window head which mark out the principal figures of the design; from these the minor and more strictly decorative parts of the stone work may be distinguished under the title of *Form pieces.*

Decorated window tracery has been generally divided into two chief varieties, Geometrical and Flowing; the former consisting of geometrical figures, as circles, trefoils, quatrefoils, curvilinear triangles, lozenges, &c. &c.; while in flowing tracery, these figures, though still existing, are gracefully blended together in one design. In its most perfect state, geometrical tracery invariably exhibits some large figure of a distinct and decided character, which occupies the entire upper part of the window-head.

Fig. 4 represents a quatrefoil window, fig. 5, a pointed trefoil in outline; with the centres of the different circles indicated, and such lines as may be necessary to explain the way in which they are described. These forms and modifications of them, will be found of general application in traceried windows. Fig. 6 represents two forms of circular windows, or roses tournantes.

Fig. 7 represents an example of the earlier decorated tracery window-head, consisting of two foiled lancets, with a pointed quatrefoil in the spandrel between them. One half of the windows in this, as in some of the following figures, is drawn in skeleton to explain their construction.

Fig. 8 is another example of Decorated tracery.

Fig. 9 is an example of the English leaf tracery; fig. 10 of the French flamboyant. The difference between the two styles is, that while the upper ends of the English loops or leaves are round, or simply pointed, the upper ends of the latter terminate like their lower ones, in angles of contact, giving a flame-like form to the tracery bars and form pieces.

In England the Perpendicular style succeeded the Decorated; the mul-

PLATE XIV.

Fig. 1.
Fig. 2.
Fig. 3.
Fig. 5.
Fig. 6.
Fig. 4.
Fig. 8.
Fig. 7.
Fig. 9.
Fig. 10.
Fig 11.
Fig. 12.
Fig. 15.
Fig. 13.
Fig. 14.

PLATE XV.

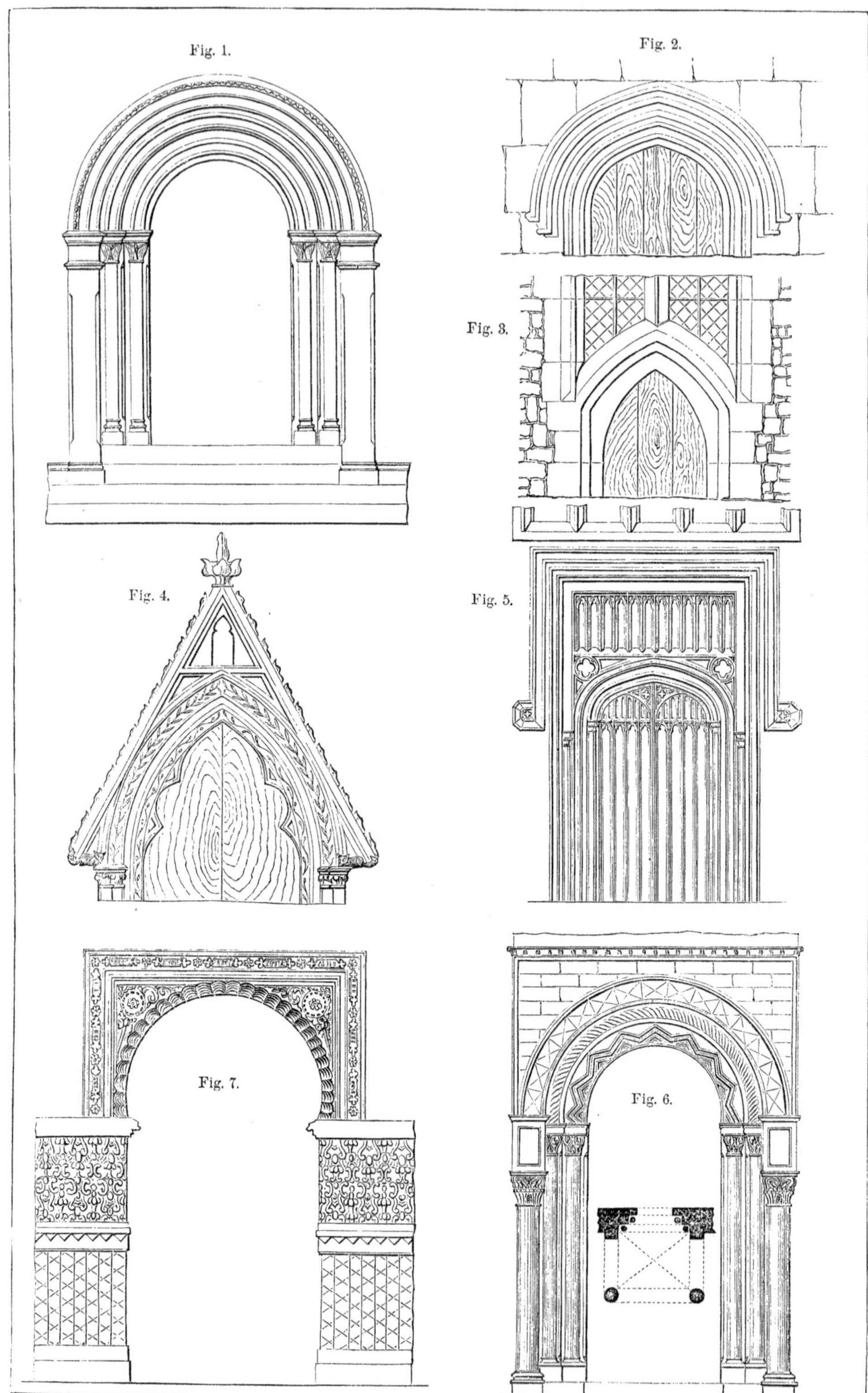

lions instead of diverging in flowing or curvilinear lines, are carried up straight through the head of the windows; smaller mullions spring from the head of the principal lights, and thus the upper portion of the window is filled with panel-like compartments. The principal as well as the subordinate lights are foliated in their heads, and large windows are often divided horizontally by transoms. The forms of the window arches vary from simple pointed, to the complex four-centred, more or less depressed.

Fig. 11 is an example of Perpendicular windows.

Fig. 12 is a square-headed window, such as were usual in the clere stories of Perpendicular architecture.

Figs. 13 and 14 are quadrants of circular windows, used more especially in France, for the adornment of the west ends and transepts of the cathedrals.

Besides the tracery characteristic of Gothic architecture, there is a tracery peculiar to the Saracenic and Moorish style, of which fig. 15 may be taken as an example—it being a window of one of the earliest mosques. The general form of the window and door-heads of this style is that of the horse-shoe, either circular or pointed.

Doorways.—Plate XV. fig. 1, represents the half of a circular-headed doorway, which may be considered the type of many entrances both in Romanesque, Gothic, and later styles. It consists of two or more recessed arches, with shafts or mouldings in the jambs. In the earlier styles the arches were circular, in the later Gothic, generally pointed, but sometimes circular; in the earlier, the angles in which the shafts are placed are rectangular; in the later, the shaft is often moulded on a *chamfer* plane, that is, a plane inclined to the face of the wall, generally at an angle of 45°; often the chamfer and rectangular planes are used in connection.

Fig. 2 is a simple head of a depressed four-centred or Tudor-arched doorway, with a hood moulding. Fig. 3 represents the incorporation of a window and doorway. Sometimes the doorway pierces a buttress; in that case, the buttress expands on either side forming a sort of porch. The Gothic architects placed doors where they were necessary, and made them subservient to the beauty of the design.

Fig. 4 is an example of a gabled doorway with crockets and finials. Fig. 5, of a Perpendicular doorway, with a gable above, and ornamented spandrels.

Fig. 6 is an example of a Byzantine, and fig. 7 of a Saracenic doorway.

The Renaissance style succeeded the Gothic, being, originally, but the revival or a fair rendering of the classical orders of architecture, with ornaments from the Byzantine and Saracenic styles.

It was in Italy that this revival took place, and Garbett divides this style into three Italian schools, the Florentine, Venetian, and Roman, exhibiting a certain analogy to the three orders of ancient architecture. The Florentine, corresponding to the Doric, admits of little apparent ornament, but any degree of real richness, preserving in its principal forms severe *contrast;* powerful masses self-poised without corbelling, without arching; *breadth* of every thing, of light, of shade, of ornament, of plain wall; *depth* of recess in the openings, of perspective in the whole mass, of projection in the cornice. To these add a sort of utilitarianism, or absence of features useless to convenience or stability, an absence of sacrifice of *material*, admitting of great plainness, of very florid enrichment. On the whole, the Florentine may be called the plain, common-sense school.

Very different in principle was the Venetian school, which, like its prototype, the Corinthian, superseded its sober rivals. Its aim was splendor, variety, show, and ornament; not so much real as effective ornament. Thus, it rarely contains so much carving or minute enrichment as the Florentine admits; but it has larger ornaments, constructed (or built) ornaments, great features useless except for ornament, as inaccessible porticoes, detached columns, and architraves supporting no ceiling, towers built only for breaking an outline. Its decoration is spread equally over the whole work. Rectangular severity gives place to curved elegance, in arches, domes, circular and oblique-angled plans, true grandeur to effect, intellectual sense of fitness to eumorphic beauty.

The Roman school, holding the same place as the Ionic, is intermediate in every respect between the two other schools. It is better adapted to churches than to any other class of buildings. This fitness arises from the grand, simple, and unitory effect of one tall order, generally commencing at or near the ground, and including, or rather obliterating, the distinction of two or three stories, making a high building appear a single story.

To describe these schools technically, the Florentine is mostly astylar, the style of finistration and rustic quoins; the Roman, the style of pilasters; and the Venetian, that of columns. In calling the Florentine astylar, a total absence of external orders is not implied, but their absence as main features, or on a considerable scale. Their chief application is to windows and doors, and the greatest orders never include so much as the height of a single story. In the Roman school, the great scale of the principal order renders it chiefly an order of pilasters. The outer pilasters of the great order were often filled in with smaller and columnar ones, in two tiers, while a still smaller set decorated the openings. As the Venetians did not use such large orders, they easily made them more columnar, and introduced hanging entablatures. In this school there is (except in churches) no principal story or order, if there be more than one, all are nearly equal, or equally important.

General plan and outline, in the Florentine, is of the utmost simplicity, rendering it fitter for town than country buildings; in the Roman, slightly more varied; in the Venetian, whenever the site will admit, broken, complex, and picturesque.

We have thus briefly treated of the distinguishing features, according to Garbett, of the three modern schools; there are many other distinctive styles and names, but they may mostly be included under the one or the other of these schools, their claim for a distinctive name resting rather on the peculiar style of ornament or tracery used, than any great distinctive architectural feature.

Ornament.—Architectural ornament is of two kinds, constructive and decorative. By the former is meant all those contrivances, such as capitals, brackets, vaulting shafts, and the like, which serve to explain or give expression to the construction; by the latter, such as mouldings, frets, foliage, &c., which give grace and life, either to this actual constructive forms, or to the constructive decoration. It is to the latter class that we wish to call attention; mouldings of the different styles have been already treated of; we therefore propose to give now what are even more merely decorations of a style.

First, as to Grecian orders. By reference to Plate IX. we see that the Doric has the triglyph mutules and guttæ. By reference to Plate X., the Ionic, we find various mouldings of the cornice frieze, abacus, and neck of the column enriched. The principal ornament of the neck of the column is the anthemion, commonly known, in its most simple form, as the honeysuckle or palmetto; in the anthemion as represented in the figure, the palmetto alternates with the lily or some analogous form. The ornament of the abacus is the egg and dart, shown on a large scale, fig. 9, Plate XVI., where may be found also the ornament of the frieze and cornice, fig. 7. Fig. 99, the fret, and fig. 100, the guilloche, are also common Greek ornaments, used to adorn the soffits of beams, and ceilings. The acanthus is the distinctive ornament of the Corinthian, of which a leaf is represented on a large scale in front and side view, figs. 1, 2, 3, Plate XVI. These figures illustrate, also, the way in which ornaments of

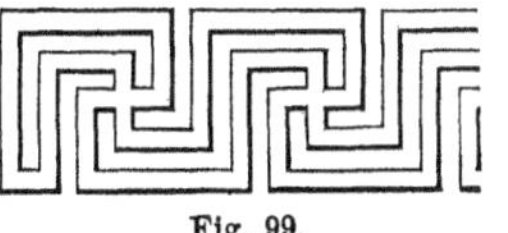

Fig. 99.

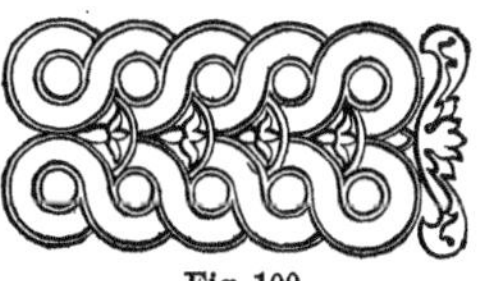

Fig. 100.

irregular figure are copied by the draughtsman. Thus, suppose it were required to draw fig. 2, and in a reversed position; circumscribe around the given figure, a parallelogram; divide this parallelogram into any number of equal squares, and in the position required for the copy, as fig. 3 for instance, construct a similar parallelogram. For convenience of reference, we have marked the vertical divisions of the squares by letters, *a*, *b*, *c*, *d*, *e*, *f*, *g*, and the horizontal divisions by figures, 1, 2, 3, 4; this is done with both parallelograms. But it must be remarked, that if the copy is to be a reverse of the original, the figures marking the horizontal divisions of the copy must be the reverse of the original, as may be seen in figs. 2 and 3. Now mark on the different vertical and horizontal lines of the corresponding squares, the relative positions of the parts of the leaf, and through these points thus established, construct the leaf required. A similar method may be used in constructing a copy to an enlarged or to a reduced size of the original, by enlarging or reducing the comparative sizes of the squares of the parallelogram of the copy on a scale proportioned to the enlargement or reduction required. In general, the intersections of the portions of the leaf, or other figure, with the vertical or horizontal lines, are measured and transferred by the eye; the larger the number of squares, therefore, the greater probability of the copy coinciding with the original. Figs. 4, 5, and 6, are the side elevation, front elevation, and section of a Greek bracket, the principal ornaments of which are taken from the anthemion and acanthus.

Fig. 1, Plate XVII., is an elevation of a portion of an enriched cornice from the temple of Jupiter Stator at Rome, of the Corinthian order of architecture. Fig. 2, is the under side of the modillion.

The chief characteristic of Roman ornament, is its uniform magnificence. As a style it is not original, but rather an enlargement or enrichment of the Greek. There is, further, this distinction between the two styles, that the most rarely used elements among the Greeks are the most characteristic of the Roman decorations, the scroll and the acanthus. Indeed, every form which will admit of it, is habitually enriched with acanthus clothing or foliations. The acanthus of the Greeks is the narrow prickly acanthus; that of the Roman, the soft acanthus. For capitals the Roman acanthus is commonly composed of conventional clusters of olive leaves. The Greek scroll is seldom elaborated, but the Roman is seldom without acanthus foliations. Fig. 3, represents a Roman acanthus scroll.

The free introduction of monsters and animals is likewise a characteristic of Greek and Roman ornament, as the sphinx, the triton, the griffin, and others; they occur however more abundantly in the Roman.

Fig. 3.
4 3 2 1
Fig. 1.
Fig. 2.
1 2 3 4
g
f
e
d
c
b
a
Fig. 4.
Fig. 5.
Fig. 6
Fig. 7.
Fig. 8.
Fig. 9.

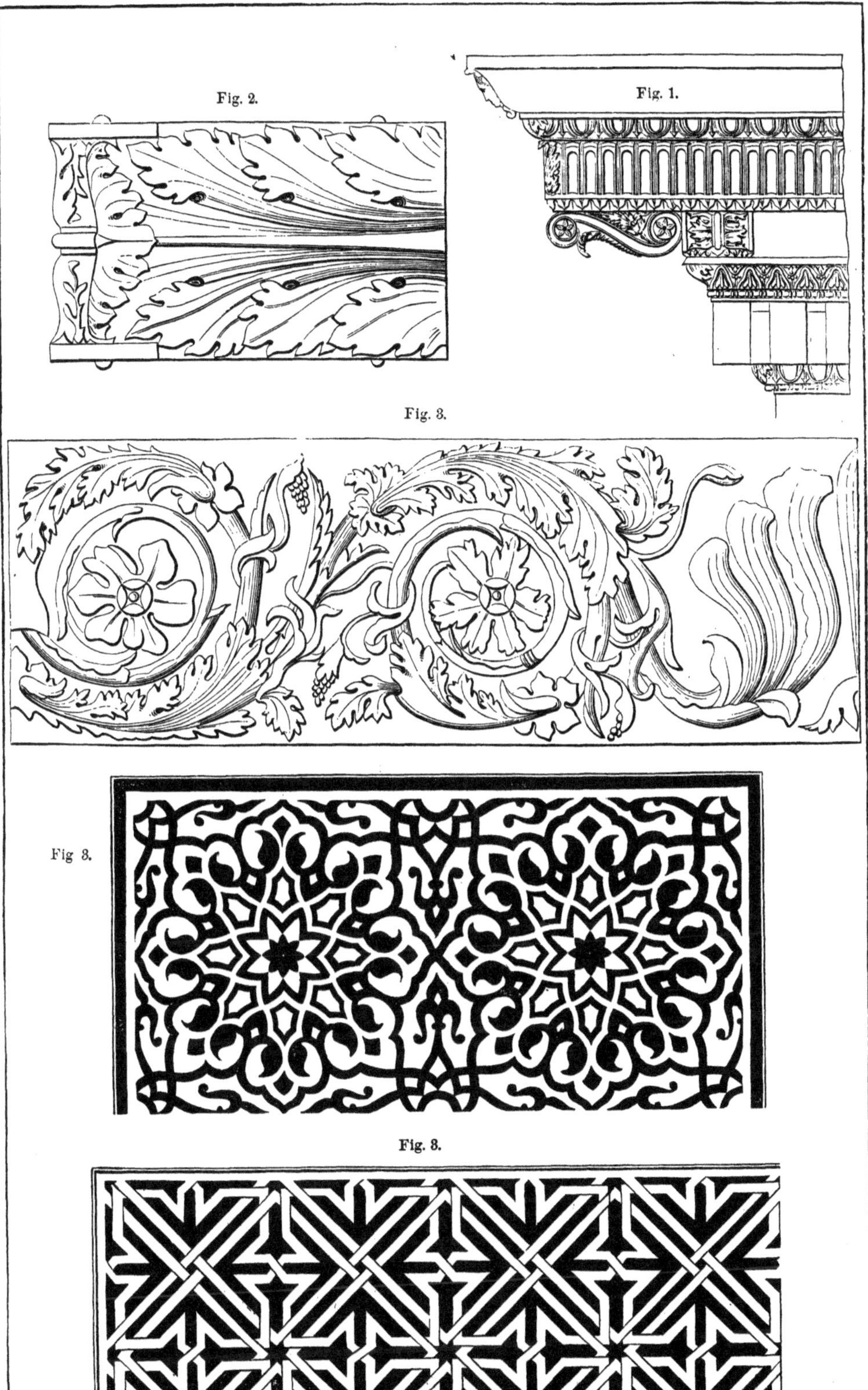
Fig. 2.
Fig. 1.
Fig. 3.
Fig 3.
Fig. 3.

As the Christian art succeeded the Pagan, symbols became the foundation of decorations in the Byzantine and Romanesque. The early symbols were the monogram of Christ, the lily, the cross, the serpent, the fish, the aureole, or vesica piscis, and the circle or nimbus, the glory of the head, as the vesica is of the whole body. These are very important elements in Christian decoration, especially the nimbus, which is the element of the trefoil and quatrefoil; the first having reference to the Trinity, the second to the four Evangelists, as the testimony of Christ, and to the Cross, at the extremities of which we often find four circles, besides the circle in the centre, which signifies the Lord. Occasionally the symbolic images of the Evangelists, the angel, the lion, the ox, and the eagle, are represented within these circles.

The hand in the attitude of benediction, and the lily (the fleur-de-lis), the emblem of the virgin and purity, are common in Christian decoration. This last symbol was eventually elaborated into the most characteristic foliage of Byzantine and Romanesque art. Conspicuous in their foliage also is a peculiar formed leaf, somewhat resembling the leaf of the ordinary thistle. The serpent figures largely in Byzantine art as the instrument of the fall, and one type of the redemption.

As paganism disappeared, their ornaments, under certain symbolic modifications, were admitted into Christian decorations. Thus the foliations of the scroll were terminated by lilies, or by leaves of three, four and five blades, the number of blades being significant; and in a similar way, the anthemion and every other ancient ornament. In the Byzantine the symbolism is seldom or ever absent, however much it may be modified or disguised. An important feature, always to be observed in the Byzantine, is that all their imitations of natural forms were invariably conventional; it is the same even with animals and the human figure, every saint had his prescribed colors, proportions and symbols.

The Saracenic was the period of gorgeous diapers, for their habit of decorating the entire surfaces of their apartments was highly favorable to the development of this class of design. The Alhambra displays almost endless specimens, and all are in relief and enriched with gold and color, chiefly blue and red. The religious cycles and symbolic figures of the Byzantine are excluded. Mere curves and angles or interlacings were now to bear the chief burden of a design, but distinguished by a variety of color. The curves however very naturally fell into standard forms and floral shapes, and the lines and angles were soon developed into a very characteristic species of tracery, or interlaid strap work, very agreeably diversified by the ornamental introduction of the inscriptions, which last custom of elaborating inscriptions with their designs was peculiarly Saracenic. Although flowers were not palpably admitted, yet the great mass of the minor details of Saracenic designs are composed of flower forms disguised, the very inscriptions are sometimes thus grouped as flowers; still no actual flower ever occurs, as the exclusion of all natural images is fundamental to the style in its purity.

Fig. 3, is a specimen of Alhambra diaper.

All the symbolic elements of the Byzantine are continued in the Gothic. Ornamentally, the Gothic is the geometrical and pointed element elaborated to the utmost; its only peculiarities are its combinations of details; at first the conventional and geometrical prevailing, and afterwards these combined with the elaboration of natural objects in its decoration. The Byzantines never did this, their ornaments are purely conventional; while in the finest gothic specimens, not only the traditional conventional ornaments, but also elaborate imitations of natural plants and flowers are found. The most striking feature of all Gothic work is the wonderful elaboration of its geometric tracery; vesicas, trefoils, quatrefoils, cinquefoils, and an infinity of geometric varieties besides. The tracery is so paramount a characteristic, that the three English varieties, the early English, the decorated, and the perpendicular, and the French flamboyant, are distinguished almost exclusively by this feature. See Plate XIV.

Under the head of Gothic, the Norman is often included, but it is rather a transition style between the Romanesque or Byzantine, and the Gothic. The ornamental mouldings used in the decorative details of this style are numerous, among which the more common is the chevron or zig-zag, (fig. 1, plate XVIII.,) simple as the indented, or duplicated, triplicated or quadrupled; the billet, the prismatic billet, the square billet, and the alternate billet (fig. 2); the double cone, the fir cone; the cable, fig. 4; the embattled, fig. 5; the nail head, fig. 6. In the early English style we find the dog-tooth, fig 7; a kind of pyramid-shaped flower leaves; the ball flower, fig. 8, and the serpentine vine scroll, are the most characteristic ornamental mouldings of the decorated style. The mouldings of the perpendicular are not peculiar; they are less enriched than the preceding styles, and the same panelling which is found in the windows is spread over every surface of the building.

In the early English we have the first development of geometrical tracery, flying buttresses, crocketed pinnacles, columns clustered, and an extensive application of foliage with the trefoil leaf, as the most characteristic ornament; sometimes formed as a clover leaf, at other times very irregularly formed.

PLATE XVIII.

The early English is characterized, besides its tracery, by the ogee and the pinnacled canopied recesses of its buttresses and other parts producing a prominence of diagonal lines. There is also more copying of nature in its ornamental details.

In the Perpendicular, the new features are the horizontal line and the panellings, and the substitution of perpendicular for flowing tracery.

The crocket, in its earliest form, was the simple arrow head of the Episcopal, pastoral staff; subsequently finished with a trefoil, and afterwards still further enriched. Figs. 9 and 10 are early English crockets; fig. 11 a decorated one. Fig. 12 is a finial of the same style; both finials and crockets in detail display a variety of forms; some resembling the botanical productions of one class, some of another.

The Parapets of the early English style are often a simple horizontal course, supported by a corbel table, sometimes relieved by a series of sunk blank trefoil-headed panels; sometimes a low embattled parapet crowns the wall. In the decorated style, the horizontal parapet is sometimes pierced with trefoils, sometimes with wavy flowing tracery (fig. 13). Grotesque spouts or gargoyles discharge the water from the gutters. The parapets of the perpendicular style are frequently embattled, (14) covered with sunk or pierced panelling, and ornamented with quatrefoil, or small trefoil-headed arches; sometimes not embattled but covered with sunk or pierced quatrefoils in circles, or with trefoils in triangular spaces as in fig. 15.

Amongst the varieties of ornamental work, the mode of covering small plain surfaces with diapering (fig. 16), was sometimes used; the design being in exact accordance with the architectural features and details of the style. The rose, fig. 17, the badge of the houses of York and Lancaster, is often met with in the perpendicular style; and tendrils, leaves and fruit of the vine, are carved in great profusion in the hollows of rich cornice mouldings, especially on screen work in the interior of a church. Fig. 18, in its original type, a Byzantine ornament, an alternate lily and cross, is a common finish to the cornice of rich screen work in the latest Gothic, and is known under the name of the Tudor flower.

Figs. 19, 20, 21, are examples of ornamental crosses used as finials, either for spires or pinnacles.

The Ornaments of the Renaissance.—The term Renaissance is used in a double sense; in a general sense implying the revival of art, and specially, signifying a peculiar style of ornament. It is also sometimes, in a very confined sense, applied in reference to ornament to the style of Benvenuto Cellini; or, as it is sometimes designated, the Henry II. (of France) style.

The mixture of various elements is one of the essentials of this style. These elements are the classical ornaments; unnatural and natural flowers and foliage, the former often of a pure Saracenic character, man and animals, natural and grotesque; cartouches, or pierced and scrolled shields, in great prominence; tracery independent, and developed from the scrolls of the cartouches; and jewel forms. Fig. 1, Plate XIX.

The Elizabethan is a partial elaboration of the same style, the only difference being that what we now term the Elizabethan exhibits a very striking preponderance of strap and shield work, but the earlier and pure Elizabethan is much nearer allied to the continental styles of the time; classical ornaments but rude in detail, occasional scroll and arabesque work, and strap work, holding a much more prominent place than the pierced or scrolled shields. Figs. 2 and 3 are examples of the two styles.

Of the earliest and transition styles of Renaissance ornament, are the Tricento and the Quatrecento; the great features of the first are its intricate tracery and delicate scroll work of conventional foliage, the style being but a slight remove from the Byzantine and Saracenic. Of the second are, in addition, elaborate natural imitations of fruit, flowers, birds or animals (fig. 4), all disposed simply with a view to the ornamental; also occasional cartouches, or scrolled shield work.

In all these styles, the evidence of their Byzantine or Saracenic origin is constantly preserved, in the tracery, in the scroll work and foliage, and in the rendering of classical ornaments. The Renaissance is, therefore, something more approximative to a combination of previous styles than a revival of any in particular. Yet it is a style that was developed solely on æsthetic principles, from a love of the forms and harmonies themselves, as varieties of effect and arrangements of beauty, not because they had any particular signification, or from any superstitious attachment to them as heirlooms.

Fig. 5 is an example of ornament in the Cinquecento style. The arabesque scroll work is the most prominent feature of the Cinquecento, and with this in its elements, it combines every other feature of classical art, with the unlimited choice of natural and conventional imitations from the entire animal and vegetable kingdom, both arbitrarily disposed and combined. Absolute works of art, such as vases and implements, and instruments of all kinds, are prominent elements of the Cinquecento arabesque, but cartouches and strap work wholly disappear from the best examples. Another chief feature of the Cinquecento is the admirable play of color in its arabesques and scrolls, and it is worthy of note that

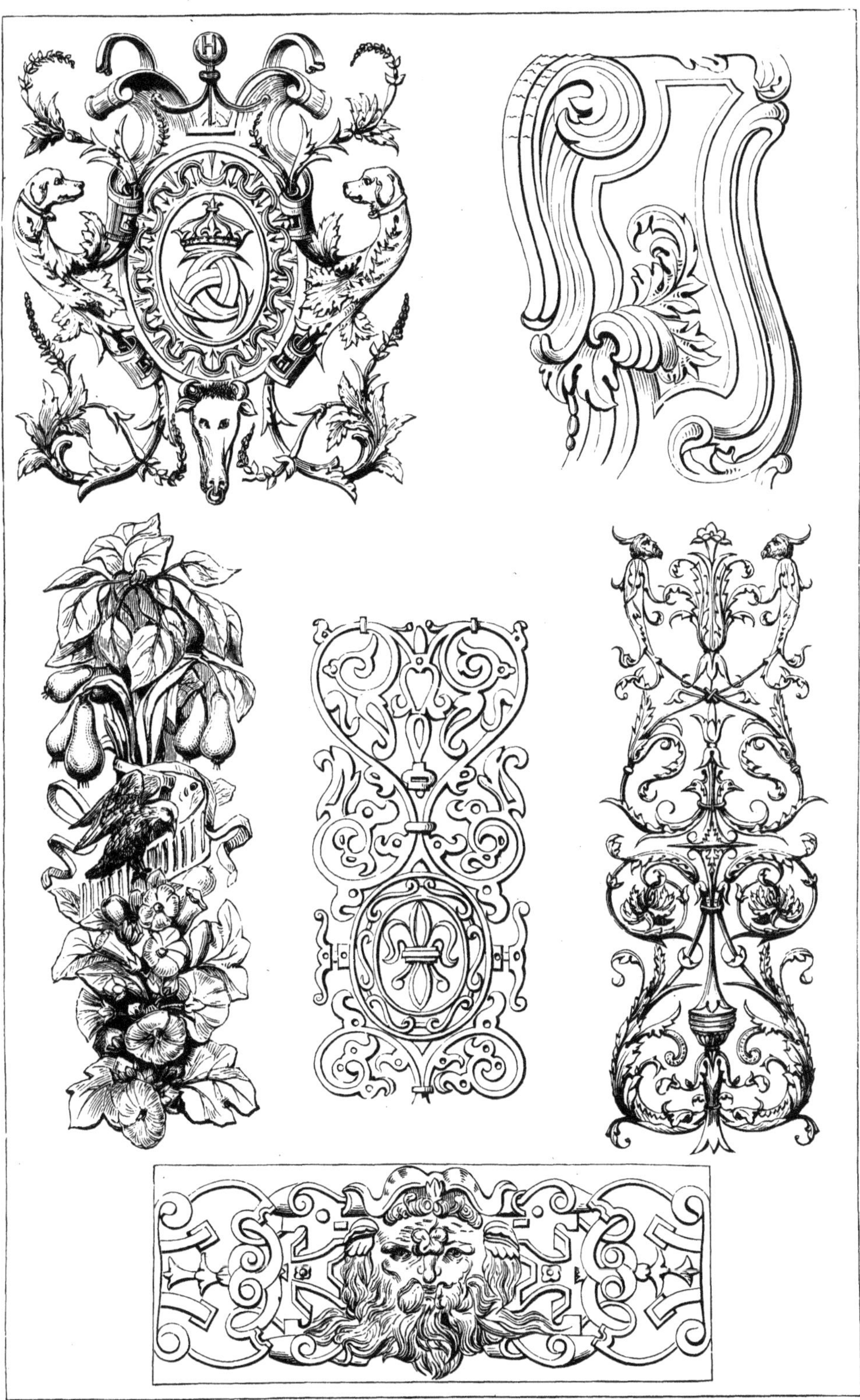

the three secondary colors, orange, green, and purple, perform the chief parts in all the colored decorations.

Fig. 6 is an example of the Louis Quatorze style of ornament. The great medium of this style was gilt stucco work, and this absence of color seems to have led to its most striking characteristic, infinite play of light, of shade; color, or mere beauty of form in detail, having no part in it whatever. Flat surfaces are not admitted; all are concave or convex: this constant varying of the surface gives every point of view its high lights and brilliant contrasts.

The Louis Quinze style differs from that of Louis Quatorze chiefly in its absence of symmetry; in many of its examples it is an almost random dispersion of the scroll and shell, mixed only with that peculiar crimping of shell work, the coquillage.

The ornaments of which we have thus given examples are, in general, applied to interior decorations, to friezes, pilasters, panels, architraves, the faces and soffits of arches, ceilings, &c., to furniture and to art manufactures in general. For exteriors these ornaments are sparingly applied; shield and scroll work, of the later Elizabethan or Renaissance style, is sometimes used, but very seldom tracery.

Of common exterior ornament, the baluster is peculiarly modern, with all the refinement of a classic model. Balustrades are sometimes of real use in building, and at other times merely ornamental. Such as are intended for use, as when they are employed on steps or stairs, before windows, or to enclose terraces or other elevated places of resort, must always be nearly of the same height, from three to three and a half feet, so that a person of ordinary height may, with ease, lean over them without the danger of falling. But those that are principally designed for ornament, as when they finish a building; or even for use and ornament, as when they form the railing over a large bridge, should be proportioned to the architecture they accompany, and their height ought never to exceed four-fifths of the entablature on which they are placed; nor should it be less than two-thirds, without counting the plinth, the height of which must be sufficient to leave the whole balustrade exposed to view.

Fig. 101. Fig. 102. Fig. 103. Fig. 104.

Figs. 101, 102, 103, 104, 105, and 106, represent various figures of balusters and of various proportions, suited to the various orders they may serve to finish. The double-bellied balusters (figs. 101 and 102) are the lightest, and, therefore the best adapted to windows or other compositions of which the parts are small and the profiles delicate. The base and rail may be of the same profile but not so large as for single-bellied ones.

Fig. 105. Fig. 106.

In balustrades, the distance between two balusters should not exceed the half of the diameter of the thickest part of the baluster, nor less than one-third of it. The pedestals, if possible, should be at intervals of about nine balusters, but as the pedestals must be placed over the centre of the piers, the intervals must frequently contain more balusters.

Fig. 105 shows the arrangement of a baluster with inclined rails and bases.

When used in interiors, either for decoration or use, the forms of the baluster are much varied and enriched; this is especially observable in constructions in iron.

ELEVATIONS OF HOUSES.

Having thus given a brief abstract of the characteristics of various prominent styles of architecture, we continue our article on houses by giving elevations, either suited to plans already exhibited, or to other plans which will be found on the same plate as the elevations. It must be perceived that, in general, in modern constructions, pure ancient art is seldom exhibited, nor would it, in domestic architecture, be found suitable, the requirements and appliances being very different, and he may be called an architect, who, conversant with ancient and modern practice, can adapt them in unity and harmony to modern necessities.

Plate XX. represents the front elevation of a basement house with the general characteristics of the Florentine style, uniting richness and grandeur of effect, admirably suited to the locality and purpose for which it is designed, a first-class house, or even what might be termed a palatial residence. This building has been constructed in Fifth Avenue, New York, after designs of T. Thomas & Son, architects; the specifications of which will be found in a subsequent chapter.

English basement houses are generally constructed with a rusticated basement as in the preceding example, (Plate XX.) with a balustrade marking the distinction between it and the principal story. The entrance is generally raised not to exceed three steps, and seldom with a projecting porch; the intention being to make the basement subordinate to the principal story, the usual finish of the door-head is similar to that of the window. In general English basement houses are intended for narrow lots;

PLATE XX.

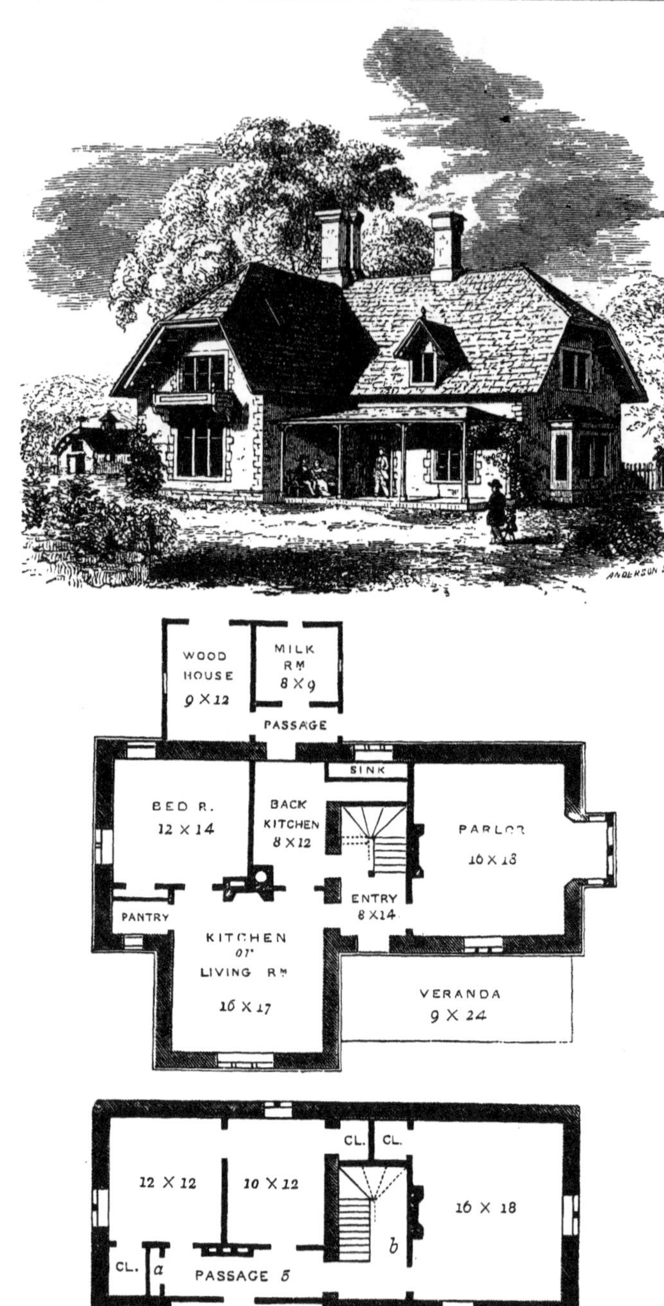
ANDERSON S.
WOOD HOUSE
9 X 12
MILK RM
8 X 9
PASSAGE
SINK
BED R.
12 X 14
BACK KITCHEN
8 X 12
ENTRY
8 X 14
PANTRY
KITCHEN or LIVING RM
16 X 17
VERANDA
9 X 24
CL.
CL.
12 X 12
10 X 12
16 X 18
b
CL.
a
PASSAGE 5
12 X 16

PLATE XXIII.

KITCHEN
C
CHINA
C
STORE ROOM
PARLOR
A
C
B
VERANDA
HALL
DRAWING ROOM
DINING ROOM
D
ENTRANCE
D

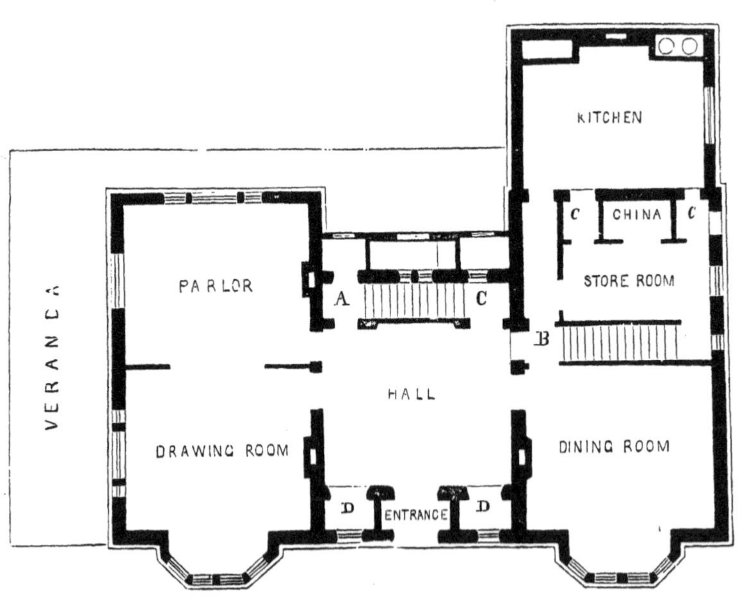

showing in front but two windows to the stories above the basement, and one basement window. Circular heads are almost invariably used for the basement openings, and for the windows above either square lintels or slightly arched. Sometimes a species of Romanesque window of clustered openings is adopted.

Plate XXI. is an elevation of a house after what is here usually termed the French style of architecture. Its peculiarities consist rather in the form of roof, its dormer window, than any distinctive feature in the main elevation or its ornaments. This style of house is well adapted both for city and country residences. It is especially popular in the neighborhood of Boston.

When the architect is not controlled by the form or size of the lot, much picturesqueness may be given by varieties of form and irregularities of outline in the construction of edifices.

Plate XXII., XXIII., XXIV. and XXV. are elevations and plans of country residences from "Downing's Country Houses," drawn in perspective, the principles of which will be given in a subsequent chapter. They may be taken as beautiful illustrations of modern constructions.

Plate XXII. are the plans and elevation of a Farm House in the English Rural Style.

Plate XXIII. is an elevation and plan of a plain timber cottage villa, after designs of Gervase Wheeler, Architect, of Philadelphia. "The construction, though simple, is somewhat peculiar. It is framed in such a manner that on the exterior the construction shows. At the corners are heavy posts, roughly dressed and chamfered, and into them are morticed horizontal ties, immediately under the springing of the roof; these, with the posts and the studs and the framing of the roof showing externally. Internally are nailed horizontal braces at equal distances apart, stopping on the posts and studs of the frame, and across these the furring and lathing cross diagonally in different directions. On these horizontal braces, the sheathing composed of plank placed in a perpendicular position is supported and retained in its place by battens, two and a half inches thick, and made with a broad shoulder. These battens are pinned to the horizontal braces, confining the planks, but leaving spaces for shrinking and swelling, thus preventing the necessity of a single nail being driven through the planks. A representation is given (fig. 107) of the batten B, and the mode of framing.

Fig. 108 represents the usual form of vertical boarding, which is less expensive than the first illustration, and, in general, will be found sufficiently secured for the class of buildings to which it is applied.

Plate XXIV. is a villa in what Mr. Downing designates as the Rural

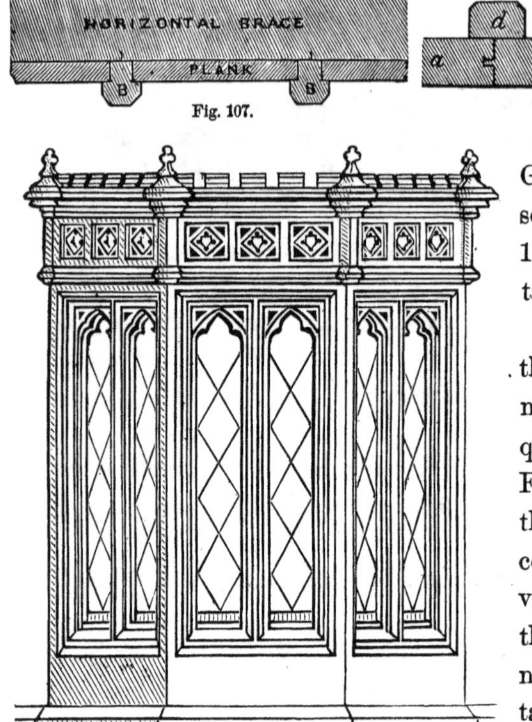

Fig. 107.

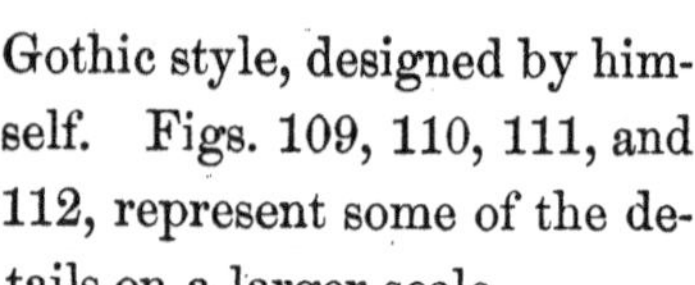

Fig. 108.

Fig. 109.

Gothic style, designed by himself. Figs. 109, 110, 111, and 112, represent some of the details on a larger scale.

Fig. 109 is an elevation of the bay window with a balcony over it, to the scale of one-quarter of an inch to the foot. Fig. 110, the *verge board* of the small gable over this balcony. Fig. 111, part of the verge board of the gable over the porch. Fig. 112 are chimney tops, such as can be obtained of Garnkirk clay.

Fig. 110.

Fig. 111.

PLATE XXIV.

ANDERSON SC

VERANDA
DRAWING
17 X 27
DINING
17 X 22
PANT.
KITCHEN
15 X 17
GREEN-H.
W.C.
PORCH
LIBRARY
16X20
HALL
BOUDOIR
PORCH

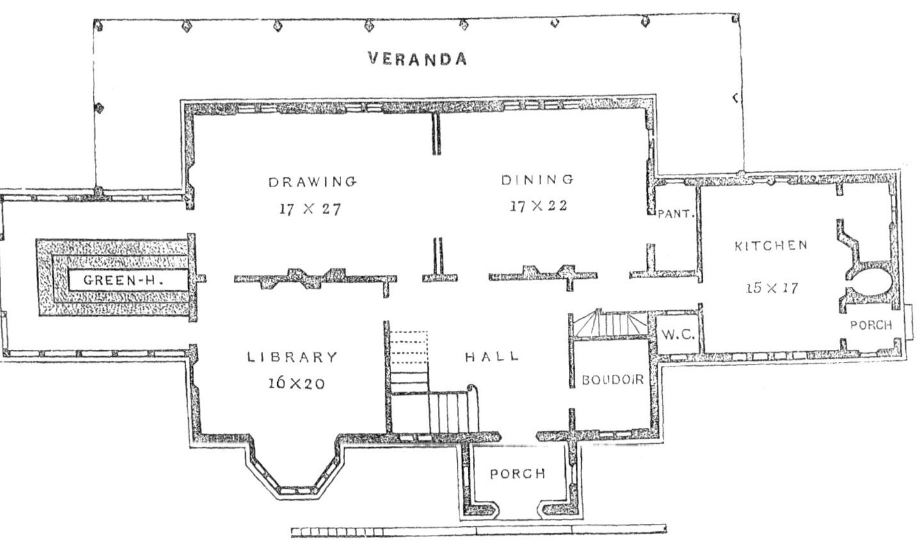

Fig. 112.

Fig. 113.

Plate XXV. is the elevation and principal floor plan of a villa in the Italian style, as constructed after plans of Mr. Upjohn. "It is one of the most successful specimens of the Italian style in the United States."

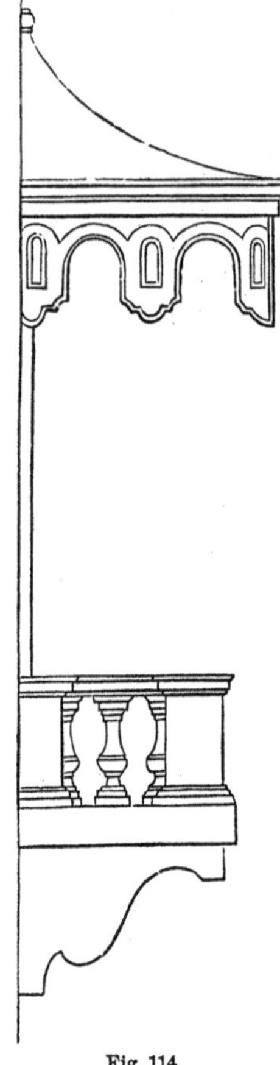
Fig. 114.

This villa is built of brick, painted externally of a light freestone color, and the window dressings, string courses, cornices, brackets, &c., are all freestone. Figs. 113 and 114 are the front and side elevation of the balcony window in the front of the house, drawn to a scale of one-quarter of an inch to a foot.

Figs. 115 and 116 are the first and second story plans, and Plate XXVI. an elevation in perspective of a tenant house, built by the New York Workingmen's Home Association, after designs by John W. Ritch, architect.

The plans are admirably suited to the purpose designed, a separate house as it were for each tenant; sufficient for the wants, and within the means of the laboring classes, especially adapted for the population of large cities. In its construction it is almost entirely fire proof; the staircases are of iron, the hall floors are constructed with iron beams, brick arches, and blue flagging; the dividing floors and walls are deafened; every alternate wall is of brick; every window has inside shutters, and every room is well ventilated, having air flues from each to the roof.

In the lower story are large stores, with vaults in front. On the south is a spacious flagged court yard, 22 by 188 feet, which is used by the inmates for washing and drying their clothes—the families on each floor having the exclusive use of it for specified days of the week. The yard connects with the main hall, by cross halls, and is shut off from the streets by high gates that are kept closed, except fuel is brought to the premises, when carts can be driven to each tenant's cellar, and at once deposit their loads. The cellar is divided into 94 compartments, that is, one for each tenement, with a lock and key for each.

On the upper floor are two large adjoining rooms, measuring together 53 by 50 feet, which can be thrown into one, or disconnected at pleasure. They are designed for lectures, concerts, or moral and educational uses for

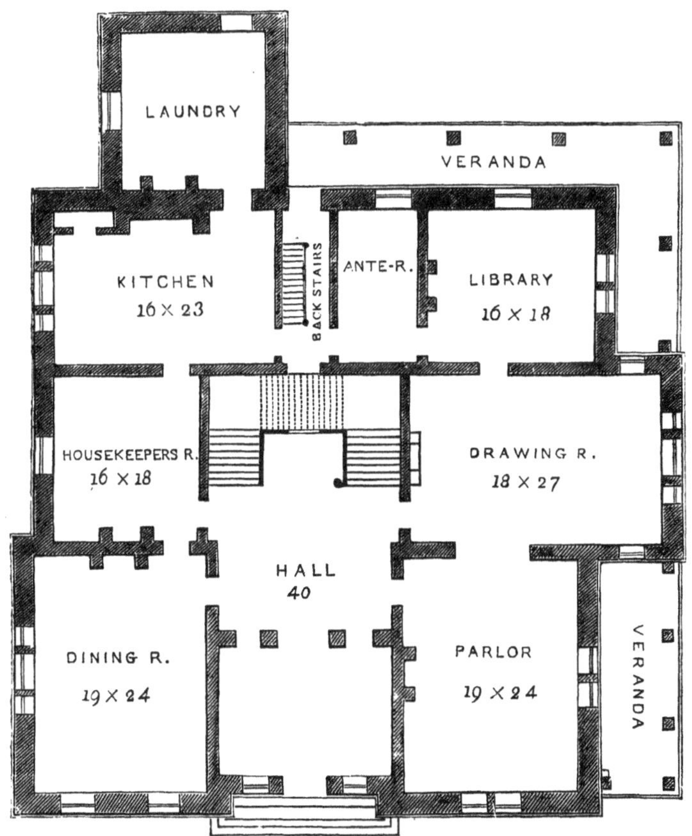
LAUNDRY
VERANDA
KITCHEN
16 X 23
BACK STAIRS
ANTE-R.
LIBRARY
16 X 18
HOUSEKEEPERS R.
16 X 18
DRAWING R.
18 X 27
HALL
40
DINING R.
19 X 24
PARLOR
19 X 24
VERANDA

PLATE XXVI.

Fig. 115.

Fig. 116.

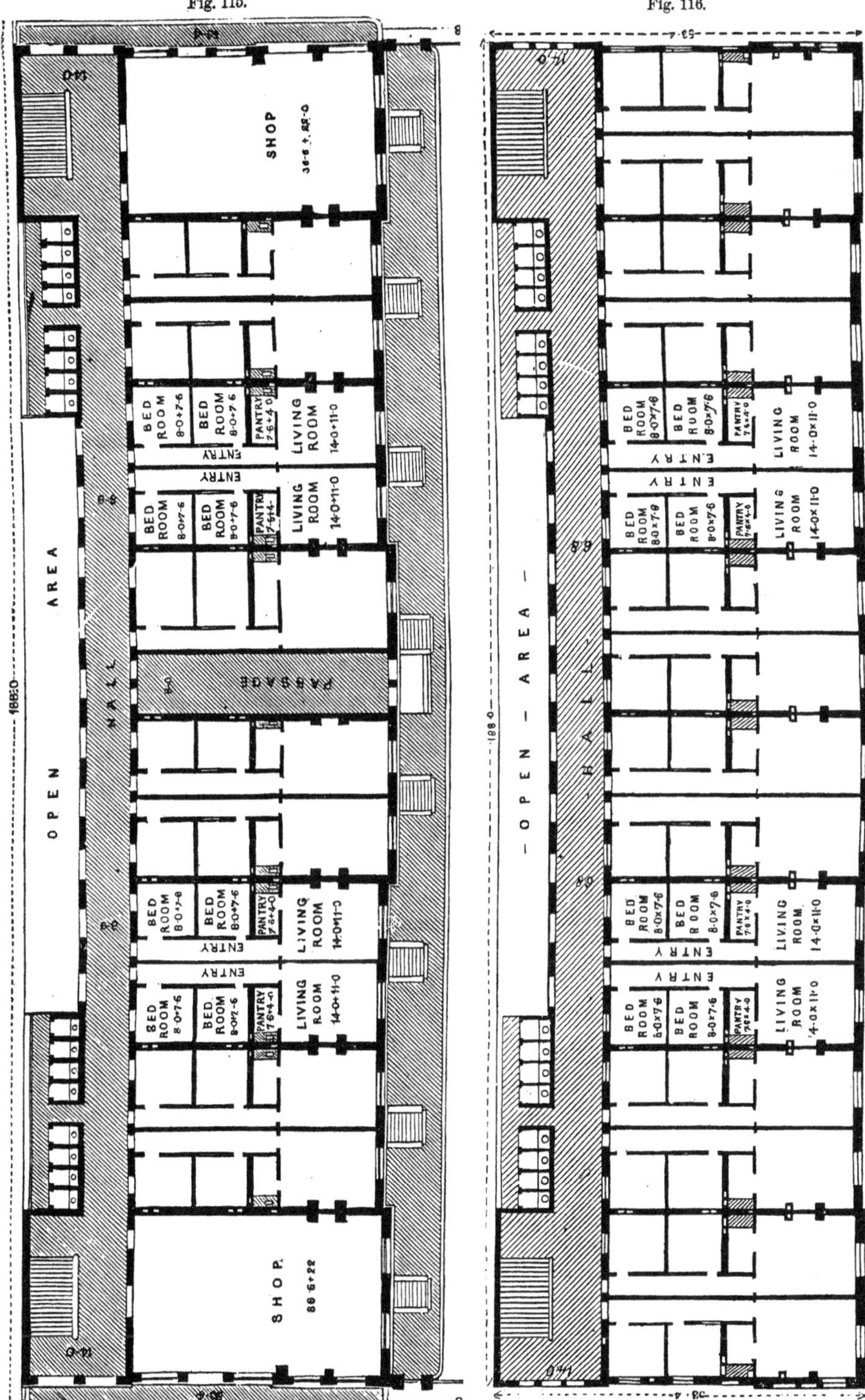

the inmates during the week, and for Sunday school and religious observances on the Sabbath.

The exterior is of brick with brown stone window-sills, and in its style is an excellent example of the architectural effect that may be produced in our most common materials, and in an unpretending edifice, by breaking up the monotony of façade by even slight projections, by the clustered and circular heads of the windows, and by an appropriate and varied cornice. This style is becoming very popular and is particularly applicable to the construction of mills and workshops.

Store and Warehouses.—Plate XXVII. is an elevation of a store front, and figs. 117 and 118 plans of first story and basement.

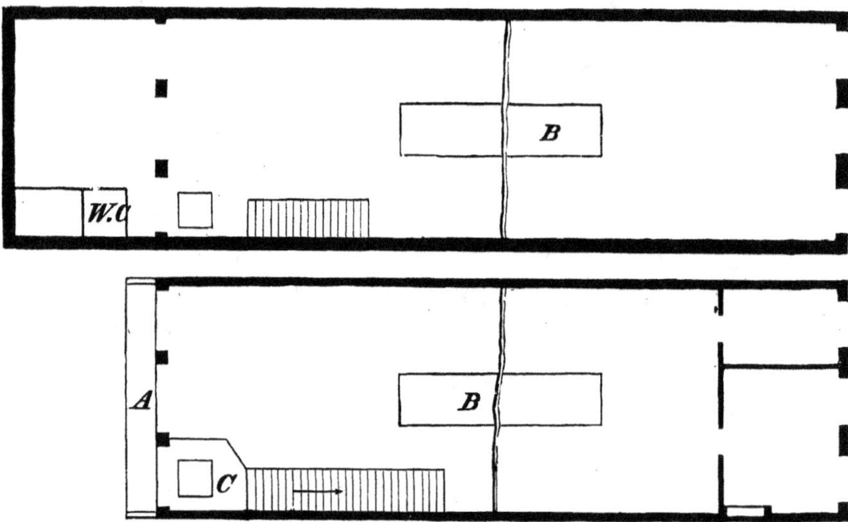

These plans may be taken as a type of the general class of large wholesale or retail stores covering but one lot. In this city there is usually beneath the sidewalks two stories, the basement and sub-cellar. These are generally let with the first story, and the upper stories together by themselves. The depth of the stores are mostly from 100 to 200 feet, on an average about 150 feet. The centre is lighted by a skylight in the roof, and by well-holes, B, beneath, in the several floors. In front of the entrance is a platform, A, which is either an iron grating, or, when the basement extends through into the front vaults, covered with patent vault lights. To protect the vaults from moisture the walls are laid hollow, and the outside covered with asphalte. The hoistway to basement and subcellars, is by a trap in the grating front of the window, usually a platform supported by chains at the four corners, and raised vertically, often

PLATE XXVII.

by a car sliding on an incline, if there are outisde stairs leading to the basement. In the rear an area of some ten to fifteen feet in width is dug out, and the two lower stories show full. All the rear windows are protected by iron shutters.

The floor of the first story is often laid with a rising grade, of about 1 foot in 100 towards the rear, to prevent the appearance which a long level sometimes has of descending, and to afford more light in the rear to the basement. The offices are in the rear on this floor. The safe is sometimes built into the wall, or into a projection from it, or the safe is movable; or, what is rare at present, a book vault is made in the front vault. The front windows and doors are mostly protected by revolving shutters rolling up like a curtain in the box lintels above. Separations are made between tenants occupying different floors by iron framed skylights over the well-holes.

C is the entry way to the second story, separated from the store by a glass partition protected by a wrought iron screen or guard. Above this entrance in the second floor, is the hoistway for goods, generally about five feet square. The second floor does not differ in plan from the first, and so with the stories above, except in some cases the well-holes are wider in the upper stories. The floors are all level.

The water closets are mostly on the third floor, and in the front basement vault. The heating is either by stoves, hot air furnaces, or steam. The shelvings, counters and other furniture depend, of course, on the class and kind of business.

Front Elevation.—Various styles are adopted, but in one particular there is almost an uniformity; that is, the whole front is supported on posts of cast iron in the first story, with iron lintels and cornice; the great object being to get as much light as possible in this story. These posts are sometimes square or rectangular in plan, with a small sunk panel on the face, and shield-like ornaments containing the number of the store, and capitals at the top; sometimes a sort of Corinthian column, and sometimes two posts, the inside one circular, and the outside square. As there is but little chance for ornament, the building seldom assumes any distinctive expression till it reaches the second story. The great ornament of the first story is the plate glass. The elevation and plans represent the usual form of the wholesale stores with but three openings in the first story —one window and two doors. In the retail stores occupying a full lot there are generally four openings, the door to the first floor, central between two windows, and the side door leading to the second story; but where all the stories are occupied by the same trade, the side door is usually omitted. The door of the retail store is generally recessed, with show windows at the sides to admit of the greater display of goods. The glass of the windows are sometimes of one plate, as large as 8 × 14 feet even, but more usually in four squares; seldom more in number.

Above the first story, the front begins to assume an architectural expression, though seldom perhaps very significant of any intention or design for a specific purpose inside. The example selected may be considered a fair average of the class. It is to be remarked that where various businesses are to be carried on in the same building, and where large signs may be necessary to designate them, there will be but little room, as there will but little necessity, for much ornamental detail.

Plate XXVIII. is an elevation of a store front as designed and executed in cast iron by D. D. Badger & Co. of this city. This is the type of a class of buildings coming into extensive use, and is, as far as we can judge, the handsomest of the class. The style is Venetian, and when the front is more than fifty feet in width, the effect is imposing. It is rather more appropriate for stores with offices above, or for stores designed for but one purpose, as signs larger than could be placed in the panels would mar the effect. Iron was first introduced for house fronts by Mr. Bogardus, and it has much to recommend it. Ornaments can be applied profusely, and at the same time cheaply, and in durability it exceeds our common freestones. The chief objection at present lies in this, that few wish to go to the expense of new patterns: the result is that the forms become too stereotyped, especially objectionable when much ornament is used. The color which it should be painted has been a subject of much discussion; the prevailing tint at present is a sort of cream color, with brown trimmings of the windows.

School Houses.—Plate XXIX. contains a plan and elevation of a district school house, with seats for forty-eight scholars. There are two entrances, one for each sex, with ample accommodations of entry or lobby room for the hanging up of hats, bonnets and cloaks. A side door leads from each entry into distinct yards, and an inside door opens into the school-room. The desk, T, of the teacher, is central between the doors, on a platform, P, raised some six or eight inches above the floor. In the rear of the teacher's desk is a closet or small room, for the use of the teacher. The seats are arranged two to each desk, with two alleys of eighteen inches, and a central one of two feet; the passages around the room are three feet. The scale is eight feet to the inch. The elevation is in a very plain Romanesque style, to be constructed of brick with hollow walls.

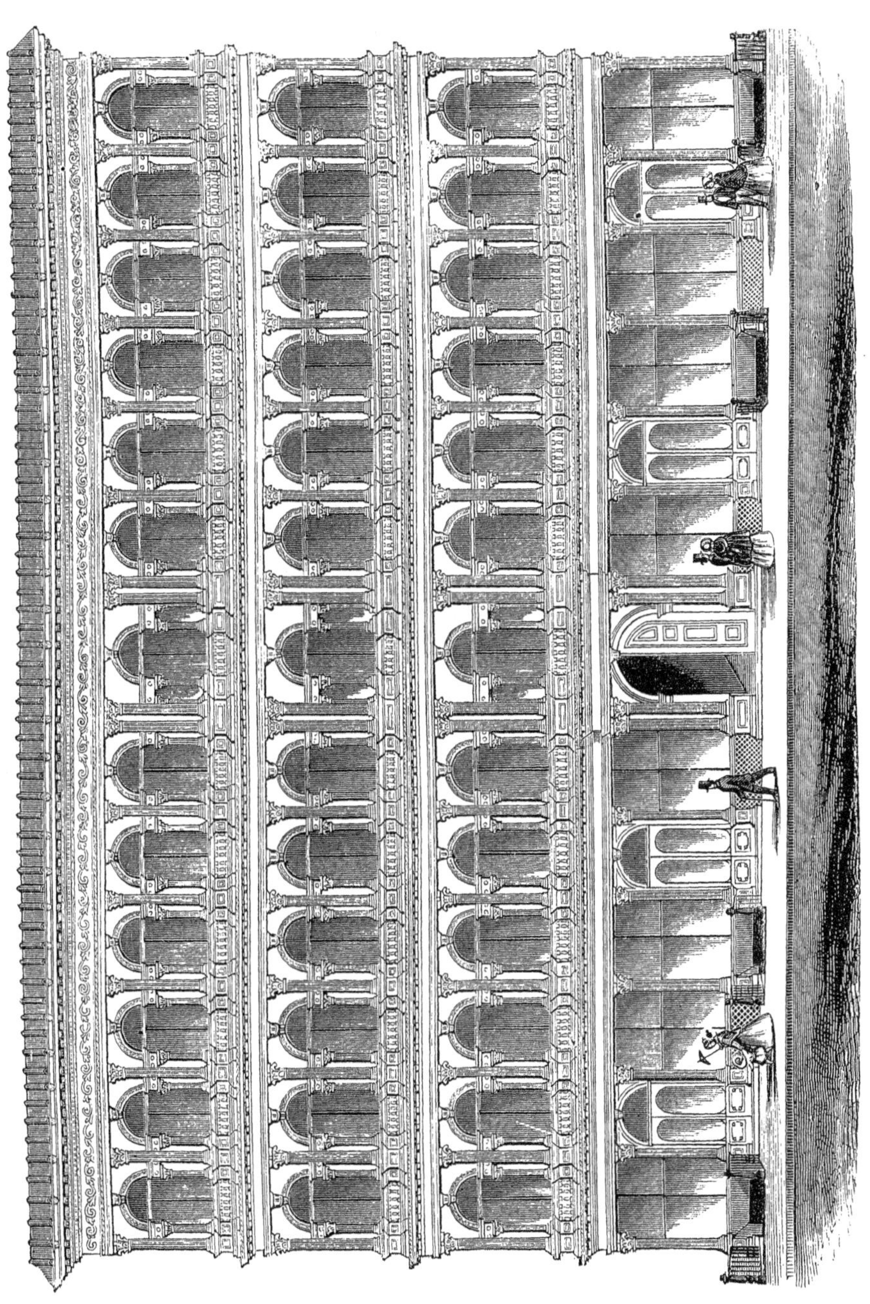

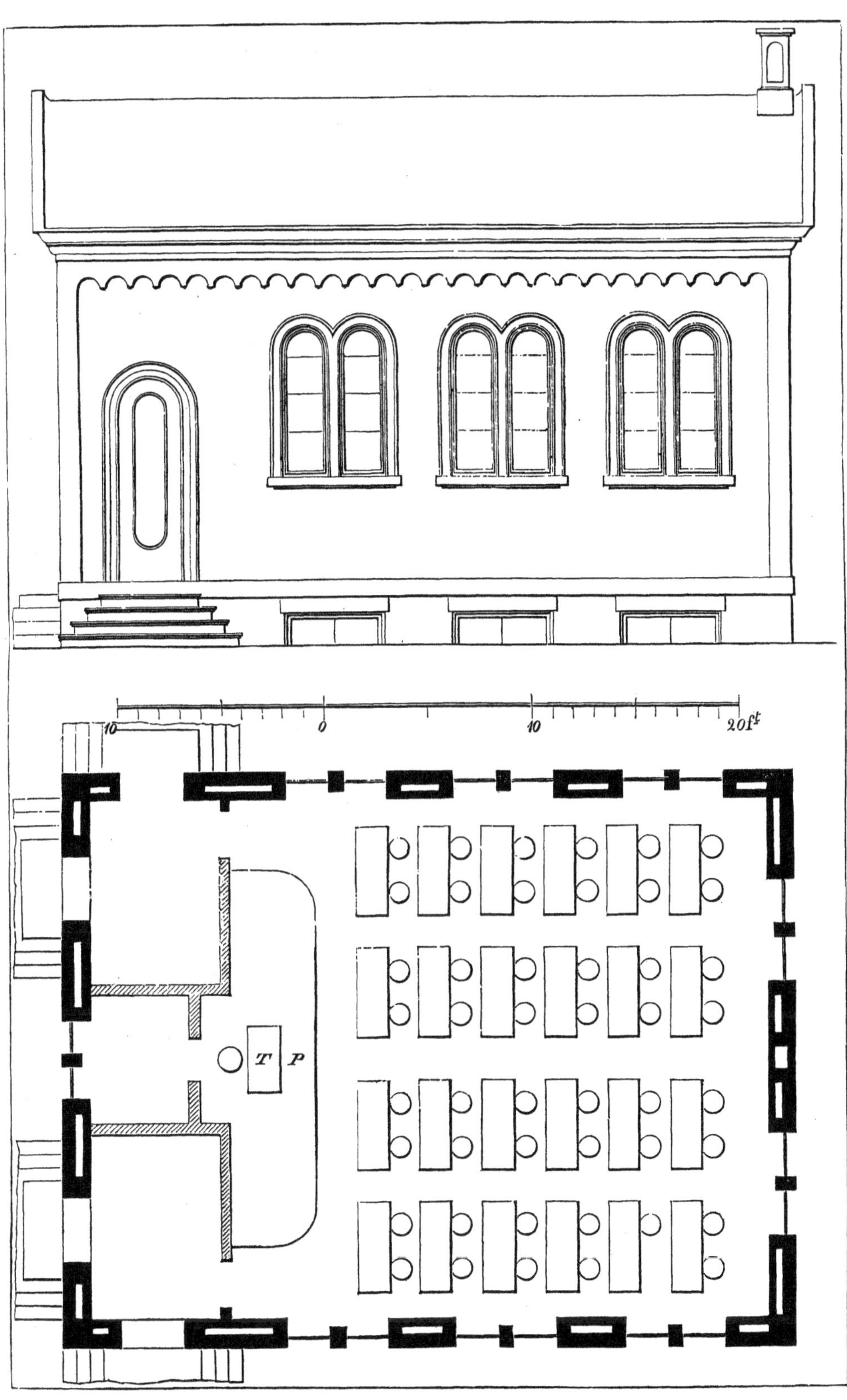
10
0
10
20ft
T
P

On the Requirements of a School-House.—Every scholar should have room enough to sit at ease, his seat should be of easy access, so that he may go to and fro, or be approached by the teacher without disturbing any one else. The seat and desk should be properly proportioned to each other and to the size of the scholar for whom it is intended. The seats as furnished by the different makers of school furniture, vary from nine to sixteen inches in height; and the benches from seventeen to twenty-eight inches; measuring on the side next the scholar. The average width of the desk is about eighteen inches, and is formed with a slope of from one and a half to two and a half inches, with a small horizontal piece of from two to three inches at top. There is a shelf beneath for books, but it should not come within about three inches of the front. The width of the seat varies from ten to fourteen inches, with a sloping back, like that of a chair; it should, in fact, be a comfortable chair. It will be observed that, in the plate, two scholars occupy one bench; fig. 119 represents another arrangement, in which each scholar has a distinct bench; and, in many respects it is preferable, but is not quite so economical in room. In primary schools, desks are not necessary; and in many of the intermediate schools, the seat of one bench is formed against the back of the next bench; but distinct seats are preferable. The teacher's seat is invariably on a raised platform, and had better be against a dead wall than where there are windows. The best light is undoubtedly a skylight, but as this is seldom convenient, the lights at the side should be high above the floor. Blackboards and maps should be placed along the walls. Care should be taken in the warming and ventilation; the room should not be less than ten feet high; the best method of heating is by furnaces in the cellar, warm air should be introduced in proportion to the number of scholars, and ventiducts should be formed to carry off the impure air.

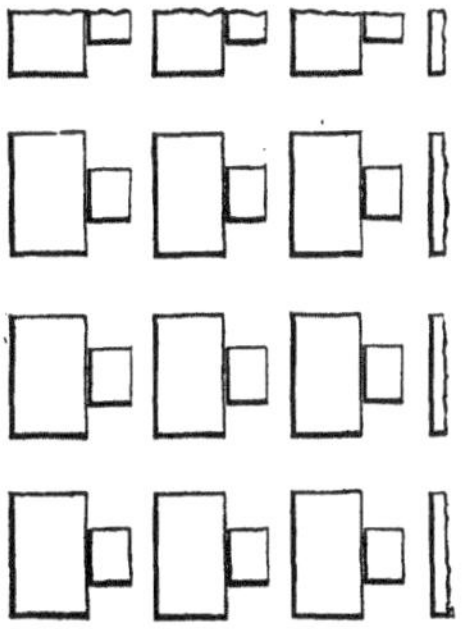

Fig. 119.

In cities the school-houses are made of a number of stories—the primaries being in the lower stories, and, in some cases, play rooms also, and the grammar schools occupying the whole floor above. In these cases the teachers are numerous, and separate rooms are prepared for the hearing of recitations. The style of interior finish should always be simple; in the exterior various styles have been adopted. We know of none more suitable than brick school-houses, with Romanesque or circular window-heads and coved cornices, as given in the plate, or similar to the Home, Plate XXVI.

Lecture Rooms, Churches, Theatres, Legislative Halls.—To the proper construction of rooms or edifices adapted for these purposes some knowledge of the general principles of acoustics, and their practical application, is necessary. In the case of lecture rooms and churches, the positions of the speaker and the audience are fixed; in theatres, one portion of the enclosed space is devoted to numerous speakers, and the other to the audience; in legislative halls, the speakers are scattered over the greater part of the space, and also form the audience.

The transmission of sound is by vibrations, illustrated by the waves formed by a stone thrown into still water; but direction may be given to sound, so that the transmission is not equally strong in every direction; thus, Saunders found that a person reading at the centre of a circle of one hundred feet in diameter, in an open meadow, was heard most distinctly in front, not as well at the sides, but scarcely at all behind. Fig. 120 shows the extreme distance every way at which the voice could be distinctly heard: ninety-two feet in front, seventy-five feet on each side, and thirty-one feet in the rear. The waves of sound are subject to the same laws as those of light, the angles of reflection are equal to those of incidence; therefore, in every enclosed space, there are reflected sounds more or less distinct, according to the position of the hearer, and to the form and condition of the surfaces against which the waves of sound impinge. Thus, of all the sounds entering a parabolic sphere, the reflected sounds are collected at the focus. Solid bodies reflect sound, but draperies absorb it. As, in all rooms, the audience can never be concentrated at focal points, nor is it possible in any construction to make calculation for all positions, it is in general best to depend on nothing but the direct force of the voice, and not to construct larger than can be heard directly without aids from reflected sounds.

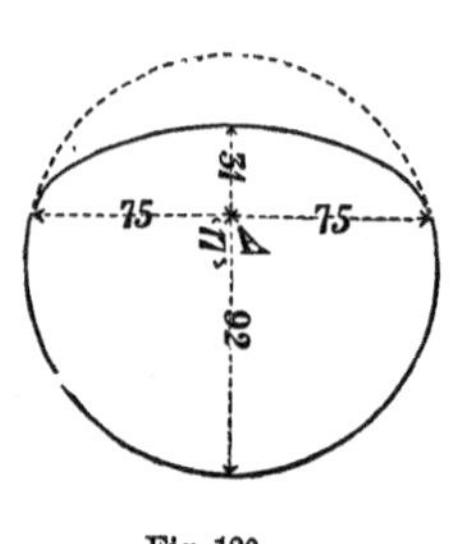

Fig. 120.

There is great difference in the strength of voice of different speakers; the limits as given in the figure are for ordinary reading in an open space. In enclosed spaces, owing to the reflected sounds or some other cause, there are certain pitches or keys peculiar to every room, and to speak with ease, the speaker must adapt his tone to those keys. The larger the room, the slower and more distinct should be the articulation.

It has been observed, that the direction of the sound influences the extent to which it may be heard. The direction of the currents of air through which the sound passes effects the transmission of the sound, and this may be made useful when the rooms are heated by hot air, by introducing the air near the speaker, and placing the ventilators or educts at the outside of the rooms, and by placing their apertures rather nearer the bottom of the room than at the top. It would seem much better and easier to make a current of air a vehicle of sound rather than depend on reflection.

The best form for a lecture room is the semicircle, or three-fifths of a circle, fig. 120, the speaker in the one case at the centre, in the other, at the point A, on a platform raised some two or three steps above the floor, the audience being ranged in concentric seats, rising from the centre outwards. The room should be no higher than requisite for beauty or for ventilation. The ceiling should be slightly curved, not flat nor half globe.

On the space occupied by seats in general.—A convenient arm-chair occupies about twenty inches square, the seat itself being about eighteen inches in depth, and the slope of the back two inches. Eighteen inches more affords ample space for passage in front of the sitter: this accommodation would be ample. In the arrangement of seats at the Academy of Music the bottom turns up, and twenty-nine inches only is allowed for both seat and passage, and eighteen inches for the width of seat, which may be taken as the average allowance in width to each sitter in comfortable public rooms. In lecture rooms stalls are often used, the space there occupied by seat and passage being about two feet six inches. The alleys should be at the sides of the room, with two intermediate, dividing the seats into three equal benches, and not one in the centre, except in very large rooms, as the space thus left is the best for hearing and seeing the speaker.

In the earlier churches, ceremonies and rites formed a very large part of the worship, the sight was rather appealed to than the hearing, and for this purpose, churches were constructed of immense size, and with all the appliances of ornament and construction, with pillars, vaults, groins and traceried windows. In the churches of this country, the great controlling principle in the construction of a church, is its adaptation to the comfortable hearing and seeing the preacher. In this view alone, the church is but a lecture room: but since even the character of the building may tend to devotional feelings in the audience, and since certain styles and forms of architecture have long been used for church edifices, and seem particularly adapted for this purpose, it has been the custom to follow these time-honored examples, adapting them to the modern requirements of church worship.

Fig. 121, is a plan of an ancient basilican or Romanesque church; fig. 122, a sectional elevation of the same. Fig. 123 is a plan of a Gothic

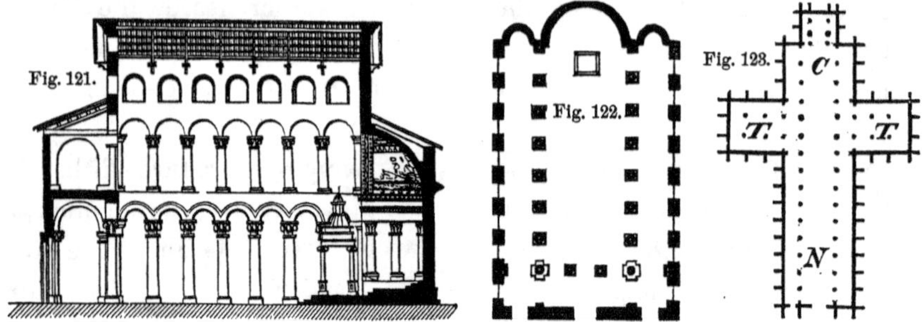

church in which C is the chancel, usually at the eastern extremity, TT the transept, and N the nave. In general elevation the Gothic and Romanesque agree; a high central nave and low side aisles. In the later Romanesque the transept is also added.

The basilicas aggregated within themselves all the offices of the Romish church. The circular end or apex, and the raised platform, or dais in front of it, was appropriated entirely to the clergy; beneath was the crypt or confessional where were placed the bodies of the saints and martyrs, and pulpits were placed in the nave, from which the services were said or sung by the inferior order of clergy.

The plan, fig. 123, is that of the original Latin cross, the eastern limb or chancel being the shortest, and the nave the longest. Sometimes the eastern limb was made equal to that of the transepts, sometimes even longer, but never to exceed that of the nave. In the Greek cross all the limbs are equal. In most of the French Gothic churches the eastern end is made semicircular, often enclosed by three or more apsidal chapels, that is, semi-cylinders, surmounted by semi-domes.

The Byzantine church consisted internally of a large square or rectangular chamber, surmounted in the centre by a dome, resting upon massive piers; an apse was formed at the eastern end. Circular churches were built in the earlier ages for baptisteries, and for the tombs of saints and emperors.

Having thus briefly treated of the general form of ancient churches, we proceed now to the consideration how far they may be applied to the requirements of modern church services. The prime necessities are those of the lecture room; comfortable seats, convenient for hearing and seeing the preacher; and proper provision for ventilation. In addition, an eligible position for the choir, a small withdrawing room for the clergyman, and a room suitable for Sunday Schools and for parish meetings.

Seats are arranged by pews or stalls, the width of each pew being in general about two feet ten inches. The length of pews is various, being generally of two sizes, adapted to either small or large families, say from seven feet six inches, to eleven feet six, eighteen inches being allowed for each sitter. In arrangement it is always considered desirable that there should be a central aisle, and if but four rows of pews, two aisles against the wall; if six rows, one row on each side will be wall pews. Few churches are now without an organ; its dimensions should of course depend on the size of the church. In form it may be adapted somewhat to the place which may be appropriated to it. In general it is oblong in form, the longer side being with the keys. The dimensions suited to a medium sized church are about nine feet by fifteen, and twelve feet in height. The withdrawing room for the clergyman may be but of very small dimensions, and should be accessible from without. The Sunday School, in general, requires in plan about half the area of the church.

As city residences differ from those in the country, from the same necessities do the city churches differ from the rural ones. A very common form of city church is, in plan, that of the Latin cross, with extremely short transepts and chancels; sometimes the roof is supported by pillars, with imitated vaults in plaster, but often with a double pitch roof, and open timber finish in the inside. The organ loft is sometimes in one of the transepts, sometimes at the back of the congregation over the door of entrance.

A sort of basilican church is also very common: rectangular in form with a small semicircular niche behind the preacher, and small withdrawing rooms or vestries at each side of it. The ceilings are finished after the Greek style, with sunk panels, sometimes coved, with pilasters but seldom pillars, except short ones, to support the galleries which are adopted in this style of buildings, but not so commonly in the Gothic. The rooms for Sunday Schools are almost invariably in the basement of the city churches.

The basilican form is evidently the most economical in its occupation of land; if the church be situated at the corner of two streets, it can cover the whole lot, one side, or a portion of one side being left blank of windows. If an elevation similar to fig. 122 be adopted, the light can be taken in at clere-story windows. But this form is objectionable as requiring pillars in construction, which, unless made of iron, and of small size, very much interfere with sight and hearing.

The position of our city churches is usually as we have said at the corner of streets, but if they can be placed so far in the centre of a lot as to receive the light from the back areas, the position is preferable as removed from the noise of passing vehicles. In that case the church proper is approached by a long aisle, above which may be the room for the Sunday School. This room should be fitted with water-closets, in fact they would be often of great convenience connected with all churches.

In elevation, city churches are Greek with porticoes in front, Romanesque and Gothic, occasionally Byzantine. The Greek have no tower but often a spire above the portico; the Romanesque and Gothic generally one tower, over the central door of entrance, or at one corner; sometimes two, one at each side of the principal door, almost invariably surmounted by spires, high and tapering, usually of wood, but in some instances of stone.

Plate XXX. is an elevation in perspective of a church in the Romanesque style, colored to represent the materials of which it is composed, viz: brick with mouldings of freestone. Plate XXXI. is an elevation of a church in the English Decorated Gothic style. The tower as we have stated before was not attached to the earlier Roman churches, but were generally separate campaniles or watchtowers. According to the requirements of modern architecture, whatever be the style, they are usually placed at the extremity near the main entrance, either centrally or at the sides, or with two towers, one at each side. It will be observed in the Gothic that there is a side entrance with its appropriate gable; in a similar way, small edifices may be attached to the main one, for necessary offices, parsonages, or Sunday schools, adding much to the picturesque effect, and particularly appropriate to country churches.

With regard to the windows of churches, it is the custom, in Episcopal churches, to place the chancel at the eastern end, and very often to make a large window at this extremity. This is very objectionable, as the light falls directly in the eyes of the congregation; if a window is indispensable at this end, it is better that it should be a side or top opening, to give light to the clergyman, whenever he is placed within the recess—a very beautiful effect is produced by skylight in the apse of the Romanesque church, which, being high above the congregation, does not interfere with them, and affords the best light to lead the services. The light in churches should not be garish, but well diffused, which will be best effected by light by windows placed as high up as possible. A single north window, in many small churches, would be sufficient for all purposes, would not injure the eyes of the congregation by cross lights, and were the walls painted in fresco or distemper, would add very much to the effect. Were suitable means provided for ventilation no other windows would be necessary. In some city churches the light in the daytime is taken entirely from skylights, and gas burners being placed in the roof of the church,

the roof of the church, and reflected below through the same apertures in the ceiling.

Theatre.—The requirements of theatres and opera houses, differ essentially from those of lecture rooms and churches, in that the audience themselves form an important part of the exhibition. It is not only necessary that the audience should have a good position for hearing and seeing the performance upon the stage, but also to see each other. The most approved form, now, for the body of the house, is a circular plan, the opening for the stage occupying from one-fourth to one-fifth of the circumference, the sides of the proscenium being short tangents. The circular form is well adapted for both hearing and seeing, and also for lighting.

In the general position of the stage, proscenium, orchestra, orchestra seats, parquette, and boxes, but one plan is followed. We proceed to give briefly the usual arrangements of seats, and some other requirements, and a small table of the proportions of different houses. The line of the front of the stage, at the foot lights, is generally slightly curved, with a sweep, say, equal to the depth of the stage, and the orchestra and parquette seats are arranged in circles concentric with it: of the space occupied by seats we have already spoken. The entrance to the parquette may be through the boxes, near the proscenium, and often centrally, but better at the sides, dividing the boxes into three equal benches; the seats in the boxes are usually concentric with the walls, and more roomy than those of the parquette. The orchestra seats are of a height to bring the shoulders of the sitter level with the floor of the stage, and the floor of the parquette rises to the outside, 1 in 15 to 18. The floor of the first row of boxes is some 2 to 3 feet above the floor of the parquette at the front centre, and rises by steps at each row, some 4 inches; in the next tier of boxes the steps are considerably more in height, and so on in the boxes above. In general, three rows of boxes are all that is necessary; in front, above the second, the view of the stage is almost a bird's eye view. The floor of the stage descends to the footlights at the rate of about 1 in 50. In large theatres it is of the utmost importance that all the lobbies or entries should be spacious, and the means of exit numerous and ample. The staircases broad, in short flights and square landings, and not circular, as, in case of fright, the pressure of persons behind may precipitate those in front the whole length of the flight. Ladies' drawing rooms should be placed convenient to the lobbies, of a size adapted to that of the theatre, arranged with water closets; there should also be provided rooms for the reception of gentlemen's canes and umbrellas, with water closets attached. The box-office should be, of course, near the entrance, but so arranged as to interfere as little as possible with the approach to the doors of the house. At the entrance there should be a very spacious lobby, or hall, so that the audience may wait sheltered against the weather; if possible, there should be a long portico over the sidewalk, to cover the approach to the carriages. But single entrances are necessary to distinct parts of the house, but the greater the number of, and the more ample places for exit, at the conclusion of the piece, the better.

COMPARATIVE TABLE OF THE DIMENSIONS OF A FEW THEATRES.

NAME AND LOCATION.	DISTANCE, IN FEET.						HEIGHT, IN FEET.	
	Bet. boxes and foot-lights.	Bet. foot-lights and curtain.	Bet. curtain and back of stage.	Greatest breadth of pit.	Breadth of curtain.	Breadth of stage bet. side walls.	From floor of pit to cornice.	From floor of pit to centre of ceiling.
Alexandre, St. Petersburg, . .	65	11	84	58	56	75	58	58
———, Berlin, ...	62	16	76	51	41	92	48	47
La Scala, Milan, ...	77	18	78	71	49	86	60	64
San Carlo, Naples, ...	77	18	74	74	52	66	81	83
Grand Theatre, Bordeaux, . .	46	10	69	47	87	80	50	57
Salle Lepelletier, Paris, . . .	67	9	82	66	48	78	52	66
Covent Garden, London, . . .	66*		55	51	82	86	54	
Drury Lane, " . .	64*		80	56	82	48	60	
Boston, Boston, ...	53	18	68		46	87	55½	58
Academy of Music, New York, . .	74	18	71	62	48	88	74	
Burton's (New), " . .	53		40	62			52	62
Opera House, Philadelphia, . .	61	17	72	66	48	90	64½	74

* These dimensions include the distance between the foot-lights and curtain.

Although much has been written about the construction of legislative halls, in relation to acoustic principles, there yet seems to be great disagreement in practical examples, and in the deductions of scientific men. The Chamber of French Deputies was constructed after a report of most celebrated architects, in a semicircular form, surmounted by a flat dome, but as the member invariably addresses the house from the tribune, at the centre, in its requirements it is but a lecture room. Mr. Mills, Architect, of Philadelphia, recommends for legislative or forensic debate, a room circular in its plan, with a very slightly concave ceiling. Dr. Reid, on the contrary, in reference to the Houses of Parliament, gave preference to the square form, with a low, arched ceiling. The Hall of Representatives nearly completed at Washington, is 139 feet long, by 93 feet wide, and about 36 feet high, with a spacious retiring gallery on three sides, and a reporter's

PLATE XXXII.

gallery behind the Speaker's chair. The members' desks are arranged in a semicircular form. The ceiling is flat, with deep sunk panels, openings for ventilation, and glazed apertures for the admission of light. The ventilation is intended, in a measure, to assist the phonetic capacity of the Hall, the air being forced in at the ceiling and drawn out at the bottom.

In reviewing the general principles of acoustics, it will be found that those rooms are the best for hearing in which the sound arrives directly to the ear, without reflection; that the sides of the room should not be reflectors, not sounding boards, and that surfaces absorbing sound are less injurious than those that reflect. Slight projections, such as ornaments of the cornices and shallow pilasters, tend to destroy sound, but deep alcoves and recessed rooms produce echoes. Let the ceiling be as low as possible, and slightly arched or domed; all large external openings should be closed; as M. Meynedier expresses it, in his description of an opera house, "Let the hall devour the sound; as it is born there, let it die there."

Crystal Palaces.—Plate XXXII. represents a perspective view of the interior of the New York Crystal Palace, figs. 125, 126 a half plan of the ground floor and of the galleries. This building originated from that of London, of which some of the details of construction have been already given. These buildings are composed wholly of iron, glass and wood, but no large pieces of either material are used; in this consists their great peculiarity. Stiffness and tenacity of material are applied rather than mass, to counteract incidental strains; and, on this account, they are not as suitable as walls of brick and stone for permanent structures, nor are they as cheap; and in this respect, an improvement has been made in the French exhibition building; but for a structure easily moved and put together, as it was intended, and for green or hot-houses, it seems especially adapted; and as a practical example of the application of iron, and an economical application, it has been of great importance.

Before concluding the article on architectural drawing it may be appropriate to speak briefly of materials as applied in the exteriors of edifices. Sufficient has already been said of their strength, we now refer merely to their fitness to architectural ornament.

Brick in cities is by far the most common of all materials, nor do we know of any more suited to workshops and factories, for appropriateness, economy, and durability (when hard burned), nor do we know of any style of architecture more fitted to the material than the Romanesque, as in Plate XXVI. Stone in the rough or rubble walls, laid in cement or mortar, are often used for these structures, but in that case the lintels should be square, and if possible of a different shade of stone.

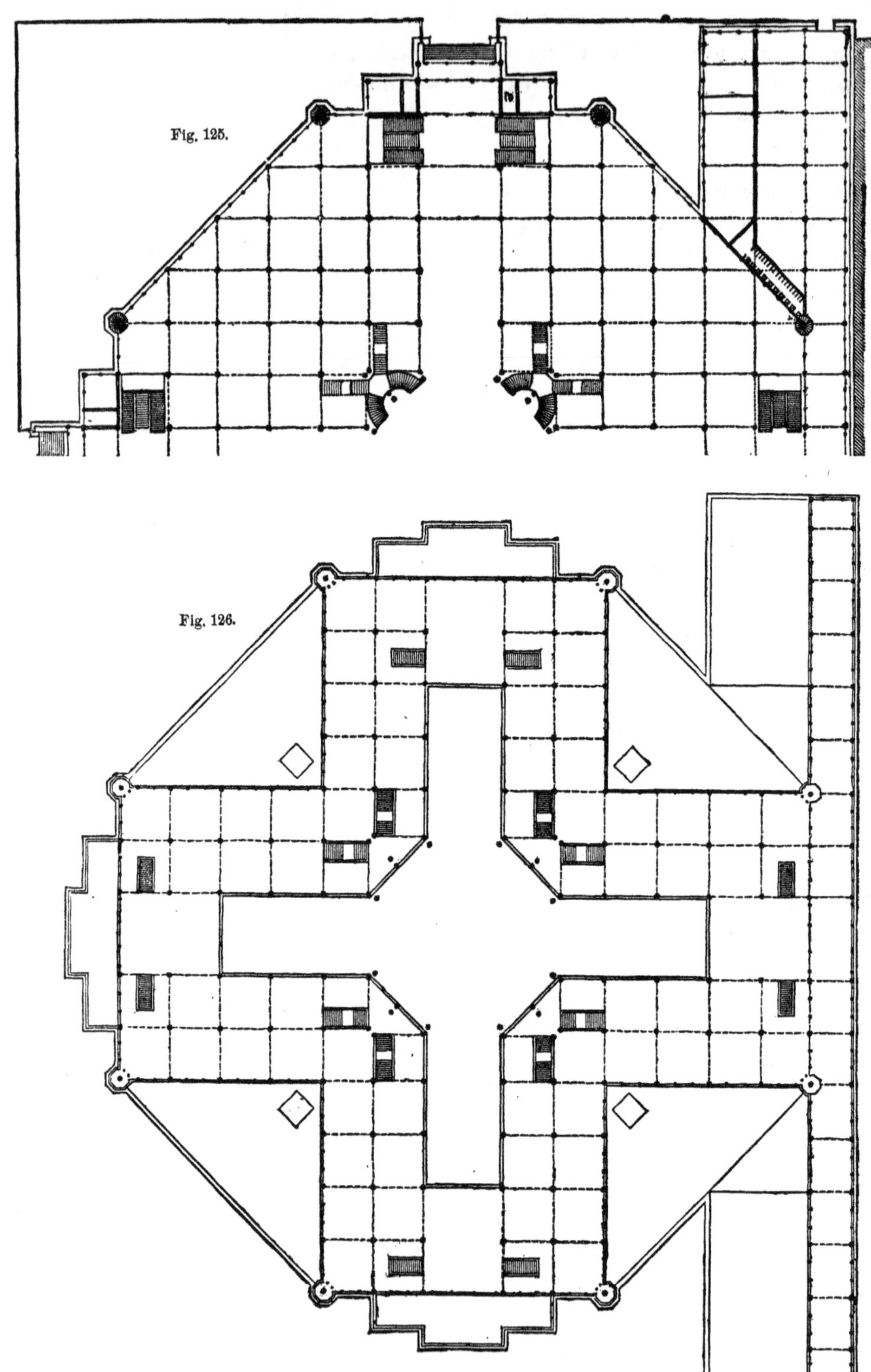
Fig. 125.
Fig. 126.

For city residences, and stores, the exteriors are composed of all sorts of building materials, with the exception of wood, from its insecurity in case of fire; brick, with marble, freestone, iron or terra cotta lintels and sills for openings, red brick and straw-colored bricks, brick on rusticated basements, and sometimes brick in alternate stripes with marbles; freestone in a great variety of shades, mostly of a reddish brown, often fawn and drab; marbles white and veined; native and foreign granite; and iron, the use of which in fronts is the invention of our age, and is destined to modify our style of architecture.

All materials are suited for country residences except iron; stone houses may be kept in their native color, but brick or wood should be painted. We extract from Downing the following on the color of country houses. "We think all buildings in the country should be of those soft quiet shades called neutral tints, such as fawn, drab, gray, brown, etc., and that all positive colors, such as white, yellow, red, blue and black should always be avoided; neutral tints harmonizing best with nature and, positive colors most discordant.

In the second place, we would adapt the shade of color as far as possible, to the expression, style or character of the house itself. A large mansion may receive a somewhat sober, dignified hue; a house of moderate size, a lighter and more pleasant tone; small cottages should always have a cheerful, lively tint, not much removed from white. Country houses thickly surrounded by trees, should always be of a lighter shade than those standing exposed. In proportion as a house is exposed to view, let its hue be darker; and where it is much concealed by foliage, a very light shade of color is to be preferred.

"A species of monotony is produced by using the same neutral tint for every part of the exterior of a country house. A certain sprightliness is bestowed on a building in neutral tint by painting the bolder projecting features of a different shade. The simplest practical rule that we can suggest for effecting this in the most satisfactory manner, is the following: if the tint selected for the body of the house be a light one, let the facings of the windows, cornices, etc., be painted several shades darker of the same color. The blinds may either be a still darker shade than the facings, or else the darkest green. If on the other hand, the tint chosen is a dark one, then let the window dressings, etc., be painted of a much lighter shade of the same color."

Thus far Mr. Downing. Most persons must be struck with the justness of his remarks in general, but all are not prepared entirely to ignore white as a color for country houses. We have always fancied in contemplating an extensive landscape that jottings of white enlivened the scene, and prefer a whitewashed cottage, carrying an air of cleanliness, to the least admixture of neutral tint: neither seems it high art to harmonize always with nature, it often makes a very flat picture.

However we build, or whatever built of, let the building express the purpose, and let the material be suited to it. Let those which are intended for time be of lasting materials, but those that are temporary, be of that most convenient; let not one imitate the other.

Ventilation and Warming.—To the proper construction of all edifices some knowledge of the principles of ventilation and warming are necessary, as the arrangements for this purpose are to be made in planning the building. Air is deteriorated in apartments by the respiration and perspiration of people, and by combustion in heating and lighting. At least 3 cubic feet per minute of fresh air should be supplied for each person occupying the room, this quantity being deteriorated by respiration and perspiration. As to combustion, 1 pound of carbon or charcoal, in burning, consumes 2.6 pounds of oxygen, which is that contained in between 13 and 14 pounds of atmospheric air; and 1 pound of hydrogen, consumes 8 pounds of oxygen, which is that contained in about 40 pounds of atmospheric air. Now tallow, wax and oil contain upon the average from 77 to 80 per cent of carbon, and from 11 to 14 per cent. of hydrogen: the per centage of carbon in anthracite and bituminous coal is more various, but the same calculations may be used. 100 cubic feet of air weighs about 7 pounds, so from the above data the approximate consumption of oxygen by any given quantity of the above combustibles, is easily calculated. The combustion of coal gas generally spoils thrice its bulk of oxygen, or, fifteen times that of air.

The methods of warming most generally practised in this country are by hot air furnaces; in which coal is consumed, in furnaces inclosed within a brick chamber into which the fresh air is introduced from out of doors, heated, and conveyed usually by tin conductors to the various rooms of the building. In this case it will not of course be necessary to find how much air is required for the combustion of the fuel, as the air for this purpose is introduced from the cellar: it is only requisite to determine how much may be deteriorated by persons occupying the rooms, and how much by the lighting. Having determined this quantity, we make provision for introducing the amount through a cold air box to the hot air chamber of the furnace. The velocity of the current in this box, to determine the size of the box, we call 4 feet per second. This box is provided with a slide valve, to regulate the amount of air furnished; in extremely cold weather the air may pass too rapidly through the chamber without becoming sufficiently heated. The size of the conductors is less in proportionate area than that of the air box, usually not more than half, depending somewhat on the vertical length of the conductor. The higher the conductor the stronger the current, and the less the necessary area. All hot air flues should be removed at least two inches from wood work. Having provided means for the introduction of air, it is necessary also to provide means of egress. In general the cracks of doors and windows provide some little outlet, but hardly adequate to the requirements of public rooms. There should be ventilating flues, somewhat larger than the hot air flues. It is the general practice to introduce the hot air into the room at or near the bottom, and there is considerable disagreement where the openings of the ventilators should be, whether at top and bottom, or top only or bottom only. In the English Houses of Parliament, the hot air is introduced at the floor, and the ventilating flues are in the ceiling; in our House of Representatives exactly the opposite course is to be pursued, the hot air is forced in by a fan into the top of the room, and taken out at the bottom; probably as long as sufficient air can be got into and foul air out of the room, it matters little whether it is introduced at top or bottom. It is evident that in common rooms, when the current is not influenced by the ventilating arrangement, the nitrogen of the vitiated air rises to the ceiling, whilst the carbonic acid falls to the bottom, and as the former is more in quantity, the uppermost stratum of air is the foulest; and in our view, if the foul air be drawn off at a height but little above the height of the persons in the room, it would seem sufficient for ventilation, and if the fresh air be introduced into one side of the room, and the foul air taken out at this height on the other, there would be a warm current of air circulating at the height most effectual for warming the occupants of the room.

All ventilating flues should be provided with valves or regulators; thus when it is not necessary to change the air, by retaining it the heat is retained, and if the cold air from the room can be supplied to the air chamber of the furnace so as to establish a current, the heat will be much economized. The previous remarks on ventilation belong more appropriately to the heating and ventilating of public edifices, and rooms occupied by numbers of people; in private houses, in general, there are but few, and the amount of air deteriorated but small, and if heated with open fire-places and grates, the cracks of the doors and windows supply plenty of air for ventilation; but the objection to this are the draughts of cold air. The most perfect way for heating private houses is by a small furnace or hall stove, taking a supply of fresh air from outside and warming the halls, and open fires in the occupied rooms. In a sanitary point of view no arrangement of ventilation and warming can supply the place of a radiant fire; but in view of the inconvenience of numerous fires, the next best thing is heating by low steam, or by hot water pipes, a coil being placed in air chambers in the cellar, with a fresh air supply, and coils in all the necessary rooms. No room in a house should be without a flue, or movable fanlights over the door for ventilation, and if an air tube can be carried into a flue which is always heated, a current is secured. Steam is now used extensively to heat factories and workshops, and is decidedly the most cleanly. The general arrangement is in rows of $\frac{3}{4}$ or 1 inch pipe against the walls of the room; one foot in length of $\frac{3}{4}$ inch pipe being the length considered adequate to heat fifty cubic feet of space. If there are many windows in the room, as they are very cooling surfaces, and also very seldom tight, more length of pipe should be allowed. Steam is used at various pressures, but low or exhaust steam is preferable, as the pleasantest to the occupant, being in this respect like hot water. The desideratum in all warming apparatus is to heat with a surface not exceeding the heat of boiling water. The objection to water lies in its expense, and the danger if not kept constantly at work in the winter of freezing. It is not therefore adapted to places which are to be heated intermitingly.

Ventilators.—Although flues may be made for ventilation, still it is not always certain that there will be an ascending current; often chimneys draw but poorly. In public buildings an artificial draught is created by a fire or by a fan, as has been done in the English House of Parliament. The usual expedient in this country, is by some of the common cowls for smoky chimneys, but the best appears to be Emerson's Ventilator.

Much has been written on the subject of ventilation and warming, and many expedients, undoubtedly adequate in themselves, have failed, from the carelessness of servants and from want of attention. The grand requisite seems to be, something that will be sure, and will not get out of order. It is now but a half a century since gas was introduced for lighting; it has now been applied for cooking and warming, but not to a large extent economically; whether it may be brought into general use for this purpose is a problem yet to be solved; but steam, as now applied in most New England factories, from a central set of boilers, could easily be applied to the warming and ventilation of many houses, and for many culinary purposes, from one set of boilers; and with gas would supply all requirements.

SPECIFICATIONS.

THE following blank Specifications for Mason's and Carpenter's work are intended as illustrations of the usual forms of such papers.

Specification for Mason work. To be performed in building, erecting and finishing a Dwelling House; to be situated on , between , for Agreeably to drawings made and prepared by , Architects.

Date.

Size of Building.—..

Excavation.—Dig out and cart away all the ground (that may be necessary), for Basement, Cellar, Areas, Drains, Cesspools, and footings for foundations, and cart away all the superfluous rubbish that may be made during the progress and at the completion of the building.

Materials and Workmanship.—All the several materials used in or about this Building, are to be of the very best quality, and all the work to be done in the best and most workmanlike and substantial manner, under the direction and to the satisfaction of the architects.

	ft.	in.	
Height of Stories.—Under Cellar,	..	..	All to be in the clear between floors and ceilings when finished.
Basement,	....	..	
First Story,	....	..	
...... Story,	..	..	

The roof to pitch ....

Base Courses.—All the base courses to be of the best .... stones, and to be .... wide to all the walls and piers throughout, and all to be .... thick, laid close and solid, and of parallel thickness.

Blue Stone Walls.—Build up all the stone walls agreeably to the drawings and figures thereon, with the best quality of .... stones (in cement), properly hammered square and straight, laid close and level, well bonded and flushed in.

The face of all the stone walls that are in sight, are to be neatly pointed.

All the stone walls that come in contact with the ground, are to be properly coated on the outside with Hydraulic Cement.

Concrete.—The whole of the cellar is to be concreted with broken stones and Hydraulic lime laid .... thick in the very best manner.

Coal Slide.—Build a coal slide, as per plan, and cover the same, both top and bottom, with .... flag stones, well laid and bedded in cement, and to a proper grade.

Brick Work.—Build up all the brick walls agreeably to the drawings and figures thereon.

The chimney of brests fire places in Kitchen and Laundry, and chimney stacks above roof, and all the rear front, are to be faced with the best quality of .... pressed bricks of uniform deep red color. All laid in running bond and white putty mortar, and tuck-jointed.

All the residue of the brick work throughout the premises to be done with the best, well burnt, hard, ... bricks, all the brick walls in Basement and Areas to be built in cement.

Build Piers and Arches in cellar, and Piers and Arches under hearths, and build proper Ash-pits as shown on plan. Build all necessary flues, turn trimmer-arches to all the fireplaces, arches to all the openings of the width of the openings. Parge the flues and scrape the same at the completion.

Build up the hot air pipes as shall be directed. Leave indents in walls for hot air tubes, &c. The side walls are to be carried up two courses of brick above the roof planking to receive the tin, and then two courses on the tin, laid in cement, to receive the coping.

All the fireplaces are to have brick inner hearths. All brick walls that come in contact with the ground, are to be well cemented on the outside.

Cut away for, and make good after Plumbers, Furnacemen, Gasmen, &c., and finish all the brick work complete in the best manner.

All the front plain Ashlar is to be backed in with .... wall built in ....

Drain.—Build a drain, to sewer on .... street, in the best manner, and all to be properly cemented; also make all necessary blind drains, and put in proper traps, &c., complete, and cover the drain with flagging, and all to be done in the best manner and as shall be directed.

Build cesspools, ... diameter and .... deep, in 4 inch brick work as shall be directed.

Flagging.—All the flagging to be done with the very best quality of .... flagging, and not to be less than .... thick and .... super., on the face, and to be well smoothed off.

Flag all the .... lay and bed in the concrete, and join neatly and perfectly tight.

Flag the sidewalk on .... with large sized strong flagging, ... thick, squared and fine axed, out of wind, and the joints laid solid in mortar, and the walk to be .... stones in width—have blue cut stone curbs, ... by ...., and cut gutters .... by .... agreeable to city ordinances.

Lay the hearths in Kitchen and Laundry with blue stone flagging, as shown on plans, to be .... wide and .... thick, and polished.

CUT-STONE WORK.

All the Cut-Stone work is to be done with the very best quality of Stone, of close, fine grain and of uniform color. Cut and set in the very best manner, with oil putty, and agreeably to working drawings, pointed and cleaned off, and all to be polished except what is mentioned to be tooled.

The Chimney Stacks and Flues are to have caps as per elevation, cramped and leaded.

Cope the wall to both sides of main building with tooled coping, 3 inches by 14 inches, cramped and leaded, and bedded in cement.

All the windows to rear of building to have sills .... by .... washed and throated and moulded lintels .... by .... to doors and windows. Sills to doorways ....by ..... Water table to be .... by ..... Copings to gratings .... by ..... Have jambs and mantels to Kitchen and Laundry fireplaces: jambs .... by ...., cut in the usual way.

Front Work.—All the windows to front on . . . . to have architraves, pilasters, and trusses and cornice, as shown on elevation—moulded sill .... by ....and blocks under.

Provide and put up the rusticated ashlar to first story .... thick, and the cornices, panels and balusters over a moulded water table to first story, and balusters and moulded sill course supported by heavy consols.

The rusticated ashlar to be in courses, as shown on drawings, not less than .... bed, and .... reveals to windows, and cramped, resting upon moulded sill course. The plain and rusticated ashlar to return .... in the doorways, and all the front area walls and under stoop throughout to be faced with ashlar, and to average .... bed. Coping to area walls .... by ..... Coping to receive railing .... by .... and moulded. Moulded steps .... by .... Sills to basement doorways to be .... by ....

All the front on ———, above first story, is to have plain ashlar, and not to be less than .... inch bed, properly cramped with two cramps to each stone, and all the architraves to all the windows are to have .... inch reveals.

Front Steps and Door Piece.—Put up the steps and door piece as per drawings and working drawings, moulded steps, and moulded solid strings, and panelled ashlar both sides, and pedestals, rails and balusters complete.

Provide and put up the cornice properly cramped and anchored, and cut grooves in top for copper.

Iron Work.—Provide a sufficiency of anchors, ties, and cramps; and anchors for cut-stone work, and iron rims and covers to flues for stove pipes, and registers in kitchen, laundry and chimney brest; have gratings to areas as per plans, one grating to be made to fold open with chain, fastenings, and gratings to small cesspools. Provide proper plate, chain, and fastenings to Coal Slide. Provide and set wrought-iron guard bars to all the basement windows in rear.

All the residue of the windows in basement to front on ——— are to have ornamental wrought-iron panels to fill up the whole size of the windows.

Provide and put up, strong iron lintels to all openings in walls shown on the plans. Provide and fix iron doors and frames to ash-pits and flues in cellar.

Finish and paint all the iron work twice over; brown stone color and sanded.

Plastering.—All the lathing to be done with narrow laths, free from sap, reversing the heading joints every 18 inches.

The mortar for the two first coats to be made up with the very best quality of .... lime and sharp grit sand, and the best long fresh cattle hair.

All the hard finishing work to be done with the best lump .... lime and pure white marble dust, all the works to be properly gauged with plaster of Paris.

Lath, scratch-coat, brown and hard finish, all the walls, ceilings, partitions, studs, and furring of every description, throughout the building, except walls of under cellar, which will be whitewashed twice over.

The browning to be made plumb and straight, and to be properly hand floated, the hard finishing to be trowelled hard and smooth in the best manner. The ceilings of cellar to have one thick coat, and hard finished.

Cornices.—The bed, bath and dressing rooms, to have a moulded cornice to girt .... inches.

The drawing room, dining room, library, hall, and vestibule on first story, to have a large moulded and cove cornice with one row of large enrichments.

The reception room ceiling to be groined, and put up large moulded cornice, finished plain for painting, the niches to be finished with a rule joint.

Form a dome over centre of staircase, in panels, with enriched mouldings. All the ceilings of principal story, are to be formed out in various panels, and large raised enriched mouldings.

Put up a centre piece in hall, ... diameter, and one ...., and ....

Working drawings at large will be given for all cornices, &c. Make good all damages during the progress and at the completion of the work. And should any blisters, cracks or defects appear during the progress or within six months after the completion of the building, the same is to be rectified without any extra charge.

.... story floors, are to be deafened with the best quality of deafening.

Provide materials for setting all the mantels, and all the grates. (The grates and mantels will be furnished by the owner.)

Make good after plumbers, bellhangers, gasmen, and other works necessary to be done in the mason's department. And finish all the several works complete to the true meaning and intention of the drawings and this specification, leaving all the works sound, clean and perfect, at the completion of the building; and the building is to be properly cleaned out at any and all times when directed by the architects, and if neglected by the contractor, the architect shall have the power to have it cleaned out, and the expense charged to the contractor.

Specification for Carpenters' Work. To be performed in building, erecting, and finishing a dwelling house, to be situated on ......, for ...... Agreeably to the drawings made by .... Architects.

Date.

Size of Building.—..

Materials and Workmanship.—All the several materials used in the erection and finishing of this building are to be of the very best quality. Timber to be well seasoned white pine free from all defects. All the lumber for joiners' work, to be clear white pine, and well seasoned, and free from all defects, and all the works throughout to be done in the best, most workmanlike, and substantial manner, under the direction and to the satisfaction of the architects.

Height of Stories.—..

Floor and Roof Beams.—Basement beams .... by ...., and .... from centres. First, ..., ... story beams, ... by ...., and .... from centres. Roof beams, ... by .... from centres.

All the trimmers and headers to be .... thick, by the depth of the beams in each tier.

All the beams are to be properly framed and wedged, for fireplaces, staircases, skylights, &c., and to be well laid solid on the walls. No blocking will be allowed.

Have .... rows of double cross bridging to each tier of beams, and springing pieces for arches, and strong anchor strips.

The ceilings of basement, and .... stories are to be cross furred with inch furring 2 inches wide, and to be 12 inches from centres. The basement, ... story floors to be prepared for deafening.

Partitions.—Put up all the partitions throughout, agreeably to the drawings, all to be properly framed and bridged in the strongest manner, as shall be directed. All the partitions are to have door studs and heads .... by ...., sills and plates .... by ...., filling in studs .... by .... and .... from centres; all to have upright blockings and templates.

Furrings, Wall Strips, &c.—Stud out for boxing and sliding shutters, niches and circular corners, with studs .... by ...., and .... from centres; fur out all the walls with inch furring 2 inches wide and 12 inches from centres.

Put up lintels to all the openings .... thick by their respective widths, provide a sufficiency of yellow pine planks, wall strips, plates and wood blocks, and such other timber that may be required to complete all the furrings as shall be directed.

Dome and Ceiling Joist.—Form the dome over principal staircase with .... and framing as shall be directed, bracketed out for panels, cornices, &c.

The reception room ceiling is to be groined, and form a square dome and soffits.

Provide all necessary brackets and furrings for circular soffits, and cradlings for plasterers, centres for arches, and turning pieces for apertures; all the centres to be made in a strong and substantial manner.

Roofs and Skylights.—All the roof is to be covered with merchantable planed, grooved, and tongued planks, free from large or loose knots and other defects, laid in courses, and form proper gutters as shall be directed. Provide and put up an iron scuttle to roofs, ... by ...., hung with strong, wrought straps, hinges, and iron curbs; put on chain, hasp, staple and padlock.

provide and fix an iron hipped skylight over .... by ...., with proper capping and ventilation, worked with pulleys, weights, and cords. Provide and fix a horizontal skylight in dome as shall be directed.

Floorings.—Lay the basement floor with the best quality 1¼ inch Yellow Georgia pine, narrow planks, and the ...., ... story floors, with the best quality of narrow, clean, 1¼ inch white pine planks, not to exceed 3½ inches wide, all to be planed, grooved, and tongued, laid in courses, and blind nailed. All the floors are to be neatly cleaned off at the completion, put borders to hearths, and saddles to doorways.

Sashes and Frames.—All the sashes and frames are to be made agreeably to drawings, all the windows to the .... are to have French casements, hung with ....butts, and .... sash fastenings. All the residue of the windows are to have ovolo sashes, double hung with cords, axle pulleys, weights, and box frames, sunk sills, ... sash fastenings. All the sashes in partitions are to be made, hung and finished, as shall be directed. All the rear sashes are to be made imitation French.

Put up rough grounds for all bases, doorways, and windows, throughout, for mason to finish plastering to.

ATTIC.

Bases.—All the rooms, entries and landings, are to have 1¼ inch moulded bases, ... inches high. Closets to have inch headed bases, ... inches high.

Windows.—All the windows are to have 1¼ inch framed and moulded backs, plain linings, and moulded architraves.

Doors.—All the doors are to be .... inches thick, four panel, moulded both sides, hung with .... inch butts, and city-made mortise locks, single rebated jambs, and architraves as described to windows. And put up in all the closets iron hooks, and shelves in each, and beaded rails. All the bedroom doors are to have fan lights and to swing on a pivot, and put up the large closets and trunkroom as shall be directed by the owner, with wide shelves and iron pins.

THIRD STORY.

Bases.—........ ....

Windows.—..

Doors.—. ....

Closets.—..

SECOND STORY.

Bases.—All the rooms, entry, and landing, throughout, are to have .. inch sunk plinth,.. inches high, and moulded base to girt ...., and the plinths to be grooved and tongued into the floors.

Windows.—All the windows on this story are to have boxing and sliding blinds, and the architraves ....

Doors.—All the doors on this story are to be .... thick, panelled and raised mouldings both sides, hung with .... wide butts and .... mortise locks—1¼ inch rebatted jambs and architraves, as described to windows.

The sliding doors are to have brassways, shieves, stops, and .... mortice locks, complete, and double set of furniture.

Closets.—The closet doors are to be .... All to be fitted with jambs and narrow moulded architraves inside.

Fit up all the closets with drawers, shelves, locks, knobs, and folding doorways, large brass hanging pins and porcelain heads, complete, to suit the owner.

All the wide jambs and soffits to have moulded panels to match the doors.

All the closets in dressing rooms, private room, to be fitted up with ....

Water Closets and Baths.—Fit up the water closet with red cedar seats, risers, and clamped flaps, hung with 3 inch brass butts, and 1¼ inch dovetailed cistern; and put up moulded panel framing to baths, and put up pilasters, caps, cornice, and arches complete.

Fit up all the wash stands with moulded and bead and butt dwarf panel doors and hinges, knob and brass spring catches, and shelves complete, as shall be directed.

PRINCIPAL STORY.

Bases.—....... ....

Windows.—..... ....

All the window shutters to rear to be lined with iron in the neatest manner.

The sliding shutters to rear windows in library to be .... thick, in two thicknesses, panelled and moulded both sides, with iron in between, and have proper brass ways, shieves, astragals, stops, bolts, and mortice latches with flush handles, complete. The bay window to have inside folding blinds, hung with strong hinges, bolts and fastenings, and to fold back into a box.

ors.—All the folding doors to be .... thick, and raised mouldings both sides, hung with $5\frac{1}{2}$ inch wide plated butts, 6 inch city made mortice locks and large furniture, and plated flush bolts to the vestibule doors.

The sliding doors to be .... thick, panelled, and mouldings both sides, and to have brass ways, .. inch shieves, double astragals and stops; mortice locks, flush crank handles, and double set of furniture, and all plated.

All the doors to have .. inch double rebated, moulded and panelled jambs; moulded .... architraves .... wide, and plinth blocks.

Closets.—..

Wainscotting.—The dining room and library are to be wainscotted all around with panelled framing, and moulded capping, 3 feet 6 inches high.

Dumb Waiter.—Put up a dumb waiter from basement to first story, with all its apparatus complete, of the latest and most approved construction; with dwarf panel moulded doors, locks and knobs complete. And the butler's pantry is to be fitted up with pilasters, caps, cornice, and arches complete in the neatest manner.

BASEMENT.

Bases.—..

Windows.—..

Doors.— ....

The doors leading from the laundry to the yard, and also from laundry to kitchen, and from kitchen to hall and pantry, and the front entrance doors in basement, to be made sash doors, and to have proper bolts and mortice locks; and sliding doors to rear to be lined with iron, with shieves, way stops, bolts, mortice locks and rings complete.

The sashes in the front entrance door in basement are to be hung, and put in iron lattice work the size of the panel.

Closets and Pantries.—..

The kitchen and laundry walls and partitions all around, will be lined with narrow clear boards, planed and grooved tongued and beaded, 2 feet 10 inches high and properly capped.

Fit up the laundry with wash tubs made perfectly water tight, with lids complete.

Fit up the water closets and wash stands.

Under Cellar.—All the openings in cellar are to have $1\frac{3}{4}$ inch bead and butt folding sash doors, proper frames hung with 4 inch butts, and thumb latches, and proper bolts.

Cut away, and make good after plumbers, and case all the pipes.

Fit up the cellar with coal bins, &c., as shall be directed by the owner.

STAIRCASES.

Put up the principal staircase agreeably to drawings, $1\frac{3}{4}$ inch .... treads, moulded and returned noseings, $1\frac{1}{4}$ inch rises; moulded, carved and panelled front strings, ... sunk wall strings, all to be housed and wedged, put upon strong carriages, and rough bracketed. Have .... moulded and double beaded hand rails, and newels, and balusters, all to be of the best ....; the balusters and strings to be varnished .... times over, and the rails and newels to be polished.

Put up the other staircases of white pine, with proper treads, risers, rails and balusters complete in the usual way; as shall be directed.

Bay Window.— ....

Entrance Doorway.—Put up the principal entrance doorway as per elevation, of .... the door to be made folding, and of two thicknesses; moulded both sides, hung .... and lock, and two mortice bolts.

Cornice.—Put up a handsome block cornice to rear of building, as per working drawings, put up in the best manner.

Working drawings at large will be given for all moulded works.

Furniture.—All the knobs of every description throughout the ...., to be ....

All the residue of the furniture and knobs throughout the building, to be of ....

All the locks and fastenings throughout the building to be the best manufacture.

Speaking Tubes.—Provide and put up .... speaking tubes, from .... to ...., with .... mouth-pieces and covers.

Tin Work.—Tin the roof with the best quality of single cross tin, properly soldered. Put up leaders .. inches diameter, made of strong double cross tin, and have 6 inch strong copper socket pipe from gutters, and globe basket cover. The lower length of the leader to be of cast iron, with a shoe.

Scrape off all the rosin, and paint all the tin work three times over with the best white lead and oil.

The top of cornices and gutters are to be lined with .. ounce copper.

Bells.—Provide and hang .. pulls of bells, with strong copper wire and tin tubes, all to have lever chain pulls and proper cranks; .. pulls to be plated, and all the residue to be of porcelain.

Blinds.—The rear windows are to have outside venetian blinds, moulded both sides, and painted French green, hung with strong hinges and patent fastenings and catches.

Painting.—Paint all the woodwork throughout, both exterior and interior, three times over in the best manner, including all the rear stairs, shelves, etc., with pure white lead and oil.

All the woodwork in basement and attic throughout, and bath rooms, and butler's pantry, to be grained in imitation of oak, and varnished twice over with the best varnish; also panelling under wash basins; and all the rear wood cornices to be painted brown stone color and sanded.

All the vestibule doors and trimmings to be grained in imitation of dark oak, and varnished .... over.

Glazing.—Glaze all the front windows throughout on all the stories, and lights to entrance doorway, and vestibule doors, with .... plate glass.

Glaze all the windows of .... with ....

All the residue of the glazing to be done with ...., except under cellar.

The outer skylight to be glazed with extra double thick ribbed glass.

Glaze all the sash doors throughout, and sashes in partitions, with ornamented enamelled glass, to cost not less than .... per foot.

All to be left whole and clean at the completion of the building.

The skylight over the principal stairs to be glazed with stained glass to cost not less than $...

The skylight over reception room to cost not less than $.., and one over the private stairs to cost $...

Size of the glass to be obtained from the drawings.

The owner to have the privilege of furnishing the stained glass, and the contractor to deduct the amount specified.

Finish and complete all the carpenters' work to the true meaning and intention of the drawings, and this specification; leaving all the works sound, clean, and perfect at the completion of the building. All the floors and stairs are to be properly scrubbed before the last coat of paint is put on.

Conditions which may be inserted in both Contracts.

The .... work is to be commenced on or before the .. day of ...., and the building to be completely finished and delivered to the owner by the ....

The owner shall be held harmless, either in suits at law or otherwise, from all damages to the property of other person or persons arising during the progress of the work. And he shall not be responsible for any of the materials to be used in the erection of the building that may be lost or stolen, or destroyed by fire, beyond the amount of any insurance that he may have on the building, until the last instalment on the contract is paid. Such insurance would be equally for the benefit of owner and contractor, *pro rata.*

SHADING AND SHADOWS.

LIGHT is diffused through space in straight lines, and the lines of light are called *rays*. When the source of light is situated at a very great distance from the illuminated objects, as in the case of the sun with relation to the earth, the rays of light do not sensibly diverge, and may be regarded as *exactly parallel* to each other. Such is the case in mechanical drawings, where the objects to be represented are always regarded as illuminated by the solar light.

Light is called *direct* when it is transmitted to an object without the intervention of any opposing medium. But as all bodies subjected to the action of light possess, in a greater or less degree, the property of giving out a certain portion of it to the surrounding objects, this *reflected light* becomes in its turn, though with greatly diminished intensity, a source of illumination to those objects which are deprived of direct light.

Everything which tends to intercept or prevent the direct light from falling in upon a body, produces upon the surface of that body a degree of obscurity of greater or less intensity; this is called a *shade* or *shadow*. Such effects are usually classified as *direct shadows* and *cast shadows*.

The shade proper, or *direct shadow*, is that which occurs on that portion of the surface of a body which is situated opposite to the enlightened part, and is the natural result of the form of the body itself, and of its position with regard to the rays of light. The cast shadow, on the other hand, is that which is produced upon the surface of one body by the interposition of another between the former and the source of light; thus intercepting the rays which would otherwise illuminate that surface. An illustration of this distinction is afforded in the pyramid represented at fig. 1, Plate II, where the shade proper is shown upon that half of the figure which is denoted by the letters D′ E′ G′ F′ in the plan, while the cast shadow occupies the space comprised between the lines D′ *e* and F′ *d* on the horizontal plane of projection. Cast shadows may also obviously be produced upon the surface of a body by the form of the body itself; as, for example, if it contain projecting or concave parts.

The limit of the direct shadow in any body, whatever may be its form or position, is a line of greater or less distinctness, termed *the line of separation between light and shade;* or, more shortly, *the line of shade;* this line is, of course, determined by the contact of the luminous rays with the surface of the body; and if these rays be prolonged till they meet a given surface, by joining all the points of intersection with that surface, we obtain the *outline of the shadow cast* upon it by the part of the body which is deprived of light.

The rays of light being regarded as parallel to each other, it is obvious that in the delineation of shadows, it is only necessary to know the direction of one of them; and as that direction is arbitrary, we have adopted the usual and confessedly the most convenient mode of regarding the rays as in all cases falling in the direction of the diagonal of a cube, of which the sides are parallel to the planes of projection. The diagonal in projection upon the vertical and horizontal planes lies at an angle of 45° with the ground-line; and thus the light in both elevation and plan appears at the angle of 45°. In illustration, let R, R′ (fig. 1, plate I) be the projections of a ray of light in elevation and plan; and let A, A′, those of a point of which the shadows are required to be projected upon the vertical plane X Y. Draw the straight lines A *a*, A′ *a*′, parallel to the lines R, R′, and from *a*′, where the line A′ *a*′ meets the plane X Y, draw the perpendicular *a*′ *a* to meet the oblique line A *a;* then the intersection *a* is the position of the shadow of the point A.

In the following illustrations, the same letter accented, is employed in the plan as in the elevation, to refer to the same point or object.

The projections of the diagonals of the imaginary cube which denote the direction of the rays of light being equal in both planes, it follows that in all cases, and whatever may be the form of the surface upon which the shadow is cast, the oblique lines joining the projections of the point which throws the shadow, and that which denotes it, are also equal. Thus the line A *a* in the elevation is equal to the line A′ *a*′ in the plan. Hence it will in some cases be found more convenient to use the compasses instead of a geometrical construction; as, for example, in place of projecting the point *a*′ by a perpendicular to the ground-line, in order to obtain the position of the required shadow *a*, that point may be found by simply setting off upon the line A *a* a distance equal to A′ *a*′.

Plate I, fig. 1.—*Required to determine the shadow cast upon the vertical wall* X Y *by the straight line* A B.

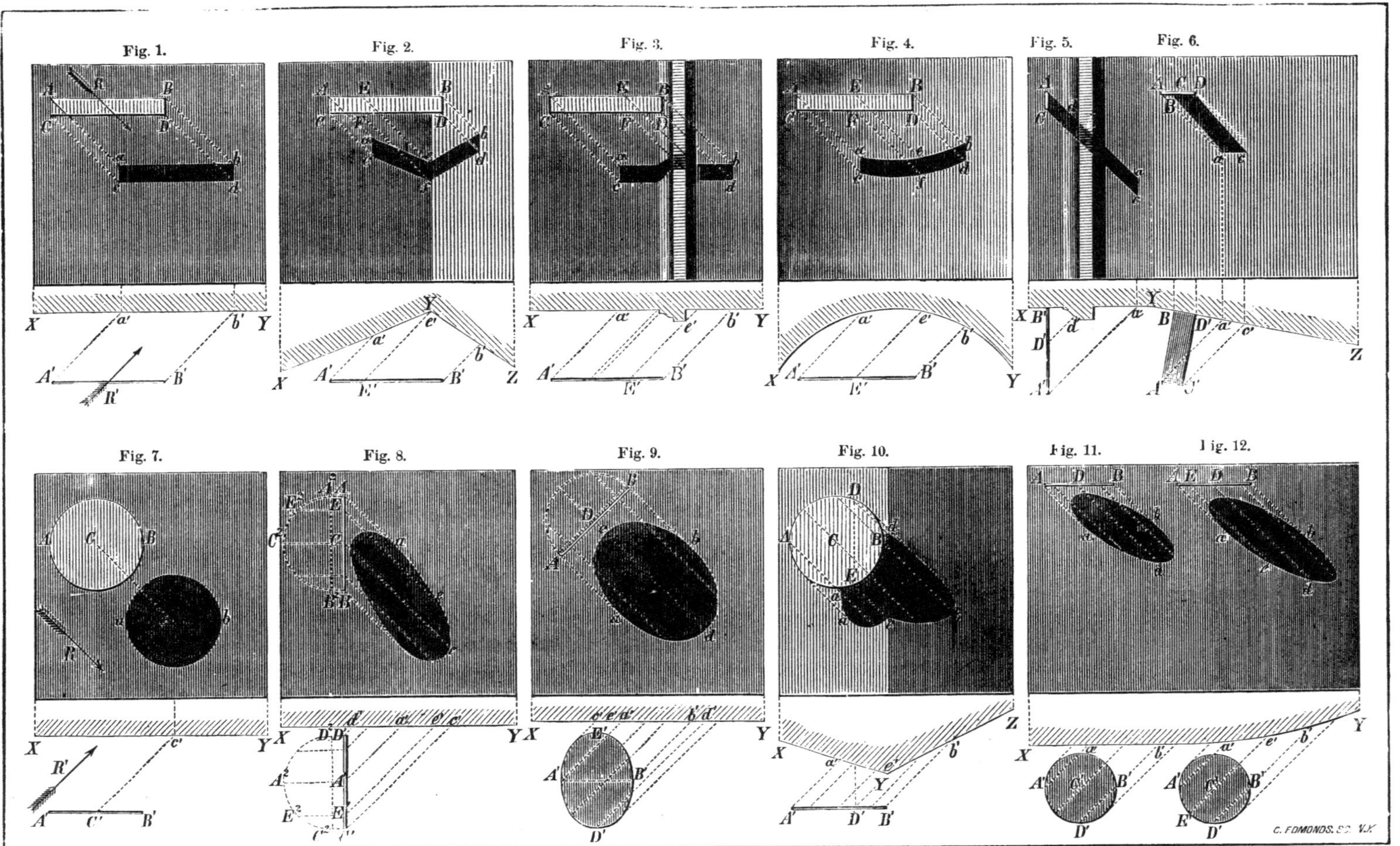
Fig. 1.
Fig. 2.
Fig. 3.
Fig. 4.
Fig. 5.
Fig. 6.
Fig. 7.
Fig. 8.
Fig. 9.
Fig. 10.
Fig. 11.
Fig. 12.
C. EDMONDS SC. N.Y.

It is obvious that in this case the shadow itself will be a straight line; hence, to solve the problem, it is only necessary to find two points in that line. We have seen that the position of the shadow thrown by the point A is at *a;* by a similar process we can easily determine the point *b*, the position of shadow thrown by the opposite extremity B of the given line; the straight line *a b*, which joins these two points, is the shadow required.

It is evident from the construction of this figure, that the line *a b* is equal and parallel to the given line A B; this results from the circumstance that the latter is parallel to the vertical plane X Y. Hence, *when a line is parallel to a plane, its shadow upon that plane is a line which is equal and parallel to it.*

Suppose now that, instead of a mere line, a parallel slip of wood or paper, A B C D, be taken, which, for the sake of greater simplicity, we shall conceive as having no thickness. The shadow cast by this object upon the same vertical plane X Y is a rectangle *a b c d*, equal to that which represents the projection of the slip, because all the edges of the latter are parallel to the plane upon which the shadow is thrown. Hence, in general, *when any surface*, whatever may be its form, *is parallel to a plane, its shadow thrown upon that plane is a figure similar to it, and similarly situated.* This principle facilitates the delineation of shadows in many cases. In the present example, an idea may be formed of its utility; for, after having determined the position of any one of the points *a*, *b*, *c*, *d*, the figure may be completed by drawing lines equal and parallel to the sides of the slip, without requiring to go through the operations in detail.

Fig. 2.—When the object is not parallel to the given plane, the cast shadow is no longer a figure equal and similarly placed; the method of determining it remains, however, unchanged; thus, take the portion A E of the slip A B, which throws its shadow on the plane X Y; draw the lines A *a*, E *e*, C *c*, F *f*, and A′ *a*′, E′ *e*′, parallel to the rays of light; make A *a* and C *c* equal to A′ *a*′; and E *e* and F *f* equal to E′ *e*′; connect *a e f c*, and we have the outline of the shadow of the slip A E.

By an exactly similar construction we have the shadow of the portion E B on the plane Y Z, which being inclined to the plane of projection in a direction contrary to X Y, necessarily causes the shadow to be broken, and the part *e d* to lie in a contrary direction to *a f*.

Fig. 3 still further illustrates the determination of the shadow of the slip upon a moulding placed on the plane X Y parallel to the slip.

Fig. 4.—*To find the shadow cast by a straight line* A B *upon a curved surface, either convex or concave, whose horizontal projection is represented by the line* X *e*′ Y.

It has been already explained, that the shadow of a point upon any surface whatever is found by drawing a straight line through that point, parallel to the direction of the light, and marking its intersection with the given surface. Therefore, through the projections A and A′ of one of the points in the given straight line, draw the lines A *a*, A′ *a*′, at an angle of 45°; and through the point *a*′, where the latter meets the projection of the given surface, raise a perpendicular to the ground-line; its intersection with the line A *a* is the position of the shadow of the first point taken; and so for all the reversing points in the line.

If it be required to delineate the entire shadow cast by a slip A B C D, by the construction above explained, trace two equal and parallel curves *a e b*, *c f d*, which will represent the shadows of the sides A B and C D; while those of the remaining sides will be found denoted by the vertical straight lines *a c* and *b d*, also equal and parallel to each other, and to the corresponding sides of the figure, seeing that these are themselves vertical and parallel to the given surfaces.

Fig. 5.—When the slip is placed perpendicularly to a given plane X Y, on which a projecting moulding, of any form whatever, is situated, the shadow of the upper side A′ B′, which is projected vertically in A, will be simply a line A *a* at an angle of 45°, traversing the entire surface of the moulding, and prolonged unbroken beyond it. This may easily be demonstrated by finding the position of the shadow of any number of points such as D′, taken at pleasure upon the straight line A′ B′. The shadow of the opposite side, projected in C, will follow the same rule, and be denoted by the line C *c*, parallel to the former. Hence, as a useful general rule: *in all cases where a straight line is perpendicular to a plane of projection, it throws a shadow upon that plane in a straight line, forming an angle of* 45° *with the ground-line.*

Fig. 6 represents still another example of the shadow cast by the slip in a new position; here it is supposed to be set horizontally in reference to its own surface, and perpendicularly to the given plane X Y. Here the shadow commences from the side D B, which is in contact with this plane, and terminates in the horizontal line *a c*, which corresponds to the opposite side A C of the slip.

Plate I, fig. 7.—*Required to find the shadow cast upon a vertical plane* X Y *by a given circle parallel to it.*

Let C, C′, be the projections of the centre of the circle, and R, R′, those of the rays of light.

It has been already shown, that when a figure is parallel to a plane, its shadow cast upon that plane is a figure in every respect equal to, and symmetrical with it; therefore the shadow cast by the circle now under consideration will be expressed by another circle of equal radius; consequently, if the position of the centre of this new circle be determined, the problem will be solved. Now the position of the shadow of the central point C, according to the rules already fully developed, is easily fixed at *c;* from which point, if a circle equal to the given circle be described, it will represent the outline of the required shadow.

Fig. 8.—When the circle is perpendicular to both planes of projection, its projection upon each will obviously be represented by the equal diameters A B and C′ D′, both perpendicular to the ground-line. In this case, to determine the cast shadow, describe the given circle upon both planes, as indicated by the figures, and divide the circumference of each into any number of equal parts; then, having projected the points of division, as A^2, C^2, E^2, &c., to their respective diameters A B and C′ D′, draw from them lines parallel to the rays of light, which, by their intersection with the given plane, will indicate so many points in the outline of the cast shadow.

Fig. 11.—If the given circle be horizontal, its shadow cast upon the vertical plane X Y becomes an ellipse which must be constructed by means of points, as indicated by the figures referred to above; that is to say, that in the circumference of the circle a certain number of points are to be taken, such as A′ D′ B′, &c., which are to be projected successively to A, D, B, on the line A B, and through each of these points lines are to be drawn parallel to the direction of the rays of light, and their intersection with the given plane determined. The junction of all these points will give the ellipse *a d b*, which is the contour of the required shadow.

Fig. 9 represents a circle whose plane is situated perpendicularly to the direction of the luminous rays. In this example the method of constructing the cast shadow does not differ from that pointed out in reference to fig. 11, provided that both projections are made use of. But it is obvious, that instead of laying down the entire horizontal projection of this circle, all that is necessary is to set off the diameter D′ E′ equal to A B, because the shadow of this diameter, transferred in the usual way, gives the major axis of the ellipse which constitutes the outline of the shadow sought, while its minor axis is at once determined by *a b*, equal and parallel to A B.

Fig. 10 exhibits the case of a circle parallel to the vertical plane of projection, throwing its shadow at once upon two plane surfaces inclined to each other. To delineate this shadow, all that it is necessary specially to point out is, that the points *d* and *e* are found by drawing from Y a line Y D′, parallel to the rays of light, and projecting the point D′ to D and E.

Fig. 12 represents constructions similar to the foregoing, for obtaining the form of the shadow cast by a horizontal circle upon a vertical curved surface.

We may here remark, that in every drawing where the shadows are to be inserted, it is of the utmost importance that the projections which represent the object whose shadow is required should be exactly defined, as well as the surface upon which this shadow is cast; it is therefore advisable, in order to prevent mistakes and to insure accuracy, to draw the figures in China ink, and to erase all pencil marks before proceeding to the operations necessary for finding the shadows.

Plate II, fig. 1.—*To find the outline of the shadow cast upon both planes of projection by a regular hexagonal pyramid.*

In these figures it is at once obvious, that the three sides A′ B′ F′, A′ B′ C′, and A′ C′ D′ alone receive the light; consequently the edges A′ F′ and A′ D′ are the lines of shade. To solve this problem, then, we have only to determine the shadow cast by these two lines, which is accomplished by drawing from the projections of the vertex of the pyramid the lines A *b′* and A′ *a′* parallel to the ray of light, then raising from the point *b′* a perpendicular to the ground line, which gives at *a′* the shadow of the vertex on the horizontal plane, and finally by joining this last point *a′* with the points D′ and F′; the lines D′ *a′* and F′ *a′* are the outlines of the required shadow on the horizontal plane. But as the pyramid happens to be situated sufficiently near the vertical plane to throw a portion of its shadow towards the vertex upon it, this portion may be found by raising from the point *c*, where the line A′ *a′* cuts the ground-line, a perpendicular *c a*, intersecting the line A *b′* in *a*; the lines *a d* and *a e* joining this point with those where the horizontal part of the shadow meets the ground-line, will be its outline upon the vertical plane.

Fig. 2.—*Required to determine the limit of shade on a cylinder placed vertically, and likewise its shadow cast upon the two planes of projection.*

The lines of shade on a cylinder situated as indicated, are at once found by drawing two tangents to its base, parallel to the ray of light, and projecting through the points of contact lines parallel to the axis of the cylinder.

Draw the tangents D′ *d′* and C′ *c′* parallel to the ray R′; these are the outlines of the shadow cast upon the horizontal plane. Through the point of contact C′ draw the vertical line C′ C′; this line denotes the line of shade upon the surface of the cylinder. It is obviously unnecessary to draw the

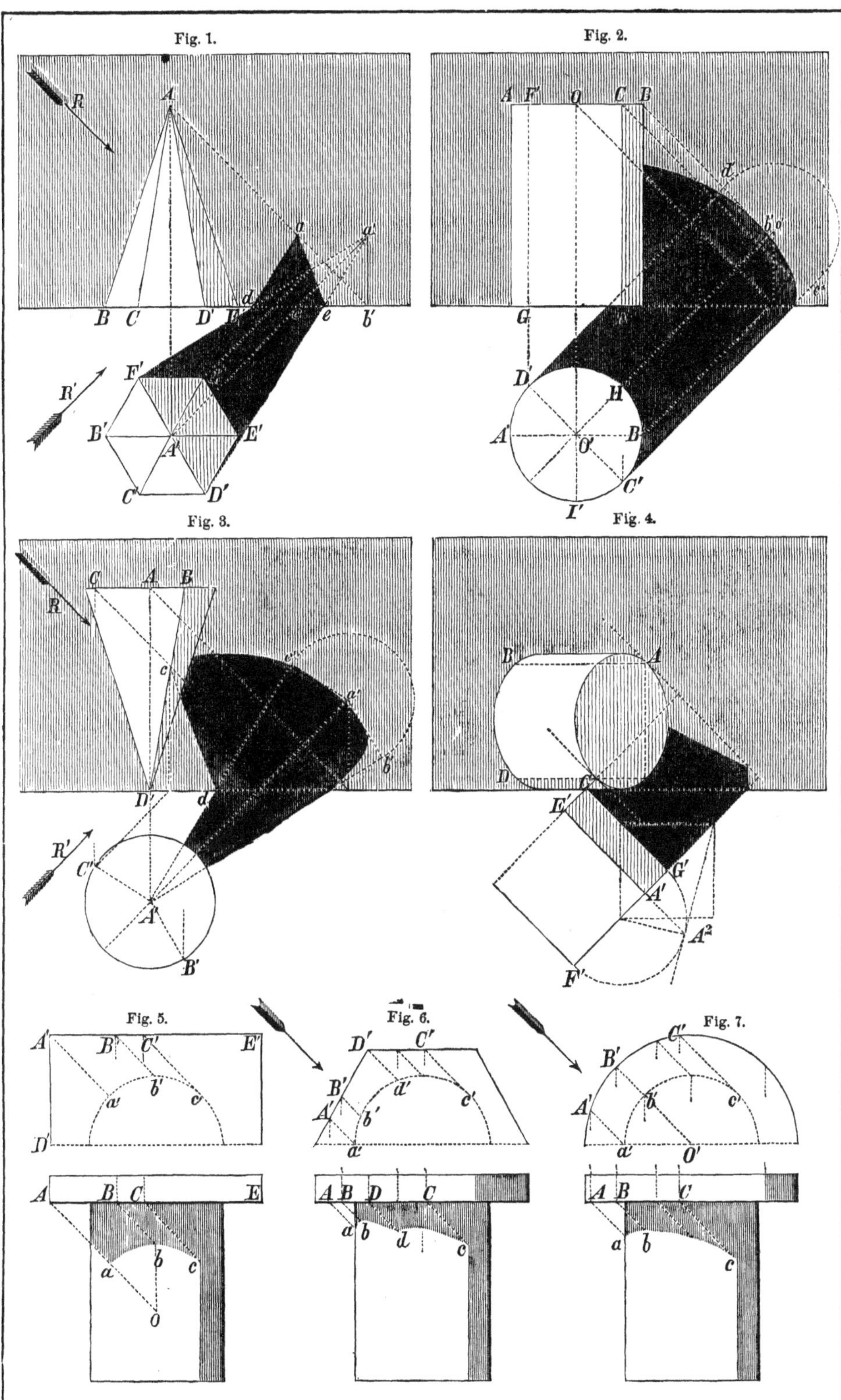
Fig. 1.
Fig. 2.
Fig. 3.
Fig. 4.
Fig. 5.
Fig. 6.
Fig. 7.

perpendicular from the opposite point D′, because it is altogether concealed in the vertical elevation of the solid. In order to ascertain the points C′ and D′ with accuracy, draw through the centre O′ a diameter perpendicular to the ray of light R′.

Had this cylinder been placed at a somewhat greater distance from the vertical plane of projection, its shadow would have been entirely cast upon the horizontal plane, in which case it would have terminated in a semicircle drawn from the centre *o*′, with a radius equal to that of the base. But as a portion of the shadow of the upper part is thrown upon the vertical plane, its outline will be defined by an ellipse drawn in the manner indicated in fig. 11, plate I.

Fig. 3.—*To find the line of shade in a reversed cone, and its shadow cast upon the two planes of projection.*

From the centre A′ of the base draw a line parallel to the ray of light; from the point *a*′ where it intersects the perpendicular, describe a circle equal to the base, and from the point A′ draw the lines A′ *b*′ and A′ *c*′, touching this circle; these are the outlines of the shadow cast upon the horizontal plane. Then from the centre A′ draw the radii A′ B′ and A′ C′ parallel to *a*′ *b*′ and *a*′ *c*′; these radii are the horizontal projections of the lines of shade, the former of which, transferred to B D, is alone visible in the elevation. But in order to trace the outline of that portion of the shadow which is thrown upon the vertical plane, it is necessary to project the point C′ to C, from which, by a construction which will be manifest from inspection of the figures, we derive the point *c* and the line *c d* as part of the cast shadow of the line C′ A′. The rest of the outline of the vertical portion of the cast shadow is derived from the circumference of the base, as in fig. 2.

Fig. 4.—When the cylinder is placed horizontally, and at the same time at an angle with the vertical plane, the construction is the same as that explained (fig. 2); namely, lines are to be drawn parallel to the ray of light, and touching the opposite points of either base of the cylinder, and through the points of contact A and C the horizontal lines A E and C D are to be drawn, denoting the limits of the shade on the figure. The latter of these lines only is visible in the elevation, while, on the other hand, the former, A E alone, is seen in the plan, where it may be found by drawing a perpendicular from A meeting the base F′ G′ in A′. The line A′ E′ drawn parallel to the axis of the cylinder is the line of shade required. Project the shadow of the line A E on the vertical plane as in previous examples, and the construction will define the outline of the shadow of the cylinder.

The example here given presents the particular case in which the base of the cylinder is parallel to the direction of the rays of light in the horizontal projection. In this case, all that is required in order to determine the line A′ E′ is to ascertain the angle which the ray of light makes with the projection of the figure. Draw a tangent to the circle F′ A^2 G′ (which represents the base of the cylinder laid down on the horizontal plane), in such a manner as to make with F′ G′ an angle of 35° 16′, and through the point of contact A^2 draw a line parallel to the axis of the cylinder; this line E′ A′ will be the line of shade as before.

Fig. 5 represents a cylinder upon which a shadow is thrown by a rectangular prism, of which the sides are parallel to the planes of projection. The shadow in this case is derived from the edges A′ D′ and A′ E′, the first of which, being perpendicular to the plane of projection, gives, according to principles already laid down, a straight line at an angle of 45° for the outline of its shadow, whereas the side A′ E′ being parallel to that plane, its shadow is determined by a portion of a circle *a b c*, described from the centre *o*.

Figs. 6, 7.—If the prism be hexagonal, or a cylinder be substituted for it, the mode of construction remains the same. But it should be observed, that it is best in all such cases to commence by finding the points which indicate the main direction of the outline. To ascertain the point *a* at which the shadow commences, draw from *a′* the line *a′* A′ at an angle of 45°, which is then to be projected vertically to *a* A. Then the highest point *b* (fig. 7) should be determined by the intersection of the radius O′ B′ (drawn parallel to the ray), with the circumference of the base of the cylinder on which the required shadow is cast; and finally, the point *c*, where the outline of the cast shadow intersects the line of shade, should be determined by a similar process.

Fig. 1 represents a hexagonal prism upon which a shadow is thrown by a rectangular prism. Determine the point *a* as in fig. 5, plate II.; draw from the angular points *b′*, *c′* lines parallel to the direction of the light, intersecting the edge of the rectangular prism at B′, C′; project these points, and draw the lines B *b*, C *c;* their intersections with the edges of the hexagonal prism will be the limiting points *b*, *c*, of the required shadow.

Fig. 2 represents a hexagonal prism upon which a shadow is cast by another hexagonal prism. The construction is precisely similar to the preceding. Lines parallel to the direction of the light are drawn from the angular points of both interior and exterior prisms; these points are projected, and the limiting points *a*, *b*, *c*, *d*, of the shadow are determined.

Fig. 3 represents a hexagonal prism upon which a shadow is cast by a cylinder, a variety of the preceding; but as in this case the outline of the shadow is curved, in addition to the lines from the angular points

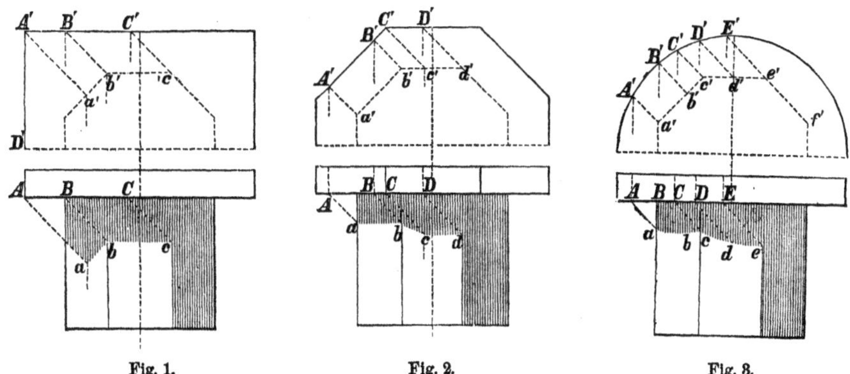

Fig. 1. Fig. 2. Fig. 3.

of the prism, parallels are also drawn from as many intermediate points b' d', as may be necessary to determine the outline of the curved shadow.

Plate III., fig. 7.—*To define the shadows cast upon the interior of a hollow cylinder in section by itself and by a circular piston fitted into it.*

The example shows a steam cylinder, A, in section, by a plane passing through its axis, with its piston and rod in full.

Conceive, in the first instance, the piston P to be removed; the shadow cast into the interior of the cylinder will then consist, obviously, of that projected by the vertical edge B C, and by a portion of the horizontal edge B A. To find the first, draw through B′ a line B′ b' at an angle of 45° with B′ A; the point b', where this line meets the interior surface of the cylinder, being projected upwards to fig. 7, gives the line $b\,f$ as the outline of the shadow sought. Then, parallel to the direction of the light, draw a tangent at F′ to the inner circle of the base; its point of contact being projected to F in the elevation, marks the commencement of the outline of the shadow cast by the upper edge of the cylinder. The point b, where it terminates, will obviously be the intersection of the straight line $f\,b$ already determined, with a ray B b from the upper extremity of the edge B C; and any intermediate point in the curve, as e, may be found by taking a point E′, between B′ and b', projecting it to E, and causing rays E e, E′ e', to pass through these points. The outline of the shadow required will then be the curve F e b and the straight line $b\,f$. Suppose now the piston P and its rod T to be inserted into the cylinder as shown. The lower surface of the piston will then cast a shadow upon the interior surface of the cylinder, of which the outline D d h o, may be formed in the same way, as will be obvious from inspection of the figures, and comparison of the letters of reference. The piston-rod T being cylindrical and vertical, it casts also its shadow into the interior of the cylinder; it will obviously consist of a rectangle *i j l k* drawn parallel to the axis, and of which the sides *i j* and *k l* are determined by the tangents I′ *i′* and K′ *k′*.

Figure 4.—This example consists of a hollow cylinder, surmounted by a circular disc or cover, sectioned through the centre, where it is also penetrated by a cylindrical aperture. The construction necessary for finding the outlines of the cast shadow will obviously be the same as already laid down. In this case, however, it is proper to know beforehand what parts of the upper and lower edges of the central aperture cast their shadows into the interior of the cylinder; if, then, we take the trouble to construct the shadows of each of these edges separately, we shall find that that of the upper edge is a curve *b c f*, and that of the lower a similar curve *a c e*, cutting the former in *c*. This point limits the parts of each curve which are actually visible; namely, the portion *b c* of the first, and the portion *e c* of the second; hence it follows, that in order to avoid unnecessary work, we should first determine the position of the point of intersection, *c*, of the two curves, which is in fact the cast shadow of the lowest point C in the curve D C, previously laid down in the circular opening of the cover, in the manner indicated in fig. 7, plate III.

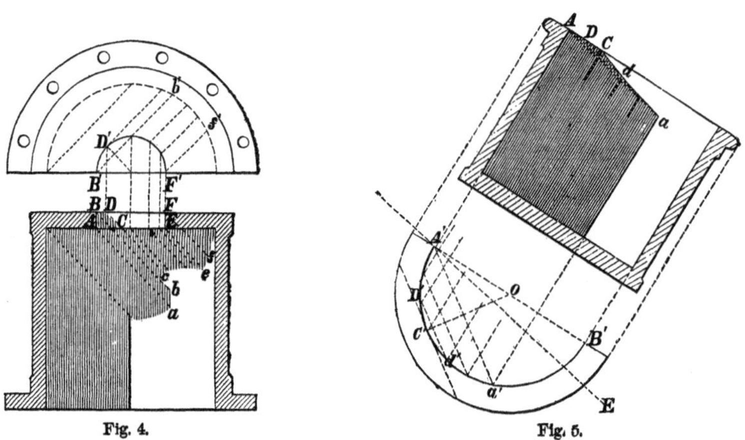

Fig. 4. Fig. 5.

Fig. 5.–Let a cylinder in section to be set at an inclination to the horizontal plane. To find the outline of the shadow cast into its interior, describe upon the prolongation of the axis of the cylinder a semicircle A′ *a′* B′, representing its interior surface, and then, in any convenient part of the paper, draw the diagonal *m o* parallel to the line of light A′ E′, and construct a square $m\,n\,o\,p$ (fig. 6); from one of the extremities, o, draw the line $o\,r$ parallel to A′ B′, and through the opposite extremity, m, draw a perpendicular $r\,s$ to this line, and set off on the perpendicular the distance $r\,s$ equal to the side of the square, and join $s\,o$. Now, draw through the point A′, in the original figure, a line A′ a', parallel to $s\,o$, intersecting the circle A′ a' B′ in the point a', which being projected by a line parallel to the axis of the cylinder, and meeting the line A a, drawn at an angle of 45°, gives the first point a in the curve C d a. The other points will be obtained in like manner, by drawing at pleasure other lines, such as D′ d', parallel to A′ a'.

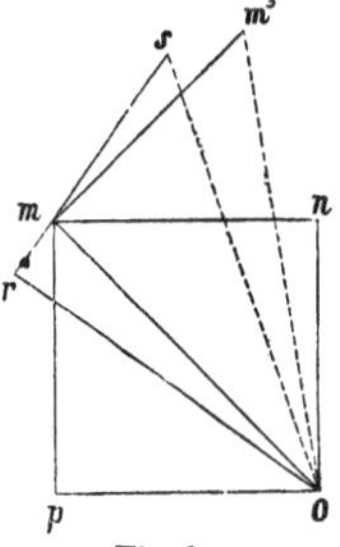

Fig. 6.

To find the outline of the shadow cast into the interior of a hollow hemisphere.

Let A B C D (fig. 7) represent the horizontal projection of a concave hemisphere. Here it is sufficiently obvious, that if we draw through the centre of the sphere a line perpendicular to the ray of light A C, the points B and D will at once give the extremities of the curve sought. Construct the square (fig. 6), making $m\,o$ the diagonal parallel with A C′ at m; erect the perpendicular $m\,m^3$, making $m\,m^3$ equal to one side of the square; connect $m^3\,o$. Take now upon the prolongation of the line B D any point O′, from which, as a centre, describe a semicircle with the radius A O, and from the point A′ draw the straight line A′ a' parallel to $o\,m^3$; the point a' of its intersection with the circle A′ a' C′, projected to a, will be another principal point in the outline of the shadow.

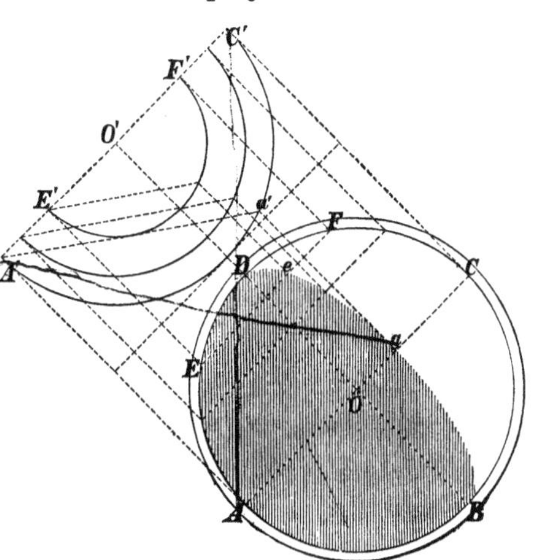

Fig. 7.

By imagining similar sections, such as E F parallel to the former A C, and laying down in the same way semicircles E F corresponding to them, and drawing through E′ lines parallel to $o\,m^3$, and projecting their intersection with their semicircles to the corresponding sections E F on the plan, the remaining points in the curve sought may be obtained. But as this curve is an ellipse, of which the diameter D B is the major axis, and the line O a the half minor axis, it follows that this last line being determined, the curve may be constructed by the ordinary methods for ellipses.

There will now be no difficulty in constructing the cast shadow in the interior of a concave surface (fig. 8), formed by the combination of a hollow semi-cylinder and a quadrant of a hollow sphere, called a niche, as we know the mode of tracing the shadows upon each of these figures separately. Thus, the shadow of the circular outline upon the spherical portion is part of an ellipse $i\ c$ D, whose semi-axis major is O D; the semi-axis minor is obtained by describing the semicircle B² i' E with the radius O B, drawing from the point B² the straight line B² i' parallel to a line $o\ m^3$, found by a construction as before (fig. 6), and finally projecting the point of intersection i' to i on the straight line B O. The point e, where this ellipse cuts the horizontal diameter A F, limits the cast shadow upon the spherical surface; therefore all the points beneath it must be determined upon the cylindrical part. Through A′ in the plan draw the line A′ a' parallel to the ray of light; project a' till it intersects the line of light A a in the elevation at a. The line of shadow below a is the shadow of the edge of the cylinder, and must therefore be a straight line. The line of shadow between a and e is produced by the outline of the circular part falling on a cylindrical surface, and is established as in previous constructions, by drawing lines parallel to the rays of light through different points, as B in the curved outline, and similar lines through the corresponding points B′ in the plan, and projecting their intersections b' with the semicircle till they intersect the first line at b as points in the line of shadow.

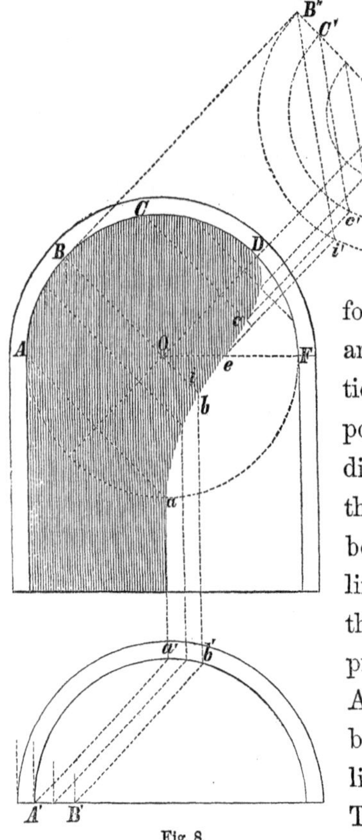

Fig. 8.

Plate III., figs. 1, 2.—*To find the line of shade in a sphere, and the outline of its shadow cast upon the horizontal plane.*

The line of shade in a sphere is simply the circumference of a great circle of which the plane is perpendicular to the direction of the luminous ray, and consequently inclined to the two planes of projection. This line will, therefore, be represented in elevation and plan by two equal ellipses,

PLATE III.

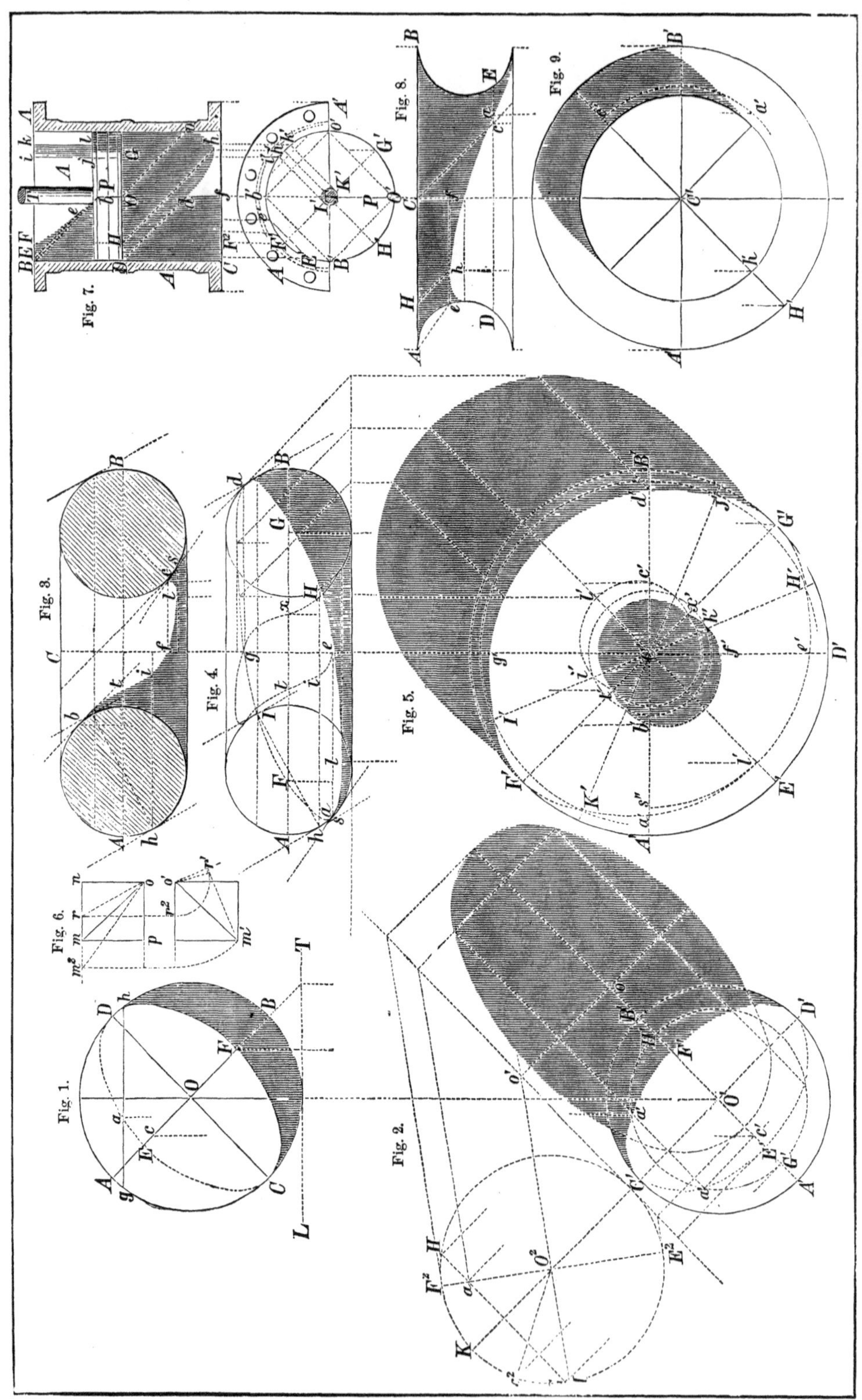

the major axes of which are obviously the diameters C D and C′ D′, drawn at an angle of 45°.

To find the minor axes of these curves, assume any point O^2, upon the prolongation of the diameter of the perpendicular C′ D′ (fig. 2), draw through this point the straight line O^2 o', inclined at an angle of 35° 16′, to A′ B′ or its parallel, and erect upon it the perpendicular E^2 F^2. The projection of the two extremities E^2 and F^2 upon the line A′ B′, will give, in the plan, the line E′ F′ for the length of the required minor axis of the ellipse, i. e. of the line of shade in the plan; and this line being again transferred to the elevation, determines the minor axis E F of the line of shade in the elevation.

Supposing it were required to draw these ellipses, not by means of their axes, but by points, any number of these may be obtained by making horizontal sections of the sphere. Thus, for example, if we draw the chord G H, parallel to A′ B′, to represent one of these sections, and from the point *a*, where it cuts the diameter E^2 F^2, if we draw a perpendicular to A′ B′, the points *a′ a′*, where it intersects the circumference of a circle representing the section G H in plan, will be two points in the line of shade required. These points may be transferred to the elevation, by supposing a section *g h* to be made in fig. 1, corresponding to G H in fig. 2, and projecting the points *a′ a′* by perpendiculars to *g h*, the line representing the cutting plane.

The outline of the shadow cast by the sphere upon the horizontal plane is also obviously an ellipse; it may be constructed either by means of its two axes, or by the help of points, in the manner indicated in the figure.

Figs. 3, 4, and 5.—*To draw the line of shade on the surface of a ring of circular section, in vertical section, elevation, and plan.*

We shall first point out the mode of obtaining those primary points in the curve which are most easily found, and then proceed to the general case of determining any point whatever.

If tangents be drawn to the circles represented in figs. 3 and 4, parallel to the ray of light, their points of contact, *a*, *b*, *c*, *d*, will be the starting points of the required lines of shade.

Again, the intersections of the horizontal lines *a e*, *d g*, *c f*, drawn through these points, with the axis of the ring, will give so many new points *e*, *g*, *f*, in the curve. These points are denoted in the plan (fig. 5), by setting off the distances *a e* and *c f* upon the vertical line *g′* D, on both sides of the centre C′.

Farther, the diameter F′ G′, drawn at an angle of 45°, determines, by its intersections with the exterior and interior circumferences of the ring, four other points F′, t', x', and G′, in the curve in question; these points are all to be projected vertically upon the line A B.

And, lastly, to obtain the lowest points $l\ l$, construct the two squares (fig. 6), making the diagonals $o'\ m'$ and $o\ m$ parallel severally to the ray of light in plan and elevation; revolve $o'\ m$ upon the point o' until it becomes parallel with the vertical plane of projection; project to m^2, and connect $o\ m^2$; draw tangents to the circles represented in figs. 3 and 4, parallel to the line $o\ m^2$, and transfer the distances between the points of contact, s, s, and the axis of the ring, to the radius E′ C′ (fig. 5), where they are denoted by $l'\ l'$; these latter points are then to be projected vertically to l, l, upon the horizontal lines drawn through the same points s, s (figs. 3 and 4).

The curves sought might now, in most instances, be traced by the points thus obtained; but should the ring be on a large scale, and great accuracy be required, it may be proper to determine a greater number of points. For this purpose, draw through the centre C′, a straight line I′ H′, in any direction, draw through o', one of the angular points of the cube at fig. 6, a straight line or parallel to I′ H′, and from the opposite point m' draw a perpendicular $m'\ r'$ to $o'\ r'$. Then, having revolved the point r' to r^2 by means of a circular arc, in order to admit of this last point being projected to r, we join $o\ r$.

Applying this construction to the figures before us, we now draw tangents to the circles represented in figs. 3 and 4, parallel to the line $o\ r$, and, taking as radii the distances from their respective points of contact, h and I, to the axis of the ring, we describe corresponding circles about the centre C′, fig. 4. We thus obtain four other points in the curves required, namely, I′, i, h, and H, which may also be projected upon the horizontal lines drawn through the points h or I.

By drawing the straight line J′ K′ so as to form with F′ G′ the same angle which the latter makes with the line H′ I′, we obtain, by the intersection of that line with the circles last named, four other points of the curves in question.

Figs. 8 and 9.—*Of the shadows cast upon the surfaces of grooved pulleys.*

The construction of cast shadows upon surfaces of the kind now under consideration is founded upon the principle already announced, that *when a circle is parallel to a plane, its shadow, cast upon that plane, is another circle equal to the original circle.*

Take, in the first place, the case of a circular-grooved pulley (figs. 8 and 9); the cast shadow on its surface is obviously derived from the circumference of the upper edge A B. To determine its outline, take any

PLATE IV.

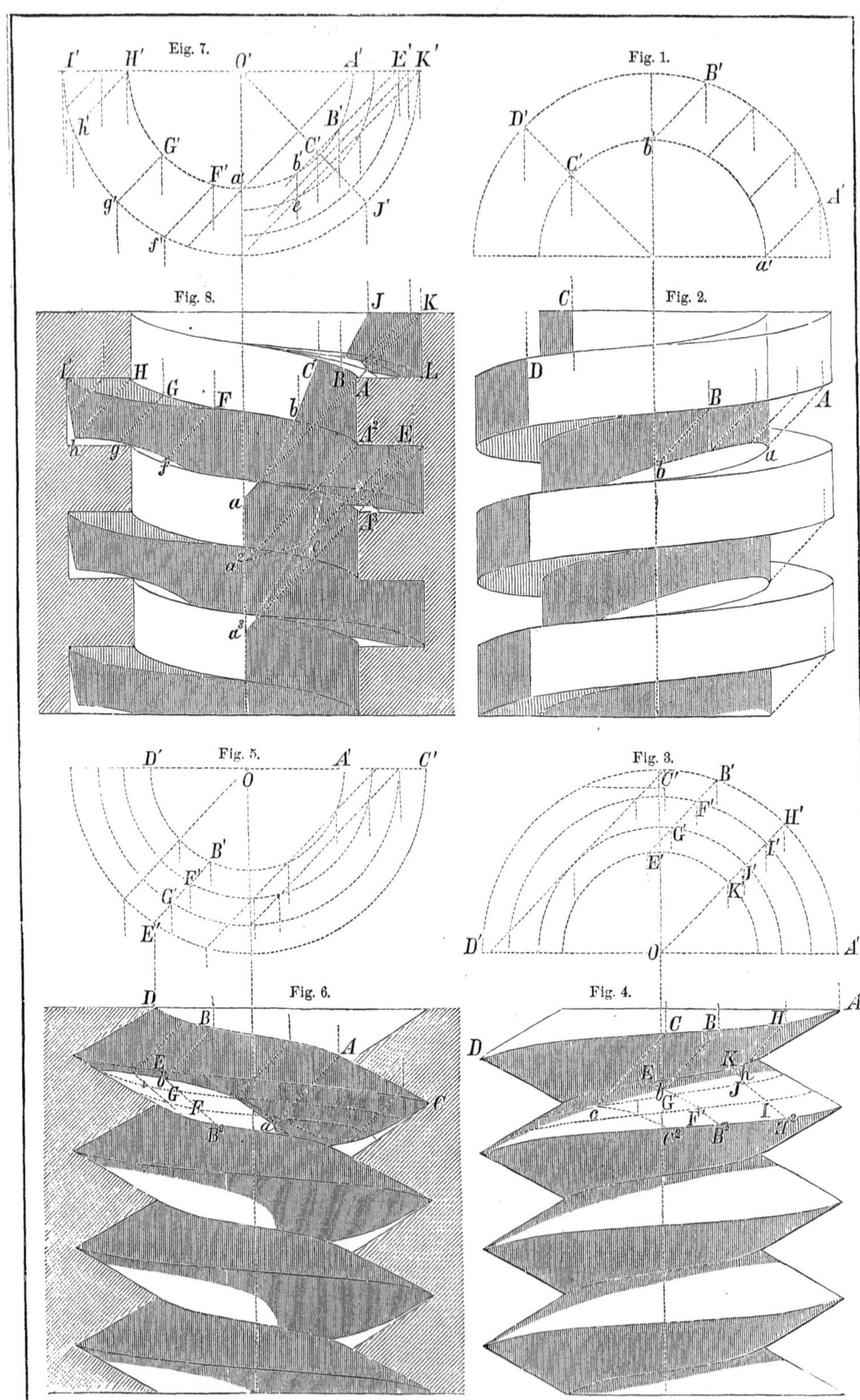

horizontal line D E upon fig. 8, and describe from the centre C′ (fig. 9) a circle with a radius equal to the half of that line; then draw, through the same centre, a line parallel to the ray of light, which will intersect the plane D E in *c*; lastly, describe from the point *c*′, as a centre, an arc of a circle with a radius equal to A C; the point of intersection, *a*′, of this arc, with the circumference of the plane D E, will give when projected to *a* (fig. 8), one of the points in the curve required.

To avoid unnecessary labor in drawing more lines parallel to D E than are required, it is important, in the first place, to ascertain the highest point in the curve sought. This point is the shadow of that marked H on the upper edge of the pulley, and which is determined by the intersection of the ray C′ H′ with the circumference of that edge in the plan; and it is obtained by drawing through the point A (fig. 8) a straight line at an angle of 35° 16′ with the line A B, and through the point *e*, striking a horizontal line *e f*, which by its intersection with the line H *h*, drawn at an angle of 45°, will give the point sought.

In fig. 9, the pulley is supposed to be divided horizontally in the centre, and the shadow represented is derived from the smaller circle I K, and is easily constructed by methods above described.

Plate IV.—*To trace the outlines of the shadows cast upon the surfaces of screws and nuts, both triangular and square-threaded.*

Figs. 1 and 2 represent the projections of a screw with a single square thread, and placed in a horizontal position, A′ *a*′ being the direction of the ray of light. In this example, the shadow to be determined is simply that cast by the outer edge, A B, of the thread upon the surface of the inner cylinder; therefore its outline is to be delineated in the same manner as we have already pointed out, in treating of a cylinder surmounting another of smaller diameter (page 320).

Figs. 3 and 4.—The case of a triangular-threaded screw does not admit of so easy a solution as the above, because the outer edge A C D of the thread, in place of throwing its shadow upon a cylinder, projects it upon a helical surface inclining to the left, of which the generatrix is known. Describe from the centre O (fig. 3) a number of circles, representing the bases of so many cylinders, on the surfaces of which we must suppose helical lines to be traced, of the same pitch with those which form the exterior edges of the screw (see fig. 4). We must now draw any line, such as B′ E′, parallel to the ray of light, and cutting all the circles described in fig. 3 in the points B′, F′, G′, E′, which are then to be successively projected to their corresponding helical lines in fig. 4, where they are denoted by B^2, F, G, and E. Then, transferring the point B′ (fig. 3) to its appropriate position B on the edge A C D (fig. 4), and drawing through the latter a line B b at an angle of 45°, its intersection with the curve B^2 G E will give one point in the curve of the shadow required. In the same manner, by constructing other curves, such as H^2 J K, the remaining points, as h, in the curve may be found.

Figs. 5 and 6.—The same processes are requisite in order to determine the outlines of the shadows cast into the interior surfaces of the nut corresponding to the screw last described, as will be evident from inspection of figs. 5 and 6. These shadows are derived not only from the helical edge A B D, but also from that of the generatrix A C.

Figs. 7 and 8.—The shadow cast by the helix A B C upon the concave surface of the square-threaded nut is a curve a b C, which is to be determined in the same way as that in the interior of a hollow cylinder. The same observation applies to the edges A A^2 and A^2 E, as well as to those of the helix F G H and the edge H I. With regard to the shadow of the two edges J K and K L, they must obviously follow the rules laid down in reference to figs. 4 and 6, seeing that it is thrown upon an inclined helical surface, of which A L is the generatrix.

The principles so fully laid down and illustrated in the preceding pages will be found to admit of a ready and simple application to the delineation of the shadows of all the ordinary forms and combinations of machinery and architecture, however varied or complicated; and the student should exercise himself, at this stage of his progress, in tracing, according to the methods above explained, the outlines of the cast shadows of pulleys, spur-wheels, and such simple and elementary pieces of machinery. It must be observed, that the student should never copy the figures as here represented, but should adopt some convenient scale somewhat larger than our figures, and construct his drawings according to the description, looking to the figures as mere illustrations; in this way the principles of the construction will be more surely understood, and more firmly fixed in his mind.

MANIPULATION OF SHADING AND SHADOWS.—METHODS OF TINTING.

The intensity of a shade or shadow is regulated by the various peculiarities in the forms of bodies, and by the position which objects may occupy in reference to the light.

Surfaces in the light.—Flat surfaces wholly exposed to the light, and at all points equidistant from the eye, should receive a uniform tint.

In geometrical drawings, where the visual rays are imagined parallel to the plane of projection, every surface parallel to this plane is supposed to have all its parts at the same distance from the eye; such is the vertical side of the prism *a b c d* (fig. 4, plate V).

When two surfaces thus situated are parallel, the one nearer the eye should receive a lighter tint than the other. Every surface exposed to the light, but not parallel to the plane of projection, and therefore having no two points equally distant from the eye, should receive an unequal tint. In conformity, then, with the preceding rule, the tint should gradually increase in depth as the parts of such a surface recede from the eye. This effect is represented in the same figure on the surface, *a d f e*, which, by reference to the plan (fig. 1), is found to be in an inclined position.

If two surfaces are unequally exposed to the light, the one which is more directly opposed to its rays should receive the fainter tint.

Thus the face *e′ a′* (fig. 1), presenting itself more directly to the rays of light than the face *a′ b′*, receives a tint which, although graduated in consequence of the inclination of this face to the plane of projection, becomes at that part of the surface situated nearest to the eye fainter than the tint on the surface *a b*.

Surfaces in shade.—When a surface entirely in the shade is parallel to the plane of projection, it should receive a uniform dark tint.

When two objects parallel to each other are in the shade, the one nearer the eye should receive the darker tint.

When a surface in the shade is inclined to the plane of projection, those parts which are nearest to the eye should receive the deepest tint.

The face *b g h c* (fig. 4), projected horizontally at *b′ g′* (fig. 1), is situated in this manner. It will there be seen, that towards the line *b c* the tint is much darker than it is where it approaches the line *g h*.

If two surfaces exposed to the light, but unequally inclined to its rays, have a shadow cast upon them, that part of it which falls upon the surface more directly influenced by the light should be darker than where it falls upon the other surface.

Exemplifications of the foregoing rules may be seen on various figures in the plates.

In order that these rules may be practised with proper effect, we shall give some directions for using the brush or hair-pencil, and explain the usual methods employed for tinting and shading.

The methods of shading most generally adopted are either by the superposition of any number of flat tints, or by tints softened off at their edges. The former method is the more simple of the two, and should be the first attempted.

Shading by flat tints.—Let it be proposed to shade the prism (fig. 4, plate V.), by means of flat tints. According to the position of the prism, as shown by its plan (fig. 1), the face *a b c d* (fig. 4) is parallel to the plane of projection, and therefore entirely in the light. This face should receive a uniform tint either of Indian ink or sepia. When the surface to be tinted happens to be very large, it is advisable to put on a very light tint first, and then to go over the surface a second time with a tint sufficiently dark to give the desired tone to the surface.

The face *b g h c* being inclined to the plane of projection, as is shown by the line b' g' in the plan (fig. 1), should receive a graduated tint from the line *b c* to the line *g h*. This graduality is obtained by laying on a succession of flat tints in the following manner:—First, divide the line b' g' (fig. 1) into equal parts at the points $1'$, $2'$, and from these points project lines upon, and parallel to, the sides of the face *b g h c* (fig. 4). These lines should be drawn very lightly in pencil, as they merely serve to circumscribe the tints. A greyish tint is then spread over that portion of the face *b g h c* (fig. 2), between the lines *b c* and 1, 1. When this is dry, a similar tint is to be laid on, extending over the space comprised within the lines *b c* and 2, 2 (fig. 3). Lastly, a third tint covering the whole surface *b c h g* (fig. 4) imparts the desired graduated shade to that side of the prism. The number of tints designed to express such a graduated shade depends upon the size of the surface to be shaded; and the depth of tint must vary according to this number.

As the number of these washes is increased, the whole shade gradually presents a softer appearance, and the lines which border the different tints become less harsh and perceptible. For this reason the foregoing method of representing a shade or graduated tint by washes successively passing over each other is preferable to that sometimes employed, of first covering the whole surface *b g h c* with a faint tint, then putting on a second tint *b* 2 2 *c*, followed, lastly, by a narrow wash *b* 1 1 *c;* because, in following this process, the outline of each wash remains untouched, and presents, unavoidably, a prominence and harshness which, by the former method, are in a great measure subdued.

The face *a d f e* is also inclined to the plane of projection, as shown by the line a' e' in the plan (fig. 1); but as it is entirely in the light, it should be covered by a series of much fainter tints than the surface *b g h c*, which is in the shade, darkening, however, towards the line *e f*. The gradation of tint is effected in the same way as on the face *b g h c*.

Let it be proposed to shade a cylinder (fig. 12), by means of flat tints:

In shading a cylinder, it will be necessary to consider the difference in the tone proper to be maintained between the part in the light and that in

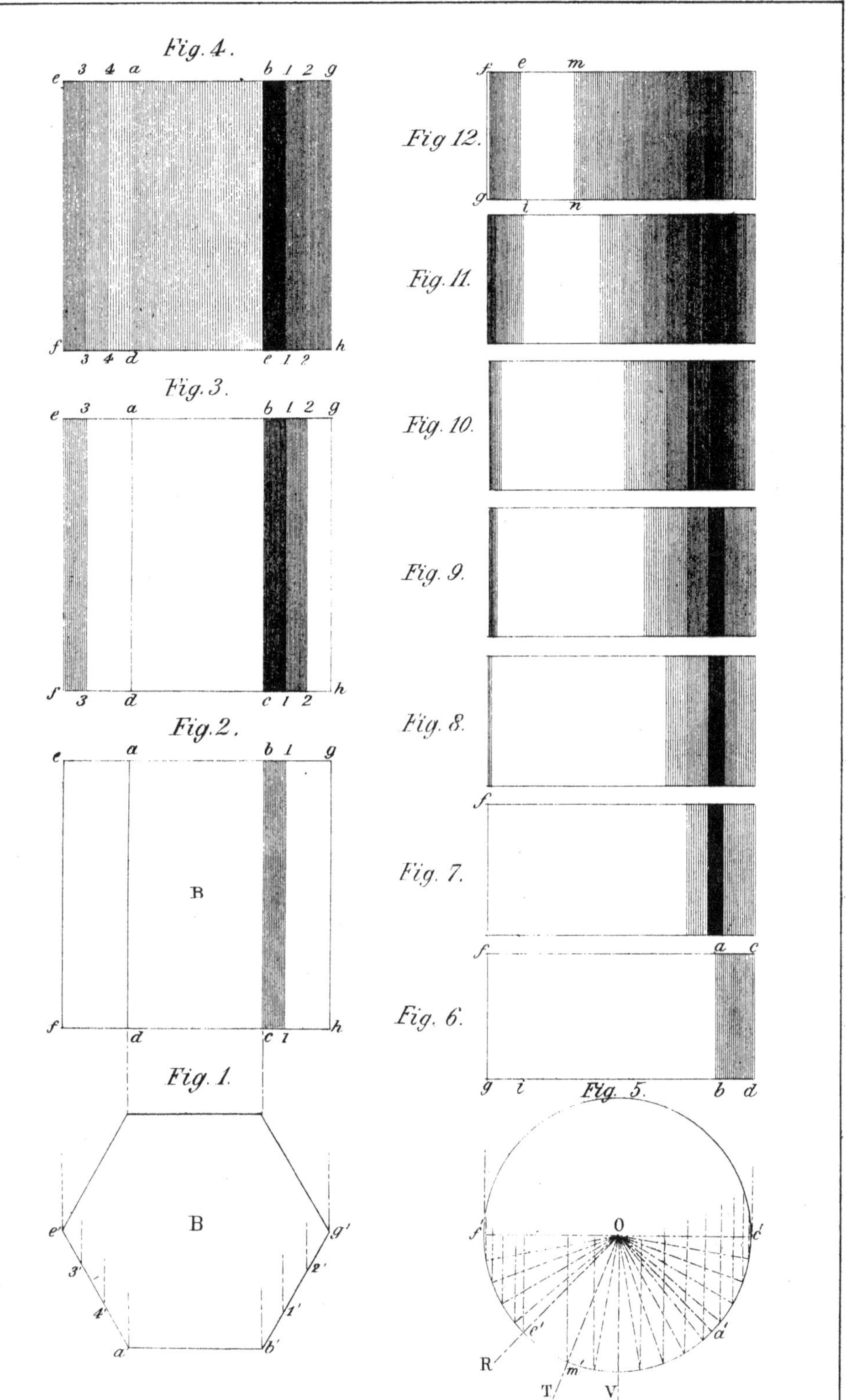
Fig. 4.
e 3 4 a b 1 2 g
f 3 4 d c 1 2 h
Fig. 3.
e 3 a b 1 2 g
f 3 d c 1 2 h
Fig. 2.
e a b 1 g
B
f d c 1 h
Fig. 1.
B
e' 3' 4' a' b' 1' 2' g'
f e m
Fig 12.
g i n
Fig. 11.
Fig. 10.
Fig. 9.
Fig. 8.
f
Fig. 7.
f a c
Fig. 6.
g i b d
Fig. 5.
O
f' c'
e' a'
R m'
T V

the shade. It should be remembered that the line of separation between the light and shade *a b* is determined by the radius O *a′* (fig. 5), drawn perpendicular to the rays of light R O. That part, therefore, of the cylinder which is in the shade is comprised between the lines *a b* and *c d*. This portion, then, should be shaded conformably to the rule previously laid down for treating surfaces in the shade inclined to the plane of projection. All the remaining part of the cylinder which is visible presents itself to the light; but, in consequence of its circular figure, the rays of light form angles varying at every part of its surface, and consequently this surface should receive a graduated tint. In order to represent with effect the rotundity, it will be necessary to determine with precision the part of the surface which is most directly affected by the light. This part, then, is situated about the line *e i* (fig. 12), in the vertical plane of the ray of light R O (fig. 5). As the visual rays, however, are perpendicular to the vertical plane, and therefore parallel to V O, it follows that the part which appears clearest to the eye will be near this line V O, and may be limited by the line T O, which bisects the angle V O R and the line R O. By projecting the points *e′* and *m′*, and drawing the lines *e i* and *m n* (fig. 12), the surface comprised between these lines will represent the lightest part of the cylinder.

This part should have no tint upon it whatever if the cylinder happen to be polished: a turned iron shaft or a marble column for instance; but if the surface of the cylinder be rough, as in the case of a cast-iron pipe, then a very light tint—considerably lighter than on any other part—may be given it.

Again, let us suppose the half-plan of the cylinder *f′ m′ a′ c′* (fig. 5), to be divided into any number of equal parts. Indicate these divisions upon the surface of the cylinder by faint pencil lines, and begin the shading by laying a tint over all that part of the cylinder in the shade *a c d b* (fig. 6). This will at once render evident the light and dark parts of the cylinder. When this is dry, put on a second tint covering the line *a b* of separation of light and shade, and extending over one division, as shown in fig. 7. A third tint should be spread over this division, and one on each side of it, as in fig. 8. Proceed in this way until the whole of that part of the cylinder which is in the shade is covered. The successive stages of this process may be seen in figs. 9, 10, and 11.

Treat in a similar manner the part *f e i g*, and complete the operation by covering the whole surface of the cylinder—excepting only the division *e m n i* (fig. 12)—with a very light tint; the cylinder will then assume the appearance presented by fig. 12.

Shading by softened tints.—The great advantage which this method possesses over the one just described, consists in imparting to the shade a much softer appearance; the limitations of the different tints being imperceptible. On the other hand, it is considerably more difficult, requiring longer practice, and greater mastery over the movements of the brush to accomplish it with tolerable precision.

Let it be proposed to shade by this method the segment of the hexagonal pyramid (fig. 8, plate VI.)

The plan of this figure is similar to that of the prism (fig. 4, plate V.) Its position in reference to the light is also the same. Thus the face *a b c d* should receive a unform flat tint. If, however, it be desired to adhere rigorously to the preceding rules, the tint may be slightly deepened as it approaches the top of the pyramid, seeing that the surface is not quite parallel to the vertical plane.

The face *b g h c* being inclined and in the shade, should receive a dark tint. The darkest part of this tint is where it meets the line *b c*, and gradually becomes lighter as it approaches the line *g h*. To produce this effect, apply a narrow strip of tint to the side *b c* (fig. 6), and then, qualifying the tint in the brush with a little water, join another strip to this, and finally, by means of another brush moistened with water, soften off this second strip towards the line 1, 1, which may be taken as the limit of the first tint. This is shown in fig. 6.

When the first tint is dry, cover it with a second, which must be similarly treated, and should extend beyond the first up to the line 2, 2 (fig. 7). Proceed in this manner with other tints, until the whole face *b g h c* is shaded, as presented in fig. 8.

In the same way the face *e a d f* is to be covered, though with a considerably lighter tint, for the rays of light happen to fall upon it almost perpendicularly.

It may be observed, that consistently to carry out the rules we have laid down, the tint on these two faces should be slightly graduated from *e a* to *f d*, and from *c h* to *b g*. But this exactitude may be disregarded until some proficiency in shading has been acquired.

It is now proposed to shade the cylinder (fig. 4) by means of softened tints. The boundary of each tint being indicated in a manner precisely similar to that shown by fig. 5, plate V., the first strip of tint must cover the line of extreme shade *a b*, and then be softened off on each side, as shown in fig. 13. Other and successively wider strips of tint are to follow, and receive the same treatment as the one first put on. The results of this process are shown in figs. 2, 3, and 4.

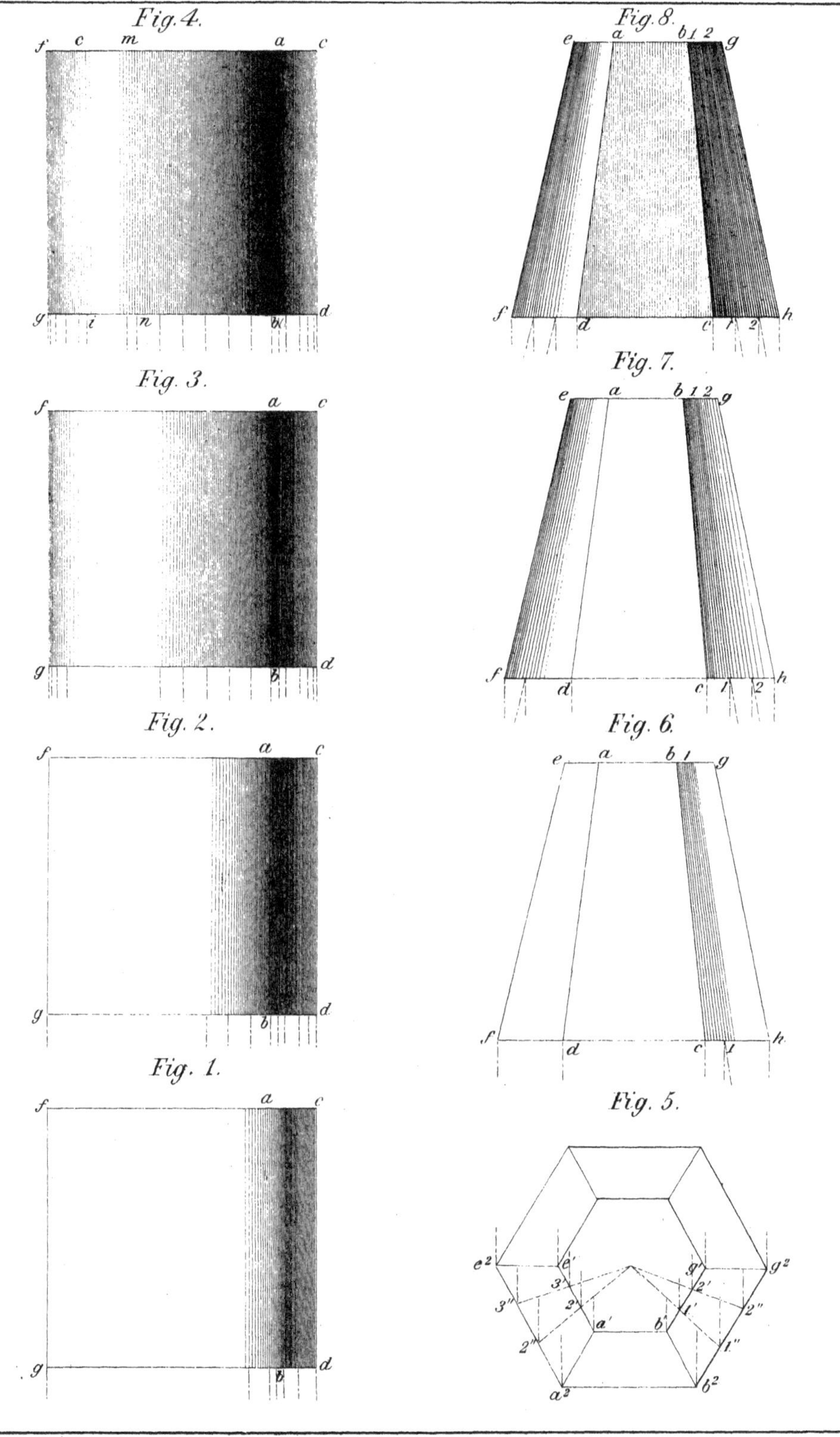
Fig. 4.
f c m a c
g i n b d
Fig. 3.
f a c
g b d
Fig. 2.
f a c
g b d
Fig. 1.
f a c
g b d
Fig. 8.
e a b 1 2 g
f d c 1 2 h
Fig. 7.
e a b 1 2 g
f d c 1 2 h
Fig. 6.
e a b 1 g
f d c 1 h
Fig. 5.
e²
e'
g'
g²
3'
2'
3"
2'
1'
2"
a'
b'
2"
1"
a²
b²

As this method requires considerable practice before it can be performed with much nicety, the learner need not be discouraged at the failure of his first attempts, but persevere in practising on simple figures of different sizes.

If, after shading a figure by the foregoing method, any very apparent inequalities present themselves in the shade, such defects may be remedied in some measure by washing off redundancies of tint with a brush or a damp sponge, and by supplying a little color to those parts which are too light.

Dexterity in shading figures by softened tints will be facilitated in practising upon *large* surfaces; this will be the surest way of overcoming that timidity and hesitation which usually accompany all first attempts, but which must be laid aside before much proficiency in shading can be acquired.

ELABORATION OF SHADING AND SHADOWS.

Thus far the simplest primary rules for shading isolated objects have been laid down, and the easiest methods of carrying them into operation explained. It is now proposed to exemplify these rules upon more complex forms, to show where the shading may be modified or exaggerated, to introduce additional rules more especially adapted for mechanical coloring, and to offer some observations and directions for effectively shading the drawing of machines in their entirety.

Whatman's best rough-grained drawing-paper is better adapted for receiving color than any other. Of this paper, the *double elephant* size is preferable, as it possesses a peculiar consistency and grain. A larger paper is seldom required, and when the drawing to be made happens to be small, a *portion* of a double elephant sheet should be used.

The paper for a colored drawing ought always to be strained upon a board with glue or strong gum. Before doing this, care must be taken to damp the *face* of the paper with a sponge well charged with water, in order to remove any impurities from its surface, and as a necessary preparation for the better reception of the color. The sponge should merely touch the paper lightly, and not rub it. The whole of the surface is to be damped, that the paper may be subjected to a uniform degree of expansion, thereby insuring, as it dries, a uniform degree of contraction. Submitted to this treatment, the sheet of paper will present, when thoroughly dry, a clean smooth surface, not only agreeable to work upon, but also in the best possible condition to take the color.

The size of the brushes to be used will, of course, depend upon the scale to which the drawing is made. Long thin brushes, however, should be avoided. Those possessing corpulent bodies and fine points are to be preferred, as they retain a greater quantity of color, and are more manageable.

During the process of laying on a flat tint, if the surface be large—though this is seldom the case except in topographical drawings—the drawing may be slightly inclined, and the brush well charged with color, so that the edge of the tint may be kept in a moist state until the whole surface is covered. In tinting a small surface, the brush should never have much color in it, for if it have, the surface will unavoidably present coarse rugged edges, and a coarse uneven appearance throughout. A moderate quantity of color in the brush, well though expeditiously rubbed into the paper, is the only method of giving an even close-grained aspect to the surface. In fact, for mechanical drawings, there is rarely occasion for well charging the brush with color. The tint in the brush may be very dark or very light, but there should seldom be much of it.

As an invariable rule let it be remembered, that no tint, shade, or shadow is to be passed over or touched until it is quite dry.

In the examples of shading which are given in this work, it may be observed that all objects with curved outlines have a certain amount of reflected light imparted to them. It is true that all bodies, whatever may be their form, are affected by reflected light; but, with a few exceptions, this light is only appreciable on curved surfaces. The judicious degree and treatment of this light is of considerable importance for the acquirement of an effective style of shading.

All bodies in the light reflect on those objects which surround them more or less light according to the situation. Wherever light extends, reflection follows. If an object be isolated, it is still reached, by reflected light, from the ground on which it rests, or from the air which surrounds it.

In proportion to the degree of polish or brightness in the color of a body, is the amount of reflected light which it spreads over adjacent objects, and also its own susceptibility of illumination under the reflection from other bodies. A polished steam-cylinder, or a white porcelain vase, receives and imparts more reflected light than a rough casting or a stone pitcher.

Shade, even the most inconsiderable, ought never to extend to the outline of any smooth circular body. On a polished sphere, for instance, the shade should be delicately softened off just before it meets the circumference, and when the shading is completed, the body color intended for the sphere may be carried on to its outline. This will give a transparency to

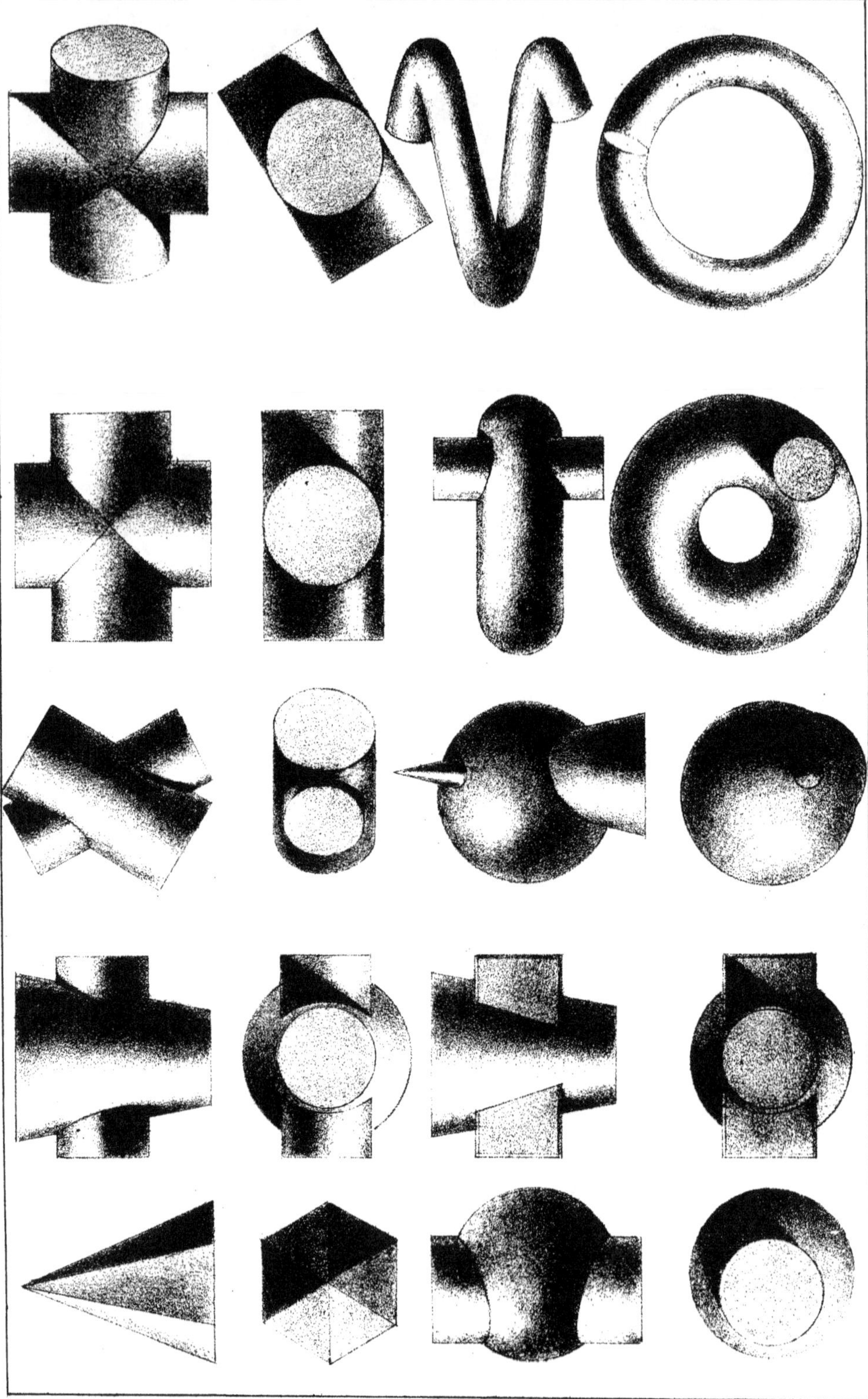

that part of the sphere influenced by reflected light, which it could not have possessed if the shade tint had been extended to its circumference. Very little shade should be suffered to reach the outlines even of rough circular bodies, lest the coloring look harsh, and present a coarse appearance quite at variance with its natural aspect. Shadows also become lighter as they recede from the bodies which cast them, owing to the increasing amount of reflection which falls on them from surrounding objects.

Shadows appear to increase in depth as their distance from the spectator diminishes. In nature this increase is only appreciable at considerable distances. Even on extensive buildings, inequalities in the depth of the shadows are hardly perceptible; much less, then, can any natural gradation present itself in the shadows on a machine, which, supposing it to be of the largest construction, is confined to a comparatively small space. It is most important, however, for the effective representation of machinery, that the variation in the distance of each part of a machine from the spectator should at once strike the eye; and an exaggeration in expressing the varying depths of the shadows is one means of effecting that object. The shadows on the nearest and most prominent parts of a machine should be made as dark as color can render them, the colorist being thus enabled to exhibit a marked difference in the shadows on the other parts of the machine as they recede from the eye. The same direction is applicable in reference to shades. The shade on a cylinder, for instance, situated near the spectator, ought to be darker than on one more remote; in fact, the gradation of depth for the shades follows that which depicts the shadows. As a general rule, the color on a machine, no matter what it may be intended to represent, should become lighter as the parts on which it is placed recede from the eye.

Plates VII. and VIII. present some very good examples of finished shading.

Plate VII. represents, both in elevation and plan, different solids variously penetrated and intersected. The rules for the projection of these solids have been given under the head of *Geometrical Projection*, and illustrated in plates IV., V., VI., and VII. They are selected with a view of exhibiting those cases which are of most frequent occurrence, and at the same time elucidating the general principles of shading.

Plate VIII. presents examples of shading and shadow.

Fig. 1 represents a hexagonal prism surmounted by a fillet. The most noticeable part of this figure is the shadow of the prism in the plan view. It presents a good example of the graduated expression which should be given to all shadows cast upon plain surfaces. Its two extremities are remarkably different in their tone. As the shadow nears the prism, it increases rapidly in depth; on the contrary, as it approaches the other end, it assumes a comparatively light appearance. This difference is doubtlessly a great exaggeration upon what it would naturally display. Any modification of it, however, in the representation would destroy the best effect of the shadow.

The direction which the shades and shadows take in all the plans of the figures in this plate, is from the left hand lower corner. This is rigorously correct, supposing the objects to remain stationary, whilst the spectator views them in both a vertical and horizontal position. Nevertheless, to many, this upward direction given to the shadows has an awkward appearance, and, perhaps, in the plan of an entire machine, the shadows may *look* better if their direction coincide with that which is given to them in the elevation. If, however, the shadows be correctly projected, their direction is an arbitrary matter, and may be left to the taste of the draughtsman.

Figs. 2, 3, and 6 exemplify the complex appearance of shade and shadow presented on concave surfaces. It is worthy of particular notice, that the shadow on a concave surface is darkest towards its outline, and becomes lighter as it nears the edge of the object. Reflection from that part of the surface on which the light falls most powerfully causes this gradual diminution in the depth of the shadow, the greatest amount of reflection being opposite the greatest amount of light.

It may be as well to remark here, that no *brilliant or extreme* light should be left on concave surfaces, as such lights would tend to render it doubtful at first sight whether the objects represented were concave or convex. After the body-color—which shall be treated in a subsequent section—has been put on, a faint wash should be passed very lightly over the whole concavity. This will not only modify and subdue the light, but tend to soften any asperities in the tinting, which are more unsightly on a concave surface than on any other.

The lightest part of a sphere (fig. 4) is confined to a mere point, around which the shade commences and gradually increases as it recedes. This point is not indicated on the figure referred to, because the shade tint on a sphere ought not to be spread over a greater portion of its surface than is shown there. The very delicate and hardly perceptible progression of the shade in the immediate vicinity of the light point should be effected by means of the body-color of the sphere. If, for instance, the material of which the sphere is composed be brass, the body-color itself should be

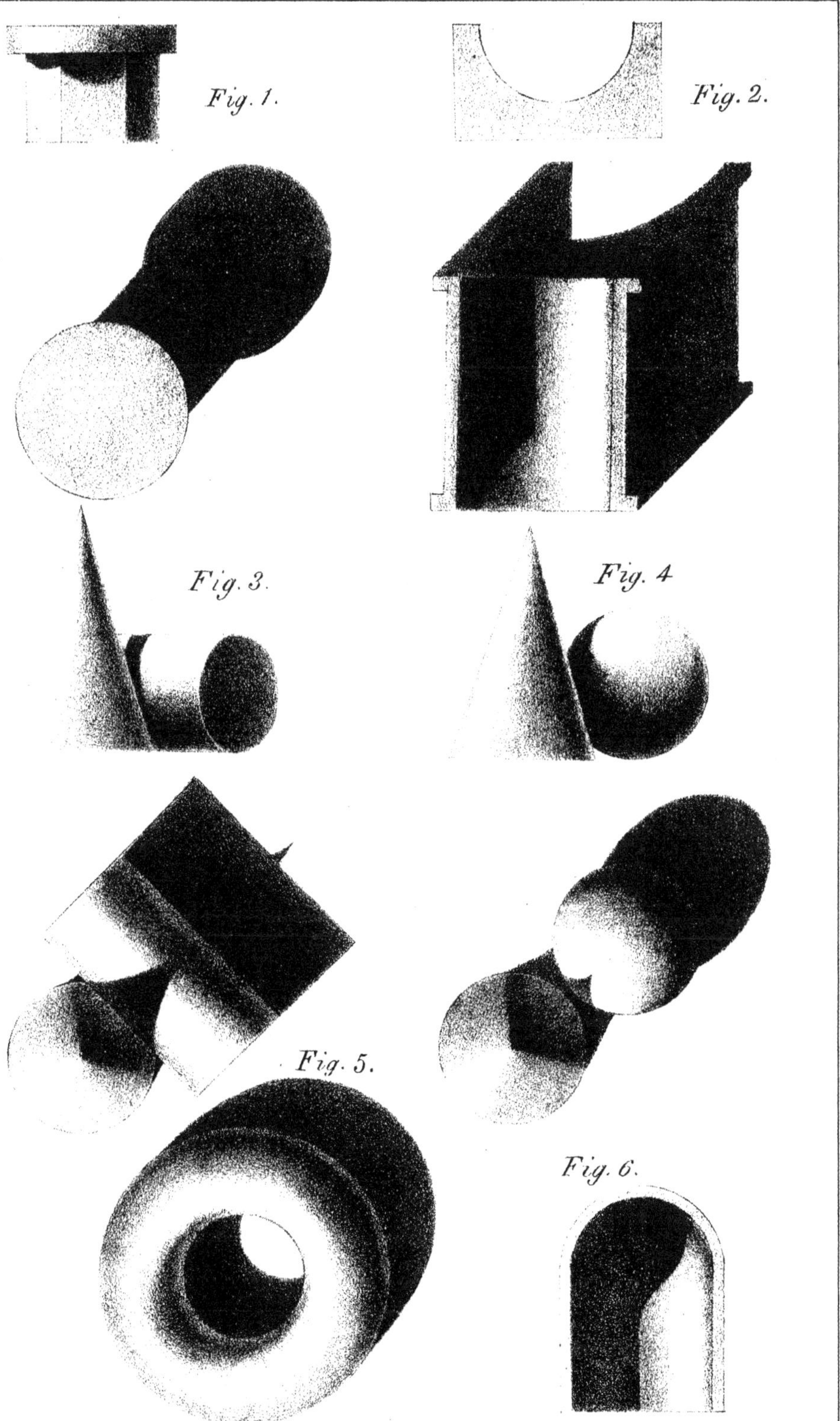
Fig. 1.
Fig. 2.
Fig. 3.
Fig. 4
Fig. 5.
Fig. 6.

lightened as it nears the light point. In like manner all polished or light-colored curved surfaces should be treated; the part bordering upon the extreme light being covered with a tint of body-color somewhat fainter than that used for the flat surfaces. Again, if the sphere be of cast-iron, then the ordinary body-color should be deepened from the light point until it meets the shade tint, over which it is to be spread uniformly. Any curved unpolished surface is to be thus treated; the body-color should be gradually deepened as it recedes from that part of the surface most exposed to the light. Considerable management is necessary in order to shade a sphere effectively. The best way is to put on two or three softened-off tints in the form of crescents converging towards the light point, the first one being carried over the point of deepest shade.

A ring (fig. 5) is a difficult object to shade. To change with accurate and effective gradation the shade from the inside to the outside of the ring, to leave with regularity a line of light upon its surface, and to project its shadow with precision, require a degree of attention and care in their execution greater, perhaps, than the shade and shadow of any other simple figure. The learner, therefore, should practise the shading of this figure, as he will seldom meet with one presenting greater difficulties.

Figs. 7 and 8 show the peculiarities of the shadows cast by a conical form on a sphere or cylinder. The following fact should be well noted in the memory:—That the depth of a shadow on any object is in proportion to the degree of light which it encounters on the surface of that object. In these figures very apt illustrations of this fact may be remarked. It will be seen by referring to the plan (fig. 7), that the shadow of the apex of the cone happens to fall upon the lightest point of the sphere, and is, therefore, the darkest part of the shadow. So also the deepest portion ot the shadow of the cone on the cylinder in the plan (fig. 8) is exactly where it coincides with the line of extreme light. *Flat* surfaces are similarly affected, the shadows thrown on them being less darkly expressed, according as their inclination to the plane of projection increases. The body-color on a flat surface should, on the contrary, increase in depth as the surface becomes more inclined to this plane.

Another notable fact is exemplified by these figures:—that reflected light is incident to shadows as well as to shades. This is very observable where the shadow of the cone falls upon the cylinder. It may likewise be remarked, though to a less extent, on other parts of these figures. The reflected light on the cone from the sphere or cylinder is also worthy of observation. This light adds greatly to the effect of the shadows, and indeed to the appearance of the objects themselves. Altogether, these figures offer admirable scope for study and practice.

The concentration within a small space of nearly all the peculiarities and effects of light, shade, and shadow, may be seen on plate IX., in the examples of screws there given.

The parts of a highly-finished colored drawing of a machine are always affected by a certain degree of indefinableness in their outline.

Notwithstanding the most careful exertions of the colorist to keep every feature of a machine clear and distinct, some amount of uncertainty, resulting unavoidably from the proximity and natural blending of the different parts, will pervade the lines which separate its component members. For practical working purposes, therefore, a completely colored drawing of a machine is unsuitable. On the other hand, a mere outline, although, perhaps, intelligible enough to those who are familiarly acquainted with the machine delineated, has an undecided appearance. As complete coloring renders it difficult for the eye to separate the various parts of a machine, owing to an apparently *too* intimate relationship between them; a line drawing, on the contrary, perplexes the eye to discover any relation between them at all, or to settle promptly their configuration. The eye involuntarily asks the question, is that part round or square, or is it even a distinct part of the machine at all? As a means of avoiding the indefiniteness presented by the outline in the former case, and the want of adequate coherence and doubtfulness in the form of the different parts amenable to the latter, recourse is not unfrequently had to a kind of semi-coloring, or rather mere shading of the parts of a machine. Exemplifications of this practical style of representing machines may be observed in plates XXVIII. to XXXI. inclusive, "Drawing of Machinery," pages 204 and 206. Every figure looks complete without elaboration, and is clearly delineated without degenerating into the bareness of a mere skeleton. Outlines and forms are at once apprehended, and every member of the machine is adjusted without hesitation to its proper place.

In such drawings shading only is allowed, and therefore but slight scope is permitted for imparting effects; and it is advisable to follow a direction previously given, and to modify the color on every part according to its distance from the eye. It may be as well also, for the purpose of maintaining harmony in the coloring, and of equalizing its appearance, to color less darkly large shades than small ones, although they may be situated at an equal distance from the eye. No very dark shading is permissible on this species of drawing; indeed the tint should be very considerably lighter than on finished colored drawings. Besides presenting too violent a contrast between the parts colored and those without any color at all, dark shading would produce, in some measure, the indistinctness which is objectionable in completely tinted drawings.

FINISHED COLORING.

As shades and shadows have been copiously treated of, attention will now be directed to the body-colors best adapted for depicting the various materials employed in the manufacture of machinery; to their composition and mixture; to the best way of laying them on; and to the various effects to which they may be made subservient.

The coloring of drawings representing machinery requires a special study, the process of its development being, in many essentials, very different from that pursued in the artistic expression of other objects.

The parts of a machine being usually constructed with mathematical accuracy, and always presenting a well-defined rigid outline, the same unmistakable definiteness should be maintained in any attempt to picture such an object on paper. There should be no "blending" of different colors, no doubtful finish to a tint, no softening off into the imaginative; every part should present at once to the eye its form and position; should, in fact, supply the place of a *model* of the machine. So important a feature is this in mechanical coloring, that when correct shadows would materially obscure any part of a machine, they should either be entirely suppressed, or, when such an omission would be very striking, so modified as to lessen as much as possible the obscurity thus produced.

The color of cast-iron fresh from the foundry is commonly a very dark bluish black, having blended with it an almost imperceptible brownish-green tint or cast. To represent the casting on paper to the best advantage, the following colors should be employed:—Indian ink and indigo, with a very slight admixture of lake. This last ingredient is necessary; for Indian ink, being actually only a very dark brown, it would, in conjunction merely with a blue, impart *too* green a cast to the tint sought to be realized. As near an approximation to the natural tint of cast-iron as can be obtained by the process of printing in colors, is shown on plate X.

Great care should be taken in mixing these colors. First, the lake—crimson is preferable—should be rubbed on the pallet; about half-a-dozen turns of the hand are sufficient, as too much of this color would impart a rusty appearance to the desired tint. The indigo may then be added, and lastly the Indian ink. The quantity of lake being very inconsiderable, about two-thirds of the mixture should be composed of Indian ink, and the remaining third of indigo. This proportion, however, will be best ascertained by occasionally trying the tint on a scrap of drawing-paper during the process of mixing. When the tint appears to have approximated as near as possible, according to the colorist's judgment, to the tint described above, its ingredients should be well mixed together with the brush. The more intimate this intermixture of the colors can be rendered, the better; for if any considerable number of particles of the same color remain together, the tint, when essayed, will present a streaky, semi-party-colored appearance. The tint being thus prepared, should be left for a short time untouched, so as to allow the grosser particles of color to settle at the bottom of the saucer. No fear need be entertained of getting the tint too dark, or of mixing too much; on the contrary, it is better to compound a considerable quantity and very dark in one saucer, and then gently pour a little into one or two others, in which, with varying quantities of water, different gradations of tint may be produced. The tint left in the first pallet should be preserved for shading or for shadows, and when it has become dry, should by no means be discarded, as it will always be serviceable, and indeed preferable for imparting the lesser dark effects to various parts of the drawing.

With one or two exceptions, which will be pointed out later, this tint, variously modified, is the only one to be employed for the representation of cast iron. It is adapted as well for expressing the shades and shadows as for depicting the body-color. If the shades and shadows be indicated by Indian ink alone, the small amount of "brilliancy" which cast iron naturally enjoys will disappear wherever covered with Indian ink, and even the effect of the body-color will be very sensibly diminished.

The first parts of the drawing of a machine which it is usually most judicious to color are those of a circular form—cylinders, the more important shafts, &c. The rods and smaller shafts, especially where they cross other parts of the machine, may be left until the other work is finished.

Taking for granted that the learner has practised the art of shading according to the simple methods previously described, and, therefore, that he is somewhat acquainted with the use of the brush, let him now proceed to color a circular casting, it being with *cast iron* only that we have to do at present.

Imagine this casting to be a large cylinder. First draw two faint pencil lines, to indicate the extremes of light and shade on its surface. Pass the brush, moderately full of the *darkest* tint, down the line of deepest shade, spreading the color more or less on either side, according to the diameter of the cylinder; then, if possible, before this layer of tint is dry, towards the line of extreme light, beginning at the top, and encroaching slightly over the edge of the first tint, lay on another not quite so dark, but about double its width. It may be observed, that it is not very essential to put on the second tint before the *first* is dry, for the latter should be so dark and thick, that its edges may be easily softened at any time. Whilst this second tint is still wet, with a much lighter color in the brush, proceed in the same manner with a third tint, and so on, until the line of extreme light is nearly attained. Repeat this process on the other side of the first tint, approaching the outline of the cylinder with a very faint wash, so as to represent the reflected light which progressively modifies the shade as it nears that line. Then let a darkish narrow strip of tint meet, and pass along the outline of the cylinder on the other side of the extreme line of light, after which gradually fainter tints should follow, treated in a manner similar to that which has been already described, and becoming almost imperceptible just before arriving at the line of light.

This is a very expeditious way of shading a cylinder; but even to the most experienced colorist, it is not possible, by the above-described means alone, to impart a sufficient degree of well-regulated rotundity to the appearance of such an object. Superfluities and deficiencies of color will appear here and there. It will be necessary, therefore, to equalize to some extent, by a species of gross stippling, the disparities which present themselves. This is done by spreading a little color over the parts where it is deficient, and then passing very lightly over nearly the whole width of the shade, with the brush supplied with a very light wash. This process may be repeated to suit the degree of *finish* which it is desired to give the drawing. In the same manner the shading of all curved surfaces is to be treated.

Recourse is often had to what is called "washing" or "sponging," in order to impart softness and circularity to certain forms. Beyond a very limited extent, this is a most injudicious system. It robs the shade of all the lightest and most brilliant particles of color, the natural position of which is on the surface; it destroys that "crisp" freshness, so essential towards the beautiful appearance of all coloring; and, what is still worse, spreads a dirty appearance not only over the whole surface of the coloring, but more or less on all the paper which surrounds it. Sponging should never be adopted, and if a slight washing with the brush be sometimes attempted, it should be done very lightly, and, except on rare occasions, not allowed to pass beyond those parts of the drawing covered with color, otherwise that sharp cleanly appearance, which so enhances the effect of a colored drawing, will be lost. Let it, then, be remembered, that the less the color, whether as a shade, shadow, or tint of any kind, is touched *after* it has reached the paper, the better. The system of shading by numerous tints laid one over the other—a system which almost universally prevails —is no doubt a very easy, and, therefore, advantageous one for the initiation of beginners into a dexterous use of the brush and the grosser mysteries of coloring; but no highly effective mechanical drawing can be produced in this manner.

The principal shadows are the next parts of the coloring which will now claim attention. The outline of any shadow being drawn in pencil, along its inner line—the line which forms a portion of the figure of the object whose shadow is to be represented—lay on a strip of the darkest tint, wide or narrow, according to the width of the shadow, and then, before it is dry, soften off its outer edge. This may be repeated as often as the taste of the colorist may dictate, but the color should not spread itself over much more than half the space occupied by the shadow. These preliminary touches will add to the intensity of the proposed shadow, and neutralize a certain harshness of appearance inevitable to all shadows made equally dark throughout. The effect they give to the drawing is very pleasing, and is, moreover, quite natural, for, as previously explained, the greatest depth of a shadow is invariably that part of it immediately contiguous to the object shadowed forth.

The representation of the casting is now to be completed by laying on the body-color. This might be done by a single wash of tint if the appearance of cast iron were as light as it is usually depicted; but its natural color being, on the contrary, very opaque and heavy, two and sometimes three washes are necessary, the first tint being rather darker than those which follow. Each tint should pass over the shades and shadows when they occur, care being taken to manœuvre the brush at such parts very lightly.

The most conspicuous fault observable in the generality of colored mechanical drawings is a deficiency in the depth of the tints employed. There appears to exist an undefinable fear of transferring to paper the naturally dark appearance of iron; the result is the production of tame, ineffective representations, which, instead of looking as they should, like models of iron machines, present mere faint shadows of such objects, or, at best, machinery constructed of some unknown, light, and rather dirty materials.

The sectional surfaces of cast-iron are to be indicated by *one light tint* of indigo.

The next most extensive and important component used in the manufacture of machines is wrought iron. Precisely the same colors are to be employed to represent this material as have been pointed out for cast-iron. The difference in the appearance of these metals is produced by altering the proportion of the two principal colors,—Indian ink and indigo. These ingredients should be mixed, and *well* mixed, in about equal proportions, a very small quantity of crimson lake being first rubbed in the saucer. See plate X., Wrought iron.

The same methods of shading and of laying on the shadows prescribed for cast iron are to be adopted in the case of wrought iron, keeping, however, all parts of the latter lighter, particularly the body-color. The direct and reflected lights must also present themselves more distinctly, and to a much greater extent. Polished and semi-polished surfaces invariably afford greater contrasts of light and shade than other surfaces. The steps or rather glidings from one extreme to the other are, moreover, softer and more delicately graduated, and, therefore, greater care is requisite in representing them on paper. These remarks are very effectively illustrated by the fragments of large screws shown on plate IX.

For the parts of wrought iron in section a light tint of Prussian blue is most suitable. This is the only service for which Prussian blue can properly be made available in coloring drawings of machinery. In conjunction with Indian ink or indigo its inherent brightness entirely disappears; an ill-assorted union with the former producing a dirty color, in appearance not unlike that presented by the surface of a stagnant pool; and with the latter creating a tint bearing a striking resemblance to soiled glass. For mechanical drawings, then, this color must never be used in combination.

Brass, except in small quantities, seldom makes its appearance in machinery. This is fortunate for the colorist, as there is no metal more difficult to represent than brass. The body-tint is composed either of gamboge and burnt sienna, or gamboge and crimson-lake; the shading and shadows being best expressed by burnt umber. See plate X., Brass.

The most delicate and careful treatment is needed in making use of these colors; for, when on the paper, they are all of them very soft, and therefore highly sensitive to every touch of the brush. For this reason the shadows are best put on *after* the body-color, otherwise their edges will inevitably present a smeary, indefinite appearance.

For representing brass and copper, the method of coloring we have described in this section is particularly suitable. To attempt the production of a shade with burnt umber, by means of a succession of tints, would merely realize a complicated smear. We find, therefore, that the shades and shadows of brass are usually represented by Indian ink; but as gamboge almost invariably enters as an ingredient into the body-color of brass, the result is that the bright gamboge over the brown-black Indian ink exhibits a species of green, to which we cannot find any thing comparable, but which commonly has a very unpleasant effect to the eye.

In shading circular surfaces great management is requisite. "Washing" is here entirely out of the question, for even the necessary softening off with the brush is attended with much difficulty. The brush should not pass heavily or often over the shade tint, lest unseemly deficiencies and streaks of color present themselves here and there, which prove rather difficult blemishes to repair. The utmost care and experience, nevertheless, cannot wholly insure the colorist against the perplexities of such partial failures. The only way to manage these defects is by delicate stippling; suiting the depth of tint to the various degrees of shade affected, and then passing a soft brush, filled moderately with dark body-color, very lightly over the whole shade.

A light tint of gamboge is to be used for the sections of brass.

The directions which we have given for the most advantageous treatment of the colors representing brass, are equally applicable to those which exhibit the nearest approach to copper, the colors to be used for this metal opposing nearly an equal amount of difficulty in their management. A mixture of orange chrome and lake, or red-lead and lake, best represent this metal; its shades and shadows being indicated by sepia, whilst its sectioning is shown by a light tint of orange chrome. See plate X., Copper.

Such are the colors, and such is the manner of treating them, employed for depicting on paper each of the principal metals used in machinery.

Having explained in detail the tinting of machinery in reference both to its shading and body-color, we propose to complete our remarks on mechanical coloring with a few suggestions for imparting some peculiar effects to the representations of masses of machinery.

We have already noticed that the shades and shadows of a machine are modified in intensity as their distance from the eye increases. Its body-color should be treated in a similar manner, becoming lighter and less bright as the parts of the machine which it covers recede from the spectator.

When the large circular members of a machine have been shaded, the shadows, and even the body-color on those parts furthest removed from the eye, are to follow, and the proportion of Indian ink in the tint used should increase as the part to be colored becomes more remote. A little washing, moreover, of the most distant parts is allowable, as it gives a pleasing appearance of atmospheric remoteness, or depth, to the color thus treated.

The amount of light and reflection on the members of a machine should diminish in intensity as the distance of such objects from the spectator increases. As it is necessary, for effect, to render, on those parts of a machine nearest the eye, the contrast of light and shade as intense as possible, so, for the same object, the light and shade on the remotest parts should be subdued and blended according to the extent or size of the machine.

A means of adding considerably to the definiteness of a colored mechanical drawing, and of promoting, in a remarkable degree, its effective appearance, is obtained by leaving a very narrow margin of light on the edges of all surfaces, no matter what may be the angles which they may form with the surfaces that join them. This should be done invariably; we do not even except those edges which happen to have shadows falling on them; in such cases, however, this margin, instead of being left quite white, which would have a harsh appearance, may be slightly subdued. The difficulty of achieving this effect, of imparting a clear, regular, unbroken appearance to these lines of light, seems very formidable, and, indeed, nearly insuperable. The hand of the colorist may be as steady and confident as a hand can be, and yet fail to guide the brush, at an almost inappreciable distance from a straight or circular line, with that precision and sharpness so requisite for the accurate delineation of this beautiful effect. We shall, however, explain a novel and effective method of arriving at this most desirable result.

Suppose the object about to receive the color to be the elevation of a long flat rod or lever, on the edge of which a line of light is to be left. Fill the drawing pen as full as it will conveniently hold with tint destined to cover the rod or lever, and draw a broad line just within, but not touching, the edge of the lever exposed to the light. As it is essential for the successful accomplishment of the desired effect that this line of color should not dry, even partially, until the tint on the whole side of the lever has been put on, it will be as well to draw the pen again very lightly over the same part, so that the line may retain as much tint as possible. Immediately this has been done, the brush, properly filled with the same tint, is to pass along and join the inner edge of this narrow strip of color, and the whole surface of the lever filled in. Thus a distinct and regular line of light is obtained, and, in fact, the lever, or whatever else the object may be, covered in a shorter time than usual. A still more expeditious way of coloring such surfaces is to draw a second line of color along and joining the opposite edge of the lever or other object, and then expeditiously to fill in the intermediate space between the two wet lines, by means of the brush. In this manner a clear uniform outline to the tint is obtained, which could not be effected in any other way. As celerity in the movements of the colorist is very necessary to carry out properly this method of leaving a light edge to the boundaries of flat surfaces, and as confidence in possessing the requisite ability to perform it must precede success, a little practice is desirable before essaying it on any drawing of importance. The blades of the drawing pen must not be sharp, and the pen should be used with great precaution and delicate lightness, otherwise the blades will cut more or less the paper and leave their course visible—an unsightly betrayal of the mechanical means employed to obtain such regularity in the coloring. Flat circular surfaces may be treated in the same manner, by using the pen-compass in place of the drawing pen. When such surfaces are rather extensive, it will be judicious to color them in halves, or in quadrantal spaces, taking great care, when joining the parts together, that they may overlap or fall short of each other as little as possible. The appearance of these junctions may be obliterated by slightly washing them, or by going over the whole surface with a very light tint, and, in passing, gently rubbing the seams with the brush. By similar means the line of light on a cylinder, shaft, or other circular body, may be beautifully expressed. To indicate this light with perfect regularity is highly important, for if a strict uniformity be not maintained throughout its whole length, the object will look crooked or distorted. After having marked in pencil, or guessed the position of the extreme light, take the drawing pen, well filled with a just perceptible tint, and draw a line of color on one side the line of light, and almost touching it; then with the brush, filled with similar light tint, join this line of color whilst still wet, and fill up the space unoccupied by the shade tint, within which the very light color in the brush will disappear. Let that part of the object on the other side of the line of light be treated in the same way, and the desired effect of a stream of light clear and mathematically regular will be obtained. The effectiveness and expedition of this method will be most obvious in coloring long circular rods of small diameter, where the want of accuracy is more immediately perceptible. The extreme depth of shade, as well as the line of light in such rods may, with great effect, be indicated by filling the pen with dark shade tint, and drawing it exactly over the line representing the deepest part of the shade. On either side and joining this strip of dark color, another, composed of lighter tint, is to be drawn. Others successively lighter are to follow, until, on one side, the line of the rod is joined, and on the other the lightest part of the rod is nearly reached. The line of light is then to be shown, and the faint tint used on this occasion spread with the brush lightly over the whole of that part of the rod situated on either side of this line, thus blending into smooth rotundity the graduated strips of tint drawn by the pen.

We have treated of the proper tints of metals as belonging to drawings of machines, as they are in general the important elements in their construction; but there are other materials as wood, brick and stone, which are almost always necessary as components, or supports for machines, and require to be represented. These materials are the important ones in architectural drawings. The best general rule to be observed, is to imitate in the drawings the natural colors of the material, and, if necessary to the proper understanding, put small marginal blocks of color for reference.

The elevation of wood, supposing it to be of a light color, may be tinted with burnt sienna or burnt umber; if it be of a dark character, as oak, a little sepia should be added to the umber. A mixture of Indian red and Indian ink is well adapted for shading wood, and for the shadows which fall upon it.

The best representative for granite and gneiss and like stones, is a very light tint of Indian ink; for the shading and shadows Indian ink is also preferable. On some occasions a very small quantity of Indian red will impart a pleasing effect to the shade or shadows. For the red sand stones this color will serve very well as the body color.

The tint for brick work must be varied to suit the color of bricks used. For the elevation of ordinary red brick work, gamboge and burnt sienna with more or less of crimson lake, in proportion to the degree of redness which the bricks present, is a very appropriate mixture. Indian ink and Indian red compound a tint well suited for the shades and shadows, and a light tint of pure lake exhibits the section of brick work most naturally.

In all tinted drawings the more important parts, whether the machinery or the structure, should be more conspicuously expressed than those parts which are mere adjuncts. Thus, if the drawing be to explain the construction of the machine, the tint of edifice and foundations may be kept lighter and more subdued than those of the machine; and if the machine, on the contrary, be unimportant, it may be represented quite light, or better still in mere outline, whilst the edifice is brought out conspicuously in color.

Plate XI. represents the elevation of an horizontal stationary engine upon a heavy cast iron frame, placed on a stone coping of a brick wall, each part being represented in colors appropriate to the materials of which they are severally composed.

For further illustrations of the applicability of shade and color in the elaboration of drawings, see "Architectural Drawing," Plates XXI. XXX. and XXXI., and "Isometrical Drawing," Plate III.

PLATE I.

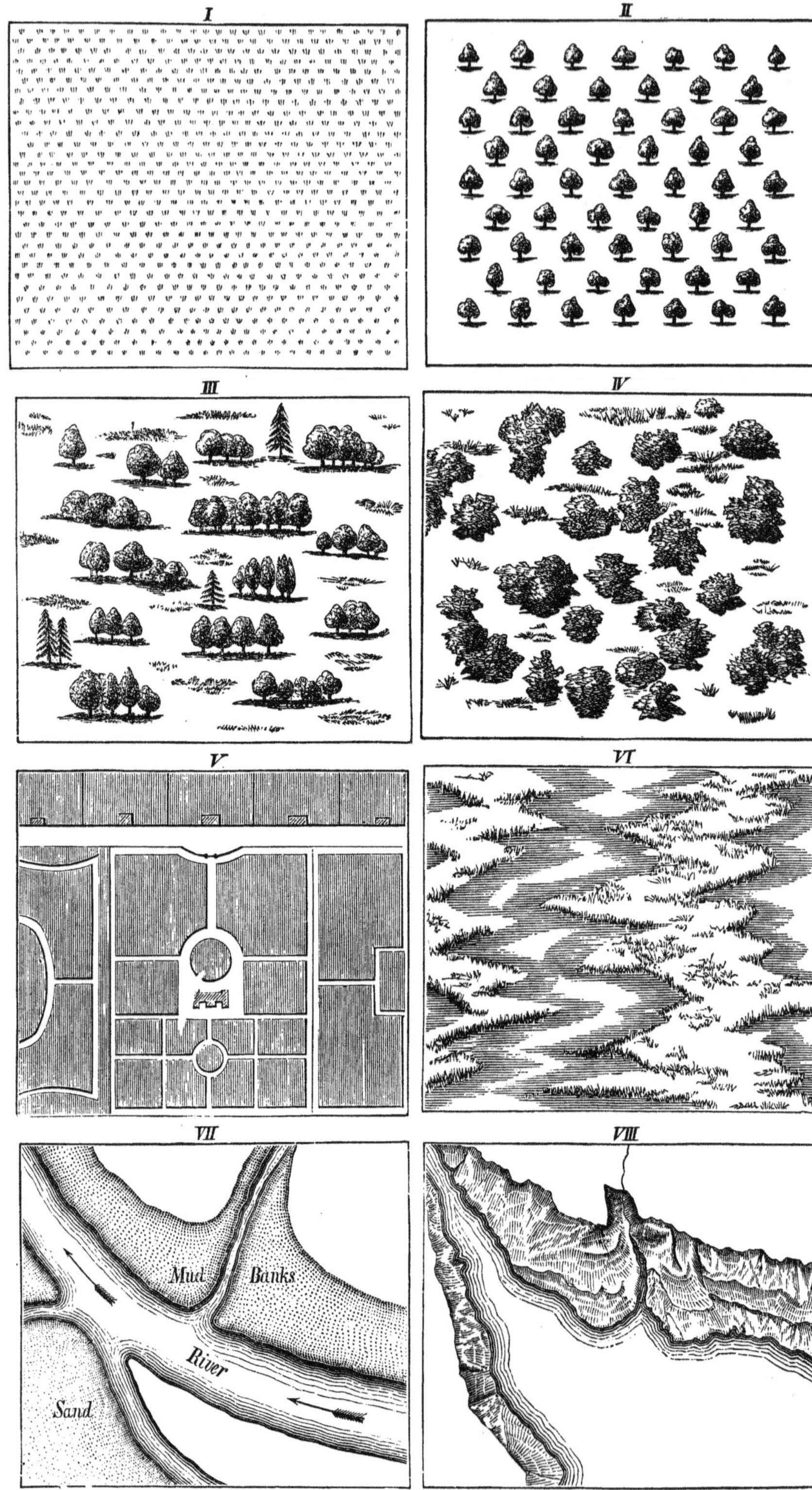

TOPOGRAPHICAL DRAWING.

TOPOGRAPHICAL DRAWING is the delineation of the surface of a locality, with the natural and artificial objects, as houses, roads, rivers, hills, etc., upon it in their relative dimensions and positions; giving, as it were, a miniature copy of the farm, field, district, etc., as it would be seen by the eye moving over it. Many of the objects thus to be represented can be defined by regular and mathematical lines, but many other objects, from their irregularity of outline, it would be very difficult thus to distinguish; nor are the particular irregularities necessary for the expression. Certain conventional signs have therefore been adopted in general use among draftsmen, some of which resemble, in some degree, the objects for which they stand, whilst others are purely conventional. These signs may be expressed by lines, or by tints, or by both. We commence with those in lines, and in the latter part of our treatise, finish with examples in color.

Plate I., fig. I., represents meadow or grass line, the short lines being supposed to represent tufts of grass; the base line of these tufts should always be parallel to the base of the drawing, no matter what may be the shape of the enclosure. Fig. 1 expresses the same thing on a larger and coarser scale.

Fig. 1.

Fig. II. represents an orchard; fig. III. a forest or clump of forest trees. In both these examples, the trees are represented in elevation; this is a very common method of representation, but not consonant with the other parts of the plan. It seems better that trees should be represented in plan, as in fig. IV. Orchards may be represented thus (fig. 2), and forests, on a larger scale, by a sort of distinctive foliage, according to the kinds of trees; thus fig. 3 may represent chestnut, fig. 4, oak, fig. 5, pine and fir. When trees occur upon a hill-side, the shading lines of the hill-side should be interrupted to receive the body of the tree, but not its shadow, which may be drawn independently of them when the slope is slight, but when it is steep the shadows may be omitted, and the trees shaded nearly as dark as that of the slope, but the foliage should be represented rather sparse.

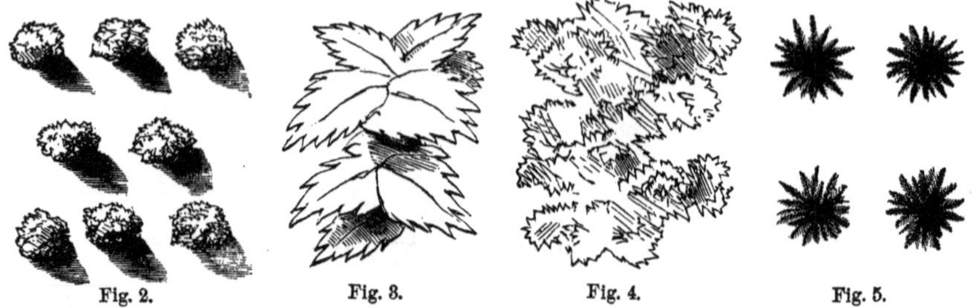

Fig. 2. Fig. 3. Fig. 4. Fig. 5.

Fig. V. represents a house and cultivated ground; the walks and roads are in white, the buildings are marked by diagonal lines. The cultivated land by parallel rows of broken and dotted lines, supposed to be furrows. Sometimes signs are used to represent the crops.

Fig. VI. represents marsh land, water and bog. Fig. VII., a river with mud and sand banks. Sand is represented by fine dots made with the point of the pen; mud in a very similar way, but the dots should be much closer together. Gravel is represented by still coarser dots, and stones by irregular angular forms, imitating their appearance, as seen from above.

Fig. VIII. represents a bold shore bounded by cliffs. Water is almost invariably represented in the same way, except in connection with bogs (fig. VI.), by drawing a line parallel to the shore or coast, following its windings and indentations, and as close to it as possible; then another parallel a little more distant, a third still more so, and so on. Small ponds are sometimes represented by parallel horizontal lines, but usually by the curved lines of shore. Brooks, and even rivers, when the scale is small, are represented by one or two lines. The direction of the current is shown by arrows.

Fig. 6 represents a turnpike. If the toll-bar and marks for a gate be omitted, it is a common highway. Fig. 7 represents a road as sunk or cut through a hill. Fig. 8, one raised upon an embankment. Fig. 9 is a

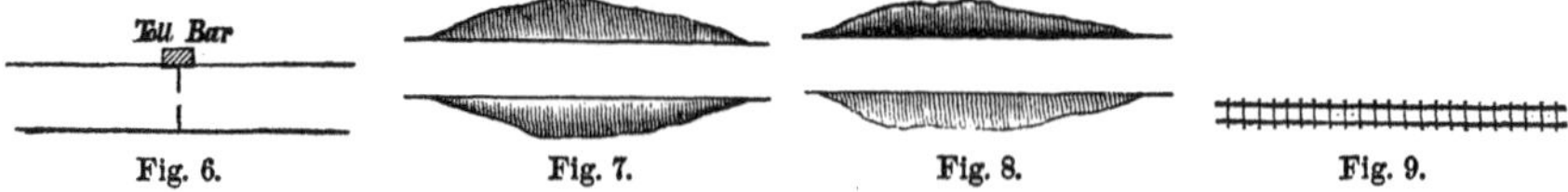

Fig. 6. Fig. 7. Fig. 8. Fig. 9.

railroad, often represented without the cross-tie, by two heavy parallel lines, sometimes by but one.

A
B
C
D
E
F.

Fig. 10 represents a bridge with a single pier. Fig. 11, a swing or

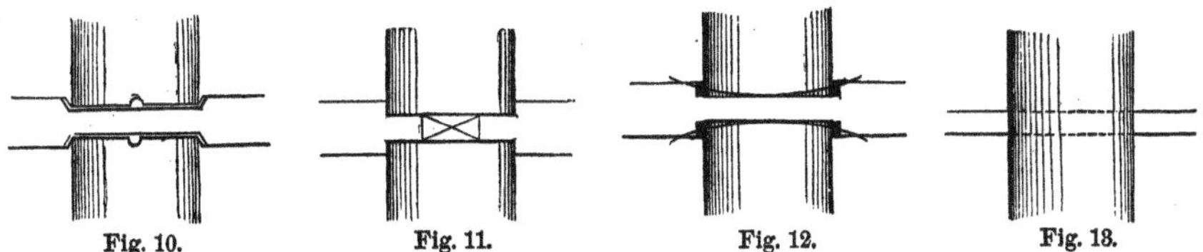

Fig. 10. Fig. 11. Fig. 12. Fig. 13.

draw bridge. Fig. 12, a suspension bridge, and fig. 13 a ford. Fig. 14, a lock of a canal. Canals are represented like roads, except that in the latter the side from the light is the shaded line, in the former, the side to the light.

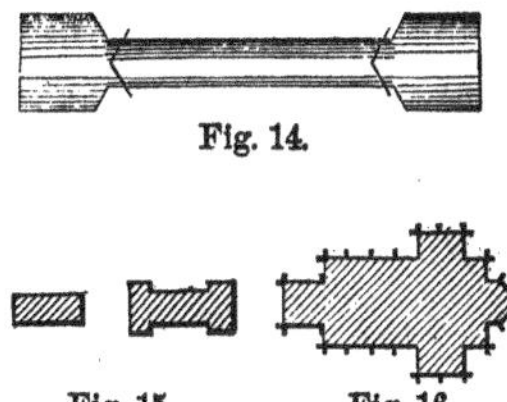

Fig. 14. Fig. 15. Fig. 16.

Fig. 15 represents dwellings, or edifices of any sort; they are often made distinctive of their purpose by some small prefix, as a pair of scales for a court-house, an elevation of a sign-post for a tavern, a letter for a post-office, a horseshoe for a smithy, a small water-wheel for a water-mill, and a chimney for a steam-mill.

Fig. 16 represents a church or cathedral; this is sufficiently expressed by its plan; but usually, churches are represented according to their own plan, with the distinctive prefix of a cross or a steeple.

The localities of mines may be represented by the signs of the planets, which were anciently associated with the various metals, and a black circle for coal. Thus ☿ Mercury, ♀ Copper, ♄ Lead, ☽ Silver, ○ Gold, ♂ Iron, ♃ Tin, ● Coal.

On the Representation of Hills.—The two methods in general use for representing, with a pen or pencil, the slopes of ground, are known as the

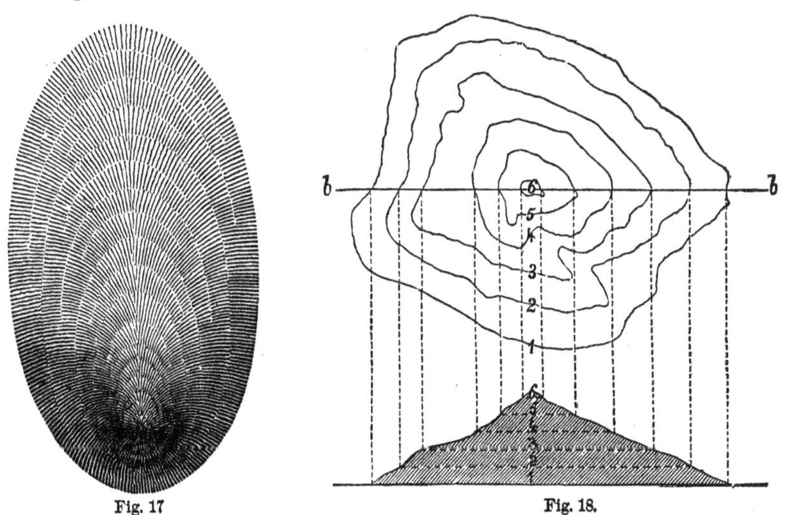

Fig. 17 Fig. 18.

vertical and the horizontal. In the first (fig. 17), the strokes of the pen follow the course that water would take in running down these slopes. In the second (fig. 18), they represent horizontal lines traced round them, such as would be shown on the ground by water rising progressively by stages, 1, 2, 3, 4, 5, 6, up the hill. The last is the most correct representation of the general character and features of the ground, and when vertical levels or contours have been traced by level at equal vertical distances over the surface of the ground, they should be so represented; or when, by any lines of levels, these contours can be traced on the plans with accuracy, the horizontal system should be adopted; but where, as in most plans, the hills are but sketched in by the eye, the vertical system should be adopted: it affords but proximate data to judge of the slope, whereas, by the contour system, the slope may be measured exactly. It is a good maxim in topographical drawing, not to represent as accurate any thing which has not been rigorously established by surveys. On this account, for general plans, when the surface of the ground has not been levelled, nor is required to be determined with mathematical precision, we prefer the vertical to the horizontal system of representing slopes.

On drawing hills on the vertical system, it is very common to draw contour lines in pencil as guides for the vertical strokes. If the horizontal lines be traced at fixed vertical intervals, and vertical strokes be drawn between them in the line of quickest descent, they supply a sufficiently accurate representation of the face of the country for ordinary purposes. It is usual to make the vertical strokes heavier the steeper the inclination, and systems have been proposed and used, by which the inclination is defined by the comparative thickness of the line and the intervening spaces.

In describing ground with the pen, the light is generally supposed to descend in vertical rays, and the illumination received by each slope is diminished in proportion to its divergence from the plane of the horizon. Thus in fig. 19, it will be seen that a horizontal surface receives an equal portion of light with the inclined surface resting upon it, and as the inclined surface is of greater extent, it will be darker than the horizontal in proportion to the inclination and consequent increase of the surface, and on this principle varied forms of ground are represented by proportioning the thickness of stroke to the steepness of the slope.

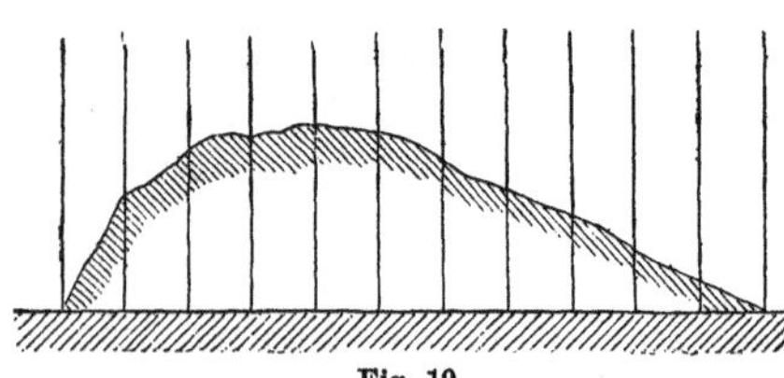

Fig. 19.

In the German system as proposed by Major Lehmann, of representing the slopes of ground by a scale of shade, the slope at an angle of 45°, as reflecting its light horizontally, is supposed to be the greatest ever required to be shown, and is represented by black, whilst the horizontal plane reflecting all rays upward is represented by white, and the intermediate slopes by different proportions of black in the lines to white in the spaces intervening. We have not thought it necessary to give an illustration of this scale of shade, as it does not discriminate between slopes of greater inclination than 45°, preferring the modification as proposed for the U. S. Coast Survey, adapted to the representation of all necessary slopes, and consonant with the demonstration, fig 19. Fig. 20 represents this scale of

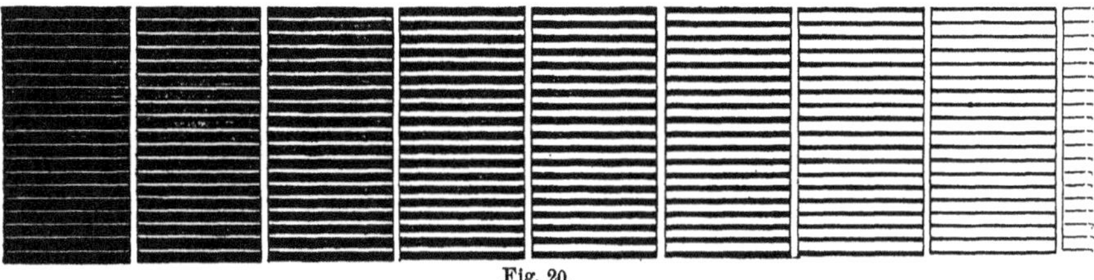

Fig. 20.

shade tabellated, the following are the proportions of black and white for different inclinations, and the construction may be easily understood from fig 20. Thus form eight parallel rectangles according to the number of slopes to be represented; divide each of these rectangles into eleven parts, then the proportion of white to black in a slope of 2½° will be to make one of these parts black; of 5° two parts, of 10° three, and so on. Now thicken the lines according to this proportion, and copy the strokes till the hand becomes habituated to their formation, and the eye so practised, that the graduation for all practical purposes may be performed without direct reference to the scale.

Slope.	Proportion of	
	Black.	White.
2½° or 2¾°	1	10
5° or 6°	2	9
10° or 11°	3	8
15° or 16°	4	7
25° or 26°	5	6
35°	6	5
45°	7	4
60°	8	3
75°	9	2

On Drawing Hills by Contours.—Draw first the curves which have been traced on the ground by levels, and these should be distinguished from the other lines by color, as red, or by size of lines. It should be observed that whatever point has been actually established by survey, it should not be confounded with sketching by eye. If there are no such lines, but it is merely intended to sketch the hills as in the usual vertical style, lay off the curves at equal vertical intervals, say 10, 20, 50 or 100 feet, according to the scale, and then proceed to fill in. The ground between these fixed curves or sections, is supposed to slope uniformly. Divide the space therefore equally, and draw within each set of curves as many lines as may be suited to the scale of the map, and the vertical intervals between the curves. Draw the lines with firmness, and let them have a length varying from one to three fourths of an inch, according to the greater or less degree of the slope. When the hill is steep the lines should be short and heavy, growing longer and lighter as the inclination becomes less. The lines should nearly touch each other, so as to appear almost consecutive, but not overlap, nor with a determinate interval between their ends. Fig. 21 represents the half of the hill, fig. 18, and at double scale, completed by drawing the intermediate contour lines.

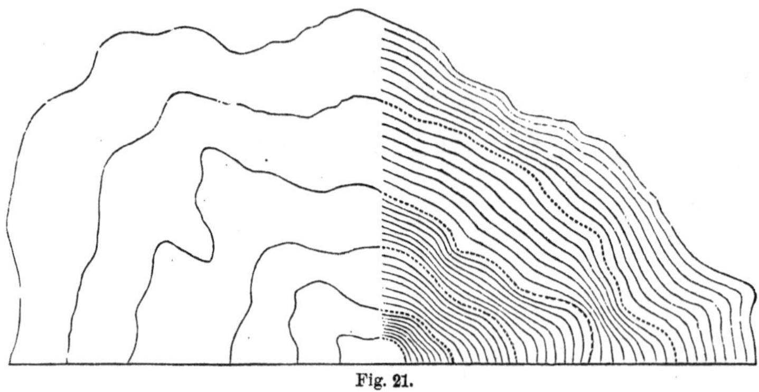

Fig. 21.

Drawing hills by contours is of comparatively late introduction, and is generally practised abroad, but little used here; it is more difficult for the draughtsman, and no more expressive of the features of the ground than the vertical system, and has little to recommend except where actual lines have been traced, and it becomes a record of facts. Certain lines in pencil are necessary for the proper drawing according to the vertical system, but when the drawing is complete, an implied line is merely left. Hills are much more effectively expressed by the brush than the pen, and much more readily, of which illustrations will be given further on.

In our list of conventional signs we have given but few, and these only the most prominent. It is useless to tax the memory with many, as the purposes for which an edifice or locality is intended will supply some characteristic by which they are easily distinguished; as in case of mills already given, or as in case of a graveyard by a tombstone, a quarry by a stone-hammer, a battle field by crossed swords, &c. When there is no obvious characteristic, the positions may be lettered or numbered and explained by marginal notes, if there be not room on the plan in its appropriate locality.

PLOTTING.

Plotting is the making of the plan on paper from the measurements taken in the field.

The rough sketch is usually made in the field-book, that is, the book kept in the field, in which all the steps or observations of the survey are noted on the spot. The field-book is generally ruled with a middle column, from one half to one inch in width. This middle column is intended to represent the station line itself; and all lines crossing the station line are not drawn directly across the middle column, but arrive at one side and leave it on the other, at points precisely opposite. The middle column is reserved entirely for the angles and measures, made in direction of the station line. All measurements of offsets or angles other than those on the direct line are entered in the marginal spaces at each side of the middle column, according to the side of the station line on which they are taken. The stations are marked thus ⊙, and the notes commence at the bottom of the page.

Scales.—The choice of the scale for the plot depends in a great measure on the purpose for which the plan is intended. It should be large enough to express all the details which it is desirable, modified by the circumstances, whether the map is to be portable, or whether space can be afforded for the exhibition of a large plan. We must adapt our plan for the purposes which it is intended to illustrate, and the place it is to occupy.

Plans of house lots are usually named as being so many feet to the inch; plots of farm surveys, as so many chains to the inch; maps of surveys of States, as so many miles to the inch, and maps of railway surveys, as so many feet to the inch, or so many inches to the mile.

For farm surveys, if of small extent, two chains to the inch is a convenient scale; for larger farms three chains to the inch. This last scale is that prescribed by the English Tithe Commissioners for the first-class maps. One acre laid out in the form of a square, to the scale of

1	chain	to the inch	occupies	3.16	inches	square.
1½	"	"	"	2.10	"	"
2	"	"	"	1.58	"	"
3	"	"	"	1.05	"	"

and so on.

Knowing how much is the area of the ground to be plotted, if the form is square we can easily determine the side of the square occupied, by multiplying the square root of the area in acres by 3.16, and dividing the product by the number of chains to the inch in the scale assumed. Thus if 50 acres were to be plotted in a square, to the scale of 3 chains to the inch $= \sqrt{50} = 7.07$. $7.07 \times 3.16 = 22.34$. $\frac{22.34}{3} = 7.45$ inches, side of the square of the plot on a scale of 3 chains to the inch. This rule will assist the draughtsman in selecting a scale for figures not very irregular in form.

State surveys are of course plotted on a smaller scale than those of farms. On the U. S. Coast survey all the scales are expressed fractionally and decimally. The original surveys are generally on a scale of one to ten or twenty thousand, but in some instances the scale is larger or smaller. The public surveys embrace three general classes:—1. Small harbor charts. 2. Charts of bays, sounds, &c. 3. General coast charts.

The scales of the first class vary from 1 : 5,000 to 1 : 60,000, according to the nature of the harbor and the different objects to be represented.

The scale of the second class is usually fixed at 1 : 80,000. Preliminary charts are, however, issued of various scales, from 1 : 80,000 to 1 : 200,000.

Of the third class the scale is fixed at 1 : 400,000 for the general chart of the coast from Gay Head to Cape Henlopen, although considerations of the proximity and importance of points on the coast may change the scales of charts of other portions of our extended coast.

On all plots of large surveys, it is very desirable that the scales adopted should bear a definite numerical proportion to the linear measurement of the ground to be mapped, and that this proportion should be expressed fractionally on the plan, even if the scale be drawn or expressed some other way, as chains to the inch. The decimal system has the most to recommend it, and is generally adopted in government surveys.

For Railroad Surveys, the New York general railroad law directs the scale of map which is to be filed in the State engineer's office, to be 500 feet to one-tenth of a foot, 1 : 5,000.

For the Canal Maps, a scale of 2 chains to the inch, 1 : 1584 is employed. In England, plans and sections for projected lines of inland communication, or generally for public works requiring the sanction of the Legislature, are required, by the "standing orders," to be drawn to scales not less than 4 inches to the mile, 1 : 15,840, for the plan, and 100 feet to the inch, 1 : 1,200, for the profiles.

In the United States engineer service, the following scales are prescribed:

General plans of buildings, ...	10 feet to the inch,	1 : 120
Maps of ground with horizontal curves 1 foot apart,	50 " "	1 : 600
Topographical maps 1½ miles square, . . .	1 mile to 2 feet,	1 : 2,640
" " comprising 3 miles square, .	1 " 1 foot,	1 : 5,280
" " " bet. 4 and 8 miles,	1 " 6 in.,	1 : 10,560
" " " 9 miles square, .	1 " 4 "	1 : 15,840
Maps not exceeding 24 miles square, . . .	1 " 2 "	1 : 31,680
" comprising 50 " " . . .	1 " 1 "	1 : 63,360
" " 100 " " . . .	1 " ½ "	1 : 126,720
Surveys of roads and canals, ...	50 feet to 1 "	1 : 600

The description of various scales and the principles of their construction will be found at pp. 17 and 18, to which the reader is referred.

In plotting from the field book, the first lines to be laid down are the outlines or main lines of the survey. If the survey has been made by triangles, the principal triangles are first laid down in pencil by the intersection of their sides, the length being taken from the scale and described with compasses; if the lines are longer than the reach of the compasses, or the extent of the scale, lay off the length on any convenient line, and measure and describe with beam compasses. The principal triangles being laid down, other points will be determined by intersections in the same manner as measured on the ground. In general, when the surveys have been conducted without instruments to measure the angles, as the compass or theodolite, the position of the points on paper are determined by the intersection and construction of the same lines as has been done in the field.

Surveys are mostly conducted by measuring the inclination of lines to a meridian or to each other by the compass, or by the theodolite. In the surveys of farms, where great accuracy is not required, the compass is most used. The compass gives the direction of a line in reference to the magnetic meridian. The variation from the true meridian, or a direct north and south line, varies considerably in different parts of the country. In 1840, the line of variation in which the needle pointed directly north, passed in a nearly straight direction from a little west of Cape Hatteras, N. C., through the middle of Virginia, about midway between Cleveland, Ohio, and Erie, Pa., and through the middle of lakes Erie and Huron. At all places east of this line the variation is westerly, that is, the needle points west of the line north. West of this line the variation is easterly.

Fig. 22 represents the field notes of a survey by compass. Fig. 23 a plot of the same, with the position of the protractor in laying off the angles. In this way of plotting, a meridian is laid off at the intersection of each set of lines. Sometimes the angles are plotted directly from the determination of the angle of deflection of two courses meeting at any point, without laying down more than one meridian: Figure 24. When the first

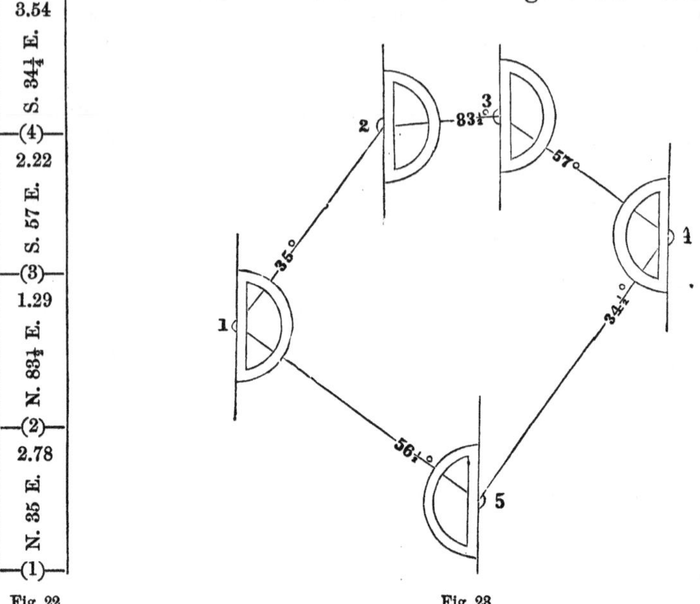

Fig. 22. Fig. 23.

letters of the bearing are alike, that is, both N. or both S., and the last letters also alike, both E. or both W., the angle of deflection C B B′ will be the difference of the bearings, or, in this instance, 20°.

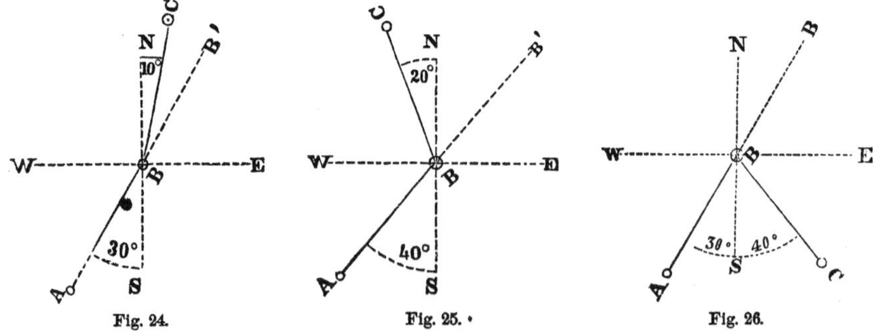

Fig. 24. Fig. 25. Fig. 26.

Fig. 25. When the first letters are alike and the last different, the angle C B B′ will be the sum of the two bearings.

Fig. 26. When the first letters are different and the last alike, subtract the sum of the bearings from 180° for the angle C B B′: when both the first letters and last are different, subtract their difference from 180° for the angle.

Instead of drawing a meridian through each station, or laying off the angle of deflection, by far the easiest way is to lay off but a single meridian near the middle of the sheet; lay off all the bearings of the survey from some one point of it as shown in fig. 27, and number to correspond with the stations from which the bearings are taken, and then transfer them to the places where they are wanted by any of the instruments used for drawing parallel lines. For the protracting of the rough plan, sheets of drawing paper can be bought with protractors printed on them. When the plans are large, it is often convenient to lay out two or three meridians on different parts of the sheet and lay off the bearings of lines adjacent to each meridian upon them.

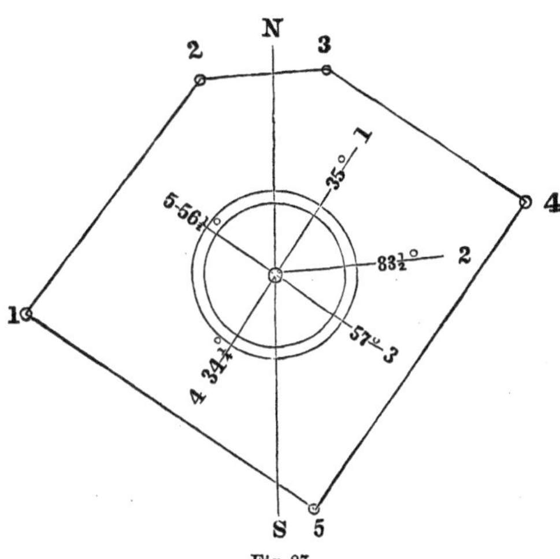

Fig. 27.

In plotting from a survey by a theodolite or transit, it is generally usual to lay off the angles of deflection of the different lines as taken in the field, plotting all the tie lines as corrections.

When the plot of a survey does not close, that is, come together, or return to the point of commencement, as it seldom does exactly, it may be corrected or forced; but first be sure that the bearings and distances as given in the field book are laid down accurately, and then proceed to correct as follows: thus, let A B C D E, fig 28, be the boundary lines plotted according to the notes, and suppose the last course comes to E instead of ending at A as it should. Suppose also that there is no reason to suspect any error more in one line than another, that the measures and bearings of all are equally cer-

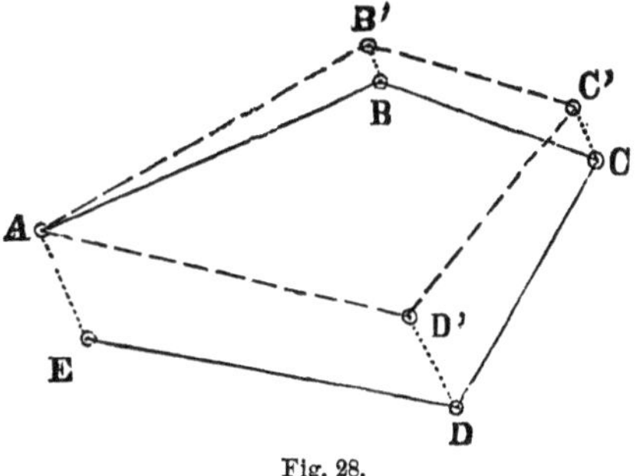

Fig. 28.

tain; then the inaccuracy must be distributed among all the lines in proportion to their length. Each point, B, C, D, E, must be moved in a direction parallel to E A, by a certain distance. Thus add together the length of all the lines, and this sum is to the line A B, as the error A E is to the correction B B′; for the next point, the whole sum is to A B, B C, as the error is to the correction, E C; and so on; obtaining the second term of the proportion by adding consecutively the different lines. This calculation may be much simplified by the use of the sector, according to the rule given for finding a fourth proportional (p. 23). Take the error A E from the plan, and open the sector until this quantity becomes the transverse distance of the first term or sum of the lines; then the distance between the points corresponding to the consecutive sums will be the corresponding error.

The best way of correcting errors and of plotting a survey, whether made by compass or by theodolite, is by balancing the survey, or correcting the latitudes and departure of the courses so that they shall be equal. For the method of doing this, we refer to any of the recent works on surveying. From Gillespie on Land Surveying, we have taken most of the preceding on the plotting of angular surveys, and the following paragraph on balancing.

Sta.	Total Latitude from Sta. 1.	Total Departure from Sta. 1.
1	0.00	0.00
2	+ 2.21 N.	+ 1.55 E.
3	+ 2.36 N.	+ 2.83 E.
4	+ 1.15 N.	+ 4.69 E.
5	− 1.78 S.	+ 2.69 E.
1	0.00	0.00

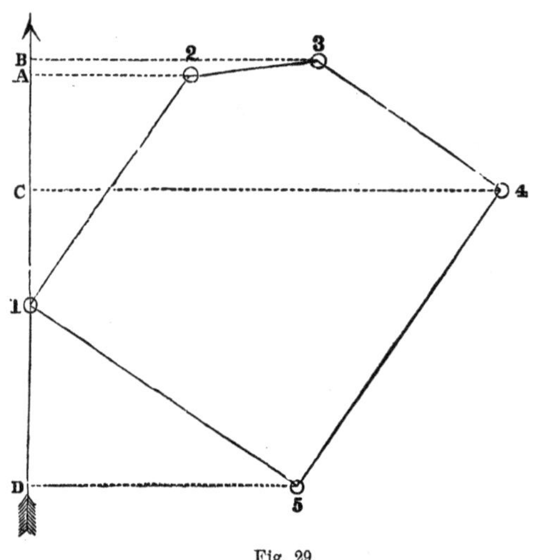

Fig. 29.

This table represents the survey as given, fig. 22, balanced.

To plot from this table, draw a meridian through the point taken for station 1, as in fig. 29. Set off upward from this along the meridian the latitude 2.21 chains north to A, and from A to the right or E. set off the departure 1.55 chains. This gives the point or position of Station 2, join 1 and 2. From A again set off upward 2.36 chains, and from B to the right perpendicularly set off 2.83 chains, which gives position of Station 3, join 2 and 3: and so proceed setting off North latitudes upwards, and South downwards, East departures perpendicularly to the right, and West perpendicularly to the left.

In balancing surveys made by a theodolite, a meridian is assumed, generally one of the lines of the survey. The most convenient will be some long line of which the survey lies all to one side.

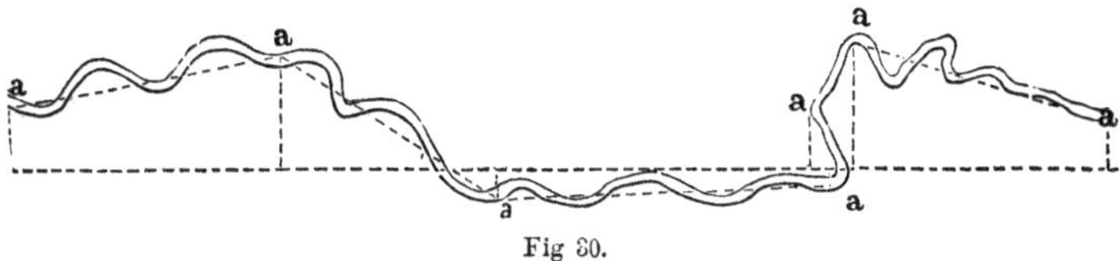

Fig 30.

The advantages of this method of plotting are its accuracy, rapidity, the impossibility of an error in one point affecting the others, and the certainty of coming together.

The above explains the method of plotting the main lines of the survey; the filling in is from points established from these main lines, either by the construction of triangles, by measure, or by angles, or by perpendiculars. In case of unimportant lines, as the crooked brook for instance, fig. 30, offsets are taken to the most prominent angles, as, *a*, *a*, *a*, and the intermediate bends are sketched by eye into the field book. In copying them on the plan a similar construction is adopted.

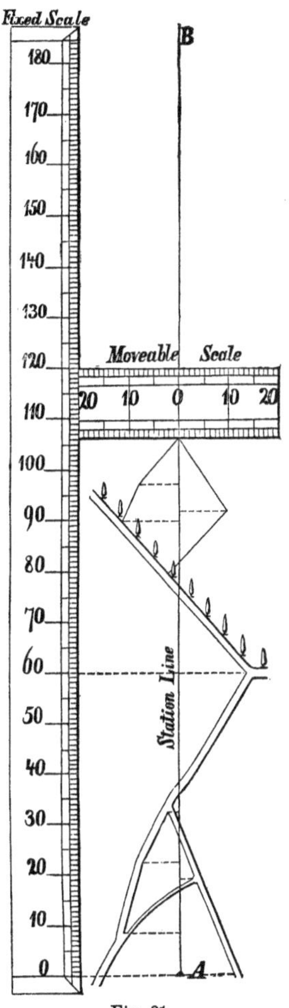

Fig. 31.

The most rapid way of plotting the offsets, is by the use of a plotting and offset scale, fig. 31—the one being fixed parallel to the line A B from which the offsets are to be laid off, at such a distance from it, that the zero line on the movable scale coincides with it, whilst the zero of its own scale is on a line perpendicular to the position of the station A from which the distances were measured. It is to be observed that in the field book all the measures are referred to the point of beginning on any one straight line. Having placed the plotting scale, move the offset scale to the first distance by the scale at which an offset has been taken, mark off now on the offset scale the length of the offset on its corresponding side of the line. Proceed then to the next distance, establishing thus repeated points, join the points by lines as they are on the ground.

The plotting and offset scale must of course be of the same scale as the rest of the drawing, on which account it may not always be possible to obtain such scales adapted to those of the plan; but they may be easily constructed of thick drawing paper or pasteboard.

When a great deal of plotting to one scale is necessary, as in government surveys, the offset scale may be made to slide in a groove upon the plotting scale.

In protracting the triangles of an extended trigonometrical survey in which the sides have been calculated or measured, it is better to lay down the triangles from the length of their sides rather than by measuring the angles, because measures of length can be taken with more accuracy from a scale, and transferred to the plan with more exactness than angles can be pricked off from a protractor; but for ordinary surveys, the triangulation is most frequently and expeditiously plotted by the means of a protractor.

The outlines of the survey having been balanced and plotted in, and the subsidiary points, as established by offsets and by triangles, the filling in of the interior detail is done by copying from the field book the natural features of the ground, in their appropriate position, and according to the conventional signs already described.

In many surveys, as of roads, rivers, canals, and boundaries, the plot to be made is but a single line, with a few of the nearest local objects on either side. In some instances the angles at each intersection are taken merely with reference to the two lines forming the angle, and are therefore to be plotted as shown in fig. 23, by laying the protractor at each intersection; but in other instances, by the method of surveying, the directions of all lines are referred to the first as meridian, or if the survey is extensive, to some number of lines, and the plotting is then expeditiously performed as in fig. 27. In this system of surveying, instead of fixing the vernier at zero, for every back angle the preceding forward angle is retained except for those lines intended as meridians.

Surveys for railways, like those above, are of lines extensive in length but of very little width. In the surveys of preliminary or trial lines, the curves at the intersection of lines are seldom introduced; and in plotting it is but the usual method of plotting surveyed lines, by either of the methods, according as the survey may have been conducted, with the theodolite, or with the compass.

In plotting curves on a line of location, lay off from the intersection of tangents, as C, fig. 32, the distance of the tangent points A and B, and find the centre O of the curve, by the erection of perpendiculars to these

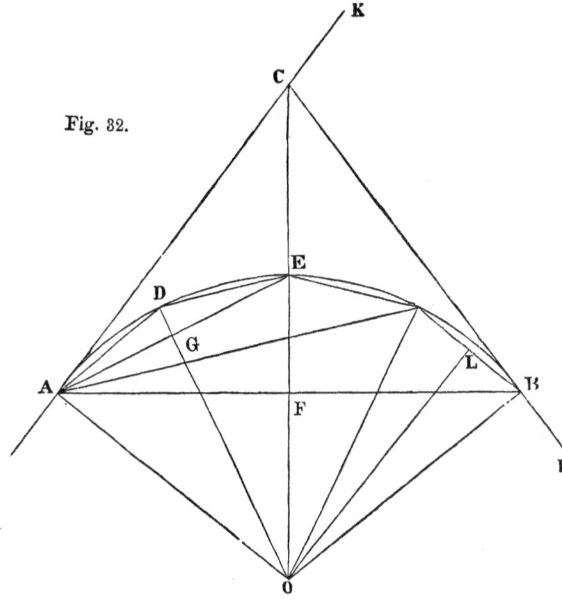

Fig. 32.

Degree.	Radii, ft.	Central Ordinate.
1°	5729.65	0.218
2°	2864.93	0.436
3°	1910.08	0.655
4°	1432.69	0.873
5°	1146.28	1.091
6°	955.37	1.309
7°	819.02	1.528
8°	716.78	1.746
9°	637.27	1.965
10°	573.69	2.183

two points, or if the radius of the curve is known, by describing arcs with this radius from the same points. Railway curves are designated by degrees or a curve of 1°, 2°, 3°, according to the angle of deflection made by two chords of 100 feet each, as the angle A D E, if the chords A D, D E each represent 100 feet.

Two curves often succeed each other having a common tangent, at the point of junction. If the curves lie on opposite sides of the common tangent, they form a reversed curve, A B C, (fig. 33,) and their radii may be the same or different. If they lie on the same side of the common tangent and have different radii, they form a compound curve, A B D. When the radii of curvature are known, the determination of the centres is obtained easily, by describing arcs with the established radii from the tangent points.

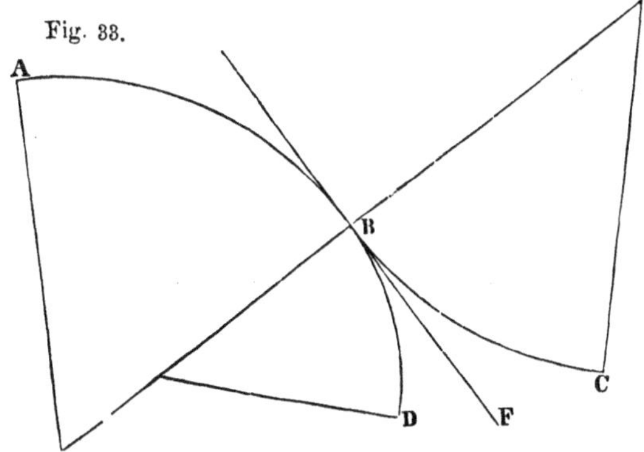

Fig. 33.

If the radii of curvatures are not known, and it is required to plot a compound or reversed curve which shall be tangent at the points A and D or C to other straight lines, the change of curvature taking place at B, then at A erect a perpendicular to the given line, find some point on this perpendicular which is equally distant from A and B, and this point will be the centre of the curve A B; through this point and B draw an indefinite line, its intersection by the perpendicular to the tangent at D will be the centre for the other portion of the compound curve; and its intersection by the perpendicular to the tangent at C will give the centre for the reversed. The centres of curves tangent to each other must lie in a straight line, passing through their point of connection.

When the curves are larger than can be described by the dividers or beam compasses, they can be plotted as shown in geometrical problems, or points of a curve may be obtained by calculation of their ordinates, and the curves drawn from point to point by sweeps and variable curves. Approximately, knowing the central ordinate of the curve between two points, the central ordinate of one half that curve will be one quarter of the first. Thus, fig 32, G D is about one quarter of E F, hence by subdivisions as many points as are necessary may be obtained; but it should be observed, that the greater the number of degrees in the arc, the less near to the truth the rule.

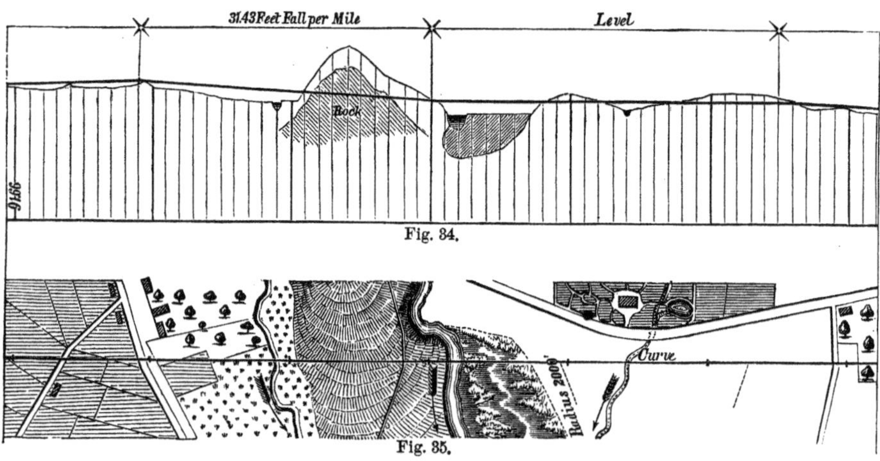

Fig. 34.

Fig. 35.

Fig. 35 represents a plot of a railway line; in this plot the curve is represented as a straight line, the radius of curvature being written in. This method is sometimes adopted when it is desirable to confine the plot within a limited space upon the sheet, and it is convenient when plotted thus directly beneath the profile or longitudinal section (fig. 34).

In plotting the section, a horizontal or base line is drawn on which are laid off the stations or distances at which levels have been taken; at these points perpendiculars or ordinates are erected, and upon them are marked the heights of the ground above the base, and the marks are joined by straight lines. To express rock in a cut, it is generally represented by diagonal lines; rivers are represented in section by cross lines or colored in blue; the depth of the sounding in a mud bottom by masses of dots.

Since it would be in general impossible to express the variations of the surface of the ground in the same scale as that adopted for the plan, it is usual therefore to make the vertical scale larger than that of the horizontal lines one, in proportion of 10 or 20 to 1. Thus, if the horizontal scale of the plan be 400 feet to the inch, the vertical scale would be 40 or 20 feet to the inch.

For the purpose of facilitating the plotting of profiles, profile paper is prepared, on which are printed horizontal and vertical lines; the horizontal lines being ruled at a distance of $\frac{1}{30}$ of an inch from each other, every fifth line being coarser, and every twenty-fifth still heavier than the others. Each of the spaces is usually considered one foot. The vertical lines are one quarter of an inch distant from each other, every tenth line being made more prominent than the others; these spaces in general represent a distance of 100 feet, the usual distance between stations on a railroad. Much time is saved by the use of this paper, both in plotting, and in reading the measurements after they are plotted.

In the plotting of sections across the line, which are extended but little beyond the line of the cut or embankment, equal vertical and horizontal scales are adopted; these plots are mostly to determine the position of the slope, or to assist in calculating the excavation. To facilitate these, cross section paper is prepared, ruled with vertical and horizontal lines, forming squares of $\frac{1}{10}$ of an inch each. Every fifth line in each direction is made prominent. When cross sections are extended to show the grade of cross road, or changes of level at considerable distance from the line of rail, the same scales vertical and horizontal are adopted as in the longitudinal section or profile.

It will be observed in fig. 34, that the upper or heavy line represents the line of the rail, the grades being written above; this is the more usual way, but sometimes, as in fig. 36, the profile and plan are combined; that

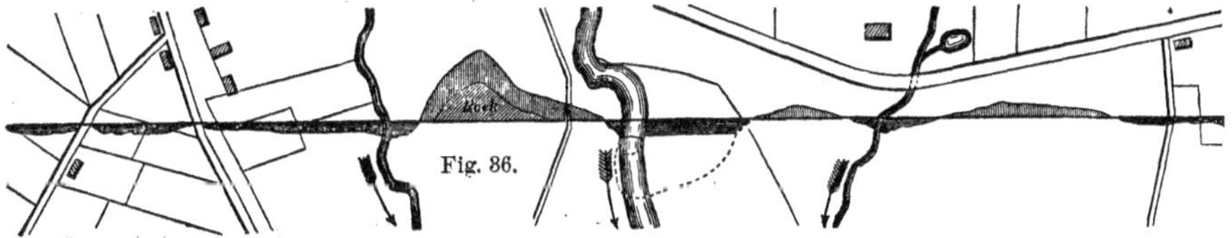

Fig. 36.

is, the heights and depths above and below the grade line of the road are transferred to the plan, and referred to the line in plan, which becomes thus a representation both in plan and elevation.

Cross sections, for grades of cross roads, etc., are usually plotted beneath or above the profile; they may, if necessary, be plotted across the line when plan and profile are combined.

Besides the complete plans as above, giving the details of the location, land plans, so called, are required, showing the position and direction of all lines, of fences and boundaries of estates, with but very few of the topographical features. The centre line of road is represented in bold line, and each side, generally in red, are represented the boundaries required for the purposes of way. In general, a width of five rods is the amount of land set off, lines parallel to the central line being at a distance of two and one half rods on each side; but when, owing to the depth of the cut or embankment, the slopes run out beyond this limit, the extent is determined by plotting a cross section and transferring the distances thus found to the plan, and enclosing all such points somewhat within the limits as set off for railway purposes. These plans are generally filed in the register's office for the county through which the line passes.

For Railway plans prepared for the English Parliament certain regulations are defined.

The plan must be upon a scale of at least four inches to a mile, and must describe the line or situation of the whole of the proposed work, and the lands through which the same will be made, and also any communication to be made with the proposed work. If the plan is on a scale less than ¼ of an inch to every 100 feet, there must be an additional plan upon that scale (1 : 4,800) of any building, yard, and of any ground cultivated as a garden.

The plan to exhibit thereon the distances in miles and furlongs, from one of the termini, with memoranda of the radii of all curves less than one mile in length, noted on the plan in chains where the curve occurs. When a tunnel is intended to be constructed, it must be marked in by a dotted line on the plan.

Each distinct property, divided by any visible boundary from another property, should have a separate number; with this exception, that any collection of buildings and grounds within the curtilage of a building, belonging to one person and in one occupation, may be described under one number; thus, farm house, yard, &c. When it is necessary to interpose a number, a duplicate number should be added; thus, 8*a*, 3*a*. The numbering should recommence in every parish.

All lands included within the limit of deviation, shown by lines drawn on plan, and all lands which those lines touch, must be numbered and described. Public roads, and private roads if fenced out, should have a separate number. Navigable and mill streams must be separately numbered.

It is sometimes usual, at the completion of a railway, to make plans of the works as finished; and, if a profile of the line, to represent the different strata or rocks in the cuts, with their dip or inclination. This is more properly a geological profile; the different rocks are usually distinguished by different colors and explained by marginal notes and squares, sometimes by marks, dots, and cross hatchings, as fig. 37, often by color in ad-

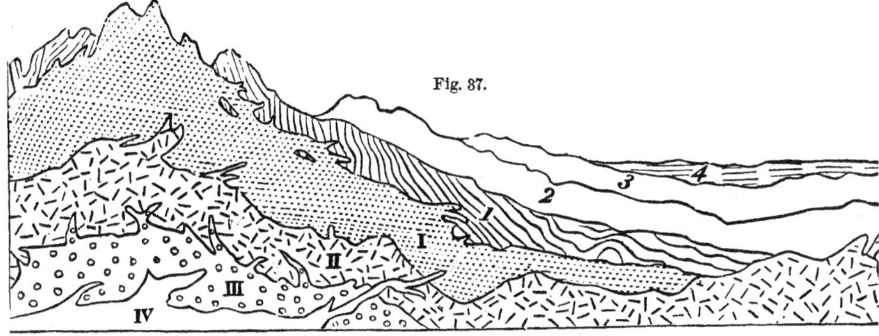

Fig. 37.

dition. Figs I., II., III., IV., represent the primary, secondary, tertiary, and recent plutonic rocks. Fig. 1 represents the primary fossiliferous strata; figs. 2, 3, 4, the secondary, tertiary, and recent strata. In the plots of geological sections, it is especially requisite that the different strata should be accurately represented.

In plotting hydrometrical or marine surveys, the depths of soundings are not expressed by sections, but by figures written on the plan, expressing the sounding or depth below a datum line, generally that of high water. The low water line is generally represented by a single continued line. The soundings are generally expressed in fathoms, sometimes in feet.

It is usual, in plotting from a field book, to make first but a rough draft, and then make a finished copy on another sheet. In the first, many lines of construction, balances of survey, and trial lines are drawn which are unnecessary in the copy; outlines of natural features are sketched roughly, but the plotting of surveys, and such lines and points as are to be preserved in the copy, must be plotted with accuracy.

The most common way of transferring, for a fair copy, is by superposition of the plan above the sheet intended for the copy, and pricking through every intersection of lines on the plan, and all such points as may be necessary to preserve. The clean paper should be laid and fastened smoothly on the drawing board, the rough draft should be laid on smoothly and retained in its position by weights, glue, or tacks. The needle must be held perpendicular to the surface of the plan, and pressed through both sheets; begin at one side and work with system, so as not to prick through each point but once, nor omit any; make the important points a trifle the largest. For the irregular curves, as of rivers, make frequent points, but very small ones. On removing the plan select the important points, those defining leading lines; draw in these, and the other points will be easily recognized from their relative position to these lines. When any point has not been pricked through, its place may be determined by taking any two established points adjacent to the one required, and with radii equal to their distance, on the plan, from the point required, describing arcs, on the copy, on the same side of the two points, their intersection will be the point desired. In this way, as in a trigonometrical survey, having established the two extremes of a base, a whole plan may be copied. For this purpose the triangular compasses (p. 27) will be found very convenient. In extensive drawings it is very common to prick off but a few of the salient points, and fill in by intersections, as above, or by copying detached portions on tracing paper, and transferring them to the copy; the position of each sketch being determined by the points pricked off, the transfer is made by pricking through as above, or by transfer paper placed between the tracing and the copy.

Tracing paper is a thin, transparent paper, prepared expressly for the purpose of making copies of drawings. Placed above the drawing, every line shows through, and is traced directly with the pen, in India ink. These tracings are used mostly to preserve duplicates of finished drawings. As tracing paper is of too slight a texture to bear much handling, cotton cloth is prepared and sold under the name of "vellum tracing paper." When it is necessary to use tracing paper drawings to work by, it is usual to attach them to sheets of white paper, which serves both to bring out the lines and to strengthen the paper.

Duplicates of drawings are now very neatly executed, and of course accurately copied, by the Photographic process, but it is more applied to mechanical and architectural drawings than topographical.

An accurate and rapid way of tracing, on drawing paper, plans of small extent, is by means of an instrument called a copying glass. It consists of a large piece of plate glass set in a frame of wood, which can be inclined at any angle in the same manner as a reading or music desk. On this glass is first laid the original plan, and above, the fair sheet, and the frame being raised to a suitable angle, a strong light is thrown by reflectors or otherwise on the under side of the glass, whereby every line in the original plan is seen distinctly through the fair sheet, and the copy is made at once, in ink, as on tracing paper, and finished while being traced. This same process, on a small scale, is adopted by putting the plans upon a pane of glass in a window.

Plans of great extent cannot be conveniently copied by means of the copying glass. Moreover, being often mounted on cloth, which renders them opaque, they do not admit of being traced in this way. In such cases the copy may be made by means of transfer paper. The plan is first traced in ink on tracing paper or cloth, black leaded or transfer paper is then placed on the fair sheet, and the tracing paper copy is placed above. All is steadied by numerous weights along the edges, or by drawing pins fixed into the drawing board. A fine and smooth point is then passed over each boundary or mark on the tracing with a pressure of the hand sufficient to cause a clear, pencilled mark to be left on the fair sheet by the black leaded or transfer paper. The whole outline is thus obtained, and afterwards drawn in ink. The copyist should be careful in his manipulations, so as not to transfer any other lines than those required, nor leave smutches on the fair sheet.

Plans may be copied on a reduced or enlarged scale by means of the pentagraph, but the more usual way is by means of squares. Draw on the plan to be reduced, a series of parallel and equi-distant lines, with others perpendicular to them at similar intervals, thus covering the whole surface with equal squares. On the clean sheet draw a similar set of squares, but with their sides to the desired reduced scale; one-half, one-third, &c., as the case may be. Then copy into each small square all the points and lines in the corresponding square on the plan, in their true position relative to the sides and corners of the square, reducing each distance, by proportional dividers, or by eye as may be necessary, in the given ratio. In reducing by the camera lucida, squares on the plan are brought apparently to coincide with squares in the copy, and the details as seen through the prism of the instrument, are then filled in with the pencil. This instrument is used in the U. S. Coast Survey office, but it cannot reduce smaller than one-fourth without losing distinctness, and it is very trying to the eyes.

Finishing the Plan or Map.—In general, in topographical as in architectural and mechanical drawings, the light is supposed to fall upon the surface in a diagonal direction from the upper, left-hand corner. This rule is not uniform: by some draughtsmen the light is introduced at the lower left, and hills are mostly represented under a vertical light, although the oblique adds more to the picturesque effect. The plan is usually so drawn that the top may represent the north, and the upper left-hand corner is then the north-west.

In inking in, commence first with the light lines, since a mistake in these lines may be covered by the shade lines. Describe all curves which are to be drawn with compasses or sweeps before the straight lines, for it is easier to join neatly a straight line to a curve than the opposite. Ink in with system, commencing say at the top; ink in all light lines running easterly and westerly, then all light lines running northerly and southerly, then commence in the same way and draw in the shade lines. It will of course be understood that elevated objects have their southern and eastern outline shaded, whilst depressions have the northern and western; thus in conventional signs roads are shaded the opposite to canals. Having inked in all lines that are drawn with a ruler or described with compasses, commence again at one corner to fill in the detail, keeping all the rest of the plan except what you are actually at work upon covered with paper, to protect it from being soiled. The curved lines of brooks, fences, &c., are sometimes drawn with a drawing pen, sometimes with a steel pen or goose quill. The latter are generally used in drawing the vertical lines of hills.

Boundary lines of private properties, of townships, of counties, of states, &c., are indicated by various combinations of short lines, dots and crosses, thus: —— —— —— —— ——·——·——·——·——· ——···——···——···——···——.

All plans should have meridian lines drawn on them, also scales. Plate I. represents several designs for meridians. In these diagrams it will be observed that both true and magnetic meridians are drawn; this is desirable when the variation is known, but in many surveys merely the magnetic meridian is taken; in these cases this line is simply represented with half of the barb of the arrow at the north point, and on the opposite side of the line from the true meridan. Scales are drawn or represented in various forms, as may be seen in the following plates, or the proportion of the plan to the ground is expressed decimally, as the number of feet, chains, etc., to the inch.

Lettering.—The style in which this is done very much affects the general appearance of the plan. Great care must be taken in the selection and character of the type, and in the execution. The usual letters are the

ROMAN.

ABCDEFGHIJKLMNO

PQRSTUVWXYZ&

PLATE II.

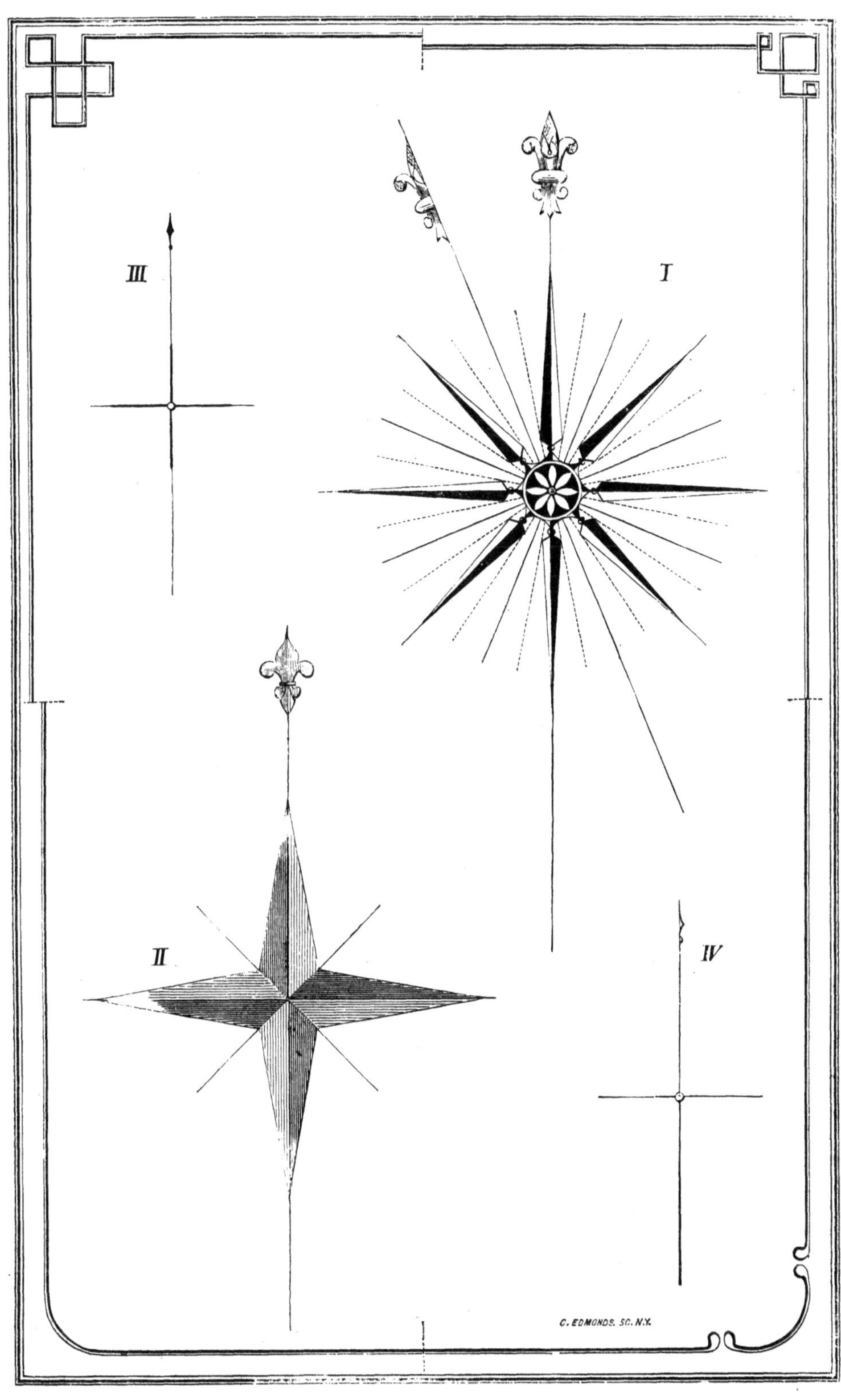

SMALL ROMAN.

abcdefghijklmnopqrstuv
wxyz,;:.

1234567890

ITALIC.

A B C D E F G H I J K L
M N O P Q R S T U V W
X Y Z &

abcdefghijklmnopqrst
uvwxyz;:

GOTHIC, OR EGYPTIAN.

ABCDEFGHIJKLMN
OPQRSTUVWX
YZ&,;:.

OLD ENGLISH SCRIBE BLACK.

ABCDEFGHIJKLMNOP

QRSTUVWXYZ&

abcdefghijklmnopqrstuvwxyz

1234567890,;:.

GERMAN TEXT.

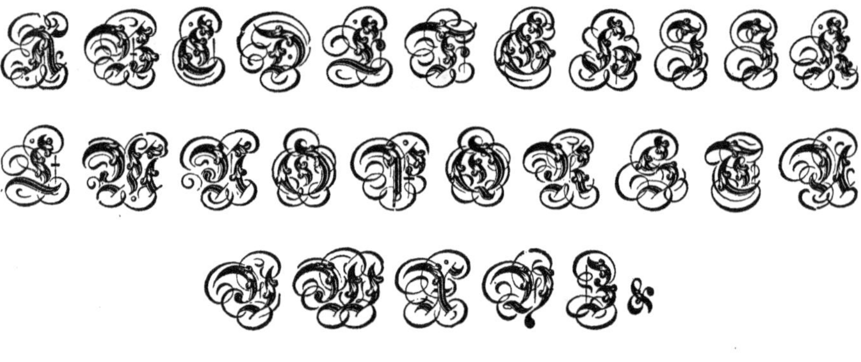

abcdefghijklmnopqrstuvwxyz,;:.

1234567890

CLARENDON.

ABCDEFGHIJKLMNOP

QRSTUVWXYZ&

SMALL CLARENDON.

abcdefghijklmnopqrstu
vwxyz,;:.

GRECIAN.

ABCDEFGHIJKLMNOPQRST
UVWXYZ& :,..

OLD ENGLISH.

ABCDEFGHIJKLMN
OPQRSTUVWXYZ&
abcdefghijklmnopqrstuvwxyz
1234567890 ,;:.

ABCDEFGHIJKLMNOP
QRSTUVWXYZ&,;:.

ABCDEFGHIJKLMNOPQRSTUVW
XYZ&,;:.

ENGLISH OUTLINE.

ABCDEFGHIJKLMNOPQRSTU
VWXYZ&,;:.

Plate III. represents a mechanical method of constructing letters and figures. This plate should be copied by the draftsman, and on a much larger scale, by drawing first the system of squares or parallelograms, and then sketching in the letters; in this way well formed and proportioned letters can always be made, and from a selection of alphabets the lettering may be selected and transferred to the plan.

Plate IV. are examples of titles, intended merely as an illustration of the form of letters and their arrangement, the scale being much smaller than that used on plans, except such as are drawn to a very small scale. It will be observed that the more important words are made in prominent type. The lower part of the title should always contain, in small character, the name of the party making the survey, and also the name of the draftsman, with date of the execution of the plan: if the survey was made some time previous, the date of the survey should be given. If the plan is compiled from several surveys, the authorities should, if possible, be given. The lettering of the title should be in lines parallel to the bottom of the plan, and, in general, the great mass of lettering in the body of the plan is formed in similar lines; but curved lines are often not only essential, but they materially contribute to the beauty of the plan. Thus on crooked boundaries on outlines of maps, the lettering should follow the general curve of the boundary; also on crooked rivers, lakes, seas, &c.; on irregular or straggling pieces of land, in order to show the extent, connection, or proprietorship thereof, the lettering should follow the central line of such a tract; and if pieces of land be very oblong in form but regular in outline, the lettering will be central in the direction of the longest side. The lettering of roads, streets, &c., is always in the direction of the line of road. Curved lines of lettering are often introduced into extended titles to take off the monotonous appearance presented by a great number of straight lines of writing.

The direction of all lettering should be so as to be read from left to right. If shades or shadows are introduced to give relief or break up the monotony, they should be uniform with the rest of the plan.

On the Spacing of Letters.—It will be observed that letters vary very considerably in their width, the *I* being the narrowest, and the *W* the

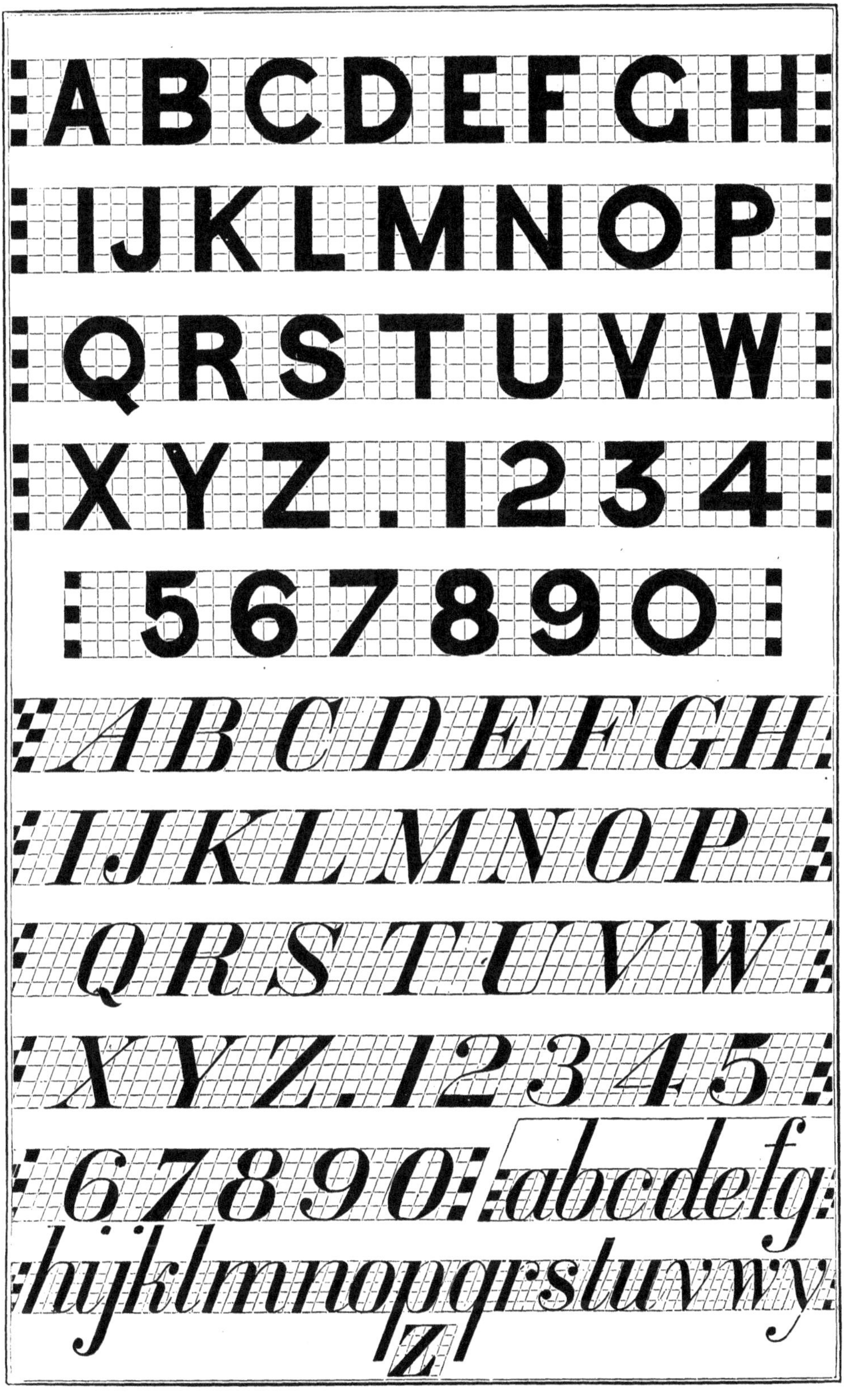

ABCDEFGH
IJKLMNOP
QRSTUVW
XYZ.1234
567890

ABCDEFGH
IJKLMNOP
QRSTUVW
XYZ.12345
67890 abcdefg
hijklmnopqrstuvwy
z

PROPOSED RAIL ROAD

BETWEEN

NEW-ROCHELLE & NEW YORK.

THE ESTATE OF

HENRY HALL, ESQ.

in the Town of

YONKERS.

Surveyed & drawn by

John Smith, C. E.

Scale of Chains:

May, 1857.

widest: if therefore the letters composing a word be spaced off at equal distances from centre to centre, the interval or space between the letters will be more in some cases than in others. Thus, in the word

R A I L W A Y

To avoid this, write in first one letter, and then space off a proper interval, and then write in the next letter, and then space off the interval as before, and so on, thus,

R A I L W A Y

When, as frequently happens, the words are very much extended, in order to embrace and explain a large extent of surface or boundary, and the space occupied by the letter is small in comparison with the interval, the disparity of intervals will not be noticed, and the letters may be then laid off at equal spaces from centre to centre, thus:

R A I L W A Y

When the lines of lettering are curved, the same rules for spacing are to be observed as above. If the letters are upright, as Roman or Gothic, the sides of each letter are to be parallel to the radius drawn to the centre of the letter, and the bottom and top lines at right angles to it. If the letters be inclined as Italic letters, then the side lines of the letters must be inclined to the central radial line, as on a horizontal line they are inclined to the perpendicular.

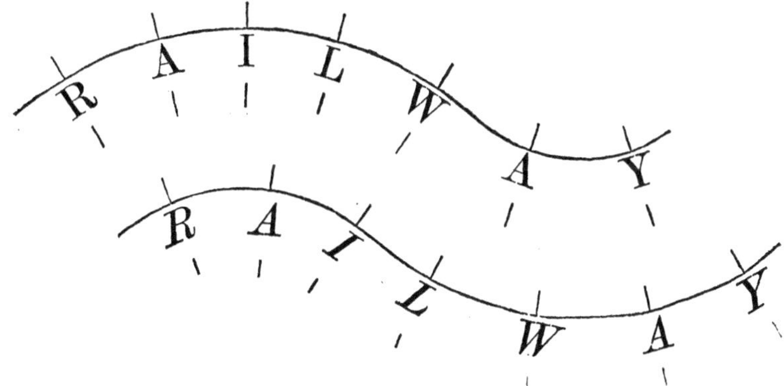

In laying off letters by equal intervals, it is usual to count the number of letters in the word, and fix the position on the plan of the central one, and then space off on each side: this is particularly important in titles, when it is necessary that many lines should have their extremities at uniform distances from the centre line. In laying off the title, we determine what is necessary to be included in the title, the space it must occupy, the number of lines necessary, and the style and arrangement of characters to be used. Thus, if the title were, plan of a proposed terminus of the Harlem Railroad at New York, 1857, knowing the space to be occupied, we can write the title thus:—

Plan

of the

Proposed Terminus

of the

Harlem Railroad,

at

New York,

1857.

We now draw parallel lines at intervals suited to the character of the type we intend to employ for the different words. *Harlem Railroad* is the line to be made most prominent; this, calling the interval between the words one letter, includes 15 letters; or, if we consider *I*, with its proper interval, but half a letter, (which will be found a very good rule in spacing,) 14½; hence the centre of the line will be 7¼ letters from the beginning, or ¼ of the space occupied by the letter *R* and its interval. Draw a perpendicular line at the centre, and write in *R* in such a character as may suit the position to be filled, and lay off by letters and spaces the other letters. The line *Harlem Railroad* is intended to occupy the whole length of space; that is, it must be the longest line in the title, and the lines above and below must gradually diminish, forming a sort of double pyramid. *Proposed Terminus* includes 16½ letters, the *I* and interval between the words being rated as above, we find the centre to be nearly midway beween the words. These words including more letters, and being confined within less space, must be in smaller character than the preceding; and as a further distinction, a different style should be adopted. Having determined this, we proceed to write in the letters as before, and in the same way with the other lines, the prepositions as unimportant are always written in small type.

Plan

of the

PROPOSED TERMINUS

of the

HARLEM RAILROAD

at

NEW YORK

1857

In general it is better that letters should be first written on a piece of paper, distinct from the plan, as repeated trials may be necessary before one is arranged to suit the draughtsman. Having formed a model title, it may be copied in the plan by measures or by tracing and transfer paper. There are some words, such as Plan, Map, Section, Scale, Elevation, &c., which, as they are of constant occurrence, may be cut in stencil; sometimes whole alphabets are thus cut and words compounded. It will be found very convenient for a draughtsman if he makes tracing or copies of such titles as he meets with, and preserves them as models; for there is no manipulation on a plan that contributes more to the effect than good lettering and arrangement of titles, and considerable practice should be expended in acquiring a facility in lettering, and for the first start, perhaps nothing will be found more valuable than tracing good examples.

We have treated of mechanical methods by which most persons can learn to form letters and words; but it must be borne in mind that the distances between letters on the plan are only intended to suit the eye; if therefore a person accustom himself to spacing, so that his eye is correct, there will be no necessity of laying off by dividers; in this mode, such letters as A and V, L and T are brought nearer each other than the regular interval. In general it may be observed in reference to to the lettering of Topographical Drawings, stiff letters like those of stencil should not be introduced, but there should be such variety, incident on construction by the pen, as may be consonant with the rest of the drawing.

TINTED TOPOGRAPHICAL DRAWING.

We have hitherto treated of the representation of the features of the country by the pen only, but it may be done full as effectively and much more expeditiously by means of the brush and water colors, either by India ink alone, or by various tints, or by the union of both.

The most important colors for conventional tints are, (besides India ink), Indigo (blue), Carmine (or crimson lake), and Gamboge (yellow), used separately or compounded. Besides these, Burnt Sienna, Yellow Ochre, and Vermilion are sometimes used, although the three first are susceptible of the best combinations, and the others are generally used alone.

The following conventional colors are used by the French Military Engineers in their colored topography. Woods, *yellow;* using gamboge and a very little indigo. Grass land, *green;* made of gamboge and indigo. Cultivated land, *brown;* lake, gamboge, and a little India ink; "Burnt Sienna" will answer. Adjoining fields should be slightly varied in tint. Sometimes furrows are indicated by strips of various colors. Gardens are represented by small rectangular patches of brighter *green* and *brown.* Uncultivated land, marbled *green* and light *brown.* Brush, brambles, &c., marbled green and yellow. Heath, furze, &c., marbled *green* and *pink.* Vineyards, *purple;* lake and indigo. Sands, a light *brown;* gamboge and lake; "Yellow Ochre" will do. Lakes and rivers, light *blue,* with a darker tint on their upper and left hand sides. Seas, dark *blue,* with a little yellow added. Marshes, the *blue* of water, with spots of grass *green,* the touches all lying horizontally. Roads, *brown;* between the tints for sand and cultivated ground, with more India ink. Hills, *greenish* brown; gamboge, indigo, lake and India ink. Woods may be finished up by drawing the trees and coloring them green, with touches of gamboge towards the light, (the upper and left hand side,) and of indigo on the opposite side.

In addition to the conventional colors, a sort of imitation of the conventional signs already explained are introduced in color with the brush, and shadows are almost invariably introduced. The light is supposed to come from the upper left hand corner, and to fall nearly vertical, but sufficiently oblique to allow of a decided light and shade to the slopes of hills, trees, &c. The shadow of any object will therefore surround its lower right hand outlines. After the shadow has been painted, the outline of the object is strengthened by a heavy black line on the side opposite the light. The flat tints are first laid on as above, and then the conventional signs are drawn in with a pencil and colored in with appropriate and more intense tints; the shadows are generally represented in India ink.

Hills are shaded, not as they would appear in nature, but on the conventional system of making the slopes darker in proportion to their steepness: the summit of the highest ranges being left white. This arrangement, though obviously incorrect in theory, has the advantage of being generally understood by those not accustomed to plan drawing, and is also easy of execution. Wash the surface first with the proper flat tint, trace in with a pencil, outlines; then lay on in India ink tints proportioned in intensity to the height of the hills and steepness of the slopes. To soften the tints two brushes are used, one as a color brush, the other as a water brush: the tints are laid on with the first, and softened by passing the water brush rapidly along the edges. The water brush must not have too much water, as it would in that case, lighten the tint to a greater extent than is intended, and leave a ragged harsh edge. Tints may be applied in very light shades, one tint over another, with the boundary of the upper tint not reaching the extreme limit of the tint below it. When depth of shade is required, it is best produced by application of several light tints in succession: no tint is to be laid over the other until the first is dry, and a little indigo mixed with the India ink improves its color and adds to the richness of effect.

When woods have to be represented, the shading used for the trees instead of interfering with the shadows due to the slopes, may be made to harmonize with them, and contribute to the general effect by presenting greater or less depth, according to the position of the woods on the sides, or summits of the hills.

An expeditious and effective way of representing hills with brush, a species of imitation of hills drawn with a pen on the vertical system, is effected by pressing out flat the brush to a sort of comb-like edge; drawing this over a nearly dry surface of India ink, and then brushing lightly or more heavily between the contours, according to the steepness of the slope, each of the comb-like teeth making its mark.

Rivers and masses of water may be shaded in with a color and water brush as above, or by superposition of light tints, a shadow may be thrown from the bank towards the light, and the outline of this bank strengthened with a heavy black line. The tints are to be in indigo, the shadows in India ink.

Topographical drawings may be made in water color with but one tint, as India ink, or ink mixed with a little sepia. The conventional signs are in imitation of pen drawings, the hills in softened tint, or drawn with the comb-edged brush, and the rivers shaded with superposed tints.

Most artistic and effective drawings are made of hills as they would appear in nature, under an oblique light: the sides of the hills next the light receiving it more or less brilliantly, according as they are inclined more or less at right angles with its rays, and the shades on the sides removed from the light increasing in intensity as the slopes increase in steepness. This style may be rendered most expressive by a skilful draughtsman, especially when the character and strike of the hills are favorable to the direction of the light, but with this style of representation the hills are generally made to partake more or less of the same character, appearing almost uniformly steepest on the sides removed from the light. It partakes therefore more of the artistic character, more difficult to execute, and conveying information in a more vague manner than by the common topographical conventionalities. As a picture it must be left to explain itself; the writing and outline necessarily introduced on the plan contribute to mar its effect.

In preparing the paper for a tinted drawing it must be damp-stretched upon the drawing board in such a manner that the moisture of the color will not cause undulations or blisters on the surface: this process is previously described at page 37. Having prepared a sheet of paper according to the directions there given, first draw in the lines in pencil, and afterwards repeat them with a very light ink line: a soft sponge well saturated should then be passed quickly over the surface of the drawing, in order to remove any portions of the ink which would be liable to mix with the tint and mar its uniformity. When the paper is dry proceed to lay on the conventional tints.

Great care is necessary in preparing and combining the different colors, and attention to certain mechanical conditions and rules must be observed in order to insure neatness and despatch in execution. The cakes of color are quite brittle, and it is well to moisten the end and allow it to soften slightly before using, then rub upon a perfectly clean palette, with a few drops of pure water, a sufficient quantity of color to tinge to the proper intensity as much water as will be required for the whole drawing, This should be thoroughly mixed with the brush, and as often as the brush is filled, to insure uniformity in the tint.

Previous to applying the tint, it is well to moisten the surface to be colored with clean water, which will prevent the tint from drying too rapidly at the edges. In tinting never allow the edge to dry until the whole surface is covered: leave a little superfluous color along the edge whilst filling the brush. Great caution is necessary in approaching the outlines of the drawing, and the point of the brush should be used so as not to overrun the lines.

In applying a flat tint to large surfaces, let the drawing board be inclined upwards at an angle of 5 or 6 degrees, so as to allow the color to flow downwards over the surface. With a moderately full brush commence at the upper outline, and carry the color along uniformly from left to right and from right to left in horizontal bands, taking care not to overrun the outlines, in approaching which the point of the brush should be used, and at the lower outline let there be only sufficient color in the brush to complete the tinting.

No color should be allowed to accumulate in inequalities of the paper, but should be evenly distributed over the whole surface.

Too much care cannot be given to the first application of color; as any attempt to remedy a defect by washing or applying fresh tints will be found extremely difficult, and to generally make bad worse.

Erasers should never be used on a tinted drawing to remove stains or patches, as the paper when scratched, receives the tint more readily, and retains a larger portion of color than other parts, thereby causing a darker tint.

Marbling is done by using two separate tints, and blending them at their edges. A separate brush is required for each tint; before the edge of the first is dry, pass the second tint along the edge, blending one tint into the other, and continue with each tint alternately.

In reference to the general effect to be produced in tinted topographical drawings, as to intensity, every thing should be subordinate to clearness, no tint should be prominent or obtrusive. Tints that are of small extent must be a little more intense than large surfaces, or they will appear lighter in shade. Keep a general tone throughout the whole drawing. Beginners will find it best to keep rather low in tone, strengthening their tints as they acquire boldness of touch.

In lettering tinted drawings, let the letters harmonize with the rest of the plan; let them be in tint more intense than the topography, prominent but not obtrusive.

Flourishes around the titles may be used on handsome estate maps, and on engraved maps of countries. They should be used in proportion to the degree of finish bestowed on the rest of the map; and while they give grace and elegance to the title when used in moderation, care should be taken to prevent their having too prominent an appearance.

Plate V. is a map of the Harbor and City of New Haven, reduced from the charts of the U. S. Coast Survey, without the depth of soundings or the marks of shoals.

Plate VI. is a representation of map drawing as executed by the brush in India ink only. The hills are drawn with a comb-edged brush in nearly dry color, as already described; in the following plate they are in blended tint.

Plate VII. a similar map in color, represented according to the conventional signs, and executed as described in the previous pages.

Plate VIII. contains plan and sections of strata of a lead mine copied from Greenwell's "Mine Engineering," intended as illustrations in this department of the profession. On geological maps sections are similarly represented, and plans are colored in patches according to the formation. Shades of India ink usually represent coal measures; of blue, limestone; of pink, the igneous rocks, as trap, granite, &c. In all cases, there are small blocks of color at the margin of the map, to designate the mineral represented by each.

In all the departments of drawing, we have thus tried to illustrate as fully as the limits of this work would admit, the general principles of representation and the rules of projection; but in addition, we would recommend to every one who wishes to make himself a perfect draughtsman, that he should collect good charts and drawings, study them, and in his leisure moments copy them. In this way he will acquire a readiness of manipulation, and ease and freedom of expression.

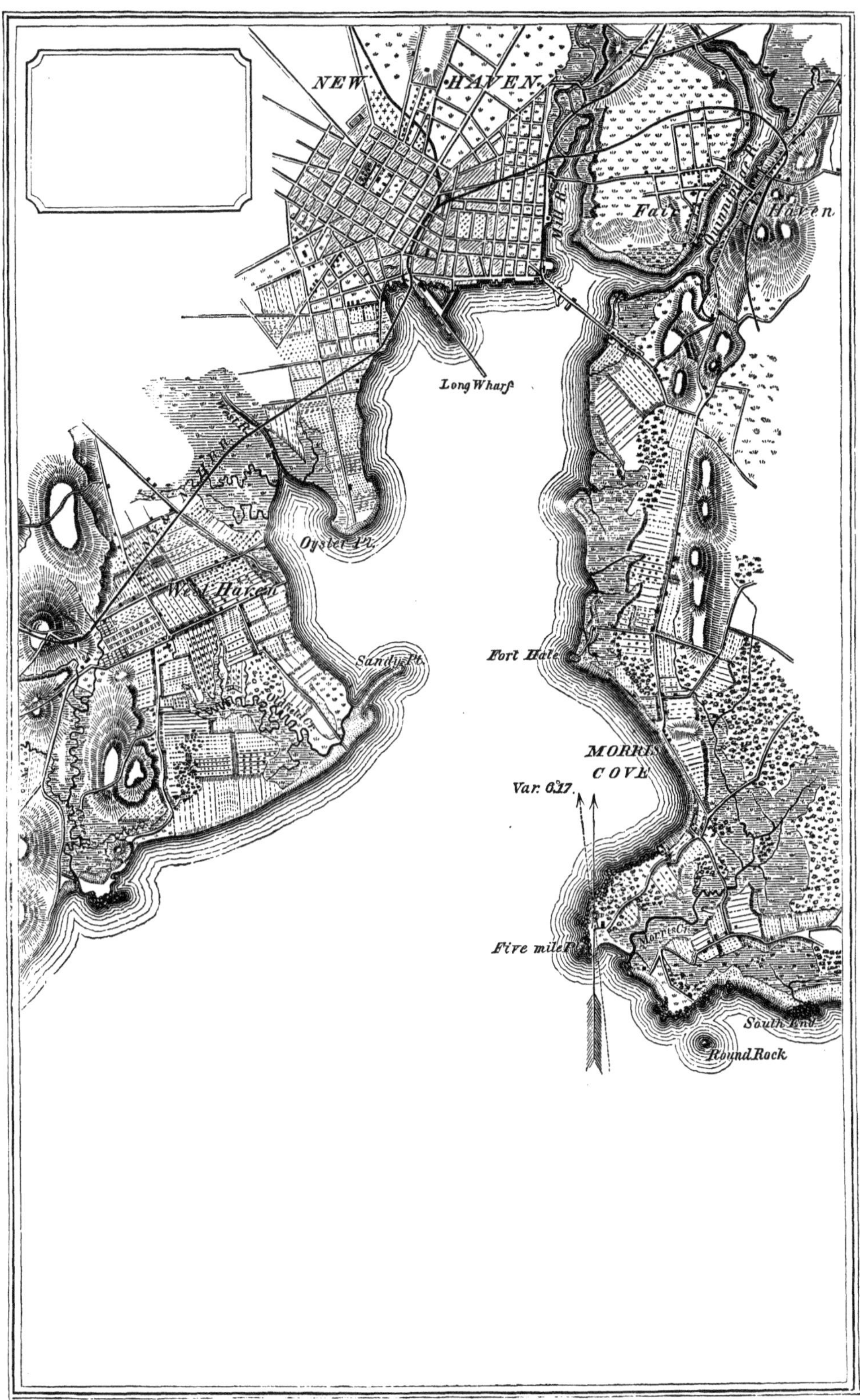
NEW HAVEN.
Haven
Long Wharf
Oyster Pt.
West Haven
Sandy Pt.
Fort Hale
COVE
Var. 6°17'.
Five mile Pt.
Round Rock

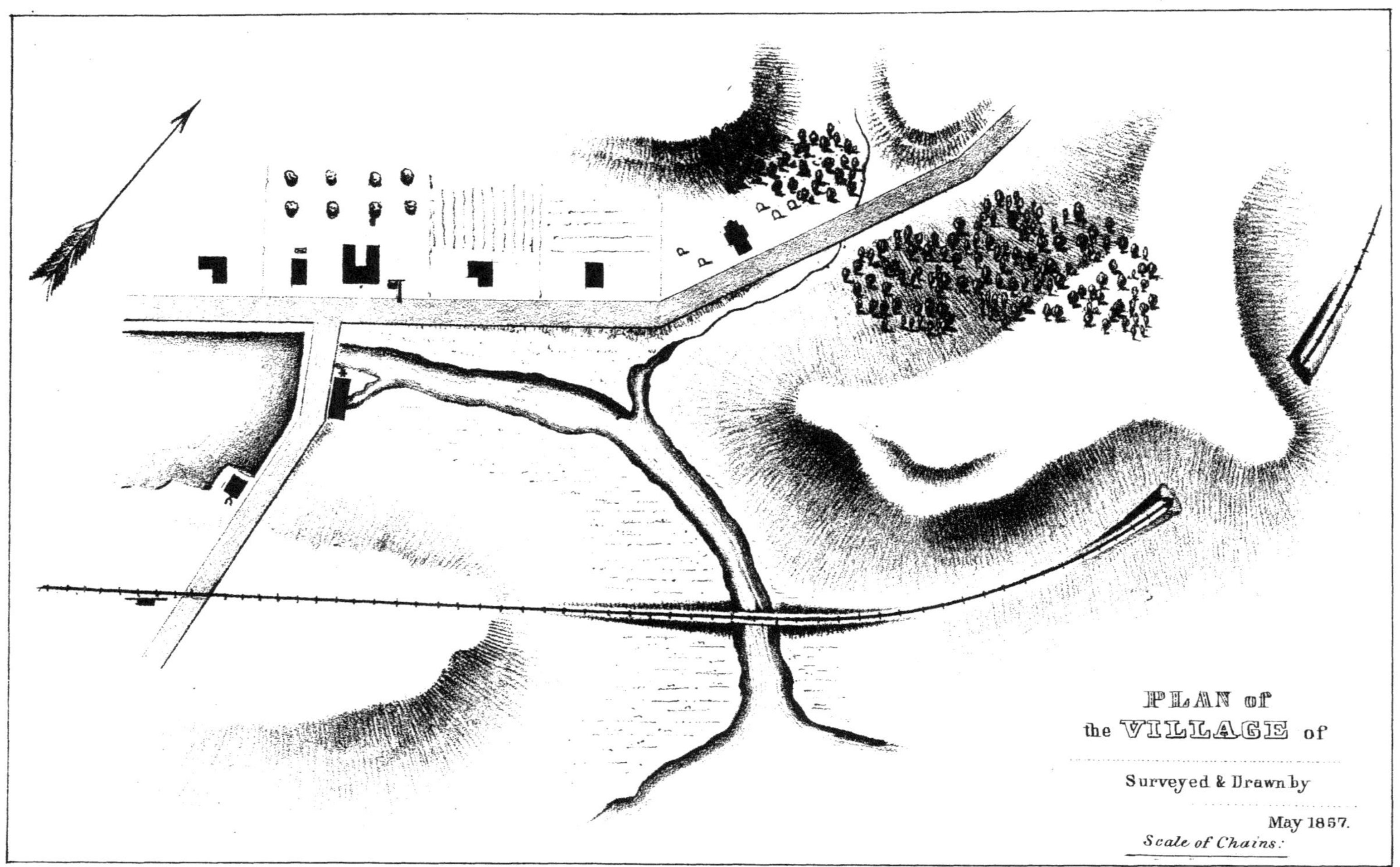
PLAN of
the VILLAGE of
Surveyed & Drawn by
May 1857.
Scale of Chains:

COPYING OF DRAWINGS BY PHOTOGRAPHY.

As it is now quite common to make copies of drawings by Photography, it seems not out of place to give a brief abstract of the process as taken from the "Manual of Photography" by Robert Hunt.

The most simple method of obtaining sun pictures is that of placing the drawing to be copied on a sheet of prepared paper, pressing it close by a piece of glass, and exposing the arrangement to sunshine; all the parts exposed darken, while those covered are protected from change, the resulting picture being white on a dark ground: such pictures are called *negative photographs*. *Positive* photographs, those which are correct copies of the drawing, are obtained by the super-position of the negative upon another piece of prepared paper. Some kind of copying frame is an indispensable requisite to the photographer; it is used for copying all objects by transmission, and for multiplying the original pictures obtained by means of the camera obscura from nature. Some prefer two plates of stout plate glass pressed very closely together with clamps and screws; but as the intention is to bring the object to be copied and the sensitive paper into the closest possible contact, numerous mechanical contrivances will suggest themselves for the purpose to the ingenious.

Select a paper of a uniform texture, free from spots and of equal transparency, choosing the oldest rather than the newest varieties. In the preparation of paper, the only apparatus required are some very soft sponge brushes and large camel-hair pencils, (no metal should be employed in mounting the brushes, as it decomposes the silver salts,) a wide shallow vessel capable of receiving the sheet without folds, a few smooth planed boards sufficiently large to stretch the paper upon, and a porcelain or glass slab; also some good *white* blotting paper, soft linen or cotton cloth, a box of pins, a glass rod or two, some porcelain capsules, and some beaker glasses, graduated measures, scales and weights.

I would advise the amateur to start upon his studies with but three solutions: 1st, chloride of sodium; 2d, nitrate of silver; 3d, hyposulphite of soda.

Muriated Papers, as they are termed, are formed by producing a chloride of silver on their surface, by washing the paper with the solution of the chloride of sodium, (*muriate of soda*,) or any other chloride, and when the paper is dry, with a solution of nitrate of silver. Take some flat deal boards perfectly clean, pin upon them by their four corners, the paper to be prepared, observing the two sides of the paper, and selecting that side to receive the preparation which presents the hardest and most uniform surface. Then, dipping one of the sponge brushes into the solution of chloride of sodium, a sufficient quantity is taken up by it to moisten the surface of the paper without any hard rubbing, and this is to be applied with great regularity. The papers being "salted," are allowed to dry: a great number of these may be prepared at a time, and kept in a portfolio for use. To render these sensitive, the papers being pinned on the boards or carefully laid upon folds of white blotting paper, are to be washed over with the nitrate of silver, applied by means of a camel-hair pencil, observing the instructions previously given as to the method of moving the brush upon the paper. After the first wash is applied, the paper is to be dried, and then subjected to a second application of the silver solution. Thus prepared, it will be sufficiently sensitive for all purposes of copying by application. The second wash is applied for the purpose of insuring an excess of the nitrate of silver in combination, or more properly speaking, mixed with the chloride. The proportions in which the chloride of sodium have been used are exceedingly various; in general, the solutions have been made too strong, but several chemists have recommended washes that are as much too weak. For copies of engravings or drawings the following proportions should be used:

Chloride of sodium, twenty-five grains to an ounce of water. Nitrate of silver ninety-nine grains to an ounce of distilled water.

The paper is first soaked in the saline solution, and after being carefully pressed between folds of blotting-paper and dried, it is to be washed twice with the solution of silver, drying it by a warm fire between each washing.

Of all the fixing agents, the hyposulphite of soda is decidedly the best.

The picture, or as many of them as there may be, is to be soaked in warm water, but not warmer than may be borne by the finger; this water is to be changed once or twice, and the pictures are then to be well drained, and either dried all together, or pressed in clean and dry blotting-paper to prepare them to imbibe a solution of the hyposulphite of soda, which may be made by dissolving an ounce of that salt in a quart of water. Having poured a little of the solution into a flat dish, the pictures are to be introduced one by one; daylight will not now injure them; let them soak for two or three minutes, or even longer if strongly printed, turning and moving them occasionally. The remaining unreduced salts of silver are thus thoroughly removed by soaking in water and pressing in clean blotting paper alternately; but if time can be allowed, soaking in water alone will have the effect in twelve or twenty-four hours, according to the thickness of the paper. It is essential to the succees of the fixing process, that the paper be in the first place thoroughly penetrated by the hyposulphite, and the sensitive matter dissolved; and next, that the hyposulphite compounds be effectually removed.

The hyposulphite of silver being formed, it has to be dissolved out of the paper, the fibres of which hold it with a strong capillary force; and it is only by very long continued soaking that all can be removed. The slight mechanical aid afforded by dapping the surface of the paper with a soft sponge well filled with water, greatly accelerates the removal of the salt; and when the paper ceases to *taste sweet*, we may depend upon the permanence of the photograph.

PERSPECTIVE DRAWING.

The science of Perspective is the representation by geometrical rules, upon a plane surface, of objects as they appear to the eye, from any point of view.

All the points of the surface of a body are visible by means of luminous rays proceeding from these points to the eye. Thus, let the line A B (fig. 1) be placed before the eye, C, the lines drawn from the different points 1, 2, 3, 4, &c., represent the visual rays emanating from each of these points. It is easy to understand that, if in the place of a line a plane or curved surface is substituted, the result will be a cone of rays.

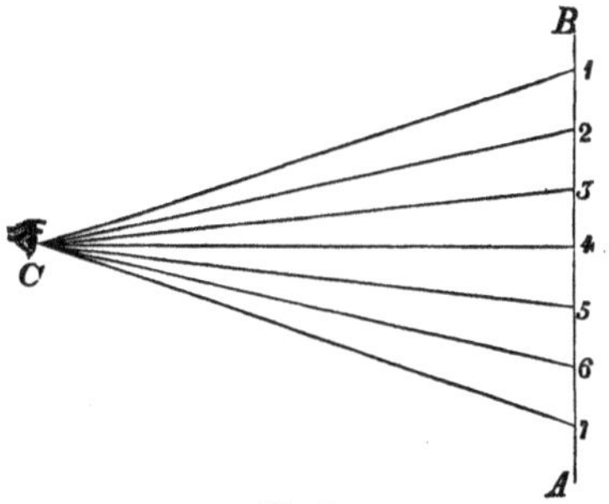

Fig. 1.

Let A B (fig. 2) be a straight line, and let the globe of the eye be represented by a circle, and its pupil by the point C. The ray emanating from A, entering through C, will proceed to the retina of the eye, and be depicted at *a*. And as it follows that all the points of A B will send rays, entering the eye through C, the whole image of A B will be depicted on the retina of the

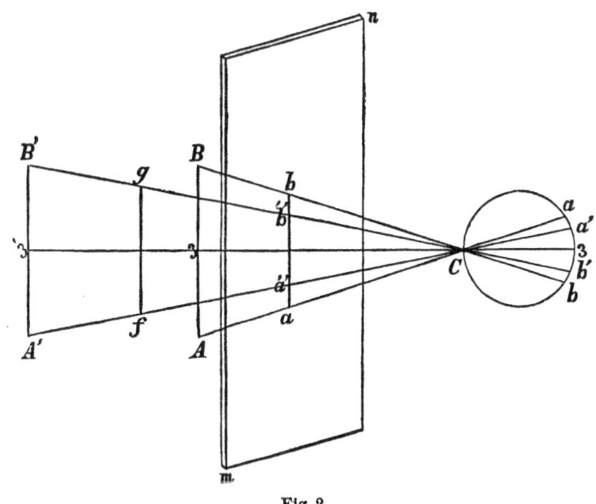

Fig. 2.

eye in a curved line *a* 3 *b*. Conceive the line AB moved to a greater distance from the eye, and placed at A′ B′, then the optic angle will be reduced, and the image *a′* 3 *b′* will be less than before; and as our visual sensations are in proportion to the magnitude of the image painted on the retina, it may be concluded that the more distant an object is from the eye, the smaller the angle under which it is seen becomes, and consequently the farther the same object is removed from the eye the less it appears.

Observation has rendered it evident, that the greatest angle under which one or more objects can be distinctly seen, is one of 90°. If between the object and the eye there be interposed a transparent plane (such as one of glass *m n*), the intersection of this plane with the visual rays are termed perspectives of the points from which the rays emanate. Thus *a* is the perspective of A, *b* of B, and so on of all the intermediate points; but, as two points determine the length of a straight line, it follows that *a b* is the perspective of A B, and *a′ b′* the perspective of A′ B′.

It is evident from the figure that objects appear more or less great according to the angle under which they are viewed; and further, that objects of unequal size may appear equal if seen under the same angle. For draw *f g*, and its perspective will be found to be the same as that of A′ B′.

It follows also, that a line near the eye may be viewed under an angle much greater than a line of greater dimensions but more distant, and hence a little object may appear to be much greater than a similar object of larger dimensions. Since, therefore, unequally sized objects may appear equal in size, and equally sized objects unequal, and since objects are not seen as they are in effect, but as they appear under certain conditions, perspective may be defined to be a science which affords the means of representing, on any surface whatever, objects such as they appear when seen from a given point of view. It is divided into two branches, the one called linear perspective, occupying itself with the delineation of the contours of bodies, the other called aerial perspective, with the gradations of colors produced by distance. It is the former of these only, that is proposed here to be discussed.

The perspective of objects, then, is obtained by the intersection of the rays which emanate from them to the eye, by a plane or other surface (which is called the picture), situated between the eye and the objects.

From the explanation and definition just given, it is easy to conceive that linear perspective is in reality the problem of constructing the section, by a surface of some kind, of a pyramid of rays of which the summit and the base are given. The eye is the summit, the base may be regarded as the whole visible extent of the object or objects to be represented, and the intersecting surface is the picture.

A good idea of this will be obtained by supposing the picture to be a transparent plane, through which the object may be viewed, and on which it may be depicted.

In addition to the vertical and horizontal planes with which we are familiar in the operations of projection, several auxiliary planes are employed in perspective, and particularly the four following:

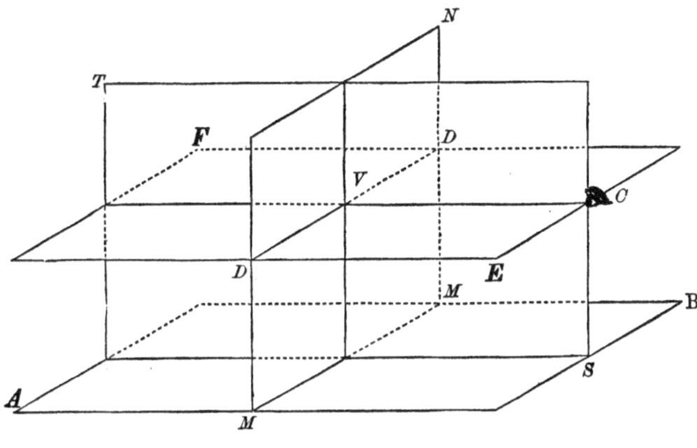

Fig. 3.

1. The horizontal plane A B (fig. 3), on which the spectator and the objects viewed are supposed to stand, for convenience supposed perfectly level, is termed the *ground plane.*

2. The plane M N, which has been considered as a transparent plane placed in front of the spectator, on which the objects are delineated, is called the *plane of projection* or the *plane of the picture.* The intersection M M of the first and second planes is called the line of projection, the *ground*, or *base line of the picture.*

3. The plane E F passing horizontally through the eye of the spectator, and cutting the plane of the picture at right angles, is called the horizontal plane, and its intersection at D D with the plane of the picture is called the *horizon line*, the *horizon* of the picture, or simply the *horizon.*

4. The plane S T passing vertically through the eye of the spectator, and cutting each of the other planes at a right angle, is called the *central plane.*

Point of view, or *point of sight*, is the point where the eye is supposed to be placed to view the object, as at C, and is the vertex of the optic cone. Its projection on the ground plane S is termed the *station point.*

The projection of any point on the ground plane is called the seat of that point.

Centre of view (commonly, though erroneously, called the point of sight), is the point V where the central vertical line intersects the horizon line; a line drawn from this point to the eye would be in every way perpendicular to the plane of the picture.

Points of distance, are points on the horizontal line, as remote from the centre of view as the eye.

Vanishing points, are points in a picture to which all lines converge that in the original object are parallel to each other.

Parallel perspective.—An object is said to be seen in parallel perspective when one of its sides is parallel to the plane of the picture.

Angular perspective.—An object is said to be seen in angular perspective when none of its sides are parallel to the picture.

To find the perspective of points, as the points *m*, *s*, (fig. 4) in the ground

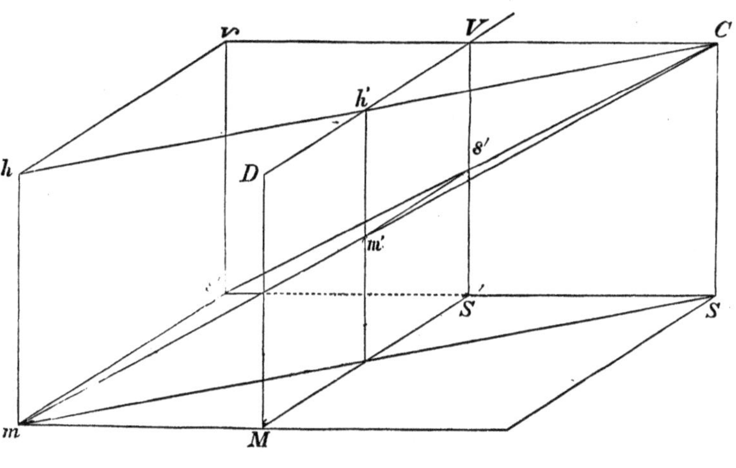

Fig. 4.

plane, the same letters designating similar planes and points as in fig. 3. From the point *m* draw a line to the point of sight C, and also to the station point S, at the intersection of the line *m* S with the base line M S′, erect a perpendicular cutting the line *m* C, the intersection *m′* will be the perspective projection of the point *m*, on the plane of the picture M V. The point *s* being in the central plane, its projection must be in the intersection of that plane by the plane of the picture, as the point *s′* the intersection of the central vertical line by the line *s* C. The point *v* being both in the central and horizontal plane, its projection in the plane of the picture must be in the intersection of all three planes, or at the point of view V. The point *h* being in the horizontal plane, its projection must be in the intersection of this plane with the plane of the picture, or the intersection *h'* of the horizon line by the line *h* C. The points *h* and *m* being in the same vertical line, the points *h'* and m' must also be in the same vertical line in the plane of the picture, and the position of *h'* might be determined by the intersection of *h* C by the perpendicular to the base line at its intersection by *m* S.

Connect the points *h v s m*, and also their projected perspective points *h'* V *s' m'*, and we find that *when an original line is parallel or perpendicular to the base of the picture, the perspective of that line* will also be parallel or perpendicular to it.

Fig 5. Draw the diagonals M *s* and *m* S', project as in preceding figure the points *m* and *s* into the plane of the picture, draw M *m*, M S' and S' *m'*; now since *m* and M are the extremities of a line perpendicular to

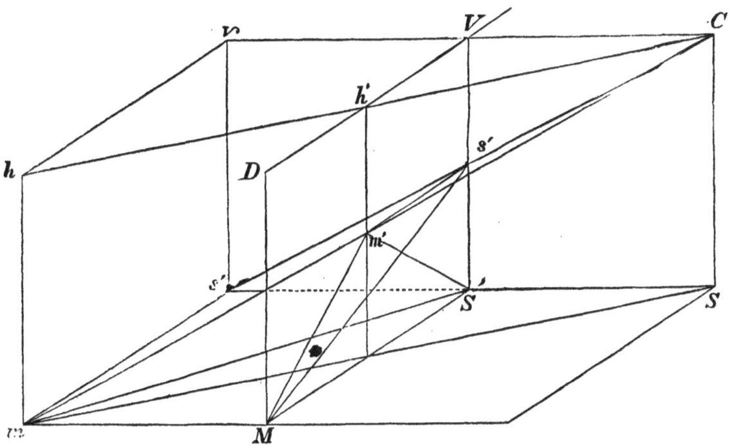

Fig. 5.

the plane of the picture, the line *m'* M must be the projection of this line on the plane of the picture, and if this line be extended it will pass through V, which may be demonstrated of all lines perpendicular to the plane of the picture; *hence the perspective direction of lines perpendicular to the picture is to the centre of view.*

If the line *m'* S' be extended, it will pass through the point D, and if M *s'* be extended it will pass through a point in the line of the horizon at a distance from V equal to V D; by construction D V has been made equal to V C, and as this demonstration is applicable to other similar lines, and since M *m s* S' is a square; hence *the perspective direction of all lines, making an angle of 45° with the plane of the picture, is towards the point of distance.*

Having thus illustrated the rules of parallel perspective, we now proceed to apply them to the drawing of a square and cube, Plate I. The same letters are employed in similar position as in preceding figures.

It is necessary to premise that the student should draw these examples at least three times the size of those in the plate.

Let A and B (fig 1,) represent the plan, or situation upon the ground, of two squares, of which a perspective representation is required. First draw the line M M, which represents the base line of the picture; make S the station point or place of the observer, and draw lines or rays from all visible angles of the squares, to S; then draw the lines S M, parallel to the diagonal lines of the squares. Now draw M′ M′ parallel to M representing the base line of the picture in elevation; then draw S′ V, the vertical line immediately opposite the eye; let the distance, S′ V, be the height of the eye from the ground, and draw D D the horizontal line; V being the centre of view; let fall perpendicular lines from the angles *a* and *b* of the plan of the square A, and also from the point *c*, where the ray from the angle *e* intersects the base line, M M, and from *a′* and *b′*, where *a a′* and *b b′* intersect the base or ground line M′ M′, draw lines to the centre of view, V; and *e′* where the perpendicular line from *c* intersects the line *b′* V, will give the apparent or perspective width of the side *b e*; from *e′* draw a line parallel to *a′ b′*, and the perspective representation of the nearest square A, is complete. In order to prove the accuracy of this performance, it is necessary to try if the diagonal lines, *a′ e′*, and *b′ f′*, incline respectively to the points of distance, D D, on the horizontal line: if so, it is correct. The square B is drawn in precisely the same manner, and will be easily understood by observing the example.

The plans of the two cubes C and D, are the same as the plans of the squares A and B. As neither of these cubes appears to touch the plane of the picture M M, it will be necessary to imagine the sides *l g*, and *k h*, to be continued until they do so; now draw down perpendicular lines from where the continuations of these sides intersect the base line, and set off on them from the line M′ M′, the height of the cube, as 1—2 which is the same as the width, and complete the square shown by the dotted lines: from all four angles of this square draw lines to the centre of view —this will give the representation of four lines at right angles with the picture carried on as far as it would be possible to see them; then it only remains to cut off the required perspective widths of the cubes by the perpendicular lines from the intersection of the visual rays with the plane of

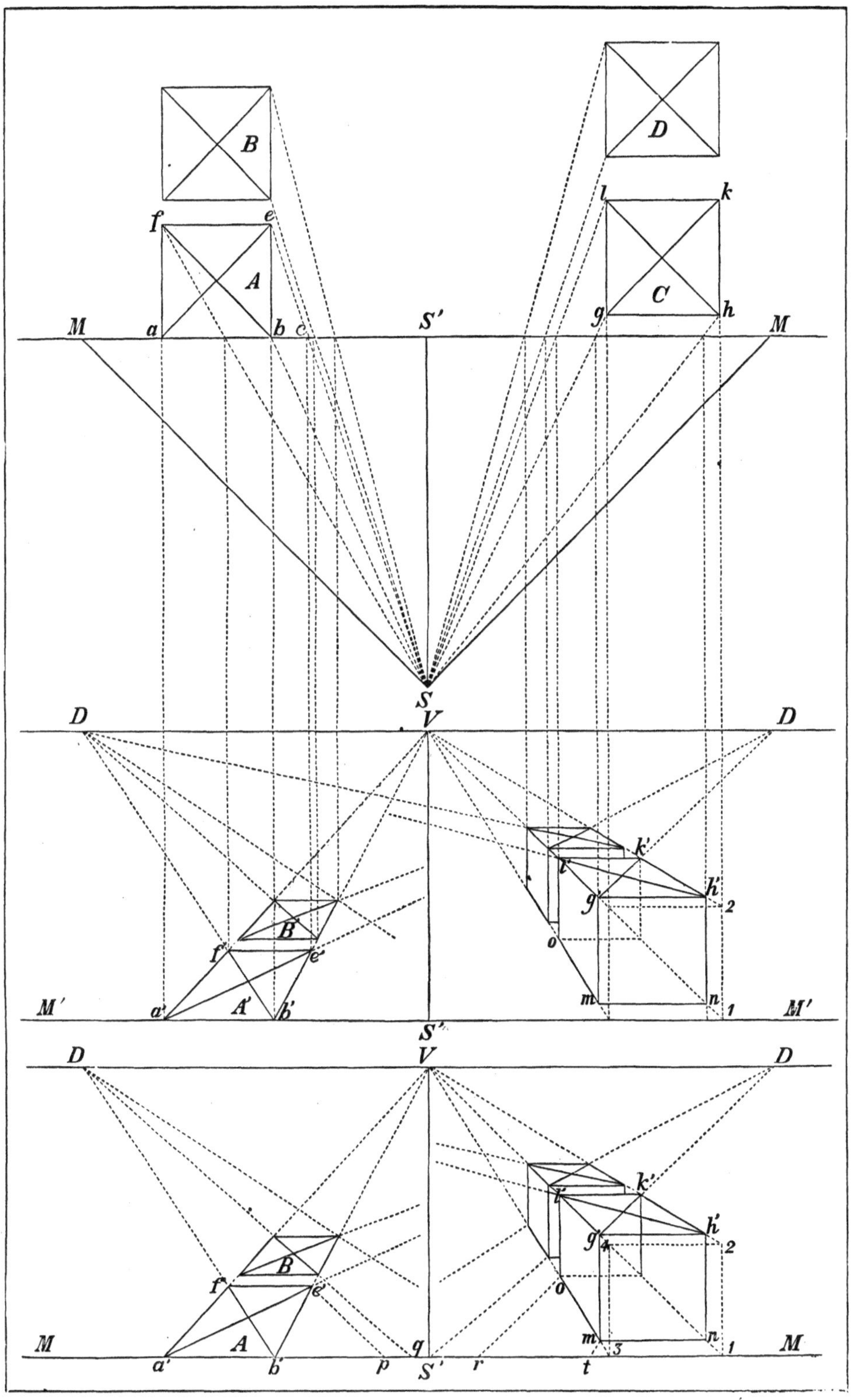
B
D
f
e
l
k
A
C
M
a
b
c
S'
g
h
M
S
D
V
D
k'
l'
h'
g'
2
B'
f'
e'
o
M'
a'
A'
b'
m
n
1
M'
S'
D
V
D
l'
k'
h'
g'
4
2
B
f'
e'
o
M
A
m
3
n
1
M
a'
b'
p
q
S'
r
t

the picture: the completion of this problem will be very easy, if the drawing of the squares is well understood.

In such simple objects as these it will not be necessary to draw a plan; when one side is parallel to the picture, and dimensions are known. In fig. 2, the same objects as those in fig. 1 are drawn without a plan thus:—

Draw the ground line M M, then the vertical line S′ V, and the horizontal line D D, at the height of the eye; making D D the same distance on each side of V, that the eye is from the transparent plane; for drawing the squares mark off from S′ to *b′*, on the ground line, the distance that the square is on one side of the observer; let *b′ a′* be the length of one side of the square; from *b′* and *a′* draw lines to V, which represent the sides of the square carried on indefinitely; to cut off the required perspective width of the side *b′ e′* of the square, lay off the width, *a′ b′*, from b′ to *p*, then draw from *p* to D on the left, and the point *e′* where the line D *p* intersects *b′* V, will give the apparent width required; then draw *f′ e′* parallel to *a′ b′*, and the square is complete: this may be proved in the same way as in fig. 1. The further square may be obtained in a similar manner, setting off the distance between the squares from *p* to *q*, and the width of the square beyond that, and drawing lines to D as before: some of the lines in this plate are not continued to the ground line, in order to avoid confusion. Proceed with the cubes by the same rule. Let 1, 2, 3, 4, be the size of one side of the cube if continued until touching the picture; from these points draw rays to V: from 3 to *t* set off the distance the cube is from the picture, and from *t* to *r*, the width of the cube; draw from these points to D on the right, and their intersection of the line 3 V in *m*, *o*, will give the perspective width and position of that side of the cube: draw lines perpendicular to the ground line from *m* and *o*, and lines parallel to 4—2 from the angles of the cube, *l′*, *g′*, *m*; then draw the side *n h′*, and the cube is complete. The operation of drawing the other cube is similar, and easy to be understood.

From the drawing of a square in parallel perspective, we deduce rules for the construction of a scale in perspective. Let D M M D, (fig 6,) be the plane of the picture, the same letters of reference being used as in preceding figures. From S′ lay off the distance *o* S′ equal to some unit of measure, as may be most convenient; from *o* draw the diagonal to D the point of distance; now draw 1 1′ parallel to the ground line M M, again draw from 1′ the diagonal 1′ D, and lay off the parallel 2 2′, proceed in the same way with the diagonal 2′ D and the parallel 3 3′, and extend the construction as far as may be necessary. It is evident *o* S′ 1 1′, 1′ 1 2 2′, 2′ 2 3 3′ are the perspective projectors of equal squares, and therefore *o* S′, 1 1′, 2 2′ 3 3′, etc., and S′ 1, 1 2, 2 3, etc., are equal to each other, and that if *o* S′ is set off to represent any unit of measure, as one foot, one yard, or ten feet, &c., each of these lines represents the same dis-

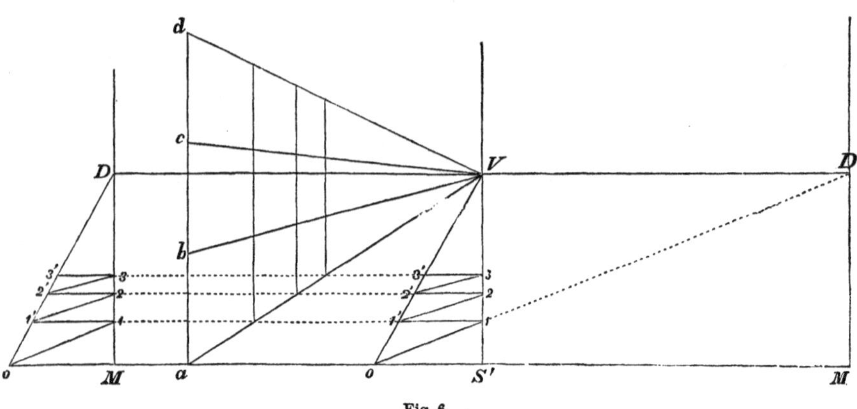

Fig. 6.

tance, the one being measures parallel to the base line, the others perpendicular to it. In making a perspective drawing a scale thus drawn will be found very convenient; but as in the centre of the picture it might interfere with the construction lines of the object to be put in perspective, it is better that the scale be transferred to the side of the picture *a* M *o*, the diagonals to be laid off to a point to the right of D equal to the point of distance.

The scales thus projected are for lines in the base or ground plane; for lines perpendicular to this plane the following construction is to be adopted; upon any point of the base line removed from S′, as *a* for instance, erect a perpendicular, *a d;* on this line, lay off as many of the units *o* S′ as may be necessary; in this example three have been laid off, that is, *a d* =3 *o* S′. From *a* and *d* draw lines to the centre of view, and extend the parallels 1 1′, 2 2′, 3 3′; at the intersection of these lines with *a* V erect perpendiculars. The portions comprehended between the lines *a* V and *d* V will be the perspective representations of the line *a d*, in planes at distances of 1, 2, 3, *o* S′ from the base line, and as *b*, *c*, *d* are laid off at intervals equal to *o* S′, by drawing the lines *c* V and *b* V six equal squares are constructed, of which the sides correspond to the unit of measure, *o* S′.

To determine the Perspective Position of any point in the Ground Plane. Thus (fig. 7), to determine the position of the point *p*, which in plane would be six feet distant from the plane of the picture, M M, and ten feet from the central plane, to the left.

Lay off from S′, to the left, the distance *a* S′, equal to six feet on the scale adopted; draw the diagonal to the point of distance D, on the right; at its intersection a' with the vertical line V S′, draw a parallel to M M the base line; lay off from S′, S′ b equal to ten feet, draw b V; the intersection of this line p, with the parallel previously drawn, will be the position of the point required.

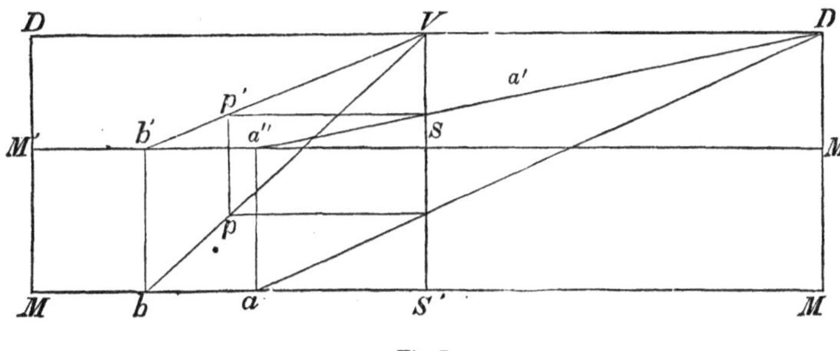

Fig. 7.

By a similar construction the position of any point in the ground plan may be determined. It is not necessary that the distances should be expressed numerically; they may be shown on the plan and thence be transferred to the base line, and thrown into perspective by the diagonals and parallels. As the intersections of the various lines of the outlines of objects are points, by projecting perspectively these points, and afterwards connecting by lines, the perspective of any plane surface, on the ground plane, may be shown.

If the point p were not in the ground plane, but in a position directly above that already assumed, that is, the distances from the plane of the picture, and the central plane being the same, but its distances above the ground plane were, say, five feet; then at b erect a perpendicular, and lay off $b\ b'$ equal to five feet, connect b' V, at p erect another perpendicular, and its intersection p' with the line b' V will be the position of the point required.

Or the plane of the point p' might be assumed as the position of the ground plane, M′ M′ becoming the base line, and laying off from S″, S″ a'' and S″ b'—equal respectively to six and ten feet; drawing the diagonal a'' D and b' V and the parallel as before, the point p' will be determined.

To draw an Octagon in Parallel Perspective.—Let A (fig. 8) represent the plan of an octagon. Draw M M, S′ V, and D D, as before; from the points M, a, b, c, draw rays to V. Set off on M M from c to the right the distances $c\ e$, $c\ d$, $c\ f$, from which draw diagonals to D on the left, and at their intersection with the ray c V, draw parallels $e'\ g'$, $d'\ h'$, $k'\ l'$, to the base line; these points will correspond to the angles on the plan. Now connect the angles on the perspective view, in the proper succession, and the perspective projection is complete.

It will be observed, that in this construction the plan has been placed forward of the plane of the picture, contrary to the position it should occupy, which should be the same relative position back of this plane; but it will be found much simpler in construction than if it were placed as in Plate I., and the points were all projected to the base line; it is, of course, equally correct in its perspective projection.

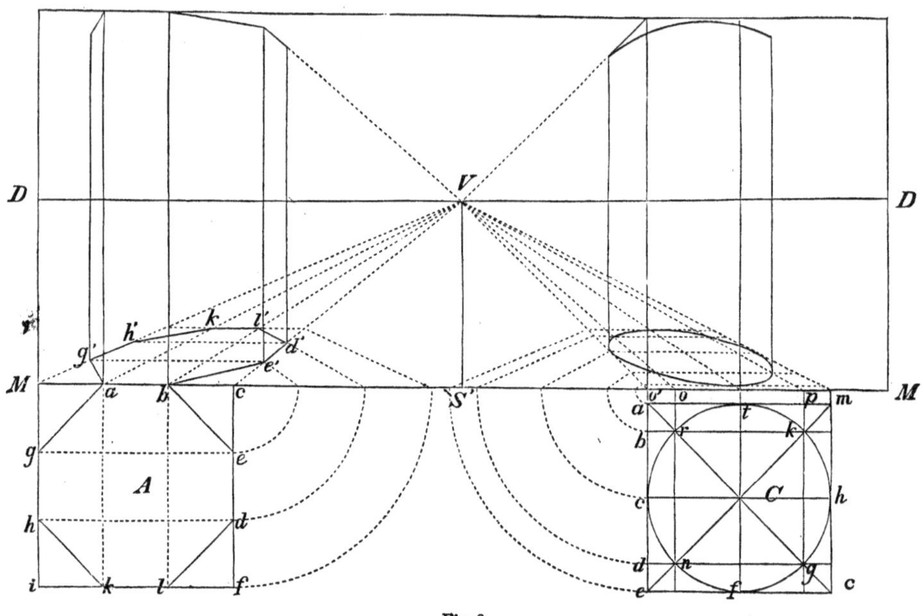

Fig. 8.

To draw a Circle in Parallel Perspective.—Let C, (fig. 8) represent the plan of a circle, round which let the square *a e c m* be described, two of its sides being parallel to the base line M M; draw diagonals across the square, and where these intersect the circumference of the circle draw the lines *b k* and *d g* parallel to the base line, and the lines *o n* and *p g* at right angles thereto. Draw also the lines *f l* and *c h* at right angles to each other through the centre of the circle, project the points *a*, *o*, *l*, *p*, *m*, to the base and draw rays to V; set off from *a'* to the left the distances *a' a*, *a'b*, *a'c*, *a'd*, *a'e*, and draw diagonals to the point of distance D on the right; at their intersection with the line *a'* V draw horizontal lines, or parallels to the base, and there will be projected in perspective the square *a e c m*, with all the lines of parallels and perpendiculars; connect the intersections corresponding to the points *c*, *n*, *f*, *g*, *h*, *k*, *l*, *r*, and we have the perspective projection of the required circle, which will be an ellipse.

To erect upon the octagonal base A an octagonal pillar or tower. This construction resolves itself into simply constructing another octagon on an upper plane, and connecting the visible angles by perpendiculars, or perpendiculars may be erected at the points M, *a*, *b*, *c*, and the heights of the tower laid off upon them, and from these extremities rays drawn to the centre of view; the intersection of these rays by perpendiculars from the angles of the octagon beneath will determine the projection of the upper surface of the pillar; represent in full lines all visible outlines, and the projection is complete.

In the same manner a pillar may be erected on the circular base. If the pillars be inclined, the first method of projecting the upper outline on a plane assumed at the height of the pillar, must be adopted.

To draw a Pyramid in Parallel Perspective.—Let A (fig. 9) be the plan of a pyramid, the diagonal lines represent the angles, and their intersection the vertex; project the plan as in previous examples of squares. Draw diagonal lines from M to *b*, and *a* to *c*, their intersection gives the perspective centre of the square; upon this point raise a perpendicular line which is the axis of the pyramid; draw a perpendicular line *e f*, in

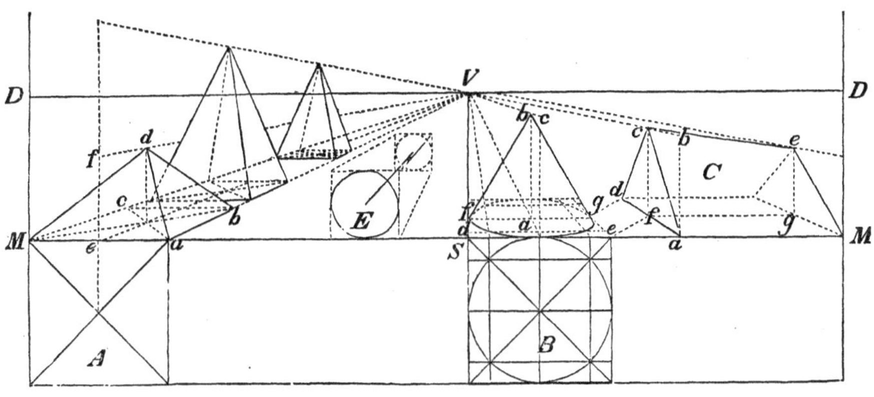

Fig. 9.

the centre of the line M *a*, upon which set up the height of the pyramid *e f*; from *f* draw a line to V, and its intersection of the axis of the pyramid at *d* will give the perspective height; complete the figure by drawing lines from *d*, the apex, to M, *a*, *b*, the three visible angles. The other two pyramids are drawn in a similar manner, by setting their distances from the plane of the picture off from *a*, on the ground line to the right, and drawing diagonals to the point of distance on the left.

To draw a Cone in Parallel Perspective.—Let B (fig. 9) represent the plan of a cone, apply the same lines of construction as to C (fig. 8); and draw the perspective view of a circle, upon the perspective centre of which draw a perpendicular line, *a*, *b*; on the centre of the line *d e*, raise a perpendicular, upon which set up the height of the cone, from the ground line to *c*; from *c* draw a ray to V, and the point where this line intersects the axis of the cone *a b*, in *b*, will give the perspective height of the axis; from *b* draw lines to *f* and *g*, and the figure is complete.

To draw the prism, C, which consists of two triangular ends and three rectangular sides, place the length of the side *a* M upon the ground line, and draw lines to V; mark off the width of one end from *a* to the left upon the ground line, and draw to the point of distance on the right, which gives the perspective width, *a d*; find the perspective centre *f* of the side in the same way, and from *f* and *d* draw horizontal lines until they intersect the line from M V; upon *f* and *g* draw perpendiculars; set up the height *a b*, of the end of the prism, and from *b* draw a line to V, and the point where it intersects *f c*, in *c*, will give the perspective height of the end of the figure; from *c* draw *c e*, parallel to *a* M, from *c* draw *c d*, and *c a*, and the visible end is complete; the other end is dotted in to show the process only.

E is the representation of a cylinder, with one end towards the spectator; its projection will be easily understood by examination.

To draw a Square and Cube in Angular Perspective. Plate II. Let A (fig. 1) be the plan of the square, and B the plan of the cube, M M the base or ground line, and S the station point. Draw M′ M′, and D D′ parallel to M M, the one being the ground line and the other the horizon of the plane of the picture; project the point *d* on M M to *d′*, on M′ M′. It has been shown in parallel perspective that the vanishing points of diagonals of squares lie in the points of distance; if through the station point S, in any of the preceding figures, lines be drawn parallel to the diagonals, they will intersect the base lines at distances from the central plane equal to the points of distance. In like manner to find the vanishing points of lines in the ground planes, or in planes parallel to the ground plane, inclined to the plane of the picture, through the station point S draw lines parallel to the inclined lines, and project their intersection with the base line to the horizon of the picture; thus, in the present example draw S M, S M parallel to *a d*, *e h*, and to *d c*, *h g*; project their intersections M, M, with the base line to D, D′, the horizon of the picture, and D, D′, will be the vanishing points of all lines parallel to *a d* and *d c*. Draw *d′* D and *d′* D′, the perspective projection of *d a* will lie in the former of these lines and

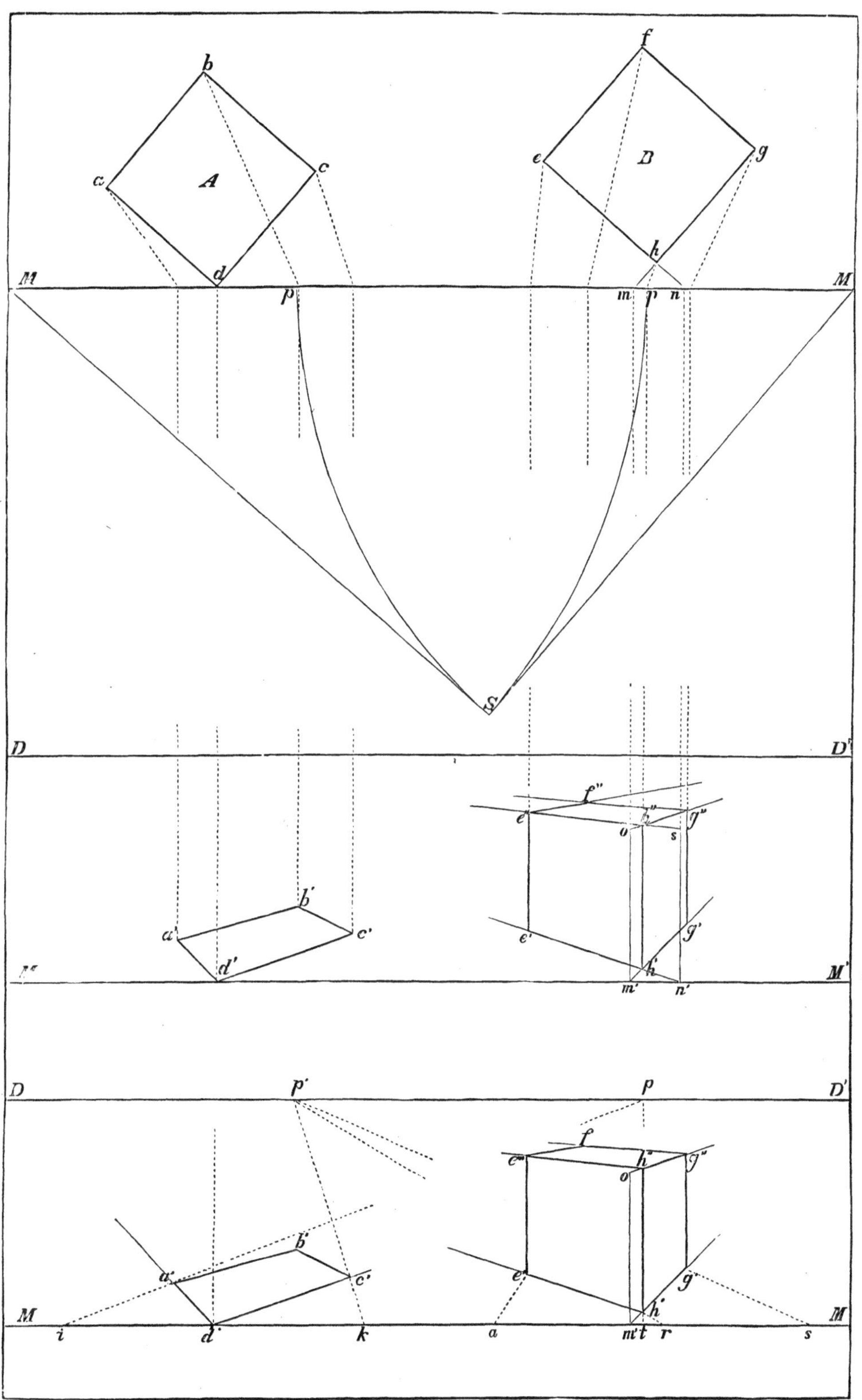
b
a
A
c
d
f
e
B
g
h
M
p
m
p
n
M
S
D
D'
f''
e''
h''
g''
o
s
b'
a'
c'
e'
g'
d'
h'
m'
n'
M'
D
p'
p
D'
f
e''
h''
g''
o
b'
a'
c'
e'
g'
h'
M
i
d'
k
a
m't
r
s
M

d c in the latter. To determine the perspective position of the points *a* and *c*, or the length of these lines, draw the rays *a* S and *c* S, project their intersection with the base M M, upon the lines *d'* D and *d'* D', and their intersections *a'*, *c'* will be the perspective projection of the points *a* and *c*. To complete the projection of the square, draw the lines *a'* D' and *c'* D, their intersection will be the perspective projection of the point *b*, and the square is complete. To prove the construction, draw the ray *b* S and project its intersection with the base M M, and if the construction be correct it will fall upon the point *b'*.

As the cube is placed at some distance from the plane of the picture, it will be necessary to continue either *e h* or *g h*, or both, till they intersect the base line M M at *n* and *m*; drop perpendiculars or project these points upon M M' at *n'* and *m'*; on these perpendiculars set up the height of the cube *m' o* and *n' s*, draw the lines *m'* D', *o'* D' and *n'* D, *s* D; connect the intersections *h'* and *h''*; draw the rays S *e* and S *g*, and project their intersections with M M, to *g' e'*; draw the lines *e''* D' and *g''* D; if the construction be correct, the projection of the intersection of the ray S *f* with the base will fall upon *f'*, and of the ray S *h* will fall upon *h''* and *h'*.

To Solve the Same Problem by a Different Construction.—Let A and B, (fig. 1,) be as before the plans of the square and of the cube; to project them perspectively on the plane of the picture M D D' M, (fig. 2).

From the point M and M, (fig. 1,) set off distances equal to M S, M S, to *p* and *p'*; project these points upon D D' fig. 2, the point *p*, fig 2, will be that from which any number of parts may be laid off on lines vanishing in D'; the point *p* will be the corresponding point for lines vanishing in D. These points may be called the points of division. In parallel perspective the points of distance were the points of division, the one for the other. To illustrate their application in the present example, project the point *d*, (fig. 1,) to *d'* (fig. 2,) draw *d'* D and *d'* D', from *d'* on either lay off a distance *d' i*, *d' k* equal to the side of the square *a d*. Now since *p* is the division point of lines vanishing in D from *i*, draw the line *i p*, and its intersection with *d'* D cuts off a line *d' a'* equal perspectively to the line *d' i* or *a d* measured on the base line. Again since *p'* is the division point of lines vanishing in D', the line *k p'* cuts off on *d'* D', a line *d' c'* equal perspectively to the line *d' k*, or *a d* measured on the base: having *a' d' c*, the square is completed by drawing the lines *c' b'* towards D, and *a' b'* towards D'.

To construct the cube, project the point *m*, (fig. 1,) to *m'*, (fig. 2); lay off on the perpendicular forming the projection, the height *m' o'* of the cube; draw the lines *m'* D' and *o'* D'. Lay off the distance *m' r* equal to *m h*, (fig. 1,) and draw the line *r p′*, its intersection with *m′* D′ will cut off *m′ h′*, equal to *m h*, (fig. 1,) and establish the angle *h* of the cube. From *r* lay off *r s*, equal to *h g*, (fig. 1,) draw *s p′*, and its intersection with *m′* D′ establishes the angle *g′*. From *h′* draw a line vanishing in D. Through *h′* extend a line *p h′* to *t*, from *t* lay off to the left *t a*, equal to the side of the cube *h e*; draw *a p*, and its intersection with the line *h′* D, establishes a third point *e* of the cube. Upon these points *h′ g′ e′* erect perpendiculars; those upon *h′* and *g′* will, by their intersection with *o′* D, determine *h″ g″*. Draw *h″* D′, its intersection with the perpendicular at *c* determines *e″*. Draw *g″* D′ and *e″* D to their intersection, and the cube is complete.

To Draw the Perspective Projection of an Octagonal Pillar in Angular Perspective.—Plate III. Let A, (fig. 1,) be the plan of the pillar. Enclose it by a square. Let M M be the base line, and S the station point; determine the position of the vanishing points for the sides of the square as in Plate II., and project the square upon the plane of the picture M D D′ M′ by either of the methods already explained. These lines of construction are omitted, as on the necessarily small diagrams they would confuse the student; but in drawing these examples to the scale recommended, they might be retained. From the angles of the octagon visible to the spectator draw rays to the station point S project their intersection with the base line M M, to the perspective square, (fig. 2,) which will thus determine on the sides of the square the positions of the points *a′*, *b′*, *c′*, *d′*, *e′*, corresponding to the visible angles of the octagon; connect these points by lines. To construct the pillar upon this base, upon the perpendicular let fall from the corner *f* of the square upon M M′ at *f* set off the height of the pillar; from this point *f* draw lines to the vanishing points D, D′, and construct three sides of an upper square similar to the lower one. The lines of this square will determine the length of the sides of the tower, which are the perpendiculars let fall upon *a′ b′ c′ d′ e′*.

To Construct a Circular Pillar in Angular Perspective.—Plate III. Let B, (fig. 1,) be the plan of the base; enclose it with a square whose sides are parallel respectively to S M and S M; project this square upon the plane of the picture, (fig. 2,) divide the plan into four equal squares by lines parallel to the sides; draw rays through the points *h* and *i*, and project their intersection with M M upon the perspective square. From the points *h′* and *i′* thus formed, draw lines to vanishing points D′ and D, and the perspective square is divided similarly to the original, and there are four points of the circle established: through these draw the perspective of the circle. By the division of the base into smaller squares more points of the curve might be determined, but for the present purpose they are unnecessary.

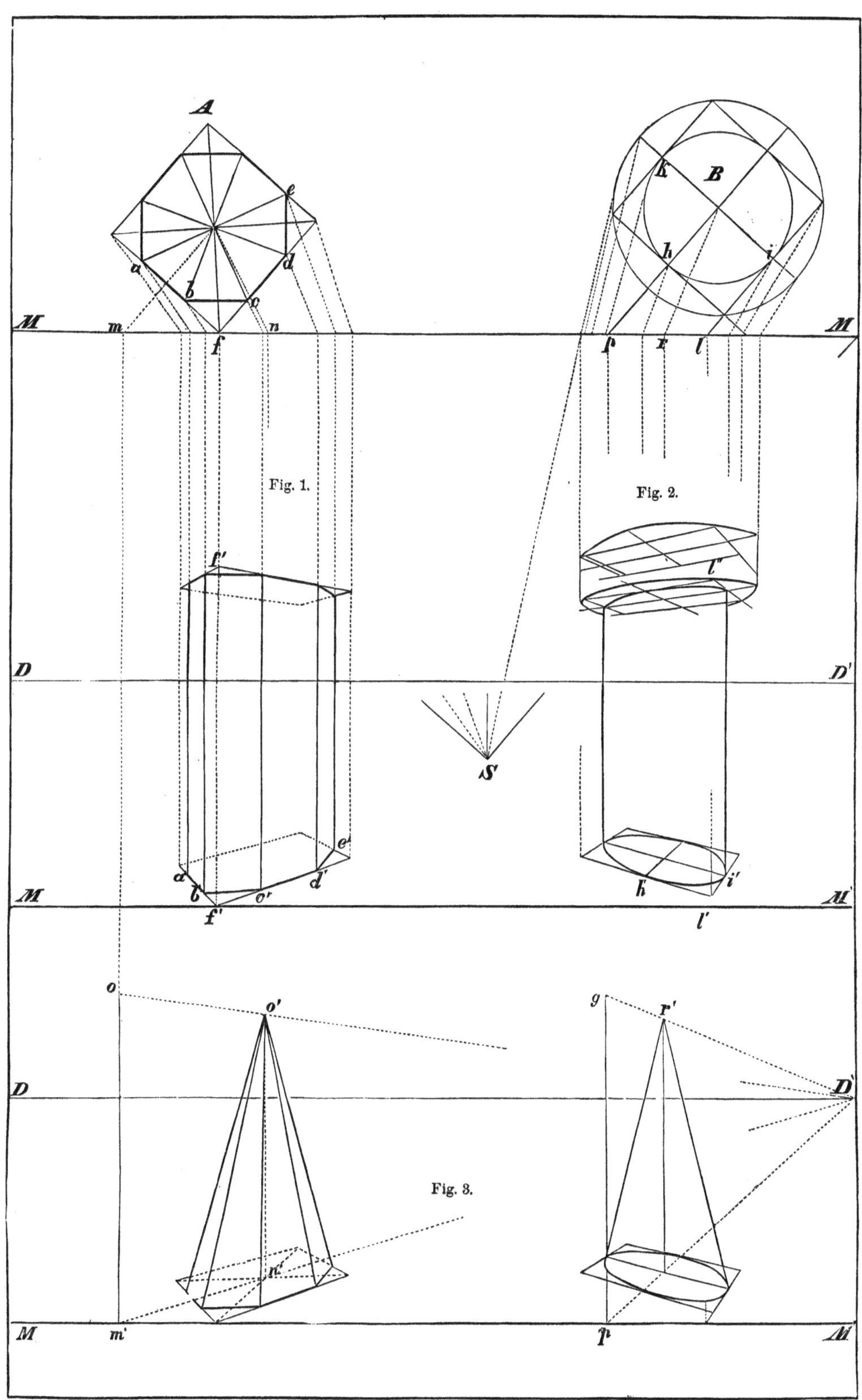
A
B
k
h
i
a
b
c
d
e
M
m
f
n
M
f
r
l
M
Fig. 1.
Fig. 2.
f'
l''
D
D'
S
e'
a'
b'
c'
d'
h'
i'
M
M'
f'
l'
o
o'
g
r'
D
D'
Fig. 3.
n'
M
m'
p
M'

To determine the outline of the pillar, draw from S rays tangent to the sides of the plan at *k* and *i*, the perpendiculars let fall from their intersection with M M will be the outline of the cylinder. To cut them off to the proper height, and to determine the top of the cylinder, upon the perpendicular let fall upon *i*, set off the height of the cylinder *l′ l″*, and upon this plane project the square as before, and draw in through the points thus determined the outline of the curve. As a still further elucidation of the principle of projection, an enlarged cap is represented on the pillar, of which the circumscribing circle (fig. 1,) is the plan. In this by extending the central lines of the square, both in plan and perspective, we are enabled to project readily eight points in the larger circle through which the curve may be drawn.

To Draw an Octagonal Pyramid in Angular Perspective.—Plate III. Let *f*, (fig. 1,) be the base of the pyramid; project upon the plane of the picture, (fig. 3,) the visible angles of the base, as in the case of the pillar. Through the centre of the plan draw a line parallel to one of the sides and intersecting M M at *m*; from this point let fall a perpendicular to *m′* on M M′, (fig. 3,); on this perpendicular set off the height of the pyramid *m′ o* from *m′* and draw lines to D′. From the centre of the plan draw a ray to S, and project its intersection with M M, upon the line *o* D′, its intersection *o′* with this line will be the apex of the pyramid: from this point draw lines to the angles of the base already projected, and the pyramid is complete.

To Draw a Cone in Angular Perspective.—Plate III. Let the inner circle B, (fig. 1,) be the base of the cone project its visible outline to fig. 3, as in case of the cylinder. To determine its height extend one of the diameters of the plan to the base line at *p*; from this point let fall a perpendicular to *p′* on M M′, and set off upon it *p′ g*, the height of the cone; from *p′* and *g* draw lines to the vanishing point D′. From the centre of the plan, (fig. 1,) draw rays to S, and project its intersection with M M, upon *r′* on the line *g* D′, and *r′* will be the apex of the cone: connect the apex with the extremities of the perspective of the base, and the projection of the cone is complete.

To Draw the Elevation of a Building in Angular Perspective.—Plate IV. For example, take the school-house, Plate XXIX. of architecture. Plot so much of the plan of the building at it as may be seen from the position of the spectator at S. Draw a base line, and through the station point draw parallels to the sides of the building cutting the base as at M M: draw M M′ for a base, and D D′ for the horizontal line of the picture. Project M and M to D and D′, for the vanishing points, the one of the lines parallel to *a c*, the other to *a b;* extend *a c*, *a b;* project *d*, *e*, to *d'*, *e'*, and on *d' d* set off the height of the eaves *d' o*, and of the ridge *d n;* from *d'*, *o* and *n* draw lines to D′, and from *e* to D, draw rays from *c* and *b* to S′, and project their intersection with the base to the vanishing lines just drawn. To find the perspective of the ridge draw a ray from the centre of *a b*, and project its intersection with the base to *r* on the line *n* D′, the point is the apex of the gable, the line *r* D will be the perspective of the ridge; to determine its length erect a perpendicular at the intersection of *t* D′ and *s* D, draw the sloping lines of the roof, and the outline of the building is complete. The filling in of the details will be readily understood; it will only be necessary to keep in mind, that all lines parallel to *a b* must meet in D′, those to *a c* in D: all measures laid off on any lines of the plan must be connected with the point of sight S, and their intersections with the base projected. All vertical heights must be laid off on the line *d' d*, and referred to the proper position by lines to D or D′, as the case may be.

As an example of the other method of constructing this same problem, let the scholar lay off to the double of the present scale the plane of the picture M D D′ M′, and the division points *p'* and *p*, and without drawing plan or elevation take the dimensions from Plate XXIX. of architecture.

To Draw an Arched Bridge in Angular Perspective.—Plate V. Let A and B, (fig. 1,) be the plans of the piers; on the line *a h*, one of the sides of the bridge, lay down the curve of the arch as it would appear in elevation, in this example an ellipse. Divide the width of the arch as at *b. c. d. e. f. g. h.*, carry up lines perpendicular to *b h* until they intersect the curve of the arch, and through these points, draw lines parallel to *b h* as *k. l. m.;* let *o r* be the height of the parapet of the bridge above the spring of the arch. Through the station point draw lines parallel to the side *a h* and end *a a* of the bridge, till they intersect the assumed base line M M: project these intersections to the horizon line of the picture for the vanishing points D, D′ of perspective lines parallel to *a h* and *a a*. Let fall a perpendicular from *a* to *a'*, and on this perpendicular set off from *a'* the heights *s k*, *s l*, *s m*, and *s t;* from *a'* and *r'* draw lines to D and D′, and from the points *m'*, *l'*, *k'* to D′. Draw rays from the points *a. b. c. d. e. f. g. h.* to the station point S, and project their intersection with the base lines to the perspective line *a'* D′ as in previous examples: the intersection of the lines *k'* D′, *l'* D′, *m'* D′ by the perpendiculars thus projected, will establish the points of the curve of the arch on the side nearest the spectator. To determine the position of the opposite side of the arch, from *a''*, the perspective width of the bridge, draw *a''* D′, and from *h'* draw lines to D;

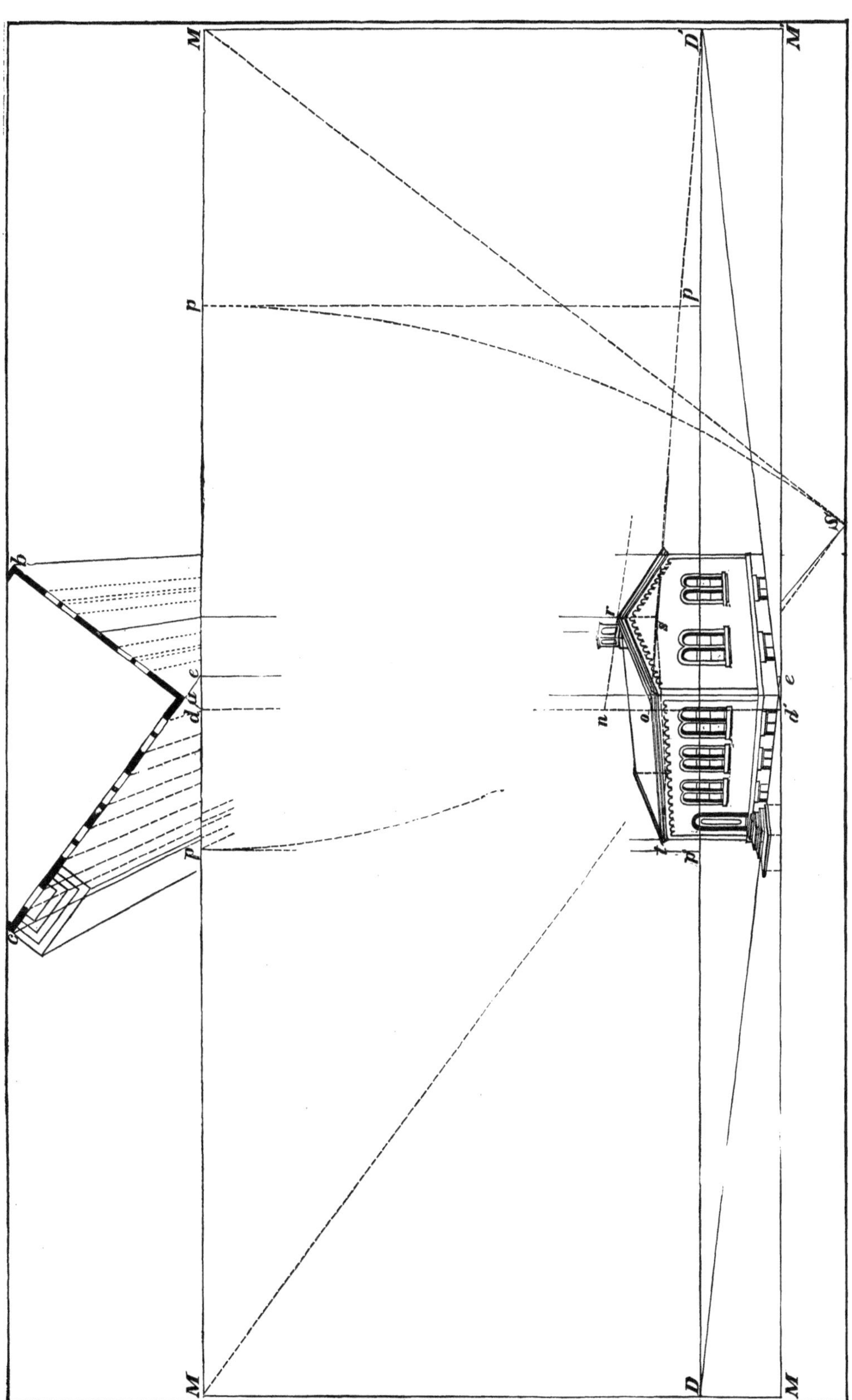

PLATE V.

r
r
B
i
h
g
o
f
m
l
k
e
s
a
d
c
A
b
M
M
a
D
D'
r
m'
l'
k'
a'
p'
g''
f
g'
b'
i''
b''
c'
d'
e'
M
M
a'
S
f
d
e
V
D
D'
a'
i
M
S'
M

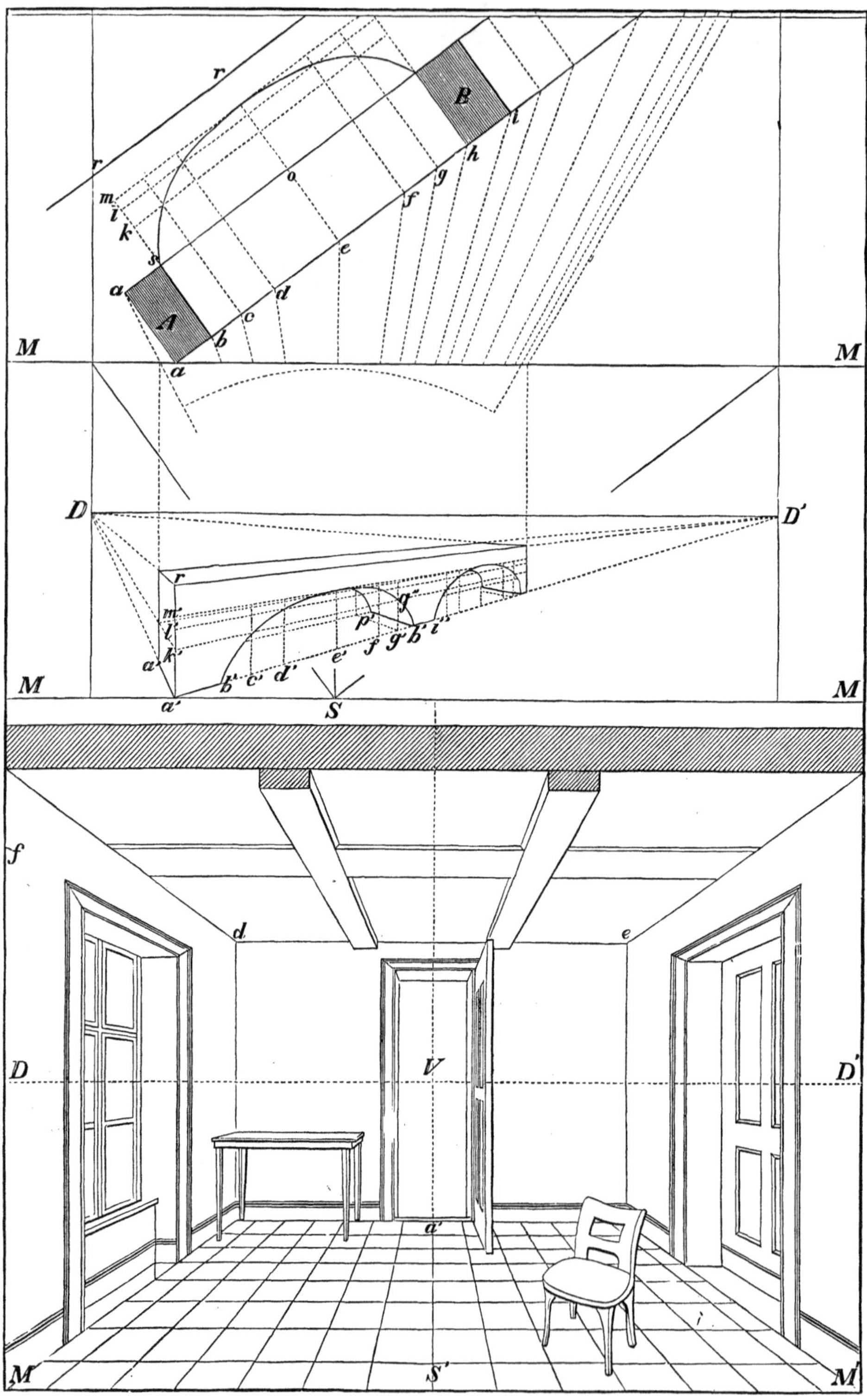

the line $h' p'$ will be the perspective width of the pier; draw k' D; and from k'', k'' D; from g'' the intersection of the curve of the arch by the perpendicular to g', draw g'' D, the intersection with k'' D$'$ will be one point in the curve of the arch on the opposite side of the bridge: in the same way, from any point in the nearer arc draw lines to D, and the intersection with lines in the same planes on the opposite side of the bridge, will furnish points for the further arch: all below the first only will be visible to the spectator.

To Draw in Parallel Perspective the Interior of a Room.—Plate V. We propose to construct this by scale without laying down the plan. Draw the horizon line D V D$'$, and the base M M$'$, making D and D$'$ the point of distance. Let the room be 20 feet wide, 14 feet high, and 12 feet deep; on the base M M$'$, lay off the rectangle of the section in our figure on a scale of 8 feet to the inch, 20 feet × 14 feet. From the four corners draw lines to the centre of view V; from S$'$ lay off to the right or left on M M$'$ 12 feet, and through this point draw lines to D$'$ or D as the case may be: through the point of intersection a' of this line with S$'$ V draw a line parallel to M M$'$; at the intersections of this line with M V and M$'$ V erect a perpendicular, cutting the vanishing lines of the upper angle of the room at d and e; connect $d\ e$ and the perspective of the room is complete. To draw the aperture for a door or window on the side, measure off from S$'$ the distance of the near side from the plane of the picture, and in addition thereto the width of the aperture; from these two points draw lines to the proper point of distance, and at their intersection with S$'$ V, draw parallels to M M$'$, cutting the lower angles of the room, and erect perpendiculars, the height of which will be determined by a line drawn from f, the height of the window above the floor measured on M D. Should the window be recessed, the farther jamb will be visible; extend the farther parallel to M M$'$, and cut it by a line g V. M g being the depth of the recess, the rest of the construction may be easily understood by inspection of the figure. At the extremity of the apartment a door is represented half open, hence as the plane of the door is at right angles to the plane of the picture, the top and bottom lines will meet in the point of view; if the door were open at an angle of 45°, these lines would meet in the points of distance; if at any other angle, the vanishing points would have to be determined by constructing a plan, drawing a line parallel to the side of the door through the station point, and projecting it upon the horizon line. The chair in the middle of the room is placed diagonally, and the table parallel to the plane of the picture; their projection is simple.

To Draw in Perspective a Flight of Stairs.—Plate VI. Lay off the base line, horizon, centre of view, and point of distance of the picture, construct the solid *a b c d*, *e f g h*, containing the stairs, and in the required position in the plane of the picture, divide the rise *a c* into equal parts according to the number of stairs, four for instance; divide perspectively the line *a b* into the same number of parts; at the points of division of this latter erect perpendiculars, and through the former draw lines to the centre of view; one will form the rise and the other the tread of the steps. From the top of the first step to the top of the upper continue a line *a d*, till it meets the perpendicular S′ V prolonged in *v*; this line will be the inclination or pitch of the stair; if through the top of the step at the other extremity a similar line be drawn, it will meet the central perpendicular at the same point *v*, and will define the length of the lines of nosing of the steps, and the other lines may be completed. As the pitch lines of both sides of the stairs meet the central vertical in the same point, in like manner *v* will be the vanishing point of all lines having a similar inclination to the plane of the picture. The projection of the other flight of stairs will be easily understood from the lines of construction perpendicular to the base line or parallel thereto, lying in planes.

To Find the Reflection of Objects in the Water.—Plate VI. Let B be a cube suspended above the water; we find the reflection of the point *a*, but letting fall a perpendicular from it, and setting off the distance *a′ w* below the plane of the water equal to the line *a w* above this line; the line *w f′* will also be equal to the line *w f*; find in the same way the points *b′* and *e′*, through these points construct perspectively a cube in this lower plane, and we have the reflection of the cube above.

To find the reflection of the square pillar D removed from the shore: suppose the plane of the water extended beneath the pillar, and proceed as in the previous example.

It will be observed that those lines of an object which meet in the centre of view V, in the original; their corresponding reflected lines will converge to the same point. If the originals converge to the points of distance, the reflected ones will do the same. To find the reflection of any inclined line, find the reflection of the rectangle of which it is the diagonal, if the plane of the rectangle is perpendicular to the plane of the picture; if the line is inclined in both directions enclose it in a parallelopided and project the reflection of the solid.

To find the Perspective Projection of Shadows.—Plate VII. Let the construction points and lines of the picture be plotted. Let A be the perspective projection of a cube placed against another block, of which the face is parallel to the plane of the picture: to find the shadow upon the

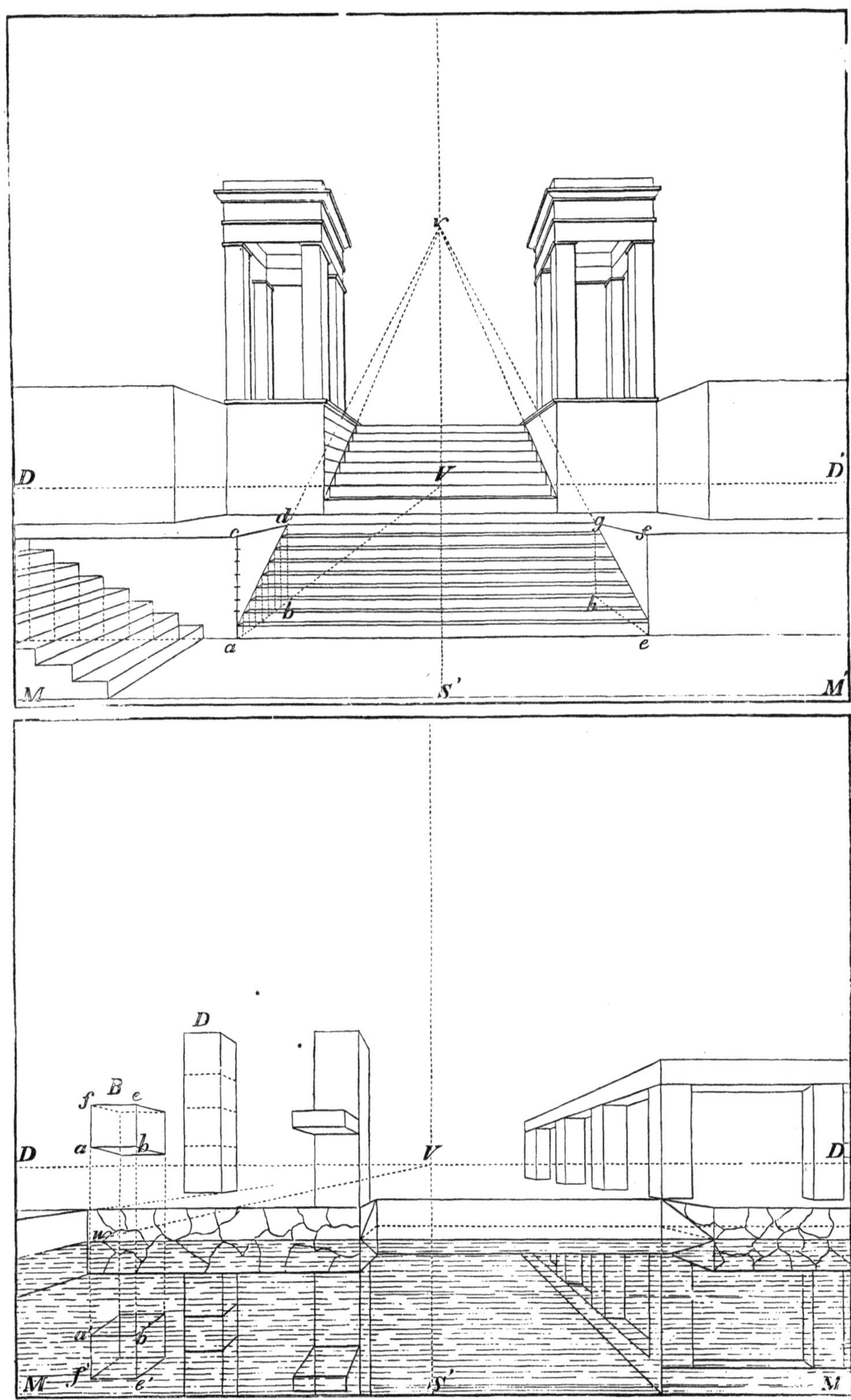
r
D
V
D'
c
d
g
f
b
h
a
e
M
S'
M'
D
f
B
e
a
b
D
V
D
u
a'
b'
M
f'
e'
S'
M

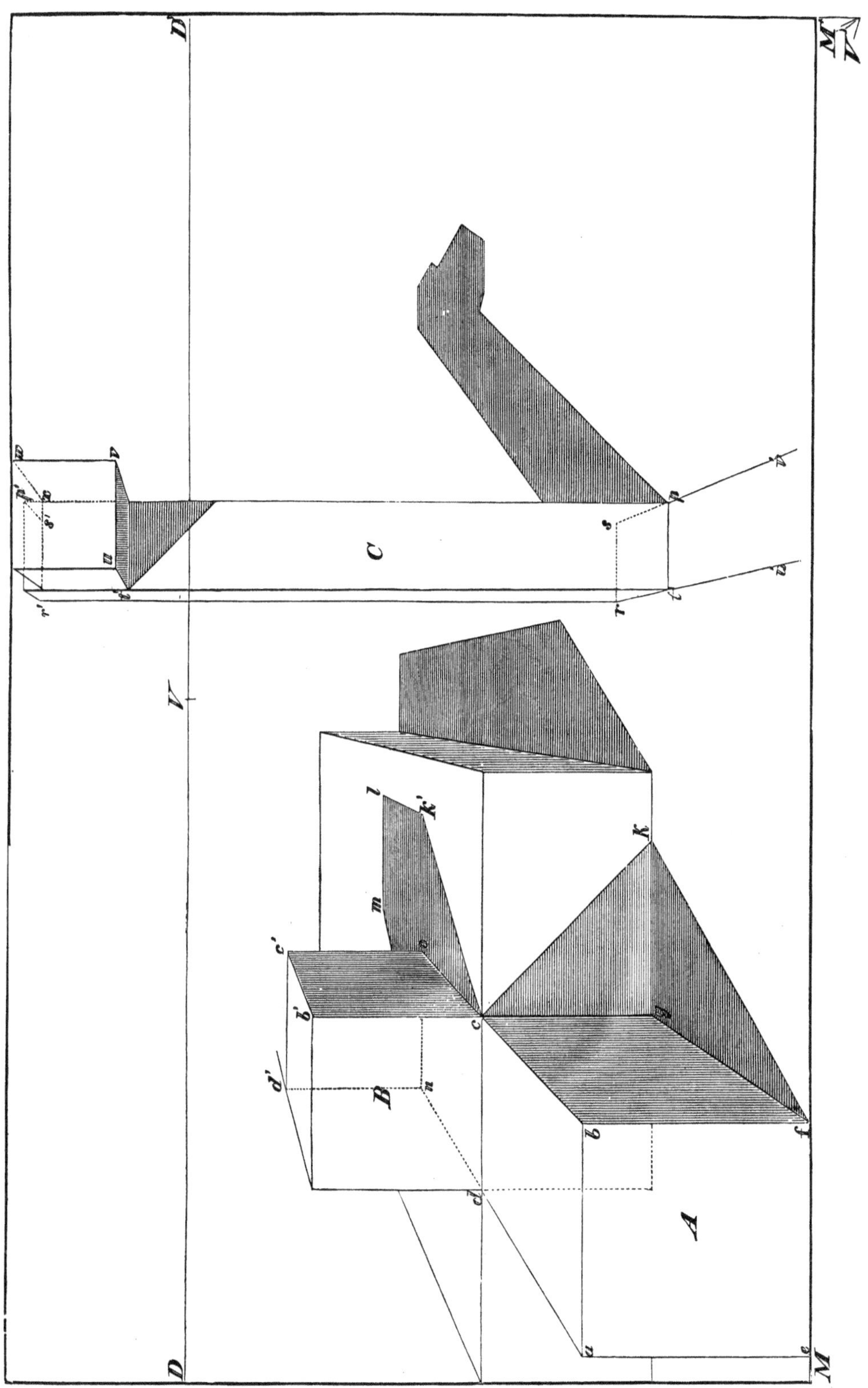

block and upon the ground plane, supposing the light to come into the picture from the upper left-hand corner and at an angle of 45°. Since the angle of light is the diagonal of a cube, construct another cube similar to A, and adjacent to the face *d c g;* draw the diagonal *b k*, it will be the direction of the rays of light, and *k* will be the shadow of *b;* connect *f k* and *c k*, *f k* must be the shadow of the line *b f*, and *c k* of *b c;* the one upon the horizontal plane and the other in a vertical one: the former will have its direction, being a diagonal, toward the point of distance D′, the other being a diagonal in a plane, parallel to that of the picture, will be always projected upon this plane in a parallel direction.

Let B be a cube similar to A; to find its projection upon a horizontal plane, the shadow of the point *b′* may be determined as in the preceding example, but the shadow of the point *c′*, instead of falling upon a plane parallel to the picture, falls upon a horizontal one; its position must be determined as we did before by *b*. Construct the cube and draw the diagonal *c′ l;* in the same way determine the point *m′* the shadow of *d′;* connect *c k′ l m n*, and we have the shadow of the cube in perspective on a horizontal plane.

On examination of these projected shadows, it will be found that as the rays of light fall in a parallel direction to the diagonal of the cube, the vanishing point of these rays will be in one point V′ on the line D′ M′ prolonged, at a distance below D′ equal V D′; and since the shadows of vertical lines upon a horizontal plane are always directed towards the point of sight, the extent of the shadow of a vertical line may be determined by the intersection of the shadow of the ground point of the line by the line of light, from the other extremity. Thus, the point *k*, cube A, is the intersection of *f* D′ by *b* V′; the points *k′*, *l*, *m* are the intersections of *c* D′, *o* D′, *n′* D′ by *b′* V′, *c′* V′ by *d′* V′. Similarly on planes parallel to that of the picture, *k*, cube A is intersection of the diagonal *c k*, by the ray of light *b* V′.

Applying this rule to the frame C, from *r*, *s*, *p*, draw lines to D′ from *r′*, *s′*, *p′*, draw rays to V′; their intersections define the outline of the shadow of the post. To draw the shadow of the projection, the shadow upon the post from *t* will follow the direction of the diagonal *c k*. Project *u* and *v* upon the ground plane at *u′* and *v′;* from *t′ u′ v′* and *p* draw lines to D′; from *t*, *u*, *v*, *w* and *x* draw rays to V′, and the intersection of these lines with their corresponding lines from their bases will give the outline required; as *v* and *w* are on the same perpendicular, their rays will intersect the same line *v′* V′.

With reference to the intensity of "shade and shadow" and the necessary manipulation to produce the required effect, the reader is referred to the article on this subject.

In treating of Perspective it has been considered not in an artistic point, as enabling a person to draw from nature, but rather as a useful art to assist the architect or engineer to complete his designs, by exhibiting them in a view such as they would have to the eye of a spectator when constructed. In our examples, owing to size of the page, we have been limited in the scale of the figures, and in the distance of the point of view, or distance of the eye from the plane of the picture, and as it was unimportant to the mathematical demonstration, few of the figures extend above the line of the horizon. In these particular points it is unnecessary that the examples should be copied. The most agreeable perspective representations are generally considered to be produced by fixing the angle of vision M S M′, at from 45 to 50°, and the distance of the horizon above the ground line at about one-third the height of the picture.

Linear perspective is more adapted to the representation of edifices, bridges, interiors, &c., than to that of machinery; it belongs, therefore, rather to the architect than to the engineer or the mechanic; for the purposes of the latter we would recommend Isometrical Perspective, uniting accuracy of measures with graphic perspective representation.

ISOMETRICAL DRAWING.

PROFESSOR FARISH, of Cambridge, has given the term Isometrical Perspective to a particular projection which represents a cube, as in fig. 1. The words imply that the measure of the representations of the lines forming the sides of each face are equal.

The principle of isometric representation consists in selecting for the plane of the projection, one equally inclined to three principal axes, at right angles to each other, so that all straight lines coincident with or parallel to these axes, are drawn in projection to the same scale. The axes are called isometric axes, and all lines parallel to them are called isometric lines. The planes containing the isometric axes are isometric planes; the point in the object projected, assumed as the origin of the axes, is called the regulating point.

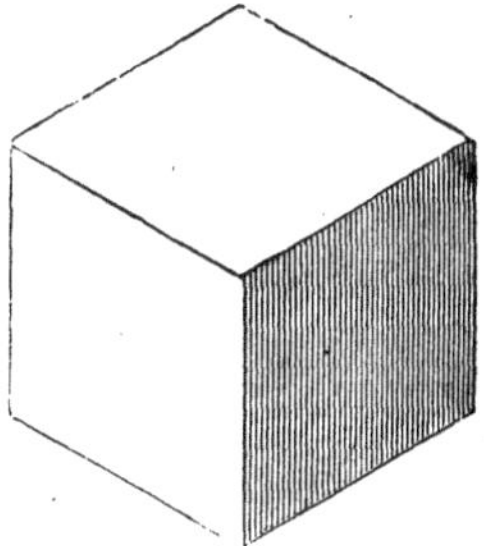

Fig. 1.

To draw the isometrical projection of a cube, (fig. 2,) draw the horizontal line A B indefinitely; at the point D erect the perpendicular D C, equal to one side of the cube required; through D draw the line D *b* and D *f* to the right and left, making *f* D B and *b* D A each equal an angle of 30°. Consequently the angles F D *f* and F D *b* are each equal to 60°. Make D *b* and D *f* each equal to the side of the cube, and at *b* and *f* erect perpendiculars, making *b a* and *f e* each equal to the side of the cube; connect F *a* and F *e* and draw *e g* parallel to *a* F, and *a g* parallel to F *e*, and we obtain the projection of the cube.

If from the point F, with a radius F D, a circle be described, and commencing at the point D radii be laid off around the circumference, forming a regular inscribed hexagon, and the points D *a e* be connected with the centre of the circle F, we have an isometrical representation of a cube. The point D is called the regulating point.

If a cube be projected according to the principles of isometrical perspective, in a similar manner as we have constructed one according to the rules of linear perspective, the length of the isometrical lines would be to the original lines as .8164 to 1, but since the value of isometrical perspective as a practical art lies in the applicability of common and known scales to the isometric lines, in our constructions we have not thought it necessary to exemplify the principles of the projection, but have drawn our figures without any reference to what would be the comparative size of the original and of the projection, transferring measures directly from plans and elevations in orthographic projections, to those in isometry. It will be observed that the isometric scale adopted applies only to isometric lines, as F D, F *a* and F *e* or lines parallel thereto; the diagonals which are absolutely equal to each other, and longer than the sides of the cube, are the one less, the other greater; the minor axis being unity, the isometrical lines and the major axis are to each other as, 1. $\sqrt{2}$. $\sqrt{3}$.

Understanding the isometrical projection of a cube, any surface or solid may be similarly constructed, since it is easy to suppose a cube sufficiently large to contain within it the whole of the model intended to be represented, and as hereafter will be farther illustrated, the position of any point on or within the cube, the direction of any line or the inclination of any plane to which it may be cut, can be easily ascertained and represented.

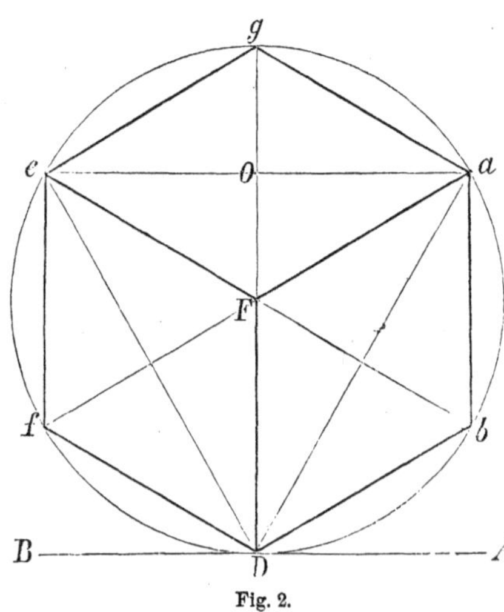

Fig. 2.

In figs. 1 and 2 one face of the cube appears horizontal, and the other two faces appear vertical. If now the figures be inverted, that which before appeared to be the top of the object, will now appear to be its under side.

The angle of the cube formed by the three radii meeting in the centre of the hexagon, may be made to appear either an internal or external angle; in the one case the faces representing the interior, and in the other the exterior of a cube.

Figs. 3, 4, 5, illustrate the application of isometrical drawing to simple combinations of the cube and parallelopipedon. The mode of construction

Figs. 3, 4, 5.

of these figures will be easily understood by inspection, as they contain no lines except isometrical ones.

To draw Angles to the Boundary Lines of an Isometrical Cube.

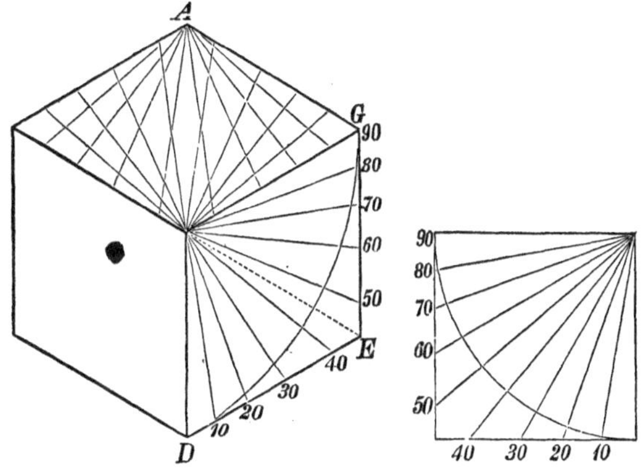

Fig. 6, 7.

Draw a square C (fig. 6,) whose sides are equal to those of the isometrical cube A, and from any of its angles describe a quadrant, which divide into 90°, and draw radii through the divisions meeting the sides of the square. These will then form a scale to be applied to the faces of the cube; thus on D E, or any other, by making the same divisions along their respective edges.

As the figure has twelve isometrical sides, and the scale of tangents may be applied two ways to each, it can be applied therefore twenty-four ways in all. We thus have a simple means of drawing, on the isometrical faces of the cube, lines, forming any angles with their boundaries.

Figs. 1, 2, 3, 4, 5, 6, Plate I., show the section of a cube by single planes, at various inclinations to the faces of the cubes. Figs. 7, 8 are the same cube, but turned round, with pieces cut out of it. Fig. 9 is a cube cut by two planes forming the projection of a roof. Fig. 10 is a cube with all of the angles cut off by planes, so as to leave each face an octagon. Fig. 11, represents the angles cut off by planes perpendicular to the base of the cube, forming thereby a regular octagonal cylinder. By drawing lines from each of the angles of an octagonal base to the centre point of the upper face of the cube, we have the isometrical representation of an octagonal prism.

As the lines of construction have all been retained in these figures, they will be easily understood and copied, and are sufficient illustrations of the method of representing any solid by enclosing it in a cube.

We have now to consider the application of this species of projection to curved lines.

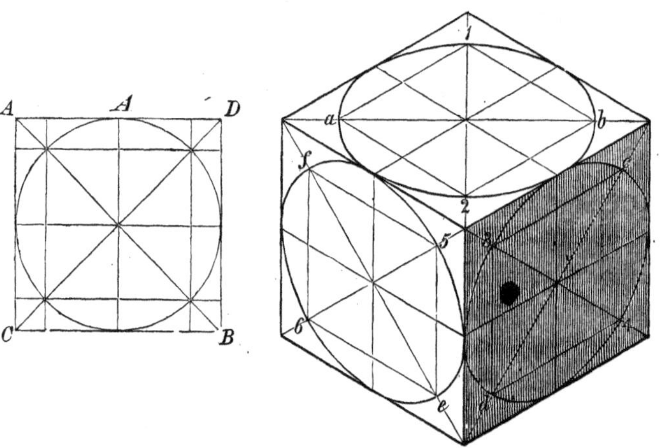

Figs. 8, 9.

Let A B (fig. 8,) be the side of a cube with a circle inscribed; and suppose all the faces of the cube to have similarly inscribed circles. Draw the diagonals A B, C D, and at their intersection with the circumference lines parallel to A C, B D. Now draw the isometrical projection of the cube, (fig. 9,) and lay out on the several faces the diagonals and the parallels; the projection of the circle will be an ellipse, of which the diagonals being the axes, their extremities are defined by their intersections *f* 6,

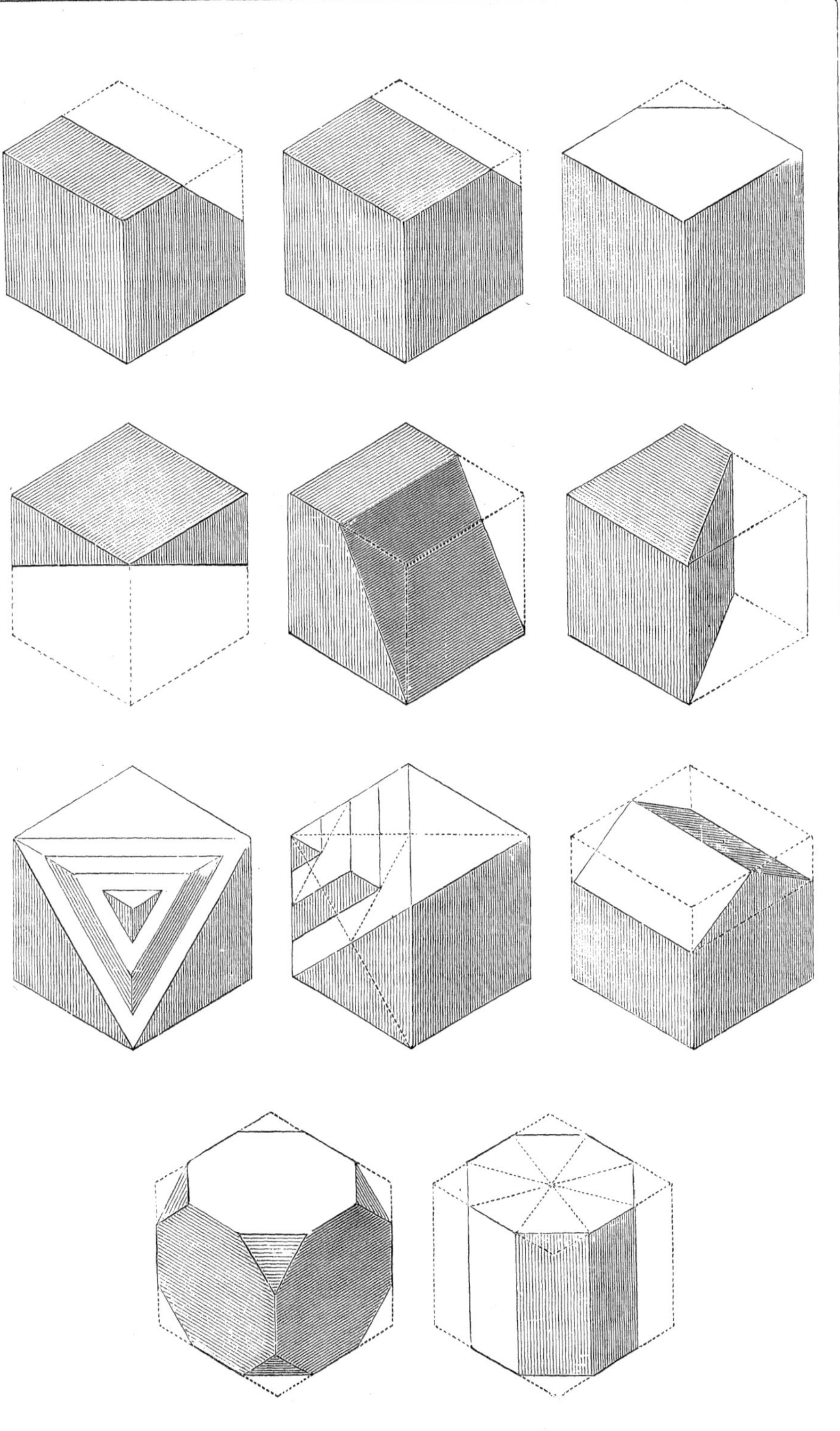

PLATE II.

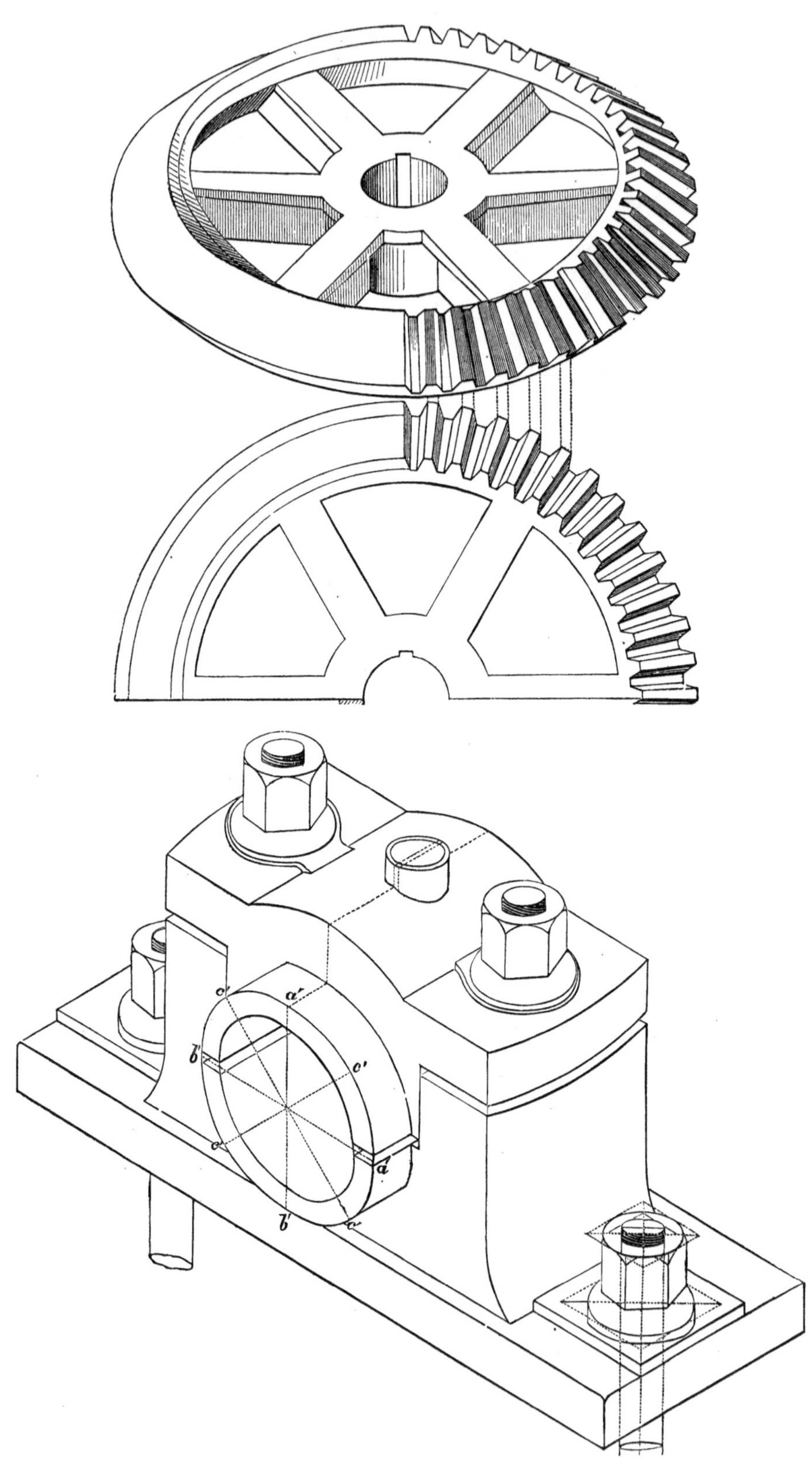

PLATE IV.

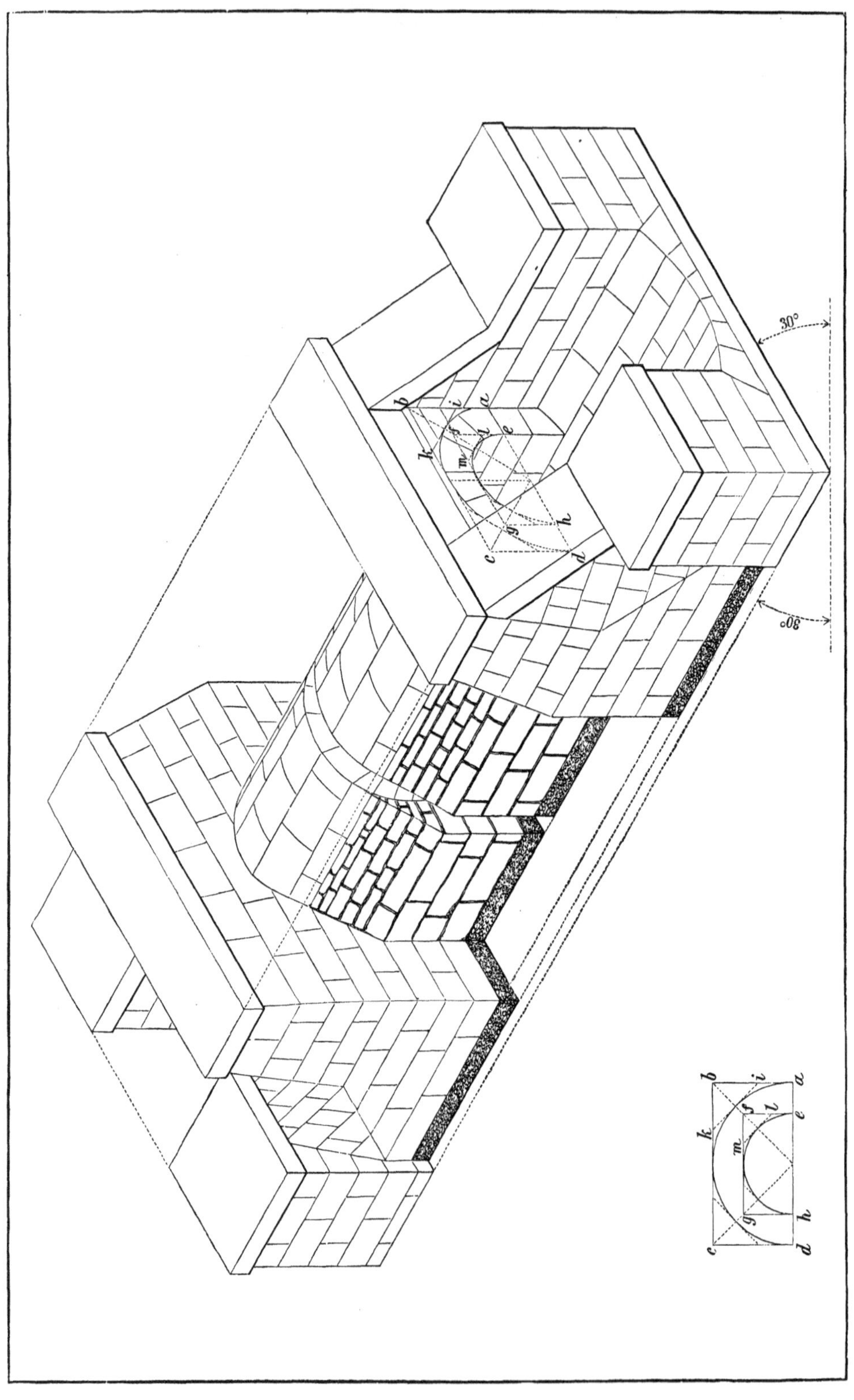

$e\,5$, $a\,2$, $b\,1$, $d\,3$, $c\,4$, by the parallels; having thus the major and minor axis, construct the ellipse by the trammel, or since the curve is tangent at the centre of the sides, we have eight points in the curve; it may be put in by sweeps or by the hand.

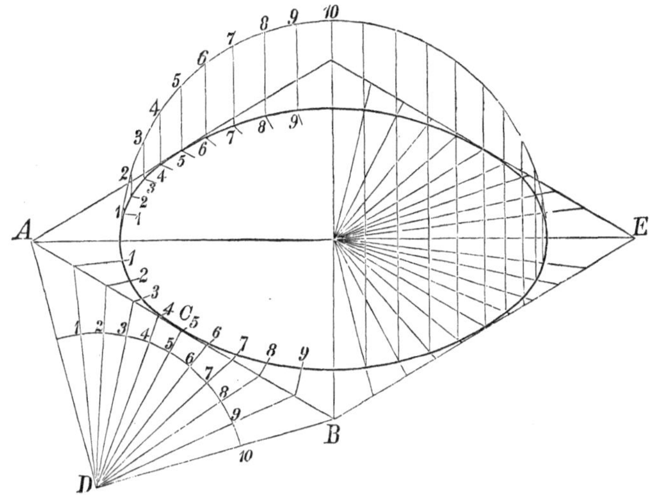

Fig. 10.

To Divide the Circumference of a Circle.—First method. On the centre of the line A B erect a perpendicular C D, making it equal to C A or C B; then from D, with any radius, describe an arc and divide it in the ratio required, and draw the divisions radii from D meeting A B; then from the isometric centre of the circle draw radii from the divisions on A B, cutting the circumference in the points required.

Second method. On the major axis of the ellipse describe a semi-circle, and divide it in the manner required. Through the points of division draw lines perpendicular to A E, which will divide the circumference of the ellipse in the same ratio. On the right hand of the figure both methods are shown in combination, and the intersection of the lines give the points in the ellipse.

The drawing of the mitre-wheel, (fig. 1, Plate II.) is given as an illustration and example for practice.

Fig 2, Plate II., represents a pillow block.

Plate III. represents various combinations of framing met with in architectural and mechanical constructions.

Plate IV. represents a culvert such as were constructed beneath the Croton Aqueduct.

The Plates and figures thus represented show the applicability of this method of projection to various examples. Many others might be introduced, but the principles of this perspective are so easy and intelligible, that to multiply examples would be entirely unnecessary.

Isometrical projection is especially valuable to the mechanical draughtsman, embracing as it does the applicability of a scale with pictorial representation. For drawings for the Patent Office it is especially desirable, yet when pictorial representation alone is intended, it is not as truthful as a drawing in linear perspective. Its office is rather practical than ornamental.

A LIST OF
NEW WORKS IN GENERAL LITERATURE,

Published by D. APPLETON & CO., 346 & 348 Broadway, New York.

Complete Catalogues, containing full descriptions, to be had on application to the Publishers.

Agriculture and Rural Affairs.

Boussingault's Rural Economy, 1 25
The Poultry Book, illustrated, 5 00
Waring's Elements of Agriculture, 75

Arts, Manufactures, and Architecture.

Appleton's Dictionary of Mechanics. 2 vols. 12 00
Appleton's Mechanics' Magazine. 3 vols. each, 3 50
Allen's Philosophy of Mechanics, 3 50
Arnot's Gothic Architecture, 4 00
Bassnett's Theory of Storms, 1 00
Bourne on the Steam Engine, 0 75
Byrne on Logarithms, 1 00
Chapman on the American Rifle, 1 25
Coming's Preservation of Health, 75
Cullum on Military Bridges, 2 00
Downing's Country Houses, 4 00
Field's City Architecture, 2 00
Griffith's Marine Architecture, 10 00
Gillespie's Treatise on Surveying,
Haupt's Theory of Bridge Construction, 3 00
Henck's Field-Book for R. R. Engineers, 1 75
Hoblyn's Dictionary of Scientific Terms, 1 50
Huff's Manual of Electro-Physiology, 1 25
Jeffers' Practice of Naval Gunnery, 2 50
Knapen's Mechanics' Assistant, 1 00
Lafever's Modern Architecture, 4 00
Lyell's Manual of Geology, 1 75
" Principles of Geology, 2 25
Reynold's Treatise on Handrailing, 2 00
Templeton's Mechanic's Companion, 1 00
Ure's Dict'ry of Arts, Manufactures, &c. 2 vols. 5 00
Youmans' Class-Book of Chemistry, 75
" Atlas of Chemistry. cloth, 2 00
" Alcohol, 50

Biography.

Arnold's Life and Correspondence, 2 00
Capt. Canot, or Twenty Years of a Slaver, 1 25
Cousin's De Longueville, 1 00
Croswell's Memoirs, 2 00
Evelyn's Life of Godolphin, 50
Garland's Life of Randolph, 1 50
Gilfillan's Gallery of Portraits. 2d Series, 1 00
Hernan Cortez's Life, 38
Hull's Civil and Military Life, 2 00
Life and Adventures of Daniel Boone, 38
Life of Henry Hudson, 38
Life of Capt. John Smith, 38
Moore's Life of George Castriot, 1 00
Napoleon's Memoirs. By Duchess D'Abrantes, 4 00
Napoleon. By Laurent L'Ardèche, 3 00
Pinkney (W.) Life. By his Nephew, 2 00
Party Leaders: Lives of Jefferson, &c. 1 00
Southey's Life of Oliver Cromwell, 38
Wynne's Lives of Eminent Men, 1 00
Webster's Life and Memorials. 2 vols. 1 00

Books of General Utility.

Appletons' Southern and Western Guide, 1 00
" Northern and Eastern Guide, 1 25
Appletons' Complete U. S. Guide, 2 00
" Map of N. Y. City, 25
American Practical Cook Book,
A Treatise on Artificial Fish-Breeding, 75
Chemistry of Common Life. 2 vols. 12mo.
Cooley's Book of Useful Knowledge, 1 25
Cust's Invalid's Own Book, 50
Delisser's Interest Tables, 4 00
The English Cyclopaedia, per vol. 2 50
Miles on the Horse's Foot, 25
The Nursery Basket. A Book for Young Mothers, 38
Pell's Guide for the Young, 38
Reid's New English Dictionary, 1 00
Stewart's Stable Economy, 1 00
Spalding's Hist. of English Literature, 1 00
Soyer's Modern Cookery, 1 00
The Successful Merchant, 1 00
Thomson on Food of Animals, 50

Commerce and Mercantile Affairs.

Anderson's Mercantile Correspondence, 1 00
Delisser's Interest Tables, 4 00
Merchants' Reference Book, 4 00
Oates' (Geo.) Interest Tables at 6 Per Cent. per Annum. 8vo. 2 00
" " Do. do. Abridged ed. 1 25
" " 7 Per Cent. In'st. Tables, 2 00
" " Abridged, 1 25
Smith's Mercantile Law, 4 00

Geography and Atlases.

Appleton's Modern Atlas. 34 Maps, 3 50
" Complete Atlas. 61 Maps, 9 00
Atlas of the Middle Ages. By Kœppen, 4 50
Black's General Atlas. 71 Maps, 12 00
Cornell's Primary Geography, 50
" Intermediate Geography,
" High School Geography,

History.

Arnold's History of Rome, 3 00
" Later Commonwealth, 2 50
" Lectures on Modern History, 1 25
Dew's Ancient and Modern History, 2 00
Kœppen's History of the Middle Ages. 2 vols. 2 50
" The same, folio, with Maps, 4 50
Kohlrausch's History of Germany, 1 50
Mahon's (Lord) History of England, 2 vols. 4 00
Michelet's History of France, 2 vols. 3 50
" History of the Roman Republic, 1 00
Rowan's History of the French Revolution, 63
Sprague's History of the Florida War, 2 50
Taylor's Manual of Ancient History, 1 25
" Manual of Modern History, 1 50
" Manual of History. 1 vol. complete, 2 50
Thiers' French Revolution. 4 vols. Illus. 5 00

Illustrated Works for Presents.

Bryant's Poems. 16 Illus. 8vo. cloth, 3 50
" " cloth, gilt, 4 50
" " mor. antique, 6 00
Gems of British Art. 30 Engravings. 1 vol. 4to. morocco, 18 00
Gray's Elegy. Illustrated. 8vo. 1 50
Goldsmith's Deserted Village, 1 50
The Homes of American Authors. With Illustrations, cloth, 4 00
" " cloth, gilt, 5 00
" " mor. antqe. 7 00
The Holy Gospels. With 40 Designs by *Overbeck. 1 vol. folio. Antique mor. 20 00
The Land of Bondage. By J. M. Wainwright, D. D. Morocco, 6 00
The Queens of England. By Agnes Strickland. With 29 Portraits. Antique mor. 10 00
The Ornaments of Memory. With 18 Illustrations. 4to. cloth, gilt, 6 00
" " Morocco, 10 00
Royal Gems from the Galleries of Europe. 40 Engravings, 25 00
The Republican Court; or, American Society in the Days of Washington. 21 Portraits. Antique mor. 12 00
The Vernon Gallery. 67 Engr's. 4to. Ant. 25 00
The Women of the Bible. With 18 Engravings. Mor. antique, 10 00
Wilkie Gallery. Containing 60 Splendid Engravings. 4to. Antique mor. 25 00
A Winter Wreath of Summer Flowers. By S. G. Goodrich. Illustrated. Cloth, gilt, 3 00

Juvenile Books.

A Poetry Book for Children, 75
Aunt Fanny's Christmas Stories, 50
American Historical Tales, 75

UNCLE AMEREL'S STORY BOOKS.

The Little Gift Book. 18mo. cloth, 25
The Child's Story Book. Illus. 18mo. cl. 25
Summer Holidays. 18mo. cloth, 25
Winter Holidays. Illus. 18mo. cloth, 25
George's Adventures in the Country. Illustrated. 18mo. cloth, 25
Christmas Stories. Illus. 18mo. cloth, 25

Book of Trades, 50
Boys at Home. By the Author of Edgar Clifton, 75
Child's Cheerful Companion, 50
Child's Picture and Verse Book. 100 Engs. 50

COUSIN ALICE'S WORKS.

All's Not Gold that Glitters, 75
Contentment Better than Wealth, 63
Nothing Venture, Nothing Have, 63
No such Word as Fail, 63
Patient Waiting No Loss, 63

Dashwood Priory. By the Author of Edgar Clifton, 75
Edgar Clifton; or Right and Wrong, 75
Fireside Fairies. By Susan Pindar, 63
Good in Every Thing. By Mrs. Barwell, 50
Leisure Moments Improved, 75
Life of Punchinello, 75

LIBRARY FOR MY YOUNG COUNTRYMEN.

Adventures of Capt. John Smith. By the Author of Uncle Philip, 38
Adventures of Daniel Boone. By do. 38
Dawnings of Genius. By Anne Pratt, 38
Life and Adventures of Henry Hudson. By the Author of Uncle Philip, 38
Life and Adventures of Hernan Cortez. By do. 38
Philip Randolph. A Tale of Virginia. By Mary Gertrude, 38
Rowan's History of the French Revolution. 2 vols. 75
Southey's Life of Oliver Cromwell, 38

Louis' School-Days. By E. J. May, 75
Louise; or, The Beauty of Integrity, 25
Maryatt's Settlers in Canada, 62
" Masterman Ready, 63
" Scenes in Africa, 63
Midsummer Fays. By Susan Pindar, 63

MISS McINTOSH'S WORKS.

Aunt Kitty's Tales, 12mo. 75
Blind Alice; A Tale for Good Children, 38
Ellen Leslie; or, The Reward of Self-Control, 38
Florence Arnott; or, Is She Generous? 38
Grace and Clara; or, Be Just as well as Generous, 38
Jessie Graham; or, Friends Dear, but Truth Dearer, 38
Emily Herbert; or, The Happy Home, 37
Rose and Lillie Stanhope, 37

Mamma's Story Book, 75
Pebbles from the Sea-Shore, 37
Puss in Boots. Illus. By Otto Specter, 25

PETER PARLEY'S WORKS.

Faggots for the Fireside, 1 13
Parley's Present for all Seasons, 1 00
Wanderers by Sea and Land, 1 13
Winter Wreath of Summer Flowers, 3 00

TALES FOR THE PEOPLE AND THEIR CHILDREN.

Alice Franklin. By Mary Howitt, 38
Crofton Boys (The). By Harriet Martineau, 38
Dangers of Dining Out. By Mrs. Ellis, 38
Domestic Tales. By Hannah More. 2 vols. 75
Early Friendship. By Mrs. Copley, 38
Farmer's Daughter (The). By Mrs. Cameron, 38
First Impressions. By Mrs. Ellis, 38
Hope On, Hope Ever! By Mary Howitt, 38
Little Coin, Much Care. By do. 38
Looking-Glass for the Mind. Many plates, 38
Love and Money. By Mary Howitt, 38
Minister's Family. By Mrs. Ellis, 38
My Own Story. By Mary Howitt, 38
My Uncle, the Clockmaker. By do. 38
No Sense Like Common Sense. By do. 38
Peasant and the Prince. By H. Martineau, 38
Poplar Grove. By Mrs. Copley, 38
Somerville Hall. By Mrs. Ellis, 38
Sowing and Reaping. By Mary Howitt, 38
Story of a Genius. 38
Strive and Thrive. By do. 38
The Two Apprentices. By do. 38
Tired of Housekeeping. By T. S. Arthur, 38
Twin Sisters (The). By Mrs. Sandham, 38
Which is the Wiser? By Mary Howitt, 38
Who Shall be Greatest? By do. 38
Work and Wages. By do. 38

SECOND SERIES.

Chances and Changes. By Charles Burdett, 38
Goldmaker's Village. By H. Zschokke, 38
Never Too Late. By Charles Burdett, 38
Ocean Work, Ancient and Modern. By J. H. Wright, 38

Picture Pleasure Book, 1st Series. 1 25
" " " 2d Series, 1 25
Robinson Crusoe. 300 Plates, 1 50
Susan Pindar's Story Book, 75
Sunshine of Greystone, 75
Travels of Bob the Squirrel, 37
Wonderful Story Book, 50
Willy's First Present, 75
Week's Delight; or, Games and Stories for the Parlor, 75
William Tell, the Hero of Switzerland, 50
Young Student. By Madame Guizot, 75

Miscellaneous and General Literature.

An Attic Philosopher in Paris, 25
Appletons' Library Manual, 1 25
Agnell's Book of Chess, 1 25
Arnold's Miscellaneous Works, 2 0
Arthur. The Successful Merchant,

D. Appleton & Company's List of New Works.

A Book for Summer Time in the Country, 50
Baldwin's Flush Times in Alabama, 1 25
Calhoun (J. C.), Works of. 4 vols. publ. each, 2 00
Clark's (W. G.) Knick-Knacks, 1 25
Cornwall's Music as it Was, and as it Is, 63
Essays from the London Times. 1st & 2d Series, each, 50
Ewbanks' World in a Workshop, 75
Ellis' Women of England, 50
" Hearts and Homes, 1 50
" Prevention Better than Cure, 75
Foster's Essays on Christian Morals, 50
Goldsmith's Vicar of Wakefield, 75
Grant's Memoirs of an American Lady, 75
Gaieties and Gravities. By Horace Smith, 50
Guizot's History of Civilization, 1 00
Hearth-Stone. By Rev. S. Osgood, 1 00
Hobson. My Uncle and I, 75
Ingoldsby Legends, 50
Isham's Mud Cabin, 1 00
Johnson's Meaning of Words, 1 00
Kavanagh's Women of Christianity, 75
Leger's Animal Magnetism, 1 00
Life's Discipline. A Tale of Hungary, 63
Letters from Rome. A. D. 138, 1 90
Margaret Maitland, 75
Maiden and Married Life of Mary Powell, 50
Morton Montague; or a Young Christian's Choice, 75
Macaulay's Miscellanies. 5 vols. 5 00
Maxims of Washington. By J. F. Schroeder, 1 00
Mile Stones in our Life Journey, 1 00

MINIATURE CLASSICAL LIBRARY.

Poetic Lacon; or, Aphorisms from the Poets, 38
Bond's Golden Maxims, 31
Clarke's Scripture Promises. Complete, 38
Elizabeth; or, The Exiles of Siberia, 31
Goldsmith's Vicar of Wakefield, 38
" Essays, 38
Gems from American Poets, 38
Hannah More's Private Devotions, 31
" " Practical Piety. 2 vols. 75
Hemans' Domestic Affections, 31
Hoffman's Lays of the Hudson, &c. 38
Johnson's History of Rasselas, 38
Manual of Matrimony, 31
Moore's Lalla Rookh, 38
" Melodies. Complete, 38
Paul and Virginia, 31
Pollok's Course of Time, 38
Pure Gold from the Rivers of Wisdom, 38
Thomson's Seasons, 38
Token of the Heart. Do. of Affection. Do. of Remembrance. Do. of Friendship. Do. of Love. Each, 31
Useful Letter-Writer, 38
Wilson's Sacra Privata, 31
Young's Night Thoughts, 38

Little Pedlington and the Pedlingtonians, 50
Prismatics. Tales and Poems, 1 25
Papers from the Quarterly Review, 50
Republic of the United States. Its Duties, &c. 1 00
Preservation of Health and Prevention of Disease, 75
School for Politics. By Chas. Gayerre, 75
Select Italian Comedies. Translated, 75
Shakespeare's Scholar. By R. G. White, 2 50
Spectator (The). New ed. 6 vols. cloth, 9 00
Swett's Treatise on Diseases of the Chest, 3 00
Stories from Blackwood, 50

THACKERAY'S WORKS.

The Book of Snobs, 50
Mr. Browne's Letters, 50
The Confessions of Fitzboodle, 50
The Fat Contributor, 50
Jeames' Diary. A Legend of the Rhine, 50
The Luck of Barry Lyndon, 1 00
Men's Wives, 50
The Paris Sketch Book. 2 vols. 1 00
The Shabby Genteel Story, 50
The Yellowplush Papers. 1 vol. 16mo. 50
Thackeray's Works. 6 vols. bound in cloth, 6 00

Trescott's Diplomacy of the Revolution, 75
Tuckerman's Artist Life, 75
Up Country Letters, 75
Ward's Letters from Three Continents, 1 00
" English Items, 1 00
Warner's Rudimental Lessons in Music, 50
Woman's Worth, 38

Philosophical Works.

Cousin's Course of Modern Philosophy, 3 00
" Philosophy of the Beautiful, 62
" on the True, Beautiful, and Good, 1 50
Comte's Positive Philosophy. 2 vols. 4 00
Hamilton's Philosophy. 1 vol. 8vo. 1 50

Poetry and the Drama.

Amelia's Poems. 1 vol. 12mo. 1 25
Brownell's Poems. 12mo. 75
Bryant's Poems. 1 vol. 8vo. Illustrated, 3 50
" " Antique mor. 6 00
Bryant's Poems. 2 vols. 12mo. cloth, 2 00
" " 1 vol. 18mo. 63
Byron's Poetical Works. 1 vol. cloth, 3 00
" " " Antique mor. 6 00
Burns' Poetical Works. Cloth, 1 00
Butler's Hudibras. Cloth, 1 00
Campbell's Poetical Works. Cloth, 1 00
Coleridge's Poetical Works. Cloth, 1 25
Cowper's Poetical Works, 1 00
Chaucer's Canterbury Tales, 1 00
Dante's Poems. Cloth, 1 00
Dryden's Poetical Works. Cloth, 1 00
Fay (J. S.), Ulric; or, The Voices, 75
Goethe's Iphigenia in Tauris. Translated, 75
Gilfillan's Edition of the British Poets. 12 vols. published. Price per vol. cloth, 1 00
Do. do. Calf, per vol. 2 50
Griffith's (Mattie) Poems, 75
Hemans' Poetical Works. 2 vols. 16mo. 2 00
Herbert's Poetical Works. 16mo. cloth, 1 00
Keats' Poetical Works. Cloth, 12mo. 1 25
Kirke White's Poetical Works. Cloth, 1 00
Lord's Poems. 1 vol. 12mo. 75
" Christ in Hades. 12mo. 75
Milton's Paradise Lost. 18mo. 38
" Complete Poetical Works, 1 00
Moore's Poetical Works. 8vo. Illustrated, 3 00
" " " Mor. extra, 6 00
Montgomery's Sacred Poems. 1 vol. 12mo. 75
Pope's Poetical Works. 1 vol. 16mo. 1 00
Southey's Poetical Works. 1 vol. 3 00
Spenser's Faerie Queene. 1 vol. cloth, 1 00
Scott's Poetical Works. 1 vol. 1 00
" Lady of the Lake. 16mo. 38
" Marmion, 37
" Lay of the Last Minstrel, 25
Shakspeare's Dramatic Works, 2 00
Tasso's Jerusalem Delivered. 1 vol. 16mo. 1 00
Wordsworth (W.). The Prelude, 1 00

Religious Works.

Arnold's Rugby School Sermons, 50
Anthon's Catechism on the Homilies, 06
" Early Catechism for Children, 06
Burnet's History of the Reformation. 3 vols. 2 50
" Thirty-Nine Articles, 2 00
Bradley's Family and Parish Sermons, 2 00
Cotter's Mass and Rubrics, 38
Coit's Puritanism, 1 00
Evans' Rectory of Valehead, 50
Grayson's True Theory of Christianity, 1 00
Gresley on Preaching, 1 25
Griffin's Gospel its Own Advocate, 1 00
Hecker's Book of the Soul,
Hooker's Complete Works. 2 vols. 4 00
James' Happiness, 25
James on the Nature of Evil, 1 00
Jarvis' Reply to Milner, 75
Kingsley's Sacred Choir, 75
Keble's Christian Year, 37
Layman's Letters to a Bishop, 25
Logan's Sermons and Expository Lectures, 1 13
Lyra Apostolica, 50
Marshall's Notes on Episcopacy, 1 00
Newman's Sermons & Subjects of the Day, 1 00
" Essay on Christian Doctrine, 75
Ogilby on Lay Baptism, 50
Pearson on the Creed, 2 00
Pulpit Cyclopædia and Ministers' Companion, 2 50
Sewell's Reading Preparatory to Confirmation, 75
Southard's Mystery of Godliness, 75
Sketches and Skeletons of Sermons, 2 50
Spencer's Christian Instructed, 1 00
Sherlock's Practical Christian, 75
Sutton's Disce Vivere—Learn to Live, 75
Swartz's Letters to my Godchild, 38
Trench's Notes on the Parables, 1 75
" Notes on the Miracles. 1 75
Taylor's Holy Living and Dying, 1 00
" Episcopacy Asserted and Maintained, 75
Tyng's Family Commentary, 2 00
Walker's Sermons on Practical Subjects, 2 00
Watson on Confirmation, 06
Wilberforce's Manual for Communicants, 38
Wilson's Lectures on Colossians, 75
Wyatt's Christian Altar, 38

Voyages and Travels.

Africa and the American Flag, 1 25
Appletons' Southern and Western Guide, 1 00
" Northern and Eastern Guide, 1 25
" Complete U. S. Guide Book, 2 00
" N. Y. City Map, 25
Bartlett's New Mexico, &c. 2 vols. Illus., 5 00
Burnet's N. Western Territory, 2 00
Bryant's What I Saw in California, 1 25
Coggeshall's Voyages. 2 vols. 2 50
Dix's Winter in Madeira, 1 00
Huc's Travels in Tartary and Thibet. 2 vols. 1 00
Layard's Nineveh. 1 vol. 8vo. 1 25
Notes of a Theological Student. 12mo. 1 00
Oliphant's Journey to Katmandu, 50
Parkyns' Abyssinia. 2 vols. 2 50
Russia as it Is. By Gurowski, 1 00
" By Count de Custine, 1 25
Squier's Nicaragua. 2 vols. 5 00
Tappan's Step from the New World to the Old, 1 75
Wanderings and Fortunes of Germ. Emigrants, 75
Williams' Isthmus of Tehuantepec. 2 vols. 8vo. 3 50

Works of Fiction.

GRACE AGUILAR'S WORKS.

The Days of Bruce. 2 vols. 12mo. 1 50
Home Scenes and Heart Studies. 12mo. 75
The Mother's Recompense. 12mo. 75
Woman's Friendship. 12mo. 75
Women of Israel. 2 vols. 12mo. 1 50

Basil. A Story of Modern Life. 12mo. 75
Brace's Fawn of the Pale Faces. 12mo. 75
Busy Moments of an Idle Woman, 75
Chestnut Wood. A Tale. 2 vols. 1 75
Don Quixotte, Translated. Illustrated, 1 25
Drury (A. H.). Light and Shade, 75
Dupuy (A. E.). The Conspirator, 75
Ellen Parry; or, Trials of the Heart, 63

MRS. ELLIS' WORKS.

Hearts and Homes; or, Social Distinctions, 1 50
Prevention Better than Cure, 75
Women of England, 50

Emmanuel Phillibert. By Dumas, 1 25
Farmingdale. By Caroline Thomas, 1 00
Fullerton (Lady G.). Ellen Middleton, 75
" " Grantley Manor. 1 vol. 12mo. 75
" " Lady Bird. 1 vol. 12mo. 75
The Foresters. By Alex. Dumas, 75
Gore (Mrs.). The Dean's Daughter. 1 vol. 12mo. 75
Goldsmith's Vicar of Wakefield. 12mo. 75
Gil Blas. With 500 Engr's. Cloth, gt. edg. 2 50
Harry Muir. A Tale of Scottish Life, 75
Hearts Unveiled; or, I Knew You Would Like Him, 75
Heartsease; or, My Brother's Wife. 2 vols. 1 50
Heir of Redclyffe. 2 vols. cloth, 1 50
Heloise; or, The Unrevealed Secret. 12mo. 75
Hobson. My Uncle and I. 12mo. 75
Holmes' Tempest and Sunshine. 12mo. 1 00
Home is Home. A Domestic Story, 75
Howitt (Mary). The Heir of West Wayland, 50
Io. A Tale of the Ancient Fane. 12mo. 75
The Iron Cousin. By Mary Cowden Clarke, 1 25
James (G. P. R.). Adrian; or, Clouds of the Mind, 75
John; or, Is a Cousin in the Hand Worth Two in the Bush, 25

JULIA KAVANAGH'S WORKS.

Nathalie. A Tale. 12mo. 1 00
Madeline. 12mo. 75
Daisy Burns. 12mo. 1 00

Life's Discipline. A Tale of Hungary, 63
Lone Dove (The). A Legend,
Linny Lockwood. By Catherine Crowe, 50

MISS McINTOSH'S WORKS.

Two Lives; or, To Seem and To Be. 12mo. 75
Aunt Kitty's Tales. 12mo. 75
Charms and Counter-Charms. 12mo. 1 00
Evenings at Donaldson Manor, 75
The Lofty and the Lowly. 2 vols. 1 50

Margaret's Home. By Cousin Alice,
Marie Louise; or, The Opposite Neighbors, 50
Maiden Aunt (The). A Story, 75
Manzoni. The Betrothed Lovers. 2 vols. 1 50
Margaret Cecil; or, I Can Because I Ought, 75
Morton Montague; or, The Christian's Choice, 75
Norman Leslie. By G. C. H. 75
Prismatics. Tales and Poems. By Haywarde, 1 25
Roe (A. S.). James Montjoy. 12mo. 75
" To Love and to Be Loved. 12mo. 75
" Time and Tide. 12mo. 75
Reuben Medlicott; or, The Coming Man, 75
Rose Douglass. By S. R. W. 75

MISS SEWELL'S WORKS.

Amy Herbert. A Tale. 12mo. 75
Experience of Life. 12mo. 75
Gertrude. A Tale. 12mo. 75
Katherine Ashton. 2 vols. 12mo. 1 50
Laneton Parsonage. A Tale. 3 vols. 12mo. 2 25
Margaret Percival. 2 vols. 1 50
Walter Lorimer, and Other Tales. 12mo. 75
A Journal Kept for Children of a Village School, 1 00

Sunbeams and Shadows. Cloth, 75
Thorpe's Hive of the Bee Hunter, 1 00
Thackeray's Works. 6 vols. 12mo. 6 00
The Virginia Comedians. 2 vols. 12mo. 1 50
Use of Sunshine. By S. M. 12mo. 75
Wight's Romance of Abelard & Heloise. 12mo. 75

Useful Engineering Works, etc.

I.

FIELD-BOOK FOR RAILROAD ENGINEERS,

Containing Formulæ for laying out Simple, Reversed and Compound Curves, Parabolic Curves Vertical Curves, Determining Frog Angles and Radii of Turnouts and Crossings, Levelling, Setting Slope Stakes, Elevating Outer Rail on Curves, Curving Rails, &c., &c.; together with many Miscellaneous Problems, and a New System of Earth-Work. Also, Tables of Radii, Ordinates, Chord, and Tangent Deflections, Ordinates for Curving Rails, Long Chords, Elevation of Outer Rail, Frog Angles, Properties of Materials, Magnetic Variations, Squares, Cubes, Square Roots, and Cube Roots, Logarithms of Number, Logarithmic Sines, Cosines, Tangents, and Cotangents, Natural Sines, and Cosines, Natural Tangents and Cotangents, Rise per mile of Grades, &c.

By JOHN B. HENCK, Civil Engineer.

One volume with fifty-eight Diagrams, pocket-book form, $

II.

TEMPLETON'S ENGINEER, MILLWRIGHT, AND MECHANIC'S POCKET COMPANION,

Comprising Decimal Arithmetic, Tables of Square and Cube Roots, Practical Geometry, Mensuration, Strength of Materials, Mechanic Powers, Water Wheels, Pumps, and Pumping Engines, Steam Engines, Tables of Specific Gravity, &c., &c. Also a series of

MATHEMATICAL TABLES.

NEW EDITION, REVISED, CORRECTED, AND ENLARGED.

One neat volume, pocket-book form, $1 25.

III.

GENERAL THEORY OF BRIDGE CONSTRUCTION,

CONTAINING

DEMONSTRATIONS OF THE PRINCIPLES OF THE ART, AND THEIR APPLICATION TO PRACTICE,

WITH PRACTICAL ILLUSTRATIONS.

By HERMAN HAUPT, A.M., Civil Engineer.

One volume 8vo., pp. 268, engravings, $3.

IV.

A CATECHISM OF THE STEAM ENGINE,

Illustrative of the Scientific Principles upon which its operation depends, and the practical details of its structure, in its application to Mines, Mills, Steam Navigation and Railways,

WITH VARIOUS SUGGESTIONS OF IMPROVEMENT.

By JOHN BOURNE, C. E.

One neat vol. 16mo., pp. 288. Price, 75 cents.

V.

TREATISE ON MARINE AND NAVAL ARCHITECTURE;

Or, THEORY AND PRACTICE BLENDED IN SHIP BUILDING.

By JOHN W. GRIFFITHS,

MARINE AND NAVAL ARCHITECT.

Fourth edition, one volume 4to, with over fifty engravings, $10

www.ingramcontent.com/pod-product-compliance
Lightning Source LLC
LaVergne TN
LVHW021221110826
845150LV00002B/213

* 9 7 8 1 4 2 5 5 6 4 3 1 5 *